Mystical Recognition

Carl ALBRECHT

Mystical Recognition

Gnoseology and Philosophical Relevance of the 'Mystical Relation'

TRANSLATED, INTRODUCED AND ANNOTATED BY

Franz K. Woehrer

A Herder & Herder Book
THE CROSSROAD PUBLISHING COMPANY
NEW YORK

A Herder & Herder Book
The Crossroad Publishing Company
www.crossroadpublishing.com

© 2020 by Franz K. Woehrer

Translated from the German edition of *Psychologie des Mystischen Bewußtseins*. Mainz: Matthias-Grünewald-Verlag, 1976 (ISBN 3-7867-0563-1), which is the identical reprint of the original edition published by Carl Schünemann, Bremen, in 1951.

© For the texts of the English translation, the general introduction and the annotations: 2018 Franz K. Woehrer, franz-karl.woehrer@univie.ac.at and Crossroad Publishing Company, New York. All rights reserved. No part of this publication may be reproduced or transmitted in any form or by any means, electronic, mechanical, photocopying or otherwise, without prior permission in writing from both the translator-editor and the publisher.

Crossroad, Herder & Herder, and the crossed C logo/colophon are registered trademarks of The Crossroad Publishing Company.

All rights reserved. No part of this book may be copied, scanned, reproduced in any way, or stored in a retrieval system, or transmitted, in any form or by any means, electronic, mechanical, photocopying, recording, or otherwise, without the written permission of The Crossroad Publishing Company. For permission please write to rights@crossroadpublishing.com.

In continuation of our 200-year tradition of independent publishing, The Crossroad Publishing Company proudly offers a variety of books with strong, original voices and diverse perspectives. The viewpoints expressed in our books are not necessarily those of The Crossroad Publishing Company, any of its imprints or of its employees, executives, owners. Although the author and publisher have made every effort to ensure that the information in this book was correct at press time, the author and publisher do not assume and hereby disclaim any liability to any party for any loss, damage, or disruption caused by errors or omissions, whether such errors or omissions result from negligence, accident, or any other cause. No claims are made or responsibility assumed for any health or other benefits.

The text of this book is set in 11/14 Sabon LT Pro.

Composition and cover design by Sophie Appel
Cover illustration 'Transcendence' by Liz W, Firestone Colorado (2016)

Library of Congress Cataloging-in-Publication Data
available upon request from the Library of Congress.

978-0-8245-9802-0 paperback
978-0-8245-9801-3 cloth
978-0-8245-9711-5 ePub
978-0-8245-9712-2 mobi

Books published by The Crossroad Publishing Company may be purchased at special quantity discount rates for classes and institutional use. For information, please e-mail sales@crossroadpublishing.com.

Translated from the German edition of *Das Mystische Erkennen. Gnoseologie und Philosophische Relevanz der Mystischen Relation.* Mainz: Matthias-Grünewald-Verlag, 1982 (ISBN 3-7867-0986-6), which is the reprint of the original edition, published in 1958 by Carl Schünemann (Bremen, Germany).

[Note: Gnoseology (alternatively spelt gnosiology). From Greek *gnōsis*, meaning 'knowledge'. It refers to any philosophy or branch of philosophy concerned with solving problems about the nature and possibility of knowledge; also, it denotes delivering knowledge of ultimate reality, especially insofar as this is not available to sense-experience. Today 'gnoseology' is an archaic term; in the first instance, it has been replaced by 'epistemology', and in the latter sense by the term 'metaphysics'. – Cf. Honderich, Ted. *The Oxford Companion to Philosophy*. 2nd ed. Oxford: OUP, 2005. s.v. "gnoseology" – FKW]

TABLE OF CONTENTS

ACKNOWLEDGMENTS	vii
PREFACE by Simon Peng-Keller	xi
PREFACE by Alicja Sakaguchi	xvii
GENERAL INTRODUCTION by F. K. Woehrer	xxix
FOREWORD by Carl Albrecht	1
INTRODUCTION *Pseudomysticism*	7
Occultism	9
'Spirit-Seers' and 'Spirit-Researchers': The Cognitive Experience of 'Higher Worlds'	20
Cosmic Consciousness	45
PART ONE *The Structure of Mystical Experience*	63
Experiencing, Cognitive Perception and Beholding	65
The 'Object Arriving' and 'the Experience of Being Acted Upon'	69
Pictorial Visions	75
Allegorical Visions	92
Graphic Visions of the Devil and of Angels (Teresa of Avila and 'Lucie Christine' [aka Mathilde Boutle, 1844–1908])	100
The Vision of Christ	117
The Vision of Light	121
Light Adhering to an Object Beheld in 'Inner Sight'	122
Light as Such	126

Light as the Medium of 'Inner Sight'	146
The Transfiguration of the Perceiver	153
The Cognitive Awareness of Presence	157
The 'Beholding' of a Presence	168
Awareness of the Presence	177
The Non-Spatial Recognition of the Presence	181
Mystical Insight	183
Numinous Perception	195
The Vision of the 'Majestas'	208
The Perception of Mystical Effects	215
Review and Future Direction of Our Enquiry	225
The Glimpse of God	234
Manifestation of Self-Expressive Gestures and Appearances	237
The Basic Structure of the 'Imageless Vision'	247
The 'Inward Vision' Directed at the Invisible	254
The End of the State of 'Vision'	263
The Spectrum of the 'Mystical Vision'	273
Auditory Mystical Experience	276
The Sense of Being 'Touched': Somatic Modes of Mystical Perception	284
The Sense of 'Being Directed' by an Overwhelming Power	288
Person-like Features of the 'All-encompassing'	291
The Experience of the Mystical Relation	303
Critical Considerations	313
The Mystical Relation	324
The Concept of the 'Ultimate Phenomenon'	328

PART TWO *Gnoseology of Mysticism*	333
Delusion and Error in the Context of Mystical Experience	336
The Gnoseological Pyramid	370
Error and Delusion in the Overall Structure of Mystical Experience	374
Critical Analysis of the Structure of Mystical Recognition	378
PART THREE *The Philosophical Relevance of the Mystical Relation*	401
Anthropology	404
Hermeneutics of "Dasein"	416
CONCLUSION	461
BIBLIOGRAPHY	467
INDEX	479

ACKNOWLEDGMENTS

Since the early 1980ies eminent scholars in the English-speaking world in the field of mysticism, such as Bernard McGinn and Harvey Egan, have expressed their regret that the pioneering empirical studies on mysticism by the German medical doctor, psychotherapist and mystic Carl Albrecht are not available in English translation. It has taken nearly forty years for this deficiency to be removed—first with the publication of *Psychology of Mystical Consciousness* by Crossroad in 2019, and now with the release of the present annotated English edition of *Das Mystische Erkennen* entitled *Mystical Recognition*. Without the discerning judgement of Chris Myers and Gwendolyn Herder from Crossroad Publishing this project would never have been realized. They recognized the ground-breaking relevance of Albrecht's research for the cross-cultural study of mysticism and the understanding of the spiritual nature of man and paved the way for bringing out Albrecht's works in English. I owe special thanks to Julie Boddorf, production coordinator with Crossroad Publishing, for patiently supervising the publishing process of this voluminous study and for speeding up procedures even when confined to working from home-office during the pandemic. I thank you all for your continued trust, prudent advice, untiring support, and discreet reminders.

Furthermore, I am especially grateful to the Albrecht family, represented by Dr. Harald Albrecht and Carl Albrecht's daughter, Adelheid Haas, for their constant encouragement, fruitful cooperation, and generous financial support.

Special thanks go to the American artist from Firestone, Colorado, known to me only by the pseudonym Liz W, who generously supplied the high-resolution image of her painting 'Transcendence' for the cover illustration.

I also wish to thank Simon Peng-Keller, professor of Spiritual Care at the University of Zurich, one of the leading experts on Albrecht in Europe, for writing a preface, and to Alicja Sakaguchi for providing another preface from the critical perspective of a linguist.

Last but not least, I wish to thank my wife Herta and my 'boys' Sebastian and Nico for their patient tolerance and benevolent understanding for the husband and father's enduring spells of absent presence in the past two years.

PREFACE

Simon Peng-Keller
(Translated by F. K. Woehrer)

Today, the research of meditative practices is mainly focussed on the neuronal corollaries of mindfulness and on the influence of these practices on mental health and well-being. Research in this area has undoubtedly made significant progress in recent years and led to a considerable increase in knowledge. Though psychological approaches and experimental research in neuroscience surely have their merits, there are also aspects that remain eclipsed or are overlooked. By strictly focussing on the mental effects of the practice of mindfulness, it is often ignored that it is a phenomenon of life that is explored, and as such it is one that can be analysed and described from different (including non-behaviourist) perspectives. Carl Albrecht opted for a philosophical approach in his study *Mystical Recognition*. His methodology is perfectly consonant with the prevailing discourse in this field and may be traced throughout the 20th century.[1] Yet despite the many diverse philosophical approaches to mysticism in the 20th century, they shared the endeavour to relate different kinds of mystical experience to modes of cognitive perception and categories of knowledge. Mystical experiences have been

---

1 For a representative survey on this issue see McGINN, Bernard. *Die Mystik im Abendland*. Vol. I. *Ursprünge*. Freiburg i. Br.: Herder & Herder, 1994. 415–60.

assessed differently, depending on the nature of the approach: either as something that is incompatible with rational comprehension, as something that causes its implosion, an experience that is ineffable and located beyond the confines of categorical knowledge or as a form of intuitive cognition, which is esteemed as the apex of the 'degrees of knowledge'.[2] If we wish to locate Albrecht's point of view in the present book within the spectrum of these two poles, it is to be located (as the title suggests) closer to the pole of 'intuition'. For Albrecht's endeavour is to demonstrate that genuine mystical experience, whatever its mode of manifestation, is inalienably imbued with intuitive cognition. Mystical perception (unlike familiar modes of perception) is not directed at some specific content, but at a Presence that is entirely imageless. Hence 'mystical recognition' means 'cognitive perception of the All-encompassing'. Albrecht tries to show that this core-experience is intertwined with numerous facets of mystical experience. Together the individual modes of mystical perception are combined into a complex experience which, however, is tinged also with 'subjective knowledge' originating from the perceiver's religious belief. This means that the act of mystical recognition is always entwined with the act of 'comprehending in faith'.

The question that needs to be asked is why Albrecht was so keen on probing into the elements of knowledge inherent in mystical experience. Why was he not just satisfied with the psychological insights that he gained in his earlier book *Psychologie des Mystischen Bewußtseins (1951)*, in which he describes in detail a wide variety of mystical phenomena? What can the numerous analyses and classifications in the second book (which make for difficult reading at times) contribute to the understanding of this pivotal phenomenon of life? Valuable clues to an answer are supplied if we look at it from the perspective of Albrecht's biography.[3] After he had completed his first study in 1950, Albrecht was clearly aware that the goals of his

---

2   Cf. MARITAIN, Jacques. *Die Stufen des Wissens*. Mainz: Matthias Grünewald, 1953.

3   Cf. PENG-KELLER, Simon. *Gottespassion in Versunkenheit. Die Psychologische Mystikforschung Carl Albrechts aus Theologischer Perspektive*. Würzburg: Echter, 2003.

empirical investigation could never be achieved by means of a psychological-phenomenological approach. The psycho-dynamic processes involved in various modes of mystical experience could not be fully embraced by psychological phenomenology, however subtle and minute its differentiations and classifications. Albrecht was vehemently opposed to reductionist psychological enquiries. For this reason, he took great pains to substantiate his central claim that genuine mystical experience is rooted in an 'ultimate phenomenon', i.e., that it is an experience that cannot be dismissed as an epi-phenomenon, which can be traced to and explained by some psychic process.

When Albrecht had finished *Mystical Recognition* two years later, he was confident that he had succeeded in corroborating the claim that mysticism is indeed an 'ultimate phenomenon'. The extreme strain and sacrifice that this endeavour had imposed on him personally and the great relief he experienced after having completed the book are openly addressed by him in a letter to one of his companions, written in 1956:[4]

> When you read this book, which has been completed at long last, you will understand why I have for a long time withdrawn into silence. And you will realize that this silence has not resulted from negligence. Now I have reached the end: my passionate aspiration has finally reached its goal. What I felt impelled to reflect on, from humble beginnings building a structured edifice to the very roof-top. As I had told you already when we met in Bremen, this was for me an arduous enterprise, in fact a catharsis, and at times I felt as if in purgatory. I leave it to you to judge whether this endeavour has any objective value or has a place in objective reality; it does have subjective significance to me now, not least because I am still rather close to the experiences encountered. I now look forward to a simple and unpretentious life. On March 27, I will travel to Greece and stay there for four weeks. After this sojourn, I will be ready to resume my social communication, which has been incumbered for the past seven years. I will seek my friends again.

---

4 The letter was written to the Italian philosopher Ernesto Grassi (1902–1992), who (for several years) taught philosophy at the universities of Freiburg and Berlin. Grassi was, like Albrecht, deeply influenced by Heidegger's existentialist philosophy. – Quotation from: PENG-KELLER, Simon. *Gottespassion in Versunkenheit. Die Psychologische Mystikforschung Carl Albrechts aus Theologischer Perspektive.* Würzburg: Echter, 2003. 68–69. (Translated by FKW).

Before Albrecht departed for Greece, however, he gathered his large family in his home to celebrate the 'feast day of the book'. In his thanksgiving address he vindicates the purpose of his research and explains the insights gained during the painstaking years of his enquiries:

> Both books, which are in fact one, have something to do with the reality of God. Truly, man ought to acknowledge this reality and abandon himself to it in faith, pure and simple, and immerse himself in this reality without resorting to rational reasoning. However, this is not the path taken by man in the 20th century, or let us put it this way: it is not my path, since I as well have been inoculated by the 'zeitgeist' of the 20th century and been exposed to the maladies of the 20th century, or perhaps I was at the same time gratified by it – depending on how you look at it. It is impossible for me simply to situate myself naively into a reality without reflecting on this reality as thoroughly as this is possible for me. Once having pondered every aspect of what this reality is, I will be better prepared to acknowledge what the real call is for me.[5]

Mystical Recognition is Albrecht's effort to gain self-assurance about the realness of 'all-encompassing Reality', couched in philosophical language. The very fact that he decided to publish this clarifying study suggests that he was aware that the self-assurance conveyed in the book might be helpful to others. Yet the question that may be asked is whether or not Albrecht's avowal is still valid today, more than half a century after the book was first published. One might also wonder if the renewed publication of this book is merely a tribute to a rare research enterprise of the past, one that is only of historical interest. The critical reader of the 21st century may, admittedly, consider Albrecht's use of mystical texts somewhat carefree and his concept of recognition not sufficiently defined in scientific terms. These deficiencies notwithstanding, the careful reading of the book will provide ample proof that Albrecht was aware of the shortcomings and limitations of his scientific and scholarly

---

5 Quotation from: PENG-KELLER, Simon. *Gottespassion in Versunkenheit. Die Psychologische Mystikforschung Carl Albrechts aus Theologischer Perspektive.* Würzburg: Echter, 2003. 69. [Translated by FKW.]

approaches. He makes it clear that this monograph does not presume to be the intellectual achievement of a philosopher, or that the book has been written for an academic readership, but he admits that it is to be taken as the work of a medical doctor who for many years had sacrificed his scarce spare time to pursue his research into the nature of mystical experience. The fact that the book is worth reading more than six decades after its first release may be accounted for by the extraordinary circumstances of its genesis: several of the concepts and insights were conceived and achieved in the meditative state of 'quiet alertness' ("Versunkenheit"). Though it is true that other philosophical works of the modern era are likewise informed by moments of instant inspiration occurring in a pre-reflective stage of the 'waking consciousness', the situation is different with Albrecht: in his case we are concerned with enquiries in which the 'quiet state of alertness' was consciously utilized as a source of clarification throughout. It falls to the individual reader to judge whether, or to what extent, the meditative process underlying the book can be noticed. Yet one thing is certain: Albrecht's method of intertwining 'meditative mindfulness' in the 'quiet state of consciousness' with philosophical and phenomenological thinking was unparalleled in the humanities in the 20th century. These distinctive features of the book's genesis need to be borne in mind when assessing Albrecht's achievement: he has supplied a highly differentiated classification of diverse varieties of mystical experience and a most sensitive, highly ramified cartography of mystical perception.

Univ. Prof. Dr. Simon Peng-Keller
Zurich, 24 December 2019
Chair of Spiritual Care
University of Zurich, Switzerland

PREFACE

Alicja Sakaguchi
(Translated by F. K. Woehrer)

More than sixty years have passed since the publication of Carl Albrecht's pioneering study *Das Mystische Erkennen* (1958; reprinted in 1982 and forthcoming in 2020), but it is only now that this groundbreaking work has been translated and published in an annotated English edition.

Carl Albrecht (1902–1965) was a medical doctor and psychotherapist who, over many years, engaged in innovative empirical research in the field of psychological phenomenology and, more specifically, in the realm of mystical consciousness. He is one of many empirical scientists in the West who tried to widen the thresholds of science by probing more deeply into the domain of mysticism. The path Albrecht embarked on was long, painstaking and fraught with difficulty, since mystical experience and the study of written testimonies of the same are only accessible to a very limited extent to empirical enquiry and the methodologies of science. Before Albrecht, the first attempt in Europe to explore the nature of 'mystical (viz., 'prophetic') experience' had been undertaken by Abraham Joshua Heschel in the 1930s.[1] Albrecht's meticulous investigations were largely carried out

---

1   Cf. HESCHEL, Abraham Joshua. *Die Prophetie*. Kraków: Polska Akademia

between the late 1940s and the early 1960s and resulted in a comprehensive phenomenology of mystical experience. In fact, Albrecht was able to establish tangible phenomenological criteria for discerning authentic from bogus mystical experience. The present book not only demonstrates Albrecht's profound and illuminating insights, but also his expert knowledge of Christian and eastern mystical writings and traditions and his wide reading in philosophy (especially existentialist philosophy). Another unique feature of his research is the fact that it is also grounded in his own mystical experiences and informed by his long-term practice of meditation.

Mystical Recognition is a sequel to Albrecht's first study, *Psychologie des Mystischen Bewußtseins* (1951; reprinted 1976, 1990, 2019, and currently available in English translation),[2] in which he offers a full systematic psychological phenomenology of mystical consciousness based on long-term empirical research and authentic records of mystical experience. Grounded in the findings of Albrecht's earlier study, *Mystical Recognition* aims—as the title indicates—to provide a 'gnoseology' of mystical experience, that is, an analysis of the cognitive content transmitted to a perceiver in a genuine mystical event. Albrecht, approaching mysticism as a scientist, is careful to focus only on empirical and cognitive aspects of mysticism and

---

Umiejętności, 1936. (*The Prophets*. New York: Hendrickson, 1962; rpt. 2007.) The book is based on Heschel's doctoral thesis, submitted at the Friedrich-Wilhelm-University Berlin in 1932, but approved only in 1935 owing to the political turmoil of the time, when National Socialists had seized political power. In this study Heschel analyses the 'prophetic consciousness' of the Hebrew prophets of the preexilic era as documented in the scriptures; he explores such thematic issues as the individual prophets' self-awareness, their perception of creation, and their mission in this world. Heschel's enquiry into the spiritual nature of the prophetic writings was innovative but conflicted with received teaching and the views held by contemporary Jewish scholars and exegetes. Heschel continued to propagate his mystical conception of religious experience after his emigration to the USA, despite ongoing criticism by conservative scholars who remonstrated that he was more interested in spirituality and mysticism than in critical textual exegesis.

2   ALBRECHT, Carl. *Psychology of Mystical Consciousness*. Trans., introd. and annotated by F. K. Woehrer. New York: Crossroad, 2019.

not on the faith-related questions or theological issues germane to it, nor does he speculate on the religious relevance or metaphysical implications of mystical experience. Albrecht is aware of the limitations of his strictly empirical approach, which relies largely on accounts of subjective mystical events supplied by mystics, but also on personal reports by practitioners of meditation and on Albrecht's personal mystical experiences. Albrecht admits that "the concept *experiential mystical knowledge* refers to knowledge derived from various mystical events reported by mystics and individual subjects; hence the only source of mystical knowledge is the collated corpus of records of subjective mystical experiences." The 'visions', 'experiential modes of cognition' and 'areas of knowledge' dealt with in this study are part of empirical reality, which however largely elude objective scientific verification and fall outside the realm of everyday life experience. Albrecht, however, succeeded in developing a method of 'introspection' termed "Versenkung" (a meditational method derived from Autogenic Training), by which the subject can advance to a serene, vacated and perfectly calm state of consciousness termed "Versunkenheit" (named 'quiet state of alertness' in English). In this state of consciousness, the capacity of 'inner sight' ("Innenschau") is released; it is a state of 'receptive openness' permitting the perceiver to observe phenomena 'arriving' in the vista of the 'inner eye', including phenomena experienced as 'arriving' from a domain beyond the confines of the 'individual self', which alone qualify as potentially mystical ones.

Albrecht's meticulous analysis of numerous records by acknowledged mystics from various mystical traditions resulted in the discovery of a new 'Ur-phenomenon' or 'ultimate phenomenon': that of the 'mystical relation', i.e., the existence of an empirical relationship between a perceiving subject while absorbed in the 'quiet state of alertness' and (what Albrecht calls) 'the All-encompassing' (to avoid a religious or philosophical term for the transcendental Otherness encountered) revealing itself in the vista of the 'inner eye'. The testimonies of male and female mystics and visionaries from different historical epochs and mystical traditions analysed by Albrecht include texts by Pseudo-Dionysius Areopagita, Hildegard of Bingen, the Hesychasts, Meister Eckhart, Johannes Tauler, Teresa of Avila,

John of the Cross, Jacob Böhme, Angela of Foligno, 'Lucie Christine' (i.e., Mathilde Boutle), and Katharina Emmerich; from eastern traditions, accounts by the Hindu Yogi Yogananda Paramahansa and the Zen Buddhist Taisetz Suzuki. Altogether Albrecht examined nearly a hundred texts in view of the reliability of their mystical claims and in view of identifying their cognitive content and phenomenological characteristics. These analyses yielded invaluable insights into the nature of mystical experience, disclosing as a major core-phenomenon the shattering, life-transforming impact on the recipient. Thus, a mystical encounter is considered genuine if its effects and aftereffects continue to persevere throughout the recipient's life, positively affecting his/her future existence, even though the significance of the mystical event is not instantly recognized but comprehended only later in the mystic's life.

Albrecht's enquiry of the 'cognitive content' of mystical experience is situated between the disciplines of transpersonal psychology and linguistics. He introduces new concepts and neologisms, of which some are admittedly vague and obscure. For instance, it is difficult to discern the subtle differences between such concepts as 'mode of perceiving', 'form of vision', 'vision of allegory' ("Schau der Allegorie"), 'pictorial vision' ("bildhafte Schau"), 'imageless vision' ("bildlose Schau") and 'visual perception of appearances'; all these terms refer to different modes of mystical perception. They tend to overlap, however, so that their distinctive qualities are difficult to grasp. Not all these concepts refer, strictly speaking, to specific modes, phases or the content of mystical experience, but rather denote modes of speaking about mystical phenomena. In fact, these expressions point to rhetorical and stylistic means of telling about mystical experience. In any case, considerations of further linguistic aspects (e.g., the issue of speech acts) in analysing different types of mystical texts would have been a helpful epistemological premise. After all, the textual corpus examined by Albrecht includes such diverse types of utterances as spiritual confessions, descriptions of mystical experience, explanations, assertions, justifications and complaints. For the mystic language is a medium of communication of great importance, especially when trying to convey spiritual and mystical states in writing which are very difficult to describe (e.g., the stage of the purification of the self), and ultimately ineffable. It is obvious that language is, as such, not a medium of mystical perception – or, to put it more specifically, not a medium of prophetic inspiration, mystical intuition, mystical insight, or even of mystical knowledge. From this follows that it is principally not the experience as such that is 'image-based' or 'imageless', 'personal' or 'apersonal', but the mystics themselves bring a great variety of language forms to light by which the many different types of texts are produced.[3]

In individual mystical traditions, the occurrence of a concrete mystical event is considered the culmination of a spiritual progress, even if it is expressed in very different ways. Thus, in Jewish mysticism, the climactic mystical occurrence is variously termed *visio Dei, prophetic experience* (or *high/inner calling*); in the tradition of Gnosis, the mystical event is termed *spiritual awakening* and identified with the *attainment of gnosis*; in Christianity, the experiential encounter with God has variously been termed *cognitio Dei experimentalis* or *transformatio mystica;* in Hinduism, it is named *experience of Brahman* (or *Atman*); in Buddhism, the seeker's initial mystical event is identified with *spiritual awakening* or *enlightenment*, or *satori* in Zen Buddhism. A mystical experience discloses aspects of the invisible, trans-material world and imparts in the perceiver a special capacity for "panoramic" knowledge and for religious awakening. In his analyses of mystical texts Albrecht demonstrates that mystics participate in unique experiences which they feel compelled to communicate to others. The language used for describing the encounter with the Divine derives its lexical material or external 'linguistic garment' from the language of the given cultural and religious context. However, in the context of mysticism, such mundane words as *light, desert, death, dying, freedom,* and verbs like *hearing, seeing, watching, receiving,* or *tasting* are imbued

---

3 It should be mentioned that every verbal account of an authentic mystical experience is rooted in a mystical perception, a mystical recognition or moment of understanding (*epignosis*). The primary event is a spiritual mystical experience, whereas the linguistic testimony of this experience is a secondary act. Hence a mystical record is inevitably recalled from memory; the verbal record thus always lags behind a given mystical event.

with special spiritual meaning. Words and idioms of common speech are transferred from the worldly object- and sense-related domain to the transcendental sphere and assume specific mystical meaning. Metaphors and pictorial expressions like *magnificent splendour, flash of illumination, fire of love, magic charm, dark night, narrow gate,* or *ascension to heaven* thus denote a distinct quality of a mystical experience. Similarly, symbols of revelation may indicate the revelatory and cognitive nature of a mystical event (e.g., *flash of lightning, voices, thunder, the eagle, a star* or *an angel*). The same applies to paradoxical expressions such as *luminous cloud, learned ignorance, dazzling darkness,* and *sweet affliction,* and to anthropomorphic expressions like *countenance and shape of a new person,* "He [God] granted me to prosper and augmented my capacity of knowledge". Expressions of this kind are typically employed to describe different mystical states, specific qualities of a mystical event or of a spiritual change (e.g., 'mystical conversion', 'illumination'). The inventory of such words and phrases that have mystical or spiritual import are the core of 'prophetic speech'.

Undoubtedly, language, with its stereotypical expressions and connotations, limits man's scope of cognition. Mystics go beyond this boundary and overcome the frailties of human language. In order to depict the totally different spaces of reality in which they have become immersed, they use very specific modes of linguistic expression, in which they resort especially to pictorial images ("Begriffsbilder"), analogies, metaphors, parallelisms, chiasmi, antitheses, allegories, paradoxes, symbols or parables.[4]

The Gnostics in late antiquity termed the eternal, uncreated and universal source of being the *pre-existent Throne of God;* the Quran and Islamic mystics (Sufis) refer to it in terms of *Divine Wisdom, the Lustre of the Light of God Sublime* or *immovable Essence.* C. G. Jung, by contrast, identified ultimate Reality with the universal consciousness termed *Collective Unconscious* ("*das kollektive*

---

4 Cf. SAKAGUCHI, Alicja. *Sprechakte der Mystischen Erfahrung. Eine Komparative Studie zum Sprachlichen Ausdruck von Offenbarung und Prophetie.* (*Speech Acts of Mystical Experience. A Comparative Study of the Linguistic Expression of Revelation and Prophecy.*) Freiburg and Munich: Alber, 2015. 360–443.

Unbewusste"). In the Christian Middle Ages, the German mystics referred to the supreme Essence by which creation is sustained and in which it is rooted, *the Ground of Being*. Earlier, St. Augustine claimed that *"God gave form to formless matter"* (*Confessiones* XII, 12). Using such expressions, mystics try to endorse the claim that these concepts do not derive from rational reflection but are manifestations of a domain transcending human thought.

The fundamental features of genuine mystical experience are thus not directly reflected by the concepts, images and technical terms used for describing a mystical event, but refer to the 'ur-phenomena'[5] (in Albrecht's terminology) or *'sacralia'*[6] underlying a mystical experience: it is these 'ur-phenomena' (or 'ultimate phenomena') that constitute the perennial archetypal core of mysticism and the ultimate stage of religiosity. Albrecht shows persuasively in this book that 'ur-phenomena' are a 'given', i.e., an existential facticity, even though 'ur-phenomena' elude scientific verification and cannot be traced to any preceding natural cause. 'Ur-phenomena' can only be cognitively grasped in an act of *'spiritual perception'*. The mystic's persistent capacity for transcendental perception thus provides a hermeneutic key to the understanding of the mystical experiences of all generations. Mystical experience and the language by which it is conveyed is thus unique: it cannot be compared to any other experience, and the language of the realm of mysticism and prophecy differs significantly from the literal meaning of ordinary speech. Therefore, the reader of today who is unfamiliar with the mystics' idiolect will consider the language of the mystics obscure, or abstruse and unintelligible. Hence such metaphoric expressions as *the path of fire* (Blaise

---

5   By 'ur-phenomenon' Albrecht understands a phenomenon that cannot be inferred from any other natural phenomenon or be explained rationally by causation. An 'ur-phenomenon' or 'ultimate phenomenon' is a proven and evident fact of human existence, though its origin is unknown and ultimately inexplicable. 'Ur-phenomena' include, for instance, 'love', 'spirit', 'freedom', 'life' and are an existential 'facticity'.
6   The term *'sacralia'* refers to archetypal elements of (prophetic) inspiration that emerge in a mystical experience and are peculiar expressive means in sacred (mystical and prophetic) texts (see SAKAGUCHI, A. *Sprechakte der Mystischen Erfahrung*. Freiburg and Munich: Alber, 2015. 360ff.).

Pascal) or *the dark night of the soul* (John of the Cross) are censured as vague and incomprehensible. However, a reader familiar with mysticism and the writings of prophets and mystics knows that these metaphors and symbolic expressions in mystical texts refer to the stage of spiritual purification by which the mystic is enabled to achieve complete detachment from this world and thus from discursive (conditioned) thinking. In mystical theology the perfect state of spiritual detachment from this world is termed *mystical death*. This metaphor suggests that in this state man has entered a space beyond language and (discursive) thinking. Albrecht has termed this spiritual condition "Versunkenheitsbewusstsein" ('consciousness of perfect calmness and alertness'). It is a mental state in which the mystic is temporarily set apart from the realm of multiplicity. In this state he can use the language differently than outsiders.

Since a mystic's unconventional mode of expression springs from a unique mode of perception of reality, a mystic's language may best be approached from the perspective of apophatic (negative) theology[7]. An apophatic mode of expression articulates in negative terms what is ultimately ineffable, employing such epithets as *incomprehensible, inexplicable, mysterious, unintelligible, ineffable, infinite, timeless, absolute, non-spatial*, or expressions like *unfathomable Nothingness*, or *the Void*. The mystical discourse about the trans-intelligible Otherness is thus couched in terms of apophatic negation. Apophatic theology is a branch of theology which is based on the conviction that God endures beyond all existence, and that divine perfection exceeds all human dimensions. Apophatic theology ('mystical theology') stipulates that God encompasses, and at the same time transcends, the entire realm of being; this manifests God's perfection, and conversely, man's finiteness and imperfection. In apophatic theology mysticism

---

[7] The term 'apophatic' or 'negative theology' and the complementary notion of 'affirmative' or 'positive theology' can be traced to Pseudo-Dionysius Areopagita. The former term derives from Greek *apophatikos* ('ineffable', 'unspeakable', 'stating something by way of negation'); the antonym originates from Greek *kataphatikos* ('affirmative', 'stating something in positive terms'). The terminological differentiation between 'negative' and 'positive theology' is, however, rarely used in contemporary Christian theology.

is seen as the highest stage of faith; 'symbolic theology', by contrast, is assigned the lowest level of religious belief. An authentic mystical experience transcends any known experience and surpasses anything that can be imagined or grasped rationally in this world. In order to describe such an experience, apophatic theology resorts primarily to rhetorical devices of negation. Albrecht's concepts of 'personal mysticism' versus 'a-personal mysticism' can be said to correspond to the notions of cataphatic versus apophatic modes of expression.

In this context we should also mention that in mysticism and folk-religion some identical expressions can be found. For example, the terms *purgatory*, *resurrection* and *ascension* are not only used in mystical writings but appear also in vernacular religious texts. The meaning of these terms, however, differs significantly between mystical and vernacular devotional traditions. We should, moreover, be aware that mystics were often forced by the church, or by secular institutions controlled by the church, to adapt their testimonies to conform to accepted theological teaching. Personal records of mystical experience generally required the approval of the spiritual counsellor or were even modified by the mystic's spiritual advisor(s). Evidence of this practice is, for instance, reflected in the recurrent use of theological concepts like *Faith, Son of God, Christ, Holy Communion*, and recurrent references to the persons of *the Holy Trinity*. This means that records of mystical experience by Christian mystics are revised versions of the original account of a mystic's personal experience. And often retractions and apologetic annotations were inserted to meet the demands of doctrinal authority. Teresa of Avila, for instance, concludes her final work *The Interior Castle* with the apologetic avowal: "If these writings contain any error, it is through my ignorance; I submit in all things to the teachings of the holy Catholic Roman Church, of which I am now a member, as I protest and promise I will be both in life and death."[8]

Mystics generally reiterate their own smallness and humble existence in the face of God's majesty and omnipotence. They emphasize

---

8   TERESA of AVILA. *The Interior Castle or The Mansions*. Ed. and trans. Benedict Zimmerman. 3rd ed. Grand Rapids, MI: Christian Classics Ethereal Library, 1921. 300.

throughout that they are incapable of verbalizing adequately what has been revealed to them in the visions and spiritual experiences. They also emphasize throughout the inability to know God in His fullness. They insist that only a few aspects of the mystical encounter with the Divine are open to cognitive perception, and thus to verbal expression. What the mystics are generally willing to confess – albeit with due humility and reverent awe – is the overwhelming impact that the encounter with the Divine has had on their whole being. The charismatic mystics testify that the encounter with the 'divine mysteries' has had persevering life-transforming effects though the experience as such is ultimately ineffable. The latter claim can be found, for instance, in the personal testimony of Al-Ghazali (1058–1111), one of the most important Islamic mystics:

> [Dear reader, I beg you to] ... ask forgiveness for me for anything wherein my pen has erred, or my foot has slipped. For it is a hazardous thing to plunge into the fathomless sea of the divine mysteries; and hard, hard it is to assay the discovery of the Lights Supernal that are beyond the Veil.[9]

Not all the testimonies of mystics are as eloquently couched as Al-Ghazali's; there are numerous accounts, particularly by female mystics, that are rendered in a rather simple, almost childlike language. This applies especially to situations in which the mystic or visionary is transported into states of ecstasy, struggling to find adequate expression for the ineffable bliss, splendour and uniqueness of the overwhelming experience with which he/she has been gratified.

Despite the great variety on the level of linguistic expression in mystical writings – with its plethora of symbols, metaphors, analogies, personifications, hyperboles, paradoxes, allegories and parables – resulting from the mystics' attempts to convey what is ultimately inexpressible, the underlying experience of these mystical texts is in part accessible to psychological enquiry. Albrecht has successfully examined a large corpus of mystical records from different periods and cultural and religious traditions in his endeavour to elucidate phenomenologically the core of mystical experience.

---

9   AL-GHAZALI. *Mishkât Al-Anwar.* (*The Niche for Lights*). Trans. and introd. by William Gairdner. London: Royal Asiatic Society, 1924. 175.

In this context I would also like to call attention to the studies of Adolf Reinach (1883–1917), a German phenomenologist and law theorist who contrasted social acts that originate from the highest religious experiences to the type of 'trans-worldly acts' ("überirdische Akte"), to acts of social behaviour rooted in the secular sphere ('worldly acts', "irdische Akte") (Reinach [1916/1917]).[10] Reinach inaugurated a new approach to religion, which had been widely displaced in western thought before the 20th century.

Finally, it should be added that Albrecht introduced a considerable number of neologisms and idiosyncratic technical terms for which there is no exact equivalent in English. Hence several of Albrecht's concepts required paraphrasing in English translation. Yet, on the whole, the semantic meanings of Albrecht's German terms have been adequately rendered in English. The author of this Foreword is confident that the English edition of *Das Mystische Erkennen* will arouse a great deal of interest in the English-speaking world and provide new incentives for the cross-cultural and interdisciplinary study of mysticism and the spiritual nature of man.

Alicja Sakaguchi
November 2019
Poznań University, Poland

---

10 REINACH, Adolf. [*Religiöse*] *Aufzeichnungen*. (1916/1917). *Sämtliche Werke*. 2 vols. Ed. Karl Schuhmann and Barry Smith. Munich: Philosophia, 1989. 589–611.

GENERAL INTRODUCTION

Franz K. Woehrer

"... mit dem ougen, da inne ich got sihe, daz ist daz selbe ouge, dâ inne mich got siht: min ouge unde gotes ouge daz ist ein ouge und ein gesiht und ein bekennen und ein minnen." [1]
["The eye with which I see God is the same eye with which God sees me: my eye and God's eye are one eye, one seeing, one knowing, and one love."[2]]
Meister ECKHART (c. 1260–1328)

"By truly emptying the self, the field of consciousness can reflect an object just as it is."
Kitaro NISHIDA (1870–1945)[3]

"When reposing in the 'quiet state of alertness', this hyper-lucid and vacated condition of consciousness affords the medium in which thinking may occur autonomously and without being disrupted by any other mental process. Thinking thus acquires the quality of an immaculate tool enabled to achieve the highest capacity possible ..."
Carl ALBRECHT (1902–1965)[4]

---

1 ECKHART, Meister. *Deutsche Predigten und Traktate*. Ed. Franz Pfeiffer. 2nd ed. Göttingen: Vandenhoeck & Ruprecht, 1908. Sermon XCVI (*Qui audit me, non confundetur*. Eccles. 24:30). 309.
2 WALSHE, Maurice O'C., Ed. and Trans. *The Complete Mystical Works of Meister Eckhart*. New York: Crossroad, 2009. Sermon 57, 298.
3 NISHIDA, Kitarō. *Kitarō Zenshū* [*Complete Works of Nishida Kitarō*]. Tokyo: Iwanami, 1987–89. Vol. IV, 221.
4 ALBRECHT, Carl. *Psychology of Mystical Consciousness*. Trans., introd. and annotated by F. K. Woehrer. New York: Crossroad, 2019. 214.

Bernard McGinn was one of the first scholars in the English-speaking world to proclaim that Albrecht's psychological studies into the nature of mysticism are 'outstanding'. In his monumental study *The Presence of God* he draws special attention to "... Carl Albrecht, physician, philosopher, and mystic, [who] stands out amongst recent German thinkers [who] have written directly on the meaning of mysticism ... though his writing is little known outside Germany."[5] McGinn refers explicitly to Albrecht's *Das Mystische Erkennen* (1958) and the monograph study *Das Mystische Wort: Erleben und Sprechen in Versunkenheit* (1974)[6], which is partly a scholarly study on Albrecht and partly a lengthy postscript by Albrecht on his research. Neither of these two books has previously been translated. Albrecht's first book, *Psychologie des Mystischen Bewußtseins* (1951), not expressly mentioned by McGinn, has meanwhile appeared in English translation.[7] Whereas Albrecht's studies have had a significant influence on the study of mysticism in German-speaking countries to this very day, they have gone largely unnoticed outside Germanophone academia.

The reception of Albrecht in central Europe was widespread from the early 1970s onward. It was spearheaded by the charismatic Jesuit spiritual counsellor Hugo Enomiya-Lassalle (1898–1990). He was the first to recognize the heuristic potential of Albrecht's innovative empirical enquiries into mysticism. He was not only impressed by the scope and detailed conception of Albrecht's psychology of mystical

---

5 McGINN, Bernard. *The Presence of God. A History of Christian Mysticism.* Vol. I, *The Foundations of Mysticism.* London: SCM, 1991. Quotations 313; bibliographical references to *Das Mystische Erkennen.* Bremen: Schünemann, 1958, and *Das Mystische Wort: Erleben und Sprechen in Versunkenheit.* Mainz: Grünewald, 1974. 433.

6 ALBRECHT, Carl. *Das Mystische Wort. Erleben und Sprechen in Versunkenheit.* Ed. and introd. Hans A. Fischer-Barnicol. Preface by Karl Rahner. Mainz: Grünewald, 1974.

7 The annotated English edition of ALBRECHT, Carl, *Psychologie des Mystischen Bewußtseins* (1951, reprinted in 1958, 1990 and 2019) has been published by Crossroad: ALBRECHT, Carl. *Psychology of Mystical Consciousness.* Trans., introd. and annotated by F. K. Woehrer. New York: Crossroad, 2019.

consciousness, but also by its sound, unprecedented empirical foundation. Unlike other studies in this field, Albrecht's research was based not only on a representative corpus of mystical records from western and eastern mystics, but also on the scientist's own mystical experiences, which were, over and beyond this, not merely recorded from memory, but documented directly from 'spontaneous mystical utterances' spoken *during* an ongoing mystical encounter. These immediate 'mystical utterances', simultaneously recorded manually by a confidante (and/or on tape), provided empirical data of supreme immediacy and authenticity.

Enomiya-Lassalle spent nearly half of his life as a Christian missionary in Japan, where he acquired firsthand knowledge of Zen-Buddhist meditation. On one of his visits home after World War II, he came across two of Albrecht's books: *Psychologie des Mystischen Bewußtseins* and *Das Mystische Erkennen*. He immediately recognized the striking affinities between Albrecht's phenomenological description of specific states of consciousness and the method of self-emptying deep relaxation applied by Albrecht (termed "Versenkung") and the practice of Zen-meditation. Both mental practices are aimed at the withdrawal of the mind from stimuli of the external world for the purpose of overcoming the scattered 'waking consciousness' in favour of a serene, calm and emptied state of mind. Albrecht's meditational method is based on J. H. Schultz's 'Autogenic Training'[8], which has psychosomatic and mind-expanding effects comparable to those induced by Zen meditation. Enomiya-Lassalle first drew attention to these affinities in *Meditation als Weg zur Gotteserfahrung* (1972).[9] By that time he had become a distinguished spiritual counsellor not only in Catholic Europe but also in India. Over and beyond this, he had become a highly respected Zen master in Japan and Europe. In *Zen und Christliche Spiritualität* (1987)[10] he

---

8 SCHULTZ, J. H. *Das Autogene Training (Konzentrative Selbstentspannung). Versuch einer Klinisch-praktischen Darstellung.* Leipzig: Thieme, 1932.
9 ENOMIYA-LASSALLE, Hugo, S.J. *Meditation als Weg zur Gotteserfahrung. Eine Anleitung zum Mystischen Gebet.* Mainz: Grünewald, 1972.
10 ENOMIYA-LASSALLE, Hugo, S.J. *Zen und Christliche Spiritualität.* Munich: Kösel, 1987.

reiterates his appraisal of Albrecht, stating that the German psychologist has established "... a concept of mysticism that does not only embrace Christian mysticism and the mysticism of non-Christian religions, but one that can also be accepted by science" (27).

Enomiya-Lassalle's appreciative assessment of Albrecht alerted another eminent Jesuit theologian to the pioneering research of the German medical doctor Karl Rahner. Rahner even met Albrecht in the 1960s and was impressed by his sincere commitment to the research of mysticism. He praised Albrecht's exceptional capacity for subtle phenomenological analysis of mental processes and mystical states of consciousness in a public speech delivered in 1976. In this lecture Rahner included Albrecht among the distinguished Christian mystics who shared with him the rare ability of minute introspective psychological analysis:

> Mystics are witnesses of a spiritual experience, and basically there is no reason why we should not deem the testimony of their experience as a whole incredible ... if we ... consider that amongst the mystics of the mystical tradition there have always been individuals of extraordinary sobriety endowed with a highly acute sense of observation; this can be traced throughout the centuries until the present to the days of Carl Albrecht, the mystic, who was at the same time an excellent medical doctor, psychologist, philosopher and empirical scientist. This much is certain: there are human beings who are courageous enough to testify to us credibly their experience of the Spirit.[11]

Shortly before Rahner gave this speech at a conference, he had complied with the request of Hans A. Fischer-Barnicol, the editor of *Carl Albrecht. Das Mystische Wort* (1974), to write a preface to the book. In this preface Rahner again praised the heuristic value of Albrecht's studies for both theology and the understanding of mysticism, stating that his books are "... important contributions to the conception of a theology of mysticism, which has as yet to

---

11 Rahner's public speech on the 'Experience of the Holy Spirit' was published in 1978, four years after the publication of *Das Mystische Wort*. Cf. RAHNER, Karl. "Erfahrung des Heiligen Geistes." *Schriften zur Theologie*. Vol. 13. Zurich: Benziger, 1978. 226–51. Passage quoted: 230.

be developed."¹² This aside, he appreciated Albrecht's insights as a much-needed critical corrective to the ongoing process of secularization and to the spiritual deprivation in western society, as well as to the zealotry of esoteric movements within and outside the Roman Catholic Church.

The late Cardinal Hans Urs von Balthasar was another noted Jesuit theologian who responded positively to Albrecht's empirical approach to mystical experience. He considered Albrecht's conception of mysticism fully compatible with the tenets of mystical theology. For von Balthasar, Albrecht's studies do not conflict with the theological conception of mysticism, since Albrecht categorically denies that mystical experience could ever be generated deliberately by personal effort. The meditational method of self-emptying applied by Albrecht is merely a method of transforming consciousness from the scattered condition of the 'waking state' into the emptied, lucid and 'quiet state of alertness'¹³ ("Versunkenheit" in Albrecht's terminology). This, however, is not a mystical state, but only the ideal mental setting for *witnessing* a mystical event, if it 'arrives' in consciousness. Albrecht insists that a mystical encounter may occur at any time, in any individual and in any state of consciousness – a claim that is entirely consonant with the theology of grace. Albrecht's insistence on the 'givenness' of a mystical event is understood by von Balthasar as a psychologist's version of the theological notion of *gratia gratis data*. The 'living God', von Balthasar states, is free to reveal Himself *ad libitum* anytime and anywhere, irrespective of the recipient's given state of mind or disposition, which means that God is free to reveal Himself in the self-induced state of "Versunkenheit" just as in the state of ecstasy, the 'waking state', or in any other state of consciousness. Von Balthasar was convinced that "[s]omething of

---

12   ALBRECHT, Carl. *Das Mystische Wort. Erleben und Sprechen in Versunkenheit*. Ed. Hans A. Fischer-Barnicol. Mainz: Grünewald, 1974. xiv. (English translation provided.)

13   The term 'quiet state of alertness' was coined in the 1960s by the American psychologist Roland Fischer. Cf. FISCHER, Roland. "State-Bound Knowledge: 'I Can't Remember What I Said Last Night, but It Must Have Been Good'." Ed. Richard Woods. *Understanding Mysticism*. London: Athlone, 1981. 306–11.

this kind [i.e., an encounter with the 'living God' in the state of "Versunkenheit"] must have occurred to Carl Albrecht, who on the basis of these experiences has found his way into the Catholic Church."[14]

The first full-length study of Albrecht was the doctoral thesis of Simon Peng-Keller, published in 2003 as *Gottespassion in Versunkenheit. Die Psychologische Mystikforschung Carl Albrechts aus Theologischer Perspektive*. Peng-Keller, at the time professor of Spiritual Care at the university of Zurich, assesses Albrecht's empirical investigations into mystical consciousness from a theological perspective. He acknowledges the exceptional epistemological and heuristic significance of Albrecht's research for theology and the interdisciplinary study of mysticism. Peng-Keller has recently created the website <christliche-kontemplation.ch>, in which Albrecht is given ample space. A succinct appraisal of Albrecht's achievements is provided by Peng-Keller in the preface to the present book and (with a different focus) in his preface to *Carl Albrecht. Psychology of Mystical Consciousness*.[15]

Albrecht's reception in Europe can be traced throughout the late 20th and early 21st centuries. A representative example is the encyclopaedic study *Die Mystik in den Religionen der Welt* by Eleonore Bock, first published in 1991 and, in a revised edition, in 2009.[16] Bock, though a chemist by profession, devoted most of her life to the cross-cultural study of world religions and mysticism. She had expert

---

14 VON BALTHASAR, Hans Urs. "Zur Ortsbestimmung Christlicher Mystik." In Werner BEIRERWALTES, Hans Urs von BALTHASAR and Alois M. HAAS. *Grundfragen der Mystik*. Einsiedeln: Johannes, 1974. 37–71. The passage quoted in the German source reads: "Man kann zwar, mit Jacques Maritain, der Meinung sein, in 'transzendentaler Meditation' könne der Mensch dazu gelangen, seine eigene Seelensubstanz zu gewahren; aber niemand kann es dem lebendigen Gott verwehren, sich dem Menschen, falls es ihm so gefällt, in dieser Schau kundzutun. Derartiges muß doch wohl Carl Albrecht widerfahren sein, der aufgrund solcher Erfahrungen den Weg zur katholischen Kirche fand" (46-47).
15 ALBRECHT, Carl. *Psychology of Mystical Consciousness*. Trans., introd. and annotated by F. K. Woehrer. New York: Crossroad, 2019. xiii–xx.
16 BOCK, Eleonore. *Die Mystik in den Religionen der Welt*. 1991. 2nd ed. Münster: Principal, 2009.

knowledge of Albrecht's works and considered his findings so important that she dedicated a full chapter to his research: "Carl Albrecht: Psychologie der Mystik" (531–44). In this chapter, Bock offers a balanced evaluation of Albrecht's psychology of mysticism and draws special attention to his unique methodology, which enabled him to probe more deeply into the 'core' of mysticism than any other study to date. She emphasizes that, owing to the unprecedented method of verbalizing ongoing mystical experience, Albrecht was able to disclose features of the 'core' of mystical experience which she claims are shared by 'all varieties of mystical experience across time and space':

> Carl Albrecht's psychological investigation of varieties of mystical experience have confirmed the pivotal issues described by many mystics of all mystical traditions and religions, even though his perspective is that of the modern Western scientist. This is seen as an important indication that there is indeed a 'common core' to all varieties of mystical experience across time and space (543). [English translation provided – FKW.]

One of the more recent academic studies in which Albrecht's works are used as an epistemological reference-frame for the interpretation of mystographical and prophetic texts is *Sprechakte der Mystischen Erfahrung*[17] by the Polish linguist Alicja Sakaguchi. In this voluminous philological study, the comprehensive corpus of mystical and prophetic texts is examined from a linguistic perspective in which Albrecht's findings provide a viable heuristic fundament for the hermeneutics of idiosyncratic tropes in mystical writings.

Outside the Germanophone world, the reception of Albrecht has been rather sparse. The only notable exception in the English-speaking world – except for Bernard McGinn – has been Harvey Egan, a professor of theology at Boston College. Egan, like Rahner and Enomiya-Lassalle, a Jesuit, has recognized the potential of Albrecht's studies for exploring mysticism and commends them in *Christian Mysticism*.

---

17 SAKAGUCHI, Alicja. *Sprechakte der Mystischen Erfahrung. Eine Komparative Studie zum Sprachlichen Ausdruck von Offenbarung und Prophetie*. Freiburg im Breisgau: Alber, 2015.

The Future of a Tradition.[18] He expresses his regret, though, that "... the studies on mysticism by the German psychologist and physician Carl Albrecht ... have been undeservedly neglected" (252). He appreciates Albrecht's empirical approach, as it is aimed at truth and objectivity and because it is – unlike many scientific studies in this field – neither inherently sceptical, nor reductionist, nor tainted by ideological bias:

> Albrecht's careful phenomenological studies show that mysticism cannot be reduced to intrapsychic processes. Although certain phases of the mystical ascent may involve some regression, neither regression nor pathology explains it. For Albrecht, the mystical consciousness is a 'phenomenological state' (sic!).[19] This means that it cannot be reduced to anything else, because it contains an irreducible essence that must be studied for its own right. Although science can and must study this irreducible essence, it demands of its very nature a theological and religious explanation as well. In short, scientific investigation alone cannot do sufficient justice to the mystical consciousness. (Egan 252–53)

After the publication of *Psychology of Mystical Consciousness* in 2019 and the current release of *Mystical Recognition*, Albrecht's main works are finally available in English and thus accessible on a global scale in the *lingua franca* of the sciences and humanities.

Readers of the present book who are not yet familiar with *Psychology of Mystical Consciousness* may, however, wonder why Albrecht's research should still be relevant in 2020, considering that his empirical studies were carried out some seventy years ago. And since the 1950s a plethora of scholarly and scientific books on mysticism have, after all, been published worldwide, so that it would seem reasonable to suppose that Albrecht's books and insights have meanwhile become obsolete. This, however, is not the case. Therefore, it is worth considering the possible reasons for the enduring value of Albrecht's studies.

---

18   EGAN, Harvey, S.J. *Christian Mysticism. The Future of a Tradition*. New York: Pueblo, 1984.

19   This is obviously Egan's flawed translation of the German term "Phänomenletztheit", which is correctly rendered as 'ultimate phenomenon' in English.

There are several reasons why the results of Albrecht's research have stood the test of time, the first being the rare coincidence that the meticulous scientist, medical doctor and originally religious sceptic was turned into a mystic in the course of his enquiries into the nature of mystical consciousness. The awe-inspiring impact of the mystical experiences encountered during his scientific enterprise turned Albrecht into a deeply religious Christian mystic. The effects of these mystical encounters – as well as of their loss – had an enduring effect on his life that lasted until his death.

The second major reason for the enduring value of Albrecht's insights is the fact that they are grounded in a double test of truth: Albrecht's findings do not just rely on critical reflection and the rational analysis of a large corpus of records by approved mystics, but are also the result of a dual test of verification. One test was imposed by Albrecht's ethics as a scientist, which demanded that all empirical data had to be screened for their objectivity and truthfulness. The second test was levied by the 'cleansing fire of mystical conscience' (as Albrecht puts it): all of his personal mystical experiences were only allowed to be articulated in 'mystical utterances', if the wording conformed truthfully to the underlying experience. The 'mystical utterances' were, in other words, subjected to a rigorous process of purification by the function of 'mystical conscience'.

This unique method of transforming mystical experience into 'spontaneous verbal utterances' during an ongoing mystical event is the primary reason for the exceptional authenticity and unparalleled immediacy of the empirical data upon which Albrecht's findings are based. Before he began his investigations into mystical consciousness, Albrecht had adapted J. H. Schultz's method of 'Autogenic Training' for therapeutic uses in his practice as a psychotherapist. The introspective method of deep-relaxation ("Versenkung") turned out to be not only an effective therapy against stress, neurotic disorders, states of restlessness and depression, but also an efficient method for transforming the scattered state of the 'waking consciousness' into a fully homogeneous, calm, clear and emptied mental condition. By 'emptying' the mind, a serene state of consciousness can be attained, one marked by enhanced inner clarity, inner peace and increased alertness to 'incoming' phenomena in the vista of the 'inner eye'. In phenomenological terms, the state of "Versunkenheit" corresponds closely to what in eastern mystical traditions is known as 'mindfulness'. In this lucid and vacated mental state, the only active function remaining is the capacity of the 'inner eye' ('inner sight', "Innenschau"). This exceptionally clear mental state differs from any other state of consciousness available to man, notably from both states of increased arousal (like the normal 'waking state', and various stages of the 'ecstatic consciousness') and states of decreased arousal (somnambulist states, daydreaming, hypnosis, deep-sleep and various drug-induced states). "Versunkenheit" is phenomenologically defined as "… a fully integrated, homogeneous, hyper-lucid and vacated state of consciousness; in it the flow of experience is slowed down; it is sustained by the persevering mood of calmness, and the only active function remaining in the otherwise entirely passive 'experiencing I' is the capacity of 'inner sight'."[20]

Yet the mere fact that Albrecht has identified and phenomenologically described in detail the state of "Versunkenheit" is not the pioneering achievement for which he deserves acclaim. The state of 'mindfulness' is, after all, an altered state of consciousness which has from time immemorial been reported by mystics and ancient sages as the desired goal of meditation or of related techniques of transforming the state of consciousness, such as contemplation, spiritual prayer, yoga, Zazen, or Dervish-dancing (to name only a few). The purifying, emptying and calming effects of these meditational methods have, in other words, long been common knowledge amongst contemplatives and mystics across cultural traditions. Though numerous antecedents of Albrecht's concept of "Versunkenheit" might be quoted here, only a few may suffice to corroborate this claim.

In Christian mysticism, a description that has evident affinities with Albrecht's practice of "Versenkung" and its progress toward the state of "Versunkenheit" can be found as early as the fourth century in the teaching of Evagrius of Ponticus (ca. 345–399). Evagrius was one of the first Christian contemplatives to employ the method of self-emptying by spiritual prayer. His advice to an adept has obvious

---

[20] ALBRECHT, Carl. *Psychology of Mystical Consciousness*. Trans., introd. and annotated by F. K. Woehrer. New York: Crossroad, 2019. 162.

psychological similarities with Albrecht's psychological-phenomenological account of the secular practice of "Versenkung":

> When you are praying, do not shape within yourself any image of the Deity, and do not let your mind be stamped with the impress of any form; but approach the Immaterial in an immaterial manner ... Prayer means the shedding of thoughts ... Blessed is the intellect that has acquired complete freedom from sensations during prayer.[21]

Two centuries after Evagrius, Pseudo-Dionysius promoted a similar method of spiritual prayer as a 'natural' preparation for the supernatural gift of 'infused contemplation'. The teaching of Pseudo-Dionysius became the prevailing method of 'contemplation' in the apophatic tradition of Christian spirituality, which can be traced from the sixth century through the Middle Ages and the modern era to the present.[22] Similarly, in Hinduism, diverse methods of vacating the mind had been developed from ancient times. If a 'mystic' wishes to attain the state of 'mindfulness', "[a]ll the mystic has to do is to empty his mind from thoughts, images and forms, what is called *nirvikalpa* in all the traditions of Yoga."[23] In Buddhism, the adept is taught to 'withdraw from this world' and to empty the mind by passing through the four (in other traditions six) stages of *jhana*.[24] In Zen Buddhism, an analogous notion is expressed in the teaching of the 20th-century Zen master Nishida: "By truly emptying the self, the field of consciousness can reflect an object just as it is."[25]

Albrecht's psychological phenomenology of "Versenkung" and of the state of "Versunkenheit" is thus perfectly consonant with

---

21 Source: McGINN, Bernard, and John MEYENDORFF, eds. *Christian Spirituality I. Origins to the Twelfth Century*. New York: Crossroad, 1985. 399.

22 Cf. WOEHRER, Franz K. "*The Cloud of Unknowing*: A Late Medieval Example of Apophatic Spiritual Guidance." *Studies in Spirituality* (Louvain, Belgium) 7 (1997): 113–44.

23 BÄUMER, Bettina, ed. *Mysticism in Shaivism and Christianity*. New Delhi: Printworld, 1997. xiv.

24 Cf. CONZE, Edward. *Buddhist Meditation*. London: Unwin, 1972. 48; 113–18.

25 NISHIDA, Kitarō. *Kitarō Zenshū* [*Complete Works of Nishida Kitarō*]. Tokyo: Iwanami, 1987–89. Vol. IV, 221.

received teaching on the effects of spiritual prayer and the practice of meditation in eastern and western mystical traditions. Hence Albrecht's findings are indirectly corroborated by the teachings of the mystics across cultures, just as, conversely, his empirical insights corroborate the veridical claims of the latter.

The congruity of Albrecht's state of "Versunkenheit" with descriptions of the analogous state of mystics by spiritual counsellors and mystics across mystical traditions may be extended to the concept of 'inward perception' ('inner sight', "Innenschau"). This concept refers to the capacity of inward perception, which reaches its highest potential in the serene state of 'quiet alertness' (viz., 'mindfulness'). It consists of the heightened receptivity to phenomena 'arriving' in the vista of the 'inward perception'. Amongst the phenomena appearing in its vista are such as are perceived as surfacing from within the 'individual self', and such as are perceived as 'arriving' from a domain beyond the confines of individual self. The former are entirely intra-subjective phenomena that do not qualify as instances of genuine mystical perception. The latter, by contrast, are perceived as intruding from an unknown trans-subjective domain and qualify potentially as mystical phenomena. They can be approved as such if they have revelatory import and are perceived as 'arriving' from an unknown, unfathomable sphere and experienced (in the widest sense) as an 'encounter' with 'the All-encompassing' or with unfathomable 'ontic Reality' (whatever its concrete mode of manifestation). When an 'encounter' of this kind occurs in the 'quiet state of alertness', the state of consciousness is transformed into a mystical state. Though a genuine mystical encounter is ultimately ineffable and incomprehensible, this does not fully apply when the mystical event occurs in the calm and serene state of 'quiet alertness'. In this mental condition the perceiver is able to grasp cognitively and phenomenologically some of the pivotal features of the 'mystical Otherness' when it appears in the vista of 'inner sight'. A mystical experience on this level may, for instance, be perceived as an encounter with 'unfathomable, all-encompassing Space', or with an ineffable 'Nothingness', a 'Loving Thou', or may consist of the 'awareness of an invisible numinous Presence', or the presence of an 'unfathomable Power' acting upon and within the perceiver. The mystical event is, in other words, experienced as an encounter with 'ontic Reality', which may take many different (personal and non-personal) forms. When the encounter is genuine, it has inevitably a transforming impact on the perceiver that lasts for a lifetime. Albrecht's pioneering contribution here is the claim that a mystical event can be acknowledged as genuine if it is sustained by the concurrent awareness that the perceiver has here and now become immersed in a living *'mystical relation'* with 'the All-encompassing'.

At the very beginning of his enquiries, Albrecht was dissatisfied with the circumstance that he had to rely only on records of mystical experience from the traditional canon of mystical writings, and thus on empirical data that were entirely subjective and likely to have been transformed by post-experiential interpretation. To overcome these epistemological deficiencies, he developed an empirical method that enabled him (and fellow practitioners) to speak during the ongoing process of self-emptying as well as when absorbed in the state of 'quiet alertness', including 'mystical states'. He knew from his therapeutic use of hypnosis that man's capacity to speak is retained in any state of consciousness (except for the state of cerebral coma). He also knew that speech can be elicited subconsciously in the state of "Versunkenheit" if the express intention to verbalize inner experience is 'programmed' in the practitioner's mind before embarking on the meditative process of "Versenkung". In this way Albrecht was able to bypass the mediating functions of reason and memory in obtaining records of inward experience. This methodological stratagem allowed him to verbalize ongoing experience and to have these 'spontaneous utterances' ("Versunkenheitsaussagen") chronicled simultaneously by a confidante in writing or recorded on tape.[26]

Albrecht distinguished between two kinds of 'spontaneous mystical utterances'. The first is a descriptive variety in which the perceiver's state of mind and response(s) to 'the All-encompassing' are verbalized. In this case, the 'mystical utterance' is prompted by the

---

26 Albrecht's 'spontaneous utterances' were recorded in writing by an eye-witness, usually his wife, his daughter or another trusted person. Some utterances were recorded on tape. "Versunkenheitssaussagen" spoken by fellow practitioners were all recorded by Albrecht.

mode of revelation of 'the mystical Object' in 'inner sight'; here the 'spontaneous utterance' is a spoken testimony of the living relationship between the perceiver and the 'mystical Object' perceived. The second variety (which is often intertwined with the former type) originates from the opaque phenomenon of the 'birth of the mystical word' (or of a sequence of words) in the mind of the perceiver when absorbed in the 'state of quiet alertness'.[27] In this case, a 'word' is perceived as 'arriving' in consciousness either intuitively, or aurally, or visually, or in a composite experience in which visual, auditory and cognitive modes of perception are intertwined. In a genuine event the experience is always interlinked with the simultaneous awareness of an existing mystical relationship with 'all-encompassing Reality' – for instance, the 'non-visual awareness of a numinous Presence'. In this complex experience the living 'mystical relation' between perceiver and the 'mystical Presence' becomes (as it were) incarnate in the 'mystical word', articulated in the perceiver's idiom, a concurrent 'mystical utterance'. Albrecht offers a succinct description of this elusive experience in *Psychology of Mystical Consciousness*,[28] and again in explanatory letters published in *Das Mystische Wort*.[29] The fact that the encounter with 'the all-encompassing mystical Presence' does not only become manifest in visions, auditions and numinous feelings, but also in tactile and somatic modes of mystical perception, and in moments of verbal and pre-verbal 'intuition' and 'spiritual illumination', may be difficult to grasp for a scholar of the 21st century. However, if viewed from a historical anthropological and cross-cultural perspective, the phenomenon of 'the birth of words' in a mystical event is less mysterious than it appears at first sight: 'inspired speech', 'the speaking in tongues', and instances of 'glossolalia' and related phenomena can be found across all religious and

---

27 This important variety of mystical experience claimed to be genuine by Albrecht is unfortunately not acknowledged as empirical fact by the linguist Sakaguchi in her 'Preface' to this study.

28 Cf. ALBRECHT, Carl. *Psychology of Mystical Consciousness*. Ed., trans. and annotated by F. K. Woehrer. New York: Crossroad, 2019. 219–20; 309–10.

29 Cf. ALBRECHT, Carl. *Das Mystische Wort. Erleben und Sprechen in Versunkenheit*. Ed. Hans A. Fischer-Barnicol. Mainz: Grünewald, 1974. 190–96.

cultural traditions. 'Inspired speech' is based on 'words infused' in altered states of consciousness. The phenomenon is an integral part of countless experiences of mystics and charismatics and documented in the sacred scriptures of world religions. The phenomenon may arguably be extended to the 'mantic speech' of the Delphic priestesses of classical antiquity, though in this context the mantic speech-acts appear to have occurred in a trance-like state induced by psychedelic drugs and not in a calm, hyper-lucid mental state equivalent to the 'quiet state of alertness'. Still, the fact remains that throughout the history of humanity, mystics, prophets, saints and sages were chosen to function as 'channels' for the Sacred Word to enter this world.[30]

Albrecht explains that when a 'word' surfaces in the mystical consciousness, the recipient is inevitably bound to transmit it truthfully in his/her personal idiom. The transfer from the pre-verbal intuition to the word articulated in the perceiver's linguistic code does not allow any interpretation because this process is surveiled by 'mystical conscience'. Any volitional intervention on the part of the perceiver would instantly terminate the mystical event. Due to the express summons to verbalize truthfully any intuition or an aural locution, 'mystical utterances' are usually replete with neologisms, unusual metaphoric descriptions and original lyrical expressions.

---

30 Cf. the gift of 'pneumatic speech', 'glossolalia', the ability of 'speaking in tongues' as witnessed by Paul in Christianity. – For studies in this field, see, for instance, FORBES, Christopher. "Early Christian Inspired Speech and Hellenistic Popular Religion." *Novum Testamentum* 28 (1986): 257–70. – STANLEY, Gordon, W. K. BARTLETT, and Terri MOYLE. "Some Characteristics of Charismatic Experience: Glossolalia in Australia." *Journal for the Scientific Study of Religion* 17 (1978): 269–77. – DARŌCZI, Anikó. "Ein Spiel der Worte, in dem das 'Urwirkliche' Atmet. – The Birth of the Mystical Word According to Carl Albrecht." In MIKLŌS, Vassányi, Enikő SEPSI, and Anikó DARŌCZI, eds.: *The Immediacy of Mystical Experience in the European Tradition*. New York: Springer Berlin Heidelberg 2017. 231–38. – From a theological perspective, the anagogic reading of the Prologue of the Gospel according to John 1.1–2 ("In the beginning was the Word, and the Word was with God, and the Word was God. (2) The same was in the beginning with God." *Authorized Version*) implies that the Divine Logos may become manifest also in the spiritual 'word' perceived by the mystic.

To facilitate understanding of this rather opaque phenomenon of the 'birth of the mystical word', it is illuminating to consider a striking analogue found in Tantric Shaivism. The affinities between Albrecht's account and the conception of the 'birth of the mystical word' in the writings of the Shaivist mystic Abhinavagupta (fl. 950–1020) are indeed astonishing. Of course Albrecht could not have known the works of Abhinavagupta, as they were unknown in Europe when Albrecht wrote his books. Only a few of Abhinavagupta's writings have so far been translated from Sanskrit into German, yet none before the 1990s.[31]

The Shaivist mystic distinguishes four hierarchical stages in the katabasis of the 'transcendental word' from transcendental reality into this mundane world: The 'transcendental (mystical) word', termed *parā vāc* in Sanskrit, reveals itself in the incipient stage visually (*paśyantī*) and intuitively on a subverbal level. Next, the 'mystical word' descends to the level of thought, entering the domain of the perceiver's cognitive and linguistic capacities. On this level, the 'mystical word' is transformed into the 'mediated word' of the recipient (*madhyamā*). Finally, on the fourth level, the mediated 'mystical word' is articulated aloud (*vaikharī*). When voiced, the 'mystical word' becomes part of this world of illusion, and as such inevitably refers back to its transcendental origin and triggers a process of spiritual recognition.[32]

The parallels between Abhinavagupta's conception of the 'mystical word' and Albrecht's description of the 'birth of the mystical word' are astonishing. Albrecht and the Hindu mystic appear to have identified the same elusive phenomenon independently across different cultural and historical contexts. This can be taken as evidence that Albrecht's claim that 'language' is a distinct mode of mystical experience is true. The Shaivist mystic's conception of 'mystical language' may, moreover, serve as a cogent reference-frame for the understanding of the 'mystical utterances' transmitted by Albrecht

---

31 BÄUMER, Bettina. *Abhinavagupta. Wege ins Licht. Texte des Tantrischen Sivaismus aus Kaschmir.* Zurich: Benziger, 1992.

32 Cf. BÄUMER, Bettina. *Abhinavagupta. Wege ins Licht. Texte des Tantrischen Sivaismus aus Kaschmir.* Zurich: Benziger, 1992. 91.

and provide a pre-emptive epistemological corrective to potential reductionist readings of the same.

Albrecht was clearly aware that the written accounts of his 'spontaneous mystical occurrences' are vulnerable to misunderstanding and misuse. For this reason, he destroyed most of them before his death; the few surviving documents are kept in the private archives of the Albrecht family. During his lifetime, he allowed only a small selection to be published, not least because these testimonies are imbued with intimately personal religious responses to his mystical encounters. In the documents that he released for publication he carefully removed all religious concepts and tokens of personal faith. The example quoted below, however, is an exception in this respect: it is a testimony taken from the archives of the Albrecht family that was originally not selected for publication, but allowed to be published by Albrecht's son thirty years after his father's death:[33]

> Tief begründet bin ich als Mensch. Der geheime Atem flutet als Leben in meinem Leibe und wenn ich jetzt den Urraum der Mystik wieder betrete, überkommt mich das Wundern darüber, dass ich einerseits in meiner menschlichen Gestalt das durchlichtete Leben so bluthaft gesund erfühle und dass andererseits der Raum der Gnade ohne jeden Inhalt ist. Die Leere ist nicht quälend ... Es ist sogar wohltuend in dieser Leere zu atmen, und mein Herz möchte jubeln – darüber dankbar sein, dass in diesem wunderbaren Raume niemals etwas geschehen kann, das nicht reines Eigentum Gottes ist. Jedes Wort, das ich hier spreche, ist aus der Selbstsicherheit des Wahrseins geboren.

---

33   Before his untimely death in 1965 at the age of 63, Carl Albrecht ordered most of the 500 spontaneous 'mystical (and non-mystical) utterances' that he had compiled over a period of twenty-five years to be destroyed. He allowed only a small number to be published in the appendix to *Das Mystische Wort* (245–78). Albrecht was obviously keen on preserving his privacy and on protecting these unique mystical documents from profane eyes. The documents were sacred to him, valued as tokens of divine grace. The passage quoted is from a 'mystical utterance' dated 3 March 1948. It was first published from the private archives by the Swiss theologian Peng-Keller, who was given access to the surviving documents by Ernst Albrecht, Carl Albrecht's son, when he worked on his doctoral thesis. Cf. PENG-KELLER, Simon. *Gottespassion in Versunkenheit. Die Psychologische Mystikforschung Carl Albrechts aus Theologischer Sicht.* Würzburg: Echter, 2003. 315–16.

[As a human being, I am deeply rooted in the Unfathomable. The secret breath permeates my life, flowing through my body; and now, as I enter again the primeval space of mysticism, I am, on the one hand, overwhelmed by wondrous awe as I may again feel life permeated by light so vividly and healthily in my human body; on the other hand, I perceive the room of grace, albeit entirely devoid of any content. This emptiness, however, is not painful ... It is even wholesome to breathe in this emptiness, and my heart desires to rejoice – to be grateful that in this miraculous room nothing can occur that is not entirely the property of God. Every single word I am speaking here has been born from the self-assured certainty of its truthfulness. (Translation provided – FKW).]

This passage is replete with religious concepts and indications of personal religious belief. Yet irrespective of these religious elements, this 'mystical utterance' reveals clearly that the controlling instance of reason is suspended and that every single word has been articulated only after having passed through the gates of 'mystical conscience'. What is eventually verbalized is a veridical 'mystogram' of the underlying experience while the perceiver is abiding in the 'sacred room of grace'.

In the subsequent example of a 'mystical utterance', dated 23 March 1949, a surprisingly intelligible account of the elusive experience of the 'birth of the mystical word' is given. The syntax of the 'mystical utterance' suggests, however, that only a part of the testimony (i.e., passages in present tense) was spoken while the perceiver was immersed in the 'state of quiet alertness', whereas the passages rendered in preterite tense appear to have been reported retrospectively from memory. This part cannot, therefore, be properly classified as a 'spontaneous mystical utterance':

> Ich war versunken – herausgelöst aus allem, was mir vertraut war. Ich glaubte knien zu müssen und horchte auf jede Regung, die in dieser seltsamen Stille zu mir herüber wehte. Ich fühlte diesen Hauch, der aus dem innersten Geheimnis dessen herüberkam, den ich als ein Nichts in meiner Hand gehalten hatte - diesen sorgsamen Hauch, der meine Ordnung zerschmolzen hat. Dann aber wurden Ehrfurcht, Dankbarkeit und Liebe so klar in mir, dass ich es wagte schutzlos vor Dem zu stehen, was mich verwandelte. Ich muss es zulassen, dass meine Augen aufgetan werden. In meiner Nacktheit stand ich da. In mir zittert etwas, was ich nicht verstehe. Und ich kann mich nicht bergen vor dem Übermass scheuer Worte. Es sind Worte, die aus einem neuen und

noch unverstandenen Wissen kommen und die irgendwie in der geheimsten Kammer meiner Liebe verborgen waren.³⁴

[I was absorbed by the calmness within – inwardly alert and entirely removed from everything that was familiar to me. I felt the desire to kneel down and to listen attentively to every single stirring in this mysterious hush and silence that emanated from the innermost depth of the Mystery and drifted softly toward me. It was a Mystery that I had held in my hand as a Nothingness which has melted away my ordered existence. But then reverent awe, gratitude and love became so clear to me that I ventured to stand exposed, defenceless before the One who has transformed me. I must allow my eyes to be opened. I was standing there in my nakedness. Something is shivering within me that I do not understand. I am unable to escape the gush of timid words [by which I am inundated]. It is words that come from a realm of knowledge that is new and unknown to me; these words seem to have been hidden somehow in the innermost secret chamber of my love. (Translation provided – FKW).]

The unfaltering sense of the realness and saneness of the experience, and especially the sense of certainty by which it is sustained, derives from the recognition that the 'experiencing self' is here and now engrossed in a living relationship with an 'unfathomable Mystery', which subsequently reveals Itself as a person-like 'mystical Presence' – 'the One'. The cognitive perception of the 'mystical relation' is the hallmark of any genuine mystical encounter and is identified by Albrecht as an 'ultimate phenomenon'.³⁵ The experience of the 'word' emerging from the depths of the 'unfathomable Mystery' is intertwined with the cognitive awareness of the 'mystical Presence'.

As 'spontaneous mystical utterances' are inherently revelatory in nature, they contain intellectual insights that cannot reasonably

---

34 Source: PENG-KELLER, Simon. *Gottespassion in Versunkenheit. Die Psychologische Mystikforschung Carl Albrechts aus Theologischer Perspektive*. Würzburg: Echter, 2003. 317.

35 The concept of the 'ultimate phenomenon' ("Phänomenletztheit") is explained by Albrecht in several places of the present book. The term refers to a primordial phenomenon which cannot rationally be accounted for, nor traced scientifically to a definitive origin. Despite their unfathomable origin, 'ultimate phenomena' are unquestionably real: they include, for instance, 'life', 'love', 'spirit', 'consciousness' and 'language'. Another 'ultimate phenomenon' identified by Albrecht is the 'mystical relation'. (This is further elaborated below.)

be explained as originating from the perceiver's store of knowledge. A 'spontaneous mystical utterance' is therefore best understood as a verbalized experience triggered by 'intuitions' instilled from a domain beyond the confines of the 'individual self'. From the evidence of the mystics, and of his own experience, Albrecht concludes that human beings are 'vessels' ("Gefäße") for the 'entrance of the Mystery' into the 'soul'. In a letter written a few months before his death he states: "Die Seele des Menschen ist erwählt, Durchgangsraum zu sein für den Eintritt des Geheimnisses in die Welt." ['The soul of man has been chosen to be a passageway for the entrance of the Mystery into the world.'[36]] In other words, Albrecht claims that every individual may be chosen to function as a 'channel' or 'medium' for transpersonal Reality to reveal itself.

The notion of a human being serving as 'channel' or 'medium' for the Logos to enter the world may be speculative and esoteric, but the notion has been an integral part of man's cultural and religious heritage. Numerous mystics of eastern and western mystical traditions might be quoted that support the realness of such a phenomenon. Surprisingly, it is even endorsed by an unexpected area of science: The German physicist and Nobel Laureate Werner Heisenberg expresses a similar view, insisting that 'spiritual illumination' is an empirical fact, albeit one confined to a few specially gifted individuals. In an essay published from his literary remains only in 2019, Heisenberg maintains that 'spiritual illumination' is a vital, inalienable source of any original creative achievement. He is adamant that the creative ingenuity of specially gifted individuals (e.g., great geniuses of the arts, literature, music and the sciences) does not spring from the creative capacity of the genius alone but from a cooperative artefact triggered and directed by 'spiritual illumination' ("geistige Erleuchtung"). For Heisenberg, 'spiritual illumination' is a rare gift vouchsafed to persons of great talent and promise by which they are empowered to produce artefacts of supreme artistic and/or intellectual value. When an act of 'spiritual illumination' occurs, he insists, the recipient has become the chosen 'medium' of a higher Power operating within and through him/her. It is a rare mystical event in which the recipient is

---

36 ALBRECHT, Carl. *Das Mystische Wort. Erleben und Sprechen in Versunkenheit.* Ed. Hans A. Fischer-Barnicol. Mainz: Grünewald, 1974. Letter dated 19 June 1964. 190.

infused with knowledge, intuitions, inspirations, illuminations and creative energy that enable him/her to produce artefacts that he/she could otherwise never have achieved:

> Die Menschen, in denen dies geschieht, sind eben nicht mehr nur Menschen, sondern sie sind die Werkstätten, in denen die schöpferischen Kräfte sichtbar wirken und Zeugnisse schaffen, die über alles Menschliche hinausweisen. Was in dieser obersten Schicht der Wirklichkeit entsteht, ist zugleich das Objektivste und das Subjektivste: Das Objektivste, denn der betreffende Mensch ist sich in jedem Augenblick des Schaffens bewusst, dass er hier im Auftrag einer anderen Welt handelt, die durch ihn hindurch schafft, und das Subjektivste, denn das Geschaffene konnte allein von diesem einen Menschen so gesagt oder geschrieben oder gedacht werden.[37]
>
> [Those special human beings ... [i.e., talented individuals blessed with the gift of 'spiritual illumination'] are not ordinary human beings any longer when they are instilled with 'spiritual illumination' but are converted into 'workshops' of creative powers which operate in them, producing testimonies that point beyond what is naturally human. Anything that originates from this highest layer of reality is most objective and most subjective at the same time. It is the most objective thing because the individual concerned is instantly clearly aware that he is acting at the summons of 'another world', which is creating through him. It is, on the other hand, the most subjective thing, because what is created could never have been achieved, written or thought by any other person than by the one special individual who has been gratified with the experience. (Translation provided – FKW).]

In light of these considerations it should come as no surprise that the results of Albrecht's research have stood the test of time. His psychological phenomenology and gnoseology of mysticism have proved to be consonant with concepts of mysticism across eastern and western mystical traditions. The pivotal insights gained in long-term empirical enquiries are epitomized in *Mystical Recognition* in ninety-seven propositions or 'key-findings' (called "Thesen" by Albrecht) which, taken together, offer a profound innovative epistemological foundation for any serious future research in mysticism.

Yet given these ground-breaking achievements, there are some provisos and limitations to be added to the appraisal of Albrecht's

---

37 HEISENBERG, Werner. *Ordnung der Wirklichkeit*. Ed. K. Kleinknecht. Munich: Springer, 2019. 183–84.

achievement. He has, of course, not achieved the impossible – a complete phenomenology, gnoseology of mystical experience within the confines accessible to empirical research. Though he has stretched empirical enquiry to the utmost thresholds of science, the introspective methodology applied by him imposed obvious limitations. This method permitted only reliable access to mystical phenomena occurring in the state of "Versunkenheit", whereas mystical experiences encountered in the state of 'ecstatic consciousness' can be covered only to a very limited extent, i.e., confined to phenomena perceived in the incipient stage of 'ecstasy'. Albrecht's phenomenology of mysticism is thus limited to phenomena perceived in the clear, calm, vacated and hyper-alert state of "Versunkenheit", in which the capacity of 'inward perception' is most highly developed; it is also the mental state most highly resilient to error and delusion. This 'quiet state of alertness' is the clearest and most unified state of consciousness available to man, and this is why the subject-object division can most clearly be perceived in it. It is in the 'quiet state of alertness' that the 'experiencing self' is able to distinguish unambiguously between phenomena that have surfaced from within the 'sphere of the self' and phenomena 'arriving' from a realm beyond the individual self. This capacity of discretion is by comparison impaired in the 'ecstatic consciousness', and entirely annulled in the ultimate stage of 'mystical ecstasy'. For this reason, Albrecht declined to expand his enquiries into the realm of 'ecstatic consciousness'.

Apart from the limitations imposed by empirical method, Albrecht levied limiting ideological parameters on the scope of his research. As a meticulous empirical scientist, he considered it imperative not to transgress into the disciplines of theology and metaphysics. He confined his enquiries to the disciplines of empirical psychology, psychological phenomenology and anthropology. Only in the final part of *Mystical Recognition* did he allow himself to roam into the domain of existentialist philosophy, as he considered it necessary to challenge Heidegger's concept of the hermeneutics of Dasein and his conception of fundamental ontology. Especially Heidegger's claim that 'care' is the primary 'existential' of human 'Dasein' is not shared by Albrecht. Although he acknowledges that 'care' is an 'existential' of human existence and as such an 'ultimate phenomenon', Albrecht insists that 'care' can be mitigated and even overcome if an individual is gratified with a genuine mystical event. If this happens, the individual experiences that there is a reassuring and persevering bond between him/her and the 'all-encompassing mystical Presence'. Thus, the cognitive awareness of a living 'mystical relation' becomes the primary 'existential' replacing that of 'care'. This aside, Albrecht questioned, as a matter of principle, that existentialist philosophy is an adequate approach to the ontological foundation of 'being-in-this-world'.

Mystical Recognition is basically an empirical study of mystical discretion extended to the thresholds of science. Albrecht had previously supplied a comprehensive psychological study on mysticism in *Psychology of Mystical Consciousness*. The present book is a sequel to the first study, in which Albrecht expanded his research into the domain of 'ontic Reality'. He tried to establish viable criteria for answering the fundamental question as to whether a mystical event is indeed the result of an empirical encounter with 'ontic Reality', or if claims of having experienced such an 'encounter' can be shown to be entirely delusory. If it is possible to trace alleged mystical events exclusively to intra-psychic phenomena, originating, for instance, from the unconscious, the subconscious, the imagination, or corollaries of a pathological condition (e.g., an epileptic seizure), or from side-effects of psycho-somatic, neurophysiological or neurochemical processes, such phenomena would have to be dismissed from the realm of genuine mystical experience. If this applied, mystical experiences would indeed be merely delusory fabrications of the human brain.[38] In the Foreword to the present book, Albrecht states that his ambitious goal in *Mystical Recognition* is to engage in a critical interdisciplinary study of 'mystical discretion':

> The goal of the present study ... is to go beyond the threshold of psychological phenomenology and probe more deeply into the core of mysticism.

---

38 Claims of this kind have been propagated from Freud through contemporary misotheism, spearheaded by Richard Dawkins and his Neo-Atheist disciples. For Dawkins, a mystical experience is merely a delusory occurrence, "a by-product of the misfiring of several modules ... [of the brain]." Cf. DAWKINS, Richard. *The God Delusion*. London: Bantam, 2006. 179.

[This book] ... focuses on two crucial interrelated questions: (1) Is it possible to ascertain that mysticism, after having been described and fully embraced phenomenologically, ... involves an encounter with an 'ultimate phenomenon' which cannot be traced further to any other source? And (2) if the first question can be answered affirmatively, the important ensuing question is: What is the relevance of mysticism for philosophical thinking?

To achieve this ambitious goal, Albrecht has analysed not only several hundred 'spontaneous mystical utterances', which he had compiled in more than two decades of research, but also three dozen records of mystics from western and eastern mystical traditions. The testimonies of the mystics were supplemented by accounts of paranormal experiences, such as reports of occult occurrences, descriptions of extrasensory perception and of other parapsychological phenomena, and accounts of experiences of the 'spirit world' by Rudolf Steiner ("Land der Geister").[39] The corpus of texts includes, furthermore, records of pseudo-mystical experience induced by mescaline and other psychedelic drugs (e.g., experiments reported by William James in *Varieties of Religious Experience*)[40] and experiences of 'cosmic consciousness' reported by R. M. Bucke.[41]

Overall, these paranormal phenomena are assigned to the category of 'pseudo-mysticism' by Albrecht. This, however, is no derogatory term, because pseudo-mystical experiences are, as Albrecht contends, part of empirical reality. Pseudo-mystical experiences are not *a priori* bogus, delusory or pathological, not least because such preternatural phenomena are often addressed in records of approved mystics and visionaries. Albrecht claims that a 'seer of spirits' like Steiner, or a perceiver of occult phenomena, has access to layers of empirical reality that are beyond the pale of normal sense perception. Paranormal experiences can, in a sane perceiver, be aroused by extraordinary sense perceptions and

---

39   Cf. STEINER, Rudolf. *Theosophie: Einführung in Übersinnliche Welterkenntnis und Menschenbestimmung*. New ed. Freiburg i. Br.: Novalis, 1946. 115–39.

40   Cf. JAMES, William. *Varieties of Religious Experience. A Study in Human Nature. Being the Gifford Lectures on Natural Religion Delivered at Edinburgh in 1901–1902*. [1902]. New York: Random House, 1929. 248–50; 377–84.

41   Cf. BUCKE, Richard M. *Cosmic Consciousness. The Evolution of the Human Mind*. New York: Dutton, 1901. 2.

be interlaced with paranormal inner perceptions. Apart from a hybrid visionary experience of this kind, there are occult experiences that are exclusively perceived by the 'inner eye' and subsequently projected onto the external world. Compared to a 'pictorial mystical vision', 'occult visions' are composed of objects and personages that are known from the external world and not grounded in an ineffable encounter with 'all-encompassing Reality', or 'an unfathomable Presence', or a 'loving Thou'. Over and beyond this, an 'occult experience' does not – like a genuine mystical event – arouse an overwhelming sense of bliss, ineffable joy, love, sacred awe, or a cognitive awareness of an extant 'mystical relation' between the perceiver and an 'unfathomable mystical Object'. An 'occult experience' thus has none of the pivotal characteristics of a genuine epiphanic 'mystical vision'.

In the first fifty pages of the book, Albrecht singles out the domain of 'pseudo-mysticism' for critical assessment by contrasting it to genuine varieties of mystical experience. In the succeeding part of the book, he focuses on diverse types of genuine mystical experiences, starting with pictorial visions and followed by non-pictorial (imageless) mystical visions. The detailed phenomenological and gnoseological analyses of about one hundred textual passages from mystical records comprise more than two hundred pages of the book. On the basis of these empirical data and his own recorded testimonies, Albrecht supplies a most comprehensive phenomenology and gnoseology of a broad range of visual, aural, non-visual (imageless), numinous, cognitive, somatic and verbal modes of mystical experience.

Albrecht's psychological phenomenology and gnoseology of mysticism is, for methodological reasons, strictly confined to varieties of *introvertive* mystical experience and, amongst these, to phenomena occurring in the state of "Versunkenheit".[42] The domain of *extrovertive* mystical experience (i.e., natural mystical experience and 'apparitions' perceived as occurring in external space) is excluded from Albrecht's concept of mysticism. 'Apparitions' are classified as phenomena in the 'twilight zone' between paranormal sensory perception and (pictorial) mystical vision. Although 'apparitions' are

---

42 Note: The terms 'introvertive' and 'extrovertive' mystical experience were introduced by STACE, Walter T. *Mysticism and Philosophy*. London: Macmillan, 1960.

acknowledged as potentially genuine varieties of mystical experience in traditional mystical typology and categorized as *visio corporalis*,[43] Albrecht excluded them from his concept of mysticism, which is defined thusly: "Mysticism is the 'arriving' of an 'All-encompassing' in the 'quiet state of alertness'."[44]

An additional methodological stricture on Albrecht's research is imposed by the fact that in empirical reality mystical occurrences consist of intricate structures with variously intertwined phenomenological patterns and modes of perception. The interlaced patterns of a singular mystical event must, however, be disentangled in scientific analysis and dealt with separately.

The first type of mystical experience examined is *pictorial visions* (equivalent to *visio imaginaria* or *visio spiritualis* in traditional mystical typology), followed by non-pictorial visions, notably 'visions of light' and other non-pictographic mystical perceptions. The latter include the 'sense of Presence' and other imageless modes of mystical perception, such as mystically 'infused' intuitions (corresponding to *visio intellectualis* in traditional typology) and the perception of the 'aura' of 'the all-encompassing Presence', as well as tactile, somatic, auditory, verbal and emotional varieties of mystical experience. The arduous process of segregating critically dozens of mystical phenomena individually resulted in ninety-seven 'key findings'. The most significant insight is the discovery of the 'mystical relation' ("mystische Relation") and its identification as a new 'ultimate phenomenon'.

---

43 In Christian mystical tradition, the hierarchically structured tri-partite division of 'mystical visions' into *visio corporalis*, *visio imaginaria* or *spiritualis*, and *visio intellectualis* can be traced to Augustine's *De Genesi ad Litteram*, XII, 7. – Cf. RUH, Kurt. *Geschichte der Abendländischen Mystik*. 2nd ed. Vol. 1. Munich: C. H. Beck, 2001. 104.

44 ALBRECHT, Carl. *Psychology of Mystical Consciousness*. Ed., trans. and annotated by F. K. Woehrer. New York: Crossroad, 2019, 373. – This is the definition of Albrecht's 'narrow concept of mysticism'; the wider, less stringent concept includes the realm of ecstatic mystical experience: "Mysticism is both the experience of an 'All-encompassing' 'arriving' in the 'quiet state of alertness', and the 'ecstatic' experience of an 'All-encompassing'." Cf. ALBRECHT, Carl. *Psychology of Mystical Consciousness*. Ed., trans. and annotated by F. K. Woehrer. New York: Crossroad, 2019. 374.

The 'mystical relation' is, as Albrecht insists, an indispensable component of any genuine mystical event.

In Part Two, Albrecht offers a detailed gnoseological analysis of the kinds of mystical experience identified in the foregoing chapters. Each variety is subjected to thorough scrutiny in regard to its potential propensity or resistance to error and delusion. Albrecht insists that in a genuine mystical event some vestiges of the 'whatness' ("Washeit") of the 'mystical Object' encountered can be grasped, even though mystical experience is inalienably co-determined and tinged by the perceiver's subjective self, notably by ideas, beliefs, concepts and expectations that the recipient holds prior to a mystical occurrence. Albrecht concludes from this that a mystical encounter is the more susceptible to error and delusion, the more it is imbued with notions, concepts and phenomena originating from the 'experiencing self'. Stated more specifically, the more a mystical experience is colored by variables such as the perceiver's personality, the given social, cultural, historical and religious contexts, the more is it vulnerable to delusion. Conversely, the less it is shaped by the recipient's personality and the given cultural and religious contexts, a mystical occurrence is more likely to be genuine and less susceptible to delusion and the less the perception of the 'mystical Object' is imbued with sensory qualities. In other words, the sparser and less subjective the 'content' of a mystical experience, the more the 'whatness' of the 'mystical Object' becomes manifest, and the less is the experience susceptible to delusion (see Albrecht's key findings 95 to 97). Relying on these insights, Albrecht proposes a hierarchically structured model of 'mystical recognition' termed the 'gnoseological pyramid' ("Gnoseologische Rangpyramide"). In this 'pyramid', individual types of mystical perception are assigned a specific rank, depending on their propensity to error and delusion. Thus, pictographic mystical visions are commonly rich in visual detail and, therefore, less resilient to error than imageless modes of mystical perception. They are for this reason allocated the lowest rank, whereas the latter are assigned the top rank on the 'gnoseological pyramid'.

In Part Three, Albrecht reflects on the potential 'philosophical relevance' of his claim that the 'mystical relation' is an 'ultimate phenomenon'. If it is acknowledged as an ontological fact, this epistemological premise should usher in a 'Copernican turn' in philosophical thinking.

Albrecht critically reviews Heidegger's existentialist philosophy (which dominated European philosophy when Albrecht wrote the book). In particular, he considers Heidegger's 'hermeneutics of Dasein' with its staunch emphasis on 'care' as the primary 'existential' of human 'Dasein' as too rigorous. If the 'mystical relation' is placed instead of 'care' as the primary 'existential' of human 'Dasein', man's existence in this world will be acknowledged to be inherently mystical. The acceptance of this proposition would result in a complete change in philosophical thinking: instead of viewing man as a being 'thrown into this world', estranged from the 'ultimate ground of Being', human 'Dasein' would be recognized as an existence that is *a priori* and perennially rooted in the eternal bond of the 'mystical relation'. Hence Albrecht calls for a philosophical approach to humanity, one that acknowledges this 'trans-worldly relationship' as an ontological fact. In his 'Conclusion', Albrecht abandons the diction of the scientist and adopts the lyrical parlance of the mystic when he envisages the ideal path of philosophical thinking: Philosophical thinking that is truly guided by the 'mystical relation' and immersed in the mystical stream of 'ontic Reality' has become mystical itself. Conventional philosophical thinking is speculative metaphysics or else 'mystology' – thinking *about* mysticism. Philosophical thinking, however, that has itself become *mystical* is permeated by spiritual illumination and sustained throughout by 'mystical intuition'. Mystical thinking can alone advance to the ultimate limits of human thinking and mystical recognition until, at the final threshold, it is bound to subside, abandoning to silence and facing the Unfathomable, and abide in reverent awe until it is overwhelmed by the influx of Love Ineffable.

It is hoped that this outline of Albrecht's research and his pioneering achievements as a scientist and mystic have provided some impression of the great importance of *Mystical Recognition* for the future research of mysticism. Yet the book is not only recommended reading for scholars and scientists; it is also addressed to readers around the globe interested in the cross-cultural study of mysticism and the spiritual nature of man.

FOREWORD

Carl Albrecht

This book is the sequel to *Psychologie des Mystischen Bewußtseins*, an empirical study on mystical states of consciousness first published in 1951.[1] The methodological approach of the first book was strictly confined to psychological phenomenology. The earlier scientific enquiry has resulted in a psychological definition of mysticism: "Mysticism is the 'arriving' of an 'All-encompassing' in the 'quiet state of alertness'." This definition has been derived from a wide range of empirical data, notably from phenomena and psychological structures retrieved from introspective empirical research as well as from records of mystics, which could be identified as instances of authentic mystical states. The distinctive psychological features of a mystical experience involve an event that occurs in a calm, empty and lucid state of consciousness [termed "Versunkenheit", viz., 'quiet state of alertness'], in which the only active function is that of inward perception, i.e., the capacity of 'inner sight', by which the 'arrival' of mystical phenomena can be observed; 'mystical phenomena' are related to the 'mystical Object' and are perceived as coming from a domain beyond

---

1 [Note: *Psychologie des Mystischen Bewußtseins* reprinted in 1976 and again in 1990 and 2019. The first English translation was published by Crossroad in 2019. – FKW.]

the boundaries of the individual consciousness and experienced as 'all-encompassing' and ultimately unfathomable in essence.

For a better understanding of the present book,[2] we need to call to mind the three key concepts of mystical consciousness:

1) The 'quiet state of alertness' ["Versunkenheit"] is a pure and lucid state of consciousness which is fully integrated, coherently structured and emptied of all content [i.e., vacated from any perceptual and discursive content featuring in the normal 'waking consciousness']; in it the stream of experience is slowed down to near stasis; it is fully imbued with calmness and the only active function operating in the passively receptive 'experiencing I' is that of 'inner sight' ["Innenschau"].

2) The concept of 'arriving' refers to the experience of an 'all-encompassing Essence' or 'Presence' 'arriving' in consciousness and perceived intuitively as coming from a sphere beyond the individual self and which tends to reveal Itself (usually) in a sequence of successive events.

3) The item that 'arrives' qualifies as a genuine mystical phenomenon if it is perceived as something unknown, unfathomable and 'all-encompassing' in nature. The crucial quality of a genuine mystical event is that of being 'all-encompassing'. A subject who is absorbed in the 'quiet state of alertness' perceives 'the All-encompassing' ["das Umfassende"] as an entity that is ultimately incomprehensible, overwhelming and 'arriving' from an unknown sphere beyond the threshold of the individual consciousness.

We should add, in parenthesis, that our earlier study was focussed on phenomena discerned during the subjective perception of the 'mystical Object' in 'inner sight'. This enquiry has moreover also disclosed so called 'ultimate phenomena' ["Phänomenletztheiten"][3],

---

2 [Note: *Das Mystische Erkennen*, first published in 1958. – FKW.]

3 [Note: 'Ultimate phenomenon of consciousness' is the English translation of the German term "Phänomenletztheit", which is a neologism coined by Albrecht. By

most of which are part of everyday life and anthropological reality, but cannot be rationally explained or traced to any final source. 'Ultimate phenomena' such as love, spirit, thinking, or language are an integral part of human existence and recognized in normal states of consciousness. The enquiry has however disclosed another 'ultimate phenomenon', which becomes manifest only in a mystical event and thus in a 'mystical state of consciousness'; it consists of the experience of a living 'mystical relation' between the experiencer and 'the All-encompassing'.

The psychological definition of mysticism suggests that mysticism is a unique experiential phenomenon, which must be distinguished from spurious paranormal or preternatural phenomena which are often falsely claimed to be instances of mystical experience. In *Psychologie des Mystischen Bewußtseins* a sound inventory of many varieties of mystical experience is provided by which a critical differentiation between mystical and pseudo-mystical phenomena can be achieved. It thus offers a reliable epistemological foundation for the empirical study of mysticism. The goal of the present study, by contrast, goes beyond the limitations of psychological enquiry and endeavours to probe more deeply into the core of mysticism and to enlarge upon the implications of the insights thus gained for philosophy and anthropology. It is two crucial questions to which the present study tries to give a viable answer: 1) Is it possible to ascertain that mysticism, after having been defined in psychological and phenomenological terns, involves a genuine encounter with an 'ultimate phenomenon' which cannot be traced to any intelligible source or phenomenon? 2) If this question can be answered affirmatively, the ensuing pivotal question is: What is the relevance of this new 'ultimate phenomenon', identified as the 'mystical relation', for philosophical thinking?

---

this concept he understands phenomena of human existence that cannot be traced to, or explained by, any prior experiential source. An 'ultimate phenomenon' is an inalienable empirical fact and thus a facticity of the human condition; it is a universal phenomenon of humanity, such as spirit, love, thinking, desire for freedom, or the 'mystical relation'. The latter has been disclosed by Albrecht as a new 'ultimate phenomenon' (which will be elaborated later in the book). – FKW.]

In empirical reality the three main constituents addressed in the psychological definition of mysticism – the 'quiet state of alertness', 'arriving' and 'the All-encompassing' – are closely interrelated. They refer strictly speaking primarily to the subjective 'pole' of the experience. The objective 'pole' is that of the 'mystical Object' experienced as 'arriving' in the perceiver's consciousness from beyond the boundaries of the self. But since the 'mystical Object' reveals Itself and establishes a living relationship with the 'experiencing I', this relationship refers to a real bond experienced individually by diverse emotional, cognitive and/or somatic phenomena and responses. This means that any mystical encounter is unique and has a deep impact on the perceiver, which may last for a lifetime. If the 'mystical relation' can be shown to be an event of this kind, it can indeed be acknowledged as an 'ultimate phenomenon'.

Viewed from a rational perspective, the 'mystical relation' is surely something elusive and obscure. In order to probe more deeply into its essence, we need to establish at least one element that is accessible to close phenomenological analysis. We can only explore the 'mystical relation' from the experiencer's point-of-view, notably, from the impact it has on the perceiver. If we apply this approach, we shall see that we may also gain some insight into the nature of the 'mystical Object', because any genuine experience of the 'mystical relation' has some cognitive import. Hence the perception of a genuine pictorial vision, a vision of light, the sense of Presence, an imageless vision, or of an auditory mystical experience is not only shaped and coloured by the subject's consciousness and personal response, but also determined by the mode in which the 'mystical Object' reveals Itself in a given mystical event. Thus, any genuine mystical event can be claimed to have gnoseological import. This corroborates the claim that our gnoseological enquiry is methodologically consistent; this is why the book has been named 'mystical recognition'.

In the introductory chapter we are going to examine the area of 'pseudo-mysticism' and explain why diverse paranormal and preternatural phenomena, which have erroneously been classified as 'mystical', can be dismissed from the realm of genuine mystical experience. In the main section (Part One), we shall scrutinize in depth a wide variety of mystical experiences reported by mystics from different epochs and mystical traditions as well as some 'spontaneous mystical utterances' spoken by subjects while immersed in mystical states of consciousness. This provides a sound epistemological foundation for the ensuing considerations and analyses. In Part Two a detailed gnoseological analysis of various types of mystical experience is provided, and in Part Three the implications of the discovery of the 'mystical relation' for philosophy and anthropology are considered.

It is important to add that the results of this study have emerged successively and cumulatively during the investigation. This study has not started from a specific research hypothesis but is rather the result of reflections on research data that have emerged in the course of the progress of the enquiry. The study has been motivated by the endeavour to verify as to whether the 'mystical relation' is, or is not, a universal anthropological phenomenon. The individual chapters have for this reason not been arranged systematically beforehand, but each part presents a specific stage in the progress of the enquiry. Thus, the reader is required to take part in the quest for the new 'ultimate phenomenon' of the 'mystical relation' and is exposed to the vicissitudes, vagaries and dead ends encountered on the way.

INTRODUCTION

Pseudomysticism

Occultism[1]

The term *occultism* refers to a domain of human experience inhabited by a wide variety of phenomena which elude rational explanation or cannot be accounted for by the science of psychology or by any other discipline of the natural sciences, though the followers of occultism claim that it is an area of science. In the past few decades, numerous studies have been published that are intended to corroborate that claim. In these studies, the attempt is made to arrange occult phenomena systematically, and research has been devoted to exploring potential causes of occult phenomena. A large number of case studies have been compiled and critically analysed,[2] and meticulous empirical investigations based on experiments have been carried

---

1 Cf. BENDER, Hans. *Parapsychologie – Ihre Ergebnisse und Probleme*. Bremen: Schünemann, 1953. DRIESCH, Hans. *Leib und Seele. Eine Untersuchung über das Psychophysische Grundproblem*. Leipzig: Reinicke, 1923. DRIESCH, Hans. *Parapsychologie: Die Wissenschaft von den 'Okkulten' Erscheinungen*. 3rd ed. Zurich: Rascher, 1952. MOSER, Fanny. *Der Okkultismus: Täuschungen und Tatsachen*. 2 vols. Munich: Reinhardt, 1935. RHINE, J.B. *Die Reichweite des Menschlichen Geistes: Parapsychologische Experimente*. Ed. R. Tischner. Trans. Karl Hellwig. Stuttgart: Deutsche Verlags-Anstalt, 1950. RHINE, J. B. *Neuland der Seele*. Trans. Hans Driesch. Stuttgart: Deutsche Verlags-Anstalt, 1938. TISCHNER, Rudolf. *Ergebnisse Okkulter Forschung*. Stuttgart: Deutsche Verlagsanstalt, 1950. TYRRELL, George N. *The Personality of Man. New Facts and Their Significance*. West Drayton: Penguin, 1948. WALTHER, Gerda. *Phänomenologie der Mystik*. 2nd ed. Freiburg i. Br.: Olten, 1955.

2 *Proceedings of the Society of Psychical Research*. [Note: Albrecht only gives the title of the periodical, but does not indicate volume number, issue year or page numbers. The periodical was first published in 1885, with annual volumes appearing annually throughout the 19th and 20th centuries, and on to the present. – FKW.]

out for the purpose of providing a sound empirical foundation for further critical enquiries.[3]

There is yet another technical term used to refer to preternatural phenomena and experiences: *parapsychology*. This term suggests a scientific concept, but it is in fact only a flawed and inadequate concept, one even more fuzzy than the term 'occultism'. It is so, first because it has obvious metaphysical connotations and implications, and second because it covers only a fraction of the occult phenomena encountered in empirical reality, as it does not include para*physical* phenomena.

The experience of paranormal phenomena is often equated with *supernatural experience* ["übersinnliche Erfahrung"]. The latter term indicates clearly that this is an empirical occurrence in which occult phenomena are encountered, but which have not been transmitted by natural sense perceptions. This term does not, however, specify if or how a supernatural experience differs from other cognitive experiences, which are caused by other paranormal perceptions. First of all, it has to be stated that both supernatural and parapsychological experiences are inner experiences: they consist of the inner perception of factual occurrences in consciousness and of the responding observation of the singular supernatural experience. This aside, spiritual seers and adherents of esoteric schools claim to have special recourse to supernatural experiences – a claim that may or may not be true – but whichever applies, these ghost-seers and exponents of supernatural experience must be placed phenomenologically into a different category from 'occultism', because the realm of their objects differs significantly from the modes of occult experience.

We are now going to classify the rather diffuse area of para-phenomena for the purpose of our enquiry. We shall establish criteria which should allow us to distinguish mystical phenomena from occult and other paranormal or pseudo-mystical occurrences. We should add, however, that our classification of occult phenomena does not claim to be exhaustive. (It would surely have gone beyond

---

3 Cf. RHINE, J. B. *Die Reichweite des Menschlichen Geistes: Parapsychologische Experimente.* Ed. R. Tischner. Trans. Karl Hellwig. Stuttgart: Deutsche Verlags-Anstalt, 1950. RHINE, J. B. *Neuland der Seele.* Trans. Hans Driesch. Stuttgart: Deutsche Verlags-Anstalt, 1938.

the purpose and scope of this study to provide a full taxonomy of occult phenomena.)

One group of occult phenomena comprises *paraphysical appearances*. Their occult nature is based on the fact that the theorems of the natural sciences cannot provide a stringent answer or rational explanation for their existence, even though real, natural physical and/or chemical phenomena appear to be involved in eliciting them. A case in point is the phenomenon of *telekinesis*, i.e., the ability to move objects at a distance merely by the use of mental power. Thus, physical objects can be moved merely by the power of the mind at a distance, and without any physical contact between the object moved and the person causing the object to move. Familiar examples reported from participants in occult séances include the sound of someone knocking at the door though no human being is in front of the door; the mysterious rumbling of the floor without apparent cause, a glass or a jar cracking or breaking instantly – which are all paraphysical phenomena occurring without an apparent natural cause but claimed to have been produced by a 'medium'. Persuasive evidence for the realness of such phenomena has been provided by the mass-experiments of J. Rhine[4], the most famous of which was the experiment of casting dice, in which a dice was moved by telekinesis consecutively by several test-persons with the aim of achieving a predicted result. – Another phenomenon is *teleplastia*, i.e., the real or (supposed) materialization of psychic, or certain paranormal phenomena such as evoking effigies and shape-like images from a distance.

Transnormal, paraphysical phenomena of this kind may provide a foundation for us in our endeavour to understand some of the paraphysical phenomena and preternatural sensations recorded by mystics and religious yogis. Mystics have usually valued such paraphysical phenomena as corollaries of their mystical experiences and understood them to be likewise tokens of special grace, whereas yogis generally acknowledge them as an indication that they have reached a 'higher state of consciousness'. Especially in the lives of Eastern mystics, we often encounter paraphysical phenomena as corollaries and/or integral parts of (genuine) mystical experiences. A most extraordinary, though also most contentious, phenomenon that has often been reported as

---

4 [Note: See footnote 3 above. – FKW.]

experienced by advanced Indian yogis (though no positive proof has ever been provided) is *levitation*, i.e., the alleged ability of a yogi to hover in the air for some time when he has been transported into the state of ecstasy; another variety of levitation is that of inanimate objects being elevated and flying around in a room or open space. A further paraphysical phenomenon reported particularly by contemporary Eastern gurus[5] is the ability to materialize, or to de-materialize substances (i.e., the phenomenon is thus termed *materialization*, viz., *de-materialization*)[6]. Paraphysical phenomena further include *occult sensations of light*, a *gust of wind* arising near a yogi or a saint, the phenomenon of being *impervious to fire*, or of being *safeguarded against starving* indeterminately after having stopped eating. All these phenomena are part of a mysterious paranormal 'reality' which cannot be explained by science and are allocated beyond the threshold of the 'natural order' of physical phenomena. Paraphysical phenomena are therefore to be placed in the twilight zone between delusion, suggestion, and genuine empirical fact. As such they are part of occultism, because these phenomena can in part be explored experimentally by science, but they cannot provide any deeper insight into the nature of mysticism, nor can they advance our enquiry into the cognitive potential of the 'mystical relation'.

The second category of paranormal occult phenomena can be described by the term *parapsychological appearances*. But I think that this term has obvious metaphysical connotations and is for this reason even less suitable than the term paraphysical phenomena; this aside, the term does not apply appropriately to all parapsychological phenomena. The area extending beyond the sphere of the psyche – hence the domain of the trans-psychical – is a realm that transcends reason and thus encompasses a transrational sphere which can only be rendered intelligible if

---

5 Cf. PARAMHANSA [sic], Yogananda. *Autobiographie eines Yogi*. Munich: Barth, 1950. – [Note: The correct appellation of the Bengali yogi is Paramahansa Yogananda (1893–1952), though in western publications – like in the one used by Albrecht – the yogi's name is sometimes given as "Paramhansa Yogananda". – FKW.]
6 [Note: Here Albrecht may have had the Indian guru Sathya Sai Baba (1926–2011) in mind (whose real name was Sathya Narayana Raju Ratnakaram), who became famous in the West in the 1950s for his astonishing capacity to materialize and de-materialize objects. – FKW.]

metaphysical assumptions are granted. The realm of trans-physical phenomena, by contrast, cannot only be compared to the realm of physical reality but also explored by analogy with physical phenomena.

From amongst the various parapsychological appearances taking place in occult occurrences, those are of special interest for our enquiry into the realm of mysticism which have been classified as phenomena of *extrasensory perception,* now commonly referred to as ESP. The two main phenomena of ESP are telepathy and clairvoyance. *Telepathy* can be subdivided into two types: 'telepathy of sending' and 'telepathy of receiving'[7]; telepathy is commonly defined as the transfer of content from the consciousness of one individual to the consciousness of another, without the use of the physical sense of hearing, or of vocal speech. The communication of some content (thoughts, ideas) from one human being to another is thus transferred in a different way than the one known from normal processes of communication and is therefore an instance of extrasensory perception. The term 'content of consciousness' does not only refer to items that are concurrent with the given situation in which the telepathic experience occurs, but also to items of unconscious 'content' which has been stored in the mind, though the subject has no longer any conscious memory of these items, and thus be considered to be extra-mental items of consciousness. *Clairvoyance* is a special instance of ESP in which things and events of the external world, including as yet unknown events of the future, become instantly known without any mediation by telepathy or sense perception. Subcategories of clairvoyance are the phenomenon of cryptoscopy (i.e., the 'perceiving' of objects which are outside the scope of a medium's physical perception), and the phenomenon of telescopy (i.e., the ability to 'see' events occurring – or having occurred – at a distant location; even one that may be unknown to the occult perceiver). A controversial variety of this phenomenon, and one that has been contested by science, is prophecy (i.e., the alleged capacity of anticipating or 'divining' future events, and joined with it, the capacity of having

---

7 WARCOLLIER, Rene. *Mind to Mind.* New York: Creative Age Press, 1948; WILKENS, Sir Hubert, and Harold M. SHERMAN. *Thoughts Through Space. A Remarkable Adventure in the Realm of Mind.* New York: Creative Age Press, 1942.

access to events of the past – even of the remote past in the history of humanity). Only a few decades ago almost all the phenomena related to clairvoyance were assumed to be instances of telepathy, and clairvoyance as such has for a long time been dismissed as a potentially delusory phenomenon; recent experimental research, however, has revised this verdict and substantiated the claim that clairvoyance is a real empirical phenomenon, albeit one that eludes scientific explanation, and one that is more frequently encountered in empirical reality than has previously been supposed. Both telepathy and clairvoyance are thus affirmed phenomena, though they cannot be explained by science and are therefore appropriately to be attributed to the category of 'extrasensory perception'.

Extrasensory perceptions thus do not qualify for a scientific approach to 'transnormal reality'. ESP, however, opens up a considerable new dimension beyond the 'normal horizon' of human experience. Any telepathic experience expands the scope of individual consciousness in that it provides the perceiver with 'content' from different spheres of consciousness, which are commonly beyond the reach of his/her normal power of sense perception. This claim is even more pertinent to the phenomenon of clairvoyance: Clairvoyance expands the normal realm of human experience and the normal capacity of consciousness considerably, and it does so to a greater extent than telepathy. Yet, irrespective of these accomplishments, *the fact remains that in both telepathy and clairvoyance, the sphere in which 'objects' are perceived and grasped cognitively in ESP does not differ from the one in which objects are perceived in normal sense perception.*

Extrasensory perceptions have not been classified as 'occult phenomena' because they are assumed to admit access to a 'hidden' 'transnormal world', but rather because the 'transnormal world' is assumed to really exist beyond the familiar domain grasped by mundane human experience. In order to account for the 'reality' of this 'hidden paranormal world', numerous paraphysical and parapsychological theorems have been proposed. One of them is the claim that transnormal 'miniscule particles' are involved in evoking occult phenomena; another hypothesis is that occult phenomena are elicited by paranormal waves, and yet another one claims that occult phenomena originate from individual psychic causation, in that psychic energy radiates and emanates beyond the periphery of the individual body. These hypotheses are based on rather diverse, hardly substantiated metaphysical assumptions, which should better be replaced by clearly formulated philosophical questions. Attempts to explore occult phenomena seriously by posing sound philosophical questions have meanwhile been attempted, and occult experience been related to the irrational states of being encountered in normal modes of human experience. There is, for instance, a *hiatus irrationalis* between the somatic processes involved in sense perception, and the psychic sphere of subjective experience, and another such *hiatus* can be observed between a simple act of the will at the juncture where the psychological process switches to the somatic sphere, something that poses a fundamental philosophical problem. A similar *aporia* applies to the occult phenomena of telepathy, clairvoyance, and even telekinesis, if this irrational *hiatus* is transferred from within the realm of the body to the realm outside of the body.

For the present purpose of exploring the phenomenon of mysticism, however, the phenomena of occultism addressed above are only of marginal interest. The only thing that matters here is that we have to distinguish between an 'occult world', in which we may encounter paraphysical and parapsychological phenomena, including occult extrasensory perceptions, and the sphere of knowledge, which may be enlarged by occult experiences, but which is as such no domain of 'occultism', but one that is identical with the cognitive sphere in which empirical reality is normally perceived.

The considerations of the foregoing section have thus turned out to be more significant for the aims of our enquiry than we had previously expected, as we may infer from these considerations seven important propositions:

THESIS 1: *We must distinguish between an 'occult world', in which paraphysical and parapsychological phenomena and extrasensory perceptions are integral parts, and a 'real' 'normal world', which can, however, be expanded by the perception of occult extrasensory experiences.* [Italics in the original][8].

---

8 [Note: All passages and phrases printed in italics follow the example of the original German text throughout. Therefore, no further annotations are given when the font is shifted to italics. – FKW.]

THESIS 2: *Occult experiences do not give access to the occult world.*

THESIS 3: *The varieties of occult experience are a special paranormal path to both the inner and outer worlds of our natural modes of experience.*

These rather stringent classifications are necessary as preliminary statements and necessary for substantiating the ensuing inferences.

As the realm of mystical recognition does not contain an 'object' pertaining to either the 'natural' or the 'occult' worlds (as we may claim by anticipating later findings), we may state:

THESIS 4: *The realm of both the normal world, in which objects and phenomena of occult experience may become manifest, and the realm of the 'occult world', to which occult modes of cognitive experience have their place together with other occult phenomena, can unmistakably be distinguished from the sphere of objects encountered in the domain of cognitive mystical experience.*

THESIS 5: *Occult phenomena are entirely irrelevant for elucidating the question as to what is to be understood by the 'mystical relation'.*

This is a crucial insight. On this basis we can now affirm a few more inferences, which will advance further the progress of our enquiry:

THESIS 6: *Physical sense perceptions are not the only modes of empirical discernment.* As our investigation has shown, extrasensory occult experiences likewise qualify as a variety of cognitive empirical perception.

THESIS 7: *Exceptional experiences do not necessarily relate to extraordinary cognitive experiences of paranormal reality.* For instance, occult experiences are strictly confined to the natural world of objects. Conversely, the objective sphere of the 'occult world' can only be explored by the known empirical methods of the natural sciences.

When formulating thesis 7, I have deliberately opted for a thoroughly stringent and discerning phrasing. One might object, however, that the claim that merely the normal world; rather than a paranormal reality, is revealed in a paranormal extrasensory experience (though admittedly at a larger scope) is valid only to a limited extent. For instance, there is evidence of extrasensory experiences in which a 'telepathic message of a deceased person' is perceived, and in such an experience some aspect of a paranormal world is inevitably conveyed; over and beyond this, one might argue that ESP is not the only variety of occult experience. Objections of this kind appear not unfounded, but there are two issues to be considered in defence of the above claims:

1. Our enquiry is strictly an empirical enterprise, and as such it is imperative for it to be strictly and uncompromisingly confined to phenomena that can be verified by the methods of empirical science. Thus, the alleged telepathic bond between a human being and the 'ghost' of a deceased relative is a paranormal phenomenon that has been insufficiently explored (though considerable research materials have recently been examined)[9] by science, and the few findings are too ambivalent and diffuse to be approved by science. The empirical insights about the nature of the transnormal world and telepathic experience gained so far is still too sparse and unreliable for us to be given further consideration.

2. It is true that there is evidence that the 'aura' of a human being can be perceived in the event of a transnormal perception.[10] However, capacity of 'seeing the aura' of a person is a phenomenon that is generally attributed to the realm of occultism. Though it is a paranormal experience in which a paranormal object is cognitively grasped, it cannot be attributed to the province of extrasensory perception in the same way as this applies to telepathy and clairvoyance. The theses above have been derived from the analysis of telepathy and clairvoyance and therefore only apply to these

---

9 Cf. TYRRELL, George N. *The Personality of Man. New Facts and Their Significance*. West Drayton: Penguin, 1948. 151–206. BALFOUR, G. F., Earl of. "A Study of the Psychological Aspects of Mrs. Willett's Mediumship, and of the Statements of the Communicators Concerning Process." *Proceedings of the Society for Psychical Research* 43 (1935): 41–318. WALTHER, Gerda. *Phänomenologie der Mystik*. 2nd ed. Freiburg i. Br.: Olten, 1955. 171–74; 144–48; 213–17.

10 WALTHER, Gerda. *Phänomenologie der Mystik*. 2nd ed. Freiburg i. Br.: Olten, 1955. 105–7; 144–48; 168–170. WÜST, Joseph. "Physikalische und Chemische Grundlagen der Menschlichen Aura." *Neue Wissenschaft: Zeitschrift für Grenzgebiete des Seelenlebens* 4 (1954): 193–200; 257–66.

two varieties of extrasensory perception. But we shall see in the following chapter that there are other occult phenomena that can be experienced in different kinds of transnormal occurrences. We shall then allocate to the phenomenon of the paranormal perception of an 'aura' accordingly as an instance of occult experience. Yet we shall see later that neither the phenomenon of perceiving the ghost of a deceased person, nor that of perceiving the 'aura' of a living individual have anything to do with mysticism.

Gerda Walther[11] has elaborated a phenomenology of mysticism on the basis of insights she has gained from her studies of Husserl, Pfänder and Scheler. Walther's phenomenology encompasses a wide range of mystical and non-mystical phenomena and experiences which are assessed from different perspectives. Experiences which can be traced to the subjective realm of the 'I' of the perceiver, and which thus surface from within the sphere of the subject's consciousness, i.e., from his/her 'individual being' ["Grundwesen"],[12] are distinguished phenomenologically from experiences that are perceived as intruding from beyond the individual consciousness. The latter include 'telepathic experiences' in which the 'perceiving I' responds to the notions or intimations of a 'foreign I' and may eventually be entirely inundated by the 'foreign I'. These phenomenological characteristics reveal the fundamental difference between, on the one hand, a telepathic experience and an experience that surfaces from within the 'sphere of the individual self', and, on the other hand, a genuine mystical experience. It is only in the latter that the content of the experience originates from the unfathomable (divine) Ground of Being, 'arriving' in the 'experiencing self' so that he/she feels 'embedded' in or inundated by it.

Contrastive differentiations of this kind supplied Walther with the foundations for her phenomenology of 'arriving'. She thus

---

11 WALTHER, Gerda. "Die Innerseelische Seite Parapsychologischer Phänomene." *Neue Wissenschaft: Zeitschrift für Parapsychologie* 6 (11/12) (1956): 364–73; and 6 (13) (1957): 408–22.

12 Cf. PFÄNDER, Alexander. *Die Seele des Menschen*. Halle: Niemeyer, 1933. PFÄNDER, Alexander. *Philosophie der Lebensziele*. Göttingen: Vandenhoeck & Ruprecht, 1948.

applied as early as 1923 a similar methodological approach as the one we employed in the study *Psychologie des Mystischen Bewußtseins* (1951), albeit with the important difference that Walther used the phenomena of telepathic experience as the criteria for discerning mystical from non-mystical phenomena, whereas in our investigation it was specific criteria of the psychology of consciousness that served as the critical discernment between mystical and non-mystical experiences. The 'quiet state of alertness' was used as the pivotal mental state and phenomenological reference frame for assessing the phenomena 'arriving' in the vista of 'inner sight' as 'mystical' ones, if they were perceived as 'arriving' from beyond the domain of the individual self and 'all-encompassing' in nature, and/or related to the 'All-encompassing'. This demonstrates once more that the phenomenon of mysticism can be approached from different perspectives and explored by diverse scientific methodologies.

The aim of the introductory chapters of this study is to identify and draw special attention to the phenomenon termed the 'mystical relation' by exploring it from different perspectives. It is not only contrasted to 'occult' extrasensory phenomena, but also to varieties of 'spiritualist experience' as described by spiritism, and the 'spirit-seers' as well as investigators of 'spectres'. The central concern of this study, then, is to develop a highly differentiated, gnoseological phenomenology of a wide variety of mystical experiences. In this study (unlike in the earlier book) it is thus no longer the main concern to set off mystical experience against other modes of human experience but to explore and capture the core and pivotal characteristics of mystical experience, and, in particular, of the 'mystical relation' as an 'ultimate phenomenon'.

The studies of Gerda Walther have resulted in some findings which are equally relevant for our study:

1. The phenomenon of 'arriving' occurring in telepathic experience has some *structural* similarities with the phenomenon of 'arriving' encountered in mystical experiences. The 'forms of arriving' are by and large the same in both telepathic and mystical events. In telepathy, just as in a mystical occurrence, a subject perceives an unexpected 'impact' effected from outside him-/herself, such

as an image or a vision or 'apparition', or 'an inner voice' speaking to him/her, or he/she may be struck by 'a summons', or an 'intuition', or some impact of his/her will-power, a sense of 'being directed or guided' by a force from beyond the individual consciousness. And there is even an analogy in the domain of telepathic experience to what in mystical experience is termed 'sense of Presence'.[13]

2. Yet despite the structural affinities between telepathic and mystical modes of 'arriving', the latter can clearly be distinguished from the former. The phenomenon that 'arrives' in a telepathic experience is endowed with a distinct 'aura', characteristic of itself, one which cannot be mistaken for the 'aura' appearing in a mystical experience.[14] An error in discerning the source or provenance of the 'aura' seems practically impossible.

THESIS 8: *The telepathic experience is irrelevant for the gnoseology of mysticism. Mistaking a telepathic experience for a mystical one is unlikely ever to happen and has practically never occurred.*
For this reason, we shall bypass telepathic phenomena and telepathic experiences in our phenomenological investigation into the core of mystical experience.

'Spirit-Seers' and 'Spirit Researchers': The Cognitive Experience of 'Higher Worlds'

It is our endeavour to get insight into both modes of cognition and knowledge of the 'realities' or 'worlds' that appear to exist beyond the familiar realm of reality, and beyond the domain accessible to

---

13 Cf. WALTHER, Gerda. *Phänomenologie der Mystik*. 2nd ed. Freiburg i. Br.: Olten, 1955. 214–17. BALFOUR, Earl of. "A Study of the Psychological Aspects of Mrs. Willett's Mediumship, and of the Statements of the Communicators Concerning Process." *Proceedings of the Society for Psychical Research* 43 (1935): 90f. and 106.
14 WALTHER, Gerda. "Die Innerseelische Seite Parapsychologischer Phänomene." *Neue Wissenschaft: Zeitschrift für Parapsychologie* 6 (11/12) (1956): 364–73; and 6 (13) (1957): 408–22.

scientific research. At this stage our enquiry will enter a different area of extrasensory perception – one clearly different from the realm of 'occultism', because we can clearly define its boundaries.

In the empirical world of the 'spirit-seers' and 'spirit researchers' we encounter – contrary to the world of 'occult phenomena' – a gnoseological sphere in which the objects featuring in it differ significantly from those perceived in our familiar, everyday world. In the world of 'ghosts' and 'spirits' a rich variety of shapes, spectres and apparitions are disclosed which have dumbfounded the general public as well as scientists throughout the centuries. This unusual world of 'ghosts' and 'spirits' does not become accessible by normal modes of perception, nor is it deliberately accessible by the extrasensory modes of perception germane to 'occultism'. What is required by someone who wishes to witness the 'objects' of this paranormal world is a special capacity for extrasensory perception. This fact is, from a phenomenological point of view, a very important insight in view of our enquiry into the nature of mystical experience. We may therefore formulate:

THESIS 9: *A new mode of experiencing can open a new realm of experience, which is unique and exclusively distinctive of its own.* This new empirical world would not be accessible without a new mode of perception being at one's disposal, and this new realm of experience can observe the 'objects' becoming manifest in this paranormal world.

The question arises, however, whether it is necessary in our investigation of the nature of 'mystical recognition' to include the preternatural realm of 'ghost-seers'. The answer is clearly affirmative, as we must consider this paranormal domain – albeit only to a limited extent – not least because various extrasensory experiences have also been recorded by mystics and visionaries throughout the centuries. The mystics, however, did not distinguish in their descriptions between mystical experience and preternatural occurrences pertaining to the realm of 'spirits' or between mystical visions and spiritual apparitions, as both varieties were unanimously seen as tokens of God's special grace. If we wish to comprehend the essence of mystical perception, we have to know beforehand the distinctive features of the 'spiritual visions' of the 'ghost-seers', in order to be able to distinguish these visions from the varieties of genuine 'mystical visions', although gaining such knowledge is fraught with difficulties because the area of 'spirit researchers' is shrouded in mystery and difficult to approach with empirical methodology.

The major difficulties involved in such an endeavour are (to my mind) the following: There are only a few records and other documented data about the paranormal experiences witnessed by 'ghost-seers' and researchers in the 'spirit-world'; moreover, the sparse reliable documents that do exist are very difficult to get hold of. Over and beyond this, the few written testimonials which can be traced to reliable sources are not categorized systematically and are therefore difficult to classify scientifically. Yet limited textual availability and reliability aside, the preternatural world of 'ghosts' and 'spirits', as well as other paranormal phenomena related to it, are so diverse and unfamiliar that a representative inventory that would be needed for a scientific analysis, and which would also be acknowledged as appropriate and representative by 'ghost-seers', would go far beyond the scope of this study. For this reason, we will deal with records by 'ghost-seers' and the spiritual experiences reported by 'researchers of the spirit-world' from the perspective of an objective observer, i.e., we will analyse these writings without prejudice, without denying beforehand their veridical claims, nor the avowal of the authenticity and truthfulness of the underlying preternatural experiences. By adopting this approach, however, we are on the other hand deprived of the opportunity to acknowledge from a scholarly and scientific basis the achievements of the research undertaken in the domain termed 'science of spirits and ghosts' ["Geistes-Wissenschaft"], notably the research and achievements of Rudolf Steiner. A critical scientific assessment of this esoteric field could only have been achieved by an in-depth epistemological investigation into the validity of the phenomena and the veridical claims of the experiences involved. This could have been done, for instance, by focussing on the question of whether the phenomena encountered in the paranormal world of 'ghosts and spirits' are indeed empirical facts, or rather delusory occurrences. However, there is no need to provide an answer to this vexing question in the context of our study into the nature of mystical experience, and we can proceed with our enquiry, leaving the question above open for the time being. We shall only occasionally resort to the question as to whether and what the essential differences are between paranormal experiences of the 'spirit-world' and genuine varieties of mystical experience.

The history of the esoteric lore and teachings of 'ghost-seers', 'sages' and disciples of the 'spirit-world' goes back to times immemorial in practically all cultural traditions. There has been an unbroken tradition – outside the long-standing history of scientific and pre-scientific thinking – of esoteric writings by spiritual guides and sages dealing with the nature of the paranormal 'world' of 'spirits' and 'ghosts', as well as with instructions to neophytes, of how to cleanse the 'spiritual senses' so that one may be bestowed with the capacity of perceiving the phenomena of preternatural reality. Though it is true that the esoteric texts of spiritual guidance from different cultural backgrounds have numerous affinities and even coincide in their descriptions of distinctive phenomena, it is also possible to discern several significant differences in an in-depth critical analysis – and these differences are, I would contend, incompatible. [I will illustrate some of these differences on the basis of examples from writings of 'spirit seers' from different periods and diverse cultural and/or religious traditions:]

There is, for instance, the *Celestial Hierarchy* of *Dionysius Areopagita*,[15] a text in which the individual ranks in the hierarchy of angels are related to the hierarchical structure of the church. Dionysius describes a stairway on which clerics from the lowest tier of an officiant, through to the apostle and on to the various hierarchical ranks of angels, ranging from guardian angels to the Seraphim, and culminating in Christ, whose cognitive experience is, however, transintelligible.[16] Thus the *Celestial Hierarchy* of Dionysius Areopagita

---

15 [Note: Albrecht used the German translation of the selected writings of Pseudo-Dionysius, the so-called *Corpus Dionysiacum*, a canon of mystical and theological writings ascribed to an unknown Syrian theologian and philosopher of the late 5th c., now commonly named Pseudo-Dionysius Areopagita. He quotes from *Des Heiligen Dionysius Areopagita Angebliche Schriften Über die Beiden Hierarchien*. Ed. and trans. J. Stiglmayr. 2nd ed. Kempten: Kösel, 1911. – FKW.]

16 Cf. BALL, Hugo. *Byzantinisches Christentum*. München: Duncker & Humblot, 1923. 211.

is conceived like a hymn, which culminates in a crescendo of perfect beauty.[17] This supernatural visionary world, perceived as an integral part of the Christian's awareness of the unique and singular existence of his/her soul, differs fundamentally from the spirit-world and its spiritual hierarchies encountered by Rudolf Steiner in his visionary experiences. Steiner was bestowed with a supernatural vision of the grand panorama of spiritual beings destined for reincarnation.

A different spirit-world is portrayed by the Swedish seer Emanuel *Swedenborg*. In his visions he elaborates on the bond between the 'spiritual world of angels and spirits' and the terrestrial world of man: 'I can assure you now that the secrets of heaven have been revealed to men who have been allowed to speak with angels, that angels and spirits cannot exist without men and vice versa.' – 'It has been their express wish that I should convey to you the message and the reassurance from their own mouths, that no angel in heaven has ever been created at the beginning of creation, nor that the devil dwelling in hell has ever been an angel of light, who was later thrown into hell. All beings of heaven and hell are rather the offspring of the human race.'[18]

There is no need to quote some of the more intimate, personal accounts of seers of the spirit world here. Many of these accounts are rather idiosyncratic, like, for instance, that of the Seeress of Prevorst[19] [*aka* Frederike Hauffe (1801–1829)]:[20] Her testimony is

---

17 Cf. BALL, Hugo. *Byzantinisches Christentum*. München: Duncker & Humblot, 1923. 246.

18 SWEDENBORG, Immanuel. *Theologische Schriften*. Trans. Lothar Brieger. Jena: Diederichs, 1904. 248, 253. [Note: English translation provided. – FKW.]

19 KERNER, Justinus. *Die Seherin von Prevorst: Eröffnungen über das innere Leben des Menschen und über das Hereinragen einer Geisterwelt in die Unsere*. Leipzig: Reclam, 1930. (1st publ. 1846).

20 [Note: Frederike Hauffe, commonly known as "the seeress of Prevorst", was a German visionary and clairvoyant. For many years she was subject to convulsions and trances that caused her to remain bedridden from 1822 until her death in 1829. In this agonizing period, while suspended between life and death, she received revelations from the spirit world about the triune doctrine of body, soul, and spirit. The spirits of the dead were said to be in constant attendance on her and were, as her personal physician Justinus Kerber records in her biography, even occasionally seen

too jumbled, too incoherent, and the mental state(s) in which her spontaneous utterances were spoken are too obscure and ambivalent to permit classification, so that Prevorst's record does not allow any tangible conclusions, or any sound scientific assessment. This is why we have not included this document in our detailed analysis.

Some of the differences occurring in accounts of the 'world of spirits' may be attributed to differences in the given status and value of a particular supernatural experience. Over and beyond this, visual supernatural experiences of 'ghosts' and 'spirits' are inevitably just as exposed to error and delusion as normal sense perceptions, and thus may result in flawed conclusions. Several accounts of supernatural experiences have led to pseudo-scientific inferences and problematic findings which must all be put into proper perspective by sound scientific investigations. On the other hand, some scientific studies of such records have yielded well-founded astonishing insights. Rudolf Steiner is a major scholarly representative; he claims that his research and insights into the domain of the 'spirit world' are informed throughout by personal experience and are thus based on authentic, reliable empirical data. He exposed these extraordinary experiences to meticulous scientific analysis so that his studies must be acknowledged as sound and consistent scholarly achievements. For this reason, they provide a pertinent reference frame for our contrastive analysis of phenomena pertaining to the supernatural world of spirits, and the domain of mystical experience.

To start with, we may say that the following *summary of Rudolf Steiner's studies in the preternatural world, which was revealed to him in a series of paranormal experiences*, has been conceived with the intention of establishing links between the 'world of spirits' and to both the normal world and the 'mystical world'. This comparative analysis is expected to yield some valuable insights.

The ghost-seer does not perceive the normal world of 'objects' separately, but he/she 'sees' simultaneously in or 'behind' the physical objects of the real world, a spiritual world by means of his/her ability

---

by others. Her most remarkable gift, however, was the ability to write and speak in what she called 'the language of the spirits', a unique coded alphabet that incorporated numbers and primitive ideographs. – FKW.]

of extrasensory perception. Thus he/she may perceive, for instance, a normal human being in the shape of a multi-layered being, composed not merely of a physical body, but also of a 'living ethereal body', and, over and beyond this, an *'astral- or spiritual body rooted in the soul'*. The latter is disclosed in the special act of extrasensory perception.[21] The body of the person observed is surrounded by an *aura*,[22] which looks like a three-dimensional cloud, or the shape of a figure from which various colours seem to emanate; the 'spirit-seer' may also perceive wave-like phantasma, or circular spectres and the *flow* of spectre-like emanations from the person observed.[23]

The extrasensory phenomena which become manifest in the *aura* are attributed to various extrasensory 'spaces'. In his writings Steiner gives detailed accounts of these phenomena and paranormal experiences. Furthermore, he distinguishes between the 'land of the soul'[24] and the 'land of the spirits': the former consists of hierarchically structured regions, each of which has a system of ranks, which the soul must pass through on its ascent. After the physical death of a human being, the soul is subjected to a process of purification. The purging of the soul in the 'other world' is achieved by the 'fire of purification'; in this world of purgation the 'spiritual eye' is faced with 'ghastly creatures', whose sight is often painful, frightening and horrifying.[25] It is 'not only shadows or effigies that are seen, but real beings'; they

---

21 STEINER, Rudolf. *Theosophie: Einführung in übersinnliche Welterkenntnis und Menschenbestimmung*. New ed. Freiburg i. Br.: Novalis, 1946. 25–60; STEINER, Rudolf. *Die Geheimwissenschaft im Umriß*. New ed. Stuttgart: Freies Geistesleben, 1948. 22–51; 414–421.

22 STEINER, Rudolf. *Theosophie: Einführung in übersinnliche Welterkenntnis und Menschenbestimmung*. New ed. Freiburg i. Br.: Novalis, 1946. 151–63.

23 STEINER, Rudolf. *Theosophie: Einführung in übersinnliche Welterkenntnis und Menschenbestimmung*. New ed. Freiburg i. Br.: Novalis, 1946. 153.

24 STEINER, Rudolf. *Theosophie: Einführung in übersinnliche Welterkenntnis und Menschenbestimmung*. New ed. Freiburg i. Br.: Novalis, 1946. 87–115; STEINER, Rudolf. *Die Geheimwissenschaft im Umriß*. New ed. Stuttgart: Freies Geistesleben, 1948. 71–82.

25 STEINER, Rudolf. *Die Geheimwissenschaft im Umriß*. New ed. Stuttgart: Freies Geistesleben, 1948. 80–81.

arise from the fire of self-devouring [carnal] desires; to these desires all carnal cravings are nourishment which a human being indulges in in the mundane world. The purification of the soul is at the same time a process of its 'dissolution'.[26] In this process the spiritual being that is enclosed in the 'I' of a human being is not only liberated from his/her ethereal body but also from the astral body. Only after this the individual is granted entry into the wide expanse of the *'land of the spirits'*[27], which is likewise hierarchically structured. However, the ghost-seer is allowed already during his/her life-time to get a glimpse of the 'land of the spirits' and is able to discern its characteristics and enabled to see 'spiritual entities' and to report on these sightings. The 'spiritual entities' encountered correspond partly to human beings and objects of the natural world and are partly recognized as the causes of events and empirical facts in this world. In the supernatural world there are layers which are the homes of living spiritual beings; and they are archetypal images of all physical and animate objects and beings of our normal world. They are the creative 'beings, artificers and creators of whatever comes into existence in the physical and (also) the spiritual world.'[28]

The ghost-seer may furthermore move around in the environment of so-called 'ideational essences' ["Gedankenwesenheiten"]. He/she is able to 'see' them with his spiritual eye and may 'hear' them in an instance of 'spiritual hearing'. The spiritual luminescence is simultaneously a harmonious spiritual sound, which may evolve into the melodious harmony of the spheres. 'Ideational essences' are real spiritual entities [literally "Geister", 'spirits'] that are interconnected in many different ways, thus forming a coherent context, a living *'world of thoughts'*. Human thinking is just a 'shadow' of the supernatural

---

26 STEINER, Rudolf. *Theosophie: Einführung in übersinnliche Welterkenntnis und Menschenbestimmung*. New ed. Freiburg i. Br.: Novalis, 1946. 105.

27 STEINER, Rudolf. *Theosophie: Einführung in übersinnliche Welterkenntnis und Menschenbestimmung*. New ed. Freiburg i. Br.: Novalis, 1946. 115–39; STEINER, Rudolf. *Die Geheimwissenschaft im Umriß*. New ed. Stuttgart: Freies Geistesleben, 1948. 83–112.

28 STEINER, Rudolf. *Theosophie: Einführung in übersinnliche Welterkenntnis und Menschenbestimmung*. New ed. Freiburg i. Br.: Novalis, 1946. 116–17.

'world of thoughts', and any individual process of thinking merely the embodiment of the ideational essences originating from this primordial spiritual reality.

At an even higher level of the 'land of the spirits', we may find 'intentions', which are the spiritual 'germ' of 'ideational essences', as well as the 'seeds of life', which have arrived from even higher regions of the 'land of the spirits' and been transferred into a lower level because it is their duty and obligation to *become embodied* in an ongoing downward movement to be incorporated into an astral body, or into the corporal body of a human being.

Beyond this layer there is another region in the 'land of the spirits' in which spiritual hierarchies prevail, notably *angels*, spirits of fire, spirits of form. There are spirits of wisdom, spirits of volition, called 'thrones', which are very high-ranking spiritual beings who may exert a great *impact on the course of history in the extrasensory world*. In this way, layer is placed on layer, and the whole process is one of probing more and more deeply into ever advancing 'higher worlds', which have, however, not yet been discovered or recognized empirically, but which are nonetheless considered to be comprehensible and ultimately intelligible.

Over and beyond this, Steiner establishes a link between the entire range of 'spiritual beings' perceived by the 'spiritual eye', the perception of which is claimed to follow certain 'spiritual laws', which Steiner has elaborated in his *doctrine of reincarnation* and in his *teaching on kharma*. Over and beyond this, the beings and essences of the 'spiritual world' are embedded into a cosmic and historical panorama, which is open to be disclosed in all its details and concrete particularities.[29] Steiner's universe is sustained by a gigantic ongoing process of 'becoming', the rising and disappearing of earthly bodies, becoming manifest in the *history of the extrasensory world*: The same spiritual entity, which initially appears as the reincarnation of 'Saturn', which becomes manifest as a shape consisting of 'caloric substances', and which continues to develop through the stages of the sun and the moon, until the creation of the world, this very spiritual

---

29 STEINER, Rudolf. *Die Geheimwissenschaft im Umriß*. New ed. Stuttgart: Freies Geistesleben, 1948. 113–285.

essence is accompanied and determined by the history of the prevailing spiritual hierarchies; the entities germane to them are spiritual essences which are partly embodied in an astral or ethereal frame, or may even be incorporated entirely in a physical body, and as such will appear and disappear again.

The preternatural history of the creation of man, the spirits of the sun and the beings of the moon, are claimed to be integral parts of this ongoing supernatural process. The hostile powers and spirits which aim at disrupting this primeval process – notably the spirits of the kind of Lucifer or Ahriman – who desire to disrupt the course of preternatural history, as well as the healing, redemptive 'impulses', are vividly described. The ghost-seer has a clear awareness of the significance of the present moment, and knowledge of future events, both ones that are imminent as well as events expected to happen at a more distant future.

We are now going to consider critically the major notions and tenets of Steiner's conception of the extrasensory world from a gnoseological perspective. The descriptive details and the large number of detailed visionary experiences, as well as the many varieties of empirical 'relations' in Steiner's descriptions, are so astonishing that it inevitably provokes *the question as to their authenticity – as to whether the extrasensory experiences described are indeed genuine, i.e., based on empirical phenomena originating from real* [and not just imagined or hallucinatory] *preternatural events*. This question, however, cannot be answered within the context of our gnoseological enquiry. Steiner's veridical claims for his extrasensory experiences could only be tested by means of a comprehensive empirical investigation and would require epistemological foundations that cannot be supplied in the context of this study. There are indeed a number of pressing questions that call for an answer: Is Steiner's account really based on genuine supernatural phenomena encountered by him in experiences of extrasensory perception? Or is his account rather the result of a retrospective, speculative interpretation of the phenomena perceived, which is coloured, influenced or informed by the metaphysical theorems he held prior to such events, or has it been inspired by other systems of philosophical speculation, which he projected (perhaps unknowingly) onto the 'spiritual world', perceived when transported into modes of extrasensory perception? Could the visions, which Steiner claims to have experienced 'intuitively', be traced and qualified as projections of the metaphysical and esoteric theorems held by him surfacing from his subconscious or unconscious? Is the latter assumption not more probable than the claim that the extrasensory visionary experiences originate from the immediate cognitive perception of an experiential 'relationship' to paranormal entities? Are extrasensory experiences only accessible to the initiated ('master')? If this applies, such extraordinary events elude scientific verification. This aside, the notion of an exclusive experience of a 'master' or 'sage' is incompatible with the implied claim of the existence of a universal consciousness by which the 'spiritual world' is sustained. However, as we can neither verify nor falsify Steiner's assertions, we will acknowledge that his account is a record of subjective preternatural experience, but we shall consider the 'spiritual world' described in it only in hypothetical terms – i.e., the phenomena are understood 'as if' they were real and authentic. But we should repeat again that the question as to whether the paranormal phenomena described by Steiner are genuine or not is not vital to the methodological progress of our enquiry.

This proviso should be borne in mind, if we venture to make a valid statement about *the 'categorical structure' of the 'spirit world'*.

THESIS 10: *The sphere of objects featuring in extrasensory anthroposophical experience is part of the real world.*

The term *'reality'* is, according to Nicolai Hartmann, determined by two characteristics: 'temporality' and 'individuality'.[30] This means that the concept of 'reality' does not necessarily include the categories of 'spatiality' and 'materiality' as well, but the term only implies that whatever is considered 'real' must be endowed with the properties of 'temporality' and 'individuality', viz., 'individual uniqueness'. On the basis of this definition, all the visions and phenomena occurring in the 'spirit world' (as perceived by Steiner) qualify as 'real' visions and phenomena. They are just as real as items of the world of the psyche, i.e., phenomena of consciousness as well as individual acts and phenomena of the imagination. This fact can, from an ontological perspective, be epitomized as follows:

---

30 Cf. HARTMANN, Nicolai. *Neue Wege der Ontologie*. Stuttgart: Kohlhammer, 1947.

As the 'spirit world' is part of the real world (amongst other worlds that are part of the real world), it must be classified as an integral part of the entirety termed 'real world'. The question, however, whether the 'spirit world' is indeed a *layer* that extends beyond the known areas of the created world, or if it had better be considered as a *region*, or separate area of its own, cannot yet be answered, as this requires additional empirical enquiries.

We may infer another thesis from what has been established above:

THESIS 11: *There is in part a wide-ranging identity between the extant categories of the 'normal world' and those of the transnormal 'spirit world'.*

Most of the categories known to us from the natural world are replicated in the 'spirit world'. This statement is self-evident when applied to the so-called basic or 'fundamental categories', such as 'uniqueness', 'multiplicity', 'individuality', 'generality', 'substratum', 'relation', 'element' or 'structure'. We have already referred to the fact that the category of 'spatiality' is missing [in the 'spirit world'], whereas the category of 'temporality' is given. The fact that Steiner assigns to the spiritual beings the freedom of self-determination, as well as the properties of having 'intentions' and a 'will', suggests that a final determination is likely to be involved.

The overabundant presence of issues of finality and causality, compared to other items of determination, may result from the erroneous judgement of the spirit-seers, or else may originate from the persevering impact of the familiar reality of the natural world. What is disconcerting, however, is the fact of how closely the categories of the 'spirit world', as well as their structural coherence, coincide with those of the 'normal world'. This gives rise to the serious question: Can we indeed discover special categories in the 'spirit world' which do not exist in the 'normal world'? It seems that such special categories and their special kind of determination that are germane to the 'spirit world' can be assumed to exist. It appears that similar to the normal organic world, (which is a layer transgressing the inorganic world of empirical reality), the phenomena of 'self-regulation' and 'self-generation' become apparent as part of complex empirical processes, and this suggests that there is indeed a *'nexus organicus'*, i.e., a highly irrational, non-causal and non-final form of determination;

this means that, by way of analogy, it might be possible that in the 'spirit world' the phenomenon of reincarnation and the *karmic* law might supply the basis from which an entirely different, as yet unknown, form of determination can develop, which is exclusively a characteristic of the 'spirit world'.

These findings are significant for our investigation. Our considerations have resulted in the conclusion that although the extrasensory 'spirit world' is partly determined by categories typical of, and inherent in, the 'spirit world', this does not mean that the 'spirit world' as such is located outside the boundaries of the empirical domain of the 'normal world'. *The paranormal modes of recognition have amplified the conception of the 'normal world', but the cognitive perception of the 'spiritual world' has yielded no phenomena or perceptions that could be classified as 'wholly foreign' and positioned entirely adverse to the 'normal world'.*

The extrasensory experience of the world by the 'ghost-seers' is the experience of a world of real spiritual entities. This 'spirit world', however, becomes accessible only if *a very special apparatus* [capacity] *is available that enables extrasensory cognitive perception*:

This special capacity for extrasensory recognition is rooted in 'the soul's organs of perception'; they are located in the 'astral-body' and operate analogously to the organs of sense perception in the physical body. Just as we see things with our physical eyes and are in this way furnished with empirical data which can be utilized for scientific research, the 'ghost-seer' is similarly able to perceive extrasensory phenomena and images by the organs of spiritual perception of the soul. [Steiner] termed these preternatural shapes 'wheels', or 'lotus flowers', and attributed them to certain areas of the 'astral-body', and thus indirectly, to the physical body. The implied spatial notion of extrasensory objects of perception evidently results from the transfer by way of analogy of spiritual, non-spatial modes of being, to the way phenomena are observed in the normal world of sense perception.[31]

---

31   Cf. STEINER, Rudolf. *Theosophie: Einführung in übersinnliche Welterkenntnis und Menschenbestimmung.* New ed. Freiburg i. Br.: Novalis, 1946. 145, 154; and STEINER, Rudolf. *Wie Erlangt man Erkenntnisse der Höheren Welten?* Berlin: Philosophisch-Anthroposophischer Verlag, 1922. 136. [Note: Here as elsewhere in the book Albrecht inserts a concise summary and his own reflections on the works of Steiner and other authors. In the German original these passages are printed in smaller font-size - a practice that has been retained in the English translation. - FKW.]

[Steiner] refers to *an organ of perception that consists of sixteen 'leaves'*, which is located near the larynx; it is claimed to facilitate quasi-sensory perceptions, in which extrasensory objects, such as items encompassed by the 'aura' of a human being, appear *as if* they were real material objects:[32] For instance, 'a benign thought may appear visually by the image of a flower blossoming'.[33] There is also a *'twelve-leaved organ of perception'*, which is located 'near the heart'; it adds to the spiritual perception of abstract forms, qualities of sensate experience, which are described in thermal terms – the 'warmth' or 'coldness of the soul'[34] – thus the familiar language of sensual reality is employed to refer to what is actually experienced in a purely spiritual manner.

There is also a *'lotus-flower consisting of ten leaves'*, which is located 'near the abdomen'; the extrasensory experience enabled by it completes the modes of the cognitive perception of the preternatural world, by eliciting spiritual impressions of colours and sensations of light: to perceive a colour spiritually means to experience something that corresponds to the natural response to a given colour when seen with physical eyes.[35] 'In this way the *aura* of colours of animate beings becomes visible.'[36]

The astral organism of perceiving consists of several more 'wheel-like shapes': there are some that have only two spokes, and again others with six spokes. Their function is to establish a link between the supernatural experience of the seer and the beings of the 'higher worlds', and also to supplement the overall experience.

The rather complex organism of *astral* perception is, however, confined to items 'existing in the world of the soul'[37]; the reason for this is that organs of experience that are receptive to spiritual items alone cannot be localised in the realm of the astral body, but depend on 'special organs of spiritual perception'.[38] Such an organ

---

32 STEINER, Rudolf. *Wie Erlangt man Erkenntnisse der Höheren Welten?* Berlin: Philosophisch-Anthroposophischer Verlag, 1922. 123.

33 STEINER, Rudolf. *Wie Erlangt man Erkenntnisse der Höheren Welten?* Berlin: Philosophisch-Anthroposophischer Verlag, 1922. 124.

34 STEINER, Rudolf. *Wie Erlangt man Erkenntnisse der Höheren Welten?* Berlin: Philosophisch-Anthroposophischer Verlag, 1922. 124.

35 STEINER, Rudolf. *Wie Erlangt man Erkenntnisse der Höheren Welten?* Berlin: Philosophisch-Anthroposophischer Verlag, 1922. 55, 133.

36 STEINER, Rudolf. *Wie Erlangt man Erkenntnisse der Höheren Welten?* Berlin: Philosophisch-Anthroposophischer Verlag, 1922. 55, 133.

37 STEINER, Rudolf. *Wie Erlangt man Erkenntnisse der Höheren Welten?* Berlin: Philosophisch-Anthroposophischer Verlag, 1922. 135.

38 STEINER, Rudolf. *Wie Erlangt man Erkenntnisse der Höheren Welten?* Berlin: Philosophisch-Anthroposophischer Verlag, 1922. 138–43; STEINER, Rudolf. *Die Geheimwissenschaft im Umriß.* New ed. Stuttgart: Freies Geistesleben, 1948. 361–64.

may, for instance, prosper in the ethereal body near the region of the heart and become the centre for the flow of energy in the ethereal body; it is a shape that 'radiates spiritually, and oscillates in numerous, most iridescent colours'[39].

However, on this stairway of anthroposophical recognition, the astral organism of perception furnishes only the foundation for what is termed *'recognition by means of the imagination'*. By this Steiner understands an extrasensory mode of perception of real and concrete spiritual entities, which are grasped by means of the imagination in analogy to the mode of perception of impressions transmitted by the corporal senses. The level of imaginative recognition 'is the first variety of extrasensory visual perception, i.e., a mode of perception in which is cognitively grasped what has been perceived, though the experience as such does not involve any physical sensation and can best be described as a picture-like spiritual experience'[40].

To evolve the capacity of attaining knowledge of the 'spirit world' it is not only necessary to cultivate one's character by special training and education, and requires, in particular, to advance one's path of purification and practical mental exercise.[41] When the practitioner has reached the ability of imaginative perception, he/she is able to 'see spiritually', but this is still a long way from being capable of arriving at 'inspirational knowledge', and to discern the mysterious processes and laws going on in the 'spirit world'. Yet it is only on *the level of inspiration* that the capacity of 'spiritual vision' achieves its full potential, so that the 'spirit-seer' is enabled to 'read the hidden script'. In the event of an 'imaginative experience', he/she becomes merely aware of 'letters or sounds'; 'without the cognitive content bestowed by inspiration, the imaginative world would merely be experienced like writing looked at, but which cannot be read or understood.'[42] 'By the power of inspiration a spirit-seer is enabled to recognize the bond and relationships that exist between the entities of the higher worlds.'[43] The capacity of recognition is highest at the level of *intuition*. The

---

39   STEINER, Rudolf. *Wie Erlangt man Erkenntnisse der Höheren Welten?* Berlin: Philosophisch-Anthroposophischer Verlag, 1922. 139.

40   LAUER, Hans E. *Die Wiedergeburt der Erkenntnis in der Entwicklungsgeschichte des Menschlichen Erkenntnisstrebens*. Freiburg i. Br.: Novalis, 1946. 234.

41   Cf. STEINER, Rudolf. *Die Geheimwissenschaft im Umriß*. New ed. Stuttgart: Freies Geistesleben, 1948. 350-85; STEINER, Rudolf. *Wie Erlangt man Erkenntnisse der Höheren Welten?* Berlin: Philosophisch-Anthroposophischer Verlag, 1922. 1-42; 47-110; 115-22; 125-32.

42   STEINER, Rudolf. *Die Geheimwissenschaft im Umriß*. New ed. Stuttgart: Freies Geistesleben, 1948. 344-46.

43   STEINER, Rudolf. *Die Geheimwissenschaft im Umriß*. New ed. Stuttgart: Freies Geistesleben, 1948. 343, 348. Cf. LAUER, Hans E. *Die Wiedergeburt der Erkenntnis in der Entwicklungsgeschichte des Menschlichen Erkenntnisstrebens*. Freiburg i. Br.: Novalis, 1946. 237-38.

seer and researcher of the 'spirit world', who is gratified with intuitive knowledge, is given insight into the essence of primeval spiritual powers. These primeval spiritual powers are the origin of the 'spirit world', and it is sustained by their ongoing interaction. By the power of intuition 'a proper enquiry into the nature of reincarnation and of karma'[44] is rendered possible, because 'it is by intuition that the seer is capacitated to perceive what is revealed to him/her inwardly as he/she passes from one reincarnation to the next'[45]. The seer 'recognizes himself in the figure that he is as a spiritual being in the spirit world.'[46]

When assessing Steiner's conception of the 'spirit world' critically from the perspective of mundane reality, one will presumably be inclined to dismiss the highly sophisticated concept of cognitive perception as curious intellectual speculation, which eludes any scientific verification. However, Rudolf Steiner has indeed been able to underpin this complex theosophical framework by a monistic epistemology[47] of his own. The unique tenet of this epistemological theory is the claim that the wholeness or unity that embraces both subject and object is not transintelligible; on the contrary, it is something that can be comprehended and recognized spiritually and is as such real.

Steiner's epistemological theory is rooted in the 'philosophy of thinking'. In Steiner's view, 'thinking of thinking' is a supreme path for attaining direct [unmediated] knowledge of the identity between the object perceived in consciousness and of the subject recognizing it. When the act of thinking is itself the content of an act of thinking, the identity between the content of thinking and the act of thinking

---

44 STEINER, Rudolf. *Die Geheimwissenschaft im Umriß*. New ed. Stuttgart: Freies Geistesleben, 1948. 350.

45 STEINER, Rudolf. *Die Geheimwissenschaft im Umriß*. New ed. Stuttgart: Freies Geistesleben, 1948. 350.

46 STEINER, Rudolf. *Die Geheimwissenschaft im Umriß*. New ed. Stuttgart: Freies Geistesleben, 1948. 388.

47 STEINER, Rudolf. *Die Rätsel der Philosophie*. 2 vols., 6th ed. Dornach: Philosophisch-Anthroposophischer Verlag, 1924 and 1926; STEINER, Rudolf. *Grundlinien einer Erkenntnistheorie der Goetheschen Weltanschauung*. New ed. Freiburg i. Br.: Novalis, 1949; STEINER, Rudolf. *Wahrheit und Wissenschaft*. New ed. Freiburg i. Br.: Novalis, 1948; STEINER, Rudolf. *Philosophie der Freiheit*. New ed. Stuttgart: Behrendt, 1947.

is immediately evident. There is another important issue in Steiner's epistemology: He insists that the pivotal insights about the process of thinking become evident only in an exceptional mental state, when one is transferred into a higher (expanded) state of consciousness in which *the process of thinking is perceived as if 'seen' visually, i.e., when thinking has become a mode of 'intuition'*. At the instance of 'intuitive recognition', *the process of thinking is itself recognized as an entity embracing both subject and object*.[48]

This epistemological theory is intrinsically *monistic:* Thinking is considered an entity, the content of which are thoughts that are represented in the object, though its distinctive features remain, for the time being, concealed; on the other hand, thoughts are *identical* with the concepts found in the subject, which have been instilled by 'intuition'. This means that in Steiner's epistemological theory, subject and object are understood to be based on identical principles. The term 'entity' as understood in this context does not say anything about the mode of being on which this 'entity' is based. The question as to whether this is a real mode of being, or an ideal one, remains open. To this point, Steiner's theory is only his version of extant (monistic) epistemological theories, by which the axiomatic reliance on the phenomenon of 'the thinking of thinking' is extolled. However, Steiner advances the theory further by his astonishing twist: He insists that the all-embracing ontological unity, from which both subject and object originate and are encompassed, is not a metaphysical theorem, nor an entity that is incomprehensible or even irrational, but this 'oneness' is an entity that can be known by intuition, and thus experienced as something real. The entities that are enclosed in the 'shape' in both subject and object are identical and as such real 'spiritual beings' ["Geistwesen"]; they are inhabitants of the 'spirit world', which can be perceived in object-like form by a subject's extrasensory awareness. In an extrasensory experience, insights are revealed of the interconnectedness of every individual being with the one all-encompassing Reality. This means that a 'spirit-seer' has several layers of cognition at his/her disposal, i.e., several *cognitive relations are superimposed upon each other* in the supernatural act of cognition.

---

48 WITZENMANN, Herbert. "Intuition und Beobachtung." *Die Drei: Monatsschrift für Anthroposophie* 18.1 (1948): 36–51.

The subject experiencing the cognitive relation on the level of spiritual perception is the same as the subject who recognizes an object on the normal level of cognitive perception. However, the object perceived by the subject in a paranormal event is the same subject who has recognized the object on the normal world and thus the ontological unity of the first relation! From this notion Steiner infers the following claim: Because of the fact that in the second i.e., extrasensory relation all ontological elements and relations of the first relation, i.e., the normal relation of natural sense perception, are recognized and fully comprehended, all the gnoseological aporias connected to the paranormal relation must be suspended, and therefore the claim that these aporias can never be resolved has been proved false for all time. The aporias upheld previously are henceforth to be replaced by the true and sound knowledge retrieved from extrasensory experience.

This line of argument is evidently a version of *petitio principii*: The aporias that are inevitably part of gnoseological perception cannot be discarded by a cognitive relation: The all-embracing relation must either be a genuine gnoseological phenomenon – but if this applies, the entire range of problems covered by the first relation is entailed by it – or the all-embracing relation is only apparently a cognitive relation, whereas it is in actual fact merely a metaphysical theorem posing in the guise of a gnoseological phenomenon.

The goal of our enquiry is to clarify and expound the phenomenon of 'mystical recognition'. So far, we have made but little progress on the way. We have not even got a glimpse of the contours of the phenomenon! At the beginning of our enquiry, we had two options of pathways along which we might proceed.

The one was to begin by compiling and analysing a representative corpus of authentic records of mystical experience by approved mystics; in this way we might have got insight into the nature and the range of phenomena acknowledged as 'mystical' ones, and we might hereafter, in a second methodological step, have compared the results of the critical phenomenological analysis of the mystical records to the cognitive experiences, phenomena and modes of recognition of the 'ghost seers' and 'spirit searchers'. This would have resulted in a comprehensive contrastive phenomenology of mystical vs. esoteric/extrasensory experience.

However, we have decided to pursue a different path by opting for an approach in which the 'spirit world' and its modes of recognition are explored on the basis of insights derived from anthroposophy and scientific research in the realm of the 'spirit world'. This approach promises to supply us with seminal features of the mystical phenomenon of recognition. We have decided in favour of the latter methodology and to defer the exploration of the structural features of mysticism to the final stage of our enquiry, that is, until after the phenomenon of 'mystical recognition' has been approached from several empirical and gnoseological perspectives.

This approach, however, generates a problem which will accompany us throughout our investigation: It is imperative for our investigation to exclude the domain of the 'spirit seers' entirely from the realm of mysticism. The problem is, however, that we are not able to ascertain at this stage of our enquiry what is to be understood by the concept of 'mystical recognition', nor do we know clearly what the object of 'mystical recognition' is. This means that we are required to start by anticipating the premise that the 'mystical Object' cannot be found within the domain of objects featuring in the 'spirit world'.

It will become apparent that the following considerations will proceed cautiously and by conjecture rather than along the lines of a strict scientific investigation, and that the central concern will be addressed from diverse hypothetical perspectives rather than clearly established.

There is yet another problem that cannot be passed over silently: At this juncture of our enquiry, we do not know at all if the 'mystical relation' encompasses any components that have gnoseological import so that the 'mystical relation' can indeed be classified in terms of a 'gnoseological relation'. For it might be that a 'mystical vision', viz., 'mystical experience', is conceived in a manner that does not include the capacity of 'recognition' at all, or that the alleged cognitive import of the 'mystical relation' has been wrongly attributed to it. For this reason, the following statements have to be read in hypothetical terms, i.e., as conditional statements implying the proviso 'as-if': If there is such an empirical phenomenon as 'mystical recognition', and if the 'All-encompassing', which we have psychologically defined as an unfathomable 'object arriving' in the vista of 'inner sight', is also an object with gnoseological import, hence a genuine object of 'mystical recognition', then it is possible to elucidate in some detail the difference between the domain of 'mystical recognition' and the gnoseological domain encompassed by the experiences of the 'spirit seers'. The following four sections in our study must therefore be read with these provisos in mind. This means that the subsequent considerations cannot provide conclusive insights to permit us to propose new theses, but despite this deficiency they will furnish us with new perspectives for the enquiry into the nature of the phenomenon of 'mystical recognition'.

1. The 'All-encompassing', conceived as the ultimate 'object' of mystical perception, cannot be thought of in terms of a mere 'object' amongst any other objects of perception. In the extrasensory experience of the 'spirit-seers' we encounter a very large number of diverse objects, which are all interrelated in different ways. Although these objects are arranged hierarchically in the 'spirit world', with each of them being allocated to different levels on the hierarchical scale, but during the cognitive act of perception, every object is identified and put side by side with the other objects perceived (which are similar, more or less). Within the hierarchy of the 'acting spirits' there are 'spirits of form', which are differentiated from the 'spirits of wisdom', which again are distinguished from 'archangels', and who are again on a different tier than 'angels'. This is different in the realm of mystical experience: *In a cognitive mystical experience there is only a single object of perception.* The 'mystical Object' is the only object of perception, and not, like in extrasensory perception, one amongst several others. The 'mystical Object' is unique and the single 'all-encompassing' content of mystical perception. At this point we must refrain from resorting to metaphysical and/or ontological concepts in qualifying the unique essence of the 'mystical Object'. It is not our intention to amplify our psychological-phenomenological concept of the 'All-encompassing' by the philosophical notion of the 'All-embracing'[49]. The cognitive

---

49 [Note: Albrecht here refers to the concept of the "Umgreifende" introduced by the philosopher Karl Jaspers, which in the English editions of Jaspers's works has

realm of the 'spirit-seers' differs markedly from the realm of 'recognition' in the context of a mystical event and cannot be equated with the threshold between normal modes of recognition in this world and modes of 'mystical recognition' of transcendental Reality. We only wish to emphasize *that the object of gnoseological mystical experience is at any time and forever the same identical 'Object', which is as such unique, incomparable, not related to, or dependent on, any other 'object', hence existing alone by itself.*

2. The *concept 'world'* will be helpful for our endeavour to expand further the scope of our considerations. In this introductory chapter on 'pseudo-mysticism' we are, however, compelled to adhere to a rather narrow definition of 'world': We shall use the term exclusively in a gnoseological and not in an ontological sense. The concept of 'the world' as used here does not refer to the totality of what exists in creation, irrespective of the question as to whether a thing can become the object of a cognitive experience or not. Our concept of 'the world' is not identical either with what the term denotes in existentialist philosophy. By 'world' we thus do not understand the preordained domain of being in which every single individual is situated, but both the totality of known objects and the entirety of things that can potentially be known. 'The world' is thus the horizon within which the discerning subject may recognize his/her object. Basically, there is only one world in which we are located as individuals, who are bestowed with the faculty of recognition. Though we are occasionally inclined to speak – irrespective of this fact – of different 'worlds', we actually mean by this merely 'partial worlds', which can be removed from the wholeness of the one 'world' that is

---

been translated as 'the embracing', and/or the 'all-embracing'. Albrecht gives a concise synopsis of Jaspers's explication of the concept in *Psychologie des Mystischen Bewußtseins*, 216ff. See also the annotations on this concept and its interchangeable use with the terms 'the encompassing' in the works of Jaspers in *Carl Albrecht: Psychology of Mystical Consciousness*. Trans. and annotated by F. K. Woehrer. New York: Crossroad, 2019. 314–18. – FKW.]

accessible to recognition. For instance, we refer to the 'world of the senses', in order to distinguish it from the 'spirit world', or the 'world of the soul', which are both accessible to us by a special mode of recognition: 'intuition'. Furthermore, the sciences and the humanities likewise address different 'partial worlds' – as 'the world' of the natural sciences is clearly a different one from 'the world' of the humanities.

We may therefore argue that 'the world of the spirit-seers' is a 'partial world', which is as such an integral part of the entire sphere of human knowledge. The term 'extrasensory world' indicates that a special kind of knowledge – a paranormal one – is attributed to it. The terms 'higher world' or 'higher worlds', by contrast, refer to the hierarchical order within the 'partial worlds', and has no longer a purely gnoseological meaning, but also ontological and metaphysical connotations. The 'spirit seers', i.e., individuals who refer to themselves as 'spirit researchers' or 'spirit-scientists', insist that their 'world' of extrasensory experiences is to be acknowledged as an area of knowledge which is just as accessible to science and scientific classification as the world of normal sense perception.

By considering these facts, it becomes instantly clear *that the sphere of mystical recognition differs profoundly from any of the other 'worlds' and modes of recognition. The term 'world' is therefore entirely inadequate for describing the domain of mystical recognition.* The one and only identical 'object' cannot be a part of any of these 'worlds', because it does not have (as we may state by way of anticipation) any of the qualities by which it could be identified as an 'object' of any of these 'worlds', be placed side by side with other 'objects' of human knowledge. The psychological concept of the 'All-encompassing' has gnoseological import: The 'object' encountered in the event of 'mystical recognition' is understood not to be part of any extant structure created by any other object of knowledge. 'The world' that is thought of as an area that provides the potential for knowledge, can be explored everywhere and at any time, like a ship exploring the ocean, or a pioneering expedition exploring an unknown wilderness, i.e., by proceeding consecutively step by step. *The domain of mystical recognition, by contrast, can neither be reached through a passageway already known, nor can it be attributed to a known part of this world. The unique, identical object of a mystical vision can only be experienced in a very special manner (which will be detailed later), but this alone does not create a mystical world. The sphere of mystical recognition and the object of mystical experience are identical.* This sphere is, as it were, a dot.

The fact that the concept of 'world' founders when applied to the domain of mystical experience does not refer to the phenomenon of transcendence (which will be explored later in this enquiry), which is something entirely different. Our focus at this stage is not on a borderline experience like the one subsumed by the term 'transcendence', as we are still concerned with establishing the gnoseological characteristics germane to the 'mystical relation'. The term 'world' was useful for the purpose of differentiating the realm of mysticism from the 'spirit world' of the 'spirit seers'. The fact that the concept of 'the world' is rendered inadequate for probing into the realm of mysticism suggests *the phenomenological 'sparsity' of the phenomenon of 'mystical recognition'*. That is to say, we cannot exclude the possibility that the phenomenon of recognition cannot be fully established, or not be verified at all in the context of mysticism.

3. 'Science is the sum total of all knowledge that is coherently structured and ordered by logical principles and which is open to understanding for every human being.'[50] Rudolf Steiner's claim that his insights are sustained by the '*science* of the spirit world' is based, first, on his firm belief that the 'spirit world' is principally – though not in actual fact – accessible to every human being, because it is possible for everyone to learn and to develop the capacity for extrasensory perception; second, on the claim that the ordered structure of the extrasensory world is largely based on the same categories and principles as the order of the

---

50 [Note: Albrecht does not specify the source of this quotation. He appears to be quoting Rudolf Steiner from memory, as the exact wording of this quotation could not be traced in Steiner's works. – FKW.]

natural world, and for this reason the two worlds can be claimed to be inherently similar. This claim, however, is by no means valid for the domain of mystical recognition: *Mysticism is a phenomenon in which the gnoseological features are extremely sparse*, and thus the cognitive capacity in mysticism differs significantly from the one in other realms of experience. And *because of the inherent cognitive sparsity of mysticism, we cannot speak of a 'science of mysticism'*. However, a mystical experience can indeed instil genuine recognition, though it is unlikely that a mystical experience will convey so many different experiential features that an ordered structure of knowledge, which fulfils the demands of science, could be inferred from it.

In our enquiry we have repeatedly come across the same unique phenomenon and realized that this singular 'object' of mysticism 'does not impart any tangible knowledge', that is, none on which a 'world' or a 'branch of science' could be founded. In other words, concepts like 'world' and 'science' are too limited for an enquiry into the cognitive aspects of mystical experience.

4. At a later stage of this study, we shall probe further into the depths of mystical experience beyond the domain of gnoseology, and consider ontological issues, notably what is to be understood ontologically by the phenomenon of the 'mystical relation'. In the context of this enterprise we shall also address the established *notion of the 'mystical Eros'*. By this a special loving relationship to the mystical object is commonly understood, which reveals itself as an intense desire for the mystical object, or more specifically, as an experience in which a person feels to be irresistibly 'drawn to and attracted by' the mystical 'object'; it is an overwhelming experience which triggers, consciously and/or unconsciously, an ardent quest for the desired 'object', by 'searching all the world for it'.[51] *The avid desire to know* can indeed be an aspect of the mystical Eros, and thus be considered as a specific stage in a person's mystical development. The desire for knowledge of the unknown is likewise at the root of the 'spirit seer's'

---

51 [Note: Quotation not identified by Albrecht. – FKW.]

aspiration for entering the 'spirit world', and of the adventurous seafarer's pioneering voyage into unknown seas and alien territories – both are aspirations that can arguably be seen as [profane] manifestations of the mystical Eros. Setting out for the unknown, the desire to transcend the thresholds of the natural world, are expressions of a human being's insatiable desire for finding the 'object' of 'existential love'. However, the 'spirit seer's' spiritual quest is overtly directed at advancing to ever 'higher regions' of the 'spirit world': towards the region of the great spiritual beings and, ultimately, to the highest layer of the primeval entities, the supreme stage of the spiritual hierarchy, which is still partially accessible to cognition. However, on the path traversed by the 'spirit seer' there is hardly ever any mention of the '*mystical* Eros', for his/her primary desire for knowledge is directed at paranormal knowledge, not at Love as the sole and supreme 'object' of cognition. It is only after the 'spirit seer' has passed all the layers in the hierarchy of the 'spirit world' and realizes in the end that his/her ardent desire for knowledge has not fully satiated, that he/she becomes open to an entirely different mode of spiritual perception; that is to say, only when the 'spirit seer' has been exposed to a process of 'mystical purification' is he/she capable of eliciting the capacity for 'mystical vision'. *Though the 'mystical Object' can be searched for on the path of the 'spirit seer' as well, it can, however, be found on this way only if (to put it in terms of the language of the mystics)*[52] *the content of the impressions*

---

52 [Note: Albrecht here has the Christian teaching of 'negative spirituality', i.e., the tradition of the *'via negativa'* or apophatic mysticism of Pseudo-Dionysius (and his successors throughout the history of western mysticism, including – amongst many others – Meister Eckhart, Johannes Tauler, the 14th c. English author of *The Cloud of Unknowing*, John of the Cross, Theresa of Avila) in mind. 'Negative theology' insists that the overwhelming mystery of God is beyond human comprehension, as the Infinite can never be expressed by finite concepts, and can only be 'known by unknowing', i.e., by an intuitive awareness of the ineffable Presence of the Godhead. The negative path to the Divine requires the practitioner of contemplation to become wholly 'detached' from 'this world' and indifferent to its sensible objects and delights. The mind must moreover be purged of self-will, discard rational thinking

of the 'spirit world' transmitted by extrasensory perception, are 'forgotten' and 'put behind', when everything in this mundane 'world' is dismissed as 'naught' when seen from the single focal point at which the 'mystical eye' is directed, and which affords 'mystical knowledge' in the event of a 'mystical vision'.

Cosmic Consciousness

It will have become clear from the foregoing considerations that the term 'pseudo-mysticism', as conceived in this study, has no negative connotations at all, and has never been used in a derogatory sense. The word is rather used as an umbrella term that includes both the concept of 'occultism' and the preternatural domain of the 'spirit-seers' and 'spirit researchers'. The concept of 'pseudo-mysticism' thus embraces two areas of spiritual recognition which both differ significantly from the realm of 'mystical recognition'. The latter can thus be clearly excluded from the field of 'pseudo-mysticism'. Such a clear-cut and consistent differentiation between the domains of 'mysticism' and 'occultism' and 'spiritualism' has not been attempted in science and scholarship to date, because such an enterprise cannot easily be achieved – which becomes apparent by the fact that even the mystics themselves have often mistaken spurious for genuine phenomena and vice versa, and often conflated occult and other paranormal phenomena with genuine modes of 'mystical vision'.

We now enter another sphere of preternatural phenomena which need to be critically contrasted to the phenomena of mysticism: the sphere of the so-called 'cosmic consciousness', a term coined by R. M. Bucke.[53] The present critical discussion on 'cosmic con-

---

and the self needs to be 'annihilated' as to become fully receptive to God. Liberated and purified in this way on the 'negative path', the seeker has achieved the (incipient) stage of 'perfection'; finally, the ultimate stage of 'perfection' is accomplished when the contemplative is gratified with the gift of mystical union. – FKW.]

53 BUCKE, Richard M. *Cosmic Consciousness. The Evolution of the Human Mind*. Philadelphia: Innes, 1905. [Note: Albrecht used the German translation of the American edition entitled *Kosmisches Bewußtsein*. Trans. and ed. Elisabeth von Brasch. Celle: Kampmann, 1925. – FKW.]

sciousness' has been deliberately assigned to the current introductory chapter, although we are aware that the phenomena pertaining to the 'cosmic consciousness' are properly to be assigned to a domain placed between mysticism and pseudo-mysticism. The term 'pseudo-mysticism' does not cover the entire range of phenomena encountered beyond the sphere of the 'natural world'. As we shall see, we shall encounter several phenomena in our enquiry into the nature of 'cosmic consciousness' which also qualify as pointers at genuine mystical phenomena. This means, in other words, that we shall get a first glimpse of the space extending towards the mystical.

The methodological approach applied in our investigation into the realm of 'cosmic consciousness' is the same as the one we are going to apply when exploring 'mystical consciousness'. Basically, we shall proceed step by step in the following manner: 1. We shall define the concept(s) under discussion. 2. Each concept will be substantiated by examples and documented by quotations from authentic mystical texts. 3. A detailed psychological analysis of the mystical records will be carried out. 4. The findings of the psychological analysis of the mystical documents will be examined from a phenomenological perspective and thus lead our enquiry beyond the discipline of psychology.

As for item 2, we should add by way of explanation that I have decided to resort to the time-honoured personal records, self-confessions and testimonies of great mystics and saints, rather than to rely on the accounts of contemporary mystics as the textual bases for my psychological analysis. It seemed imperative to me to have recourse to the proven testimonies of mystics from different historical periods and mystical traditions; excluding these authentic documents would have significantly impaired the wealth of empirical data and, consequently, reduced the validity of the results of the psychological analysis; this aside, such an approach would have violated the high esteem of the great mystics and saints, and been an expression of disrespect for the authenticity and spiritual and cultural value of these texts, which have stood the test of time. Contemporary accounts of private mystical occurrences are, by comparison, often tinged by subjective notions or shaped by ideas imposed by the current trends of thinking, as reflected, for instance, in contemporary 'school-psychology', but also by psychoanalytical theories. On the other hand, the use of historical records of mystical experience is likewise fraught with pitfalls and difficulties: Mystical reports dating from past centuries are hardly ever records of spontaneous mystical utterances, but more or less elaborate accounts and interpretations of mystical experience based on religious faith. Some of the records handed down from tradition were evidently modified later in history as to conform to theological dogma. Thus, in some of these historical mystical writings we can no longer say for sure if they are indeed authentic personal accounts of genuine mystical experience. For this reason, we have confined our choice to texts which have (by circumstantial evidence) been acknowledged to be reliable and truthful testimonies of personal mystical events. The criteria for assessing mystical records as authentic are those applied by the teaching of seasoned mystical counsellors and the mystic's own critical acumen in identifying a mystical experience as genuine. Any genuine mystic feels inexorably bound to absolute truth, and most of the great representatives had the skill, knowledge and intellectual and psychological capacity to render their exceptional experiences intelligibly in words in a coherently structured manner.

As for items 3 and 4, we should add that our textual analysis will focus first on the psychological aspects and phenomena; the results will hereafter be compared to the scientific findings established in our earlier empirical study on the nature of mystical (and other altered) states of consciousness.[54] That is to say, the earlier study will serve as a scientific reference-frame as far as the domain of psychological phenomenology is concerned. But the goal of our current study is to transcend the threshold of empirical psychology and to advance into the realms of gnoseology and ontology. It is, after all, only possible to grasp the cognitive dimension of mystical experience if we succeed in discovering a range of conclusive features germane to it. Once the phenomenon of 'mystical recognition' has been identified, we shall be

---

54 [Note: The reference is to Albrecht's study *Psychologie des Mystischen Bewußtseins,* first published in 1951, reprinted in 1958, 1990, and with corrections in 2019; the first English translation appeared in 2019, entitled *Carl Albrecht: Psychology of Mystical Consciousness.* Trans., annotated and intro. by F. K. Woehrer. – FKW.]

able to realise that it is not only a phenomenon that cannot be comprehended in psychological terms alone, but that it is also one that supplies epistemological and ontological insights. Over and beyond this, we will recognize that within, or 'hidden behind' the phenomenon of 'mystical recognition', a new one becomes apparent which has all the pivotal characteristics of an 'ultimate phenomenon'.

Unfortunately, the term 'cosmic consciousness' does not adequately define what is meant by it. Introduced as early as 1905, Bucke's term has acquired some opaque meanings; thus, the concept has been used to refer to an exceptional numinous experience with cognitive import, or to signify an awe-inspiring paranormal process and/or experience.[55]

Bucke coined the concept by analogy to other sublime states of consciousness, notably the states of the 'aesthetic', the 'ethical' and the 'religious consciousness'. The qualifying epithet 'cosmic', however, refers alone to the 'content' encountered in this mental condition, i.e., it indicates that in this paranormal mental condition the boundless existence of the cosmos as a whole is perceived in an awe-inspiring experience. Such a preternatural experience of participating in the cosmic 'life of becoming' may occur spontaneously, though it is more commonly evoked by acts of sense perception, acts of the imagination, acts of thinking, or by feelings evoked by the contemplation of creation, and by acts of volition. The epithet 'cosmic' does not designate any of the specific psychological or phenomenological characteristics of the given state of consciousness. [This is a terminological deficiency which has been emended in German translations of the term, in which 'cosmic consciousness' is often

---

55   Cf. URBAN, Hubert. *Über-Bewußtsein ("Cosmic Consciousness") Nach Bucke und Walker Bearbeitet.* Innsbruck: Tyrolia, 1950; UNDERHILL, Evelyn. *Mysticism. A Study in the Nature and Development of Man's Spiritual Consciousness.* London: Methuen, 1911. [Note: Albrecht used the German translation of Underhill's study: *Mystik.* Munich: Reinhardt, 1928; here the reference is to pages 254 and 332. – FKW.]; JAMES, William. *Varieties of Religious Experience.* London: Longmans, 1902. [Note: Albrecht's source was the German translation of James's book: *Die Religiöse Erfahrung in Ihrer Vielfalt.* Trans. Georg Wobbermin. Leipzig: 1907. – FKW.]

substituted by the synonymous term "Über-Bewußtsein",[56] literally 'meta-consciousness', or 'over-consciousness', suggesting that the term has some gnoseological import that is not available in 'normal states of consciousness']. Psychologically speaking, the "Über-Bewußtsein" is a mental state in which the 'quiet state of alertness' is combined with qualities of the 'ecstatic consciousness'; it involves, in particular (like the ecstatic consciousness), the elimination of the subject-object-split. From a metaphysical perspective the 'cosmic consciousness' can be contrasted to 'the unconscious' as conceived in depth-psychology. If we applied the term 'cosmic consciousness' by analogy to the spectrum of colours we may state: the 'normal consciousness' is located between 'the unconscious' and the realm of the "Über-Bewußtsein", which corresponds to the 'normal' spectrum of colours visible to a human being which covers the range of wavelengths between ultra-red and ultra-violet. But before we can raise the question of whether the cognitive potential of 'cosmic consciousness' can indeed contribute something that would enable us to probe more deeply into the realm of 'mystical vision', we must try to comprehend somehow the essence of experiences encountered in 'cosmic consciousness'. For this purpose, I will use the account of the 'cosmic experience' of *samadhi* by the Indian yogi Paramhansa [sic] Yogananda and the personal accounts of R. M. Bucke, which are based on both his own experience and his studies of empirical records by others. Furthermore, I will refer below to the often quoted account of the German shoemaker and mystic Jakob Böhme (1575–1624).

Text 1: (A passage from the *Autobiography* of Param[a]hansa Yogananda)[57]: "My body became immovably stalled; breath was drawn out of my

---

56 URBAN, Hubert. *Über-Bewußtsein ("Cosmic Consciousness") Nach Bucke und Walker Bearbeitet*. Innsbruck: Tyrolia, 1950.

57 [Note: Albrecht's quotation is from the German translation *Autobiographie eines Yogi*. Munich: Barth, 1950. 156ff. The English translation has been supplied on the basis of the German edition of the *Autobiographie*, although a text in English translation is available. At close inspection, however, the text of the English edition (in the e-book version) of Paramahansa's *Autobiography of a Yogi*. 1946. 13th ed. Preface by W.Y. Evans-Wentz. Los Angeles, CA: Self-Realization Fellowship, 1998, is rather

lungs, as if pulled out by a huge magnet. Soul and mind instantly lost their physical bondage and streamed out like a fluid, piercing light from my every pore. My body felt like dead although I was highly alert within and instantly aware that I had never before been so filled with life. My identity was no longer confined to the body but embraced everything that surrounded me. People on distant streets seemed to be walking through my being, which had no barriers any more. The roots of plants and trees revealed themselves to me from the deep as the soil had become transparent; I was able to discern the flow of the sap inside trees and plants.

The whole surroundings were spread out visibly in front of me. The field of vision had become spatial and enabled me to comprehend everything by a single glance. Behind me I saw the people walking down the Rai Ghat Lane and could see a white cow approaching leisurely. When the cow reached the open ashram gate, I perceived her as if with my two physical eyes. Even after she had passed on behind the brick wall of the ashram's courtyard, I could still clearly see her.

In my spatial field of vision, the objects quivered and vibrated like cinematographic images. My body, the shape of my Master, the pillars of the courtyard, the furniture, the floor, trees and the sun moved more and more vibrantly, until everything melted away in a single sea of luminescent waves like a cube of sugar dissolving in a glass of water. The all-unifying light, separated from any material shape, unveiled in these transformations the laws of cause and effect operating in creation.

Bliss ineffable inundated my soul like undulating waves of the sea. I instantly knew that the Spirit of God instils felicity beyond words. The Spirit of God is a web of infinite beams of light. An ever-growing inner radiance began to embrace valleys and continents, the earth, the sun and the stars, the galactic nebulae, and beyond to the outermost Milky Ways. The entire cosmos, softly illuminated like a city at night watched from a distance, expanded all over the infinitude of my being. The clear outlines faded away at the periphery of my field of vision; farther away I discerned an immaterial radiance, the splendour of which never faded away. The planets radiated in a grosser light.

The divine cluster of rays poured forth from the Eternal Fountain, creating the galaxies, and dissolved into thousands of radiant crowns of unspeakable splendour. Again and again, I saw how the creative beams began to materialize into constellations and to dissolve hereafter into transparent tongues of fire! Myriads of worlds were again immersed – by a reversal of the rhythm – into a transparent sea of light, the entire vaulted heaven was a single infinite blaze.

---

jumbled, failing repeatedly to convey the meaning coherently and understandably. The German edition is clearly more reliable and more carefully edited. – FKW.]

I was aware that the centre of this heavenly conflagration was in my heart, it was the centre of the vision. Radiating light issued from the cells of my body and penetrated every part of the universe! Beneficial *amrita*, the nectar of immortality, pulsated through me like a bubbling well. The voice of God, the word of the creator, resounding in the syllable *AUM*, the vibration of the motion of the cosmos.

Suddenly, I began to breathe again. The disappointment was almost unbearable when I realized that the experience of unfathomable Infinity had gone." (*Autobiographie eines Yogi*, 156–57).

Paramahansa's profuse account of a personal cosmic experience is a mixture of miscellaneous phenomena (assessed from a typological perspective): Many of the singularities of the experience actually elude clear identification and classification. The individual components of the yogi's 'cosmic consciousness' are hardly ever depicted in clear conceptual and phenomenological terms, and several of the preternatural phenomena have not been encountered and assessed critically in the course of our enquiry so far (we shall come back at a later stage to such paranormal phenomena). This fact notwithstanding, we will analyse the constituent elements of the yogi's experience at this point, though our findings can, for the time being, only claim to be provisional.

In the first paragraph a *transnormal state of consciousness* is described, which appears to have switched on spontaneously; it has several of the seminal characteristics of a *clairvoyant vision*. In the second paragraph we can identify the *occult phenomenon of translucent perception*, and in the third section we can discern that the subject-object-split has largely been removed after the yogi has been transported into the state of ecstasy; at this stage he is also overwhelmed by a *visionary experience of light*. In the following paragraph emphasis is on the intense emotional response triggered by the ecstatic experience, notably *a deep feeling of ineffable bliss and ecstatic joy*. This aside, he describes some *objective features* of the vision of light. In the final section we encounter once more the phenomenon of clairvoyance, and the vision of light, the capacity of translucent vision, and the ecstatic exuberance triggered by it. There is, however, a new element as well: *the transfiguration of the yogi's own body*, which is the *corresponding subjective part of the visionary experience of light*.

The five major phenomena identified above – ecstatic exuberance, occult clairvoyance, translucent perception, visionary experience of light and awareness of one's own transfiguration – are similarly addressed in the description of R. M. Bucke, which is partly based on his own 'cosmic experience' and partly on his scholarly investigations into the nature of 'cosmic consciousness':

> Text 2 (Excerpts from R. M. Bucke's *Kosmisches Bewußtsein*)[58]:
> "It is the 'experience of the Light within'. – 'Without any premonition, one suddenly feels as if being ablaze and surrounded by a burning rose-coloured cloud, as if flames of fire would flare up from inside." – "This sensation evokes ineffable joy, bliss, a sense of assurance, and triumphant feelings." – "All the powers of the mind and intellect are illuminated." – "The cosmos is no longer perceived as dead matter." – "In a flash, the sense and purpose of creation are revealed."

Psychological considerations: Any attempt to describe 'cosmic consciousness' in psychological terms would be fragmentary if it were based alone on reports of people who had experienced states of 'cosmic consciousness', even if these reports appear to be trustworthy, authentic and conclusive. There are, however, very few records that can be approved to be reliable beyond any doubt, and these rare testimonies cannot be seen as sufficiently representative to allow a scientific analysis that could yield conclusive results. Therefore, it is helpful to rely, in addition, on critical studies like Otto Bollnow's *Das Wesen der Stimmungen*[59] [The nature of moods and emotional dispositions]. Contrary to Heidegger and his conception of the "Hermeneutik des Daseins" ['hermeneutics of being-in-the-world'] as outlined in *Sein und Zeit* (1927),[60] Bollnow focussed on exploring the happy, positive and elated moods encountered in human existence.

---

58 BUCKE, Richard M. *Kosmisches Bewußtsein*. Trans. and ed. Elisabeth v. Brasch. Celle: Kampmann, 1925. [Note: Albrecht does not give a page reference. English translation provided on the basis of the German text used by Albrecht. – FKW.]
59 BOLLNOW, Otto. *Das Wesen der Stimmungen*. 2nd ed. Frankfurt am M.: Klostermann, 1943.
60 HEIDEGGER, Martin. *Sein und Zeit*. 1927. 2nd ed. Halle a.d. Saale: Niemeyer, 1929.

Bollnow does not only assess several varieties of joyful moods and uplifted dispositions from a philosophical perspective, but also analyses them in detail from a psychological-phenomenological point of view. In this way he was able to specify the *psychological structure of the joyful state of mind*. He endorses quite persuasively the claim that *there is an essential, inalienable interlacing between the 'content' of certain experiences and of certain modes of experiencing with the basic mood of happy and blissful elation*. One of these necessary relations between a particular event and the mood evoked by it is – inevitably – time, i.e., the subjective awareness of the time having passed. The altered awareness of the sense of time in a cosmic experience is addressed in the records in expressions like 'the abiding now', 'eternal presence', or 'the influx of eternity in the flash of a moment'. These descriptions of temporality indicate that the sense of time is slowed down, or even suspended, thus come to a standstill. In some accounts time is, for instance, likened to 'the seas that have ceased to roll', in others the state of bliss is identified with 'timelessness', or 'the loss of the sense of time' is equal to perfect 'blessedness'.[61] Yet it is not only the sense of time that is altered in a 'cosmic experience', but also the sense of space: *The awareness of space is transformed and expanded*: Rooms and objects that are close to the observer are perceived enlarged and long-drawn-out: 'The small room in the cellar seemed to expand into the infinite'. Moreover, all sense perceptions are enormously intensified in a cosmic experience: 'All colours are more intense and radiant.'[62]

For the purposes of our enquiry, however, another characteristic feature is more important: *The fact that the mood of elation is interlinked with the phenomenon of translucent perception*. The subject becomes instantly aware of the perfection and meaningfulness of creation and of every single organic and inorganic 'object' in it; over and beyond this, he/she is instantly overwhelmed by the clear awareness of the perfection of the *eidos* of the soul; in this experience

---

61 Cf. BOLLNOW, Otto. *Das Wesen der Stimmungen*. 2nd ed. Frankfurt a. M.: Klostermann, 1943. 167ff.

62 BOLLNOW, Otto. *Das Wesen der Stimmungen*. 2nd ed. Frankfurt a. M.: Klostermann, 1943. 167ff.

mysteries of creation are directly revealed to the perceiver. Over and beyond this, the meaningful harmony permeating and sustaining the cosmos, flashes up and is comprehended at an instant; there is perfect concord between the perceiver and the object perceived, culminating in an ineffable sense of oneness, the perception of identity in what is normally experienced as separate.

We have after all been able to identify some of the seminal features of 'cosmic consciousness': the slowing down of the sense of time, the altered awareness of space, the increased intensity of sense perceptions, the instant capacity of clairvoyance, and the experience of primeval oneness; these experiences are all interlinked with the persevering mood of joy, bliss and elation, which culminates in an ecstatic state commonly termed 'intoxication'. As we are still concerned here with a psychological enquiry of the nature of 'cosmic consciousness', I would like to add two contrasting testimonies, which, however, transgress the scientific domain of psychology. The two examples are entirely different in kind. The first is a protocol of experiments with mescaline carried out by *Beringer*,[63] taken from Bollnow's study. The second document is a passage from *Jakob Böhme's* astonishing personal account of his great epiphanic vision.

> *Text 3:* (From the protocols of Beringer's experiments with mescaline, quoted by Bollnow).[64]

---

63 [Note: Emended from "Behringer" in Albrecht's text. Albrecht does not give the primary bibliographical source, neither in a footnote, nor in the 'List of Works Quoted'. – The reference is to Kurt BERINGER (1893–1949), German psychotherapist, neurologist and pioneer of experimental research in Europe (following William James in the United States) on the effects of mescaline and other psychedelic drugs. Beringer compared the effects of mescaline to psychosis, notably the sense of alienation from the world, altered perception of time, and depersonalization. His post-doctoral thesis *Der Meskalinrausch. Seine Geschichte und Erscheinungsweise*. Berlin: Springer, 1927, became a standard work and influenced German medical research on the effects of psychedelic drugs on the human psyche for decades to come. – FKW.]

64 BOLLNOW, Otto. *Das Wesen der Stimmungen*. 2nd ed. Frankfurt a. M.: Klostermann, 1943. 172.

"Then I directed my attention only at the meadow: I was able to see every single leaf of grass, it was clear that every single leaf had to be placed exactly where it was and to sway in the special way it did, and to cast that tiny shadow, and surely the earth was enormously delighted at this small shade. I saw a plethora of single plants ... and while I was contemplating the flowers I was suddenly overwhelmed by an awe-inspiring sensation, for I thought I could experience life itself in every plant, or even to see the spiritual ideal by which it should develop and emulate, and experienced the rhythm of growth, and its archetypal shape. And the further I looked across the meadow, the clearer the spiritual design of every plant became to me and saw the great harmony of the whole meadow."

Text 4: (A passage from the writings of Jakob Böhme [1575–1624], quoted in Martin Buber's anthology *Ekstatische Konfessionen*[65]). "When I was consumed by a deep melancholy, I gravely lifted up my spirit, of which I had hardly any understanding what it was, lifted it up to God vehemently like in a big storm, and all my heart and mind with all its thoughts and the will joining in as well, determined to wrestle relentlessly with God's love and mercy so long until he would respond and bless me, that is, until he would illuminate me with the Holy Spirit so that I would be able to know His will, and to overcome my sadness – and *then the Spirit did indeed break through*. But when I, in my surging zest and enthusiasm, was storming straight towards God and against the gates of hell, as if I had even more powers left, and been willing to sacrifice my life – which, would of course not have been in my power without the assistance of the Spirit of God – *my spirit eventually succeeded, after several stormy attempts, in breaking through the gates of hell and in penetrating even as far as the innermost origin of the Godhead*, where I was embraced with love, like a bridegroom embracing his bride.

I am unable to express in words the triumphant joy that filled my spirit at that time, nor can I compare it to anything except for the instance, where at the moment of death, new life is born, or else, this can be likened to the resurrection of the dead. In this light my spirit was at once able to see through everything and to recognize God in all creatures, herbs and grass, and enabled to know who He is and how He is, and what His will is."

---

65 BUBER, Martin. *Ekstatische Konfessionen*. Leipzig: Insel, 1921. 163. [Note: Buber does not give any reference to the sources used in his anthology of mystical 'confessions'. The passage is from Böhme's *Aurora, oder Morgenröte im Aufgang*, chapter xix. – The English translation has been supplied; italics printed as added by Albrecht for emphasis. – FKW.]

The textual examples chosen have been intended as illustrations for experiences of the 'cosmic consciousness'. They provide sufficient materials for our psychological analysis and will enable us to compare the results to the psychological phenomenology of mystical consciousness established in our earlier empirical study. The question that needs to be answered first in our comparative analysis is where the state of 'cosmic consciousness' should be located within the spectrum of states of consciousness identified by us. Does the 'cosmic consciousness' represent a pure form of the 'ecstatic consciousness', or is it rather a variety of the 'quiet state of alertness'? We may reply that all the descriptions of 'cosmic consciousness' examined by us show clearly that in a cosmic experience, consciousness is primarily inundated by feelings of exuberance and joy, as well as blessedness and/or a deep sense of blissful oneness. The elation and ecstatic joy evoked is so overwhelming that the awareness of the division between subject and object in the 'experiencing I' is almost entirely eroded; and this is a pivotal characteristic of the ecstatic state of consciousness as well. These facts notwithstanding, the 'cosmic consciousness' cannot appropriately be classified as a variety of the 'ecstatic consciousness', not least because the 'cosmic consciousness' is not a short-lived state of ecstatic elation, but rather an enduring condition in which the sense of bliss and exuberance may last several days, or even weeks. In the latter instance, this means that the state of 'cosmic consciousness' tends to be sustained, coexisting temporarily side by side with the 'waking consciousness'. This indicates that the condition of the 'cosmic consciousness' is usually not ephemeral, but a long-term state of bliss and exuberance which is not bound to the 'ecstatic consciousness' but is often intertwined with the 'quiet state of alertness' and the structure of the 'waking consciousness'.

In the reports examined, we can see that the heightened sense of alertness – a pivotal feature of the 'quiet state of alertness' – is expressly addressed. The 'experiencing I' has an advanced capacity of 'receiving' and/or responding to 'incoming' phenomena becoming apparent in the vista of 'inner sight' in a mental condition that is exceptionally lucid, calm and serene. This indicates that the 'quiet state of alertness' is involved in part. The mode of inward perception in the 'cosmic consciousness' differs, however, in degree from the hyper-lucid mode of 'inner sight' ["Innenschau"] germane to the 'quiet state of alertness'. In the latter state, contrary to the mental condition during a 'cosmic experience', all sense-perceptions are suspended, and the 'inner eye' is receptive only to phenomena perceived within. In the 'cosmic consciousness', by contrast, all sense perceptions continue to be active and responsive to external stimuli.

The faculty of 'seeing' in 'cosmic consciousness' is rather characterized as a dual mode of perception – consisting of the paranormal capacity of translucent perception, the ability of 'seeing through' things, which is intertwined with an intensified mode of sense-perception. In a cosmic experience the perceiver is enabled to see 'through' and 'behind' the objects seen by the normal sense organs. As *'translucent perception' is inevitably bound to the world of normal sense perception, and/or the world of the imagination, it differs significantly from the mode of 'inward perception', viz., the function of the 'inner eye' or 'inner sight' that is the distinctive characteristic of the 'quiet state of alertness'*. This means that 'translucent perception' as encountered in 'cosmic consciousness' consists, psychologically speaking, of a peculiar fusion of normal and paranormal sense-perceptions and intuition: Though 'translucent perception' in the state of 'cosmic consciousness' consists in part of familiar objects and impressions of normal sense perception, though these are transformed in manner and characterized by a different sense of time and space, by being more luminescent, more colourful, more graphic, but on the whole 'translucent perception' is also the perception of objective reality, which is as such similar to objective reality perceived in the normal 'waking consciousness'. The perception of objective reality is, however, intertwined with the cognitive and perceptual context of the 'clairvoyant I', and thus the 'living essence' flowing in the objects perceived is recognized by intuition with a deep subjective sense of certainty.

'Translucent perception' functions by analogy with normal sense-perception, which means that the awareness of a genuine cognitive relation is an integral part of it. But since the objects perceived by 'translucent perception' in 'cosmic consciousness' usually do not include an encounter with the 'All-encompassing', but consists primarily of finite things of objective reality as well as of phenomena of the paranormal world, *'translucent perception' is, from the viewpoint of gnoseology, generally akin to the visionary perception of the 'spirit seers', and as such does not qualify as a mode of 'mystical perception'*.

However, we may occasionally encounter amongst the phenomena appearing in the state of 'cosmic consciousness' a few that have mystical import. This is the case, for example, when a 'cosmic experience' involves a cognitive relation to an entity transcending the limitations of this world. Thus *the 'translucent perception' of the normal world can intensify and expand and culminate eventually in a visionary experience of the endless expanse of the entire cosmos. At the instant when 'translucent perception' is transported into the realm of the infinite, it assumes the quality of a mystical vision.* This surely applies to the 'cosmic vision' described by Paramahansa. He gives a vivid account of the vision of a radiant sea of light, which is unfathomable and permeating creation. He furthermore likens this visionary experience to the 'inner hearing' of the word AUM, the divine sound of the 'seas of vibrations', and also with the overwhelming non-visual awareness of the secret omnipresence of the 'All-encompassing'. The yogi's 'seeing I', immersed in the hyper-lucid state of consciousness, is overpowered by the encounter with an 'all-encompassing' Entity enfolding the cosmos: This ecstatic visionary experience of the cosmos has clearly mystical quality in that the 'object' comprehended is described in such terms as a blissful awareness of 'vibrant all-encompassing Life', and of 'primeval Light', 'Sublime Beauty', and of 'all-encompassing Love'.

When exploring 'cosmic consciousness', we have thus for the first time come across a phenomenon which clearly has mystical quality. This fact notwithstanding, we shall see later in our enquiry that the mystical phenomena featuring in 'cosmic consciousness' cannot help us to elucidate the phenomenon of the 'mystical relation': In a 'cosmic experience' occurring in the ecstatic state of 'cosmic consciousness' the mystical qualities inherent in it are so profusely intertwined with and hence obfuscated by non-mystical phenomena and non-mystical relations that they cannot be clearly identified, i.e., by the standards of empirical science. As becomes clear from the examples quoted above, in a 'cosmic experience' the awareness of the 'All-encompassing' is not only closely intertwined with 'clairvoyant visions', but the perception of the 'All-encompassing' also involves being transported into the 'ecstatic consciousness', by which the ability of clear discernment is impaired, when consciousness is inundated by intense feelings of exuberance, elation, rapture or reverent awe. Because of these overall phenomenological characteristics of 'cosmic consciousness', we can state that it falls phenomenologically outside the domain of mysticism. Its analysis, however, has provided some valuable clues and perspectives for the future course of our investigation. The visionary experience of 'primordial Light' ["Urlicht"], identified as an integral part of 'cosmic consciousness', is an especially significant phenomenon that is also encountered in genuine cognitive mystical experience (as will be shown later in this study). Moreover, some of the pivotal phenomena encountered in a 'cosmic experience' have given rise to philosophical and metaphysical notions and resulted in some mystical theorems: The experience in which the 'perceiver' feels as 'one' with the 'object perceived', and the awareness of the eternal in the temporal, in which time appears to be suspended, have resulted in the theorem that in the event of 'mystical gnosis' the perceiver, the object perceived and the act of perceiving are one. This is, in essence, the gist of the mystical epistemology of *Plotinus*: "There were not two; the beholder was one with the thing beheld; it was not a vision contemplated, but a unity apprehended. The beholder transformed by this mingling with the Supreme, must (if he can remember) carry the image impressed upon him."[66] – "And this is the true end to which the soul aspires, to touch that light, and to get a glimpse of it within itself, not to see the Light through another light, but to see it by the Light by which the soul is enabled to perceive it at all. That is to say, the Light by which the soul is illuminated, is the same Light that is comprehended."[67]

The realm of 'cosmic consciousness' has been explored in our enquiry as long as our contrastive analysis enabled us to clarify our understanding of the nature of the 'mystical vision' by distinguishing it from the 'cosmic vision'. The major findings of the foregoing comparative analysis can be summarized succinctly in the following theses:

---

66 Plotinus, quoted in BUBER, Martin. *Ekstatische Konfessionen*. Leipzig: Insel, 1921. 51. – [Note: Albrecht gives the exact location of the quote in the works of Plotinus, which is missing in Buber's anthology. Albrecht's actual source was: *Enneaden* VI.9.11, in PLOTINUS. *Plotins Schriften*. Trans. Richard Harder. 5 vols. Leipzig: Meiner, 1930–1937. Vol. I, 107f. – English translation provided. – FKW.]
67 PLOTINUS. *Enneaden* V.3.17. PLOTINUS. *Plotins Schriften*. Trans. Richard Harder. 5 vols. Leipzig: Meiner, 1930–1937. Vol. V, 91. – English translation provided. – FKW.]

THESIS 12: *'Cosmic consciousness' is, phenomenologically speaking, no pure, unadulterated state of consciousness, but an amalgamation of diverse phenomena deriving from the 'waking consciousness', the 'quiet state of alertness' and the 'ecstatic consciousness'.*

THESIS 13: *The phenomenological core of 'cosmic consciousness' consists of an intensely exulted mental state which is combined with the capacity of 'looking through' material objects, viz., 'translucent perception'.*

THESIS 14: *'Translucent perception' is something other than 'inner sight'* ["Innenschau"]; *unlike the latter it is bound to the function of* [external] *sense perception.*

THESIS 15: *'Translucent perception' of the normal world of sense perception shifts into a 'mystical mode of translucent perception', when the entire cosmos is beheld in a transparent and all-pervading manner and when the experience is accompanied simultaneously by a clear awareness of the presence of the 'All-encompassing'.*

THESIS 16: *If the 'mystical variety of translucent perception' is isolated from the overall structure of 'cosmic consciousness', and viewed separately as a phenomenon of its own, it can phenomenologically not be distinguished anymore from a 'mystical vision' proper.*

THESIS 17: *Though consisting of a typical mixture of diverse* [mystical and non-mystical] *phenomena, 'cosmic consciousness' nonetheless belongs to the peripheral sphere of mysticism. The 'mystical vision' is only one of its many individual elements.*

At this juncture we need to insert a clarifying annotation: In Zen-Buddhism we encounter a mystical experience which seems to have many shared phenomenological characteristics with 'cosmic consciousness'. Would it not be advisable then to proceed with our considerations by exploring Zen? This would seem to be even more pertinent as the experience of Zen is – unlike 'cosmic consciousness' – not a blending of various phenomena and mental states, but rather decidedly a pure, genuine, direct and unadulterated experience of the 'All-encompassing'. "Without the experience of *satori* there is no Zen ... *satori* is both the goal, meaning and the core of Zen."[68] *Satori*

---

68 HUMPHREYS, Christmas. *Zen Buddhismus*. Munich: Barth, 1951. 175, 26, 104f. [Translation provided. - FKW.]

is the supreme experience, in which the great life, the great fullness, is encountered.[69] *Satori* is the flash of enlightenment, "the instant and immediate absorption of the world within oneself, in which there is no division and the stream of life flows joyfully, unbounded and free."[70] "*Satori* is the instantaneous flashing of a truth which has previously been unknown and which is beyond comprehension. It is a kind of spiritual cataclysm, suddenly bursting in, after having accomplished many things intellectually and created great things ...".[71]

"Zen is a state of consciousness beyond any opposites. But Zen is, at the same time, the path towards the intended ultimate state of consciousness".[72] Anyone who wishes to participate in the 'great experience' of Zen is required to leave the mode of discursive thinking behind, which is determined by division and differentiation. Our enquiry, however, depends inevitably on logical reasoning and must needs apply a mode of thinking that is incompatible with Zen; it aims at exploring the 'differences' between mystical and non-mystical states of consciousness and is therefore averse to the principles of Zen. Seen from the perspective of Zen-Buddhism, our phenomenological endeavour will certainly be assessed critically and is likely to be dismissed as futile.

The teaching of Zen is not only harshly critical of an approach like the one pursued by us but, conversely, the experience of Zen is as such also inaccessible to our phenomenological method. Though the experience of Zen is undoubtedly a genuine [mystical] experience, it remains [almost entirely] beyond the compass of our empirical methodology, which depends on criteria of classification and differentiation. The mystical experience of Zen ultimately eludes phenomenological enquiry. Our methodological approach must therefore founder when applied to the ineffable experience of the one, infinite,

---

69 Cf. DÜRCKHEIM-MONTMARTIN, Karlfried Graf von. *Im Zeichen der Großen Erfahrung*. Munich: Barth, 1951. [Translation provided. – FKW.]

70 HUMPHREYS, Christmas. *Zen Buddhismus*. Munich: Barth, 1951. 80. [Translation provided. – FKW.]

71 SUZUKI, Daisetz T., quoted in HUMPHREYS, Christmas. *Zen Buddhismus*. Munich: Barth, 1951. 167. [Translation provided. – FKW.]

72 Cf. DÜRCKHEIM-MONTMARTIN, Karlfried Graf von. *Im Zeichen der Großen Erfahrung*. Munich: Barth, 1951. [Translation provided. – FKW.]

unfathomable and immutable Nothingness, which is the hallmark of Zen, though it ultimately eludes any conceptualization. Zen occurs in a domain beyond concepts. Therefore, our investigation can at best trace stages on the path of Zen, but it cannot probe into the innermost core of the experience of Zen.

It is thus important to state quite clearly: The aim of this study is not to launch a critical discussion with the claims of metaphysics, nor is it our intention to unravel the secrets of religious experience. Our goal is exclusively to disclose and classify systematically the pivotal phenomena of mystical experience, which are accessible to psychological phenomenology. This explains why our enquiry has first focussed on identifying and classifying rationally mystical phenomena, and on differentiating genuine from non-mystical and pseudo-mystical experience. For this reason, we will hold on to the contrastive analytical approach throughout our enquiry. While proceeding, we will take great care not to bypass an option that might be conducive to our search for the 'mystical relation'.[73]

---

[73] Cf. SUZUKI, Daisetz T. *Die Grosse Befreiung*. 3rd ed. Constance: Weller, 1947; HERRIGEL, Eugen. *Zen in der Kunst des Bogenschießens*. Munich: Barth, 1951.

PART ONE

The Structure of Mystical Experience

Experiencing, Cognitive Perception and Beholding

This chapter was written after the book had been finished. Inserting it was, however, considered indispensable in retrospect, as the different modes of 'mystical recognition' identified in this study have not been sufficiently expounded. There are three key concepts that refer to the three pivotal levels in which 'mystical recognition' may occur in a concrete mystical event: experiencing, comprehending cognitively and perceiving inwardly. Initially, we had doubts as to whether these terms are best suited for signifying the underlying experiential characteristics. However, due to the fact that none of these terms could appropriately denote the entire range of cognitive mystical experience individually, we abandoned the idea of using a single concept. The use of a single concept would have unduly overemphasized the cognitive component in a mystical event. It depends, after all, on the nature of a particular mystical event as to whether the concept of 'experience', or that of 'cognitive comprehension', viz., 'recognition', or the features of 'inward perception', viz., 'apperception' have relative predominance. The application of these terms in the analysis of the mystical records selected for illustration will help to clarify these concepts and reveal the phenomenological differences between them and show to what extent they tend to overlap. To begin with, a concise explanation of each of the three concepts shall be given, to indicate the cognitive import adhering to each of the three modes of mystical encounters.

1. The term 'experience', as used in science in the past decades, has been considerably expanded in scope. Further, its meaning has likewise shifted, particularly in current philosophical debate.[1]

---

1 [Note: The reference is to philosophical studies published between 1910 and

Though the 'act of experiencing' is evidently related to something that is really present, in that it is an empirical event that has a real effect or impact on the observer, the cognitive component inherent in it is usually too elusive and opaque to be qualified in terms of an experience in which a 'cognitive relation' becomes manifest. We should call to mind that there is knowledge that can be elicited during a mystical event. Any knowledge *a posteriori* originates from an act of 'experience', i.e., from the experiencer's encounter with a real object, or from a cognitive impact on the experiencer. In such an instance the 'cognitive relation' is embedded in, and sustained by, the relation of 'experiencing', which cannot be further specified gnoseologically. Experiencing thus means being affected by an 'encounter' with an 'object', and is thus a passive event, i.e., one that is 'suffered' ["Erleidnis"].[2] Experiencing thus involves, first and foremost, the passive sufferance of some impact effected by a power from outside the individual self; the 'cognitive' component, the awareness that some knowledge that has been imparted in the process is only a secondary quality. Experiencing may furthermore consist in a confrontation with an 'opposing object', which imposes limitations on the subject's will. In such a 'volitional experience' the awareness that the 'experiencing I' is confronted by an opposing 'object' or antagonistic power is immediately given. Such a confrontational encounter occurs primarily on the level of volition, in which the 'harshness of the real' is cognitively grasped.

These considerations illustrate that the term *experience* encompasses the entire range of experiencing: The concept includes not only 'encounters' with opposing 'objects' or with

---

1950. Albrecht explicitly cites the following publications: HARTMANN, Nicolai. *Zur Grundlegung der Ontologie*. 3rd ed. Meisenheim am Glan: Westkulturverlag, 1948; HARTMANN, Nicolai. "Zum Problem der Realitätsgegebenheit." *Philosophische Vorträge, Kant-Gesellschaft* 32 (1931): 1–97; FRISCHEISEN-KÖHLER, Max. "Realitätsproblem." *Philosophische Vorträge, Kant-Gesellschaft* 1 and 2 (1912): 1–98. – FKW.]

2 HESSEN, Johannes. *Religionsphilosophie*. 2 vols. Freiburg i. Br.: Chamier, 1948. Vol. II, 99.

opposing forces, but also events in which some 'content' or cognitive awareness is 'bestowed' and 'objects' revealed so that the entire experience can be placed into an intelligible context.

We shall use the term 'mystical *experience*' only rarely, but if we do, we understand by it a clearly structured mystical event in its entirety. When we speak of 'experiencing mystically', however, we always refer to a concrete 'act' of mystical comprehension, which conveys some intuitive knowledge, and which goes beyond a fleeting, opaque impact elicited by somatic and/or emotional modes of perception (e.g., the sense of being 'touched', 'moved' or 'affected' by a mystical impact). This means that we are going to use the expression 'experiencing mystically' and even more so the expression 'mode of experiencing in a mystical manner' in a way that emphasizes (or even overemphasizes) the inherent cognitive component. This terminological approach is facilitated by the fact that the cognitive awareness that a 'mystical relation' is involved in a mystical experience never occurs on its own, isolated from a given mystical event, but is always affiliated with other experiential qualities, notably the more elusive somatic and/or emotional experiences of an impact being imposed, or of being overwhelmed passively. In other words, the term 'mystical experience' should be employed for any mystical event in which the act of cognition is an integral part, albeit only a subordinate component within the more complex experiential framework.

2. The term 'comprehending', viz., 'comprehension', differs significantly from the concept of 'experiencing'. Although the two terms overlap semantically, the differences are more considerable than their shared characteristics. An experience is based on a concrete encounter with something real and true, whereas an act of 'comprehension' extends beyond the level of experience and is rooted in the realm of ideas, in the ideal state of being, and in logical connections, visionary phenomena, and mathematical configurations. There is a mode of 'comprehending' which consists entirely in an act of recognition *a priori*. Such untainted acts of 'comprehending', however, fall outside the realm of experience, and are part of the domain of 'pure cognitive comprehension'

which is not attended by an experiential occurrence. There is, conversely, a domain of experience which is not accompanied by acts of 'comprehending': This is the area of passive modes of experience, which cannot be gnoseologically specified. The term 'comprehending' is *always* rooted in an act of recognition. In a passive, i.e., receptive experience, something is 'suffered' by the subject, who, in the incipient stage, is merely dimly aware of being exposed to some opaque influence, or of being affected emotionally, or touched somatically in some inscrutable manner. In an act of 'comprehending', there is always an 'object' that is grasped cognitively.

By '*mystical* comprehension' we signify expressly a concrete empirical act of recognition, and never an act of 'comprehending' *a priori*. The term '*mystical* comprehension' thus refers to the gnoseological encounter with mystical Reality. We shall speak of 'mystical comprehension' [rather than of 'mystical experience'] if we wish to emphasize the cognitive aspect, while suspending the issue that mystical cognition is inevitably embedded in the overall context of the 'mystical relation'.

3. The various modes of mystical experience can be said to be structured in a manner that is analogous to the types of normal sense perception. The analogy is, however, only superficial, as there are obviously significant phenomenological differences between 'inward perceptions' that are bound to special [higher] states of consciousness, and sense perceptions, which is the response to external stimuli occurring in the normal 'waking consciousness' (as has been detailed in our earlier study). Yet the notion that there is some remote analogy between inner and outer perception has resulted in the effort to find a reasonably analogous term for describing the various forms of 'inner' and 'external perception'. The term considered best suited for describing all the analogous quasi-sensate inner modes of perception (visionary, auditive, tactile/somatic, olfactory, gustatory) in the context of a mystical experience was 'mystical perception' ["mystisches Gewahren"]. In our study this term is used primarily to refer to the quasi-sensory modes of perception featuring as integral parts in the whole

of a mystical experience. The term is, moreover, employed when we wish to emphasize that the perception-like character is predominant in a concrete mystical event, or when the recorded mystical experience conveys the great immediacy between the perceiver and the 'mystical Object' perceived.

It is furthermore necessary to differentiate between the concept of 'structure of mystical experience' and that of the 'ongoing process of mystical experience', although we are aware that resorting to the word 'experience' in these two concepts is not satisfactory because of its vague meaning. This aside, the use of these terms seems to have been carefully considered and can be justified. All these novel terms will be applied consistently, and each concept will be explained in some detail and critically assessed when it first occurs in the following parts of the book.

The 'Object Arriving' and the 'Experience of Being Acted Upon' ["Das Ankommende und die Gewirktheit"]

As we are now about to enter the realm of mysticism, we should call to mind the *psychological* concept of mysticism. In our previous study, *Psychology of Mystical Consciousness*, mysticism was defined as "the arriving of an All-encompassing in the 'quiet state of alertness'."[3] The terms 'arrival', viz., 'arriving', have been chosen in order to emphasize that the 'experiencing I', when abiding in the tranquillity of the 'quiet state of alertness', intent on watching with the 'inner eye' the infinite and empty space 'arriving' in consciousness, is indeed confronted with an 'object' that has neither emerged from within nor been evoked by the person perceiving it. The 'object' that 'arrives' in the field of vision of the 'inner eye' thus comes from 'outside' the 'sphere of the individual self' and is therefore appropriately termed 'object arriving'. "By the concept of the 'object arriving' we understand a wholeness that is thought to be situated outside the realm of the individual consciousness and that reveals

---

3 Cf. ALBRECHT, Carl. *Psychology of Mystical Consciousness*. Trans. F. K. Woehrer. New York: Crossroad, 2019. 373.

itself increasingly in the 'experiencing self' in a series of consecutive events."[4] I do not expect that all items that may appear in the domain of 'mystical apperception' can be identified as 'objects' that have truly 'arrived' from beyond the confines of individual consciousness. There are surely items which are not perceived as 'arriving', but which have been there subconsciously, or dwelt in memory. But the 'beholding I' may also discern items in consciousness of which he/she knows with absolute certainty that they do not originate from his/her own self but have truly 'arrived' from a realm beyond it. In other words, there are two ways of experiencing the 'extra-mental wholeness': by beholding it as an 'object arriving', and by perceiving an 'object' that has previously arrived but is now cognitively grasped as present. But we also know from the findings of our psychological-phenomenological study that the key-phenomenon of 'arriving' is not a unique feature of mystical perception but is also attached to 'objects' surfacing from within the subject's self. The latter evidently do not qualify as 'mystical Objects', as they have neither the distinctive characteristic of being 'all-encompassing', nor of 'arriving' from an alien sphere beyond the individual self. In our earlier study we have indicated the different varieties of the 'object arriving' by stating: "The 'object arriving' can either be a split-off item of the subconscious, or an item surfacing from within the self, as such representing a fraction of the self, or it can be perceived as 'all-encompassing'."[5] On the basis of these findings, we may formulate the subsequent thesis:

THESIS 18: *The phenomenon of 'arriving' is a necessary condition for qualifying a mystical event, but it is itself not a sufficient criterion for an experience to be classified 'mystical'.*

Our previous psychological-phenomenological investigation has resulted in a rather detailed description of a wide range of mystical and non-mystical phenomena that may 'arrive' in consciousness [i.e., in the special states of consciousness termed 'quiet state of alertness', and 'ecstatic state of consciousness']. In the earlier study we bypassed a rather

---

4 Cf. ALBRECHT, Carl. *Psychology of Mystical Consciousness*. Trans. F. K. Woehrer. New York: Crossroad, 2019. 304.

5 Cf. ALBRECHT, Carl. *Psychology of Mystical Consciousness*. Trans. F. K. Woehrer. New York: Crossroad, 2019. 305.

significant, albeit opaque phenomenon, because exploring it would have complicated matters further: In *Psychology of Mystical Consciousness* we tried to provide a critical phenomenological differentiation between mystical and non-mystical phenomena perceived as 'arriving' in the vista of 'inner sight' in the 'quiet state of alertness'. Achieving this goal would have been even more difficult if we had approached the problem from other disciplines and/or from additional perspectives outside the psychology of consciousness. We had to concede that the psychological concepts of the state(s) of consciousness identified were not entirely adequate for recapturing all the phenomena that might 'arrive' in the vista of 'inner sight'. In the present study, however, we are going to reach out beyond the threshold of the psychology of consciousness and include a very important though highly elusive phenomenon of 'mystical effects' termed "Gewirktheit", i.e., a tangible albeit tenuous impact on the 'experiencing self' felt to have been effected by a power from outside the individual self, and which has long-term after-effects on the life of the individual concerned. 'Mystical effects' are a vital and inalienable component of mystical experience and will therefore be given proper consideration in this study.

Phenomena 'arriving' in consciousness are psychologically classified as "gewirkt", i.e., having been 'effected' or instilled, if they are experienced with absolute certainty ["Evidenz"] as being caused or triggered by some mysterious 'foreign' power. In such an event the 'experiencing self' responds passively to the transforming impact imposed. The 'experiencing self' is certain that he/she is not the cause of the passive transformation elicited in him/her, but the event has been triggered by the 'arrival' of unfamiliar forces inflicted from outside the individual self.

As we have seen in other instances in which phenomena have 'arrived' in the vista of 'inner sight', it is not possible to decide on the basis of the phenomenon of 'arriving' alone if the 'object' that has arrived is 'mystical' or 'non-mystical' in nature. For it is possible that the 'object arriving' is a 'split-off' item surfacing from the unconscious, or else an item that has emerged from the 'sphere of the self', or it can be one perceived that has intruded from the realm beyond the individual consciousness and be experienced as 'all-encompassing'. With the phenomenon of 'mystical effects', the difficulty in discerning genuine from spurious (non-mystical) phenomena is similar: The mere awareness alone of an impact (affecting the sphere of the body, the emotions or the mind) felt as working within oneself does not allow any safe conclusions as to its provenance. The question as to whether a given impact has a mystical cause, or has merely been triggered by intra-mental causation, cannot be inferred from the mere experience of 'being acted upon', nor from the event of an 'object arriving'.

The concept of 'mystical effects' includes such phenomena as the 'sense of being acted, or operated upon', 'of being touched', 'moved emotionally', or 'the change of one's will'. The phenomenon implies that a determining relation is encountered, though this does not say anything about the nature of the relationship to the determining entity. The term 'mystical effect' is an elusive concept which comprises a wide range of related phenomena; it does not indicate, however, whether that which has been 'effected' in the 'experiencing self' has indeed had a paranormal cause; it can consist of the experience of some (after-)effect on a subject ["Wirkung"], or of the sense of 'being transformed within, or acted upon from outside' ["Einwirkung"], or be a 'side-effect' or 'corollary' ["Auswirkung"] of a mystical event; the transformation experienced can moreover be experienced as having been 'imposed' by or 'inflicted' upon by a transpersonal Being ["Bewirkung"]. These specific terms designate different varieties of experiencing and/or responding to the unfathomable encounter with an unfamiliar extra-mental power. This suggests that the phenomena addressed here cannot sharply be separated from one another, as they tend to overlap. This fact notwithstanding, the concept of "*Wirkungen*", viz., '*workings instilled in, and upon the individual*',[6] the effects

---

6 [Note: The term 'working(s)' effected by a power beyond the individual self and operating in and upon the experiencer has been derived from the writings of the anonymous 14th c. English mystic and spiritual counsellor known as the author of *The Cloud of Unknowing* (c. 1380). He was an English monk and experienced mystagogue who wrote several treatises on practical spiritual guidance in the long-standing tradition of 'negative theology', originating from the teaching of Pseudo-Dionysius, presumably a Syrian monk living in the late 5th c. and early 6th c. A.D. The affinities between Albrecht's use of "Wirkungen" and its varieties ("Einwirkung" and "Bewirkung") are best illustrated by a passage from the *Cloud*-author's later

'infused' in the recipient,[7] is still helpful for our phenomenological analysis; it is moreover often addressed in [western] mystical tradition and used here largely in line with received meaning. In Christian mystical theology, the effects achieved in a gratuitous mystical event are inevitably seen as the 'workings' of the Holy Spirit, by which the transformation of the self-will, a positive change in the emotional state, acts of purification, or flashes of 'insight' are achieved. 'Workings' of this kind are 'infused' or 'imparted' and may advance the recipient's spiritual development and prepare him/her for the mystical event of 'awakening' and/or 'conversion'. Another experience marked by the distinctive feature of 'givenness' is the (often abrupt) change of the contemplative into an altered state of consciousness, which is, as mystics insist, a token of the recipient's progress on his/her mystical path. Mystics claim that the transfer into the calm and serene mental condition which enables him/her to receive the gift of the 'mystical vision' is 'infused', and so are the items of the 'content' bestowed. The term "*Einwirkung*" (i.e., 'having an impact on the perceiver in terms of a visionary experience or an intellectual insight') refers to a phenomenon in which a pictorial vision or an intellectual

---

treatise *The Book of Privy Counselling* (88:20–26): "... I feel verily, without any error or doubt, that Almighty God with his grace is necessarily always the prime force steering and working within, either with means or without means, and you [i.e., the practitioner of contemplative prayer] ... are merely the one consenting and suffering [God's doing] ...". (Translated from the Middle English textual edition *The Cloud of Unknowing and Related Treatises*. Ed. Phyllis Hodgson. Exeter: Catholic Records Press, 1982. *The Book of Privy Counselling*, 88.) Albrecht expressly adopted the term "Wirkungen" from the medieval Christian mystical tradition; the semantically most adequate translation is by the word 'working(s)'. – FKW.]

7 [Note: Christian mystical theology differentiates between *contemplatio acquisita* (state of contemplation that is acquired by personal effort, prayer, spiritual exercises, acts of charity etc.) and *contemplatio infusa* (i.e., the state of contemplation infused by God in an act of special grace); only the latter qualifies as a mode of genuine mystical experience (*cognitio Dei experimentalis*). The terminological distinction between the two forms of contemplation can be traced to the teaching of St. John of the Cross and Teresa of Avila. Cf. LERCHER, Ludwig. "Grundsätzliches über Mystik und Theologie." *Zeitschrift für Katholische Theologie* 42 (1918): 1–45. – FKW.]

intuition occurs, which is felt to have been 'infused', thus 'arrived' from a realm outside the individual self, effected or 'imparted' by the Divine. The experience of something being 'imparted' from beyond the confines of the individual consciousness, however, does not necessarily go along with a clear awareness in the 'experiencing self' of the ontological or ideational 'essence' of the Ultimate Cause [viz., in our phenomenological terms], the 'All-encompassing'. From a psychological point of view, the sense of 'being acted upon', or of something being 'infused', eludes rational explanation; any attempt to trace it to its potential cause(s), or to discern its final purpose, is a futile endeavour. Though it is true that an item felt to be 'imposed', 'infused' or 'inculcated' in the consciousness of a perceiver inevitably involves the awareness of a direct relation between the recipient and the 'All-encompassing', the way in which such insight is instilled, or a somatic impact achieved and to be understood, however, is not covered by the concept of "Einwirkung" as defined here. The concept of *"Bewirkung"*, by contrast, implies clearly that there is a personal relation between the 'experiencing self' and a transpersonal entity conceived as a Persona, who has been moved to act within and upon the recipient. This means that when a mystical event is cognitively experienced as being rooted in a personal encounter with the 'All-encompassing' perceived as a Persona, a visionary or mystical experience can be claimed to be an instance of genuine mystical causation in terms of a "Bewirkung".

The term *"Auswirkung"*, i.e., 'corollary', or side-effect of a mystical event, is only contiguous to the concepts addressed above. "Auswirkungen" are concomitant with, or result from, mystical events; they are to be attributed to a liminal zone, because they encompass phenomena that are off-springs or side-effects, or 'emanations', or 'radiant corollaries' of a mystical event, evoked as secondary phenomena by the presence of the 'mystical It'. These mystical corollaries can be understood (as we shall explain later) as 'tokens' or 'harbingers' of the mystical Presence. At the current stage of our enquiry, it is enough to have offered only a concise, if cursory, terminological and phenomenological description of the varieties of the mystical "Gewirktheit".

Yet more important than the terminological differentiation of the varieties of 'mystical effects' is the following finding and seminal phenomenological characteristic of the awareness of the 'object arriving':

THESIS 19: *The 'object arriving' can take on a mystical quality in two ways: 1. The 'object arriving', respectively, the 'object' that has 'arrived', is itself the 'mystical Object'. 2. The 'object arriving', or the 'object' that has 'arrived', has been caused by the 'mystical It'.*

When dealing with the phenomenon of 'mystical effects', we must therefore distinguish between these two modes of 'arriving': The direct manifestation of the mystical Object in the event of the 'mystical arrival', and the perception of objects experienced as having been 'imparted' or caused by the 'mystical It'. The further distinction between various individual forms of 'mystical effects' [modes of "Gewirktheit"] is, however, phenomenologically less important than the differentiation between these two modes of 'arriving'. This will be demonstrated in the subsequent practical analysis of testimonies of the mystics.

Pictorial Visions
["Die bildhafte Schau"]

It is imperative to provide a clear definition of the concepts employed, particularly if the meaning of received concepts are too fuzzy or ambivalent and thus tend to overlap. This is even more pertinent when the terms introduced to denote individual phenomena are to be classified and linked with a superior category of phenomenological concepts. This applies in particular to the conventional differentiation between the terms 'vision' ["Vision", i.e., visionary experience] and 'beholding' ["Schau", 'inner sight', contemplation], introduced by early medieval Christian mystics [notably St. Augustine, who was the first to distinguish between *visio corporalis*, *visio imaginaria* or *spiritualis* and *visio intellectualis*].[8] One thing is certain: The term 'beholding' clearly refers

---

8 [Note: The tripartite division of *visio* into *visio corporalis* (i.e., a visionary experience in which the 'objects' seen appear in bodily likeness and perceived with the physical eyes), and *visio imaginaria* (*spiritualis*) (i.e., an inner vision beheld with the 'inner eye') and the *visio intellectualis* (i.e., the non-pictorial, imageless and purely intellectual contemplation of the Divine) can be traced to St. Augustine's com-

to the process of seeing and not to the object seen or beheld, whereas the term "vision" denotes the 'object shown' [i.e., what is revealed and beheld in a vision with the 'inner eye', or seen with the physical eyes in the case of a *visio corporalis*]. In order to be able to distinguish clearly between the process and the 'content' of a vision, we will apply the terms 'object shown' or 'object beheld' and use the term 'beholding' only when the process of seeing is meant.

The intriguing question that must be addressed first is this: Is any 'object' that is perceived to be classified a 'vision', and must every 'vision' have a visual 'object'? It seems to me that the two concepts are, on the whole, congruous, though they appear to diverge in some characteristics.

For the purpose of delineating the concept of the 'pictorial vision' clearly, it seems best to compare it to physical sense perception. This juxtaposition involves difficulties, however, because the realm covered by 'beholding' cannot unambiguously be distinguished from the area of visual sense perception. Yet in empirical reality there is a phenomenological area expanding between the poles of 'seeing' and 'beholding'. The attempt to set off the area of 'beholding' against the area of 'seeing' is bound to fail, as there are no tangible criteria that would permit us to state definitively if a visual experience has been 'seen' or 'beheld'. The distinction between 'external' and 'internal' modes of 'beholding' or 'perceiving' does not qualify as a criterion, because there are numerous examples in the mystical records examined in which images '*beheld*' inwardly have been projected into external space, thus resulting in an apparent external sense perception. The juxtaposition between corporeality and pictoriality vs. incorporeality and imagelessness does not qualify as a criterion either, because it is not reliable enough. There are, after all, pictorial images originating from the imagination which are 'beheld' inwardly, but the visionary experience described is nonetheless distinctly portrayed in terms of corporeality. On the other hand, there are mental images which are claimed to have been '*seen*' with the physical eyes and located in

---

mentary on the *raptus* of St. Paul (2 Cor. 12:2-4) in *De Genesi ad litteram*. Cf. NEWMAN, F. X. "St. Augustine's Three Visions and the Structure of Commedia." *Modern Language Notes* 82 (1967): 58-61. – FKW.]

external space. This means that the phenomenological range of the concepts of 'seeing' and 'beholding' tends to overlap, and there are transition zones in which both phenomena appear to be involved.

Jaensch[9] and his research team of psychologists carried out experiments with a series of "pictorial memories" in which each picture amongst several pictures known from memory had some clearly characteristic feature. The classification of these mental pictures was based on the fact "that there is a special section in memory in which after-images are stored, another one in which memories of perceptions are stockpiled, and there is a branch in which images surfacing from the imagination are stored. This, however, is not to be understood as a clear-cut classification of the way the storage system of memory is thought to operate, but the various mental sections are three deliberately selected stages of what in empirical reality is one coherent continuum",[10] which encompasses the complete domain of memory, ranging from sense perceptions to images originating from the imagination. The so-called *'after-image'* ["Nachbild"] is phenomenologically and physiologically closely akin to sense perception. Placed between the 'after-image' and the type of pictorial memory proper, which are not 'seen' but visually retrieved from memory, is the category of 'eidetic images': These have been recognized as important phenomena in psychological research and classified as 'subjective images of perception'. 'Eidetic images' are again differentiated from the category of images that are similar to 'after-images' in structure but have characteristics that are more closely related to pictures of the imagination. 'Perceived images' are images that are virtually *'seen'* vividly and colourfully, with special clarity and as if occurring in the outside world, while they actually originate exclusively from memory. Regardless, however, of whether these 'subjective images of perception' are fused with a realistic, objective setting and perceived simultaneously with the physical eyes, or if they are perceived as distinct from the objective impressions of the outside world, these impressions are indeed only varieties of the same phenomenon. What really matters for us in the

---

9   JAENSCH, Erich, et. al. *Eidetische Anlage und Kindliches Seelenleben.* Leipzig: Barth, 1934.

10 JAENSCH, Erich, et. al. *Eidetische Anlage und Kindliches Seelenleben.* Leipzig: Barth, 1934. 64f.

given context is the insight: The greater the phenomenological affinity between 'subjective images of perception' and 'images of the imagination' becomes, the more graphic is their plasticity and variability, and the more are they modified and accompanied by emotions. "In the borderline case in which the evocation of images is dominated by the powers of the imagination, 'subjective images of perception' are, like after-images, quite literally *visible* pictures of the imagination, which have been projected into the world outside".[11] 'Subjective images of perception' can originate from the observation of illustrations, landscapes or thematic pictorial details to which the perceiver has been emotionally deeply attached. These images can either be static, or become dynamic, modifying their appearance as to evoke some meaningful sequence. They are seen in the mind, because they do not disappear when sense perception and the external world are screened off by closing the eyes; this means that external sense impressions are transferred into the inner realm of perception, to a peripheral sphere of sensate phenomena elicited by the eyes when closed, which is a spatial domain that is clearly separate from the space of the imagination. Though it is possible for a perceiver to distinguish clearly between the space of (sense) perception and the space of the imagination, and thus to differentiate between 'seeing' and 'beholding', this distinction can scarcely be upheld when the two modes of perception become intertwined, which results in the phenomenon of *imagined external space*. There are records in which 'pictorial visions' are described, where the external setting surrounding the visionary is very clearly perceived and assumes, as it were, the function of a 'backdrop' for the 'objects' beheld. There are, moreover, instances in which it is only a sense of spatial direction that is evoked, in which the picture perceived is located, for instance, when the picture beheld is attributed at a particular place outside the visionary's self, or when the object beheld is perceived as 'arriving' from a certain direction – approaching the visionary, as it were, from a specific path. The imagined external space and the awareness of where in-coming phenomena are 'arriving' from, is thus not identical with the real external setting 'seen' in a *visio corporalis*. The external space in this hybrid visionary experience is divested of

---

11 JAENSCH, Erich. *Die Eidetik und die Typologische Forschungsmethode*. Leipzig: Quelle & Meyer, 1925. 2.

any sense of reality and is absorbed by, and assimilated with, the inner space of the visionary's imagination.

This means that the expanse of phenomena situated between genuine images of perception and genuine effigies deriving from the imagination has three stages: 1. An empirical process elicited by the imagination, which is projected onto the real world outside, and which is *seen* in a genuine mode of 'seeing', as a dynamic apparition. 2. An imaginative experience of pictorial processes not seen as occurring in external space, but which can be assumed to be *beheld* within, as occurring in the realm of the imagination, irrespective of the fact that the surrounding space perceived is identical with the imagined external space. In such an instance, the visionary, with his/her eyes being shut, does not see pictures in the domain of inward perception, but are beheld in the imagined 'space of perception'. 3. Following the former stage is the experience of phenomena of pure imaginative content emerging and 'beheld' in the space of consciousness. *The threshold between 'seeing' and 'beholding' is reached when the genuine space of sense perception is transformed into, and replaced by, the space of the imagination, which contains the space of sense perception featuring as the object of the imagination.* We may try to elucidate this liminal phenomenological area by contrasting the concepts of 'illusion' and 'hallucination': An *illusion* is the perception of an item for which there is no objective physical foundation, although genuine components of sense perception are employed in evoking it. It is true, however, that *all* sense perceptions are inevitably intertwined with items of the imagination. An apple, for instance, is not merely 'seen' as the physiological result of a sense perception [i.e., in terms of a perfectly neutral response to external visual stimuli], but the act of perception is supplemented by elements arising from the imagination. If this process is taken a step further, it is possible that phenomena are mistakenly attributed to, or projected on an object – resulting in the experience of an illusion.

A *hallucination* is an apparition that is either 'seen' or 'beheld' in external space and that is mistaken for a genuine sense perception of a real object, although there is no objective empirical foundation whatsoever for the given visual misconception. In the widest sense, the concept of hallucination includes, for example, the phenomenon of after-images, the phenomenon of 'subjective images of perception', and the phenomenon of imaginative projection, in which imagined images are falsely projected into real external space.

However, the concepts of illusion and hallucination are only helpful in the given context because they draw attention to phenomena that can be typically encountered in the crucial transitional zone between the sane range of phenomena delineated above, and phenomena featuring in pathological 'apparitions'. This means that *every visual experience of an object appearing in external space must not only be critically examined psychologically, i.e., as to whether a phenomenon might be explained as an eidetic image, and, moreover, not only if it might be the result of an error or delusion, for instance, when an object or image is falsely identified as real whereas it has indeed been projected into the external, or internal realms of perception, but any visual experience must also be scrutinized in view of its potential pathological nature.*

Thanks to the insights gained from this rather long and intricate overview, we are now able to discern the differences between delusory and otherwise bogus external visionary experiences, 'inner visions' and the 'pictorial vision'.

THESIS 20: *The phenomenological domain of 'external visions' includes the categories of physiological after-images, eidetic images and imagined inner pictures which are projected into external space, and, furthermore (from a different point of view), all kinds of illusions and hallucinations.*

THESIS 21: *'External visions' can be subdivided into those that are 'seen' with the physical eyes and those which are 'beheld'.* The type of 'external visions' which are seen set in external space has been termed 'corporeal vision' [*visio corporalis*]. The visions that are beheld inwardly as occurring in external space, and the 'inner visions' which are beheld as occurring inside the mind, can both be classified as instances of 'pictorial vision'.

THESIS 22: *The 'pictorial vision' covers a phenomenological area that transgresses the boundary between internal and external space.* Visions beheld as occurring in an external setting usually consist of images that emerge or surface within the mind but are projected into an imagined external space. They are experienced as occurring in external space (regardless of whether the physical eyes are open or shut during the event). The 'pictorial vision' is, however, prone to delusion, which means that the spurious content is falsely identified as real and the result of a real empirical act of perception.

At this stage, the following critical question is likely to arise: Could we have avoided the sophisticated phenomenological differentiation between sensory 'seeing' and visionary 'beholding'? The answer is, however, decidedly 'no': If we had not introduced this distinction, it would hardly have been feasible to render the phenomenological differences between 'beholding' and 'seeing/sensory perceiving' intelligible, nor could we have delineated the threshold between mystical and non-mystical visionary experiences. The concept of mysticism, as conceived in this study, is limited to the realm of phenomena perceived inwardly and 'arriving' in the vista of the 'inner eye', in other words, phenomena 'arriving' in 'inner sight' ["Innenschau"]. Because of this deliberate limitation of the concept of mysticism to phenomena perceived by 'inner sight', we are required to eliminate all visionary experiences from the domain of mysticism that involve sensations originating from natural sense-perceptions.

It is true, however, that we may find in many of the *vitae* and autobiographical records of religious experience of Christian mystics and visionaries not only descriptions which are undoubtedly authentic accounts of mystical experience, but also narratives of external visions which are clearly 'seen' with the physical eyes rather than 'beheld inwardly'. The chronicles of medieval abbeys and convents, and especially the records of the lives of nuns, are often replete with accounts of 'external visions'. The recorded testimonies of the 'religious sisters of Töss', and the *vita* of the 'nun of Engeltal'[12] are particularly controversial examples. In the latter we come across numerous flamboyant descriptions of corporal visions appearing in the choir of the monastery. For example, the 'external vision' of Christ, who appears in physical likeness in several shapes and several stages of his life in the choir hall: on one occasion Christ appears as an infant, at other instances he is seen teaching as a young adult, as the Redeemer and Saviour in scenes

---

12   WEINHANDL, Margarete. *Deutsches Nonnenleben. Das Leben der Schwestern zu Töss und der Nonne von Engeltal.* 2 vols. Munich: Recht, 1921.

from the Passion, and there is a vision of Christ transfigured and the scene of his Ascension. In the lavish portrayals of these 'external visions' we also encounter angels, the Holy Virgins, the Holy Mother featuring variously as *mater dolorosa*, or Mary appearing as *madonna lactans*, nursing the infant; there are furthermore picturesque accounts of vivid visionary appearances of local saints affiliated with the monastery, and even corporal visions of deceased persons who had in some way been socially linked with the nuns of the cloister. These 'external visions' – the more appropriate term would in fact be 'apparitions' – are very detailed, graphic and colourful, and the figures featuring in them are seen communicating with the visionary, complete with their typical gestures, their way of speaking and looking at the visionary, and, in one instance, the saint is even seen amidst the group of nuns. In order to be able to assess corporal visions of this kind critically, it is indispensable to consider first the given circumstances and examine if, or to what extent, subjective and/or objective causes and conditions may have elicited these 'external visions'. In our critical approach we must not rule out beforehand the possibility that even in such extravagant visionary experiences the 'All-encompassing' may be involved, even when the visions have been 'seen' with the physical eyes only. But if we wish to arrive at a reliable evaluation of the genuine or delusory nature of these visions, it is imperative to ascertain if the 'All-encompassing' has, or has not, been an integral part of the visionary experiences. When assessing these testimonies, we have several methodological options of how to account for the potential origins of these visions: These include physiological, psychological and pathological approaches. While conceding that these visions are grounded in genuine religious devotion and may involve the event of a religious encounter within the domain of an 'external vision' seen with the physical eyes, such an event cannot – from the perspective of psychological phenomenology – be qualified as a mystical occurrence. By applying criteria of psychological phenomenology, we can only infer the following insight from these accounts, and consequently state as an empirical fact:

THESIS 23: *Within the range of phenomena encompassed by 'external visionary experiences' and which are exclusively 'seen' with the physical eyes, none can qualify as a mystical phenomenon.* This means that we can examine the potential mystical import only in the variant type of 'seemingly external visions', i.e., visions which are perceived in 'inner sight', but the items of which are projected into an external physical setting. We shall deal with this variety of apparent 'external visions' later in this study. When examining the records of the nuns of Töss, however, it is impossible to discern unmistakably whether their 'external visions' were 'beheld inwardly', and subsequently projected into the external area of perception, or if these visions were actually 'apparitions', 'seen' with the physical eyes alone, or if both modes of vision were involved. Moreover, reading these accounts in terms of pathological, or quasi-pathological testimonies of events evoked by 'illusion' and/or 'hallucination', cannot be ruled out either. We are here, in fact, concerned with a phenomenological twilight zone, a liminal area of human experience, which eludes scientific verification and does not permit any final conclusions. 'Pictorial visions', both 'external' and 'internal' varieties, are indeed ambivalent, multi-layered phenomena, and only to a limited extent open to scientific enquiry. The limitations of a scientific psychological-phenomenological approach become apparent in the following analysis of the intricate visionary experience recorded by the German Augustinian Canoness *Anna Katharina Emmerich* (1774–1824).[13] Not only the extraordinary circumstances in which these

---

13 [Note: The German canoness Anna Katherina Emmerich was beatified by Pope John Paul II on 3 October 2004, which confirms that her visions and charismatic gifts were acknowledged as genuine by the Roman Catholic Church. The gifts of grace (*gratiae gratis datae*) bestowed on her include visions, stigmata, xenoglossy (which enabled her to speak and understand Latin, Hebrew and Aramaic, although, as a simple farmer's daughter, she had received only basic formal schooling); moreover, the gift of prophesy has been recorded, and the gift of sacred *anorexia*, which enabled her to live without solid food for eleven years until her death in 1824. In the final eleven years of her life the communion wafer was the only daily nourishment. Her visions and her life were first recorded by the prestigious Romantic writer Clemens Brentano (BRENTANO, Clemens, ed. *Das Marienleben. Nach den Betrachtungen von Anna Katharina Emmerich*. Munich: Literarisch-Artistische Anstalt, 1842; and BRENTANO, Clemens, ed. *Das Bittere Leiden Unseres Herrn Jesu Christi. Nach Betrachtungen der Gottseligen Anna Katharina Emmerich, Nebst dem Lebensumriß dieser Begnadigten* [sic]. Munich: Literarisch-Artistische Anstalt, 1864). His authority and critical judge-

visionary experiences occurred to her, but also the many vivid graphic images of the Saviour and His Passion, allow divergent readings, and illustrate the psychological and phenomenological ambiguities of an experience occurring in the twilight zone of human experience:

> *Text 5* (Anna Katharina Emmerich, 1774–1824): "I don't see this with my physical eyes, but, so it seems to me, as if I saw this with my heart, right in the middle of my chest. When this happens, I am instantly bathed in sweat. Simultaneously, I perceive with my sensory eyes the objects and persons surrounding me; but they do not know me, nor do I know who they are, or what their status or profession is. While I speak, I can still see and behold … For several days now I have been wavering between seeing with my physical eyes, and perceiving in a preternatural way. I have to force myself to gain control; for it may happen that in the middle of a conversation with others, I am suddenly assailed by images and see entirely different things in front of me, hearing my own voice as if it was that of a stranger, speaking to me muffled, as if from an empty casket, with a coarse and stifled sound. I also feel wobbly, as if I were intoxicated and in danger of falling. My conversations with others proceed more smoothly, but often also more lively than usual, although I do not remember afterwards what I have said, though my way of speaking has been coherent all the time. It is a great strain to me to be exposed to this dual mental state. With my physical eyes I see the surroundings dull like a person about to fall asleep when a dream is arising. The other way of perceiving tries to carry me away forcefully; it is brighter than the natural way of seeing, but whatever I perceive, it is not transmitted by the eyes."[14]

---

ment endorsed the belief in the veracity and authenticity of her extravagant visions and mystical experiences. Adverse responses questioning fundamentally the genuineness of her paranormal experiences were first voiced in the late 19th c., and critics of the 20th c. questioned the sanity of the visionary as well as the reliability of Brentano's account. At the beginning of the 21st c., however, a reappraisal began, and the genuine nature of her visions was eventually approved by the theological commission conducting the beatification process. Anna Katharina was beatified in 2004, which marked the beginning of a process of re-evaluation, which is reflected in numerous reprints of her biography and of Brentano's account of her visionary experiences, as well as in recent translations of these works into English, Spanish, Dutch, Polish and French. – FKW.]

14   BUBER, Martin. *Ekstatische Konfessionen*. Leipzig: Insel, 1921. 176f. [Note: The passage quoted by Albrecht was taken from Buber's anthology. English translation provided. – FKW.]

> "... In this peculiar waking state I can see the holy relics shining by my side, and sometimes I see the effigies of crowds of small people standing on a distant cloud beside me, hovering above the relics, and when I take great pains to concentrate, the shapes arise from the shrines and the rooms in which their radiant bones had been laid to rest."[15]

It is possible to read this passage as the description of a 'dual vision', in which visionary phenomena are 'beheld within' but projected into the external surroundings in which the visionary is placed during the event. The 'inner vision' may have been fused with sense perceptions of the real world outside. But the account of this visionary experience can also be read as a projection of visions surfacing from "the heart" of a devout religious woman, evoked by the fervent practice of 'affective devotion' to the passion of the Redeemer. If the latter applies, the visionary experience can be classified as the product of 'eidetic after-images' rather than a genuine 'pictorial vision' beheld within. Over and beyond this, it is possible to classify the visionary scenes and images as manifestations occurring in the field of 'inner vision', though the visionary's physical eyes were open during the event and may have responded to external stimuli. If this applies, we may assume that the visionary experience recorded resulted from a simultaneous 'dual vision', in which the function of 'seeing' and 'beholding' operated alternatively and/or simultaneously. Moreover, the content of the 'pictorial vision' may have exclusively been perceived inwardly, but may have originated from the visionary's imagination, and were subsequently projected into the external field of vision. Over and beyond this, it is possible that these visions were generated by a clairvoyant occult experience, i.e., a retrospective act of clairvoyance featuring the historical period in which lived the saint who was represented in the vision. Finally, the visionary experience can alternatively be classified as a potential instance of genuine mystical experience, if we presuppose that the pictographic images have been *'infused'* by an act of special grace (a phenomenon that will be dealt with in some detail later).

Our examination of the range of phenomena expanding between the realm of 'seeing' and the realm of 'beholding' has supplied a rather

---

15   SCHMÖGER, Karl E. *Das Leben der Gottseligen Anna Katharina Emmerich.* 2 vols. Freiburg i. Br.: Herder, 1870. Vol. II, 21–23. [English translation supplied. – FKW.]

reliable basis for differentiating the 'inner pictorial vision' phenomenologically from other modes of visionary perception. Grounded on this reliable basis, we can now address a further crucial question: *What are the criteria by which the entire realm of 'pictorial visions' can be subdivided into a mystical and a non-mystical domain?* It goes without saying that the mere occurrence of visual images in an 'inner vision' is not a mystical event unless other qualities are involved; in other words, the perception of a 'pictorial vision' requires some special constituent characteristics. It will be the task of the following chapters of the book to identify and to define the pivotal characteristics that qualify as genuinely 'mystical' ones.

It is not possible to discern alone from the outlines of a picture occurring in a 'pictorial vision', if it is to be identified as a 'mystical' or a 'non-mystical' one. Basically, any image that appears in a vision may have mystical import and/or involve a 'mystical relation', just as any image surfacing within can be a picture that does not involve a 'mystical relation' and thus be devoid of any mystical import. This fundamental insight does not conflict with the empirical fact that there are both objects which are hardly ever placed in a 'mystical relation', as well as objects that are almost always situated in a 'mystical relation'. Which of these options applies can be discerned on the basis of the 'mystical qualities' inherent in a visionary experience. There are two ways by which a 'pictorial vision' can be identified as a mystical one:

1. *A 'pictorial vision' can be assumed to be a genuine mystical vision, if the visionary content beheld is affiliated with the awareness that it has been 'infused' or 'effected' mystically* [i.e., perceived as 'arriving' from beyond the confines of the individual consciousness]. When such an image or picture is 'beheld within', the vision is attended by the clear awareness of its 'givenness', and as such it is experienced as something 'effected' by the 'mystical Object'. There is obviously a big difference, if the picture perceived as having been 'instilled' is a vision of the devil, or a vision of an angel, or a vision of Christ; therefore, the mere awareness that some visual object has been 'infused' into the mind of the perceiver does not suffice as a criterion. In a mystical vision the

'impact' is inalienably attributed to the 'mystical Object' [viz., the Divine], which is understood to be the ultimate cause of what has been experienced. Moreover, the images of a pictorial vision qualified as 'mystical', have a closer affinity to faith and religion than the pictures featuring in a non-mystical vision. Despite this fact, we must *not* jump to the conclusion that a vision of Christ is always an indication for a 'mystical event'; nor is it pertinent to assume that the experience of a mystical impact that has evoked a religious image in the vista of 'inner sight' is confined to the image shown, whereas the mystical effects actually extend far beyond the boundaries of the image.

2. The mystical quality, however, does not depend on the phenomenon of effects, 'instilled' or 'infused', but is coupled in a 'pictorial vision' with the cognitive awareness of the 'mystical Presence', by which the experiential awareness of the 'mystical relation' between perceiver and the 'mystical Object' perceived is further corroborated. By 'awareness of Presence' we understand the instant cognitive perception of the presence of the Numen, which is the core phenomenon of 'mystical recognition'. (This will be further elaborated later in this study.) At this stage of our enquiry it is enough, however, to indicate that there is a phenomenon termed *cognitive awareness of the mystical Presence*, the manifestation of which is *a pivotal criterion for discerning whether the picture appearing in a 'pictorial vision' is a mystical or a non-mystical one.*

We have now disclosed a new spectrum of phenomena. On the one side is a mere graphic image that is 'beheld' inwardly but which is not intertwined with the awareness of the 'mystical Presence'; on the opposite side, is the perception of a picture imbued with the 'mystical Presence', which we have termed 'epiphanic mystical apparition' ["*mystisches Erscheinungsbild*"]; here the 'mystical Object' is in some way interwoven with the picture and experienced as present. Within the two juxtaposed focal points, we may discern six types of pictorial images:

1. *The picture per se*: A picture appears in the vista of 'inner sight', which is explicit, unequivocal and like a colourful painting, which can immediately be comprehended.

2. *An ideographic image.* This is an image that is 'beheld' in 'inner sight', but which has some 'hidden' meaning, and/or symbolic import. Its silhouettes and colours are ambiguous, and it is not immediately clear to the beholder what the picture signifies, or what is represented by it, and thus calls for an interpretation. The act of interpretation thus follows on the visual perception and is an independent cognitive process. 'Beholding' an ideographic image is furthermore often linked with the phenomenon of 'inner hearing': a 'voice' perceived within the mind imparts (as it were) a verbal explication of the ideographic image.

3. *Allegorical image.* The term allegory as used here can be subsumed under the concept of 'ideographic image'. The allegorical picture featuring in a 'vision' is a concrete representation of an abstract concept; for instance, justice, power, faithfulness or love, represented by some personification, such as a goddess, Cupid, or a blindfolded woman representing *iustitia*. The meaning of the allegorical picture may or may not be immediately apparent; if the latter applies, the visionary experience requires a subsequent process of interpretation.

4. *The double phenomenon 'picture/image interlaced with the sense of a numinous presence'*: The 'beholding' of an image in 'inner sight' is accompanied by and intertwined with the sense of the presence of the Numen. The presence does not reveal itself 'in' the picture beheld, but is perceived intuitively, in a non-visual, albeit quasi-sensory mode of awareness as being there 'behind', or 'beside' the image beheld.

5. *Non-mystical appearance.* By this term we understand a picture that appears in the vista of 'inner sight', in which the object portrayed is immediately present. This visual experience is based on a dual process of recognition, one of which results from the act of

beholding, the other from comprehending of the presence of the object. This dual mode of comprehending both the object beheld and the presence in 'inner sight' occurs simultaneously, resulting in one single experience (this is the difference to the 'double phenomenon' in which the two modes of perception are contiguous). A *non-mystical* appearance is one in which neither the picture or images beheld, nor the 'object' cognitively grasped as 'present', belong to the realm of mysticism. This implies that the phenomenon termed 'sense of presence' is not unique to mystical experience but can be affiliated with non-mystical preternatural occurrences, in which case it may be elicited by the opaque awareness of the presence of 'powers', 'ghosts', or 'spectres'. There is, however, a fundamental difference between the sense of the presence of 'powers' and 'spirits' and the 'awareness of the mystical Presence': only in the latter is the 'object' encountered comprehended as unfathomable and 'all-encompassing'. Non-mystical appearances cover a diverse spectrum of phenomena which still need to be qualified and explored scientifically, not least because there are several controversial gnoseological and ontological issues involved. The findings so far established by our enquiry do not yet supply adequate empirical data or reliable criteria by which the many varieties of non-mystical phenomena which may surface in paranormal 'appearances' can be distinguished from genuine mystical phenomena. A scientifically substantiated contrastive discernment is particularly called for as both mystical and non-mystical phenomena occur also in the records of pictorial visionary experiences of acknowledged mystics and visionaries, which they claim to have had a lasting impact on their lives. Non-mystical visual appearances encompass such diverse phenomena as the Jungian archetypes (or at least a large part of them), graphic visions of the devil and of demons, and – closer to the mystical domain – appearances of angels and biblical personages. An 'appearance' is thus defined as the manifestation of a visual image within the mind, which is 'beheld' by the function of the 'inner eye' and which is instantly and with absolute certainty taken for 'real'. The deep sense of certainty of the realness of the appearance is an experiential quality that can only be understood after we have explored further the distinctive features of mystical and non-mystical varieties of the 'sense of presence'.

The mystical appearance. In a 'mystical appearance' the inner visual perception of an image or a scene derives from the sphere of religion (e.g., in Christianity, the image of Christ) and is inalienably intertwined with the cognitive awareness of the presence of the 'All-encompassing' [viz., Divine]; this means that the Numen reveals itself in the picture that emerges, or 'arrives', in the vista of 'inner sight' during the visionary experience.

6. *The image with metaphoric import.* This is a paradoxical variety of a 'visionary experience', which is added only in parenthesis, because it is an *'imageless* vision'. There are testimonies of visionary occurrences in which the 'object arriving' in the field of 'inner sight' is blank and formless, but in rendering the experience verbally the visionary resorts to metaphoric language. The pictorial quality is thus not part of the experiential content, but a medium of expression. This type of 'visionary experience' obviously differs from the six types classified above and is as such not immediately relevant for our enquiry. It has only been mentioned in passing, as metaphoric descriptions of non-visual experiences are documented in the mystical records examined.

The six types of images can be further subdivided into two groups: types 1–3 (the single picture, the ideographic image and the allegorical image) are 'beheld' independently, i.e., the visionary experience is not intertwined or contiguous with any 'sense of presence' of the Numen. Thus, their mystical quality is exclusively sustained by the cognitive and/or experiential awareness of the vision as having been mystically imparted or 'infused'. Types 4–6 (the double-phenomenon image intertwined with presence, the non-mystical appearance, and the mystical appearance) are, by contrast, not necessarily accompanied by, or rooted in, the perception of mystical effects ["Gewirktheit"]. In this case, the mystical or non-mystical quality is rather determined by the essence of what is experienced as 'present': The 'vision' is a non-mystical one, if the image revealed can be identified as arising from the realm of archetypes; it can be classified as an authentic mystical vision, if the 'sense of presence' is cognitively grasped as originating from the 'all-encompassing mystical Object' itself, hence experienced as 'sense of Presence'.

After having clarified some of the key concepts and proposed a viable phenomenological differentiation between 'external visions' and 'inner visions' and outlined a tangible juxtaposition between 'the picture as such' and 'the visual image as a mode of mystical appearance', we may now explore in some detail some written testimonies of 'pictorial visions' handed down by mystical traditions. As a proviso we should add, however, that a phenomenological analysis of any account of a visionary experience is fraught with difficulty, as the descriptions are often phenomenologically ambivalent, multi-layered as to allow divergent readings. For example, a vision of Christ can phenomenologically – depending on the given experiential constellation – be either explained or accounted for as a mere hallucination, as a pathologically induced delusion, or a mere product of the imagination, or else as a mental image elicited by the intense practice of affective devotion to the Saviour, and as such as a self-generated vision arising from within the sphere of the self; the vision of Christ could moreover be the manifestation of an archetype as conceived by C. G. Jung, or an appearance elicited by a retrospective event of clairvoyance. However, a vision of Christ can be a mystically 'infused' image, and finally, it can be a genuine mystical experience revealed in an 'epiphanic vision'.

Non-mystical visions, like the vision of the devil, have a similar, equally complex phenomenological structure as mystical visions.

In the following, we shall try to illustrate some of the phenomena addressed above on the basis of selected autobiographical records by mystics. The examples chosen here are confined to accounts of 'inner visions'. 'Apparitions' and other *external visions* are especially prone to self-delusion and largely elude reliable scientific analysis and have therefore been excluded from our enquiry. Bypassing the first image-type (addressed above) that may feature in an inner 'pictorial vision', we will start with the analysis of an 'allegorical vision' and then proceed with a record of an inner vision of the devil, and another one of angels, and finally advance to the analysis of mystical visions of Christ. This approach should be helpful in outlining some of the seminal characteristics of pictorial *mystical* visions, but it can surely not disclose the entire range of mystical phenomena encountered in empirical reality. The phenomenological structure of 'pictorial inner visions' is too intricate and complex to achieve this goal. Though the progress from the study of the plain images in pictographic visions to visionary experience of epiphanic images opens perspectives that transcend the confines of the 'pictorial vision', extending to non-visionary modes of mystical perception. Though it is true that 'behold-ing' an image in an inner visionary experience is essentially the same at different levels, the phenomenological and cognitive difference between individual events of 'inner visions' becomes apparent, when a given vision approaches the mystical domain. The series of visionary events tends to result in the gradual dissolution of the visual content and its substitution by non-visual modes of mystical perception.

THESIS 24: *The phenomenological focus of 'pictorial visions' is situated outside the realm of mysticism.* The pure type of the 'pic-torial vision' can only be encountered outside the area of mystical experience. When a 'pictorial vision' does occur within the domain of mysticism, it is either necessarily intertwined with the clear aware-ness that the picture beheld has been mystically 'infused' by some Power beyond the confines of the individual self, and/or when the 'pictorial vision' is merely an integral part of a composite experience involving several modes of mystical perception.

THESIS 25: *An authentic 'mystical vision' never consists of the vision of a single picture alone.*

THESIS 26: *A 'pictorial vision' can be an integral part of a com-posite mystical experience.*

Allegorical Visions

An allegory is a personified representation of an abstract idea, principle or an abstract concept. In the following personal tes-timony of Saint *Hildegard of Bingen* (1098–1179), allegorical pic-tures are the prevailing 'content' of her 'inner visions'. The allegorical pictures in these visions do not result from the visionary's creative imagination in describing the visionary experience, but have been, as she insists, 'infused' into her mind in a mystical event. The allegorical images are clearly 'beheld' in 'inner sight' ["Innenschau"] and explicitly perceived as having 'arrived' in consciousness and 'infused' from outside the individual self; they are clearly not experienced as something originating from the imagination, or from some other area within the visionary's subjective self. The first event refers to the act of 'beholding' an image that has surfaced in the visionary's consciousness, viz., inner field of vision. The second empirical impact provides her with the interpretation of the allegorical picture. Some scholars have dismissed Hildegard's allegorical visions as fabrications originating from the 'unconscious'. Such a sceptical reading is, however, impaired by metaphysical assumptions and as such is neither helpful nor relevant to our phenomenological enquiry.

Any 'infused' allegorical picture inevitably calls for an explication. The visionary wishes to unravel the meaning of the allegory. Such a hermeneutical process may be triggered after the visionary experience, which can be compared to a person's endeavour to interpret the meaning of a dream after having woken up. Alternatively, it is possible that the interpretation of the allegorical image is incorporated in and concomitant with the act of beholding; if the latter applies, the simultaneous cognitive experience is 'infused', and thus the overall experience is grounded in a dual experience of a mystical impact. It is easy to understand that this twofold mode of inner perception can best be identified if entirely different modes of perception (visual vs. cognitive) are involved. We may encounter other perceptual combinations, such as the intertwining of a 'pictorial vision' with the mode of 'inner hearing'. In such an event, 'inner beholding' and 'inner hearing' complement each other and are mutually related. As we shall see later in this study, this kind of intertwining is a pivotal phenomenon of mystical experience.

This, however, is not the place to elaborate on the phenomenon of 'inner hearing', though the experience of locutions is (as we shall see) just as relevant as a token of the 'mystical relation' with the 'All-encompassing' as the phenomenon of 'inner beholding'. For elucidating a 'mystical encounter', we might just as well have started with the phenomenon of 'inner hearing'. But if we had done so, we would have been provided with an entirely different set of phenomena than those identified when starting with the analysis of visionary mystical experience. We shall therefore proceed by employing a contrastive phenomenological analysis. We just need to state for purposes of clarification that irrespective of the mystical relevance of the phenomenon of 'inner hearing', the fact remains that the 'mystical relation' by which it is informed and supposedly caused is still clouded in darkness, whereas the phenomenological structure of 'inner beholding' is not inaccessible to scientific enquiry.

> Text 6 (From a vision recorded by Hildegard of Bingen, 1098–1178)[16]: "… within the mist, referred to earlier, in which many different vices were lurking, I also beheld seven vices appearing in these pictures. The first picture showed the face of a woman; her eyes were like fire, her nose dirty and her mouth shut. There were no arms, nor hands to be seen, but on each of her shoulders was a wing like that of a bat. The right wing pointed towards the east, the left one towards the west. The chest was that of a man to which were attached thighs and legs, like those of a locust, because it had no abdomen and no backbone. Neither the head nor the rest of the body were covered with hair, or any other covering; but it was immersed in the darkness mentioned above; but a very thin thread, like a golden bracelet, was stretched from the vertex across the cheeks to the chin.
> And this picture was screaming: 'I am shouting across the mountains. And who is there, who can claim to be my equal? I spread my cloak across the hills and countries, and I won't allow anyone to overcome me; for I do not know anyone who could compare to me …'." [English translation provided.]

In Hildegard's account, the voice that accompanies the vision and interprets the allegorical vision of Pride goes on to explicate the remaining six allegorical pictures revealed in this event. I have interrupted the account at this stage to draw attention to the two phenomena addressed above but will come back to this testimony shortly. The allegorical vision composed of seven 'pictures' is intertwined here with the phenomenon of 'inner hearing', that is to say, an 'inner voice' is heard which explains the meaning of the allegorical picture. Hildegard had numerous visions of this kind, and she supplies in her works detailed descriptions

---

16 HILDEGARD von BINGEN. *Schriften der Heiligen Hildegard von Bingen.* Leipzig: Insel, 1922. 229f.

of 'showings' accompanied by 'locutions', particularly in *Scivias*[17] and in the book entitled *Vom Verdienstlichen Leben*.[18] The *psychological assessment* of these allegorical visions does not appear to be difficult to me. If we compare Hildegard's visions to those dealt with above in the context of 'cosmic consciousness', which are heavily imbued with ecstatic feelings, we can clearly see that she was hardly ever transported into liminal states of ecstasy but that all her visions were mainly 'beheld' in 'inner sight' in an entirely serene, calm and lucid mental state. The awareness of the division between subject and object is clearly maintained, and the capacity of 'inner sight' is never obfuscated by ecstatic states of rapture. [In her account below we encounter only an instance of an incipient stage of elation in response to a vision of the 'living Light'.] The capacity of beholding phenomena 'arriving' in the vista of 'inner sight' is clearly and unambiguously sustained throughout. And there is yet another distinctive feature in Hildegard's 'pictorial vision': The 'beholding' of allegorical pictures is interlaced with cognitive 'insights' as well as with metaphoric and symbolic forms of visionary experience.

In view of the aim of our study, we need to enquire at this juncture whether Hildegard's account of her visionary state of consciousness also embraces phenomena which might be helpful in our quest for the core of mystical experience. As we have seen, the visions are

---

17 [Note: Albrecht does not give a bibliographical reference here to *Scivias,* the first of Hildegard's works, which contains a series of twenty-one illustrations of her initial visionary experiences. The first critical edition of the original text (written in Latin) was published by FÜHRKÖTTER, Adelgundis and Angela CARLEVARIS, eds. *Hildegardis Bingenensis Scivias*. Turnhout (Belgium): Brepols, 1978. The standard German translation is that of BÖCKELER, Maura. *Wisse die Wege. Scivias*. Salzburg: Müller, 1954. There are several English translations; the one by HART, Columba and Jane BISHOP. *Hildegard of Bingen: Scivias*. (Classics of Western Spirituality). New York: Paulist Press, 1990 – is considered standard. – FKW.]

18 [Note: There is no bibliographical reference to this book of Hildegard's in Albrecht. Albrecht appears to have used the German edition *Schriften der Heiligen Hildegard von Bingen*. Ausgewählt und Übertragen von Johannes BÜHLER. Leipzig: Insel, 1922. In the recent reprint of Bühler's edition, entitled *Wisse die Wege*. Frankfurt a. M.: Insel, 2008, the book "*Vom Verdienstlichen Leben*" is printed on pages 217–51. – FKW.]

perceived in a serene state of consciousness, which does not elicit any ecstatic feelings, and enables the visionary to behold incoming phenomena throughout with 'quiet alertness'. This provokes the question as to whether or not her visions can indeed be classified as genuinely mystical. The formal criteria for a mystical vision to be acknowledged as 'genuine', stipulated earlier in our study, demand not only that the 'content' of the vision must have some mystical import and/or be perceived as 'having been infused' from a domain outside the individual self, but the overall experience must also be intertwined with the clear 'sense of presence of the Numen'. The latter, however, cannot be affirmed in the passage quoted from Hildegard's visionary experience: What is beheld by her is not even an emblematic image of the Numen, let alone a genuine revelation of the same. Though it is true that we may discern some passing references that might be interpreted in terms of an awareness of an extant 'relationship' to the 'All-encompassing', the fact remains that the metaphoric and symbolic images in her visions refer to all 'objects' originating from this world and/or from, or transformed by, the imagination. At this stage of our analysis, Hildegard's vision does not appear to qualify to be assessed as 'mystical' from a psychological-phenomenological perspective. We must acknowledge, however, that Hildegard herself had never any flicker of doubt that they were mystically instilled [hence the result of an act of special grace]. So we need to pursue our enquiry further and probe more deeply into the complex framework of her visionary experience if we wish to ascertain if her experience is indeed sustained by a genuine 'mystical core'.

We should bear in mind that Hildegard's allegorical pictures are only an integral part of a much more complex empirical structure. Her visionary experiences include, for instance, detailed visions dealing with 'the origin of evil', with 'man and the cosmos', 'the soul', 'the choirs of angels', the 'church', and the 'edifice of salvation'.[19] The latter visionary experiences are not composed of allegorical visions proper, but rather consist of intricate symbolic images. This indicates that these 'pictorial visions' were part of a complex preternatural experience incorporating various modes of inner perception and some multifaceted 'content',

---

19   Cf. BÖCKELER, Maura. *Wisse die Wege. Scivias.* Salzburg: Müller, 1954.

covering diverse thematic and gnoseological areas: We may discern genuine clairvoyant perceptions of the world, linked with intuitions about the natural laws and the causes underlying cosmic phenomena. These cognitive items in her visions also provide new insights for our understanding of the cosmos and the origin of creation (cosmogony). The knowledge conveyed in her visions also corroborates some of the claims of Christian dogmas. Hildegard's visionary experience also includes instances of clairvoyance, which furnished her with the subject matter for impressive prophecies. This shows that visions were occasionally also fuelled by occult experiences comparable to those witnessed by 'ghost-seers' (as outlined above).

But what is missing in the quoted passage from Hildegard is a clear reference to moments of immediate encounters with, and/or the self-revelation of what we have termed 'the All-encompassing'. Because of this (apparent) deficiency, the critical reader might be inclined to dismiss her visionary experience from the class of genuine mystical visions, and, as a consequence, to question her long-standing classification as a genuine mystic and visionary. Such a verdict, however, can be shown to be premature, as a final assessment calls for additional criteria to be considered. Throughout her lifetime Hildegard was highly esteemed for her pious life and charismatic gifts and revered as a mystic and visionary. Evidence of this (amongst many other testimonials) is, for example, a letter written by Hildegard at the age of seventy-three, addressed to the Benedictine monk Gilbert of Gembloux, her spiritual advisor and *amanuensis*.[20] Her detailed description of the nature and impact of

---

20 [Note: The name of the person addressed by Hildegard's letter is given as "Mönch Witigo" by Albrecht. The correct appellation of the monk, spiritual counsellor and Hildegard's correspondent is, however, Guibert (alternatively Wibert and Gilbert) of Gembloux (1124–1213). He lived in the cloister of Bingen from 1177 to 1180, where he was Hildegard's scribe, confidant and spiritual guide. Gilbert had corresponded with Hildegard already from 1175 onward. After Hildegard's death in 1178, he returned to the Abbey of Gembloux, where he became abbot in 1194 and began to write Hildegard's *vita* (unfinished). Guibert/Wibert/Gilbert of Gembloux are the names by which he is commonly known and referred to in historical sources. Cf. NEWMAN, Barbara, ed. *Voice of the Living Light. Hildegard of Bingen and Her World*. Oakland, CA: U of California P, 1998. – FKW.]

her extraordinary visual, auditive and cognitive experiences and their impact on her well-being display seminal features of mystical experience. In this letter Hildegard gives a vivid account of her vision of a radiating 'Light' beheld 'arriving' and abiding in the vista of 'inner sight'. In this visionary experience, her mind was filled with the 'shadow of the living Light', in which the 'living Light' revealed itself in the flash of a moment. As we shall see later, this unique experience of Light will be relevant to our enquiry into the core of mystical experience.

If we examine Hildegard's visionary experience critically from a phenomenological perspective, we must first ask whether the reference to the 'light' signified as the 'shadow of the living Light' is only a metaphor for the hyper-lucid state of consciousness, in which the 'living Light' was perceived as 'arriving'. If this is the case, we need to ask further if the word 'Light' in the expression 'living Light' is likewise merely a metaphor for a phenomenon beheld in 'inner sight', which she considered most adequate for describing the visionary quality of the experience. Moreover, we are required to ask if the visionary experiences of the 'living Light' described by Hildegard differ from the vision of the 'Ur-Licht' encountered in states of 'cosmic consciousness', in which the perceiver claims to have witnessed a 'formless', 'all-encompassing Light' permeating the cosmos.

> Text 7 (From a letter of Hildegard of Bingen to [Gilbert of Gembloux][21])
> "... from my infancy onward, when my bones, nerves and veins were still feeble, I have seen this vision in my soul until now, when I am over seventy years old. And my soul may soar up in this vision, as it pleases God, to the heights of the firmament, moving through various layers of air, and may reach out to multifarious peoples living in large, distant lands and places. And because I behold all this within my soul; I can perceive it after having passed through the clouds and facing other created things. Yet I do not hear

---

21 [Note: Albrecht here again refers to "Mönch Witigo" as the addressee of Hildegard's epistle; the passage quoted has been taken from Martin Buber's *Ekstatische Konfessionen*. Leipzig: Insel, 1921, 63ff. Buber does not indicate the name of the recipient of Hildegard's letter in this edition; in a later reprint, however, entitled *Mystische Zeugnisse aller Zeiten und Völker, gesammelt von Martin Buber*. Ed. Peter SLOTERDIJK (Munich: Diederichs, 1993), the annotation is added (in German) that "the letter is addressed to Gilbert of Gembloux" (291). – FKW.]

anything with my sensory ears, nor with any other of the five senses, nor do I grasp all this with the thoughts of my heart, but everything is exclusively beheld within my soul, though my physical eyes are open all the time; I never get exhausted or benumbed by states of ecstasy, so that, being alert and awake, I can behold the vision by day and by night. However, I am constantly beset by diseases and often tormented by agonies of pain, which are so excruciating that I fear they will cause my death, but God has always saved me and spared me until the present day.

The light, however, which I behold, is not confined to a spot, and is much, much brighter than the cloud that carries the sun. I am unable to fathom its depth, breadth or length. It has been named to me 'the shadow of the living Light'. And just as the sun, the moon and the stars are mirrored in water, so are the scriptures, the orations, the capacities and the works of men reflected in this luminous vision.

Whatever I am vouchsafed to see and experience in this vision remains stored in my memory for a long time, so that I can still recall when I had received it, and what I have heard and beheld in it. At the very moment when I behold the vision, I am instantly filled with knowledge, and whatever I know is instilled in the flash of a moment. But what is not revealed to me in the vision remains barred from my knowledge, because I am no learned woman, and have only had rather poor schooling and am skilled only basically in writing and reading. What I write down when I behold the vision is exactly what I see and hear in the vision. I do not use any other words than those heard in the vision, and I express these words exactly in the plain language heard in the vision. For I have been commanded in this vision not to write like the philosophers do. And the words heard in the vision do not sound like the words articulated by the mouth of a human being but are issued forth as if by a surging flame and move like a cloud in a clear sky.

It is impossible for me to recognize the shape of this light, just as it is impossible for me to see the contours of the sun when looking straight into it. However, within this light I behold at times (albeit not very often) another light, named the 'living Light'; but I cannot tell when, or in which manner, I behold it. But whenever I do, all sadness and all misery are instantly gone, so that I adopt the habits of a foolish maid rather than behave like a decent old woman.

Because of my persevering frailty, I have qualms about expressing aloud the words and visions revealed to me. But during the time when my soul is absorbed in the visionary experience, beholding and relishing in the vision, my condition changes so drastically that (as I have said before) I become totally oblivious to all my pains and suffering. Whatever I behold and hear in this vision pours into my soul like from a fountain which is forever full and never needs to be replenished. There is not a moment when my soul does not see the light termed 'shadow of the living Light'. And I can see it just like I see a bright cloud shrouding the stars in the firmament. And in this light, I behold what I speak and reply, when I am asked about the flash of the 'living Light'." [English translation provided]

Graphic Visions of the Devil and of Angels (Teresa of Avila and 'Lucie Christine' [a.k.a. Mathilde Boutle, 1844–1908][22])

The visions recorded by Hildegard of Bingen have been used by us to try out a phenomenological approach to the category of 'pictorial visions'. We shall now enlarge our perspective and examine records of different pictographic visions supplied by diverse mystics and visionaries. As we have seen, Hildegard's visions were primarily symbolic-metaphoric and intuitive, and in terms of 'content' clearly dominated by allegorical images. The way of experiencing visions and mystical encounters depends only in part on the 'object' that 'arrives' in the vista of 'inner sight': we shall see shortly that both form and content of a visionary experience are subject to change, and both may expand independently from each other.

The allegorical pictures dealt with in the visions of Hildegard of Bingen have been dismissed from the domain of 'mystical Objects', and the same applies even more so to pictorial visions of the devil. A vision of the devil is never affiliated with a genuine 'mystical Object', whereas a vision of angels can be accompanied by the awareness of a 'mystical Object'. Visions of angels are often phenomenologically borderline cases between non-mystical and mystical visions, not least because they can be composed of characteristics of both phenomena. Thus, visions of angels are often intertwined simultaneously with a vision of Christ. It would be premature to analyse at this stage how

---

22 [Note: 'Lucie Christine' is the pseudonym under which the married French lady Mathilde Boutle (née Bertrand, 1844–1908) published her diaries and personal testimonies of mystical and visionary experience. Her real identity was unknown at the time when Albrecht wrote this book. The fact that the real author of the diaries of 'Lucie Christine' was Mathilde Boutle was established only in the late 20th century. The first detailed scholarly biography of Mathilde Boutle was published by O'BRIEN, Astrid M. *A Mysticism of Kindness: The Biography of 'Lucie Christine'*. Scranton, PA: University of Scranton Press, 2010. – FKW.]

a vision of angels and a vision of Christ are interlaced phenomenologically. But what can be said at this point is that visions of angels are, by and large, either located at the periphery, or within the sphere encompassed by mysticism, and thus they cannot be excluded from the realm of mystical experience. This claim is substantiated by the fact that visions of angels are linked to a variety of other modes of inward perception, such as can also be encountered in the context of mystical experience; for instance, the intuitive awareness of the nearness and/or of the approach of the 'All-encompassing'. The mystical vision of angels is, moreover, often intertwined with the vision of the mystical Light, and this again is usually linked with the cognitive awareness of the presence or vicinity of the 'mystical Object' [viz., 'the All-encompassing'].

These explanatory remarks are intended to sketch the boundaries of our endeavour to analyse phenomenologically a representative selection of the visionary mystical experiences recorded by St. Teresa of Avila, and by the French laywoman and mystic known as 'Christine Lucie'. Our empirical enquiry will continue to advance in two directions: The range of 'pictorial visions' will be expanded beyond the category of symbolic-metaphoric images as to include more complex visionary experiences. This means that the focus is no longer on static, ideographic or allegorical pictures, but on dynamic, self-expressive varieties of visionary experience. In our practical approach, however, we will examine the distinctive features of the images initially in the manner of the approach taken when analysing the symbolic-metaphoric visions. We shall, however, further advance towards the mystical domain, which is inevitably linked with the visionary experience of light and the cognitive 'sense of Presence' usually concomitant with it. When a pictorial vision is combined with a vision of the mystical Light and/or the awareness of Presence, the overall visionary experience obviously no longer represents the type of an allegorical or symbolic vision but must be classified as a self-expressive, potentially epiphanic 'visionary appearance'. An exemplary analysis of a vision describing the process of transformation of a static allegorical picture into a self-expressive mode of revelation will help us to considerably broaden our methodological approach to other varieties of visionary mystical experience.

A 'vision of light' is inevitably linked with the awareness of the nearness of the 'mystical Object'. This means that the visionary experience of 'light' may adhere to, or permeate, the pictorial vision of angels; or else, a vision of Christ is typically described as radiant with dazzling light. A vision of the devil, by contrast, is entirely devoid of the white and dazzling light. Thus the 'vision of light' [as specified by Hildegard] and a vision of the devil are mutually exclusive. This apodictic claim (we should add) is not invalidated by Teresa of Avila's account of her 'vision of the fiend' (quoted in text 8), in which she states that she has been protected against the impact of the diabolical vision by a luminescent 'clarity' surrounding her. As we shall see, the light perceived in her vision of the devil does not adhere to the fiend, but is expressly opposed to him, as it serves as a protective shield against diabolical temptation.

The 'sense of presence' is a phenomenon that can be encountered in both the 'vision of angels' and the 'vision of the fiend', albeit with important differences. Though the 'vision of the devil' and the awareness of the presence of the 'All-encompassing' are incompatible, the 'sense of presence' in a diabolical vision is not opposed to the fiend (unlike 'light' in a diabolical vision) but just emerges and remains hovering in a neutral or indifferent manner. That is to say, the cognitive awareness of presence is an impartial phenomenon, i.e., it may accompany (albeit in different ways) both mystical and non-mystical experiences. The 'sense of presence' may be an integral part of a vision of the devil, even when this is not only an allegorical pictorial vision, but a mode of diabolical self-revelation. In the latter instance, the visionary experience of the devil is indeed intertwined with the sensible 'awareness' of the real presence of the fiend. Such an occurrence is thus imbued with what William James has termed 'sense of reality'.[23] At the present stage

---

23 [Note: Albrecht refers to the German translation of William James's *Varieties of Religious Experience*. New York: Longmans, 1902: *Die Religiöse Erfahrung in Ihrer Mannigfaltigkeit: Materialien und Studien zu einer Psychologie und Pathologie des Religiösen Lebens*. Trans. Georg Wobbermin. Leipzig: Hinrichs, 1907. In the original English edition James elaborates on the "sense of reality" in the context of the awareness of an "objective presence", stating that "... the whole array of our instances leads to a conclusion something like this: It is as if there were in the human

of our enquiry, we cannot yet consider what is meant by 'sense of reality' in ontological terms. (This will be deferred to a later stage of our enquiry.) This suggests that a 'vision of the devil' may subjectively be experienced as a 'real encounter' with a diabolical power and is as such a complex phenomenon that requires serious consideration. In conclusion, we should add that a 'vision of the devil' does not necessarily involve a pictographic image but can also become manifest in the shape of a self-expressive apparition, an instance of satanophany, or even in the mode of an abstract intellectual vision [*visio intellectualis*].

The descriptions of 'diabolical visions' provided by Teresa of Avila seem to me best suited to the phenomenological analysis of this variety of non-mystical visions. Some of the accounts quoted below were written by Teresa herself and published in her *Vida*, while other accounts were reported by Teresa via her spiritual counsellor and confessor; together these testimonies extend over the period 1562–1581.[24] This extraordinary Spanish Carmelite nun was not only a highly gifted psychologist, but also a systematic logical thinker whose ways of thinking and empirical testimonies are accessible to the understanding of a reader today without difficulty. Though Teresa's account of her visionary and mystical experiences is, at times, lacking in immediacy and spontaneity of expression, it is distinguished by her rare intellectual ability to analyse and reflect on the extraordinary experiences in great detail. Teresa's texts have been supplemented by selections from the diary of *Christine Lucie*,[25] which are

---

consciousness a *sense of reality, a feeling of objective presence, a perception* of what we may call "*something there*," more deep and more general than any of the special and particular "senses" by which the current psychology supposes existent realities to be originally revealed." (58). – FKW.]

24 THERESIA von JESU. *Sämtliche Schriften. Neue dt. Ausgabe.* 6 vols. Munich: Kösel, 1935–1958. *Vida* (Leben) trans. Aloysius Alkofer. Vol. I. Munich: Kösel, 1952.

25 [Note: Albrecht used the German translation of the diary of 'Christine Lucie' (aka Mathilda Boutle): *Geistliches Tagebuch (1870–1908).* Ed. Auguste POULAIN. Trans. Romano GUARDINI. 3rd ed. Mainz: Grünewald, 1952. All the passages quoted by Albrecht have been translated into English, though there is an English translation of the diary: POULAIN, Auguste, ed. *The Spiritual Journal of Lucie Christine (1870–1908).* London: Paul, Trench, Trubner & Co., 1920. – FKW.]

candidly expressive of her mystical experiences and intimate visionary encounters with Christ and invaluable personal testimonies of great immediacy and emotional intensity. Christine's diary entries cover the period 1870–1908; they were published in Germany by [the Roman Catholic priest and theologian] *Romano Guardini* under the title *Geistliches Tagebuch* [1952]. She was a married French woman living at the turn of the 20th century, which is why her way of thinking and feeling as well as her terminology and psychological concepts are much closer to our own time than Teresa's. There is no need to explain or explicate her statements, or to translate her perceptive account of mystical experience into the idiom of today. Her report, rendered in clear and straightforward language, addresses a wide range of visionary and mystical experiences, including several types of 'pictorial visions', 'visions of light' and non-visual varieties of mystical experience. Christine's diary is a treasure trove of diverse varieties of mystical experience, and thus a most valuable textual source for the purposes of our investigation.

Teresa and Christine are kindred souls of the same Catholic religious mould, which becomes evident when we compare the analogies in and affinities of their records:

> *Text 8* (Teresa of Avila, *Vida*, main section 31, 295f.): "2. It so happened to me, at the time when I was in the oratory, that to my left the devil appeared to me in a hideous shape. When he accosted me, I noticed especially his extremely horrifying mouth. A big flame of fire seemed to be blazing, which was glaring brightly but did not cast a shadow. Speaking in a dreadful voice, he insinuated to me that I may have escaped his grasp just now, but would sooner or later be seized by his power …"
>
> "3. At another occasion … I saw a small, most repulsive moor standing next to me, grating his teeth frantically like a desperate man, because he had lost, where he had hoped to win …"
>
> *Text 9* (Teresa of Avila, *Vida*, main section 31, 301): "12. At times, I saw plenty of evil spirits looming all around, intimidating me, but it seemed to me that I was enclosed and screened off against them by a great lucidity, which prevented them from getting any closer …"
>
> *Text 10* (Teresa of Avila, *Vida*, main section 32, 310f.): "1. A long time after the Lord had gratified me with many of the special gifts of grace recorded earlier, and had bestowed me with many more, I thought one

day, when I was deeply engrossed in prayer, to have been abruptly transferred into hell with body and soul, without knowing how this happened ... This occurred at an instant; I will never forget this experience, even if I am granted to live for many years to come, it will be impossible for me to forget this. The doorway appeared to me like a very long and narrow passageway, looking like a very short, dark and tight furnace. Its floor appeared to me like a foul puddle, teeming with vermin, and with insufferable, pestilential stench exuding from it. At the far end was a recess in the wall, like a cabinet, into which I felt to be squeezed. The sight of all this, which I have described here only fragmentarily, was a pleasure compared to what I felt in that place.

2. I think it is impossible to express even remotely what I really had to suffer. I felt a fire blazing in my soul, which was of a kind that is beyond description. During all this I was afflicted by most excruciating headaches ... but this was nothing compared to the agonizing struggle with death. I was overcome by affliction, deep depression, and agonizing fear, and beset by such a desperate and harrowing displeasure that I am unable to render in words. If I said that I felt as if someone tried to rip the soul from my body, this would be inadequate, as in such an experience it is someone else who tries to deprive you of your life; but in the agony I had been exposed to in this mortal struggle, it is the soul itself that is tearing itself to pieces. In brief, I am totally at a loss for words to describe that raging fire within, that despair at the unbearable torture and insufferable pain. Though I could not see who it was that tortured me so, I thought that I was consumed by fire, or crushed to death. In this agony, the terrible fire blazing away within and the sense of desolation were the most excruciating tortures. In this utterly repulsive pestilential place, in which there is no hope of succour at all, you can neither sit down nor take a rest. There is no room to lie down, as I had been squeezed into a hole-like nook; the horrible-looking walls themselves seemed to crush me and everything in it seemed to smother me. There is no light, everything is thrust into pitch-black darkness; it is entirely inexplicable to me why it is possible to see everything that must be hurtful to the eyes, despite the absence of light....

... Anything else that I have heard others say about that horrid place, and whatever I have rendered and said about the various pains ... and whatever I have read about the various pains by which those doomed are tormented by evil demons ... all these impressions are nothing compared to the torments I was exposed to. The difference between the two is like that between a painting and reality ...

3. This vision has caused such a horror in me that I am shuddering even now, six years after this nightmare; as I write this record the natural warmth of my body seems to plummet and run out ..." [English translation provided.]

Admittedly, Teresa's descriptions of the vision of the devil in text 8 and of her vision of evil demons in text 9 are not particularly comprehensive and not very rich and specific in visual detail. But despite these phenomenological deficiencies, we can state that there are some close typological affinities between Teresa's visions and those described by Hildegard of Bingen. Both types of visions, the allegorical vision as recorded by Hildegard and the vision of the devil depicted by Teresa, were individually experienced in a state of consciousness that in both visionaries had the same pivotal characteristics: The 'experiencing I' is absorbed in 'inner sight' ["Innenschau"] and beholds the 'object(s)' revealed and 'arriving' there in a clear and alert mental condition. The objects become mainly manifest in a metaphorical-symbolic mode, and there are no indications that the perceiver is at some stage transported into states of ecstasy. The visionary experiences of both mystics are furthermore intertwined with the hearing of inner voices, either simultaneously or consecutively with the contemplation of the 'pictorial vision'. The inner locutions are, moreover, in both comments on, or interpretations of, the pictures and pictorial scenes beheld within.

However, there are also some differences despite these congruities: At close analysis, Teresa's vision of the devil cannot be reduced to a symbolic or ideographic vision but must be classified as a [non-mystical] 'visionary appearance' ["Erscheinungsbild"]. Teresa's account shows unmistakably that she had a clear awareness during the event that the devil was *really* present in the given location; this means that her visionary experience is distinctly intertwined with the sense of his presence, i.e., the clear awareness of the real, spatial presence of the fiend. This means that Teresa's vision is imbued with an unflagging 'sense of reality'. In fact, she was so convinced of the 'real presence' of the fiend that she ordered the nuns of her abbey to besprinkle with holy water the site where the devil appeared to her. When questioned by her spiritual counsellor, Teresa vehemently denied that the vision of the devil was an 'apparition' rather than an inner experience of the 'real presence' of the fiend, stating emphatically that the diabolical vision was not 'seen' with her physical eyes [in which case it would have to be classified as an 'apparition' set in external space] but that the devil appeared to her in an 'inner vision', beheld by the 'inward eye', and she likewise denied that this inner vision may have been projected onto the external world. Teresa reiterates throughout all her works that she had never been subjected to an 'external vision'. And there is no reason not to trust her judgement in this.

In text 10 Teresa provides a graphic description of her harrowing vision of Hell. This vision is phenomenologically much more diverse and complex than her visions of the devil. Though it is still the metaphoric-symbolic and intuitive modes that are the prevailing modes of inner perception, there are other modes of cognition that are involved as well. Couched in terms of the psychological terminology introduced in our previous study [*Psychology of Mystical Consciousness*], the vision of Hell elicits agonizing 'responding feelings', as well as 'somatic modes of perceiving', including – arguably – an 'eruption of a storm of somatic seizures'. The latter experience is recorded by Teresa as part of another mystical occurrence which we will analyse below. Here I would like to draw attention to another feature in the above account: Teresa is adamant that the visionary encounter with the devil in Hell has paradoxically been vouchsafed by God. For Teresa, the vision of Hell is thus, theologically speaking, an 'infused vision', hence an act of special grace:

> *Text 11* (Teresa of Avila, *Vida*, main chapter 29, 280ff.): "15. It pleased the Lord to gratify me in this mental state several times with the following vision: I beheld, next to me to the left, an angel in physical likeness. I have hardly ever beheld angels in this manner. Though angels appear to me quite often, I usually do not behold them physically, but in an 'imageless [intellectual] vision'. In this special vision, however, the Lord wanted me to behold the angel in bodily shape. The angel was not tall, in fact rather small and very lovely. His face was so radiant that he seemed to me to be one of the most sublime angels, who appear to be ablaze all over ... The angel that appeared to me had a long golden arrow in his hands, the iron tip of which seemed to be glowing with fire. I felt as if he was piercing my heart again and again with this fiery arrow right into the innermost core, and when he withdrew the arrow, I felt as if he extracted the deepest part of my heart with it. When he released me, I was wholly inflamed with ardent love for God. The pain of this wound was so great that I was overwhelmed by stifling sobs and wailing cries; however, this wound paradoxically also triggered exuberant feelings of bliss so that I was unable to pray to be released from it, nor could I be satisfied by anything less than God Himself. This pain, however, is not physical but entirely spiritual, even though the

body is involved in and affected by it, and surely, not in a small measure. The loving interaction between the soul and God is so delightful and sweet, that I plead to the mercy of the Lord that he should allow also others to taste it, lest they should think I am telling a lie.

16. While this exceptional state lasted, I was scampering about, as if I had been out of my senses. I was unable to see and to speak, as I only desired to remain absorbed in that pain which provided greater bliss for me than any of the things of creation. I felt this pain of love from time to time, until it pleased the Lord to transport me into raptures of ecstasy, so overwhelming that I was unable not to succumb to them, even when I was with other people ..." [English translation provided.]

The vision of Teresa's experience of transverberation had a wide-ranging and lasting impact on her. The event of the piercing of her heart was henceforth celebrated annually by the order of the Discalced Carmelites by a feast on 27 August.[26]

Teresa's description of this ecstatic visionary experience is from *a psychological perspective* surprisingly clear and conclusive. The account provides definite indications that the 'pictorial vision' occurred 'within', which is moreover confirmed elsewhere in her *Vida*. The editor [of the German edition of Teresa's *Complete Works*] has added the appropriate annotation that the sentence "Here it pleased the Lord that I should behold the angel in physical likeness" can only be understood as a statement about an 'inner vision', and definitely not about an 'apparition', because the angel in this vision was not seen with Teresa's physical eyes, "for the simple reason that the saint never had any corporal visions."[27]

The structure of the 'inner sight' in this visionary experience consists largely of pictorial components, though the visionary phenomena are accompanied throughout by 'somatic modes of perception'. The pain experienced was, as she puts it, "largely a spiritual pain, but the body was likewise affected in a considerable measure"; she furthermore

---

26 Cf. THERESIA von JESU. *Sämtliche Schriften. Neue dt. Ausgabe*. 6 vols. Munich: Kösel, 1935–1958. *Vida* (Leben) Trans. Aloysius Alkofer. Vol. I. Munich: Kösel, 1952. 281.

27 THERESIA von JESU. *Sämtliche Schriften. Neue dt. Ausgabe*. 6 vols. Munich: Kösel, 1935–1958. *Vida* (Leben) Trans. Aloysius Alkofer. Vol. I. Munich: Kösel, 1952. 280; 284.

describes in great detail the somatic experience of the transverberation of her heart by the angel's fiery arrow, and its twofold impact and long-term after-effect. The wound caused by the piercing arrow triggered both agonizing spiritual pain and, simultaneously, an upsurge in ineffable bliss. The exceptionally intense emotional response elicited by this vision of the angel, afflicting the wound of love, generates ecstatic feelings of delight, love and bliss. She confesses emphatically that during this experience she was ultimately transported into ineffable states of ecstasy: "... until it pleased the Lord to transport me into great raptures ..."

After having analysed Teresa's angelic vision from a psychological perspective, we may now consider if it contains any new elements which might advance our phenomenological enquiry. To start with, we encounter in this testimony a feature first mentioned in passing in the analysis of a 'pictorial vision' by Hildegard of Bingen: a visionary experience of light or luminescence adhering to, or emanating from, a figure from the 'other world'. The "sight of a special luminous radiance" is also linked to Teresa's vision of the angel, who is "fully ablaze." Though the light is attached here to a non-mystical, or arguably a 'semi-mystical Object', it can be attributed to the mystical sphere, as the mystical realm is somehow "present in the background." (We shall explain this later).

Furthermore, we must draw attention to the fact that Teresa insists that both the vision of the angel and the somatic experience of the transverberation of her heart by the seraphic arrow, resulting in a composite ecstatic visionary experience, have been bestowed on her by God. The visionary experience is accompanied and sustained throughout by the intuitive awareness that God has not merely caused the event, but is also directly involved in it: "The bliss caused by the excruciating pain [of transverberation] was so rapturous that it was impossible for me to plead to God to be released from it, nor could I be satisfied by anything less than God Himself." This insatiable state of bliss *can alone* be attributed to God [and can be seen as an indication of the visionary's living experiential relationship to God]. Thus, a new phenomenon of mystical recognition has become apparent here, which we are going to term 'perception of mystical effects'.

There is a third aspect that can advance our phenomenological enquiry: We have (nearly inadvertently) been provided with a further characteristic feature of our phenomenology of the 'sense of presence': In Teresa's testimony we have come across another variety of perceiving a mystical 'presence'; she refers to a mystical 'object' that is non-visual and placed (as it were) in the backdrop of the sphere in which the 'objects' of the pictorial visions are set. The 'object' cognitively grasped as contemporaneously present is not identical with the 'object' shown in the pictorial vision. In both Teresa's vision of the devil, and the vision of the angel, which occurred after the diabolical vision, a 'sense of presence' is evoked, but it is strikingly adverse: The stark 'sense of reality', which adhered to the vision of the devil, emerged from a 'sense of presence' of the same 'object' [the fiend] that appeared in the vision, and this 'object' was definitely not a 'mystical' one. The question concerning if, and how, non-mystical 'objects' such as angels, the devil, saints, or ghosts are merely symbolic or metaphoric manifestations, or if they are indeed genuine modes of self-revelation, does not yet have to be decided at this point, since it is not relevant in the given context. But what is important is the new insight, gained from and substantiated by the visionary's experience, *that the pictorial vision of an unquestionably non-mystical 'object' can be imbued with the non-visual awareness of the 'mystical presence'*. This provokes the question as to whether this special awareness of the *mystical* 'givenness' of a phenomenon, i.e., the immediately evident knowledge that a vision has been 'bestowed' or 'infused' into the visionary's mind, is indeed the only experiential quality by which the experience can be identified as a mystical one? This question cannot be answered at this stage of our enquiry, and we must be careful not to stipulate prematurely that there is a causal relationship between the phenomenon of 'mystical effects' and that of the 'sense or cognitive awareness of a presence'.

We have repeatedly strayed by now from the actual aim of this chapter: to establish on the basis of empirical accounts a comprehensive phenomenology of 'pictorial visionary experience'. The digressions above became necessary in order to determine the fact that a *pure* 'pictorial vision' is limited to the 'inner beholding' of symbolic or metaphoric images, and to demonstrate furthermore that the 'inner sight' of 'infused pictorial appearances' do not occur unless they are simultaneously intertwined with imageless modes of perception that are experienced as something 'given' or 'infused'.

THESIS 27: *In a pure pictorial vision, symbolic images are beheld which are 'infused'.*

THESIS 28: *The structure of 'inner pictorial appearances' is more complex than that of pure 'pictorial visions' and thus transgresses the confines of the latter.*

We have now sufficiently explained the reasons for anticipating some aspects that are not directly concerned with issues related to 'pictorial visions'. But before we move on with our enquiry, we should pause for a moment to recall and clarify some of the concepts introduced earlier. For it is rather disconcerting to me that the terms 'inner sight', 'vision', 'inner hearing' and 'somatic mode of perception' have been used freely in our study so that their meanings seem to have become fuzzy. In the previous book [*Psychology of Mystical Consciousness*], we have placed *all* forms of inward perception, whether visual or non-visual, within the collective concept of '*inner sight*'. As a consequence, such heterogeneous 'forms' of inner perception as 'inner hearing', 'perceiving one's own corporeality', or the 'form of self-understanding', the 'form of responding feelings' as well as 'intuition' as a cognitive mode of inner perception, have all been subsumed under the same generic concept and collectively conceived as varieties ('forms') of 'inner sight' ["Innenschau"]. Two reasons were then stated in support of this collective approach:

1. In empirical reality any experience occurring in 'inner sight' is a composite mix of several 'forms of inward perception'; this means that any mode of inward perception *can* be involved in any event of 'inner sight'. Though it is possible that in a given event visual, auditory or emotional components can prevail, it hardly ever happens that the 'overall form' is composed of only a singular 'form of inward perception'. For this reason, it has been considered appropriate to use a classifying general key-concept that encompasses several subcategories of 'inner perception'. Replacing the term 'inner sight' with the more comprehensive term 'inner experience' would have complicated matters even further, because of the special nature of 'inner experience' encountered in, and confined to, special states of consciousness: by definition, 'inner

sight' is exclusively concerned with the perception of 'objects' that 'arrive' in the vista of 'inner sight' in the special state of consciousness termed 'quiet state of alertness' – and to a very limited extent, the incipient state of the 'ecstatic consciousness' – which means that 'inner sight' embraces only a limited range of the phenomena encompassed by 'inner experience'. That is to say, the word 'sight' in the term 'inner sight' denotes only the range of phenomena that may become manifest in the clear and vacated mental state called 'quiet state of alertness' and – to a limited extent – the incipient state of the 'ecstatic consciousness'.

2. The focus of the present book is – unlike the one in the previous psychological study – on the 'gnoseology' of mystical experience. In the foregoing chapters we have moreover repeatedly resorted to such terms as 'mystical beholding' and 'mystical vision', fuzzy concepts that call for clarification: the term 'mystical beholding' is juxtaposed with two equally important modes of 'inward perception' – 'inner hearing' and the 'perception of mystical effects'. Introducing this gnoseological classification is justified by the findings of our earlier psychological study. It has been shown that the term *'sight'* refers to the composite mode of 'inward perception', which in empirical reality consists of visual perception intertwined with intuition and/or somatic and emotional modes of 'inward perception', eliciting 'responding feelings'. *'Inner hearing'* is a variety of inner perception that is less complex than 'inner sight' because it is generally affiliated only with the mode of 'responding feelings'. The 'perception of mystical effects', by contrast, i.e., *becoming aware of a mystical force or mystical impact* operating within or upon the 'experiencing I', has a considerably more complex structure. In this case, somatic and emotional alterations in the body are often combined with flashes of 'intuitive self-understanding', resulting in a type of 'inner sight' that differs strikingly from 'visual' and 'auditory' modes of 'inner perception'. However, in empirical reality the phenomenological differences between the three types of 'inner perception' outlined here tend to overlap and cannot as clearly be distinguished as described here in the theoretical analysis. But it is still important

for our enquiry to have established these three distinct 'forms of inner sight' in view of the subsequent analysis of individual records of mystical experience. Teresa of Avila's accounts of the diverse forms of 'inner sight' experienced by her are particularly rich in descriptive detail and reflect the multifarious structure of 'inward perception' operating in the overall experience. Teresa pondered carefully the events of 'inner sight', as well as the nature of the instances of 'inner hearing', the 'responding feelings' and the 'somatic modes of perception' she had been blessed with.

We may state by way of summary: The gnoseological concept of 'inner beholding' is strictly understood to refer to visual modes of inner perception. The psychological concept of 'inner sight' [viz., 'inner perception'], however, denotes a much wider range of inner perception including 'inner hearing' and the perception of somatic and emotional effects elicited by an object 'arriving' in the realm of 'inner sight'. If this strict terminological and phenomenological distinction is kept in mind, terminological confusion and misunderstanding should be obviated when reading the textual analyses and critical reflections on visionary and mystical experiences in the subsequent sections of this study.

Text number 12 is part of an account of a visionary experience of Teresa of Avila, which will bring us back to the main issue of the present chapter – the phenomenological analysis of the *'pictorial vision'*. Though this report does not address any new aspects and thus does not further advance our knowledge of the characteristics germane to the 'pictorial vision', it is still illuminating as it describes quite convincingly the changing mental condition during the Saint's visionary experience:

> *Text 12* (Teresa of Avila, Vida, main chapter 33, 330ff.): "16. ... Then I was transported into such a great state of ecstasy that I nearly lost my capacity of sense perception. I sat down and was hardly able to see how the Host was lifted during the Eucharist, nor was I capable of following holy mass, which later caused great fear and pangs of conscience in me. In this ecstatic state it seemed to me as if I was apparelled in a white, radiant garment. At the beginning I could not see who had garbed me with this attire; but soon after I became aware of our Holy Lady to the right of me, and Holy Father Joseph to the left ...

17. The beauty of Our Lady when I beheld her was overwhelming, although I did not see the detailed features of her face, but only the figure as a whole. She was clad in a white dress and surrounded by supreme radiance, which, however, was not blinding to the eyes, but pleasantly refreshing ... Then it seemed to me that I saw her ascending again to heaven, surrounded by a large host of angels. I was left behind alone, however, but full of consolation and filled with elation, so fully absorbed in prayer and so deeply affected that I thought for some time to be quite out of my mind, unable to stir, and unable to speak. I also felt a great desire to offer myself up to God, and other similar effects on me. The whole vision was of a kind that I did not doubt in the least that it had come from God, and no one could have persuaded me to believe the contrary. The after-effects that continued to persevere after this vision were a sweet sense of succour and deep inner peace." [English translation provided.]

This testimony of Teresa's is to be attributed taxonomically to the sub-category of the 'pictorial vision', termed above 'ideographic and/or symbolic vision'. As such it is a suitable link to the visions described by the 19th-century French mystic *Christine Lucie*[28] in her diary. Despite the many striking similarities between Teresa's and Lucie's descriptions of their visionary experiences, Lucie's account is more easily comprehensible to a modern reader and is also more easily accessible to critical analysis. Lucie's visionary experiences are less intricate in structure; the visual components of inner perception (including symbolic-metaphoric images) are clearly predominant so that the greater part of her visions can be classified as varieties of 'pictorial visions'.

Text 13 (Christine Lucie, diary entry dated 16 June 1903. 322f.): "The day before yesterday, on Sunday ... during mass in the afternoon, my soul was struck with awe at the sight of angels; the soul saw very many of them ..."

Text 14 (Christine Lucie, diary entry dated 18 September 1883. 141f.): "... When I was absorbed in prayer before receiving Holy Communion, I saw the Redeemer encircled by a magnificent light. The light radiated from his venerable shape, and within this light I saw many angels. They formed more than a semi-circle around the Lord. Above Him I could not see any

---

28 'CHRISTINE, Lucie'. *Geistliches Tagebuch (1870–1908)*. Ed. Auguste POULAIN, S.J. Trans. Romano GUARDINI. 3rd ed. Mainz: Grünewald, 1952.

angels; but I saw a thronging mass of very small angels crouching at a distance beneath His divine feet. On both sides were larger angels, some on their knees, others lying there prostrate. There were so many angels that they formed a long continuous queue ... My soul was filled with ineffable joy ... I was completely overwhelmed with happiness ..."

Text 15 (Christine Lucie, diary entry dated 5 January 1883. 98): "Again, the same grace was revived. I saw a flower; it was planted in my heart and blossomed in the Heart of Jesus; and Jesus showed me lovingly that the high stalk of the flower had not been broken before. But I could also see that my Heavenly Bridegroom had spread His royal cloak over the fragile stalk to protect it ..."

Text 16 (Christine Lucie, diary entry dated 17 October 1883. 198): "My soul appeared to me in the shape of a white dove. It fluttered over the venerable figure of the Divine Master settling down on His shoulder. He took the dove and moved it close to Him ...

When I was engrossed in spiritual prayer about two hours later, before going to bed, Jesus granted me the same grace again. The moment when my soul was most deeply united with God, I beheld how the dove flew from my breast into the heart of our Lord, and how it settled there. I was instantly overwhelmed by an outburst of love and joy, which was so strong that I almost lost my mind. Yet the outburst seemed to last only for a short time, whereas the peace felt within, which I had already experienced before, did not only continue, but became even more intense during this outburst.

Just as the words of God always achieve what they say, the pictorial visions likewise evoke what they display, thus the inalienable impact of *all* these visions is to intensify and amplify peace and love."

Text 17 (Christine Lucie, diary entry dated 12 March 1883. 107): "I was granted to worship Jesus in the tabernacle, and again I beheld almost instantly the white garment of light surrounding His venerable figure.

And my Lord spread out His white robe to me, wrapped me entirely up in it, and allowed me to feel His love and shelter. I saw that I was enveloped by a rare luminescence – I had seen nothing here on earth that could compare with this white and glaring radiance ..." [English translations provided.]

Christine Lucie had the capacity to perceive visions in several different ways. In the first series of examples quoted from her diary above, it is primarily visions that appear in the symbolic-metaphorical mode. We have chosen these textual examples for two reasons: The first is to illustrate that in these 'pictorial visions' mainly non-mystical phenomena become apparent – as such they provide a link to the visions of Hildegard of Bingen dealt with earlier; and second, that these textual examples are valuable sources for our preliminary analysis of another type of 'pictorial vision': the 'vision of Christ'. In texts 15 and 16 the Redeemer becomes manifest in terms of a symbolic representation. These descriptions can be seen as antecedents to the vision of Christ recorded several years later, which is quoted in text 18 below; in the latter, the symbolic vision of Christ is intertwined with the inner hearing of express locutions, which supply the visionary with an explication of the pictorial vision. Text 18 has also been chosen because it provides some persuasive arguments as to why the type of the 'symbolic-metaphoric vision' cannot be dismissed as an elementary mode of visual perception. Though in text 18 the symbolic-pictorial description of God is foregrounded, the vision as a whole is sustained by several non-visual perceptions, notably the impact of an opaque [as yet unidentified, mystical] force, which is explicitly experienced as an 'object' that has 'arrived' in the visionary's consciousness in some mysterious way [from beyond the confines of the 'individual self']. This demonstrates that a genuine mystical vision is not merely confined to visionary and/or auditory perceptions but usually has a considerably more complex structure which encompasses several other modes of 'inner perception', such as (in this case) emotional and somatic effects and/or after-effects. For this reason, it is imperative that any in-depth analysis of a mystical event must be careful not to bypass a single phenomenon within the entire phenomenological constellation of a given mystical event.

> *Text 18* (Christine Lucie, diary entry dated 16 November 1897. 312f.):
> "My soul was completely absorbed in God. Suddenly, the soul saw itself appear inside Him, like a speck of dust at the bottom of a goblet. The goblet, however, was made of a single piece of opal stone, which was perfectly pure. The brim of the goblet began to rise, when God said to me: 'I am placed between you and all things created.' And the brim of the goblet continued to rise and eventually turned into an orb, which finally enclosed my soul completely. And God said: 'I am placed between all things and yourself.' Nothing can express the inebriation and exuberant joy that was elicited by these words. God and his word are one. My soul listened to God and drank God. I appeal to the one who has vouchsafed to be drink and

nourishment to us, to pardon the boldness of my words. But there are truly no words at all that can express such things.

But my soul has indeed felt it: The mysterious orb which enclosed the soul was at the same time the sword of separation, and the detachment from all things. Then the soul surrendered ..."

It is not possible to trace here all the individual phenomenological characteristics addressed in these records of visionary experience. For our purpose it is enough to point out that we have by now entered the borderline area between the 'mystical pictorial vision' and the perception of 'mystical effects'. The main issue, however, that we wish to pursue from here, and which is of paramount importance, is to explore the phenomenological differences between the 'pictorial vision' and non-visual varieties of 'inner sight'. The phenomenological bond by which the metaphoric-symbolic vision and the 'awareness of effects' [imposed on the recipient by a power transcending the individual self] is the sense of effects being mystically instilled or inculcated ["mystische Gewirktheit"]. In other words, the perception of 'mystical impacts' is one of the two fundamental empirical phenomena which must be given, and on which any phenomenology of mystical experience must be based: The perception of a mystical impact 'arriving' in the recipient's consciousness, notably the mental condition termed 'quiet state of alertness'.

The Vision of Christ

We will now explore another type of pictorial vision: the 'vision of Christ'. In doing so, we will enter – not without deference and hesitation – a realm that is overtly religious. The (inner) picture-based vision of Christ is a phenomenon that is part of a special order of sacred values, and therefore calls for a cautious and deferential approach. This does not mean, however, that by adopting such an approach the clarity and focus of our enquiry will be impaired in any way. But we need to make two clarifying statements to begin with: 1. There is no reason to assume beforehand that by examining inner visions of Christ, we will be provided with the core of the 'mystical vision'; 2. approaching the 'vision of Christ' in a deferential and circumspect manner must not deter us from exploring its multi-layered phenomenological structure and the potential causes for this particular visionary event. Fortunately, we have already been familiarized with some of the essential features of the 'vision of Christ' by the foregoing examples and textual analyses, notably when we analysed the 'vision of angels' and its juxtaposition to the 'vision of the devil'. In this context, we have drawn special attention to the phenomenon of light, and especially the 'vision of light'; light appeared as a visual corollary in the vision of angels, but paradoxically also, with a protective function, in the 'vision of the fiend'. These phenomenological features suggested that something was looming on the horizon ahead of our enquiry. As we shall see, the phenomenon of the 'mystical Light' will become more central in our subsequent considerations, notably when we shall encounter the light adhering to and emanating from the image of Christ in an 'inner vision'. There is, moreover, the phenomenon termed 'sense of presence', which has come more and more into view. We shall be able to recognize later that there is a difference between the 'sense of presence' adhering to a pictorial vision of non-mystical Objects and the experiential awareness of the mystical presence of the 'All-encompassing', which is always an integral part of a genuine 'vision of Christ', though it is phenomenologically perceived individually, i.e., as a distinct phenomenon of its own. The manifestation of the mystical presence of the 'All-encompassing' is a most significant existential occurrence, albeit one not easily accessible to cognitive understanding. When dealing with 'pictorial visions' we are situated in the twilight zone between the metaphoric-symbolic vision and the 'mystical vision' with theophanic import, viz., 'mystical theophany'. We find ourselves in a similar twilight zone when dealing with 'visions of Christ'. It is possible, after all, for a vision of Christ to surface from fantasy or the imagination, in which case a purely iconic picture of Christ is evoked in the perceiver's mind; for instance, when a perceiver recalls the image of Christ 'the Pantocrator', holding the scales in His hands, from memory or from the imagination, the 'inner sight' is based on known portrayals of the 'Pantocrator' in famous paintings and frescoes, and is thus a purely intra-mental perception. It differs significantly from a 'mystical vision of Christ the Pantocrator' because the latter is inevitably intertwined with the awareness of its 'givenness' as well as with the perception of the visionary light adhering to Christ, and with the unwavering 'sense of presence'. The following accounts of 'visions of Christ' have been selected from the extensive textual corpus handed down from mystical tradition. In our process of selection, we have excluded accounts of merely iconic visionary representations of Christ in favour of records that can be classified as 'theophanic visions'. From amongst the passages quoted, only text 19 seems to be closer to an iconographic representation of Christ than to a 'theophanic vision':

Text 19 (Christine Lucie, diary entry dated 6 November 1881. 42f.): "While absorbed in spiritual prayer in front of the holy tabernacle, I saw with my inner eyes the outlines of the venerable countenance of our Lord Jesus Christ appearing. Though I did not notice specific features of His face, I beheld His face as a whole; it was so beautiful, so soft, so adorable, so entirely beyond human imagination. My soul was transported beyond itself by this wonderful sight; the glance [of Christ] pierced my soul to its innermost core.

[Visions like this] ... continued to occur for the next three days; that is, any time when my soul visited the tabernacle, it was gratified with this inner vision ... It so happened that I had to go to Paris during these three days. When I was approaching the city and prayed to my Lord, who was present there in all the churches, I saw how His beloved head was lifted high above the big city, which was smothered by the vapours of sin. I saw how the countenance of Jesus averted the blows of divine justice. I also beheld how the face of the Redeemer rose up over all parts of the globe and realized that His adorable head is the protective shield of all the world.

During these three days of heavenly joy, my soul felt to be too excessively happy for this world ..."

Text 20 (Christine Lucie, diary entry dated 19 September 1882. 77): "I saw that our Lord put a precious bar of gold into my soul, and wondered what that might signify, when Jesus responded: 'It means the peace of the cross, peace with everything.' These images appear in the soul quite suddenly; when it happens, the mind is inactive and all the powers of the soul are suspended. And this is what distinguishes these visions from images arising from memory or the imagination. And the word, or the light without words that accompanies these visions, does not arise from any mental effort either."

Text 21 (Christine Lucie, diary entry dated 13 November 1886. 210): "Yesterday, during the Holy Communion, my Lord appeared to me clad in a purple cloak. All over the cloak lilies were spread in abundance. The hemlines of the mantle extended a bit beyond the earth. They were decked with flowers and gems, as if they had been spread across the seams, and I did not know what that should signify. Then Jesus said to me: 'These are your achievements. You are the person who has attired me with this robe.' ..."

Amongst the large number of iconographic visions of Christ recorded by both Lucie and Teresa of Avila, only the few quoted above qualify as instances of iconographic visions, which are devoid of visionary perceptions of light and of the 'sense of presence'.

By presenting these descriptions of purely iconographic visions of Christ we wanted to illustrate that the 'mystical vision of Christ' is inherently symbolic and metaphoric. *The image beheld* [during the visionary event] *has neither any gnoseological nor ontological relevance*. This means *that nothing can be cognitively grasped by the image beheld in 'inner sight'*. The 'picture' or figure beheld in the vision is not understood by the perceiver as something or someone 'being really there'. The perceiver rather understands the image beheld within as an iconographic representation of something/someone that is absent. This means that the pictorial mode operating in a *mystical* vision qualifies as a variety of mystical experience only because it fulfils the following three criteria: 1. The state of consciousness by which the capacity of 'inner sight' is elicited, and the image appearing in the vista of 'inner sight' are perceived as 'mystically infused'; i.e., the perceiver 'is aware' that the visual object(s) that have 'arrived' in 'inner sight' have been 'effected', 'sent', 'inculcated', 'given' or 'implanted' by the 'All-encompassing'. 2. The content of the pictorial vision is related to an object located in the 'mystical sphere' – albeit only metaphorically or symbolically. 3. The phenomenon of 'inner hearing of mystical locutions' [which is usually intertwined with a pictorial visionary experience] is another token of the mystical 'givenness' of the entire visionary experience.

THESIS 29: *In a purely iconographic vision of Christ we are faced with a mystically infused symbolic or metaphoric image of Christ, but not with a theophanic self-revelation.*

THESIS 30: *The 'inner sight' of a metaphoric-symbolic picture is as such no cognitive mode of perceiving the 'All-encompassing'.*

THESIS 31: *A pictorial/iconographic vision is not an element of mystical recognition.* For this reason, iconographic mystical visions must be excluded from the realm of cognitive mystical experience, and thus also from the domain in which a 'mystical relation' can be encountered.

The Vision of Light
["Die Lichtschau"]

A 'pictorial vision' as such does not offer immediate access to the realm of 'mystical Objects'. This is not an arbitrary assertion but a categorical claim that can be proved to be valid without exception and irrespective of the type of pictorial vision. That is to say, in a 'pictorial vision' there is only an indirect relation between the perceiver and the 'mystical Object'. The act of beholding of a 'pictorial vision' qualifies as a mystical mode of 'inner sight' only if it is intertwined with the clear cognitive awareness that the visionary event has been mystically 'instilled'. Owing to these inalienable insights, we must concede that our enquiry has not yet reached the pivotal phenomenological domain of 'mystical recognition'. The express goal of our enquiry is to elucidate the phenomenon of the 'mystical relation', in which the perceiver is vouchsafed to grasp the presence of 'mystical Objects' in an act of 'mystical recognition'. This goal can only be achieved if we succeed in finding direct modes of cognitive mystical perception, i.e., varieties of 'inner sight' in which a direct relation to the 'mystical Object' becomes manifest.

We have so far been alerted to two phenomenological areas in which such a direct relation to the 'mystical Object' *might* be involved. One of which is the visionary experience of light. I have been wavering for some time as to whether the phenomenology of the 'vision of light' should be explored first, or if we should better have started with the phenomenological area of the 'cognitive awareness of presence', the second area in which a direct relation to the 'mystical Object' can be discerned. I have decided in favour of the former: First, because the 'vision of light' is another variety of an inner visionary experience, and thus linked to what has just been expounded, and second, because it became clear that the 'vision of light' contains several features which provide the foundation for a phenomenology of the 'cognitive perception of presence'.

The 'vision of light' is a multifaceted phenomenon. As stated earlier, there are different varieties of 'light' that may become apparent in a visionary event in 'inner sight': The light that adheres to an 'object' perceived within; this light is beheld simultaneously with an image, shape or figure appearing in 'inner sight'; it is a radiance or luminescence emanating from the 'object' beheld. It would have been impossible in our phenomenological analysis to isolate the image beheld within from the 'mystical Light' adhering to it, if we had not established previously that the 'mystical Light' may become manifest individually in 'inner sight' featuring as the only object of visual and cognitive perception.

In empirical reality both the 'pictorial vision' and the 'vision of Light' are often closely intertwined phenomenologically. In order to be able to establish some of the distinctive features of each, we will resort to insights gained from our analysis of the 'pictorial vision'. If we want to determine the difference between a 'vision of an iconographic image' and a 'theophanic vision' which is intertwined with phenomena of luminescence, we have to ask, first, if the light encountered in a 'vision of light' is only a metaphoric or symbolic appearance, or if it is a 'vision of Light', and as such a self-revealing [theophanic] manifestation of the 'All-encompassing'. Over and beyond this, we need to ask if the Light described by the mystics is merely a metaphor for what is experienced and cognitively perceived as 'present', or if the 'Light' is the 'mystical Object' itself. In the following we will try to unravel these complex issues as far as possible by the critical close-reading of representative personal testimonies of Teresa of Avila and Christine Lucie.

Light Adhering to an Object Beheld in 'Inner Sight'

It is helpful to begin with the analysis of mystical visions in which light is described as adhering to or emanating from a figure, image or object appearing in 'inner sight', as this phenomenon has already been addressed in passing above.

> Text 22 (Teresa of Avila, *Vida*, main chapter 28, 261; 263): "1. ... One day, when I was absorbed in prayer, the Lord granted to show me His hands on their own, which were so radiant and so wonderful that I am at a loss for words. This vision aroused great fear in me, because every new supernat-

ural grace that is bestowed in me by the Lord evokes at first such fearful feelings in me. A few days afterwards, I also saw His divine face; at the sight of it I was so filled with awe and wonder that I felt I was totally out of my mind. I could not understand at that time why the Lord was revealing Himself to me only bit by bit; it was only later that He granted me the grace to see His full shape …

2. Your grace[29] may perhaps think that beholding lovely hands and a wonderful face does not require much courage. But *His glorified body is so preternaturally beautiful, and radiant with such glory,* that one is transported into raptures of bliss at the sight of it. Therefore, I was so deeply filled with fear that I became extremely upset and distraught; but only a short time after this, I felt great reassurance and confidence, and such vigour was instilled in me that all my fears disappeared…"

"4. … even if I had endeavoured for many years to imagine something similarly beautiful, I could never have succeeded. The very *luminous radiance and brightness of this vision transcends anything* that could ever be imagined on earth. It is a splendour and a luminescence that is not dazzling or blinding, but it is of a lovely whiteness, *a radiance that has been infused,* and which is in no way painful to the perceiver but imparts utmost rapture and bliss …" [Italics as added by Albrecht for emphasis. – English translation provided.]

We shall come back to this record of Teresa's shortly, as I would like to insert here a concise explanatory comment to alert the critical reader to some special characteristics in this vision. In the second part of the quotation, Teresa shifts from the description of the 'light adhering' to Christ to the depiction of different qualities adhering to the light in her 'vision of Christ'. She addresses two phenomena that are explicitly affiliated with the vision of light: the 'vision of beauty' and the cognitive perception of Christ as *'majestas'*:[30]

Text 23 (Christine Lucie, diary entry dated 22 August 1881. 37f.): "… Then I suddenly saw with my inner eyes the garment of my divine Master. I rec-

---

29 [Note: By "Your grace" Teresa addresses one of her spiritual counsellors, of which she had eight (cf. the Institute of Carmelite Studies <https://www.icspublications.org>). – FKW.]

30 [Note: Albrecht elaborates on the notion of the *'majestas'* as the supreme numinous quality of an encounter with the presence of a 'mystical Object' perceived as a Persona, later in the book. – FKW.]

ognized its outlines and could clearly discern some of its drapes. (I am using this term as I don't know a better one.) *The garment was white and shining brightly. It was not just radiant, but it was light itself. Its material was neither of the stuff of a cloud, nor of a fabric, nor was it made of flames;* it was something entirely different. I have never seen anything like this before, and I looked at it closely, but I was unable to determine what the material was. *Its radiance was different than that of daylight, and different from the brightness of the stars* by night, and different from the shine of any other light we know. The splendour filled my eyes with its rays without making them weary. My soul was as if immersed in a *heavenly sea of light* and filled with an unfathomable sense of peace, majesty and innocence ..."

Text 24 (Christine Lucie, diary entry dated 22 March 1893. 292): "... His eyes and His holy countenance seem to be permeated by a warm light. The garment, a long white tunic, encloses His feet. It does not look like a tissue, but rather *like glowing, radiant snow*. This seems paradoxical, but it is indeed like this."

Text 25 (Christine Lucie, diary entry dated 9 March 1882. 53f.): "When I returned to my pew after receiving Holy Communion, the adorable figure of the Lord appeared to me suddenly with great majestic dignity, when I was kneeling on my pew. I completely lost all consciousness of myself as well as any awareness of what surrounded me. I saw His holy figure garbed in that *garment of light* which I had briefly seen in a previous vision. With a gesture that seemed quite superhuman, He lifted the garment slightly with His left hand. *The glance of the Lord was radiant with a splendour that surpassed anything in nature. I would have been overwhelmed with fear by His overpowering majesty,* if my gracious Master had not taken my soul close to Him, transporting me into an extasy of love ineffable.

All around the Lord there was a luminescent clarity, which was not like the light of day, or like the light of the stars at night. I had not known this clarity before; I first got a glimpse of it when I was granted to see some of the drapes of the divine garment. Whenever the Lord grants me to see His divine shape, or just His garment, I can see that luminous clarity again. Whenever my soul is vouchsafed a glimpse of this garment, all restlessness, caused by the devil, disappears instantly, and my soul is filled with profound peace ... What I have reported here lasted altogether scarcely as long as the flash of lightning ...". [Italics as added by Albrecht for emphasis, referring to the issues addressed in the given chapter. – English translations provided.]

Are the 'infused visions of Christ' recorded by Christine Lucie and Teresa not strikingly similar? Is it not remarkable that in the visionary experiences of both mystics the new phenomenon – the visual and cognitive perception of the *'majestas'* – should be explicitly addressed and identified as a distinctive experiential characteristic? Moreover, the unique quality of the light perceived in the 'vision of light' is unanimously acknowledged by both. *The light adhering to the image of Christ when perceived in 'inner sight' is a radiant and illuminating light*: The figure of Christ – and, respectively, the figures of angels and of Holy Mary referred to earlier – is radiant with this light. Light emanates not only from the entire body of Christ, but also from specific parts of it, his face and hands, as well as from his garment. To the visionaries the quality of this luminescence is experienced as something preternatural or 'other-worldly'; it is a light that eludes adequate description, though both Teresa and Christine Lucie resort to comparisons with natural sense perception. Both insist, however, that the light perceived in 'inner sight' is beyond anything known in this world and beyond anything accessible to human imagination. *The light is distinctly qualified as supernatural in essence.* The visionary experience of this paranormal light cannot be 'produced' by the perceiver. It is expressly experienced as a light 'arriving' in the vista of 'inner sight', along with the 'pictorial vision of Christ'. Thus, both phenomena are experienced as 'objects' 'infused' into the perceiver's mind. Because of these distinctive features of the 'vision of light', it represents a different type of 'vision' than that of the 'pictorial vision'. On the other hand, the vision of the non-physical light adhering to the pictorial vision of Christ also differs clearly from what mystics have termed 'intellectual vision' [*visio intellectualis*] [i.e., a non-visual experience, in which some illumination or intellectual insight is 'imparted']. Our critical enquiry is thus faced with the pivotal question of how this paranormal visionary light can be accounted for. What then is the light that is claimed to be 'supernatural' but also an 'object' of visual inner perception? It seems that we are faced here with a unique phenomenon – one that has at all times had great importance in theology (and perhaps still has). At this stage we can only state the fact that it is a rare preternatural, ultimately ineffable and incomprehensible light, the experience of which has crucial existential relevance for any perceiver.

Light as Such

The 'pure' variety of the 'vision of light' is the one in which light is the only 'object' of inner visual perception, i.e., when 'light' is not an integral part of a pictorial or other visionary experience. The experience of the light becoming manifest as the sole 'object' of 'inner sight', though ultimately ineffable and unintelligible, is still best rendered by the term 'light'. It is a sensation of a 'formless something', though some of the distinctive characteristics can phenomenologically be identified: It is an omnipresent, all-permeating and all-encompassing medium, and as such it is a 'mystical Object'. The 'vision of light' thus belong to the domain of 'mystical visions'. And we even might be inclined to speculate if the 'vision of light' is in fact not a 'vision of Light', and thus the core of mystical experience. However, if we pursue the path of science, the attempt to answer this question is fraught with difficulties, not least because the 'vision of the mystical Light' is – judging from the records of the mystics and visionaries – an encounter with an intangible, immaterial luminous essence, which in empirical reality is, moreover, often commingled with other modes of visionary and non-visual perception.

The word 'light' is itself an elusive and ambiguous term open to misconceptions and misunderstandings. Its ambivalent meaning is due to its metaphysical connotations and symbolic import in cultural, religious and philosophical history. As a consequence, the word 'light' has acquired diverse semantic meanings. Five of the major ones are the following: 1. 'light', signifying a burning flame, is associated with fire, embers, radiating warmth; 2. 'light' as a medium of visual sense perception is associated with clarity and lucid brightness; 3. 'light' is connoted with beams and rays, and may thus be associated with the sun, or lightning; 4. 'light' referring to 'limelight', or as the source of illumination pointing out the way; 5. 'light' as the source of life, the eternal fountain of growth and rejuvenation. These five major semantic fields encompassed by the word 'light' supply various options for their metaphoric use. Mystics have made ample use of the word's polysemic options. In their records we encounter, for example, such metaphoric expressions as 'the light of the heart', 'the light of love', which are used as metaphors of emotion, whereas phrases like 'the light of reason', or 'the light of truth' are employed to emphasize the special clarity and sincerity of thinking. Expressions like the 'dazzling ray of light' is an apt image for an event by which the mystic is suddenly 'struck' with awe, or petrified by the moment of illumination, or lost for words when 'struck' with the ineffable and overwhelming encounter with God. When describing the spiritual path, mystics often resort to 'light' as a metaphor of spiritual guidance, and thus 'light' is linked to both reason and volition. This illustrates that the semantic sphere of the word 'light' is so wide-ranging that it can be employed as a metaphor to every single phenomenon of consciousness, including (what has been termed) 'ultimate phenomena of consciousness'. Thus one of the distinctive features of the 'quiet state of alertness', its unique serene and hyper-lucid condition, is often described in metaphors of light. And metaphors of light are also used in descriptions of ecstatic mystical experience: When a mystic is transported into states of ecstasy becoming inundated by the ineffable 'light of Bliss' or overwhelmed by the all-consuming 'fire of Love'[31].

In addition to these semantic uses of the word 'light' by mystics, I would like to add another instance to demonstrate why the metaphysics of light could develop so rampantly and persevere in the first place.

Light is a physical concept which comprises a physiological area, which is again linked with an experiential sphere. The physical light has some qualities which have not yet been addressed: Light expands in all directions, a quality that may suggest the notion of omnipresence. Light, furthermore, may penetrate certain objects, thus suggesting transparency and translucence; light can be reflected and absorbed, thus causing reflections in a mirror, or the phenomenon of colours; the fact that Light can split up into prismatic colours suggests the notion of unity (light) enclosing multiplicity. Physical light may furthermore evoke the notion of an all-encompassing oneness, hence suggesting omnipresence and the notion of the 'ultimate origin' emanating into a process of creation that

---

31   [Note: This metaphor is used, for instance, in the autobiographical Latin treatise of the medieval English mystic Richard Rolle of Hampole (c.1300–1349), entitled *Incendium Amoris*. The work was translated into the vernacular in the late 15th c. by Richard Mysin and became known as *Fire of Love* (1434–1435); it circulated widely in England and on the European continent from the 15th to the 17th centuries; meanwhile, several critical editions have appeared in the 20th and 21st centuries. – FKW.]

is subject to time and space. Thus, any theory of emanation cannot do without resorting to the imagery of light.

There are probably more metaphoric uses of the word 'light'. The diverse applications of the word outlined above have sufficiently demonstrated that 'light' is, on the one hand, the primary metaphor in descriptions and manifestations of mystical and religious experience, but that it is, on the other hand, also an ambivalent multi-semiotic term that has caused misunderstanding and 'obfuscation' of experiential phenomena. This semantic ambivalence becomes apparent in the diversity of connotations evoked by the word 'light' in different experiential contexts: 'light' referring to a shimmering, warming flame; 'light' as a metaphor for clarity and brightness; the 'light' pointing the way, and 'light' conceived as the primeval and perennial source of life. There is, in other words, a time-honoured 'myth of light', which has inspired countless and ineradicable speculative theorems. For this reason, we wondered if we should not better avoid using the ambiguous word 'light' in our enquiry and substitute the conventional umbrella term referring to the elusive phenomenon becoming manifest in 'mystical visions' by a more appropriate term. We had to realize, however, that there is indeed no term that is more adequate to denote the experience of the 'mystical Light'. Over and beyond this, the word 'light' has for many centuries been used as a key metaphor for describing the sensation of light in mystical visions, and thus has become a firmly established concept which cannot arbitrarily be substituted. This is why we have finally adopted the term 'vision of light', but it is important to add that its use is strictly confined here to the 'light' beheld in 'inner sight'; the term thus does not refer to any physical light, nor does it refer to any other phenomenon encountered outside the domain of the 'inner mystical vision', which is conventionally depicted by metaphors of light.

The previous considerations have provided us with important criteria by which we may assess critically the nature of the 'vision of light' without plunging into the pitfalls spread out by received notions of the myth of light. We have so far established that in the realm of mystical experience the word 'light' is always just a symbolic-metaphoric mode of expression, and thus never signifies any real physical light. But the question arising from this is whether the 'light' beheld by the mystic is always the same, i.e., a recurring phenomenon, or if the 'content' of a visionary experience consists of different kinds of 'light', i.e., diverse manifestations of 'light' that are essentially different though addressed by the same word. Furthermore, we need to ask if we can indeed discern aspects of the very essence of the 'light' beheld in mystical visions, after we have removed peripheral phenomena of visionary experiences described by the word 'light', and after having focused our enquiry exclusively on the central phenomenon of the 'vision of light'. For it would seem reasonable to assume that the essence of 'light' is in some way linked to a perception that is most adequately expressed by the term 'light'. From a methodological point of view, it is for this reason advisable to approach the pivotal phenomenon of the 'vision of light' immediately, without any detour, and to explore the peripheral phenomena of light hereafter, approaching them (as it were) inside out, proceeding towards the periphery by starting from the core phenomenon. We shall begin with the 'vision of light' that may be encountered in the context of the cosmic consciousness.

To start with, I would like to ask the reader to turn again to text 1 – the passage from the autobiography of Yogananda Paramahansa, in which he describes the event of his experience of *samadhi*. The Hindu mystic insists on having been overwhelmed by the inner vision of an 'all-encompassing dazzling light', which he insists is a typical feature when immersed in a state of cosmic consciousness. This visionary experience is also intertwined with a 'clairvoyant vision' ["Durchschauung"], i.e., the capacity of 'seeing through' things:

> Text 26 (From the *Autobiography* of Param[a]hansa Yogananda). "Closing my eyes, I saw flashes of lightning; the vast space within me was a chamber of molten light. I opened my eyes and observed the same dazzling radiance. The room became a part of the infinite vault that I was beholding with interior vision.
>
> The yogi said, 'Why don't you go to sleep?'
>
> 'Sir, how can I sleep when lightning is blazing around me, whether my eyes are shut or open?'
>
> 'You are blessed to be having this experience. The spiritual radiations are not easily seen.' ..."[32]

---

32 [Note: Albrecht's quotation is from the German translation *Autobiographie eines Yogi*. Munich: Barth, 1950. 153. – The passage quoted here has been taken from the

The Indian yogi describes here an inner vision of light, which is interpreted by him in terms of a physical and meta-physiological sensation of light. This interpretation has obviously influenced his choice of words. Later in his life, Yogananda's reflections on experiences of this kind resulted in a complex physical hypothesis[33] claiming that "the essence of the cosmos is light". In his view, light is a visual phenomenon closely related to the physical notion of light consisting of waves.

I have chosen another passage in which an experience of cosmic consciousness is described albeit recorded by the western visionary R. M. Bucke, who first coined the term 'cosmic consciousness'.[34] The passage has some similarities with the visions described by the Hindu yogi; it has been chosen to show that the 'cosmic vision of light' is not bound to any specific cultural context. In Bucke's account we likewise encounter the intertwining between the 'vision of light' and the 'clairvoyant vision' of the universe, eliciting an ecstatic response culminating in an upsurge of a deep sense of bliss and joy. Furthermore, we can discern a peculiar conflation between the visionary experience of light with external (physical) sense perception of the surroundings. In fact, it is not clear from this description whether the light is perceived inwardly as an 'object' of 'inner sight', and which has afterwards been 'projected' unto external space, or if the light is to be assessed as an occult, meta-physiological phenomenon, which was seen with the physical eyes and perceived as permeating external space:

> Text 27 (From R. M. Bucke's self-testimony "First Words", 9–10)[35] "... All at once, without warning of any kind, he found himself wrapped around

---

e-book PARAMAHANSA, Yogananda. *Autobiography of a Yogi*. 1946. 13th ed. Preface by W. Y. Evans-Wentz. Los Angeles, CA: Self-Realization Fellowship, 1998. 158. – FKW.]
33 PARAMAHANSA, Yogananda. *Autobiographie eines Yogi*. Munich: Barth, 1950. 279–84.
34 [BUCKE, R. M. *Cosmic Consciousness. A Study of the Evolution of the Human Mind*. New York: Dutton, 1901. – FKW.]
35 [Note: Albrecht quotes from the German translation of Bucke's study. The English quotation has been taken from the original work: BUCKE, R. M. *Cosmic Consciousness. A Study of the Evolution of the Human Mind*. New York: Dutton, 1901. "First Words", 9–10. – FKW.]

as it were by a *flame-colored cloud*. For an instant *he thought of fire, some sudden conflagration* in the great city; the next, *he knew that the light was within himself*. Directly afterwards came upon him a sense of exultation of immense joyousness, accompanied or immediately followed by an intellectual illumination quite impossible to describe. Into his brain streamed one momentary lightning-flash of the Brahmic Splendor which has ever since lightened his life; upon his heart fell one drop of Brahmic Bliss, leaving thenceforward for always an aftertaste of heaven. Among other things he did not come to believe, he saw and knew that the Cosmos is not dead matter but a living Presence, that the soul of man is immortal, that the universe is so built and ordered that without any peradventure all things work together for the good of each and all, that the foundation principle of the world is what we call love and that the happiness of every one is in the long run absolutely certain. He claims that he learned more within the few seconds during which the illumination lasted than in previous months or even years of study, … The illumination itself continued not more than a few moments …" [Italics as provided by Albrecht.]

Bucke's 'vision of light' is, like that of Yogananda, interlaced with a 'clairvoyant vision'; the latter, however, is inevitably closely linked with sense perception. For our enquiry, the intertwining of the two phenomena poses a problem for understanding the nature of the 'light' encountered in this event. The crucial question is: Is the 'light' that is seen while the 'clairvoyant vision' is perceived a physical, viz., occult meta-physiological light, or can it be understood to be identical with the 'mystical Light' of the Hesychasts and other mystics, who claim to have beheld a 'spiritual light within', which only the Hindu mystic has interpreted in physical terms? If the 'light' is indeed a 'light' perceived inwardly, does the physical manifestation of the 'light' originate from the essence of the light beheld, or is it rather a flawed reading of the given phenomenon of light? I must concede that I am not able to answer these questions definitely on the basis of the texts examined, as both texts are not only ambivalent, but also inherently contradictory. We cannot provide a final assessment as to whether the 'vision of light' in the event of a cosmic consciousness experience is perceived in an inverted 'inward mystical vision', which has been projected into the world outside, or if the 'vision of light' originates from an unknown variety of occult experience, or if it could even be assessed as a vision akin, if not identical to, the vision of a 'ghost seer' when perceiving the 'aura' of an object or figure. None of the latter varieties of visionary light-experiences qualify as instances of genuine mystical recognition. We have thus failed in our attempt to elucidate the nature of the 'cosmic vision of light', and this is why dealing with it is pointless and will not provide any further insights into the nature of 'mystical vision'.

Advancing our enquiry, we shall now turn to records depicting the *'vision of Light' provided by the Hesychasts*. These testimonies promise to be more valuable and conclusive in our endeavour to advance to the core of the phenomenon.

Anyone who wishes to comprehend the mystical 'vision of Light' as recorded by the Byzantine mystic *Symeon the New Theologian* (c. 949–1022) does not necessarily have to be familiar with any details of the historical development, doctrines and practice of spiritual prayer of the Greek-Orthodox Church[36]; what one ought to know, however, is that the Hesychasts' way of living and thinking is seminally determined by the following three notions inherited from cultural and religious tradition: 1. the concept of Gnosis; 2. a special form of spiritual prayer; and 3. the focus on the visionary experience of Light.

Gnosis, understood here in the Christian sense, refers to the direct, non-visual (imageless) 'vision of God'. Initially, the concept of Gnosis coincided with the Neoplatonic notion of the *'nous'* [νοῦς] or *'noos'* [νόος] [i.e., divine reason, mind, intellect; regarded as first divine emanation in Neoplatonism]; it refers to the direct, imageless experiential knowledge of God. Later the concept of Gnosis was expanded to include not merely the purely intellectual knowledge of the divine, but also perceptions of God in which He revealed Himself

---

36 [Note: Albrecht himself was well read in the history and the teachings of the Greek-Orthodox Church, and the methods of spiritual prayer practised by the Hesychasts. He refers to the major sources consulted in a footnote: AMMANN, A. M. *Die Gottesschau im Palamitischen Hesychasmus: Ein Handbuch der Spätbyzantinischen Mystik*. 2nd ed. Würzburg: Augustinus, 1948. ARSENIEW, Nikolaus von. *Ostkirche und Mystik*. Munich: Reinhardt, 1943. HEILER, Friedrich. *Urkirche und Ostkirche*. Munich: Reinhardt, 1937. PABEL, Reinhold. *Athos, der Heilige Berg. Begegnung mit dem Christlichen Osten*. Münster: Regensburgsche Verlagsbuchhandlung, 1940. VILLER, Marcel, and Karl RAHNER. *Aszese und Mystik in der Väterzeit. Ein Abriss der Frühchristlichen Spiritualität*. Freiburg i. Br.: Herder, 1939. – FKW.]

in a visual manner, notably as 'Light Eternal'. Hence the knowledge of God became equal to the 'vision of Light'.

The Hesychasts practised a special method of spiritual prayer, which is based on the continuous (silent) reiteration of the formula 'Lord Jesus Christ, Son of God, have mercy on me, a sinner', commonly known as the 'Jesus prayer'.[37] The 'Jesus prayer' is usually said inwardly, and repeated incessantly not only for hours throughout the day, but day after day and throughout the believer's life. While repeating the prayer, the practitioner is also required to control his breath, breathing rhythmically, in conformity with the rhythm of the heart. For this reason, the prayer has also been termed 'prayer of the heart'. By the successful practice of the 'Jesus prayer' the state of consciousness is transformed, advancing the contemplative from the normal 'waking consciousness' to the serene state of inner peace and inward alertness. *Hesychia* [ἡσυχία] means 'silence, stillness, peace', and is the mental condition required for a contemplative to become perfectly receptive and responsive to the grace of God's Presence. The 'prayer of the heart' thus changes the condition of heart and mind, cleansing the contemplative's 'inner eye' to become perfectly receptive to the Gnostic vision of 'uncreated Light', which is God.

In the 14th century, Greek and Roman theologians expounded conflicting notions about the nature of the light/Light experienced by the Hesychasts. This resulted in a dispute known as the 'Hesychast controversy' – a theological debate between the supporters of Gregorius Palamas (1296–1359), a monk of Mount Athos and later archbishop of Thessaloniki, and the followers of the Roman (Calabrian) theologian Barlaam of Samara [Bernardo Massari] (c. 1290–1348), a priest and Thomist scholar who had moved to Constantinople. A concise summary of this controversy is provided in the study of Friedrich Heiler: "Gregory Palamas ..., following the Hesychast teaching of Symeon the New Theologian, corroborated it further by promoting the dogmatic theory that the 'Light' revealed is the eternal uncreated Light of God, which became originally manifest on Mount Tabor [at the Transfiguration of Christ], and which becomes accessible to the devout Hesychast when

---

37 Cf. SCHMIDT, Bernhard. *Das Geistige Gebet. Eine Untersuchung zur Geschichte der Griechischen Mystik*. Halle an der Saale: Karras, 1916.

absorbed in a perfect state of inner calm (*hesychia*), in a gratuitous mystical visionary experience. Palamas insists that a Hesychast, when gratified with the vision of Light, is lifted into the realm of uncreated being, transfigured and deified ... [The scholastic theologian] Barlaam of Rome refuted this doctrine, accusing Palamas of heresy as he identifies in this doctrine the essence of God with the uncreated Light beheld inwardly by the mystic. Palamas wrote several treatises in defence, in which he stated his theological position more precisely by distinguishing between the incomprehensible essence of God (*ousia*) [οὐσία] and 'uncreated energies' emanating from God; the latter may cross the thresholds of human perception."[38] This modified theory was finally confirmed to comply with orthodox teaching by the Synod of Constantinople in 1484.

> *Text 28* ('A version of the Hesychast method of spiritual prayer ... ascribed to Symeon the New Theologian'):[39] "Sitting in a quiet cell in a secluded corner, try to carry out what I am going to teach you: Lock the door, and withdraw your mind from any idle transitory object. Lower your chin and place it on your chest; direct your eyes with full concentration at the middle of the abdomen, i.e., your navel. Control your breath so that you do not respire in a random manner. Try to search the place within you where the heart is located, in which naturally all powers of the soul are dwelling. In the beginning you will only be faced by a darkness, which is dense and impenetrable; but if you persevere in your efforts by day and by night, you will find – oh what a miracle – endless joy. Because as soon as the spirit has entered and found its place in your heart, the spirit beholds instantly what it has experienced never before; because the spirit sees through the veil of the heart and is aware that it is wholly enveloped in light and perfect clarity."

The notion that the experience of the 'vision of Light' was an integral part of the 'prayer of the heart' of the Hesychasts can be traced throughout the centuries. Evidence from the 19th century is found in the mystical writings of a Russian contemplative known as 'Russian

---

38 HEILER, Friedrich. *Urkirche und Ostkirche*. Munich: Reinhardt, 1937. 405ff. [English translation provided. –FKW.]

39 PABEL, Reinhold. *Athos, der Heilige Berg. Begegnung mit dem Christlichen Osten*. Münster: Regensburgsche Verlagsbuchhandlung, 1940. 101f. [English translation provided. – FKW.]

pilgrim'.[40] In the anthology of spiritual guidance entitled *Philokalia*, the anonymous pilgrim confesses to having practised consistently the Byzantine method of spiritual prayer as taught by the monks of Athos and other Greek monasteries. This anthology was compiled in the late 18th century by Nicodemus of Naxos [also known as St. Nicodemus the Hagiorite (1748–1809)]; it contains selected mystical writings by Greek and Coptic monks, including Antonius (c. 460), Macarius the Great (c. 295–392), Symeon the New Theologian (c. 949–1022) and Gregorius Palamas (1296–1359).[41]

> Text 29 (From *Tales of a Russian Pilgrim*)[42]: "... Then I began to breathe in the Jesus prayer, thus guiding it to my heart, and to recover it again from the heart, as it is taught by St. Gregory of Sinai [c. 1260–1346], Callistus [d. 1363] and St. Ignatius of Antioch [d. c. 110]; that is to say that my spirit entered deep into the heart, took a deep breath and called to mind the first three words of the Jesus prayer: '*Lord Jesus Christ*'. Then, exhaling, I uttered the words '*have mercy on me*' silently in my mind. Initially I performed this spiritual exercise for about one hour, occasionally up to two hours; then I extended the exercise and became more and more skilled in it, until I finally got so proficient in it that I spent almost the whole day practising it."

> Text 30 (From *Tales of a Russian Pilgrim*)[43]: "About five days later, he felt a great heat inside, along with ineffable feelings of bliss and a fervent desire to remain absorbed in this prayer incessantly; the prayer elicited true love for Jesus and the ardent desire to reach perfection in it. From time to time he perceived a glimpse of a shining light within; but no objects could be recognized in this light; occasionally it seemed to him, when he was engrossed in his heart, as if a blazing flame of a candle would flare up in his heart, releasing ineffable bliss in the heart; the flame seemed to be exhaled along with the breath, illuminating and surrounding his body entirely; in the lustre of this flame he could even see distant things and events ..."

---

40   ANONYMOUS. *Erzählungen eines Russischen Pilgers*. Luzern: Stocker, 1944.
41   Cf. HEILER, Friedrich. *Urkirche und Ostkirche*. Munich: Reinhardt, 1937. 408.
42   ANONYMOUS. *Erzählungen eines Russischen Pilgers*. Luzern: Stocker, 1944. 52. [English translation provided. – FKW.]
43   ANONYMOUS. *Erzählungen eines Russischen Pilgers*. Luzern: Stocker, 1944. 128. [English translation provided. – FKW.]

The *Hymns* of Symeon the New Theologian (949–1022) contain undoubtedly numerous accounts of genuine ecstatic 'visions of Light'. However, any critical assessment of these lively descriptions is required to call to mind that these lyrical hymns are based on or informed by theorems grounded in the teaching of the Byzantine Church. This means that the distinctive characteristics of the experience described are in some measure transformed by the theological explication of the event as well as modified by the artistic form of lyrical hymnology. For this reason, it is not easy to find in the received corpus of Symeon's hymns texts that can be classified as authentic accounts of the visionary experience and the light beheld, and which render realistically the phenomenological features witnessed during the given event. There is apparently a big difference between Teresa of Avila's or Christine Lucie's detailed psychological descriptions of mystical visions and Symeon's artistic and theological rendering of the phenomena encountered in his 'visions of Light' in his *Hymns*. I must admit that I have had some reservations about including some of Symeon's texts and wondered if they are conclusive and authentic enough for elucidating visionary experiences of light. However, I finally decided to include passages from the *Hymns*, aware that this decision is open to criticism, but I finally became convinced that Symeon's portrayals of the 'uncreated Divine Light' are unique and impressive representations of the 'vision of Light' which must not be bypassed. Moreover, the authenticity of Symeon's accounts was further corroborated after having read his *Homilies*, in which he provides numerous persuasive personal accounts of his visionary experiences of 'Light'.

> *Text 31* (Symeon the New Theologian, describing the experience of a 'young novice'; [the following account is narrated from the first-person perspective of the novice]):[44] "When I had entered the room in which I used to pray, and was about reciting the Trisagion and recalled the words of the holy sage, I suddenly began to weep and was so powerfully overwhelmed with tears and a burning desire for God that cannot be expressed in words. Nor can I utter the joy and sweet consolation that filled my soul. Prostrate I fell

---

44 Quoted in ARSENIEW, Nikolaus von. *Ostkirche und Mystik*. Munich: Reinhardt, 1943. 149f. [English translation provided. – FKW.]

to the ground, my face touching the ground; I then beheld something wonderful: lo, a great light illuminated my spirit and permeated my mind and soul. I was astonished at this surprising miracle and was so overjoyed that I almost went out of my mind, oblivious of all things around me, unaware of the place where I was, and who I was ... I only kept on crying: 'Lord, have mercy on me!' – which I realized, however, only after I had come to myself again ..." [In homily 92 Symeon describes his personal experience, speaking in his own name:] 'I have been granted grace upon grace, and blessing upon blessing, fire upon fire, and flame upon flame. I have been vouchsafed progress and ascent, and at the end of the ascent – light. And adding to this light, another Light – even more radiant. Amidst that Light the blazing sun flared up, from which a beam irradiated and imbued everything. What this means, goes beyond reason. During that time, I could only shed sweet tears, being dumbfounded at the sight of the Ineffable."

Text 32 (Symeon the New Theologian, *Hymn 27*)[45]: "Again the light is radiant within me. I see the light clearly once again. It opens the gates of heaven once more to me, dispelling night. Again, the light reveals everything to me, discloses everything in the light of day. Again, I can see the light alone. Once again the light is lifting me up above everything visible, and, in doing so, it separates me from all things of sense perception. Again, the one who resides above the heavens and who has ever been seen by a human being, dwells within me. There is no need for Him to unlock heaven's door, nor to wander through the night, or does He pierce the clouds or air, or do damage to the roof of my home when He comes; no, without penetrating anything He dwells in me, the poor one, the light is radiating inside, in the middle of my cell, in the middle of my mind, in the middle of my heart. – Oh, what a venerable mystery! – When the light is within me everything remains as it is and is lifting me up above everything. And I, who am amidst all things, am at that time removed from all things, so much so that I even think to have moved out of my body. And in this state, I am fully immersed in truth, and everything around me is light, nothing but light. When I behold this, I become pure simplicity myself, and perfect without any wrinkles ..."

Text 33 (Symeon the New Theologian, *Hymn 40*)[46]: "... then, in tears, I have longed to see You. I was so distraught and full of grief that I became

---

45   SYMEON the New Theologian. *Licht vom Licht: Hymnen.* Trans. Kilian Kirchoff. Munich: Kösel, 1951. 165. [English translation provided. – FKW.]

46   SYMEON the New Theologian. *Licht vom Licht: Hymnen.* Trans. Kilian Kirchoff. Munich: Kösel, 1951. 263ff. [English translation provided. – FKW.]

oblivious of all things around me, and of all the world, ... then You revealed yourself invisibly within me in an incomprehensible and intangible manner. I beheld You purifying my soul and increasing the visionary powers of my soul; You allowed me to see Your splendour more fully and more clearly by flourishing within me, expanding Your radiant light in me. I was able to see You coming through a distant darkness, coming closer. I felt Your approach as I feel sensual things approaching; You seemed to become greater though you are indeed immutable and immovable. You appeared to increase and to take on some shape, although You are formless. It was like a blind man slowly recovering his eye-sight ... You have revealed Yourself to me and bestowed me with this light through the light of the Holy Spirit and purified my spirit. And because my spirit could now see more clearly and purely, I saw You coming towards me, and saw how You appeared to me in a radiant beam and allowed me to see the outlines of Your shape even though You are formless. Then You led me away, removed from this world, well – and I think I may justly put it this way – transmuted even out of my body. But You have denied me any conscious knowledge of this experience. Your splendour was immeasurable, overwhelming and blissful, when You revealed Yourself to me in this manner ..."

Text 34 (Symeon the New Theologian, from *Hymn 20*)[47]: "Where do You come from? How do You enter my cell, which is locked everywhere? This is a new miracle, which is beyond my capacity to tell, and beyond my ability to comprehend. That You are within me, and suddenly radiant within me, and willing to reveal Yourself to me in the semblance of Light, like the moon when it is fully ablaze, this robs me of my understanding and my power of speech, oh Christ my Lord ..."

Text 35 (Symeon the New Theologian, from *Hymn 17*)[48]: "... He came, when it pleased Him to come. At first shining clouded in mist, which descended slowly, as it seemed, on to my head so that I cried out, overwhelmed by a sense of wonder. At that instance, the fog gradually lifted, and I was left all alone. But when I searched for Him painfully, I suddenly felt Him again dwell inside me. He allowed me to behold Him in the middle of my heart, like a light comparable to the sun ..."

---

47 SYMEON the New Theologian. *Licht vom Licht: Hymnen*. Trans. Kilian Kirchoff. Munich: Kösel, 1951. 118 [English translation provided. – FKW.]

48 SYMEON the New Theologian. *Licht vom Licht: Hymnen*. Trans. Kilian Kirchoff. Munich: Kösel, 1951. 86f. [English translation provided. – FKW.]

To advance our enquiry, we need to subject the various accounts of visionary perceptions of light to our psychological-phenomenological analysis. These are the main results:

1. In these texts we can clearly discern that the 'vision of the light' evokes intense emotional responses. Joy, bliss, rapture are the primary qualities evoked. The visionary is clearly transported into ecstatic states of consciousness, which may, at times, become so intense that the ability of inward perception is suspended. The pivotal features of the prevailing state of consciousness in which the 'vision of light' occurs, however, are clearly those of the *fully integrated 'quiet state of alertness'* [viz., "Versunkenheit"]. As becomes clear from texts 32 and 33, the visions occur (at least initially) in a clear, lucid and calm mental state, which is vacated from all sense-perceptions, acts of the will and notions of the sensual world; calmness is the prevailing emotional condition, and 'inner perception' is highly alert to extramental phenomena 'arriving' in the vista of 'inner sight' ["Innenschau"].[49]

2. *It can be affirmed that Symeon's 'vision of Light' is a genuine variety of 'inner sight'* [viz., "Innenschau" as defined by Albrecht], and surely not an external 'corporal vision' [*visio corporalis*]. There are no indications either that this could be an occult experience of sensual light, or luminous phenomena witnessed by 'ghost seers'. Though it is not possible to distinguish a vision of light perceived in 'cosmic consciousness' unmistakably from an external 'corporal vision', the account of Yogi Yogananda can almost certainly be classified as a visionary experience of light perceived physically in external space, and thus not as a 'vision of light', but rather a corporal vision of light, or as an 'apparition of light'. Phenomenologically speaking, the latter is close to

---

[49] [Note: The pivotal psychological-phenomenological features of the mental state of "Versunkenheit" – translated here as 'quiet state of alertness' – have been established by Albrecht in long-term empirical research carried out over a period of more than thirty years. The results were first published in *Psychologie des Mystischen Bewußtseins* (1951). – FKW.]

physical and meta-physiological sensations of light. The 'vision of light' recorded by Symeon, by contrast, is one that clearly occurs in 'inner sight'. If Symeon refers to phenomena pertaining to the world of sense perception at all, for instance, when he indicates the splendour, exceptional brightness, and of external space, or refers to the expansion of light in space, or its 'shape', this does not mean that he *has actually seen* the surroundings with his physical eyes during the event, nor does it mean that the inner vision of light has been projected into external space, thus resulting in an experience in which inner vision and sense-perception are fused. In Symeon's report, the references to external space, such as to the direction from which the light appears to be coming, as well as the express description of light having some 'shape' and expanding, are, psychologically speaking, imagined items rather than perceptual features. For this reason, it is possible for him to juxtapose two important theological aspects which he considers to be indispensable to avoid misunderstandings for theological reasons: The 'object of light' beheld in the vision within is radiant and in some way 'shaped' and spatial, is understood to be an emanation from, and is contrasted to 'the uncreated Light', which is formless, incomprehensible, infinite, ineffable and unfathomable.

3. The word 'light' is not used in both the literal and metaphoric senses. The 'light' beheld within is evidently a genuine *visual or pictorial* form of light appearing in 'inner sight'. The expressions *'visual/pictorial'* manifestations of light suggest that a few sparse features of visual perception are still involved, which are expressed by such words as 'splendour', 'lustre', 'radiance', 'luminescence', 'brightness'; over and beyond this, the visual quality is denoted by reference to some spatial characteristics: the direction from which the light appears to be approaching, or the direction into which a 'beam' or 'ray of light' is pointing, as well as references to the expansion and formal properties of light. The terms 'visual/pictorial' indicate, second, that they do not denote a symbol or an ideographic image. *The 'light' beheld by Symeon can rather unequivocally be classified as a self-expressive image, or more properly speaking*, a visual form of [divine] self-revelation. This means

that in the visionary experience it is not just a form-like quasi-sensory light that is perceived, but, first and foremost, the instant knowledge or 'illumination' about the real presence of what in our phenomenological terminology has been termed the 'All-encompassing', is conveyed contemporaneously. It seems to me *that the experiential recognition of the presence of the 'All-encompassing', conveyed at the flash of a moment, is indeed the core of Symeon's inward experience of the light, and this is what is ultimately existentially relevant to him.* This is a new ground-breaking insight: *In Symeon's testimonies, the cognitive awareness of the presence of the 'All-encompassing' is intertwined with, or embedded in, the vision of an image-like, quasi-sensory three-dimensional light.*

4. The descriptions of Symeon confirm, moreover, another vital phenomenological feature of genuine mystical experience – the phenomenon of the 'All-encompassing' 'arriving' in the vista of 'inner sight'. At the core of Symeon's visionary event is the experience of the 'all-encompassing' Light *'arriving'* in the 'quiet state of alertness' transporting him into the heights of ecstatic bliss.

   The inner 'vision of light' is a phenomenon that can be encountered across many cultures and thus cannot be claimed to be only typical of the Byzantine Greek-Orthodox spiritual tradition. 'Visions of light' have been recorded, for instance, quite frequently in various occidental mystical traditions. We have already mentioned two western representatives above, in which the pictorial vision of Christ is merged with the sight of a preternatural light emanating from the Redeemer. Teresa of Avila, representing the monastic Christian mystical tradition in the 16th century, provides detailed testimonies of this kind, and Christine Lucie [Mathilde Boutle, a married Roman Catholic and mother of five children] representing Christian lay spirituality of late 19th-century France. Indeed, the works of the two visionaries offer several other varieties of mystical experiences of 'light', which may help us to advance our enquiry further. In her *Vida*, Teresa supplies an example of a vision of the mystical light on its own, i.e., a vision consisting solely of an illuminating 'dazzling light' permeating the visionary's consciousness, which is not combined with any pictorial vision:

Text 36 (Teresa of Avila, *Vida*, main chapter 28, 283f.): "4. ... Moreover, the dazzling light that illuminates the mind, and enables it to behold Divine Beauty, is not blinding. It is a light that differs totally from the natural light perceived on earth. Compared to this dazzling light, the brightness of the sun even appears to be so dark that you hardly wish to open your eyes just to see the sun. The two kinds of light differ as fundamentally as the clear water in a crystalline riverbed, reflecting the sun, differs from the muddy water flowing through murky ground, dulled by dense fog. By using this simile, I do not want to suggest at all that the sun is seen in this vision, nor do I wish to insinuate that this light is like the light of the sun; for the latter appears to be like an artificial light compared to natural light. It is a light that does not know the night, but one that shines permanently and can never be eclipsed. In brief, it is a light that even the brightest mind is unable to imagine, not even if he/she pondered on it throughout his/her lifetime. God, however, reveals this light so unexpectedly and abruptly, faster than you can open your eyes to see it, if that were necessary. But it is irrelevant, if the eyes are open or shut; if the Lord wants us to see this light, we will see it, even against our will. It is no use turning away, all resistance is futile, and the sight of which cannot be avoided by either reluctance or precaution. I have often experienced all this – as I will report later." [Translated from the German edition of Teresa's *Vida* used by Albrecht. – FKW.]

This detailed description of the 'vision of light' experienced by Teresa supplements and corroborates the portrayals of the Hesychasts, though it differs in some respects from the account of Symeon. Teresa perceives a 'dazzling light' which, however, is formless and not blinding; it thus differs in essence from physical light and is not identical with the visionary Light itself. Though the 'light' experienced by Teresa is, phenomenologically speaking, a light perceived in the vista of 'inner sight', it cannot be classified as a 'pictorial object'. What Teresa describes here is indeed a new variety of 'visionary light': a 'light' that has been 'infused' and inundates the mind as to become an ever-present medium of illumination, and which affords intuitive insights into the realm of mysticism that cannot be attained in any other way. If we systematically exclude in our analysis of these testimonies all the phenomena in which the word 'light' is used metaphorically, and if we furthermore take care not to confuse an account of an experience of the 'mystical Light' with one describing merely the serene, luminous condition of consciousness when the perceiver is absorbed in the hyper-lucid and 'quiet state of alertness', we are beyond doubt finally left with what can be claimed to be the phenomenological core of a genuine 'vision of Light'. In

Teresa's account this core, which is ultimately ineffable and incomprehensible, is the encounter with 'something', which is most adequately expressed metaphorically by the word 'Light'. She resorts to this metaphoric expression because this seems to be the nearest verbal equivalent to a visionary mystical experience which could not be expressed in any other way.

Before we proceed, the proviso stated previously should again be called to mind: As long as we are engaged in a psychological-phenomenological enquiry, we must not only refrain from proposing an ontological assessment of the phenomenon of light, but also from offering gnoseological assertions. Thus, we can only try to approach the question as to what the 'mystical Light' is, from the perspective of psychological phenomenology. But, as we shall see, this approach, like any other scientific approach aiming to explain the elusive and ultimately unfathomable phenomenon of the 'mystical Light', remains beyond the reach of science and is doomed to fail in the end.

However, our phenomenological analysis has enabled us to establish a few distinctive features and basic facts about the nature of visionary experiences of 'light'.

First, the 'visionary light' experienced in 'cosmic consciousness', the 'vision of Light' perceived by the Hesychasts and the 'vision of light' recorded by Teresa in text 36 represent diverse manifestations of the phenomenon. Though seemingly similar phenomenologically, the individual experiences can be shown to differ significantly despite their affinities. The 'cosmic light' is most closely akin to physical light, whereas the 'light' perceived by the Hesychasts is a visual manifestation of what in psychological phenomenology has been classified as the perception of an 'all-encompassing Light'; and the 'dazzling light' described by Teresa in text 36 is a realistic description, albeit metaphorically expressed by the word 'light', of the hyper-lucid condition of consciousness which serves as the 'medium' or 'setting' for her mystical experience of Light and other varieties of mystical experience.

Second, the visionary 'light' is perceived by all the witnesses quoted as a 'light' *'arriving'* in 'inner sight'.

Third, we also have stipulated that the 'light' experienced by the Hesychasts, as well as the 'all-encompassing Light' perceived by Teresa, qualify as manifestations of the 'mystical Light'. These visionary experiences cannot but be accounted for than as revelations of the 'primordial Light': They are encounters with the 'Ur-Light' ["Urlicht"], which is experienced as 'all-encompassing' and thus mystical in essence, and as a Light that has approached and come from a foreign sphere, and as being ultimately unfathomable and incomprehensible, and to which all past, present and future experiences are related in some inexplicable manner.[50]

The 'mystical Light' thus ultimately remains a mystery. The empirical reality of the event is evidenced by the intense emotional responses elicited by it in the 'experiencing self'. The perceiver is overwhelmed by numinous feelings of ultimate intensity as the 'mystical Light' reveals itself as both a *mysterium fascinans* and a *mysterium tremendum* at the same time. This means that *the complete range of the Numenous* is encompassed by it.

The *encounter* with the 'all-encompassing Light' is a rare, special *event*. By 'event' we understand – following *Gerhard Nebel* [51] – 'an occurrence befalling a person' ["Widerfahrnis"]. The 'Light' that 'arrives' from outside the individual consciousness is a real experiential event, one in which various other relationships are involved, notably the 'mystical relation' to a mystical 'Otherness'. The encounter with the 'mystical Light' is inalienably linked to the certain intuitive knowledge that the 'mystical vision' is a true and real empirical event.

Thus far in this book we have defined the concept of 'ultimate phenomenon' ["Phänomenletztheit"]. We have stated that an 'ultimate phenomenon' cannot be traced to any prevenient source or origin. Now the question arises as to whether the 'mystical Light' qualifies as an 'ultimate phenomenon'. If we were prepared to resort to metaphysics or theology for an explanation, the question would be answered affirmatively. In our empirical enquiry we must inevitably refrain from adopting notions derived from philosophy or theology. We shall therefore try to tackle the question within the confines of psychological phenomenology by contrasting the phenomenon of the 'mystical Light' to two other vital phenomena of mysticism, hoping that we can in this way probe more deeply into the ultimate ground of mysticism.

---

50 [Cf. ALBRECHT, Carl. *Psychology of Mystical Consciousness*. Trans., introd. and annotated by F. K. Woehrer. New York: Crossroad, 2019. 341–44. – FKW.]

51 NEBEL, Gerhard. *Das Ereignis des Schönen*. Stuttgart: Klett, 1953.

To begin with, we will pose two important questions: In which ontological terms have mystics of the mystical traditions interpreted the 'light' that manifested itself in their visionary experiences? And are there peripheral phenomena in the 'vision of Light' that might provide insights which could be helpful for advancing the progress of enquiry? Some mystics have interpreted the visual manifestation of the Light in terms of a supernatural visual appearance of the 'All-encompassing', whereas others identified the Light as the self-revelation of the 'All-encompassing' as such. In the former instance, the light perceived in the mystical vision is an 'infused image', which – although conceived as a rare exceptional visionary perception originating from outside the realms of sense perception, intellectual speculation and/or the imagination – is nonetheless identified as a 'picture' or 'shape-like object', and as such it obviously does not qualify as the self-revelation of the 'All-encompassing' itself. In the 'vision of Light', the image featuring in a visionary experience is apparently not (as the mystics seem to agree) a symbol or metaphoric representation of the 'All-encompassing', but an [epiphanic] revelation of the same. This means that the visual experience of 'Light' is intertwined by the non-visual perception of the presence of the 'All-encompassing'. The cognitive act of perceiving the 'mystical Light', in other words, is intertwined with the cognitive awareness of Presence.

In the second instance, the 'object' beheld in 'inner sight' that is termed 'Light' is claimed to be identical with the 'All-encompassing'. In this case we are not at all concerned with a 'pictorial or image-based vision of light', but rather with an entirely image-less experience of the 'All-encompassing', though visual vestiges may adhere to it which are best expressed by the metaphor of light. If this applies, the experience could no longer be classified as a 'pictorial vision', but as an 'imageless vision'. It is no longer a visual mystical experience, but a non-visual perception of 'something' unfathomable and ineffable for which the word 'light' is just as approximate a metaphor as the word 'darkness'.

The two options of interpreting the perception of 'light' in a mystical event outlined here have offered some valuable insights: The very fact that two hermeneutical options are possible in the first place, and the fact that it is impossible for us to endorse the veridical claims of neither, justifies our decision not to proceed any further in our scrutiny into the essence of the 'mystical Light', and to abstain from any attempt at an ontological interpretation. Our doubts as to whether the concept of the 'ultimate phenomenon' can justly be attributed to the phenomenon of Light. Only in the case in which 'Light' is seen as an epiphanic vision of the 'All-encompassing', the notion of the 'ultimate phenomenon' would apply. In the second instance, however, the visionary light does not qualify as an 'ultimate phenomenon', as it is part of a composite experience consisting of a luminous, albeit formless and imageless vision of the 'mystical Presence', which is intertwined with the cognitive awareness of Presence while gazing at its unfathomable 'darkness'.

Light as the Medium of 'Inner Sight"

We shall try to specify the peripheral phenomena adhering to the 'vision of light' by reflecting on the meaning of the word 'illumination'. 'Illumination' is a metaphoric term which is as ambivalent as the word 'light'. In the course of history, the term has been amplified in range and meaning. The term 'illumination' can even embrace the mystical theorem of the identity between perceiver, the object beheld and the process of beholding. These are, however, metaphysical considerations that are not part of our phenomenological investigation. We shall merely focus on phenomena of illumination that can be identified as corollaries of the core of the 'mystical vision of Light'.

In the context of phenomenology, the word 'illumination' may refer to the beams of the special 'light' beheld in 'inner sight' which emerge in the mind of the beholder – who is, as it were, the receptive 'vessel' of 'illumination'. The term, however, may also signify the hyper-lucidity 'arriving' in and inundating consciousness, and thus it becomes the medium in which 'inner sight' occurs. 'Illumination' may further be understood as a phenomenon that illumines the beholder, i.e., he/she may become visibly luminescent (as it were) and is thus transformed into an individual emanating light. 'Illumination', in this sense, refers to the phenomenon of 'transfiguration'.

The 'mystical Light' is not only a supernatural Light beheld by the perceiver [in 'inner sight']. It is also the Light in which the beholder is immersed and by which he/she is permeated; it is, over and beyond, a Light that is 'infused' in his/her body and consciousness and emanating from the person gratified by it. This means that we have been able to identify two distinct peripheral phenomena of the visionary experiences of light/Light: The light perceived as the clear luminous medium of the given state of consciousness in which the vision becomes manifest, and the Light becoming manifest in the radiant appearance of the recipient precipitating the phenomenon of 'transfiguration'; 'transfiguration' is therefore a corollary of the presence of the 'mystical Light'. It may be beheld by the 'experiencing self' him-/herself during the event, but it can also be seen by an external witness. This can be inferred from all the descriptions of the mystics examined. This suggests that these mystics were convinced that the three varieties in which the 'mystical Light' becomes manifest in a concrete mystical event were considered identical. The question, however, of whether the subjective awareness that these phenomena of 'light' are identical, and thus the cause from which the mystical theorem of identity evolved, or if this intuitive recognition was, on the contrary, the consequence of the theorem held *a priori*, must be left open. We can only suggest that the two peripheral phenomena refer to the twilight zone [between subjective awareness and objective manifestation of the 'mystical Light']. The question as to whether the two phenomena are indeed corollaries of the 'mystical Light', or if they are two different independent phenomena of light/Light, must be left pending. The fact remains, however, that these two phenomena of light are striking facts of empirical reality: All the mystics dealt with above are unanimous in their belief that the 'Light of illumination' has been 'infused' into his/her consciousness when immersed in the serene 'quiet state of alertness'. And there is no reason to doubt the testimony of these mystics.

> *Text 37* (Symeon the New Theologian, *Hymn 17*):[52] "... I am sitting in my cell by day and by night. Love is there, even if it does not reveal itself and if one is not all the time aware of it. But regardless if it is outside the creatures,

---

52 SYMEON the New Theologian. *Licht vom Licht: Hymnen.* Trans. Kilian Kirchoff. Munich: Kösel, 1951. 85. [English translation from the German text provided. – FKW.]

or felt inside them, Love is a fire, a radiance, becoming a luminous haze, or even transformed into the sun. Experienced as fire, Love offers warmth to the soul, inflames my heart and arouses in it an ardent love and desire for the Creator. And as soon as my heart has been inflamed, my soul begins to burn, Love radiates a luminescence that is spreading all around me; rays of light are infused into my soul, and at the same time my spirit is illuminated, imbued with clear-sightedness and made capable of contemplating unfathomable depths …"

In Symeon's description, the 'Light' perceived as a manifestation of the 'All-encompassing' is identified with the 'light' which 'illuminates' his spirit and releases in him the capacity of 'inner sight'. In describing the experience of 'illumination' he tends to resort to the imagery of fire and light. Therefore, it requires careful reading if one wishes to distinguish the references to 'Light' as an incoming mystical phenomenon from those referring to the condition of the 'illuminated mind' in which the 'mystical Light' is 'beheld':

> Text 38 (Symeon the New Theologian, *Hymn 34*):[53] "… Thou art the God of all things created. Thou hast shown us the immaculate splendour of thy Light. I humbly ask Thee to grant me this vision now, please do not tarry any longer. Grant me to see Thee in this Light forever like in a mirror, and to contemplate Thee, oh Word, and that I may behold and grasp Thy boundless Beauty with clarity. This Light is superior to any knowledge, it arouses awe and wonder beyond measure in my spirit, and kindles in my heart a fervent desire for Thee …"

The ability to 'see through' things [i.e., the capacity of 'clairvoyant perception'], which we have encountered above and identified as an integral part of a 'cosmic consciousness' event, is phenomenologically close to the special light experienced as the serene, hyper-lucid medium of 'inner sight'. This phenomenon is aptly described, for instance, in the *Vita et Revelationes* of the Viennese Beguine Agnes Blannbekin (c. 1244–1315):

---

53 SYMEON the New Theologian. *Licht vom Licht: Hymnen.* Trans. Kilian Kirchoff. Munich: Kösel, 1951. 224. [English translation from the German text provided. – FKW.]

Text 39 (Agnes Blannbekin, *Life and Revelations*, 17):[54] "While transported into raptures and immersed in Light Ineffable, she saw a man, more handsome than the sons of man, and in this male person and in this Light she saw the elements, the creatures and the things made of the elements, the small ones and the big ones, and they appeared with such a great clarity that every one of which, no matter how small, seemed to shine a hundred times more brightly than the sun – even the smallest grain of sand or the tiniest stone. Compared to this clarity the light of this world would appear dark as that of the moon, when eclipsed by a cloud. And the created things emerged so distinctly in this clarity that each thing had a unique quality ..."

Text 40 (Christine Lucie, diary entry dated 9 March 1884. 161f.): "Suddenly, a great Light appeared in my soul, and in this Light I saw the ugliness of my flaw; I did not see the ugliness within my soul, because it was no longer there, but I saw it in the flaw itself. Oh, how hideous! I can say it was more repulsive than anything one could imagine! *The inexorable Light permeated me so intensely that it was impossible for me to shut the eyes of my soul against it; and in the clarity of which I saw* how big seemingly small flaws really are. At this moment I felt unspeakably ashamed and deeply mortified before the Divine Majesty! All this lasted only as long as the flash of lightening, but nonetheless it remained deeply engrained in my soul ..." [Translation provided. – Italics as added by Albrecht.]

Text 41 (Christine Lucie, diary entry dated 12 April 1885. 190): "God filled my soul with a *clarity* which is nothing else but He Himself, and He said to me: 'I will show you what men of learning do not know, and what remains hidden to philosophers, human genii, scholars, scientists and men of justice as long as they rely on their natural capacities alone.' Then my

---

54   [Note: The *Vita and Revelations* of the early 14th c. Austrian visionary were first published in 1731: PEZ, Bernhard, ed. *Ven. Agnetis Blannbekin Vita et Revelationes Auctore Anonymo Ord. FF. Min. Accessit Pothonis. Liber de Miraculis Sanctae Dei Genitricis Mariae. Primum Edidit R.P. Bernardus Pez.* Vienna: Monath, 1731. Albrecht's quotation has been taken from Arseniew's anthology, albeit without a page reference. Since the time Albrecht wrote his book, the *Vita and Revelations* has been published in a modern German edition and in English translation: BLANNBEKIN, Agnes. *Leben und Offenbarungen der Wiener Begine Agnes Blannbekin* († 1315). Ed. and trans. Peter DINZELBACHER. Göppingen: Kümmerle, 1994. BLANNBEKIN, Agnes. *Agnes Blannbekin. Viennese Beguine: Life and Revelations*. Ed. and Trans. Ulrike WIETHAUS. Cambridge: D.S. Brewer, 2002. The passage quoted has been translated from the German source used by Albrecht. – FKW.]

humble soul was permeated by the Light that no one can see by his/her own power, and my soul realized that it was precisely because of its humility and smallness by which God is attracted. O Divine Goodness!" [Translation provided. – Italics as added by Albrecht.]

In another passage of her *Diary,* Christine Lucie speaks of a "light without words which accompanied the vision of God" (193) and of a light "which can reveal instantly certain truths that are enclosed in it, without any mediating ideas". These are clear references to the phenomenon of 'non-verbal illumination'. 'Illumination' here designates the event in which the mind is instantly transformed into a hyper-lucid condition and in which at the same time some knowledge of the 'attributes' of the 'All-encompassing' are conveyed, which are immediately known to be true. It is an entirely non-visual and non-verbal occurrence in which 'evident' knowledge is 'instilled' in the recipient. Lucie's description can be said to correspond closely to the phenomenon of a 'mystically *given* intuitive insight', which will be dealt with later. Explaining it and specifying the differences between Lucie's experience and the latter at this point would result in a digression of our straightforward analysis, which is why a concise clarifying remark must suffice here: The phenomenon termed *'mystically infused insight'* – when occurring in a 'pure' form, i.e., not intertwined with other phenomena – covers most adequately what is meant by the word 'illumination'. As such it is, however, psychologically and gnoseologically a highly complex and problematic phenomenon. It would require a separate chapter to examine and explicate the phenomenon from both these perspectives – a task which I have decided to defer to a later stage of our enquiry. In the given context it shall be enough to illustrate moments of 'insights' perceived as having been 'mystically infused' by a few testimonies of mystics. The examples will speak for themselves and do not require any further explication.

Text *42* (Christine Lucie, diary entry dated summer, 1879. 19f.): "One day, when I received the host at the Holy Communion I was inwardly permeated by a dazzling light, and in this magnificent splendour my soul got a glimpse of God's power and God's infinite meekness. And I knew instantly that I could never have endured the glimpse of his omnipotence, if God had not shown me his meekness at the same time.

It is in a single act of illumination like this that the soul is granted to grasp God in such a perfect manner which could never be achieved by learning or reading. This knowledge inflames the soul with love ineffable and arouses in her a great desire to serve God."

Text 43 (Christine Lucie, diary entry dated May 1879. 18): "... there I felt as if my soul had been immersed in God's own Light, and my soul beheld God in it in his unmoving essence. His venerable immutability filled me with deep admiration, and attracted my soul instantaneously by a love so enchanting that I am unable to express ..."

Text 44 (Christine Lucie, diary entry dated 21 July 1885. 194f.): "Then my soul was suddenly filled with light and saw the Wisdom of God and how His Wisdom governs all things so miraculously. God allowed me to *see* how his thoughts differ from ours ..."

Text 45 (Christine Lucie, diary entry dated 2 January 1884. 155): "These are spiritual illuminations which are entirely ineffable. If dazzling sunlight suddenly irradiated a dark dungeon, such an event could not in the least compare with what the soul experiences in such a moment of illumination. At the flash of a moment, everything is changed and transformed: It is God! What else do you need to say?" [All translations provided – FKW.]

We still need to supply a *psychological explication* of the peripheral visionary phenomenon, by which the space of consciousness is illumined, thus providing the hyper-lucid medium in which 'inner sight' usually occurs. This hyper-lucid mental state is, as empirical psychological research has shown, a pivotal characteristic of the 'quiet state of alertness'. The enhanced degree of clarity is perceived as being 'instantly given', i.e., the luminescent clarity is, metaphorically and mystically speaking, elicited by a light that has been 'infused'. This means that the 'experiencing I' knows that the condition of consciousness has suddenly become exceptionally clear and luminous – and this instant 'knowledge' is perceived subconsciously while the 'experiencing I' is immersed in the 'quiet state of alertness'. In such an event the mystic is experientially and cognitively aware of the ongoing 'influx' or 'ingression' of this unique clarity. This is evident from the records of mystics in which they speak of 'being overwhelmed by a flash of illumination', or of having experienced the 'arrival of some illuminating light'; some mystics even claim that the light that has been instilled in such an event has continued to persevere forever in consciousness. The claim that the luminescent state of consciousness can be retrieved at any time after having first been instilled, can be read in psychological terms as an avowal that an illuminated person can at any time be immersed in, or 'switch on' and 'off' the ever-present, hyper-lucid mental state termed 'quiet state of alertness'. The fact that a person is clearly aware when the 'quiet state of alertness' is switched on or off supports the view that a real cognitive process is involved and that a 'cognitive relation' is indeed involved when a person is advanced into the 'quiet state of alertness'. To obviate misunderstanding we have to emphasize that the cognitive awareness affiliated with the 'quiet state of alertness' is intuitively and/or subconsciously given and concomitant with the experience, and does not implicate, let alone result from, an act of rational reflection. These facts enable us to distinguish clearly between the 'visionary Light', conceived as a visual manifestation of the 'All-encompassing', and the 'inner light' elucidating the space of consciousness in which 'visionary mystical experience' occurs or is 'beheld'. Having established this important phenomenological difference between the two varieties of experiencing the 'visionary light within', we have proved those mystics wrong who have identified the light which is the medium of 'inner sight' with the mystical Light 'arriving' from beyond the realm of the individual consciousness, which is a mode of self-revelation of 'the All-encompassing'. The mystics who have conflated the two phenomena appear to have fallen victim to a misconception elicited by the ongoing experiential process: Many of them were overwhelmed during the event by feelings of ecstasy, by which the clarity of vision was obfuscated, so that the perception of the light permeating consciousness and 'the all-encompassing Light' 'arriving' and 'inundating' his/her mind, became to be perceived as one. It is true, however, that there are mystics who did not succumb to such a delusion. The best evidence of this is the letter written by Hildegard of Bingen to Wibert of Gembloux quoted earlier,[55] in which Hildegard clearly distinguishes between the 'shadow of the living Light', i.e., the 'light' which is merely the luminous medium of the mind, and the 'living Light', i.e., the theophanic Light revealed in the 'mystical vision of Light'.

---

55   See Text 7 quoted above.

The Transfiguration of the Perceiver

The phenomenon termed 'transfiguration' is another peripheral phenomenon of the 'visionary experience of Light'. It is a rarely documented phenomenon, and yet we have decided not to bypass it, because if we had done so we would have fragmented the entire whole in which the 'mystical Light' may reveal itself in empirical reality.

We can differentiate between an 'objective' and a 'subjective' form of transfiguration. In the event of an 'objective transfiguration', an external observer has seen the phenomenon and is thus the witness of an empirical occurrence. In the history of world religions, we may find numerous accounts of such. For our study, however, the 'subjective' form of transfiguration is more relevant and more conclusive.

We have already come across an instance of 'subjective transfiguration' in the account given by Symeon the New Theologian. It occurred to him while practising the Hesychast prayer:

> Text 28[56] (From the Hesychast method of prayer): "... As soon as the spirit has reached the location of the heart, it grasps at an instant what it has never experienced before; because the spirit sees through the veil of the heart and perceives itself to be fully wrapped in light and in perfect clarity ..."

There are several other records of 'subjective transfiguration' in Martin Buber's anthology *Ecstatic Confessions*, of which I would like to present three representative examples:

> Text 46 (Sophia of Klingnau, Convent of Töss, Switzerland, 13th or 14th c.):[57]
> "The soul was a beautiful, round and radiant light, like the sun, auburn,

---

56 PABEL, Reinhold. *Athos, der Heilige Berg. Begegnung mit dem Christlichen Osten*. Münster: Regensburgsche Verlagsbuchhandlung, 1940. 102. [Note: The numbering "Text 28" is not an error, though "Text 46" would be the number expected; the passage quoted here is taken from "Text 28" above. – English translation provided. – FKW.]

57 BUBER, Martin. *Ekstatische Konfessionen*. Leipzig: Insel, 1921. [Buber does not refer to the actual textual sources in the edition of the anthology used by Albrecht. Appropriate bibliographical references were added only in later editions of the anthology. – FKW.]

and this light was so ineffably wonderful and blissful that I cannot compare it with anything else. Even if all the stars in the sky were as bright and wonderful as the sun and all shining together, their united splendour would not be equal to the Beauty dwelling in my soul. And it seemed to me that a brightness emanated from me that illuminated the whole world, providing a blissful day around the globe. And in this light, which was my soul, I saw God shining blissfully, like a wonderful light shining from a bright, beautiful lamp; and I saw that He clung to my soul so full of love and so graciously that He became wholly united with her, and the soul fully oned with Him ..."

Text 47 (Symeon the New Theologian *Hymn 16, 76*):[58] "... He is dwelling inside me, and is like a beacon in my poor heart, dressing me all over with immortal radiance, *with a light permeating all my bones,* embracing and kissing me, He is giving Himself to me who is unworthy of this. I am saturated by His love, His beauty and filled by the bliss and sweetness of His divinity. Participating in His light, I become partaker of His glory. *My countenance is as radiant as the countenance of the one I desire. And all my limbs are radiant with light.* Then I become more beautiful than anything that is beautiful, richer than all the rich, more powerful than the mighty and greater than kings, more glorious than all the glory on earth and its treasures, no, even more beautiful than the sky and its luminaries, because the creator of all this is dwelling within me, to whom all glory and honour is due, now and for all eternity." [Italics as added by Albrecht.]

Text 48 (Symeon the New Theologian *Hymn 21, 134ff.*):[59] "And *the essence of my soul, nay, the essence of my body as well attains the splendour of God,* and pours all around it the radiance of God ... I only knew that I was carried by the light and surrounded by light and that I was guided towards an even greater Light. This Light was immeasurable and magnificent. I think even angels are unable to elucidate the essence of this Light."

These authentic accounts of experiences of 'subjective transfiguration' (chosen at random from numerous similar testimonies) show clearly that we are concerned here with a multi-layered phenomenon. Despite this fact it is possible to infer from these records some distinctive characteristics: The experience of 'subjective transfiguration'

---

58 SYMEON the New Theologian. *Licht vom Licht: Hymnen.* Trans. Kilian Kirchoff. Munich: Kösel, 1951. 76. [English translation provided. – FKW.]
59 SYMEON the New Theologian. *Licht vom Licht: Hymnen.* Trans. Kilian Kirchoff. Munich: Kösel, 1951. 124. [English translation provided. – FKW.]

is generally intertwined with unusual somatic perceptions, such as the sense of being 'weightless', or the sense of being 'luminescent', which suggest that the perceiver was transported into a state of cheerfulness and elation. Transfiguration is furthermore linked with the awareness of ongoing changes within the soul, which is understood to achieve the 'passive purification' of the soul. Transfiguration is moreover intertwined with a growing sense of bliss and love radiating from inside the perceiver and emanating from his/her body. 'Subjective transfiguration' is also linked to the awareness of the mind being cleansed, resulting in a state of supreme clarity. This clarity is perceived as something that has 'arrived' rather than surfaced from within. 'Subjective transfiguration' is furthermore embedded in a 'pictorial vision', in which the perceiver's soul is seen in the shape of light. Finally, 'subjective transfiguration' may be an integral part of a genuine 'mystical vision of Light', provided that the radiance beheld is identified with the 'Light' that is the ultimate 'ground' of the soul.

These are the major pivotal features of the phenomenon of 'transfiguration', but the list cannot be claimed to be exhaustive. Even so, the characteristics identified here are enough to derive from them two important insights: The experience of 'subjective transfiguration' is composed of somatic modes of perception, intense emotional responses, the concomitant awareness of an ongoing process of spiritual and somatic transformation, a 'pictorial vision' and a genuine 'vision of Light' – all of which are intertwined in a concrete occurrence in various ways. This implies that if we wish to subject the phenomenon of 'subjective transfiguration' to a close psychological-phenomenological scrutiny, we are required to split it up into its constituent elements.

The full complexity of the phenomenon, however, becomes apparent, if we wish to determine whether the 'light' beheld in the 'quiet state of alertness' qualifies as a manifestation of the all-pervasive and 'all-encompassing' 'mystical Light'. This cannot be ascertained from the evidence of the subjective records of transfiguration. We are exclusively provided with subjective accounts of ecstatic experiences retrieved from memory. These records tell us that in a 'subjective transfiguration' experience, the perceiver is overwhelmed by an ineffable sense of bliss and love, and instilled with the awareness of some paranormal light emanating from him/her, and that he/she is imbued during the event with a sense of light-heartedness, weightlessness, and inundated by a radiant light within, beheld in the hyper-lucid clarity of consciousness, which he/she claims to emanate from his/her body. In the state of ecstasy, the visionary perceives everything radiant with light, which is understood by him/her to be identical with the primordial, eternal Light.

Though we have so far explored extensive areas of the 'vision of light/Light', we have still not been able to advance to the core of mysticism. The mystics' encounters with the 'visionary light/Light' are still events occurring at the periphery of mysticism. We have arrived at our insights on the diverse 'visions of light/Light' by splitting the complex phenomenon up into four varieties: Our assessment of the fourth type – transfiguration – has shown that the diverse sensory experiences involved may be corollaries of the 'mystical Light' but, arguably, do not include a direct revelation of the same; the third phenomenon, the awareness of a hyper-lucid clarity being 'infused' in the perceiver's mind, does not result from the direct manifestation of the 'mystical Light', either. The first phenomenon addressed above, the preternatural light adhering to the 'mystical Object' when it 'arrives' in consciousness, is again merely a corollary of the 'mystical Light'. Thus, reviewing our analytical process, we are left with only a single core phenomenon to which we can unanimously attribute the term 'mystical': The empirical encounter with a 'Light' that is unanimously and inexorably experienced as 'all-encompassing' and intertwined with the non-visual awareness of Presence.

THESIS 32: *The light beheld inwardly can be classified as a mystical Light, if it can be identified unmistakably as 'all-encompassing'.*

THESIS 33: *The mystical Light is preternatural and trans-occult.* Neither the light that has physical characteristics nor the light that has meta-physiological characteristics belongs to the domain of the mystical Light. From this follows:

THESIS 34: *The experience of light in the context of cosmic consciousness is not a vision of the mystical Light.*

THESIS 35: *The mystical Light is an iconographic manifestation of the 'All-encompassing'.* This means that the visionary experience of the 'mystical Light' is inevitably linked with the awareness of the mystical Presence.

THESIS 36: *The vision of the mystical Light is an experience in which two modes of cognitive perception are intertwined: The awareness of the Presence of the 'All-encompassing' and the pictorial vision of an 'object' approaching, which is most appropriately expressed by the metaphor of light.*

THESIS 37: *The object-like vision of light has two distinct features: the pictorial perception of a light surfacing from the imagination, and the image-less vision of the elusive quality of the 'All-encompassing', which is sufficiently akin to the notion of light that it is most adequately expressed by the word 'light'.*

Summarizing this section about the 'vision of light', we may perhaps venture to lapse into non-scholarly parlance if we wish to epitomize what is to be understood by 'mystical Light', stating that in a 'vision of the mystical Light' 'something of', or 'in', the abiding presence of the 'All-encompassing' is experienced that is not accessible to any of the other modes of mystical perception.

The Cognitive Awareness of Presence

We have first explored the realm of 'pictorial visions' and hereafter the realm of the 'vision of light', hoping that we might be able to advance further in our search for the core of mystical experience. The intended path pursued in our enquiry was intended to move from the domain of pictorial mystical visions to the realm of mystical experience that is entirely without form and image. The 'imageless vision', in which the mystical 'object' itself is the only 'content', appeared to be the very essence of the cognitive 'mystical relation'. However, doubts have meanwhile arisen as to whether the course of enquiry has indeed been a straightforward one. The path along which our phenomenological investigation has proceeded, starting with visions of ideographic images and ending in theophanic visions, has required us to incorporate a new phenomenon encountered beyond that visionary path: the cognitive awareness of the presence of the mystical Object. This has turned out to be a pivotal phenomenon in the overall structure of any genuine mystical event, so that all conceptual decisions in our enquiry will henceforth be co-determined by it.

There is another even more significant argument by which our decision to change our approach is endorsed: The closer we get to the realm of 'imageless visions', the less the term 'vision' applies. This is because the visual mode of 'inner sight' does not prevail anymore but is merely an integral part amongst several other modes of inner perception.

On the basis of these considerations we have decided to digress briefly at this point from the path originally taken, and to deal with the experience of 'Presence'. The appropriate term applied here is 'cognitive awareness of Presence and not 'vision of Presence', because we know that 'cognitive awareness' is a collective term that includes diverse modes of inner perception, including visionary ones. This conception will prove to become increasingly important for our enquiry.

The phenomenon termed 'cognitive awareness of Presence' is a composite phenomenon which can be split up into various individual modes of cognition. But before we are going to do so, we need to survey it in its entirety.

To begin with, we must define the term 'Presence'. In the broadest sense, the word signifies that something is present for some time in the conscious experience of a subject. This general definition does not indicate, however, if the term refers to a psychological awareness of a presence featuring temporarily in consciousness, or if it is a gnoseological concept referring to the recognition of a presence, or both. For the purposes of our investigation, a concept of presence that is merely grounded in the psychology of consciousness is not viable, for the simple reason that any item appearing in consciousness is inevitably experienced as empirically present, so that we cannot infer any feasible criteria for distinguishing between mystical and non-mystical 'presence'. That is to say, it is impossible to establish criteria by which the 'content' of an 'iconographic vision' can be distinguished from what is encountered in an experience of 'presence'. 'Presence', in other words, does not refer to the merely psychological perception of the presence of some 'content' in consciousness, but *presence is a gnoseological concept*. This means that the experience of presence relies on an act of recognition in which the object is perceived as having 'arrived' or 'intruded' 'from outside' [i.e., beyond the realm of the individual self]. The gnoseological experience of presence is thus marked as an 'encounter' ["Widerfahrnis"].

An object that has 'gnoseological presence' *cannot possibly be a construct of the ideal sphere of being*. It thus must be an object that is real. An object from the realm of ideal being, by contrast, like a mathematical formula, or a particular value, is encountered in a gnoseological and/or axiological act, but the appearance of these abstract 'objects' in consciousness is not elicited by any 'encounter', nor is there any concomitant awareness of these 'becoming present' in consciousness. *The 'sense of presence', however, is not linked to the timeless essence of ideal being but rooted in the temporality and concrete individuality of real being.* Any item that is cognitively perceived as being present must be understood as a concrete entity endowed with characteristics of its own, which is known to be really present at the moment of a given encounter.

To the general concept of 'presence' does not necessarily belong the notion of spatial presence. Spatiality only adheres necessarily to an object of a sense perception. Though it is true that an object that is perceived only temporarily is not without any spatial relation, because the experiencing subject is inevitably situated in time and place, this does not mean that the object perceived must be assigned spatiality as well.

The concept of 'presence' has been conceived here in strictly gnoseological terms, and as such it is not a concept that implies any metaphysical notions, or an epistemological position. On the other hand, it must be conceded that the entire range of unresolved epistemological aporias is inevitably attached to the concept of the 'mystical Presence', although the same applies from time immemorial to any philosophical discourse on this issue.

By gnoseological awareness of the 'mystical Presence' we understand an experiential encounter with the 'mystical Object'. In such an encounter a relationship between the 'mystical Object' and the experiencing subject is intuitively grasped: The perceiver becomes instantly aware of a specific force or an impact operating on and/or within him/her. At this stage of our enquiry the distinctive features of the nature of this relationship cannot yet be further elaborated; we shall do so when dealing with the 'mystical relation' at the end of Part I. What needs to be said here in advance is that the relationship between the 'experiencing I' and the 'mystical Object' is entirely indeterminate; but we must abstain, for the time being, from attributing to it some causal or final quality.

Before we divide the domain encompassed by the cognitive awareness of 'presence' into a non-mystical area and a mystical realm, we need to delineate the sphere of this phenomenon from two adjacent areas: 1. delusive experiences of 'presence', i.e., flawed notions of a presence, which are – unlike authentic experiences of 'presence' – not sustained by an unflagging sense of certainty; 2. pathological experiences of 'presence', i.e., an obsessive, compulsive or otherwise morbid 'awareness of a corporal presence', termed "leibhaftige Bewußtheiten", a term coined by Jaspers[60]. Both these spurious varieties of 'presence' need to be further explained:

1. *Girgensohn* compiled numerous records from the participants in an experiment conducted by him in the field of the psychology of religion. The participants were asked to read religious poems and to describe their responses. The results were published in the study *Der Seelische Aufbau des Religiösen Erlebens*.[61] In several of these personal responses the phenomenon of 'presence' was addressed, referring explicitly to 'experiences of a being felt to be present' and the non-visual awareness of the presence of a religious being'.[62] Some of the participants reported that the notion of a visual presence of a religious being was evoked, others felt the presence of some non-religious being, and some felt a 'being abiding somewhere nearby'. However, close analysis of these records reveals that in all these experimentally generated notions

---

60 JASPERS, Karl. "Über Leibhaftige Bewußtheiten (Bewußtheitstäuschungen), ein Psychopathologisches Elementarsymptom." *Zeitschrift für Pathopsychologie* 2 (1913): 150–61.
61 GIRGENSOHN, Karl. *Der Seelische Aufbau des Religiösen Erlebens. Eine Religionspsychologische Untersuchung auf Experimenteller Grundlage*. Leipzig: Hirzel, 1921.
62 Cf. GIRGENSOHN, Karl. *Der Seelische Aufbau des Religiösen Erlebens. Eine Religionspsychologische Untersuchung auf Experimenteller Grundlage*. Leipzig: Hirzel, 1921. 211f.; 236; 423; 425; 432. – See also GRUEHN, Werner. *Die Frömmigkeit der Gegenwart. Grundtatsachen der Empirischen Psychologie*. Münster: Aschendorff, 1956. 265–69.

of 'presence', the sense of the realness of the 'presence' is missing. Even in the records in which the 'presence of God' is claimed to have been experienced, this awareness can be shown to derive either from the subject's imagination, or his/her religious faith; in the latter instance the knowledge of God's omnipresence has been 'grafted' upon the subject's religious response to the sacred poem. This demonstrates that the notion of 'presence' perceived by the subjects of this experiment significantly differs phenomenologically from a genuine 'cognitive awareness of presence', which is rooted in a real encounter, and thus in the cognitive awareness of a real 'mystical relation' having been established in the event.

THESIS 38: *The concept of 'presence' is inalienably linked to the sense of realness of what is perceived as 'present'; this means that the sense of realness is not necessarily to be understood psychologically in the sense that some content is perceived as present in consciousness but has to be understood in gnoseological terms.*

2. Differentiating the sane phenomenon of the 'cognitive awareness of presence' from the pathogenic varieties of the 'awareness of a corporal presence' is not so easy. 'Awareness' is a psychological concept, and it refers to some knowledge that is instilled invisibly and perceived as currently present. The more specific concept of 'the awareness of some corporal presence', viz., "leibhaftige Bewußtheiten", was introduced by Jaspers to identify a special psychopathological phenomenon.[63] The term refers to the bogus cognitive awareness of the invisible presence of an object or a human being. The apparent awareness of the physical presence of someone or something does not spring from the imagination or a sense-perception and is thus entirely non-visual. The difficulty is, however, that instances of the 'non-visual awareness of a corporal presence' are encountered in non-pathological contexts as well. For instance, a 'non-visual awareness of the presence of a person' can be the after-effect of a foregoing sense-perception: this may

---

63 Cf. JASPERS, Karl. *Allgemeine Psychopathologie*. 5th ed. Berlin: Springer, 1948. 66ff.

occur, for example, in a situation in which a person is in a room with another human being, and both are engaged in a dialogue; then the person sitting at a desk turns away and starts writing a letter; becoming absorbed in this task, the letter-writer becomes oblivious to the other person but is nonetheless still aware of his/her presence. This subliminal awareness of the presence of another person persists for as long as the other person is in the room. This means that the subconscious awareness of the corporal presence of a person is not the result of logical reasoning or of a peripheral sense-perception, nor does it spring from the imagination. It is instead a non-visual impression that intuitively perseveres.

In a pathological instance of 'the awareness of some corporal presence', however, the phenomenon is not elicited by a preceding sense-perception, or a concurrent act of subliminal sense-perception. There is no foregoing occasion by which the phenomenon could be triggered, like in the sane experience of a 'non-visual corporal presence' described above. Pathological cases of this phenomenon are either caused by so-called primary, autologous or endogenous modes of awareness: "The awareness of the reality of what is inwardly perceived is *primarily* caused by pathological processes, which have as yet remained unexplained."[64] Or, they may originate from delusive phenomena or misperceptions of consciousness. In this case, the 'awareness of corporal presence' is a flawed or erroneous impression, because no real object is involved in the event at all.

The 'mystical awareness of a Presence', by contrast, is a unique phenomenon, and markedly different in kind from the non-mystical varieties just described. Delineating the differences, however, is a demanding enterprise, as the underlying psychological structure is the same in mystical and pseudo-mystical experiences of 'presence'; it can only be achieved on the level of phenomenology and requires the whole psychological structure of the empirical event to be sifted. Hence, *an instance of a 'non-visual awareness of a corporal presence' is an element*

---

64 JASPERS, Karl. "Über Leibhaftige Bewußtheiten (Bewußtheitstäuschungen), ein Psychopathologisches Elementarsymptom." *Zeitschrift für Pathopsychologie* 2 (1913): 158. [Translation provided. – FKW.]

embedded in a pathological pattern of experience, whereas the varieties of 'mystical awareness of Presence' are elements embedded meaningfully in the overall structure of mystical recognition.

Our explanations have thus far been directed by the endeavour to clarify the concept of 'presence'. Referring to the chapter heading 'The Cognitive Awareness of Presence', we have so far only dealt with one part of the subject matter announced in it. So, we need to explain in the following section what is meant by the term 'cognitive awareness'.

To begin with, and to obviate misunderstanding, the first and most important item to be addressed is the need to distinguish between *the 'cognitive awareness of presence', i.e., the experiential recognition of 'presence', and the perception of what is present.* There is a subtle difference between the two, which, however, can only be explained after we have sorted out the phenomenological difference between the act of 'recognition' of something that is experienced to be present here and now ["Daseinserfassung", or 'isness'], and the act of comprehending cognitively the properties of an object perceived ["Soseinserfassung", or 'whatness'] in 'inner sight'. In the concrete event of a mystical encounter (or a non-mystical encounter, respectively), the cognitive awareness of the presence of an object and the cognitive awareness of the qualities of the object perceived are so closely intertwined that it is impossible to unravel their components. The need to differentiate between 'isness' and 'whatness' is, however, only necessary for phenomenological reasons. But within the realm of phenomenology, sustaining this distinction is imperative because otherwise it would be impossible to propound a phenomenology of the experience of 'presence'.

We may approach the problem of the differentiation of the two aspects of 'presence' from yet another perspective by proposing the critical question as to whether the expression 'cognitive awareness of presence' could be tautological. The fact that asking this question does make sense can be illustrated by way of analogy with the phenomenon of 'seeing': In the act of 'seeing', i.e., in the event of a real act of visual sense perception, it is taken for granted that some object is placed before the perceiver's eyes, which is really present in the given field of visual perception. And there is indeed no [sane] act of visual sense-perception in which the object perceived is not present in empirical reality. This means that in any empirical process – thus including instances of mystical experience – it is impossible to grasp cognitively something of the quality of an object, if the given object is not there. Hence the presence of the object is presupposed. This means that by perceiving the 'whatness' of an object, its presence is instantly recognized; the cognitive awareness of the presence of the object is immediately evident and turned into an inalienable part of the perceiver's knowledge.

Our effort in defining the 'pure' phenomenon of the 'cognitive awareness of presence' is by no means challenged by these critical considerations. They rather motivate us to elaborate even more stringently the distinctive features of the gnoseological and the psychological aspects of the awareness of 'presence': *The 'presence' understood as the gnoseological requirement for an act of recognition is something entirely different from the act of perceiving the 'presence' itself.* Though it is true that the awareness of a presence in consciousness can be inferred *a posteriori* by an act of reasoning (we shall refer to instances of such a mediated awareness of 'presence' from the records of mystics), it goes without saying that the immediate empirical recognition of 'presence' is the pivotal core of genuine mystical experience. What can be stated for certain is that the 'pure' awareness of a 'presence' intensifies in the same measure as the awareness of the 'whatness' of the 'presence' decreases. The ultimately pure and immediate recognition of 'presence' is imparted, if the object perceived as 'present', is something entirely foreign or unknown. When alone the 'isness' (i.e., the sole conviction of something invisible and indeterminate being present) of an object is perceived as present, while the awareness of its 'whatness' has been reduced to zero, the object is all but effaced and sensed to be an indeterminable 'something'. The 'whatness', however, is not dissolved or eroded, but 'lurking' (as it were) in the background, always ready and eager to reveal itself. This demonstrates that the full phenomenon of the 'awareness of presence' consists always and inalienably of the cognitive awareness of both the object's 'isness' and its 'whatness'.

We have by now provided enough of an empirical foundation for establishing a phenomenological grading of the various modes of the cognitive awareness of 'presence'.

1. The pure or overall cognitive awareness of 'presence', in which an unknown something is cognitively perceived as 'present'.

2. The cognitive awareness of 'presence' is intertwined with the perception of the 'whatness' of the 'object' comprehended, i.e., an experience in which an object that has been recognized is perceived as present.
    a) The cognitive awareness of the 'presence' of a non-mystical object.
    b) The cognitive awareness of the 'presence' of a mystical Object.

Strictly speaking, only the latter (2b) qualifies as mystical recognition of 'Presence' if we apply the (so-called) narrow definition of mysticism (proposed earlier). If we apply the concept of mysticism in a wider sense, however, it can be expanded to include the cognitive awareness of the presence of certain non-mystical objects (2a) as well, provided that the object perceived as being 'present' is also experienced as a phenomenon that has been 'infused' or imparted by 'the mystical It' ["das mystische Es"]. An example would be the non-visual experience of the 'presence' of angels.

Regarding item 1) The cognitive awareness of the 'presence' of an unknown 'something' is the purest and most general variety of experiencing 'presence'. It is the purest possible 'awareness of presence' because the awareness of the 'whatness' of the 'object' felt to be 'present' has shrunk to near zero. The awareness of the 'presence' of an unknown 'something' is at the same time the most general form of perceiving 'presence', if by 'general' we understand a mode of inner perception that is indiscriminately open to behold any phenomenon that might 'arrive' in the vista of 'inner sight', whatever its concrete shape, or mode of manifestation. I cannot say, however, if such a perfectly pure, uniform mode of experiencing 'presence' can really be encountered in empirical reality. I did not find any such testimony amongst the large number of mystical records examined which might have been quoted for illustration. Seen from a purely phenomenological perspective, it can be stated, however, that the cognitive awareness of a pure 'presence' can clearly be identified as a distinct feature and as an 'ultimate phenomenon' and as an overarching concept encompassing both mystical and non-mystical varieties of experiencing 'presence'. However, mystical and non-mystical modes of experiencing 'presence' can only be distinguished when the pure awareness of the 'presence' of an 'object' is intertwined with the perception of at least some aspects of its 'whatness'.

Regarding item 2a) The cognitive perception of the 'presence' of a non-mystical object could be illustrated by numerous records across all cultural traditions from various historical periods. But as this phenomenon has already been exhaustively treated by William James in his study *Varieties of Religious Experience*, we shall quote a representative example from James's book for illustration rather than provide new examples from other sources, as we could not get new insights by opting for the latter.[65]

Text 49 (Report contributed by a friend of William James, quoted in *Varieties of Religious Experience*, 59–60): "It was about September 1884, when I had the first experience [i.e., a vivid 'sense of a presence' in the room]. On the previous night I had had, after getting into bed at my rooms in College, a vivid tactile hallucination of being grasped by the arm, which made me get up and search the room for an intruder; but the sense of presence properly so called came on the next night. After I had got into bed and blown out the candle, I lay awake awhile thinking on the previous night's experience, when suddenly I *felt* something come into the room and stay close to my bed. It remained only a minute or two. I did not recognize it by any ordinary sense, and yet there was a horribly unpleasant 'sensation' connected with it. It stirred something more than the roots of my being than any ordinary perception. The feeling had something of the quality of a very large tearing of vital pain spreading chiefly over the chest, but within the organism – and yet the feeling was not *pain* so much as *abhorrence*. At all events, something was present with me, and I knew its presence far more surely than I have ever known the presence of any fleshly living creature. I was conscious of its departure as of its coming: an almost instantaneously swift going through the door, and the 'horrible sensation' disappeared.

---

65 For accounts of telepathic experiences of 'presence' see WALTHER, Gerda. "Die Innerseelische Seite Parapsychologischer Phänomene." *Neue Wissenschaft: Zeitschrift für Parapsychologie* 6 (11/12) (1956): 364–73; and 6 (13) (1957): 408–22. BALFOUR, G. W. Earl of. "A Study of the Psychological Aspects of Mrs. Willett's Mediumship, and of the Statements of the Communicators Concerning Process." *Proceedings of the Society for Psychical Research* 43 (1935): 41–318.

... On two other occasions in my life I have had precisely the same 'horrible sensation'. Once it lasted a full quarter of an hour. In all three instances the certainty that there in outward space stood *something* was indescribably *stronger* than the ordinary certainty of companionship when we are in the close presence of ordinary living people. The something seemed close to me, and intensely more real than any ordinary perception. Although I felt it to be like unto myself, so to speak, or finite, small, and distressful, as it were, I didn't recognize it as any individual being or person." [Quoted from the English edition of 1929, 59–60.[66]]

This text is well suited for illustrating essential characteristics of the cognitive awareness of the 'presence' of an unknown, invisible, non-mystical being. The passage addresses the main aspects of the stages and concrete circumstances of this variety of experiencing a 'presence'. It is not exactly a description of the 'pure' or 'general' awareness of a 'presence', though the phenomenological characteristics are to a considerable extent consonant with the 'pure' awareness of 'presence'. The 'whatness' of the 'object' perceived as 'present' remains largely, albeit not completely, unknown. The unknown "something" encountered discloses a few features of its essence: "Although I felt it to be like unto myself, so to speak, or finite, small, and distressful, as it were, I didn't recognize it as any individual being or person." This clearly indicates that the 'presence' encountered is a non-mystical 'being' or 'creature', though the perceiver was unable to identify it any further. This encounter arouses in the perceiver a deep feeling of "abhorrence".

There is another quality that can be identified, one especially important for the progress of our enquiry. We have so far consistently used the term 'cognitive awareness of a presence', and have not defined the concept, nor explained that various kinds of 'recognizing a presence' can be discerned. Thus, the term 'recognition of a presence', viz., 'cognitive awareness of a presence', refers to three potential modes of perception, which can be variously interconnected in empirical reality: 1. 'sensing a presence' [i.e., feeling a presence emotionally, and/or somatically, termed "Spüren der Präsenz"], 2.

---

66 JAMES, William. *Varieties of Religious Experience. A Study in Human Nature. Being the Gifford Lectures on Natural Religion Delivered at Edinburgh in 1901–1902*. 1902. New York: Random House, 1929.

'beholding a presence' ["Schau der Präsenz"], and 3. the 'non-visual awareness of a presence'.

The 'sense of a presence' can be shown to be a very important, albeit undifferentiated, component of diverse varieties of mystical experience. We shall deal with this issue in detail later in this study. In the example quoted by William James, it is the diffuse feeling of a presence, hence the 'sensing' of an unknown 'presence', that prevails in the overall experience. But there are other components involved as well: the perceiver is aware of a distinctly "distressful" 'atmosphere', and of a frightening, "unpleasant" 'aura' emanating from the uncanny 'presence'.

The 'Beholding' of a Presence

The second variety of experiencing 'presence' is the visionary one termed 'beholding of a presence'. The analysis of this variety will lead us back to the main path of our enquiry (for the time being). We have diverged from the main path because we were required to identify the main characteristics of the 'cognitive awareness of a presence'. In our endeavour to explore the different facets of 'beholding a presence', it is again inevitable to digress from the main path, as we will have to eliminate all the phenomena that might be mistaken for, or erroneously identified with, the 'pure' form of 'beholding a presence'. The main path of our enquiry is meant to explore varieties of visual mystical perception. We began with an enquiry into pictorial varieties and will advance towards the more opaque and elusive non-visual varieties, and, ultimately, deal with entirely formless varieties of mystical perception.

The phenomenon classified as the 'beholding of a presence' can be claimed to be rather an advanced variety of non-visual inner perception. Phenomenologically, it must be delineated on the one hand from the 'pictorial vision', and on the other hand from 'inner sight' that is entirely imageless. An event of imageless perception is again closely akin to the third mode of the 'cognitive awareness of the 'presence' of an unknown 'something''. The 'beholding of a presence' is, by definition, *almost* entirely without any image; what appears in this vision-like experience is entirely shapeless and devoid of any features that have expressive or communicative import. These characteristics must be given, otherwise this experience would not qualify as a pure experience of 'presence', but an experience involving some awareness of the 'whatness' of what is 'present'. On the other hand, the term 'beholding' signifies phenomenologically that some visual element is inevitably involved, i.e., that there is some residue of a content which is minimally visible, so that the term 'behold' is still appropriate.

THESIS 39: *The phenomenon termed 'beholding of a presence' is almost completely imageless, though there is a residue of visual content; this, however, is confined to the mere awareness of spatiality, and thus covers only a very limited zone within the full range of mystical (and non-mystical) perceptions.*

When referring to the spatial perception of a 'presence', it is inevitable that some phenomenological site must be attributed to it. In doing so one will have to consider two aspects: First, that the spatial awareness of 'presence' is just a single element of the more complex overall structure by which the 'cognitive experience of a presence' is elicited; and within this structure, spatiality is not even the most patent phenomenon; second, that spatiality is phenomenologically very close to the mode of the imageless perception of 'presence'.

Yet we need to qualify what 'spatiality' means in this context. It surely does not mean that the object perceived as 'present' has some three-dimensional appearance, let alone that it occupies some space in corporal terms; 'spatiality' rather signifies that what is perceived as 'present' is located somewhere at a certain distance from the perceiver. That is, strictly speaking, 'spatiality' is almost exclusively exhibited by a given direction, occasionally also by the characteristic of distance, but it never refers to any corporal, three-dimensional notion of space.

We stated earlier that the concept of 'presence' is inexorably linked to temporality and individuality, as these are the two experiential qualities that must be given if 'presence' is to be classified as a phenomenon of empirical reality. This does not mean, however, that 'presence' itself is necessarily a spatial entity. In fact, 'spatiality' is only a potential feature of 'presence' and may therefore be taken as a criterion by which different varieties of experiencing 'presence' can be distinguished. It is only in the realm of natural sense-perception that the spatial perception of a 'presence' is three-dimensional. The 'presence' perceived in 'inner sight', however, and thus including the awareness of a 'mystical Presence', can either be a spatial or a non-spatial one. But if the 'presence' is experienced spatially in inward perception, the awareness of spatiality is always an imagined quality, and never a corporal, three-dimensional one as in physical sense perception.

THESIS 40: *'Presence' as such refers to something real. The spatiality adhering to the perception of 'presence', however, is not real but imagined.* That is to say that in 'inner sight', the perception of 'presence' is transferred into an imagined, internal or external space.

Delineating the empirical conditions in experiencing a 'presence' is complicated even further by the fact that there is a coherent phenomenological bond between 'seeing' and 'beholding' a 'presence'. The spatial perception of 'presence' contains only fleeting residues of visual perception and is thus only marginally linked to the type of 'pictorial vision'. And it is indeed well-nigh impossible to decide in some of the records quoted (notably the one by William James) if a 'presence' is 'seen' or 'inwardly beheld'. Although the perceivers are convinced that the experience was real and not delusory, it is not possible to infer from the records if the occurrence was 'beheld in inner sight' or perceived with the physical eyes; nor is it possible to verify the avowal of the real occurrence of the event, or if the perceiver has fallen victim to some hallucination or delusion. (Later we will consider in detail the problem of flawed perception and delusion in the context of mystical and non-mystical experiences.)

The 'beholding of a spatial presence' [in 'inner sight'] needs to be divided into the same sub-categories as the ones introduced for classifying the varieties of the 'cognitive awareness of presence': In the general mode of 'beholding a spatial presence', 'something' is beheld to be 'present' in external space, yet this 'something' eludes identification, remaining entirely unknown. In some of the examples quoted, the 'presence' is either a 'mystical Object' or a non-mystical object. In texts 8, 9 and 11 above, it is non-mystical beings that are inwardly 'beheld' as being spatially 'present'. This applies to Teresa's vision of the devil, as well as to her visions of angels, saints. In these records the primary quality of these encounters with beings from the 'other world' is the clear awareness of the 'presence' of a shapeless figure. Teresa insists that these visions elicited a deep sense of reality and certainty as well as a distinct awareness of the (apparent) spatiality of the 'presence' of these figures, meaning that the spatiality was not a 'real', corporal or three-dimensional one, but an imagined one.[67] It is not necessary to comment on these visionary experiences of non-mystical 'presences' any further, as they cannot contribute any significant insights to the progress of our enquiry. We shall therefore move on to records dealing with encounters with the 'mystical Presence'.

> Text 50 (Christine Lucie, diary entry dated 12 March 1884. 162): "Suddenly the benign Master revealed Himself to me and filled me with His Light. I did not see Him with my bodily eyes (I have never seen something supernatural with my physical eyes), nor with the eyes of my soul (i.e., the eyes of the imagination), but *with a very clear, all-pervading spiritual vision, which is instilled with a much stronger sense of certainty than this is the case with impressions of sense-perception.* – I saw beyond the shadow of a doubt that the venerable person of Jesus ... *was present here on the right side of my bed.* My soul *did not see any picture* but was *united with Jesus with ineffable clarity* and sweetness. *It was a union and presence, union and vision.* I even dare to say: The supernatural Light is grafted upon the glance of faith; we behold what we believe in. All this lasted about 25 minutes." [Italics as given by Albrecht.] [English translation provided.]

> Text 51 (Teresa of Avila, *Vida*, main chapter 27, 250f.): "3. While I was absorbed in prayer on the feast-day of glorious St. Peter, I saw – or, to put it more precisely – I beheld (for I never saw anything with my physical eyes, nor with the eyes of my mind [i.e., imagination]) that Christ *was standing very close to me.* At the same time I realized that it was Him who spoke to me. I had no idea that such a vision could ever happen; therefore, I was initially stunned and overcome with such great fear that I began to cry. But as soon as the Lord had spoken just one word to soothe my mind, I was instantly restored to my accustomed state of calmness and filled with consolation and was without any fear. It seemed to me that Jesus was always present at my side; but since this was no pictorial vision, *I did not see His shape, and yet I was still clearly aware that He was walking all the time by my right side* and that He was the witness of all my actions. As soon as I had collected myself and when I was not shaken any more, I became aware of His presence next to me.

---

67   THERESIA von JESU. *Sämtliche Schriften. Neue dt. Ausgabe.* 6 vols. Munich: Kösel, 1935–1958. *Vida* (Leben) Trans. Aloysius Alkofer. Vol. I. Munich: Kösel 1952. 280; 300; 329; 478; and 496.

4. ... I say clearly that I have never seen Christ with my bodily eyes, nor with the eyes of my mind, because Christ never appeared to me in a corporal vision, nor in an imaginative one: But how can I then be aware of Him in this vision even more distinctly than if I had seen Him with my physical eyes? And how can I insist that He is present beside me? We might compare this experience to that of a blind person, or a person placed in a totally dark room unable to see anything, yet such a person would nonetheless be aware, if another person was in the same room – but still, this comparison is inadequate. Though these experiences are similar, they are surely not the same, because in this example one may rely on the evidence of the senses, for instance, when the other person speaks, or moves, and can be touched; the awareness of the presence of Christ, by contrast, does not depend on physical senses at all. Nor is there any darkness [in the presence of Christ], but *the Lord reveals Himself to the soul in a manner that is much brighter than the sun*. I do not say that one can see the sunlight, or any other brightness; *but it is a Light that illuminates the intellect without any light to be seen*, so that the soul can savour in this great Bounty. This act of special grace bestows many benefits." [Translation provided.]

At this juncture, I would like to interpolate a passage from a letter of Teresa's written in 1576 to her spiritual counsellor, Father Pedro Alvarez:

Text 52 (Teresa of Avila):[68] "And now I shall speak about the way in which this vision has been revealed to me, which information you have wanted me to provide: In this kind of vision you do not see anything, neither inwardly, nor outwardly, because it is not an imaginative vision [*visio imaginaria*]; yet the soul, without beholding anything, recognizes what it is, and how it has become manifest, and knows much better than if something had been seen, though no object has been placed before the soul ... for the soul perceives neither an inward, nor an external locution, and yet clearly knows who it is, and where He is located, and sometimes she even comprehends what He wants to communicate to her. *Though the soul does not know by what means and in what way she is able to recognize all this*, it does happen like this; nor can the soul say how long all this lasted. But when the vision is over, it is impossible for the soul to recreate the vision in the same way, even if she tried very hard, for she recognizes unmistakably if something is

---

68 THERESIA von JESU. *Sämtliche Schriften. Neue dt. Ausgabe*. 6 vols. Munich: Kösel, 1935–1958. *Vida* (Leben) Trans. Aloysius Alkofer. Vol. I. Munich: Kösel 1952. 453. [English translation provided. – FKW.]

evoked by the imagination, or when the event experienced does not exactly correspond to the real occurrence, *as this is beyond her power.*"

The following quotation follows in Teresa's *Vida* immediately on the passage quoted in text 51; it has not only been chosen because in it the cognitive awareness of 'presence' is clearly depicted, but also because it describes with remarkable clarity the difference between a genuine instance of instantaneous mystical recognition of 'Presence', and the mediated perception of the 'presence' of the 'numen', which is only inferred from the impact suffered by the perceiver:

> Text 53 (Teresa of Avila, *Vida*, main chapter 27, 251f.): "5. This vision is not like a certain consciousness of God's presence, which is especially felt quite often by those who are granted the grace of unitive prayer or the prayer of peace. For it seems, that in these instances of spiritual prayer, we may find the one with whom we wish to speak as soon as we have started to pray, and then we think that he can hear us concluding this from the effects and spiritual feelings aroused in us: These include, in particular, feelings of ardent love, strong faith, as well as motions replete with feelings of bliss. These gifts of God, it is true, are all acts of special grace, and those who are bestowed with such gratuitous feelings esteem them highly, because they are recognized as tokens of a highly advanced stage of spiritual prayer, but nonetheless these are experiences of contemplative prayer, *but not yet an experience of a vision.*
>
> In contemplative prayer the presence of God is merely deduced from the effects generated in the soul, by which His Majesty wants to make his Presence felt. Yet in a true vision [i.e., a genuine mystical vision of the Divine Presence] one recognizes unmistakably that Jesus Christ, the son of the Virgin Mary, is indeed present. *In spiritual prayer, by comparison, only some influences of the Godhead become manifest; in a vision of Presence all this can be experienced as well, but over and beyond this, one knows instantly that the most Holy Majesty is present* and willing to bestow special graces on us. My confessor asked me who it was that told me that Jesus Christ Himself was present in this vision. And I answered him: 'It was Jesus Himself who told me so repeatedly, but even before he had told me, *this knowledge had been instilled in my intellect ...*'.
>
> 6. ... Here, in this vision, I can claim with certainty that it is really Him who is present; *the Presence of the Lord is recognized so clearly – though nothing can indeed be seen –* that it is impossible (in my opinion) to have any doubt at all. For it truly is the will of the Lord that his Presence is so clearly impinged upon the mind that doubting His real Presence is even less feasible than if it had been seen with physical eyes ... there is such a deep

sense of certainty that *leaves no room for any doubt.*" [Italics as added by Albrecht; translation provided.]

If we compare now text 49 (William James) with texts 50 and 51, we may conclude that the awareness of spatiality described in James's text is more likely to derive from a perception of external space than from an interior vision, whereas the experience of spatiality as depicted by Teresa and Lucie does not relate to external space but is clearly imagined, or that the description is meant metaphorically. We may thus discern that there is a striking analogy between the varieties of perceiving space and the varieties of perceiving light in the context of a visionary experience: As we have seen, Yogi Yogananda perceived different kinds of physical light along with meta-physiological light appearing in external space. Some mystics, like Symeon the New Theologian, beheld a 'visionary Light' which is cognitively perceived as a visual token of the Divine Presence, whereas other mystics witnessed a luminescent clarity instilled in consciousness that is most appropriately rendered metaphorically by the word 'light'. There is a similar pattern between the perception of spatiality and 'presence': The experience recorded by William James's subject can almost certainly be identified as a visionary encounter with an occult presence, hence as an encounter with a non-mystical 'something' located in real, external space. Teresa and Lucie, by contrast, recognized a 'presence' in their visions in the realm of imagined spatiality. Unlike James's subject, the two female visionaries do not claim anywhere in their writings that the imageless 'presence' beheld *is indeed* (ontically) located in the real space around them but are rather clear in their explication that the experience occurred entirely within their minds. There is yet another important analogy between the perception of 'light' and the perception of 'space': In Symeon, the 'Light' can be interpreted as a mode of theophanic revelation; the same may occur when experiencing an all-encompassing 'spatial Presence' – which can likewise be conceived as a mode of Divine self-revelation.

The awareness of spatiality experienced within, albeit projected into external space, is the more distinct, the more visual and the more pictorial a given visionary experience is. Mystics like Teresa of Avila, who are accustomed to numinous encounters with the 'shape' of Jesus, are more likely to be faced with pictorial impressions of the 'mystical Object' during a concomitant non-visual experience of a 'Presence' than mystics whose inward perception is habitually devoid of visual impressions, and thus inherently imageless. If the latter applies, the Presence of Christ is felt inwardly but no image is beheld; the core of the experience is thus a vivid awareness of His spatial Presence (occasionally Jesus is even felt to be present in a specific room). This may explain why Christine Lucie compares her non-pictorial vision of Christ's Presence repeatedly with visual sense-perception by night or in darkness.[69]

The 'All-encompassing' perceived as something without 'shape' and thus as something that is imageless and without any visual features, has not got any space to which it could be allocated. Its spatial quality is therefore perceived in a different way than in a 'vision of Christ' that is beheld as 'arriving' in 'inner sight' in the twilight zone situated between pictorial and non-pictorial visionary experiences. The spatiality of the 'All-encompassing' perceived as formless thus evokes the sense of its omnipresence – a concept that refers to both the temporal and the spatial modes of perception. What is 'omnipresent' 'is' necessarily given in *any* external space and can thus be perceived in any location (or rather 'surrounding space') in terms of an intensified awareness of a 'presence'. The 'surrounding space' is the venue in which the perceiver 'beholds' the 'object arriving', or in which the 'experiencing I' perceives the somatic and/or emotional impact of the 'object' encountered.

> Text 54 (Christine Lucie, diary entry 24 October 1884. 200): "... This morning, He surrounded my soul with sweet bliss during Holy Communion. How can the soul perceive to be thus surrounded, if she does not see anything, since the vision is entirely a spiritual one? I will never be able to understand this ..."

The foregoing considerations on the imagined perception of 'external space' have paved the way for our subsequent reflections on the awareness of 'presence', in which the sense of spatiality is almost entirely suspended. As long as the awareness of spatiality is a

---

69 Cf. 'CHRISTINE, Lucie'. *Geistliches Tagebuch (1870–1908)*. Ed. Auguste Poulain, S.J. Trans. Romano Guardini. 3rd ed. Mainz: Grünewald, 1952. 250.

quality attributed to the imagination or the space of the body, it will be retained to some extent, but as an experiential characteristic that is largely to be assigned to the 'subjective side', i.e., to the experiencer rather than to the object experienced. In other words, it is rather improbable that what is perceived as omnipresent and all-pervasive is given a specific 'direction', or a space of its own within the sphere of the body, but rather that there is an 'organ' within the sphere of the body by which the perceiver is enabled to experience the Omnipresent as immanent.

> *Text 55* (Mrs. N., a contemporary female mystic, living in the 1950s): "It comes from a very remote depth, but the place in which it enters, the site of its birth, is in the region of the heart. Until recently, I *saw* it only in external space. Now it seems that what I have hitherto seen in external space, has become so 'solid' that I can only *feel* it inside. I feel a sweet weight within me. The whole cosmos is filled by it [i.e., what has 'arrived'] and will remain permeated by it. Yet the 'centre' has penetrated from outside. Whether it will stay with me, also depends on me. Now the presence is permanent. As soon as I become absorbed in this 'centre', the bond is established. However, the slightest disruption of this bond jeopardizes the relationship to endure. And this makes itself felt in this inmost site. There is all the power. From this site the power emanates. I can feel the emanation like an atmosphere surrounding me. It is as if one could 'feel' the Omnipresence abiding near the heart. It is the place affected by it.
>
> In addition to these feelings, words are spoken. But what is spoken is comprehended in the mind. Previously, I used to listen and to be attentive to what is going on within me, and it was only hereafter that 'speaking' began. But I did not know then that all my listening attention was directed at the place where the Presence dwelt. Now I can 'feel' the Presence. Sometimes I feel It in this 'centre' like pain, and then I know that I must be alert, because then the act of speaking will commence, or an act of guidance ... I know from experience that it is Omnipotence [that causes all this] ..."
> [Translation provided.]

In this report the visionary perception of 'presence' has already become rather vacant and sparse in a striking way. The metaphoric expression that the presence is 'felt' rather than 'seen' indicates that the experience is essentially somatic and emotive; the 'visionary' component has been depleted almost entirely; there are no pictorial images anymore. The visual perception of a presence has been replaced by a somatic and cognitive mode of perception: the conscious awareness of being 'touched' by the 'arrival' and 'indwelling' of a presence experienced as 'omnipotent'. We have thus established that the visual perception of presence may shift to a somatic or 'sensitive' mode of experience. This new insight should not, however, induce us to proceed with our enquiry into a different direction. The shift identified only suggests that the notion of spatiality addressed in accounts of visionary perceptions of presence is not merely metaphoric but can be acknowledged as references to a special quality adhering accidentally (though not inexorably) to the perception of presence. The testimony quoted above is clearly an account of a composite experience of a presence that is cognitively grasped as Presence, which contains faint residues of a pictorial vision, but is primarily composed of somatic perceptions and feelings. There is no need to explore the multi-layered phenomenon of the spatial experience of presence any further, as this might complicate matters even more, not least because it is one of the ambivalent phenomena of mystical experience and one likely to cause confusion.

Awareness of the Presence
["Bewußtheit von der Präsenz"]

There are three elements that can be distinguished in the entire phenomenological range pertaining to the cognitive awareness of 'presence'. Two of these elements have already been dealt with above: the 'visual awareness of presence', and the 'somatic and emotional awareness of a presence'. Now we will consider the third element: the 'non-visual, viz., formless, awareness of presence'. By exploring the imageless perception of presence, we shall take one of the most important steps forward in our investigation.

I could not find a more appropriate expression for denoting the phenomenon than 'awareness of the Presence', i.e., the mere conscious awareness of a non-visual presence that is cognitively grasped to be the Presence. The term has been taken from the psychology of consciousness. It is not an explanatory concept, though, because it does not say anything about the essence of the phenomenon. The mystical phenomenon of being aware of 'the Presence' is extremely sparse. In fact, not one of the gnoseological phenomena considered so far, which are inherent in mystical experience, has been so sparsely and elusively represented in consciousness. We have finally decided to stick to this psychological term, although we are aware that it is not particularly conclusive, as it neither specifies the essence of the phenomenon as encountered in empirical reality, nor does it denote the high existential relevance it has. Yet despite these shortcomings we have refrained from opting for a more suitable term from other disciplines, for the simple reason that they cannot supply a better alternative. This terminological quandary reveals that we have reached the confines of psychological-phenomenological enquiry for exploring mystical experience.

The term 'awareness of the presence of the It' ["Bewußtheit von der Präsenz des Es"] refers to the immediately evident knowledge, which is conveyed intuitively in an entirely imageless manner, that the mystical Object is 'present' here and now. The term 'awareness of the presence' is a general mode of recognition, whereas the phenomenon termed 'awareness of the presence of the It' is a special way of perceiving 'the Presence'. This means, psychologically speaking, that the 'awareness' of the presence of 'something' is not a corollary of recognition which has been 'there' all the time as a concomitant corollary, but that the 'cognitive awareness of the Presence' is only triggered at the moment when 'the Presence' 'arrives' in consciousness and encroaches upon the perceiver; in other words, the event of becoming aware is the mode in which 'the Presence' is experienced. *The event in which the non-visual, immediately evident knowledge of a presence is imparted is a gnoseological act* and must be understood as such. Thus the 'awareness of the Presence' is one of the three constituent elements of the cognitive perception of presence. Compared to the other two elements, we may recognize a certain phenomenological affinity between the 'awareness' and the 'visual perception of presence': Both modes of perception occur in a clear, lucid and intellectual atmosphere, and thus differ from the opaque mode of feeling and/or sensing the Presence somatically. Feelings and the sense of being touched by 'the Presence' are dark and diffuse modes of perception though they are at the same time the most prevalent ones, providing the empirical basis for all varieties of mystical experience, including the more lucid ones. The difference between the 'cognitive awareness of presence' and the 'visual perception of presence' becomes apparent only on the phenomenological level, in that the former is a non-visual spatial experience, whereas the latter is a visual and an entirely non-spatial one. Psychologically speaking, the 'vision' of the spatial presence is indeed nothing but the immediately evident non-visual knowledge that the 'mystical It' is present in a particular direction of the room. This means that the term 'vision' or 'inner sight' must inevitably reach its frontiers and must not be semantically expanded endlessly. This is why we can state: *The gnoseological phenomenon of the pure, non-visual, non-spatial awareness of Presence must be denied the term 'vision', viz., 'visual perception'. This phenomenon falls outside the domain of visual perception and must be understood (for the time being) as a mode of cognitive perception of its own.*

At this stage of our enquiry it is imperative for us to define in some detail a few more concepts. It is especially important for our investigation to explain, in particular, in what way the key concepts 'vision of the Presence', 'awareness of Presence', 'intellectual vision' and 'imageless vision' are related.

The term 'intellectual vision' [referring to the traditional concept of *'visio intellectualis'* introduced by Augustine and used ever since in Christian mystical theology],[70] *is a rather vague term, impaired by ambiguity, and is as such phenomenologically useless.* The conventional concept has three phenomenological characteristics, which are, however, casually merged rather than clearly distinguished. The reason why the three distinct qualities have been fused in the original concept appears to reside in the fact that the three pivotal phenomenological characteristics all refer to the intellectual sphere. The 'intellectual vision' thus encompasses not only the 'vision of spatial Presence' and the 'awareness of the Presence', but also the phenomenon of 'mystical intuition' [i.e., knowledge instilled in a concrete mystical event]. The first two instances are cognitive modes of perceiving the mystical Presence. However, the third one, 'mystical intuition', is a mystical mode of recognition but not a variety of mystical experience (this claim will be corroborated in the subsequent chapter).

---

70 See footnote 8 on page 77.

The 'vision of spatial Presence' is a visionary mode of perception, the second, 'awareness of the Presence', is no 'vision' at all, and the third one, 'mystical intuition', is a non-visual 'intellectual intuition'. These distinctive phenomenological characteristics support the claim that the term 'intellectual vision' is inadequate and must therefore be replaced by an (or several) other adequate concept(s).

The concept of the 'formless/imageless/non-pictorial vision', by contrast, is entirely appropriate. It will be used henceforth, after it has been distinguished from a few contiguous and apparently similar phenomena. Paradoxically, the final definition of this concept can only be given after we have established some of its indispensable criteria. By way of anticipation it can be said, however, that the term 'imageless vision' is not only viable but will prove to be the most meaningful concept relating to cognitive mystical experience. At this stage, we may portray some of the distinctive features which are already accessible. The 'imageless vision of Presence' is claimed to be formless and without any picture, which means that the focus of the 'experiencing subject's' 'inner sight' is directed at an 'object' – in this case, a formless and imageless 'something'. (We will consider later what is perceived, or rather, what it is the perceiver is looking at.) *Obviously, the spatial awareness of a presence alone does not qualify as an 'object' in an 'imageless vision'. As a consequence, the 'vision of a spatial presence' cannot be classified as an 'imageless vision'. The non-spatial awareness of a presence, however, regardless of whether it is experienced emotionally and/or in a tactile or somatic manner, or entirely intellectually as a 'cognitive awareness', is the primary empirical foundation of an 'imageless vision'.* The other contiguous phenomenon from which the 'imageless vision' must be differentiated is the 'mystical intuition'. This is a phenomenon that is not related to the sphere of the 'imageless vision': there is a clear difference in kind between the 'mystical intuition' and the 'mystical vision', because an intuition is a pure mode of intellectual recognition, which does not involve an experiential encounter with a concrete 'object' 'arriving' in the vista of 'inner sight'.

THESIS 41: *The non-spatial cognitive awareness of presence alone can be an integral part of the structure of the 'imageless vision'.* The predominant element in the 'non-spatial awareness of presence' is the lucid and formless 'awareness of a presence', though the emotional, tactile and/or somatic modes of perceiving presence can be assumed to be a sustaining element concomitant with the overall experience. Individually, neither the pure 'awareness of the Presence' nor the 'feeling or somatic perception of the Presence' are visual modes of inner perception. It is only when they are part of a non-spatial cognitive experience of Presence and become structural components of an 'imageless vision' that these joint modes of awareness may be fused with a visionary mode of inner perception, thus resulting secondarily in an overall visionary experience.

The Non-Spatial Recognition of the Presence

We shall now try to disclose the distinctive features of the non-spatial recognition of presence. The focus of the analyses of the following testimonies of diverse non-spatial experiences of 'presence' will be placed on the aspect of cognition, rather than on the question as to whether the non-spatial perception of presence is more determined by somatic/tactile/emotional qualities, or by the pure 'awareness of the non-spatial presence' alone.

> *Text 56* (Christine Lucie, diary entry 1 May 1883. 118f.): "Holy Communion. – Jesus has revealed Himself in my soul. He appears to the eyes of the soul like we perceive a person in twilight at nightfall, or, as we say in colloquial speech, between day and night. In this event, neither the splendour, nor the glory, nor the grace of the son of God are revealed, which usually happens in short moments of vision of His divine shape, or when the plaits of his garment are shown. The eyes of the soul are not captured by anything visible at all, if I may use this inadequate expression. *The soul merely perceives the pure and simple Presence of Jesus*, but irrespective of this [invisible Presence] our beloved Lord shows Himself so clearly to the soul that she has no doubt at all, neither during the time that this special grace is granted, nor any time hereafter. *And the plain awareness of the Divine Presence is enough for the soul to be transported beyond herself*, and thus to be deprived of any consciousness of her own being.
>
> The Lord has granted me this grace seven or eight times, since about a year ago. At first, I was even less able to describe the experience than I am now. It is possible that I am mistaken when I claim that there are differences between this 'sight' and the other visionary events, yet this 'sight' is especially wonderful to me *because of its simplicity and because it permits the soul to enter so deeply into God.*"

Text 57 (Christine Lucie, diary entry 10 May 1884. 166): "My God, what is it that attracts the soul, when she is *seized by an invisible and irresistible power, while abiding in the contemplation of Thy simple Presence?* There is nothing there for the imagination, nothing for the senses, and nothing for the intellect, which cannot grasp at all what it beholds. There is neither form, nor thought that could represent Thee; it is only Thou, and Thou alone, who is present in the soul. It is as if the soul would dissolve while engrossed in adoration, which becomes her life …"

Text 58 (Christine Lucie, diary entry 12 April 1885. 190): "God granted me to behold and perceive Him spiritually… *it is as if my ravished soul could embrace Him without being able to say who it is that is to be embraced; the soul only knows that it is indeed God.*"

We have already stated at the beginning of this chapter that the difference between the cognitive perception of the 'isness'[71] [i.e., the certain awareness that something is present; the fact that a thing is] and the 'whatness' of a thing is purely a phenomenological one, and that in a concrete mystical event the two phenomena are intertwined. Perceiving a 'presence' embraces inevitably some perception of its 'whatness'. The following accounts of perceptions of 'presence' will illustrate this fact. These examples provide a link between the phenomenology of the cognitive awareness of something/someone being present, and the subsequent enquiries into the recognition of the essence (i.e., the 'whatness') of the 'thing' perceived.

Text 59 (Christine Lucie, diary entry January and February 1882. 45): "One day God bestowed my soul with a pure and most forceful sight of Himself. It happened without a word, and in it no special quality of God was revealed to me, but God drew my poor and humble soul into Himself

---

71 ['Isness' is the English translation of the archaic German philosophical term "Istigkeit", which derives from the Latin term *haeccitas* coined by John Duns Scotus (1266–1308). The term refers to a non-qualitative property of a substance or thing, or its 'thisness' (*haecceitas*, from Latin *haec*, meaning 'this') as opposed to the 'whatness' of a thing (*quidditas*, from Latin *quid*, 'what'). Cf. *Stanford Encyclopedia of Philosophy* <https://plato.stanford.edu/entries/ medieval-haecceity/>. The word 'isness' appears for the first time in 1865 in English in the translation of the works of Georg Hegel (cf. etymological dictionary <https://www.etymonline.com/word/isness>). – FKW.]

and allowed her to behold and to feel what He is. This experience is entirely ineffable and thus futile even to try."

Text 60 (Christine Lucie, diary entry 5 January 1886. 202): "Suddenly my soul becomes bright and cheerful again at the wonderful self-revelation of God, our Lord Jesus Christ. His presence is recognized at an instant by a spiritual light with an assurance that cannot be compared to anything in this world. Once the soul has encountered God in this way, it is impossible for her to doubt that it has been Him; it is impossible because He reveals Himself by Himself."

Text 61 (Christine Lucie, diary entry 25 November 1887. 221f.): "When all the powers [of the body and the soul] are at peace and the soul lost in God, the soul may recognize four things: infinite space – clarity – peace – and happiness. The soul can comprehend these things somehow. But when the soul is led into the centre of *the Presence of the Divine Being and granted to behold Him silently, and when she is permeated by Him, she is overwhelmed and inflamed by a storm of love*. The rational faculties are shattered, reason is suspended, and the soul is unable to tell what she has beheld or felt. *The only words she is still able to utter are: 'It is God'. God is not only present, but He also reveals to the soul to a certain degree what He is.*"

In Christine Lucie's records the words 'behold' and 'sight' have not as stringent a meaning as in our psychological definition of 'vision'. Her words are descriptive expressions as she is trying to recount complex, ultimately ineffable, experiences of the Divine Presence and its 'whatness'.

The final examples of Christine's diary refer to a mystical experience which is not solely cognitive but a multi-layered perception of a living mystical relation. The experience comprises not only the instant recognition of the Divine Presence in the 'centre of the heart', but also the forceful, loving impact by which she is filled with 'clarity, peace, and happiness', and eventually overwhelmed and transported into states of ecstasy, in which all rational faculties are temporarily suspended.

Mystical Insight ["Die Mystische Einsicht"]

The separation of the 'cognitive awareness of presence' from the perception of the 'whatness' of an 'object' perceived in 'inner sight' is a purely theoretical one. In empirical reality any cognitive perception of a 'presence' is inevitably accompanied by some awareness of its 'whatness'. The concomitant awareness of the 'whatness' can, however, be so fleeting and ephemeral that it eludes phenomenological identification. In our enquiry, the mystical awareness of the 'isness' of the 'object' 'arriving' in 'inner sight' has so far phenomenologically been separated from its 'whatness', and – for the time being – been viewed in isolation. Now we are faced with a new situation which requires us to find the best possible approach for disclosing aspects of the 'whatness'. This shift in focus from the 'isness' to the 'whatness' of the phenomenon encountered in a mystical event is one of the most important steps in our enquiry. We may justly claim, I think, to have persuasively shown that 'the mystical experience of the presence of the 'All-encompassing" is an empirical fact. The question, however, as to whether there is at all a mystical experience, or a 'mystical vision' of the 'essence' of the 'All-encompassing', must – for the time being – be left pending. If we wish to find a viable answer to this question, we are required to analyse in detail the entire range of mystical phenomena encountered in a mystical event, and to try if we can to identify some of the veiled or covert features of the 'whatness' underlying a genuine mystical relationship. In pursuing this endeavour, I prefer to abide by the proven phenomenological method of critical segregation, in which spurious and potentially ambivalent phenomena are excluded from the realm of genuine mystical experience. Taking this approach, we shall start with phenomena situated at the periphery of mystical experience. This requires us to sift through experiential and quasi-empirical phenomena which in their entirety may supply the backdrop against which the genuine core mystical phenomenon can be singled out. This core-phenomenon has already been briefly referred to above in the context of the phenomenon of the 'imageless vision'. Its pivotal characteristics, however, are still rather in the dark. This pivotal mystical phenomenon can only come to the fore if the surrounding phenomena are identified beforehand. Thus, we shall embark on a slow and cautious path, which I think is the most reliable approach. The hazard of missing the pivotal core phenomenon by jumping to premature conclusions is indeed so big that it is more promising to search in the twilight zones first, as these are (largely) accessible to empirical enquiry. This approach is surely more efficient than a random enquiry into phenomena which can neither be grasped cognitively nor classified and which might ultimately never be captured empirically. This means that our methodological approach will proceed in circles, which revolve around the periphery of the core-area, and then advance gradually towards the centre. The first phenomenological circle at the periphery covers the realm of 'insight' ["Einsicht"], the second circle comprises the phenomena of 'numinous experience'.

To begin with, we need to define the term *'mystical insight'*: *'Insight' is an intellectual 'vision'*. This means that a 'mystical insight' is, first of all, both an intellectual and a spiritual phenomenon, and it is so not only because it is – unlike sense perceptions – an extra-sensory phenomenon, but also because the scope of an 'insight' does not extend beyond the area of the intellect, since what is recognized in a given 'insight' is always a rational facticity or a rational relation, which can even be expressed in terms of a judgement, if it consists of aesthetic, religious or moral notions. Second, a *'mystical* insight' is also classified as a form of 'inner sight', hence a 'vision', not just because it is an immediate mode of recognition and therefore differs fundamentally from discursive thinking, but also because what is perceived appears (like in any other form of 'vision') in the vista of 'inner sight' and thus is a 'given' insight beheld by the 'inner eye' in a hyper-lucid state of consciousness.

We must add an explanatory remark here: We have put the word 'vision' in single inverted commas to indicate that an 'insight' must not be equated with what is commonly understood by a 'vision'. In our strict and consistent terminology, the term 'vision' is always conceived as a mode of 'inner sight' and, therefore, it is inevitably linked to the 'quiet state of alertness'. An 'insight' is, phenomenologically, generally related to the 'waking consciousness'. Though an 'insight' is a vision-based mode of cognitive perception, it is [unlike the 'mystically infused insight'] commonly not a mode of 'inner sight'.

'Insight' – understood as a vision-like mode of cognition – *is the product of an act of 'intuition'*. An 'insight' is, psychologically speaking, the sudden and instantaneous appearance of thoughts and ideas in the mind, which become facts in consciousness although they

are not preceded by a process of thinking, feeling or imaging.⁷² An 'insight' is classified as an 'intuition' from a gnoseological perspective as well, since it provides immediate knowledge, which is instantly evident and conveyed in an instantaneous act of intellectual vision, and not gained from 'experience or intellectual reasoning'.⁷³

The term 'insight' – without the qualifying epithet 'mystical' – thus encompasses an area consisting of several spheres, which we need to examine more closely. We may distinguish between a central sphere, which displays most clearly the pivotal characteristics of an 'insight', and the adjacent peripheral spheres.

THESIS 42: *The core of the phenomenon of an 'insight' is the instant 'arrival' of imparted knowledge; an 'insight' is thus knowledge a priori.*⁷⁴ The knowledge infused by an 'insight' is a subject-matter pertaining to sphere of ideal being. The knowledge imparted in this way thus hardly differs from the evident knowledge encountered in the domain of logics and mathematics. The 'insight', for instance, that in God 'pure being and pure actuality', and thus substance and accident, infinity and the finite, are identical, is just as immediately evident as the mathematical theorem that the straight line is the shortest distance between two points, or the claim that two items which are identical with a third item must be equal as well. When an 'insight' occurs, knowledge is impinged, as it were, 'out of the blue'

---

72 Cf. ALBRECHT, Carl. *Psychology of Mystical Consciousness*. Ed. and trans. Franz K. Woehrer. New York: Crossroad, 2019. 277ff.

73 Cf. SCHMIDT, Heinrich, and Justus STRELLER. *Philosophisches Wörterbuch*. 12ᵗʰ ed. Stuttgart: Kröner, 1951. 284, 285.

74 [Note: This is one of the pivotal insights of Albrecht's research for understanding the spiritual nature of man, stipulating that man's creative inspiration (viz., 'mystical insight') is instilled spontaneously from beyond the confines of the individual consciousness. Albrecht's claim is thus diametrically opposed to reductionist approaches to mysticism, like those of Richard Dawkins and other exponents of Neo-Atheism (including Daniel Dennett, Sam Harris, and Christopher Hitchens). In his highly controversial book *The God Delusion* (2006), Dawkins categorically dismisses the notion of 'infused knowledge' deriving from beyond the boundaries of the individual mind as a blatant 'delusion', empirical impossibility, abortive speculation, and inane metaphysical *aporia*. – FKW.]

from the realm of ideal being; in an 'insight' it is thus not an object of the world of experience that is envisaged. If we further expand the concept of 'insight', it encompasses, *second, the intuitive comprehension of intelligible contexts. In this case, 'insight' is a form of intuitive understanding.* The notion that psychic phenomena originate from the soul is immediately evident and does not require a concrete psychic context to be accounted for. The phenomenon of instant 'insight', in which intuitive understanding is provided in a flash, is particularly significant in personal varieties of mystical experience.

We finally may discern a third variety of 'insight': *The phenomenon termed 'intuitive interpretation'*. This may occur, for instance, when the meaning of a vision or a metaphoric image beheld in a 'pictorial vision' is not immediately evident. The question 'what is the meaning of all this' is raised by the perceiver because he/she expects that the interpretation will be supplied by way of intuition. Here I would like to call to mind Hildegard of Bingen's allegorical visions quoted above. In Hildegard the intuitive explication of the meaning of her allegorical visions was precipitated by the inner hearing of messages (locutions), which occurred simultaneously with the 'pictorial visions'. But in general, it is not necessary that the meaning of a vision is explained by verbal messages transmitted by inner 'locutions'; an interpretation can also be intuitively 'instilled' in the flash of a moment; the meaning becomes instantly evident in an act of imparted knowledge.

THESIS 43: *An 'insight' becomes a 'mystical insight' exclusively if it is affiliated with the phenomenon of the 'mystical impact'.* This means that a 'mystical insight' is an 'insight' that is mystically 'imparted'. Christian mystics have termed this phenomenon 'infused illumination' [*infusa illuminatio*].[75] The term 'mystical insight' does not presuppose that something of the essence ('whatness') of the 'All-encompassing' is discerned along with it, or that the 'content' infused must be related to the essence of the 'All-encompassing'. What is conveyed by a 'mystical intuition', or the meaning explicated

---

75 [Note: The term '*infusa illuminatio*' was introduced by the scholastic theologian, Austin friar and mystic Richard of St. Victor (c. 1110–1173). He was born in Scotland but lived and taught in France. '*Infusa illuminatio*' is a key term in his *Beniamin maior*, a treatise of spiritual guidance and the practice of contemplative prayer. – FKW.]

by 'intuition', can also be an 'insight' about non-mystical facts, which is nonetheless imparted mystically.

The three modes of intuitive cognitive perception encompassed by the phenomenon of 'mystical insight' cover a considerable range of cognitive mystical experiences. In a 'mystical insight' it is, first of all, attributes of the 'all-encompassing It' that are grasped, which are known *a priori* and attributed to the 'all-encompassing It'. In the event of an instantaneous 'mystical insight', some personal qualities of the Numen are instantly recognized, and along with it, the person-like 'spiritual' bond between the Numen and the mystically illumined perceiver are known at a flash. Over and beyond this, in the event of a 'mystical insight' it is not only the meaning of 'pictorial visions' that is instantly understood, but also of the locutions that appear to be surfacing from opaque recesses of the mind. Thus, the phenomenon of 'mystical insight' intersects in three areas with the realm cognitive mystical experience: There is *the transition zone between 'insight' and the hearing of locutions* (which will be dealt with in detail later). At this point, we only need to know that the phenomenological sphere of 'intellectual locutions' begins where a silent (wordless) 'locution' is perceived as 'arriving' in the sphere of aural inner perception. The second *transition zone is that between 'insight' and 'pictorial vision'*, which occupies a larger area. The item 'infused' in the moment of 'insight' has the tendency to take shape visually. The phenomenological closeness between a 'vision' and an imparted 'insight' facilitates this process. It is important to know the characteristics of the *pure* phenomenon of 'insight' if one wishes to assess whether the pictorial content of a vision also contains elements of 'insight'. The third *transition zone is that between 'insight' and an 'imageless vision'*; we can, however, only refer to this transition zone here and illustrate it by examples in passing, as we have not yet explored in detail the phenomenon of the 'imageless vision'. We will come back to this issue later in this study.

Finally, we should mention that an 'insight', although it is no mode of experience, can in certain constellations be intertwined simultaneously with an experience of Presence. If this occurs, *this phenomenon is entirely accidental* and in no way contingent.

As the phenomenon of the 'mystical insight' is significant and widespread in the realm of mystical recognition, I would like to illustrate the four phenomena delineated above by textual examples. We have already encountered instances of 'mystical insight', although they have been termed moments of 'illumination' in the records of Teresa of Avila and Christine Lucie (see texts 40 and 42). In these records 'mystical insight' is an illuminating event occurring in the hyper-lucid state of consciousness, which is likewise understood as having been imparted in a mystical manner. Thus [the eminent Italian Jesuit theologian and mystagogue Giovanni Battista] Scaramelli [(1687–1752)] states (in his analysis of the visions of Teresa of Avila)[76] that 'God infuses into the soul a spiritual imagination, which is at the same time illuminated by a sublime light, by which the knowledge of these truths is perceived with great clarity.' It is this 'infused light' that enables the recipient to recognize facts at an instant and as immediately evident and true, though the same facts might also be attained by long-term syllogistic reasoning in a normal state of consciousness. Christine Lucie insists that 'the inexorable Light permeated me so intensely that I could not have closed my eyes, and it was in the clearness of this light that I beheld what appeared to me within …'.[77] In texts 42 and 44 it is specific attributes of the Deity that are consciously recognized in an intellectual illumination at the flash of a moment. 'By a single act of illumination of this kind, the soul is enabled to recognize God as perfectly as she would never have been able to do by study and learning.'[78] The content conveyed in a

---

76 [Note: Scaramelli's magisterial manual *Il direttorio mistico indirizzato a' direttori di quelle anime che Iddio conduce per la via della contemplazione* (1754) is an encyclopaedic companion of Christian mystical theology combining mystical theology, spiritual (anagogic) and typological exegesis of the Scriptures with psychological analysis of numerous testimonies of Christian visionaries and mystics, covering a period from the beginnings of Christianity to the middle of the 18th century. The Italian Jesuit's perceptive psychological and theological exploration of mystical states and experiences – in contrast to pseudo-mystical phenomena and spurious states of devotion – have stood the test of time. His *Direttorio mistico* was translated into several languages (including German, French, English, Spanish and Polish) and is still in print (in modern spelling editions). – FKW.]
77 Cf. Text 40 and Text 42 of Christine Lucie quoted above.
78 Cf. Text 42.

mystically 'infused insight' consists often of religious truths which the perceiver has previously adopted and acknowledged, but which now – in the moment of 'illumination' – surface in a visual manner and are instantly recognized to be evidently true. To obviate misunderstanding, it is important to emphasize *that the spontaneous event of infused 'intuitive mystical insight' into the truths of religious faith must not be mixed up with the genuine experience of 'beholding the All-encompassing'*. We shall come back to this issue after the exemplary illustration of the varieties of 'mystical insight'.

1. Texts depicting instances of 'mystical insight':

> Text 62 (Christine Lucie, diary entry 5 July 1882. 65): "During my prayers before receiving Holy Communion, my soul was *imbued with the contemplation of the purity of God's nature and God's infallibility*. I saw in the manner of the one who can never fail, and who is truth Himself. The sight is ineffable. After this *I beheld the Divine Will in a single eternal act*. His various actions and effects are called by us the works of God. I realized that the acts of His creatures must inevitably be extensions and ramifications of the single eternal act of God, and that sin disrupts this mysterious chain, causing a terrible void. My soul enjoyed the contemplation of the Divine Unity and would never have wished to withdraw from it ..." [Italics as added by Albrecht. Translation provided.]

Teresa of Avila was – like Christine Lucie – gratified with various 'mystical insights', but along with her descriptions, Teresa supplied a classification of each event which was derived from Christian mystical theology. For Teresa, these flashes of 'illumination' and 'mystical insight' were instances of a *visio intellectualis*:

> Text 63 (Teresa of Avila, *Vida*, main chapter 40, 450): "On one occasion during my prayers it happened that *I was overwhelmed by an imaginative, albeit formless, intuition (which passed by rather quickly)*, in which *I was shown with ultimate clarity how God comprehends and perceives all things*. I don't know how to describe this imaginative insight, though it has remained deeply engrained in my soul ..." [Italics as added by Albrecht. Translation provided.]

> Text 64 (Teresa of Avila, *The Graces of God*, Works vol. I, 496): "On the feast-day of St. Augustine, after having received the Eucharist, *I suddenly received a spiritual vision, which occurred in an inexplicable manner and passed by rather quickly, by which I was made to understand so clearly*

that I almost thought to have beheld it, how the three persons of the Holy Trinity, whose image I am carrying in my soul, have one and the same nature. This was shown to me by such a sublime representation and *by such a clear light* that *an impact was caused within me that was entirely different than any effect aroused by faith.* The consequence of this has been that I can no longer think of only one of the three divine persons without imagining all three of them at the same time ... Nevertheless, a single moment suffices for the soul to derive from this vision, without knowing how, incomparably more benefits than if it had devoted many years to meditate on these secrets." [Italics as added by Albrecht. Translation provided.]

2. An account describing the joint perception of 'mystical insight' and 'locution':

Text 65 (Teresa of Avila, *Vida*, main chapter 27, 252f.): "7. ... God puts into the innermost part of the soul those things that the soul should understand according to His will, and He presents it there without an image and without words, as I have explained in the vision before. These operations of God, by which He instructs the soul as He pleases about *great and sublime truths* and secrets as well as other things, should be carefully heeded, *because the Lord has often explained to me a vision precisely in this manner,* by which His Majesty wanted to gratify me ...
... 9. ... But in these locutions without words the soul does nothing, because even the little she did during the aural perception, namely, simply to listen, does not occur any more. The soul finds, as it were, everything ready cooked and eaten, and thus has nothing else to do than enjoy it. It is as if someone who has never learned anything, never studied, or even never bothered to learn to read, suddenly realizes that he is able to understand all sciences *without knowing how, or where from,* as he has never even bothered to learn the alphabet." [Italics as added by Albrecht. Translation provided.]

3. Examples of the blended perception of 'mystical insight' and 'pictorial vision':

Text 66 (Christine Lucie, diary entry 7 February 1884. 158): "My soul adored Jesus at the consecration of the Holy Sacrament, when she was transported into a prolonged state of ecstasy, in which she beheld Him at the bosom of His Holy Father and the Holy Spirit emanating from Him and the Holy Father. It is one thing to *believe* in the relationship of the persons of the Holy Trinity, but quite another *to really behold it in the bosom of God.*" [Italics as added by Albrecht. Translation provided.]

Text 67 (Teresa of Avila, *Vida*, main chapter 38, 389; 390): "14. ... Shortly after this, my spirit was transported into such a sublime state of ecstasy that I almost thought it had moved out of my body; I was completely unaware that it still resided in my body. In this state I beheld the Holiest [Man] of Humankind in such magnificent glory as I had never seen before. Christ was shown to *me in a miraculous act of illumination*, and I beheld Him placed in the bosom of the Father; yet I am unable to tell how he looked, because I could not see the Godhead, in whose Presence I seemed to be. I was so awestruck and stunned by this, that I was for several days out of my mind (I think); but all the time I felt as if the majesty of the son of God was present to me..."

4. Examples of the blended perception of 'mystical intuition' and 'imageless vision':

Text 68 (Christine Lucie, diary entry May 1878. 16f.): "... Then the ultimate beauty of my God was imprinted on my soul. I could not understand how this happened, but it captivated all my powers ..."

Text 69 (Christine Lucie, diary entry August 1880. 28f.): "I beheld God inwardly, who is the ground of all things, and saw how He possesses all and is the fountain of everything that is true, beautiful and good. Or rather, I saw God being the truth, goodness and beauty Himself, and that all things exist only because of Him ... *This way of knowing God can only be termed 'visionary beholding'*. Though it is surely only *a rather imperfect form of the vision of God* here in this world; it seems that God forestalls any mediating instance in order to reveal Himself to the soul [directly]. And in this the soul is like a human being stepping out from darkness into the brightness of the day. The soul feels that its glimpse is too feeble to grasp what God reveals to her, and she cannot comprehend it, and overwhelmed with admiration."

Text 70 (Christine Lucie, diary entry dated 9 March 1883. 106): "My soul moved from Jesus in the Eucharist, to Jesus in heaven, and became *enraptured* by the vision of the Divine Unity. I beheld God who is one in heaven and on earth, one in the three persons of the Trinity, God, the One and Infinite. *The mere thought, or rather the mere sight* penetrated me and annihilated all the powers of my soul; and because I was absorbed in the state in which God and the soul and prayer are one, my soul reposed in perfect union. The vision of infinite Oneness is one of the most wonderful visions that God has ever granted to my soul, *by which He is most deeply imprinted in her and nourishes her with Himself in a most pure and plain manner, without any images or any other thoughts.*" [Italics as added by Albrecht. – All translations provided.]

5. Example illustrating the joint perception of 'mystical insight' and 'Presence':

Text 71 (Christine Lucie, diary entry 29 January 1884. 157): "Jesus was present within me; I was abiding in a simple state of contemplation before Him, when suddenly Satan tried to upset me; but instantly my peace of mind was restored by the pure glance of the Godhead, my Lord. I think there is no other inner vision that could compare to the vision of the Divine Essence. My soul *was enclosed* (as it were) *by the Divine Substance* and beheld in it that essential trait that has been revealed to us by the mystery of the Holy Trinity: that both oneness and difference, the whole and the particular are enclosed in God, and I was well aware how foolish it is to search for something beyond God." [Italics as added by Albrecht. – Translation provided.]

THESIS 44: *'Mystical insight' is a mode of mystical recognition, and not a mode of mystical experience.* Thesis 44 thus ascertains the fact *that there is a fundamental phenomenological difference between a 'mystical insight' and a 'mystical vision'*: The former is a mode of cognition, the latter an experiential mode of mystical perception. A 'mystical vision' – whether it is the 'pictorial vision' or the type of 'imageless vision' – is per definition an empirical phenomenon. This implies that an 'object' must be given by which, or from which, something is experienced. For example, when a picture is looked at, the act of sense-perception requires the real presence of the picture. An 'imageless/non-pictorial [mystical] vision' is, by nature, a cognitive perception of Presence, and is thus inevitably an empirical encounter with the Numen. The phenomenological structure of an 'insight', by contrast, differs essentially from that of the 'mystical vision': An 'insight' conveys knowledge and enables the subject to comprehend something intellectually at an instant and directly, i.e., there is no experiential awareness at all of any encounter between the perceiver and the 'object' perceived. An 'insight' is thus – from the perspective of psychological phenomenology – a non-experiential mode of intellectual recognition. There are two more varieties of 'insight': 'intuitive understanding', in which the meaning of a situation, impression or context is disclosed spontaneously, and an 'illuminated interpretation', in which, for example, the meaning of an image or symbol featuring in a 'pictorial vision' is 'imparted' at an instant. *In none of these three varieties of 'insight' is the presence of the object of cognition required.* The core-phenomenon of 'insight' is thus an 'intellectual intuition', which is per se knowledge *a priori*, and knowledge *a priori* is necessarily self-sufficient and independent of an act of experience. Though it is true that the peripheral phenomena termed 'intuitive understanding' and 'illuminated interpretation' may occur within a concrete empirical event, the fact remains that the act of understanding and/or interpreting is elicited by a spontaneous 'insight' which is instilled in the flash of a moment and immediately known to be true without involving any awareness of an empirical encounter. Hence the claim holds true that none of the three varieties of 'mystical intuition' can be classified as an experiential mode of mystical perception.

Many of the mystics in mystical traditions, however, often misconceived the nature of an 'insight', which they understood to be a 'flash of illumination' bestowed by God, not least because moments of 'insight' often had stunning after-effects on their lives. Though it is true that the mystics also saw in a 'mystical insight' a cognitive mode of mystical perception, they tended to conflate it with an instance of 'illumination' about the truths of religious belief. But an 'illumination' about religious truths is a cognitive insight, which is something different from the conscious acceptance of these truths in a religious act of faith. Due to the fact, however, that an 'illumination' was valued as an 'insight' that has been *'mystically infused'*, it was exalted and attributed an especially high rank in the scale of mystical recognition. Thus, any knowledge about a specific subject matter claimed to have derived from 'mystical intuition' was assigned a higher rank than an insight on the same issue resulting from discursive reasoning. The superior status attributed to 'mystically infused insights' in mystical traditions over any other kind of knowledge poses obvious problems to any attempt to assess their gnoseological value objectively.

However, the real error made by the mystics of the past was their failure to recognize the phenomenological and gnoseological difference between two distinct phenomena of mystical recognition: The phenomenon of 'intellectual illumination', and that of the 'imageless vision'. These two phenomena were conflated and subsumed under the collective notion of *visio intellectualis*. Their failure, in other words, was to identify the 'mystical insight' as a mode of mystical experience rather than as a mode of recognition, since the 'mystical insight' is often an integral part of an 'imageless mystical vision', which is clearly a variety of mystical experience.

For this reason, the phenomenon termed 'mystical illumination' occupies a special position within the domain of mystical recognition. The fact, however, that it has been attributed an outstanding status in the history of mysticism should not induce us to attribute to it, *a posteriori*, exceptional gnoseological import. In our scientific enquiry we must adhere strictly to the criteria of discretion stated above: The cognitive insight conveyed in an instant of 'illumination' *that* the 'All-encompassing' is infinite and a single oneness is something entirely different from the cognitive awareness of the presence of the Numen, or the 'imageless vision' of the Numen as a dark abyss, which are evidently experiential modes of mystical cognition.

Numinous Perception

In our search for phenomena of which the empirical structure of the 'imageless vision' might be composed, we are now faced with a pivotal phenomenon pertaining to the realm of religion. *Rudolf Otto*[79] has explored the sphere of the Numinous and classified the concept, distinguishing numerous constituent elements and emotional states, of which all have the common characteristic that they are directed at and/or responding to (albeit in different ways) a dark impenetrable, irrational object termed the Numen.[80] Otto's concept of the 'Numen' refers to an obscure supernatural entity that is mysterious, eerie, and

---

79 OTTO, Rudolf. *Das Heilige: Über das Irrationale in der Idee des Göttlichen und sein Verhältnis zum Rationalen*. 1923. 26th to 28th ed. Munich: Biederstein, 1947. – OTTO, Rudolf. *Das Gefühl des Überweltlichen. Sensus Numinis*. Munich: 1932.

80 [Note: *Numen* means "divine spirit, presiding divinity,"; the word derives etymologically "... from Latin *numen* 'divine will, divinity,' literally 'a nod,' from *nuere* 'to nod' (assent)." (Cf. *Etymological Dictionary Online* <https://www.etymonline.com/word/numen>). – Originally the word referred to an ancient deity approving something, making its will and/or its presence known. – FKW.]

all-pervasive. The term, in other words, designates a preternatural being that eludes any further qualification.[81]

The numinous phenomenon embraces diverse aspects, which need to be dealt with and identified individually, before they can reasonably be compared to the phenomena of mystical experience. The psychological aspect opens up the broadest path to the understanding of the phenomenon and provides a tangible basis for answering the question if 'numinous perceptions' can be classified as a variety of religious experience, or if this does not apply, if it can at least be acknowledged as a mode of [religious] recognition. For Rudolf Otto, the latter – the gnoseological aspect – was considered more important than the psychological one.

We shall proceed with our enquiry strictly from the perspective of the psychology of consciousness. From this perspective the first important established fact is that 'numinous perception' is not bound to a specific state of consciousness; That is to say that the Numen can be perceived in the normal waking consciousness, just as it can be perceived in the 'quiet state of alertness', in 'ecstatic' mental states, or in any mental states in between. What is more important, however, is the fact that it is almost entirely composed of feelings and/or emotional states, though some rudimentary notions or fabrications of the imagination are often integral components, which are related to the mysterious Numen as a focal point, attributing to it certain qualities. On the emotional level a major response aroused is the 'numinous shudder' or 'tremor', by which the perceiver is overwhelmed by 'amazement' ineffable, and radically transformed in the wake of it. The perceiver knows by 'intuition' (viz., 'infused insight') that the 'shudder' and its transforming after-effects have been caused by the Numen. Other responses elicited by the Numen include the state of 'religious stupor',[82] being overwhelmed by a sense of awe,

---

81 OTTO, Rudolf. *Das Gefühl des Überweltlichen. Sensus Numinis.* Munich: 1932. 5.

82 [Note: According to Otto, "stupor" differs significantly from "tremor" (or "shudder"), which is negatively connoted. Both are ecstatic states, but 'stupor' is an expression of "blank wonder" and refers to a state of astonishment that strikes the perceiver dumb; it is amazement absolute. (Cf. *Stanford Encyclopedia of Philos-*

or becoming immersed in a state of bliss. The Numen may at times also evoke the 'feeling of utter profaneness' and of 'absolute dependence'; all these feelings are inexorably and unmistakably related to and oriented toward a mysterious otherness. The diverse emotional responses evoke, as corollaries, simultaneously different imaginative ideas in the perceiver, which Otto has variously termed *'tremendum'*, *'mirum'*, *'fascinosum'*, *'sanctum'* and *'majestas'*. All these notions refer to a religious mystery, or *'mirum'*, i.e., 'something' that is inalienably '[all-]encompassing', an unfathomable 'otherness'.

These imaginative qualities in perceiving the Numen shift the focus of the overall experience from the subjective sphere to the realm of the transcendental object. This suggests that what from the viewpoint of the psychology of consciousness is a transformation of an emotional condition, is in a peculiar way combined with concepts deriving from the perceiver's cognitive awareness of the Numen, though the individual notions may also be grounded in the personal emotional response. This means that when the Numen is perceived as a *'tremendum'* (i.e., something abysmally frightening), or else as *'majestas'* (i.e., as an absolute force and supreme authority), or as *'mirum'* (i.e., as the incomprehensible mystery of a total 'otherness'), or as a *'fascinosum'* (i.e., something ineffably blissful and wonderful), or else as a *'sanctum'* (i.e., the sacred, holy mystery), something of the 'whatness' of the focal point of a numinous event appears to have become manifest in consciousness. This shows that something seems to occur phenomenologically in such an occurrence that calls for a gnoseological assessment. Thus, we need to apply the concepts of 'experience' and 'recognition' to the critical assessment of the phenomenon of 'numinous perception'.

For this purpose, we need to call to mind what we have said about the distinctive features of emotional states. On the level of feelings, it is the current moods and feelings that are perceived as 'objects' abiding in consciousness, whereas the 'object' at which feelings are directed does not necessarily have to be present in the mind. An object may be the stimulus for an emotional response, even if it is only imagined, or if the imagined object no longer resides in

---

ophy, s.v. 'Emotions in the Christian Tradition' (2016), https://plato.stanford.edu/entries/emotion-Christian-tradition/- FKW.]

consciousness, except as an object of memory or the imagination. Thus, emotional perception, including all its diverse feelings and evaluations, reaches its climax alone, i.e., without depending on the awareness of the presence of the 'object' that has evoked the given emotions. What is perceived as empirically real and present is the current emotional state, not the object that has triggered the feelings and emotional state. This is the reason why feelings cannot be remembered, but only re-awakened; in other words, the presence of certain feelings or of a mood in consciousness can be rekindled by the memory of ideas and notions associated with these feelings. This may explain why 'numinous perception' is not tied to the real presence of the Numen, but can be aroused and transferred from one mind to another, and why it may fully erupt at any time when thoughts are directed at the Numen, and also when ideograms of the Numinous, like the hush of silence, the void, the sublime, are faced. Objects of the arts are often the triggers of numinous perception: for instance, the statue of the sphinx, the interior of a cathedral, the statue of the Buddha; but also the view of a landscape, a desert, of the grandeur and aloofness of a mountain ridge, of the elemental powers of the sea, or of borderline situations in thinking and acting, all these impressions can trigger numinous responses. In brief: anything that may function as a cypher of the unknown can trigger numinous feelings. Rudolf Otto has therefore come to the conclusion that the ability to experience numinous feelings is a genetic disposition, an emotional *a priori*, which is obscurely present in consciousness, and which is stringently and in a specific manner related to the Numen, and which can (as it were) roam about and become attached to certain objects, conditions of nature, works of art as well as to ideas that qualify as cyphers for the irrationality of the Numen and to be elevated to the level of real frames of reference of religious behaviour.

It has been imperative to elaborate in such detail on the phenomenon of 'numinous perception', because otherwise it would not have been possible to provide tangible answers to the three crucial questions our current enquiry is concerned with: 1. the question as to whether numinous feelings and perceptions can be classified in terms of an 'experience' proper; 2. in case of a negative verdict, can a 'numinous perception' be graded, if nothing else, as a mode of recognition? and 3. can a 'numinous perception' be an integral part of a mystical experience, and if so, what place can it be attributed to within the entire framework of mystical recognition?

As to question 1: We have previously stated that by 'experience' we understand the immediate cognitive encounter [of a perceiver] with a real, specific object. The term 'concrete encounter' presupposes necessarily the presence of an 'object', or at least its temporary presence; an 'encounter' is thus inexorably linked to the phenomenon of 'presence'. In the case of a 'numinous perception', by contrast, the response is directed at the Numen as its opaque focal point, which does not have to be 'present' at the time of the ongoing process of perception. Both the emotional and the cognitive perceptions of the Numen may advance towards their ultimate climax even though the intended 'object' does not disclose its real 'presence'. That this is an empirical fact can be illustrated by a scene from the life of Jesus: Christ's agony in the Garden of Gethsemane. In this event, Otto claims, we are faced with 'the tremor and devastation caused in human nature when confronted with the *mysterium tremendum*, the abysmal enigma of pure horror'.[83] This horrifying event, however, is barred from the least sense of Presence, and can as such only be understood 'in the light of, and against the backdrop of the Numinous'.[84] It is an experience of utter dereliction and desolation, which is at the same time the most extreme experience of the absence of the Presence.

If there is anything at all in a numinous event that qualifies as a *concrete* quality, it is the changing emotional condition, but surely not the Numen itself. The immediate awareness of the feelings emerging inside is, as it were, the reflective recognition of concrete conditions of the 'I'. This kind of cognitive inner awareness can be classified as a mode of inner experience.

---

83 OTTO, Rudolf. *Das Heilige: Über das Irrationale in der Idee des Göttlichen und sein Verhältnis zum Rationalen.* 1923. 26th to 28th ed. Munich: Biederstein, 1947. 100. [English translation provided. – FKW.]

84 OTTO, Rudolf. *Das Heilige: Über das Irrationale in der Idee des Göttlichen und sein Verhältnis zum Rationalen.* 1923. 26th to 28th ed. Munich: Biederstein, 1947. 100. [English translation provided. – FKW.]

THESIS 45: *We must distinguish between the experience of the Numen and the experience of numinous states of feelings.*

THESIS 46: *The perception of numinous feelings and their numinous evaluation are modes of perception, which do not qualify as modes of experience.*

As to question 2: The term 'experience' is a more narrowly defined cognitive concept than the term 'recognition'. Anyone versed in philosophy knows that there are kinds of recognition which do not depend on experience, and that there are other kinds of recognition that are based on empirical data, albeit not necessarily on data supplied by a concurrent empirical process. The latter kind of recognition makes use of results gained from prior experience. Thus, the claim that 'numinous perception' is not a mode of experience does not say anything as to whether it is – or is not – a mode of recognition.

> Text 72 (Otto, *Das Heilige*, 156 and 157):[85] "Something may be inherently known, or even *felt* to be familiar, blissful, or shattering, for which *reason* cannot account for ... Thus, the mysterious, inexplicable darkness of the Numen, which cannot be resolved by any concept, signifies that it is *unfamiliar* or *unrecognizable* ... This means that the 'Irrational' is by no means something 'unknown' or 'unrecognized'. It is rather something 'incomprehensible', 'intangible', 'inconceivable' for the intellect, though it can be experienced by 'feelings'."

Because of our narrow definition of 'experience', it would be consistent if we substituted Otto's expression 'can be experienced' above by the phrase 'can be perceived'. Yet despite this terminological nicety, it is obvious that Otto's concept of the *sensus numinis* is understood gnoseologically. Its meaning can be interpreted and epitomized as follows: The *sensus numinis* is a valid form of recognition. The kinds of feelings and items of the imagination contained in it are a genuine *a priori*. The intended object referred to, i.e., the Numen, transcends gnoseologically the confines of the individual consciousness, and is ontologically a 'thing-in-itself'. In a numinous event a part of the Numen is 'objectified', i.e., a portion of the 'whatness' of the Numen is grasped. The partial 'something'

---

85 [Note: All English translations from Otto's German works have been provided. – FKW.]

of the Numen's 'whatness', however, is (and this is an important, albeit paradoxical, annotation) its irrationality, otherness, terrifying abyss, its unfathomable mystery, irremediably dreadful or ineffably blissful.

In the following we shall quote some explications of encounters with the Numen from Otto's studies. At the beginning, the focus is on diverse emotional responses that are aroused by the Numen, to which some special gnoseological significance is attributed by the perceiver. In the subsequent quotations, the cognitive value of the numinous event is addressed:

Text 73 (Otto, R. *Das Gefühl des Überweltlichen. Sensus Numinis.* Munich: 1932. 327; 2; 3; 7): "All our knowledge emerges initially merely from emotional modes of perception. – Feeling is understood here as a pre- and/or transconceptual mode of perception that is related to an object, which, however, has some cognitive import. – [The *sensus numinis*] is not merely a subjective mood, but the perception is imbued with some opaque imaginative content, which does not emerge from fantasy, but from real (natural) circumstances. – By feeling we understand here (which analogously applies to language as well) an 'unravelled' and as yet obscure seed of the imagination, which is linked with a corresponding, albeit strange, emotional condition.

This dark unconceptual awareness of a numinous being, or a numinous power, or a numinous state of being is imbued with emotions of numinous awe or 'stupor', and 'dread' or 'tremor'. – To express it in the words of Immanuel Kant: 'The *sensus numinis* is the faculty of dark imagination given *a priori*'."[86]

"Numinous feelings are instances of knowledge *a priori*... In numinous feelings sparks of convictions and emotions are grounded, which are unique and entirely different from anything transmitted by 'natural' sense perceptions. Hence numinous feelings are *per se* no sense perceptions, but are, in their incipient stage, strange *interpretations* and *evaluations* of what can be perceived by sense perception, and subsequently at a higher level, they are affirmations of objects and beings, which are, as regards their form, apparently the products of fantasy, albeit instilled with some idiosyncratic meaning which is not derived from the world of sense perception, but which are added or projected on to them cognitively ... Thus [numinous feelings] (like Kant's concepts of 'pure reason' and his ethical and aesthetic ideas and their evaluations) refer back to a hidden, self-sufficient source of the imagination and of feelings, which is independent from any sense perception and which is located in the emotional disposition of the mind."

---

86 Cf. Otto, R. *Das Heilige: Über das Irrationale in der Idee des Göttlichen und sein Verhältnis zum Rationalen.* 1923. 26th to 28th ed. Munich: Biederstein, 1947. 13, annotation, and 133–34.

The present state of our enquiry into the phenomenology of mystical recognition requires us to consider critically Otto's statements and his conception of the *sensus numinis*. We may say beforehand that this will not result in the claim that the perception of numinous feelings has *no* gnoseological significance at all. We contend, however, that their gnoseological rank must be distinguished from their existential rank. We are only concerned here with the former. As we shall see, the existential rank of the *sensus numinis* is supreme because it is related to the ultimate 'Object', but assessed by the degree of its cognitive value, it occupies only a low rank.

In order to corroborate this claim, we have to analyse in detail the gnoseological value of the varieties of numinous perception distinguished by Otto. The first finding of this analysis is that the individual numinous events described by Otto do not occur on the same level. Because of this the varieties of numinous perception must be assessed separately. Otto insists that numinous perception is basically supported by three kinds of 'ultimate phenomena': 1. feelings; 2. the evaluation of what is perceived; and 3. the 'germ' of a thought, viz., 'a notion not yet disentangled'. The differences between individual numinous events originate from the fact that these three 'ultimate phenomena' are unequally distributed in a singular occurrence, thus shaping the nature of the *sensus numinis* in each case. Hence, I would argue that the phenomena of the *'tremendum'* and the *'fascinosum'* can be compared and identified as perceptions occurring on the same level. The terms *'tremendum'* and *'fascinosum'* denote that they clearly refer to emotional responses elicited by the Numen. If we were to express these appellations in a value judgement, it would be false to phrase it like this: 'the Numen *is* something terrifying and awe-inspiring, or something blissful'. The value judgement must rather be expressed as follows: '*I perceive it*, it affects me *as* something terrifying and unfathomable, or *as* something amazingly blissful.' Apparently, the qualities attributed (or projected on) to the Numen are a hypostasis of the feeling(s) aroused by it. This indicates that the focus of the perception and hence of the evaluation of the Numen is clearly on the subjective side – a fact that must be borne in mind and which will prove to be important for the critical evaluation of the gnoseological significance of individual perceptions of the

Numen: In emotional perceptions of the Numen, strictly speaking, nothing of the essence of the Numen can be discerned cognitively. The Numen is an obscure 'point of reference' in emotional perceptions, which remains entirely shrouded in darkness. And emotional responses that are not perceived as the effect of something known fall outside the domain of knowledge.

Another distinctive quality of perceiving the Numen is termed the *'mirum'* by Rudolf Otto. For exploring it, however, we need a different approach. Unlike *'tremendum'* and *'fascinosum'*, the *'mirum'* is a phenomenon that does not spring from the realm of feelings; hence *'mirum'* is not an emotional term, but rather a conceptual ideogram originating from the primordial knowledge that there are final thresholds to human reason and knowledge. The awareness of this liminal situation is both an existential and a gnoseological facticity. The Numen is the Mystery, the wholly Other, the 'All-encompassing', the Irrational, Transintelligible; in brief: what is ultimately inaccessible to human reason and knowledge. This subliminal awareness is reflected in the responses to the Numen resulting in states of stupefying awe and amazement. Thus, an ultimate boundary is perceived in the given numinous event. The term *'mirum'* implies an assessment of the liminal situation. The numinous Object is here the Unknowable. The very act in which the unknowability of the numinous Object is cognitively grasped, the mysterious paradox of this numinous event becomes apparent. However, the recognition of a liminal situation must not be confused with the recognition of the 'whatness' of the Numen denoted by the liminal term *'mirum'*.

Another distinctive quality in perceiving the Numen is termed *'sanctum'* by Otto. This phenomenon, however, only needs to be addressed in passing in this context, because it refers essentially to an act of evaluation, but not to an act of recognition. This is different from the quality termed *'majestas'*, which differs from all the other appellations for the Numen considered so far, in that it refers to a genuine feature of the essence of the 'All-encompassing'. Because of this the phenomenon of the *'majestas'* occupies a rare, exceptional place in probing into the nature of the Numen, and thus calls for a detailed phenomenological and gnoseological analysis, which will be supplied in a separate chapter below.

At this stage of our enquiry, it might be objected that we have not given sufficient consideration to Otto's claim that the *sensus numinis* consists of a range of feelings which can only be understood as manifestations of a genuine *a priori*, and which are, as such, related in a very special way to an object signified as the Numen. We do not challenge the view that there are good reasons to assume that there are feelings residing in a domain *a priori*; what we do challenge, however, is the claim that this *a priori* has also a gnoseological dimension. This does not mean that we question the claim that there is such a thing as an experiential relation to the Numen. This relation can be thought of in terms of an ontic relation which, however, transcends the thresholds of human knowledge. This means that it is a special kind of [ontological] relation between two entities of being. But here we have entered the realm of metaphysics, which is not part of our scientific enquiry. Hence it is none of our concern to reflect on the metaphysical secret underlying this ontological relation, nor on the question to which 'existential' of being [as conceived by Heidegger][87] this relation is tied. These questions not only fall outside the scope of this study, but any discourse on these fundamental issues will also lead to the threshold by which philosophy and theology are divided.

The phenomenon of the Numinous, however, is beyond any doubt an empirical fact. Perceptions of the Numen are a pivotal and inalienable foundation of religious life; and the significance of encounters with the Numen is evident and documented in the rise and development of all world religions in the history of humanity. The gnoseological importance of this phenomenon, however, consists merely of the fact that the liminal situation has been exalted and turned into a borderline concept, at which rare emotional responses are directed. If we assess the various attributes ascribed to the Numen in view of their cognitive value, we can see that they are merely value judgements, which can be inferred *a priori* from the given liminal situation. This means that these value judgements merely affirm that the numinous Object is entirely 'transintelligible' and that it can never be 'objectified'. We can thus endorse what has been stated above:

---

87 [Note: Albrecht elaborates his critical response to Heidegger's existentialist philosophy in some detail in Part III of this book. – FKW.]

The perception of an existential borderline situation along with the awareness of the confines of human knowledge must by no means be equated with the recognition of the essence, or 'whatness', of a Transcendental Reality.

The results of these considerations can be epitomized in the following theses:

THESIS 47: *In a numinous perception it is neither the 'isness' of the 'All-encompassing' nor its 'whatness' that are experienced, nor is the 'whatness' recognized a priori without being perceived.*

THESIS 48: *In a numinous event an existential threshold, and along with it a gnoseological frontier, emerge in a unique way.*

This threshold becomes apparent in the unique feelings of dreadful awe and love elicited by numinous mystery. This liminal existential situation is extended by thinking to a borderline concept that refers to a total 'otherness' which eludes the grasp of reason and understanding.

THESIS 49: *The recognition of a threshold does not involve any recognition of the essence of the Transcendental.*

These considerations on the gnoseological aspect of numinous perception should not be ended without having reflected critically on the semantics of the term '*sensus numinis*'.

The Latin word '*sensus*' means literally 'sense', as in the expression 'sense perception', and thus refers to a capacity of the natural senses. This notion, however, does not apply to the term '*sensus numinis*', which is why Otto's name is misleading and flawed. Sense perceptions are faculties of the sense organs, which enable the sensual perception of the 'real external world'. The '*sensus numinis*', by contrast, is elicited by inner perceptions rather than triggered by external ones. It has become a commonplace to contrast metaphorically the world of external perception to the world of inner perception. By way of analogy, it can be conceded to designate the modes of mystical experience as 'mystical sense'. What these various concepts of the 'senses' have in common is that they are all based on an empirical encounter with a concrete object, hence on an act of experience. The emotional perception of a numinous relation is, however, (as we have shown) not based on an encounter with a concrete object, and thus by definition no 'experience' but merely a diffuse mode of perception. For this reason, the usage of the word 'sense' in Otto's concept is patently flawed.

However, if the word 'sensus' is understood to signify 'feeling' in translation, Otto's term is more adequate, because in that case *'sensus numinis'* suggests an emotional relation directed at the Numen. But still, the term *'sensus numinis'* is ambivalent, not least because the 'sense of feeling' can easily be transformed as to signify an active mode of feeling, which does not apply to the *'sensus numinis'*, which is an entirely passive mode of feeling, in that the perceiver responds emotionally to the felt presence and/or nearness of the Numen. From this follows:

THESIS 50: *The term 'sensus numinis' has to be replaced by the term 'numinous perception'.*

Finally, as to question 3: Though our endeavour to classify numinous phenomena systematically for the purposes of our gnoseological enquiry is likely to provoke criticism in some of its details, on the whole the approach chosen provides pervasive criteria for placing the realm of numinous perception within the domain of mysticism. The entire range of mystical recognition is composed of a rather complex cluster of diverse modes of cognition, which are sustained by different varieties of mystical experience. We have already come across and outlined some of these varieties of mystical experience: The 'pictorial vision', the 'vision(s) of L/light', as well as auditory mystical experiences (locutions), and the experience of 'Presence'. Mystical experience thus encompasses many different modes of experiencing and is the real core of mystical recognition. Around this core, and based upon it, we may also come across within that range of mystical recognition modes of cognitive perception that can also be encountered outside the realm of mystical experience, for instance, in the area of sense perception. It is not necessary to refer to the latter individually, as they can – if at all – be classified only as secondary modes of mystical experience.

We have shown above that numinous perceptions cannot be classified as instances of 'experience', and, consequently, they cannot be a part of the core of cognitive mystical experience. However, this raises the question as to whether numinous perception, which has been attributed only a subordinate gnoseological rank, can be assigned a place within the domain of mystical recognition at all. It is true that, in mystical tradition, mystics have generally attributed to numinous encounters a very special rank: The perception of numinous feelings in a mystical event are seen by the mystics as a pivotal criterion for a mystical occurrence to be considered genuine. The crucial question as to whether a mystical experience can be proved to be authentic is answered affirmatively if a numinous response is aroused in a mystical encounter, which originates in the *a priori* awareness of the nature of the 'All-encompassing'. And, conversely, if a mystical event does not evoke a numinous response, the authenticity of a mystical event is questioned as a matter of principle.

The importance of numinous perceptions in the context of mysticism is, however, not be adequately acknowledged if they are reduced to the aspect of mystical cognition. After all, the cognitive mystical relation to the 'All-encompassing' is only an integral part of the entire structure of the mystical relation. The fact that our investigation has intentionally been confined to the cognitive aspect of the mystical relation should not prevent us, however, from expounding on the relevance of numinous perception for the existential domain of mysticism, which exists beyond the gnoseological sphere of mysticism.

The response to the Numen on the level of feelings, and the acts of interpreting and evaluating the emotional response to the Numen, are joined to result in an overall perception which inevitably surfaces in a mystical event, whenever the Numen is encountered in a concrete mystical experience – not least because this composite occurrence is also a fundamental element of any religious experience. A numinous perception does not depend on the 'sense of presence', nor on the givenness of the 'quiet state of alertness' to emerge. However, in a mystical event in which the Presence of the 'All-encompassing' is empirically grasped as real, when the 'experiencing I' is immersed in the 'quiet state of alertness', the two experiential relations become intertwined, i.e., that of the perceived religious relation and the one of the experiential mystical relation – and this is a phenomenon that for the mystic has long-term after-effects which often determine the course of his/her future existence. The deeply felt alterations in the perceiver's emotional condition, which are elicited by his/her response to the Numen, usually trigger a significant stage of the mystic's spiritual development termed 'conversion'. Without being overwhelmed with 'fear and trembling', without the 'stupor' and the 'shudder' at the mystery, without the annihilation of the self, and without being overwhelmed by bliss, there would be no mystical purification, no illumination and no process of 'conversion'.

The Vision of the 'Majestas'

The realm of emotional responses to the Numen is always alert and may surface during a mystical encounter, responding adequately and in proper proportion to the nature of the mystical event. It has been claimed that the features of the individual response to a *mystical* event are unevenly distributed, i.e., for instance, that responses of the *'tremendum'*, such as being overpowered by 'tremor' or shuddering dread, are less frequently encountered than instances of the *'fascinosum'*, like being transported into a state of ineffable bliss. I am not convinced, however, that this claim holds true. The records of the mystics rather show that mystical events are more elicited by the unexpected 'arrival' of the 'All-encompassing' in the perceiver's consciousness [translated into psychological parlance], which is more often than not a devastating experience, and thus a genuine manifestation of the *'mysterium tremendum'*; moreover, several varieties of ecstatic mystical experience do not merely consist of states of bliss, but the sense of bliss can be supplanted by the sense of being overwhelmed and annihilated by an unfathomable Power and/or Abyss.

The mystical records examined refer unusually often to the experiential quality which has been termed *'majestas'* by Otto. We shall consider this in some detail, as this is the final aspect of numinous perception we shall deal with. In an emotional numinous event, regardless of whether its prevailing qualities are those of a *'tremendum'* or of a *'fascinosum'*, it is the perceiver's subjective response to the Numen that determines the perception. The predicative epithets for describing the quality of the *'tremedum'* or the *'fascinosum'* derive from the subjective realm of feelings. In perceiving the Numen as *'majestas'*, however, an objective aspect of the Numen becomes apparent. The phenomenon of the *'majestas'* – unlike that of the *'mirum'* and perception of 'the irrational, wholly other' – does not refer to a liminal situation, as it implies a quality of the 'whatness' of the Numen. Whereas *'tremendum'* refers to the terrifying responses evoked by the Numen, *'majestas'* is a concept that derives from rudimentary forms of thinking that spring from an emotional response; it is, in other words, what has been described by Otto as 'a concept not yet disentangled'. The phenomenon of the *'majestas'* thus envisages a genuine part of the essence of the Numen; it is elicited from intimations of the Numen's overwhelming power and ultimate force; in such an event, responses such as the 'awareness of one's creaturely nature' or 'of one's utter dependence' on the *'majestas'* are evoked. This means that *'majestas' as an aspect of the Numinous differs from all other features of the Numinous in that it embraces always and inevitably a gnoseological relationship to the essence of Numen.* Somehow, the individual must *know* something about this overwhelming power before he/she can respond to it emotionally. The question as to whether this knowledge is given *a priori*, or acquired *a posteriori* is not our concern here, as the focus of our study is on the nature of mystical perception, not numinous perception. *Mystical perception is a cognitive empirical event.* This fact alone may explain why the perception of the *'majestas'* is related in a special way to modes of cognitive perception encountered in the realm of mysticism. The *'majestas'* of the 'All-encompassing' is directly experienced in a mystical encounter. All modes of mystical experience are related to the experience of the *'majestas'*: the 'mystical vision', auditory mystical experience, and the somatic modes of mystical experience. This statement calls for some further explication:

1. The *'majestas'* perceived in a 'mystical vision': In this case, the perceiver beholds a pictorial shape or person-like image of the 'All-encompassing'. In this instance, the *'majestas'* is encountered physiognomically and is revealed in expressive gestures and/or facial traits.

2. The *'majestas'* perceived by 'inner hearing': In such an event, not only the content of what is spoken or heard and the special form of locution and/or auditory perception can be the direct impact of the overwhelming power of the Numen.

3. The *'majestas'* is perceived by the somatic and/or cognitive and emotional impact on the recipient. The event is an awe-inspiring encounter with the irresistible force of mystical effects [by 'the All-encompassing'] which are inflicted and to which there is neither resistance, nor escape; in perceiving the *'majestas'* the supreme power becomes directly manifest.

There is a fourth variety of perceiving the *'majestas'*, which is, however, not a direct but a mediated one. The *'majestas'* can be the 'content' of a mystically infused 'insight'. The supreme power of the *'majestas'* is cognitively grasped in a mystical 'intuition'. Such a mystically 'infused insight' into the *'majestas'* of God affects and arouses all the other responses to the Numen.

The result of our classification of the ways in which the *'majestas'* may become manifest in a mystical event can thus be summarized: The perception of the *'majestas'* is not necessarily linked to a visionary experience. As described in text 74 below, the *'majestas'* appears to have been perceived cognitively in a moment of 'illumination', i.e., by means of a mystically 'infused insight'. This text does not allow any definitive conclusion, however, as to whether the 'illumination' was accompanied by a pictorial vision, in which the ultimate sovereignty and omnipotence of God also became apparent physiognomically. The expression "the glance of God's majesty", though, seems to suggest this. Text 75 provides a description of a mystical experience in which the 'sense of Presence' is intertwined with a 'pictorial vision', in which an awe-inspiring glimpse of the *'majestas'* is revealed to the perceiver:

> *Text 74* (Christine Lucie, diary entry 25 April 1888. 231): "This morning, during Holy Communion, my soul was gratified with *a glimpse of God's Majesty*. This Majesty was of grandeur beyond compare, and I perceived it with the illuminating light of faith, not by an external sensation, and saw how the cosmos was shaken before It…"

> *Text 75* (Christine Lucie, diary entry 3 August 1897. 310): "I humbled myself and worshipping Him with ardent devotions, saying to Him: 'My God!!!' – I had scarcely uttered these words, *when my soul was transported into His Presence and became instantly enthralled and entranced*, because *the sight* by which He revealed Himself was so elevating and overpowering." [Italics as added by Albrecht. Translation supplied.]

Text 76 is a record by Teresa of Avila of a genuine 'pictorial vision' of Christ, which she claims to have been 'infused' in her mind. In this vision features of God incarnate were revealed as well as features of God's omnipotence and sovereignty, which are described in terms of phenomena visibly perceptible, including special traits of the figure of the Redeemer:

> *Text 76* (Teresa of Avila, *Vida*, main chapter 28, 265 and 266): "6. Depending on the degree of clarity, the Lord has preferred to reveal Himself to me – what I beheld at the time appeared to be merely a picture; more often, however, it was not merely a picture, but Christ Himself seemed to reveal Himself to me ...
>
> 7. ... Sometimes (however), the Lord appears *in such a great Majesty that it is impossible for me to doubt that it is He Himself.* This happens especially after I have received Holy Communion ... Then He reveals Himself as the supreme Majesty of His abode so that the soul feels entirely annihilated, as it were, and absorbed in Christ. Oh, my Jesus, who can describe the Majesty by which Thou revealest Thyself? ...
>
> 8. ... I also declare: This vision, by which our Lord wishes to reveal a part of His Majesty, is so overpowering that I think it could not possibly be endured, if the Lord did not assist the soul in a supernatural manner, transporting her into a state of ecstatic rapture. Though the sense of being overwhelmed by this vision may later be forgotten, the Majesty and Beauty remain so deeply engrained in the soul that they can never be forgotten anymore, unless if the Lord wants the soul to suffer a spell of aridity and dereliction ... [Italics as added by Albrecht. Translation supplied.]

The experience of being overpowered arouses in the perceiver the deep awareness of his/her creaturely nature, but it also elicits the numinous feelings of dread and awe, as well as a profound sense of bliss. With these responses we have returned to the domain of responding feelings, which cannot, as a whole (as explained above), be attributed to an *experience* of the '*majestas*'.

> *Text 77* (Symeon the New Theologian, *Hymn 3*):[88] "... I behold the beauty, I behold the splendour, I am contemplating the light of your grace, and I am staring at the inexplicable flash of lightning, and I am beside myself

---

88 [Source: BUBER, Martin. *Ekstatische Konfessionen*. Leipzig: Insel, 1921. 57. – FKW.]

when I recognize what person I have been, and what a person, oh wonder, I have become: and I worship and contemplate myself; and as I worship you, I am frightened of me and confused and desperate, not knowing where I should be seated ..." [Italics as added by Albrecht. Translation supplied.]

It is reasonable to review one's own claims from time to time, and especially if new perspectives and new arguments have turned up. In my search for potential objections to the theses proposed here, some claims appear to be at variance with the findings of my earlier study. This applies especially to the claim that the emotional responses elicited by the Numen have no gnoseological import. In the earlier study [i.e., *Psychology of Mystical Consciousness*] we have discerned altogether eleven 'forms of inner sight', which correspond to eleven 'forms of arriving' [i.e., the forms in which an 'All-encompassing' can be perceived as 'arriving' in the vista of 'inner sight']. One of these 'forms of arriving' is that of 'responding feelings'. Given the fact that the 'arrival' of a non-mystical object in consciousness can be perceived in the form of 'responding feelings', the question arises as to why the perception of numinous feelings given *a priori*, which are related to the Numen in a special way, should not likewise be classified as a 'form of arriving' in which the 'All-encompassing' is distinctly perceived. By critically examining this inconsistency, we shall see, however, that this incongruity is only an apparent one and that the validity of the thesis stipulated above can be further corroborated rather than falsified:

1. In our previous study, the approach was strictly a psychological-phenomenological and not a gnoseological one. The concept 'form of arriving' is exclusively a psychological concept. In the previous study we did not go beyond the confines of the psychology of consciousness, nor did we endeavour to establish gnoseological varieties of 'inner sight'. Our enquiry aimed exclusively at establishing a systematic order of all the phenomena that are empirically encountered in the realm of inward perception, viz., 'inner sight' ["Innenschau"]. Although an emotional response to the 'All-encompassing' has as such no gnoseological value, it is empirically a 'form of inner sight' and as such a mode of 'arriving'.[89]

---

[89] [Cf. ALBRECHT, Carl. *Psychology of Mystical Consciousness*. Ed. and trans.

2. In empirical reality the structure of 'inner sight' is composed of several entwined modes of 'arriving'. It is possible that 'responsive feelings' can, psychologically speaking, prevail in a concrete empirical event; however, if this happens, what is perceived in 'inner sight' is nonetheless always intertwined with other modes of 'arriving', such as metaphoric perceptions, symbols, intuitions, and diverse somatic perceptions. The gnoseological value in perceiving the 'All-encompassing' does not result from the 'responding feelings' evoked by it, but from other concurrent modes of inward perception which do have some gnoseological import. The claim postulated in the previous study was moreover couched in sufficiently cautious terms to obviate any incompatibility with the proposition stated in this book. It says that the 'experiencing I' perceives what 'arrives' in the vista of 'inner sight' in the 'quiet state of alertness' with supreme clarity, whereby the alterations of its own mental condition appear as 'objects arriving', which are in part acknowledged as and/or attributed to distinctive qualities of the 'All-encompassing'.[90]

3. Feelings alone do not recognize anything. The function of 'inner sight' can only provide cognitive insights because cognitive modes of perception are integral parts of the entire range of its experiential capacity [along with emotional modes]. It is helpful in this context to refer (by way of analogy) to an experiment conducted by 'gestalt psychology', in which figurines are placed in a dark room and presented to subjects in different lighting conditions so that, finally, even the outlines of the figurines are eclipsed by twilight. This borderline situation in sense-perception can be likened to the stages of inward perception in relation to an 'object arriving': There is a temporal phase in which the 'object arriving' is grasped as surfacing from darkness, resulting in a vague sense of it as present; however, nothing of the 'whatness' of the 'object' known to be present can be recognized. In such a liminal situation

---

by F. K. Woehrer. New York: Crossroad, 2019. 234. – FKW.]
90 [Cf. ALBRECHT, Carl. *Psychology of Mystical Consciousness*. Ed. and trans. by F. K. Woehrer. New York: Crossroad, 2019. 251f. – FKW.]

of suspense and uncertainty responding feelings are aroused in the perceiver – notably fear, awe or wistful longing – or else blissful expectation; and these responding feelings can become so intense that they *are assumed to be* a form of recognition.

There is yet another potential objection to the seemingly controversial claim that numinous feelings have no cognitive import. This may be phrased in terms of the following interrogation: 'Are numinous feelings always merely responses to something already known, whether this is based on a borderline situation previously experienced, or on some prior knowledge of the presence and/or "whatness" of the "All-encompassing"?' This question hints at another mystical phenomenon, the one that mystics have termed 'mystical effects', or the 'impact' of a mystical encounter. Amongst the mystical 'effects' are some that reflect the impact on the perceiver's emotional condition. This means that we must distinguish carefully between phenomena effecting changes in feeling and emotional states that can be traced to responses to the Numen, and alterations in feeling and the emotional states which originate from immediate effects impinged suddenly by a mystical event. If we put both varieties of changing emotions to the test by asking if they comply with our psychological definition of 'experience', we shall see clearly that the emotions elicited by the perception of the Numen are subjective responses elicited in the perceiver in which nothing of the essence of the 'object' encountered is recognized or grasped empirically. The alterations in feeling and the emotional condition, by contrast, perceived as 'arriving' and/or intruding and permeating and overwhelming the perceiver's consciousness at the first intimations of a mystical encounter, is plainly an instance of 'experience' as the occurrence is cognitively grasped with absolute certainty as having been 'effected' by a Power from beyond the confines of the individual consciousness.

We are going to explore the phenomenon of 'mystical effects' in some detail in the next chapter. We shall refer to it by the collective term 'perception of mystical effects'. What needs to be added to the chapter above is that the foregoing considerations confirm the claim that numinous feelings have no gnoseological import concerning the nature of the Numen, whereas mystically 'infused' feelings and emotional changes do have gnoseological significance which derives from an indirect cognitive relation to the 'All-encompassing'.

The Perception of Mystical Effects
["Das Gewahren Mystischer Wirkungen"]

The preceding considerations on 'mystically infused insight' and the modes of 'numinous perception' have resulted in the verdict that neither of these two phenomena qualifies as a variety of mystical experience. In the present chapter we shall be concerned with an entirely different category of mystical experience: the perception of 'mystical effects'. Yet before we begin with our enquiry, it is helpful to briefly summarize the major findings established so far. Mystical experience encompasses numerous varieties, which are composed of various individual types of experience. Our enquiry started with visual (i.e., image-based) varieties of mystical experience. We shall now focus on the class of 'imageless mystical visions', i.e., modes of mystical perception without pictorial or visible content. Yet irrespective of this special focus of the subsequent enquiry, we shall be required to address some other modes of mystical experience as well in passing, since contrasting 'non-visual' to 'visual mystical experiences' may yield valuable insights into the phenomenological framework of both varieties.

Until now we have identified two non-visual types of mystical experience: 1. Verbal and non-verbal auditory mystical experiences, in which distinct words, or word-sequences ('locutions'), or sounds (or both) are heard inwardly. Though aural experiences differ significantly from 'mystical visions', they share some phenomenological characteristics. 2. 'Perceptions of mystical effects', i.e., the experience of some transforming on the emotional, and/or somatic, cognitive and/or mental state of the perceiver. This variety has an entirely different phenomenological structure than visual and aural mystical experiences. Unlike the former, 'mystical effects' constitute a rather opaque and veiled experience which is difficult to grasp phenomenologically. This fact, however, must not deter us from trying to elucidate the phenomenon, not least because spontaneous 'mystical effects' and life-transforming long-term 'after-effects' of mystical events are an integral part of most mystical experiences. The insights gained by an in-depth enquiry should enable us not only to understand all varieties of mystical experience better, but also to comprehend the more elusive peripheral phenomena, notably that of the 'mystical insight', and some of the 'numinous responses' evoked by a mystical event. Owing to their indefinite nature, 'mystical effects' are properly to be attributed to the peripheral domain of mysticism, i.e., the 'twilight zone' between mystical experience and the realm of numinous perception.

'Mystical visions', 'mystical auditions' and 'mystical effects' are, psychologically speaking, perceived in the vista of 'inner sight' ["Innenschau"]. These three kinds of mystical experience were classified in our earlier study, *Psychology of Mystical Consciousness*, as 'forms of inner sight' (out of a total of eleven forms identified). As stated earlier, the term *'sight'* refers to a composite mode of inward perception, in which visual phenomena prevail, though they are often intertwined with 'intuitions' and 'responding feelings'. The phenomenon of *'inner hearing'* is a less complex mode than 'inner sight' and is usually linked only with 'responding feelings'. The experience of 'mystical effects', finally, is a somatic form of perception, in which *the impact of a mystical force* is experienced as operating within or upon the perceiver from outside. This is a much more complex experience than 'visions' and 'auditions' and encompasses illuminating flashes of 'self-understanding', cognitive insights and intense emotional responses.

The term 'mystical effects' refers, in the broadest sense, to the entire range of mystical phenomena in which the perceiver experiences that something is 'infused', 'instilled' or even forcefully 'imposed' on him/her. In addition to the 'mystical effects' already referred to, they include spontaneous (and often dramatic) alterations in the state of consciousness, e.g., the spontaneous interpolation of the serene state of 'quiet alertness', or the state of ecstatic rapture, occurring 'out of the blue'.[91] We shall follow in our classification the guidelines of

---

91 [Note: The expression 'out of the blue' in this context refers to a spontaneous mystical event; it was coined by the Oxford scholar Sir Alister Hardy in his empirical study on varieties of religious and spiritual experience. See HARDY, Sir Alister. *The Spiritual Nature of Man. A Study of Contemporary Religious Experience*. Oxford:

the mystics, and thus confine the range of 'mystical effects' to ones approved by them as authentic: 'mystical effects' that cause extraordinary, and often instantaneous alterations of emotional states and the sudden upsurge of intense feelings; 'mystical effects' affecting the power of volition; and 'effects' transforming positively the perceiver's moral/religious attitudes and values, and having a lasting impact on his/her future orientation in life. Genuine 'mystical effects' can be released instantly during a mystical event, but occasionally they may become manifest only some time after the mystical event.

Owing to the opacity of the phenomenon, it is necessary to probe the nature of 'mystical effects' further. We shall explore especially the phenomenological structure of those 'mystical effects' that are encountered in *the transition zone embraced between the realm of mystical experience and 'mystical insights', on the one hand, and the sphere of 'numinous feelings', on the other*. In a 'mystical insight' something becomes known by 'intuition'. The knowledge conveyed is bestowed in the flash of a moment and does not involve any conscious empirical process. An 'insight', in other words, is recognized after the mystical event and perceived as an item of knowledge that has instantly been 'instilled'. For this reason, the term 'experience' does not apply in the narrow sense (as defined in this study). When a subject is exposed to 'mystical effects', he/she is aware of an ongoing unfamiliar occurrence and knows at the time that he/she is subjected to a 'foreign' power; he/she is unable to resist its impact on his/her will and state of consciousness. When a *'mystical insight'* is conveyed, however, some knowledge is instantly instilled without releasing a process of empirical perception. In the case of 'mystical effects', by contrast, the intellectual content is sparse and usually does not go beyond the mere awareness of emotional and somatic changes elicited by some unknown power assumed to reside outside the individual consciousness. The sophisticated phenomenological differentiation between 'mystical effects' and 'mystical insight' is indispensable for clarification. Therefore, we may now propose the following proposition: *It is an established fact that the 'content' transmitted in a 'mystical insight' cannot be experienced, whereas the 'content' of 'mystical effects' is immediately experienced in a concurrent process of perception.*

OUP, 1979. 76f. – FKW.]

As regards the phenomena of the transition zone between 'mystical effects' and 'numinous perception' we may state: *Changes in the emotional condition of the 'experiencing self', which are an emotional response to, or concomitant with a mystical event, are essentially different from the changes in feeling and emotional states that result from 'mystical effects'.* Thus, feelings evoked in response to a mystical encounter are not the result of 'mystical effects', as 'responding feelings' are – for instance, the sense of reassurance, feeling safe and secure, comforted, or joyful, being filled with ardent love, or transported into states of rapture and ecstasy elicited by the 'sight' of Supreme Beauty or the Sublime. This means that we can only speak of 'mystical effects' proper, when the feelings of joy, bliss, love and peace are consciously recognized in a concrete mystical event as emotions that have been mystically 'instilled' by the 'All-encompassing'. The phenomenological difference between 'responding feelings' and mystically 'instilled' emotions can alternatively be shown by relating them to the concept of 'perception'. When 'perceiving' numinous feelings, the surfacing of joy or love is perceived in the same way as joy and love are perceived when resulting from 'mystical effects'. The crucial difference, however, is that in a 'numinous perception' it is only the *responding feelings evoked in the given subject* that are perceived, whereas the feelings that result from 'mystical effects' are cognitively grasped to have been 'instilled' by a Power from outside the individual consciousness. Only the latter qualifies, by definition, as genuine a mode of *mystical experience.*

The perception of 'mystical effects', if considered as a single phenomenon not mingled with other phenomena, is nothing but a perceiver's passive experience of the change in his/her body and mind. This elementary form of experience becomes a mode of mystical cognition only when it is affiliated with a second phenomenon of mystical recognition: the clear cognitive awareness that the changes perceived originate from a 'mystical impact'. This knowledge about the 'mystical givenness' of the effects may surface in consciousness in two ways: it may be inferred retrospectively in a process of discursive thinking from the effects experienced, or the recognition of the mystical origin of these effects is immediately 'infused' by 'intuition' during the mystical event. In the former instance, the knowledge of the mystical provenance of these effects is inferred from the unique impact, notably the special qualities of bliss and love elicited, which cannot be compared with any previous experience in the perceiver's life. Because of these unique qualities the experience is acknowledged with great conviction as a genuine mystical event. In the case of the 'mystical intuition', however, the knowledge of its mystical origin is immediately 'instilled' and instantly evident.

It is only the latter form of acquiring knowledge that is relevant to our enquiry. We may thus claim that the experience of 'mystical effects' qualifies as genuine, if it is linked with the phenomenon of 'mystical intuition'. From these characteristics of 'mystical effects' it is evident that the phenomenological structure of this mode of mystical experience differs significantly from that of 'mystical visions', though both – seen from a gnoseological perspective – are oriented at the same final goal: To provide further insight into the essence of the 'mystical Object'. The phenomenological spectrum of 'mystical effects' is (as we have seen) considerably more multifaceted than that of 'mystical visions'. Though both can be claimed to be genuine varieties of mystical experience, 'mystical effects' are only based on a mediated relation to the 'mystical Object', whereas this relation in 'mystical visions' is an immediate one. In an experience of 'mystical effects', the cognitive relation to the ultimate Source is not directly experienced, but only grasped by way of its indirect impact on the perceiver, and in which the relation is partly grasped by means of 'intuitions' imparted by the 'mystical Object', and partly inferred rationally in a secondary process of cognition. *In an imageless 'mystical vision' an immediate cognitive relation between the perceiver and the 'All-encompassing' is given in a pure form without any intermixture with other cognitive modes of mystical experience.*

We will be able to say more about *the gnoseological significance of the perception of 'mystical effects'* if we relate this variety of mystical perception to the mystical experience of 'Presence'. In the mystical experience of 'Presence', a sense of the 'isness' and of the 'All-encompassing' is conveyed along with the awareness of its spatial presence, whereas the awareness of its 'whatness' remains sparse and obfuscated. It is our endeavour to elucidate the features of the 'whatness'. The crucial question in pursuing this aim is this one: Is it at all possible to grasp directly the 'whatness' of the 'All-encompassing'? And can there be at all a 'vision' of the essence of the 'All-encompassing'? In trying to find answers to these fundamental questions, we have come across some varieties of mystical experience in which a few features of the 'whatness' can be discerned at least *indirectly*. So far, we have discovered two varieties in which aspects of the 'whatness' become manifest: 1. auditory mystical experiences, and 2. the perception of 'mystical effects'. In the event of an auditory mystical experience, a message, or an express summons, is heard inwardly and intuitively identified as being related to, and having been issued by, the 'All-encompassing'. When perceiving 'mystical effects', a tangible impact is felt by the recipient, which is cognitively grasped as being related to the 'Presence' of the 'All-encompassing'. Jointly these mystical events expand the awareness of the 'whatness' of the 'All-encompassing'. 1. The 'imageless vision of Presence' and the concomitant intuitive knowledge of the 'Presence' of the 'All-encompassing' is linked with the inner hearing of 'locutions'. Though the 'Object' perceived cognitively as 'present' remains imageless and obfuscated, it can eventually be recognized as a 'mystical Object' on the basis of these locutions. Although it is true that there are 'locutions' that do not qualify as messages originating from the 'All-encompassing' [hence as originating beyond the realm of the individual consciousness], the mystics of [theistic] mystical traditions unanimously agree that there are 'locutions' which can, without any doubt, be identified as genuinely mystical. The intertwined experience of 'Presence' and the firm conviction of the mystical character of the auditory experience provide the overall experience with a high subjective degree of certainty. This, however, is no sufficient reason for acknowledging its veridical claim or its superior gnoseological relevance. 2. The cognitive awareness of 'Presence' is generally affiliated with the perception of 'mystical effects'. Together these two modes supply a full gnoseological structure in which the constituent elements corroborate and complement each other. This special phenomenological constellation has, however, given rise to the controversial claim that the perception of 'mystical effects' is especially suited for securing mystical knowledge, and that it must therefore be assigned a very high rank on the gnoseological scale. The view that 'mystical effects' have superior gnoseological import than visionary or auditory experiences has been upheld by mystics and used as a criterion of spiritual discernment. Thus 'mystical effects' that qualify as authentic had to be affiliated with the experience of God's Presence, whereas 'mystical effects' are identified as false and delusory, when they are destructive and can thus be traced to the impact of a demonic presence, or the presence of the Fiend. This approach to the 'discretion of spirits' seems to overrate the gnoseological rank of 'mystical effects'. Though this claim may be in line with mystical theology, it cannot be adopted by our scientific study, and for this reason we need to subject such claims by mystics to careful scrutiny. Sweeping statements like that of DeLangeac must therefore be treated with due caution: "God never reveals Himself in the noise of disquiet. If you witness such noise of unrest, you can be sure that it is not God."[92] The same holds true for the avowal of Christine Lucie: "Along with the ineffable feeling of His sweetness, the Lord infused into my soul again a deep sense of His Presence."[93] Yet on the whole it can be stated that 'mystical effects' are helpful empirical data for assessing the authenticity and cognitive value of mystical experiences.

Our analysis of joint mystical experiences of 'Presence' and 'mystical effects' has shown that their interlaced phenomenological structure is more complex than assumed at first glance. When we referred above to the immediate experience of God's Presence, we had to contrast this phenomenon from the cognitive awareness of Presence deriving from discursive thinking in the wake of perceiving 'mystical effects'. We were alerted to the fact that there are changes in the condition of the 'self' which seemed to point quite forcefully at the 'Presence' of the 'All-encompassing': These are particularly evident in a 'unitive mystical experience' in which the changes effected in the perceiver are so intense and exceptional that they cannot but be accounted for without the concurrent Presence of the 'All-encompassing'. Any person 'inundated' by the 'All-encompassing', and becoming immersed in it, or the experience of being permeated by it, experiences the 'Presence' dwelling within and no longer has any

---

92 'LANGEAC, Robert de' [Delage, Augustin]. *Geborgenheit in Gott. Aufzeichnungen eines zeitgenössischen Mystikers*. Trans. Hugo Härder. Einsiedeln: Benziger, 1952. Series Licht vom Licht, n.s. 2. 22.

93 'CHRISTINE, Lucie' [Boutle, Mathilde]. *Geistliches Tagebuch (1870–1908)*. Ed. Auguste Poulain, S.J. Trans. Romano Guardini. 3rd ed. Mainz: Grünewald, 1952. 211.

need to 'behold' it. That is, there is a mediated awareness of 'Presence', which is based on experience, but which is not an immediate recognition of 'Presence'.

After this short but important digression, we come back to the main topic of this chapter: the 'perception of mystical effects'. 'Mystical effects' are not only affiliated with the awareness of 'Presence', but also with pictorial and non-pictorial forms of 'mystical vision', which likewise expand the cognitive import of mystical events. Thus, the 'vision' of a pictorial representation of the 'All-encompassing', or the 'vision of the mystical Light', augment the reassurance that what is 'beheld' in the image of the vision is indeed the 'All-encompassing', if the 'vision' is at the same time supported by the experience of 'effects' that are intuitively grasped as 'arriving' from the 'All-encompassing'.

We have now sufficiently shown the importance of 'mystical effects' within the entire range of mystical experience. In the following, selected records by mystics are intended to illustrate 'mystical effects' resulting from the experience of 'infused love'. This is a typical and particularly convincing example for illustrating the overwhelming impact of 'mystical effects'. The encounter with 'mystical Love' allows us to recognize the devastating power and unexpected abruptness by which 'mystical effects' may intrude upon a mystic and result in a mystical event transforming the mental and emotional condition as well as the existential disposition of the recipient:

> *Text 78* (Teresa of Avila, *Vida*, main chapter 29, 277–79): "10. A short time later, the Lord began to show me more clearly (as He had promised me to do) that it is He Himself; and then *such ardent love for God began to burn in me* that I was unable to tell where it came from, for I had not made any effort to attain it; this love was rather entirely supernatural. I *saw myself* languishing with the desire to see God, and I could not think of any other way for attaining this blissful state than by death. The impulses and the impact of this love were so powerful that I was unaware of what I was doing – although they were not as strong and excruciating as the pangs and stirrings recorded previously; for nothing could satisfy me; I was unable to control myself and, in truth, I felt as if the soul were ripped off my body …
>
> 11. Anyone who has not yet experienced these forceful strivings cannot possibly understand them; for they are not like those occurring often during contemplative prayer, which upset the heart and appear to stifle the mind so that it is no longer able to control itself …

12. The stirrings and urges of which I will report now are entirely different from those occurring during contemplative prayer, as mentioned above. In this fire of love, *it is not merely us who feed it with pieces of wood, but it rather seems as if we were suddenly thrown into the fire ourselves to be consumed by the flames.* The soul does not cause the pain felt because of the absence of the Lord, but she is again and again pierced by an arrow through the innermost heart and through the entrails, so that she does not know any more what has happened and what is her will. The soul is only aware of languishing for God, and that the arrow appears to have been dipped into poison, which causes her to despise herself in favour of her love for the Lord, even so much that she desires to sacrifice her life for Him. It is impossible to tell how the Lord inflicts wounds on the soul, nor how immeasurably great the pains are she is suffering at the time. The soul does not know what is happening to her, and yet the pain is at the same time so sweet that there is no joy in this life that is more blissful. The soul desires to die from this sickness forever."

Text 79 (Teresa of Avila, Fifth Report to Padre Rodrigo Alvarez, 1576): "16. Another widespread form of devotion involves a certain kind of wounding, in which the soul believes to be pierced through the heart by an arrow, or through herself. This wound causes the greatest pain, so that the soul cannot but cry out aloud; but the suffering is also so sweet that the soul does not want to be without it anymore. This pain, however, does not affect the corporal senses ... it is rather felt in the soul only ..."[94]

'All-encompassing Love' is mystically 'infused' and thus differs – in its experiential quality – fundamentally from any kind of 'natural love'. Or, in the words of DeLangeac: "If you could only know the difference between natural love, even to Jesus, and supernatural, 'infused' love!"[95]

Text 80 (Christine Lucie, diary entry 18 August 1882. 76): "This morning, shortly after having received Holy Communion, my soul was seized by such a burning fire of love for Jesus that I thought I would pass out of my mind. But *the full power of this sacred force* lasted only a few seconds so that I did not lose consciousness. This happens now and again."

---

94 [Note: This passage has been taken from *The Life of St. Teresa of Jesus of the Order of Our Lady of Carmel. Written by Herself: St. Teresa of Avila*. Trans. from the Spanish by David Lewis. 3rd ed., London: Baker, 1904. 270. – FKW.]

95 'LANGEAC, Robert de' [Delage, Augustin]. *Geborgenheit in Gott. Aufzeichnungen eines Zeitgenössischen Mystikers*. Trans. Hugo Härder. Einsiedeln: Benziger, 1952. Series Licht vom Licht, n.s. 2. 26.

These descriptions of mystical experiences clearly show that 'mystical visions' are often intertwined with 'mystical effects' and their 'after-effects', which corroborate the perceiver's confidence that the entire mystical event has been genuine. Teresa of Avila refers repeatedly to diverse exceptional 'effects' she has been exposed to, and these effects are understood by her as irremediable 'signs' confirming that her visionary experiences have indeed been genuine.[96] In the treatise *The Way of Perfection* Teresa states: "God always enriches the soul that is visited by Him";[97] and elsewhere she says: "Those who practice contemplative prayer are (if their contemplation is genuine) always filled with great love, which may manifest itself, for example, in the form of a mighty blaze, which, however, does not destroy anything but only emanates a great radiance. If it were otherwise, we would have to be in great sorrow."[98]

The experience of 'infused love' is for the [theistic] mystic doubtless one of the most supreme divine gifts, and the one that has the most persevering impact on the recipient. For this the phenomenon of 'mystically infused love' is best suited for illustrating the nature of 'mystical effects'. Mystically 'infused love' is moreover a phenomenon by which the genuineness of a mystical event can be gauged persuasively, although there are certainly several other 'mystical effects' by which the authenticity of a mystical event can be assessed. Other criteria by which the authenticity of a mystical occurrence can be discerned include events in which the perceiver is passively overwhelmed by 'infused peace', 'mystical calmness', the instantaneous 'growth of humility', or the loss of self-awareness.

THESIS 51: *Effects are 'given' changes in feeling and volition.*

THESIS 52: *'Mystical effects' are changes in feeling and volition*

---

96 Cf. THERESIA von JESU. *Sämtliche Schriften. Neue Deutschsprachige Ausgabe.* 6 vols. Munich: Kösel, 1935–1958. Trans. Aloysius Alkofer. Munich: Kösel 1952. Vol. V, 175ff. and vol. I, 267. [Translation provided.]

97 THERESIA von JESU. *Sämtliche Schriften. Neue Deutschsprachige Ausgabe.* 6 vols. Munich: Kösel, 1935-1958. Trans. Aloysius Alkofer. Munich: Kösel 1952. Vol. VI, 192. [Translation provided.]

98 THERESIA von JESU. *Sämtliche Schriften. Neue Deutschsprachige Ausgabe.* 6 vols. Munich: Kösel, 1935-1958. Trans. Aloysius Alkofer. Munich: Kösel 1952. Vol. VI, 205. [Translation provided.]

that are 'mystically instilled'; this means that they are distinctly perceived as having been 'given', and thus understood as having been 'imparted' by the 'All-encompassing'.

THESIS 53: *The perception of effects is – from the perspective of the psychology of consciousness – composed of three modes of inner perception [viz., 'inner sight']: the somatic mode, the mode of feeling, and the cognitive mode of self-understanding.*

THESIS 54: *The cognitive experience of 'mystical effects' embraces 1. the plain perception of 'effects', and 2. the knowledge that the ultimate source of these effects is the 'All-encompassing', which is either logically inferred from the impact witnessed, or 'instilled' directly in a flash of 'mystical insight'.*

THESIS 55: *The cognitive experience of 'mystical effects' is a distinct, separate variety of mystical experience, and as such it is to be placed alongside both 'mystical visions' and 'mystical auditions'.*

THESIS 56: *The cognitive experience of 'mystical effects' is an experience of the impact of the 'All-encompassing', but it is not (as this is the case with the 'imageless mystical vision') a mode of recognition in which the 'All-encompassing' is experienced as 'present'.*

THESIS 57: *The experience of 'mystical effects' can be affiliated with any other variety of mystical experience.*

THESIS 58: *In a concrete mystical event, the various individual modes of mystical experience involved tend to sustain each other, thus endorsing the conviction of the truth of the mystical event.*

Review and Future Direction of Our Enquiry

Our enquiry both has a broad and a more specific thematic concern. The broad concern encompasses the area termed 'mystical recognition'; the more specific concern is devoted to the phenomenon of the 'mystical vision'. We have so far established that the 'mystical vision' is only one amongst several varieties of mystical experience – albeit a highly distinguished one. We also know that mystical recognition is sustained by several modes of mystical perception. The domain of 'mystical visions' can phenomenologically be divided into two categories: 'visions' with pictorial content and 'imageless (non-pictorial) visions'. The latter will now occupy us increasingly.

It has been relatively easy to determine the pivotal characteristics of a 'pictorial vision'; it is much more difficult to elucidate the essential features of 'mystical visions' that are devoid of images and any concrete visual content. As we shall see, we will be faced with a number of intricate problems. Already the term 'imageless vision' is ambivalent and oxymoronic and calls for clarification. The concept provokes the question as to how something can be perceived visually, if there is no visual 'object' to be seen.

A 'mystical vision' is, in the widest sense, a type of mystical experience in which the 'experiencing I', absorbed in the 'quiet state of alertness', 'beholds' an object in the vista of 'inner sight' ["Innenschau"] that is mystically 'infused' [i.e., perceived as 'arriving' from the realm beyond the individual consciousness]. It is an inward perception that is analogous to external sense perception. This analogy, however, does not apply to the 'content' of the visionary experience. Therefore, we need to explore the phenomenon of 'inner sight' further by juxtaposing the characteristics of the mode of inner perception in a 'mystical vision' to that of a 'mystical audition'.

Following this contrastive analysis, we shall divide the entire range of phenomena featuring typically in a 'visual' experience, and phenomena pertaining typically to an 'auditory' mystical experience. As the two modes of inner perception are intertwined in different degrees in empirical reality, there is inevitably a graded transition zone. In the outermost zone, it is either aural phenomena that prevail in the event of a pure 'auditory mystical' experience, and respectively, it is visual phenomena that occupy the realm of 'inner sight' entirely in a purely visionary mystical experience. In this case, visual and auditory mystical events are entirely separate types of experience. If we proceed towards the 'middle' of the phenomenological spectrum, there is a zone in which aural and visual mystical phenomena are interwoven. 'Auditory inner perception' is an imaginative mode of 'inner hearing', which corresponds in the realm of 'visionary perception' to the mode of 'image-based beholding'. At the phenomenological threshold of 'aural inner perception' the auditory phenomena are reduced to zero, 'inner hearing' becomes soundless, and is thus transformed into the silent awareness of 'in-coming' ideas and non-verbal thoughts. This liminal event is classified as an 'intellectual intuition'.

This corresponds in the realm of 'visions' to the mere awareness of a blank, empty mental space, i.e., a state of consciousness in which there is no 'object' anymore to be 'beheld' in 'inner sight'. The only 'content' the perceiver is aware of is 'incoming' ideas and insights; hence this imageless type of 'mystical vision' has been termed *'visio intellectualis'* in western mystical tradition.[99]

The more 'inner hearing' advances towards the pole of visionary experience, and, conversely, the more a 'vision' advances towards the opposite pole of 'hearing', the more clearly the differences come to the fore. Both are passive modes of mystical experience: the recipient is passively overcome by phenomena 'arriving' in consciousness. The 'content' of the experience is thus clearly perceived as something 'given': the words heard inwardly in an auditory mystical experience are cognitively grasped as being 'infused' or 'instilled', and the perceiver is aware of being 'spoken to'; similarly, in a 'pictorial mystical vision' the images, symbols and pictures appearing in 'inner sight' are experienced as 'objects' bestowed, or impinged on the perceiver. However, the notion of the 'givenness' of these mystical gifts is part of the mystic's religious faith: he or she knows that no 'mystical vision' and no 'locution' could be genuine unless it is imbued with the intuitive awareness that it has been 'bestowed' by God. Despite these analogies, 'auditory' and 'visionary' mystical experiences hinge on different receptive functions: auditive phenomena, whether single words, spoken instructions, a summons, prophetic or revelatory messages, are cognitively grasped by the capacity of 'inner hearing', whereas visions – whether pictorial or imageless – are 'beheld' in the vista of 'inner sight' and thus depend on the capacity of 'inner sight'.

This rather detailed phenomenological comparison between 'mystical hearing' and 'mystical vision' was necessary as it provided

---

99 [Note: The tripartite division of 'visions' in Christian mystical theology into *visio corporalis*, i.e., an apparition in bodily likeness that is seen with the physical eyes, *visio imaginaria* (or *spiritualis*), i.e., a pictorial vision perceived by the 'inner eye', and *visio intellectualis*, i.e., the imageless, purely intellectual awareness of the Divine, can be traced to St. Augustine's commentary on the *raptus* of St. Paul (2 Cor. 12:2–4) in *De Genesi ad Litteram*. – Cf. NEWMAN, F. X. "St. Augustine's Three Visions and the Structure of Commedia." *Modern Language Notes* 82 (1967): 58–61. – FKW.]

some important foundations for our understanding of another pivotal mystical phenomenon – that of 'mystical insight'. 'Mystical insight', to begin with, is not a separate variety of mystical experience, but an inevitable integral part of any genuine mystical event.

As explained above, the ultimate liminal variety of 'mystical hearing' is without words and sounds; hence the intellectual perception of an idea or of non-verbal thoughts, which are perceived as 'arriving' in consciousness from a domain outside the individual self. For instance, when the thought that the 'All-encompassing' is absolute Wholeness and the ultimate Ground of Being is mystically 'infused' in the perceiver in the 'quiet state of alertness' ["Versunkenheit"], it is phenomenologically, strictly speaking, to be classified as a mode of 'inner hearing' when the perceptive mode of 'listening-to-intimations-inside' prevails. Yet irrespective of this phenomenological fact, it is more pertinent to classify the phenomenon as 'mystical insight' when an 'insight' is imparted in a flash and instantly known to be true and perceived as originating from the realm of thought rather than from intimations listened to inwardly.

The fact that an 'in-*sight*' is in some way intertwined with a visionary experience is implied in the lexeme 'insight'. When an 'insight' arrives in the mind instantaneously, the idea or the train of thought appears, as it were, visually, albeit non-pictorially in 'inner sight', and thus the occurrence has some affinity to a visionary experience. However, what is encountered in an 'imageless mystical vision' differs nonetheless from a 'mystical insight' in that the visual element is more pronounced in it and tends to persevere. Moreover, an 'imageless mystical vision' is interlinked with the sense of Presence, and what is cognitively grasped does not originate from the realm of thinking, but from the visual awareness (however fleeting) of an elusive 'object'. The awareness of the omnipresence of God, for instance, which is cognitively grasped in a 'mystical intuition', is something entirely different from the experience of the non-visual Presence beheld inwardly in an imageless 'mystical vision'. In the former, the thought instilled by intuition *denotes* the same empirical reality which is in the latter the 'object' of the immediate experience of Presence. It is true, however, that it is very difficult to portray the differences between these two elusive mystical experiences. However, the foregoing considerations have at least yielded a few conclusive findings:

1. The further we have proceeded on our path, which has started out in the transition zone between visual sense perception and 'pictorial vision', in the direction of the domain of 'imageless vision', the sparser and more elusive the phenomenological structure of the 'mystical vision' has become. If we continue along this path, there will inevitably come a juncture at which the mystical occurrence can – phenomenologically – no longer be classified as a 'visionary experience'. But as long as we stay within the scope of the 'imageless vision', our perspective must be expanded, and we need to ask, if any phenomena are involved in an 'imageless vision', by which the concept of the 'mystical vision' as defined here might be corroborated. As we shall see, there are several phenomena that are contiguous with visionary experience and can be used for further elucidation. One of these is the 'mystical insight', which is a borderline phenomenon in which the characteristics of visionary perception can be discerned in the incipient stage, but which are eventually dissolved.

2. In the previous considerations I have refrained from linking the individual types of vision within the entire spectrum of 'visions' to the experience of 'Presence'. It has been established, however, that the experience of 'Presence' is an important component of a wide range of mystical events, and that the experiential quality of a mystical experience is 'coloured' and transformed by it. The experience of 'Presence' may thus serve as a criterion of discernment between different varieties of mystical experience. It is, however, important to remember that the experience of 'Presence' must not be mixed up with a 'mystical intuition', in which the knowledge about the 'Presence' is instilled, but not experienced, and that the experience of the mystical 'Presence' can never be divorced from an 'imageless mystical vision'. This is again different in 'auditory mystical experiences': A 'mystical locution' – even if it is wholly intellectual in nature – is always affiliated with the sense of the mystical 'Presence' abiding 'nearby'; that is to say, in an 'auditive

mystical experience' the mystical 'Presence' is perceived *indirectly* by the 'effects' it has on the perceiver. In the case of a 'mystical intuition', by contrast, the awareness that it is the result of a 'mystical effect' is so fleeting and scant that it does not really qualify to be termed a mediated experience of 'Presence'.

3. It seems pertinent to emphasize once more the important phenomenological differences between a 'mystical insight', on the one hand, and the two varieties of mystical experience termed 'mystical hearing' and 'mystical vision'. A 'mystical insight' is a mode of mystical recognition, but it is not (unlike the latter) a variety of mystical experience. Irrespective of the issue addressed in item 2 above (i.e., whether in auditive and visionary mystical experiences a cognitive perception of Presence is involved), we will now address a phenomenological feature which must be clearly distinguished from the phenomenon of a purely 'cognitive sense of Presence'. The concrete experiential encounter with a picture that is 'beheld' within, or with a 'locution' that is heard within, is something entirely different from the immediate encounter with the Numen that occurs in a cognitive mystical experience of 'Presence'. If we relate this phenomenon to the concept of the 'mystical intuition', the phenomenological difference becomes especially apparent: First and foremost, it should be affirmed that the moment of 'mystical insight' may of course – like any other cognitive modes of mystical experience – be intertwined with the cognitive experience of the mystical 'Presence'. There is no reason to wonder why a 'mystical insight' could not be 'infused' in a special mystical event, in which the 'Presence' of the Numen is experienced concurrently. However, the fact that a 'mystical insight' can be interlinked with the experience of 'Presence' in a special mystical event does not falsify the claim that a 'mystical insight' as such is not an experiential mode of mystical recognition (as explained above) and, therefore, falls outside the realm of phenomena encompassed by both 'mystical visions' and 'mystical auditions'.

These considerations make it imperative not to bypass the opaque central area within the transition zone situated between the 'mystical vision' and 'auditory mystical experience', if we wish to probe the core of mystical experience. Both 'mystical visions' and 'mystical locutions' point towards the very centre of mystical experience. It is in this core area that the cognitive experience of the mystical 'Presence' will turn out to have paramount phenomenological significance. We are going to analyse once more the spectrum of 'mystical visions' by tracing the varieties starting from the type of the 'concrete pictorial vision' in the direction of the types of 'vision' that are all but devoid of any visual content.

There is, however, a critical question that arises at this point: If the 'mystical vision' is only one variety of mystical experience amongst several other varieties, and if its distinctive features have not yet been exhaustively identified, why should the visionary mystical experience then be placed at the centre of our investigation? This question is indeed justified at this juncture, not least because we should review and explain each new step before probing more deeply into the dark, mysterious core of the mysticism.

We have now arrived in our enquiry at the stage where psychological phenomenology intersects with gnoseology. The domain of psychology could not yet be left behind entirely, but the course of the enquiry is clearly directed toward the area in which we shall be able to assess the gnoseological import of the psychological phenomena occurring in mystical experience. This approach should enable us in the end to discern the cognitive structure inherent in mystical experience. And visionary mystical experience is the experiential mode that can most easily be subjected to a gnoseological analysis. I think that the real core of mystical recognition is most reliably accessible in a visionary mystical experience, though the cognitive content is not expressed in it.

We already know that the 'mystical vision' is not only a multi-layered empirical phenomenon, but also a vague one with unclear boundaries that tend to peter out (as it were) towards adjoining phenomena as to be fused with them. The term 'vision' is admittedly an ambivalent umbrella term; it eludes a clear definition because it is a dynamic phenomenon consisting of shifting elements. We have already shown that in a 'mystical vision' other modes of mystical experience ('mystical insights' and 'mystical hearing') are incorporated.

We might have proceeded by exploring analogous phenomenological patterns between 'mystical visions' and 'mystical effects', or between the 'mystical effects' and 'mystical insights'. But we have opted for exploring the varieties of 'mystical visions' that can be discerned in the transition zone between 'pictorial visions' and 'imageless visions'. We have pursued this path and shall continue to do so. Eventually, however, we shall arrive at a threshold and encounter a visionary mystical experience which is entirely devoid of any image as well as of peripheral and contiguous phenomena, and in which a glimpse is afforded into the ultimate Mystery underlying the 'mystical encounter'.

Our enquiry began with the study of 'pictorial mystical visions', in which a concrete picture is 'infused' which has symbolic or metaphoric import but not a pictorial self-revelation of the ultimate Mystery. Thereafter we examined the type of 'vision' in which the image beheld is recognized as the self-revelation of the 'All-encompassing'; and followed it with the analysis of 'visions of Light', in which a dazzling preternatural Light is the only 'content' of the visionary experience. The latter variety has been classified in a genuine mode of self-revelation of the 'All-encompassing' and opens a path towards varieties of 'mystical visions' in which *the visual components become more and more sparse* until a stage is reached in which the 'vision' is entirely devoid of any image, form or shape. What remains in the end is alone the formal structure of the 'vision', i.e., the pure capacity for 'inner sight', which is at the same time the ultimate state of inward alertness and supreme openness to 'receive'.[100] It is, in other words, a

---

100 [Note: This mental condition corresponds to an advanced spiritual state marked by perfect 'emptiness' or 'mindfulness', which has been described across all the major spiritual traditions and religions. It is generally understood (albeit with variations in different traditions) to result from a contemplative process of purification and vacating consciousness – notably in Buddhism, Sufism, contemplative Christianity, and Hinduism. In Buddhism, 'mindfulness' is a state of complete detachment from the world of objects and sense perception, and thus is often alternatively called 'emptiness'. It refers essentially to a perfectly calm, pure and emptied state of mind, which is at the same time a state of "complete openness to experience". Cf. LEVENSON, Michael R., and Carolyn M. ALDWIN. "Mindfulness in Psychology and Religion." *Handbook of the Psychology of Religion and Spirituality*.

serene state of receptivity directed at 'visible invisibility' ["das 'sichtbare Unsichtbare'"][101]. *The process by which the visual content of the 'mystical vision' is more and more reduced and finally completely dissolved, can phenomenologically be clearly distinguished from the process in which diverse modes of mystical experience become blurred 'by flowing into each other'.*

The experience of 'Presence', however, stands out phenomenologically, as its framework is entirely different from that of both visual and auditory mystical experiences. In fact, the experience of 'Presence' is one of the indispensable pillars by which the core of mystical experience is sustained. The second pillar inalienably linked with it is expected to become manifest, when the phenomenological structure of the 'vision' has been entirely dissolved (as described above). For it is the experience of 'Presence' by which a 'vision' of an allegorical or symbolic picture is transformed into an epiphanic image [viz., imagological self-revelation of the 'All-encompassing]. The transition from the visionary experience of a symbolic image that is *'infused' by* the 'All-encompassing' to a visionary self-revelation of the 'All-encompassing', in which the 'All-encompassing' is cognitively grasped to be 'present', marks a crucial step forward on our path towards the type of the 'imageless vision'. As we shall see, the process of depleting the 'content' of visionary experience

---

Ed. PALOUTHIAN, Raymond, and Crystal L. PARK. 2nd ed. New York: Guilford Press, 2013. 580–91; passage quoted: 586. – FKW.]

101 [Note: Albrecht puts the oxymoronic expression "das sichtbare Unsichtbare" in quotation marks to indicate that it is an established traditional expression, but he does not refer to its source. The oxymoronic phrase 'visible invisibility' can be traced to Augustine's didactic phrase *'per visibilia ad invisibilia'* in *De Civitate Dei* XII, 7. It became a key concept in medieval Christian theology. The medieval theologian, mystic and Augustinian friar Richard of St. Victor (d. 1173) adopted it (amongst many Christian mystagogues) in his treatises *Benjamin Minor* and *Benjamin Major*, in which he describes the mystical ascent of the soul, guiding the contemplative through six stages from the visible world to the invisible and ineffable mystery of God. In the ultimate stage of mystical contemplation, the devout seeker is bestowed with the *visio Dei* – a mystical vision of the Invisible and Ineffable – in an act of special grace. Cf. COULTER, Dale M. *'Per Visibilia ad Invisibilia': Theological Method in Richard of St. Victor (c. 1173)*. Turnhout: Brepols, 2006. – FKW.]

progressively is not only inextricably linked with the experience of 'Presence', but the awareness of the 'Presence' will increasingly come to the fore and affect the way it becomes manifest in a mystical experience. Thus, the knowledge about the 'presence' of the 'All-encompassing' resulting from experience becomes intertwined with items of 'pictorial' and 'imageless visions', which may reveal something of the essence or 'whatness' of the 'All-encompassing'.

The Glimpse of God

Within the varieties of experiencing the 'mystical Presence', one is classified as *vision* of Presence'. This term indicates that this variety of experiencing the 'mystical Presence' contains some residue of visual perception. But looking at it strictly in phenomenological terms, the only visual element that remains is the notion of 'spatiality', i.e., the awareness of the spatial presence of the 'All-encompassing' 'nearby'. To what is perceived as 'present', or rather the 'Presence' 'beheld', is attributed some special area in space.

The 'vision of Presence' is inevitably linked to the perception of the 'whatness' of that which is present. We shall now explore the 'imageless vision' of this 'whatness' on the basis of the foregoing considerations on the types of 'pictorial vision' and the experience of 'Presence'. However, the new aspects that we are going to examine promise to shed new light on the distinctive features of the 'vision of Presence'. This claim springs from the fact that the 'vision of Presence' will be examined from the vantage point of its intersection with the 'vision' of its 'whatness'. The image-like residues consist, as stated above, exclusively of the sense of spatiality, i.e., the vestiges pointing at the direction in which something is perceived to be 'present'. However, it is possible that the spatial perception of a 'Presence' is combined with some adumbrations of a shape or figure, in which case the 'vision of Presence' is turned into a visual representation of the 'Presence' and thus disclosing some features of its 'suchness' ["So-sein"]. This means that spatiality has no physiognomic significance at all in a 'vision of Presence', but there is a crucial instant at which the plain, imageless 'vision of Presence' is transformed into a self-expressive manifestation of the essence [of the 'All-encompassing']. This may happen in two ways: 1. by way of the 'Presence' gradually assuming some shape, and 2. by means of gestures issued by the 'Presence'. This means that there is an intermediate stage in the graded transition zone between an imageless and an image-based vision of the 'whatness' of the 'Presence', in which something of its essence is encountered, albeit not in the manner of a shape, but merely physiognomically by means of a gesture.

The first phenomenon within the 'vision of Presence' that we are going to explore, and which has been explicitly addressed in the records of the mystics examined, is what mystics have termed 'the glimpse of God'. The glimpse is, phenomenologically speaking, not yet, or not exclusively, a distinct gesture, as this vision comprises also a few other illustrative features. However, the 'glimpse of God' is a mystical vision which can no longer be qualified as a visual perception of the 'All-encompassing' but has already been transformed into a visual mode of self-expression. The 'glimpse of God' is sustained by the full awareness of 'Presence' in which, over and beyond this, a very exciting quality of its 'whatness' becomes 'apparent': the awareness of the concealed presence of 'Him'. This means that the 'vision of Presence' is linked with the clear cognitive awareness that the 'Presence' has distinctly person-like characteristics [thus the essence of the 'All-encompassing' is, in other words, not experienced in this mystical event as an impersonal entity]. The characteristics of this mystical 'glimpse of God' are portrayed in the following testimonies. These textual examples address not only encounters with the 'All-encompassing' experienced as a Persona and identified as 'He',[102] but this 'glimpse' is also accompanied by a deep sense of His omnipotence and sovereignty. The 'glimpse of God' is thus cognitively perceived as a revelation of God's *majestas*:

> Text 81 (Christine Lucie, diary entry, May 1880. 24f.): "... Then the glimpse of the Lord pierced my soul like lightening ... in this hour of grace *I could not see the adorable eyes of the Lord clearly*, but I saw inwardly *His divine glimpse which irradiated with magnificent power*. This glimpse instilled in my soul such awe and reverence that it will never forget, even if the soul had to live on in this world for another hundred years. Moreover, the love of the soul was strengthened immeasurably. It truly takes a violent

---

102 [Note: This seemingly controversial claim is explained by Albrecht later in this chapter. – FKW.]

effort when one dares to speak about such a special favour of divine grace. It is obedience alone that compels us to do so. We do so timorously, trembling with awe as if by touching something sacred. But when one speaks about this, one feels ashamed because it is done so poorly – this at least is my impression – so that you feel like an inept, unskilled sculptor who aspires to create a masterpiece, but who is only able to create a clumsy, distorted object."

Text 82 (Christine Lucie, diary entry of 8 December 1882. 91f.): "My Lord granted me to *behold His divine glimpse* for some time when I was absorbed in spiritual prayer. I realised that this venerable glimpse would be enough to experience eternal bliss. It is *impossible to doubt its realness*, even though this rare glimpse was shown to me only in a concealed manner, *as if through a luminescent cloud ...*".

Text 83 (Christine Lucie, diary entry of 5 February 1883. 103): "... Then Jesus has healed my soul by *imprinting the glimpse of His love. This glimpse is experienced with a certainty that is beyond any doubt* and which cannot be compared with any other experience. And yet *there is no visual image involved*. The soul facing this loving glimpse of Jesus might be compared to a blind man, frozen stiff by the cold, being resuscitated by the light and warmth of the sun. The sun makes itself felt to the man's dead eyes and instils in him new vigour. But how inadequate is this comparison! Jesus, I think, nothing can be compared to you even in heaven, oh my God!"

Text 84 (Christine Lucie, diary entry of 25 July 1888. 237 – the entry refers to the experience recorded above, dated 5 February 1883): "The deeply moving grace originating from the periphery of the supernatural life is returning and allows the soul *to behold and feel* the divine glimpse of Jesus. *Today, however, this grace is instilled in a less intense and plainer manner* than previously. How does the soul perceive this adorable glimpse, how can the soul *behold it spiritually and yet so specifically*? This cannot possibly be explained or told – at least I, of all people, am unable to do so."

Text 85 (Teresa of Avila, *Vida*, main chapter 29, 273): "When I contemplated the ineffable Beauty in which He revealed Himself to me, and when listening to His endearing, and always so solemn words, which His sweet divine mouth spoke to me, I would eagerly have loved to see also the colour of His eyes and His figure as a whole, to be able to speak about it; but this grace has never been bestowed on me, and all my endeavours were futile and they rather caused the vision to disappear entirely. Though the Lord glances at me occasionally full of tender love, but *this special glimpse of love is so overwhelming that the soul cannot bear it*. For the soul is then transported into such a state of ecstasy that she is eventually deprived of this wonderful glimpse ..."[103]

Manifestation of Self-Expressive Gestures and Appearances ["Ausdruckserscheinungen"]

On our way towards exploring visions that are increasingly depleted of pictures, we have arrived at the variety in which any residue of an image has disappeared. In this type of vision, the visual content consists primarily of gestures and facial expressions, which are manifestations of the essence of the 'All-encompassing'. The threshold between 'pictorial vision' and 'vision of gestures' and other physiognomic appearances can be clearly drawn, when the outlines of the 'image' can no longer be traced, and the image is substituted by physiognomic expressions.

The 'glimpse of God' is a borderline phenomenon situated precisely at the boundary between 'picture-like visions' and 'physiognomic appearances', because it consists of both features of a figure and features of a self-expressive physiognomic manifestation. It depends on whether the characteristics of the former or of the latter prevail, if the visionary experience is to be classified as self-expressive 'physiognomic appearance', or a 'pictorial vision'. The 'glimpse of God' in the examples quoted is mainly focussed on the 'inner sight' of the contours or the impersonation of Christ, though the figure of Christ as such remains concealed. Christ thus appears as *pars pro toto*, which elicits in the perceiver the ardent longing to see more of the shape of Christ than merely his countenance or parts of his figure. The 'glimpse' is the visible part behind which the entire shape of Christ is invisibly 'present'; this 'glimpse' thus exemplifies a special type of pictorial items of 'content', which include, for instance: changing traits of Christ's countenance, a smile, the hand blessing, or Christ's radiant garment. On the other hand, there is also a variety in which the 'glimpse of God' is experienced in a manner that does not allow the inference that it is only part of the appearance of physiognomic features of Christ.

---

103 [Note: All translations from the German sources provided. Italics as added by Albrecht. – FKW.]

In such an event, the 'glimpse' is rather the visionary experience of the essence of the 'All-encompassing' becoming manifest in a gesture or a physiognomic expression. Thus the 'glimpse' is a very special manifestation directed at an individual perceiver.

By now a clarification of the concepts addressed here has become imperative. This applies in particular to the term 'self-expressive appearance' ["Ausdruckserscheinung"].

THESIS 59: *A self-expressive appearance is a three-dimensional inner vision; the entire appearance and its distinctive traits, gestures and movements are the physiognomic self-expression of a Presence concurrently experienced as 'being there'.*

On this side of the threshold of 'pictorial visions', we have identified two special types of pictures: the 'symbolic picture' and the 'double phenomenon' of image affiliated with the cognitive awareness of 'Presence'.

THESIS 60: *A symbolic picture is a mystically 'infused' image, which is, however, not affiliated with the simultaneous experience of the Presence of the 'All-encompassing'.*

THESIS 61: *The double phenomenon consisting of image and the experience of 'Presence' is an image that has been mystically 'infused' and which is accompanied by the simultaneous experience of the 'Presence' of the 'All-encompassing'.* This double phenomenon is phenomenologically to be placed between the symbolic image and a 'self-expressive appearance'. With the symbol this 'double phenomenon' shares the same type of image, and with the 'self-expressive appearance' it shares the simultaneous affiliation with the experience of the 'mystical Presence'. But the double phenomenon has not necessarily physiognomic import. Its distinctive characteristic is rather that it is intertwined with other accumulated items of content: the image beheld in the 'pictorial vision' is interlinked with the cognitive experience of the Presence of the 'All-encompassing'. The latter does not have to become manifest in the former: the vision of an angel appearing in radiant light, which is intertwined with the certain cognitive awareness that the Numen is 'nearby', is an example of the *pure* type of the 'double phenomenon'.

We may infer from the intermediate phenomenological position of the mystical 'double phenomenon' that it *can* assume physiognomic import, notably when the Being reveals itself as present to the perceiver, i.e., when the image is simultaneously a 'self-expressive appearance'. If the image does not merely coexist with the Presence, and if the Presence reveals itself in this very image, then the image becomes what we have termed 'pictorial appearance'.

THESIS 62 (a supplement to theses 29–31): *In a 'pictorial appearance', image, the experience of Presence and 'self-expressive appearance' are intertwined.*

This phenomenological threshold, which can only be defined in psychological-phenomenological terms, is of paramount significance for a gnoseological assessment. The 'double phenomenon', which is composed of a picture and the experience of Presence (and this also applies, in some instances, to the 'pictorial appearance') is, after all, merely an effigy and not the 'mystical Object' itself. The claim that the gnoseological significance of the 'double phenomenon' is superior to that of the 'symbolic picture' is grounded in the fact that the Numen is somehow 'present' in it as a 'backdrop', which is grasped cognitively in a mystical experience, though it is not the physiognomy of the 'All-encompassing' itself that is revealed in it.

On the other side of the threshold, there is an area in the realm of visionary experience in which an image emerges gradually, or a picture takes on contours, which is more authentic than the vision of a symbol or a concrete picture; this phenomenon is, in other words, nothing but a self-expressive revelation [of the Presence of the 'All-encompassing']. In this case, the Presence is not a phenomenon inherent in the image, but a fundamental item of the 'self-expressive appearance'. Without the experience of Presence there would be no revelation of the essence of the 'All-encompassing', and thus no experience of its 'whatness'.

THESIS 63: *The mystical vision of a 'self-expressive appearance' is a vision of the 'whatness' of the essence of what is perceived to be 'present'.*

It is important to bear in mind that in our enquiry we have had to put aside for the time being other varieties of mystical experience, since we have decided to focus first on the phenomenon of the 'mystical *vision*'. To obviate misunderstanding, we need to emphasize that visionary mystical experiences have been singled out first, although any visionary experience is inevitably intertwined with other varieties. This approach, however, has been the consequence of the scientific method chosen. The disadvantage of this approach is, admittedly, that the isolated focus on visionary mystical experience does not exactly correspond to empirical reality in that its role and rootedness in the life of the perceiver is not appropriately considered. The single focus on the 'visual content' and on the way it is transformed in a series of subsequent mystical events is, however, indispensable for elucidating the phenomenology of the experiential process that progresses from the 'pictorial vision' towards entirely imageless modes of mystical experience. The 'concrete subject matter' of a mystical vision is, in other words, progressively dissolved. This process ultimately results in the complete removal of all visual and non-visual phenomena culminating in an entirely vacated mental state. This theoretical claim provokes the question as to whether such a vacated mental condition can at all be encountered in empirical reality.

We are aware of the strictures imposed by methodology, but there is no other way of advancing further towards the threshold, from which we may get a glimpse of the formless and imageless 'core' of mysticism. Exploring the various modes of 'self-expressive appearances' is like proceeding on a stairway towards the ultimate stage from which it should be possible to get a glimpse into the sparse, but ultimately unfathomable domain of mysticism.

Appearances of self-expressive figures and effigies are genuine items of 'content' in a 'mystical vision'. Such appearances cannot be perceived by any other mode of mystical experience. However, we should remember that we have singled out this dynamic type of visionary experience for methodological reasons and separated it from the empirical web of which appearances can be an integral part. Thus, we should be aware that the phenomenological analysis focussing exclusively on 'self-expressive appearances' is a theoretical construct, which does not reflect the actual context in empirical reality.

In 'appearances of self-expressive gestures and effigies', facial expressions, movements of the hands or the head of the figure appearing in the 'vision' and other gestures are perceived. The countenance of the figure envisaged, for example, may get closer to the perceiver, or 'zoom out' (as it were), or the figure may seem to bend towards the perceiver, or stretch out an invisible hand, or indicate that he/

she wishes to embrace the perceiver. The gestures may communicate, moreover, non-verbally diverse messages: they may, for instance, signify a warning, express approval, or denial, support, consolation (to mention only a few). This means that the specific nuances in the changing countenance more of the 'whatness' of the figure appearing in the vision is revealed than in the bodily gestures. Thus, the 'mystical Other' appearing in human shape may reveal His Presence in 'a glimpse of love', or else by overpowering the will of the perceiver, or by evoking a deep sense of reverent awe, or sense of supreme sovereignty. Yet such isolated characteristics obscure the fact that in empirical reality the vision of 'self-expressive gestures and moving effigies' never occur separated from other modes of mystical perception; they are generally intertwined in various ways – for instance, with mystical locutions, the experience of somatic and emotional effects, mystical intuitions and the sense of 'Presence'. What is 'present', i.e., the unique Being that is experienced during the event as being spatially 'present', does not only reveal itself in dynamic eloquent gestures, but also in 'locutions', somatic effects, and diverse other influences on the perceiver. The 'self-expressive appearance' of the 'mystical Presence' may assume epiphanic import by emanating a special *'aura'* and *'fluidum'*, which can be sensed and cognitively grasped. The complex structure of interlinked modes of mystical experience constitutes a singular mystical event which mystics traditionally have referred to by the collective term 'vision'. The reason why mystics have opted for this term can be traced to the specific psychological-phenomenological structure germane to the 'vision of Presence': It is a variety of mystical experience in which the encounter with the 'Presence' evokes a clear sense of the spatial presence or 'nearness' of the 'mystical Other' which is intertwined with the disclosure of features of its 'whatness', signifying that the 'mystical Other' is perceived as a Persona. The 'mystical Other' reveals some of its person-like features in the 'inner vision' by means of epiphanic gestures, facial expressions and other physiognomic signs.

It rarely happens that 'self-expressive appearances' of this kind are the only 'content' of a 'mystical vision of Presence'. Even when this seems to be the case, they do not occur independently, i.e., separated from a multi-layered experiential context, but are meaningfully integrated in the entire framework of a given mystical event. This applies also to the gnoseological assessment of 'self-expressive epiphanic appearances'. To be precise, the 'rank' to which the 'self-expressive appearances' are assigned on the scale of mystical recognition can only be decided after the following specifications have been considered:

1. Pure 'self-expressive appearances' are a form of personal self-revelation [self-revelation of a Persona otherwise invisible]. When the 'experiencing I' beholds a physiognomic image or gesture in 'inner sight', the process is analogous to a visual sense perception: The 'objects' perceived in 'inner sight', as well as when external objects are seen, are limited here to the dynamic patterns and the silhouettes of the seen figure. What is experienced is, in other words, exclusively visual elements. The knowledge, however, that the visual phenomena are also instances of an act of personal self-revelation is not gained by the visual perception but originates from and depends on the concomitant act of cognitive understanding. That is to say, 'self-expressive appearances' must be interpreted to be understood. From this result two crucial conditions for assessing their cognitive import: first, the fact that the subjective understanding and/or interpretation of the vision of a 'self-expressive appearance' can be flawed and erroneous, even when the perception of the 'object' in 'inner sight' is genuine and true; and second, the fact that it is only possible to understand rationally what is intelligible. Though it is true that, on the one hand, the mystics maintain that a 'vision' of 'self-expressive appearances' elicits such an urgent and inalienable sense of their 'givenness' that an instantly evident sense of its certainty and veracity is simultaneously evoked, on the other hand, there are also numerous testimonies throughout the history of mysticism in which a lingering suspicion or explicit distrust of this type of visionary phenomena are articulated. This suggests that any rational reflection on this type of 'mystical vision' is likely to result in the insight that the essence of the 'All-encompassing' is more likely to be inscrutable and incomprehensible than accessible to rational enquiry.

2. If we try to crystallize carefully the essential 'core' of what communicates itself in a mystical vision of a 'self-expressive appearance', we will eventually arrive at an ultimate essence of the 'All-encompassing' which we have termed above by the personal pronoun 'He' (viz., 'Him'). Here we must call to mind that there are [basically] two [complementary] kinds of mysticism: a personal variety and an a-personal variety. A-personal [or monistic] mystical experience involves an encounter with the 'All-encompassing' that has no person-like qualities at all. Personal mystical experience, by contrast, typically represented by Christian and other theistic traditions of mysticism, is based on an encounter with the 'All-encompassing' perceived as Persona. In the context of Christianity there is no mystical experience in which the encounter with the 'All-encompassing' is not informed by the perceiver's prior religious knowledge that the 'Otherness' perceived is not an impersonal 'It', but a 'He' [i.e., the Triune Deity conceived as 'Father', 'Son' and 'Holy Ghost', hence traditionally referred to in male terms by 'He/Him']. This justly provokes the question of whether the 'mystical Otherness' addressed by 'He' is really encountered in such a mystical event, and if so, whether 'He' really reveals Himself in a manner that enables the perceiver to recognize or even 'see' Him with the 'inner eye', or if such a mystical event is merely the result of the [Christian] perceiver's religious interpretation of the occurrence. From a phenomenological perspective, the turning point at which an a-personal encounter with the 'All-encompassing' switches into a personal encounter occurs when the 'He' is experienced as a quality of the 'whatness' of the 'mystical Presence'.

We have not yet reached the stage at which we can enter on an epistemological discussion, since we are still occupied with compiling specific gnoseological and phenomenological characteristics. For this reason, we may propose the following assertions without examining subsequently their veridical claims. The impact of 'mystical effects' on a recipient demands logically that there must be an originator who has imparted the effects. This claim is at least valid for 'effects' which are not the consequences of natural causes, but which have been 'infused'. For instance, when 'locutions' are heard inwardly, the perceiver concludes instantly and with great certainty that a 'speaker' must be 'present' (albeit invisibly) who is the source of these 'locutions'. The experience of 'mystical effects' and the 'hearing of locutions' are phenomena that can exclusively be encountered in the domain of personal mysticism. The vision of 'self-expressive appearances' is a phenomenon thus consonant with these modes of personal mystical experience and may therefore be assessed as an integral part of cognitive mystical experience.

3. Reviewing our findings so far, we may summarize: The more detailed and picture-like a vision is, the more of the 'whatness' of the Numen is apparently disclosed. Hence, the 'vision of Christ', which is interlaced with the experience of 'Presence', can thus be assessed as a fully developed epiphanic pictorial appearance. The more signs of 'epiphanic self-expression' – such as traits of the countenance, the glimpse of the eyes, and gestures – are contained in the vision of the 'shape-like appearance', the wider is the range of its message. The experience of 'Presence' alone already has a great impact on the arousal of numinous feelings; but in an epiphanic 'self-expressive appearance' the perceiver is, over and beyond this, bestowed with the revelation of the [divine] essence, the existential relevance of which cannot be surpassed by any other event. Yet irrespective of these facts, in mystical tradition the mystics have unanimously ranked any kind of visual mystical experience gnoseologically below the vision of the Divine that is entirely without image and form. Though the mystical vision of an 'epiphanic self-expression of Christ' is beheld inwardly and cognitively grasped beyond any doubt as an image 'infused' by God, this did not change the mystics' critical attitude [to the *'visio imaginaria'*, and even more so, the *'visio corporalis'*] and the view that any 'infused image' tends to evoke subjective responses and imaginative ideas by which the original vision is likely to be modified.

This implies the claim that the more the genuine nature of a mystical experience is enhanced, the sparser the visual 'content', because the danger of falling victim to delusion is reduced to a minimum in a 'mystical vision' that is entirely imageless. The picture-like features in a vision of a 'self-expressive appearance' (e.g. colours, garment, bodily appearance, etc.) correspond to a symbolic representation and are as such the subjective medium in which the actual manifestation of the 'mystical Presence' occurs. But the visionary experience of 'self-expressive appearances' is clearly closer to the realm of imageless visions and has, for this reason, superior validity. But the crucial criterion of authenticity is whether the 'mystical Presence' is simultaneously experienced in an entirely formless invisible manner along with the vision of the 'self-expressive appearance'. *The more a 'mystical vision' is vacated of pictorial 'content', the less is the danger of flawed perception and delusion, and the more the vision will advance towards the perception of 'pure Presence'.*

One might omit quoting textual examples for illustration here. However, I decided to quote some representative examples, as they do not just corroborate what has been stated above but also provide us with the entire spectrum of phenomena encountered in empirical reality that are intertwined with epiphanic visions of 'self-expressive appearances'. The testimonies concern concrete epiphanic mystical visions and, as such, are a critical corrective against the analytical tendency of schematized classification and of highlighting selected components.

> Text 86 (Teresa of Avila, *Vida*, main chapter 27, 252): "6. ... the Presence of the Lord is known with such clear understanding, even though nothing can be seen, that it is impossible (it seems to me) to doubt it. For it is the will of the Lord that his Presence is so clearly impressed in the mind that doubting it is less likely than questioning something that is seen with physical eyes. Because if we see something with our eyes, there may at times arise the suspicion that we have been deceived; but the experience [of the Lord's Presence] elicits such a deep sense of certainty that doubt has no power at all, even if a moment of indecision should arise, ...
>
> 8. These visions and locutions are indeed so highly spiritual that there is (I think) not a flicker of disquiet in the powers of the soul, nor in the senses, by which the devil might achieve something ... but this kind of suspension of the powers of the soul happens only rarely during contemplation. But when it occurs, I trust we cannot do, or achieve anything, for it seems it is the Lord alone who is the cause of all this ..."

Text 87 (Teresa of Avila, *Vida*, main chapter 28, 266): "8. ... Though the vision described above, in which God has revealed Himself without an image, is *more sublime*, this pictorial revelation is more suitable for our weakness, because in it the divine Presence remains imprinted in our imagination and memory and enables us to recall it in a lively manner. Both types of vision occur, incidentally, almost always jointly. Yes, it is so, indeed; for it is with the eyes of the soul that we behold the magnificence, beauty and glory of the most sacred humanity of the Lord; whereas in the experience described previously *we recognize that He is God, that He is powerful* and can achieve everything, arrange everything, govern everything and permeates everything with His love."

Text 88 (Christine Lucie, diary entry of 30 January 1887. 212f.): "... We have to bear in mind that in this pictorial vision, the image revealed to the soul is an instantaneous token of grace, a visual instruction, tangible for the inner senses (as it were); however, *the grace of the union with God permeates the soul* [simultaneously] *with blessing so strong and meek that the pictorial vision is merely an accidental gift of grace*. God Himself occupies the ground of the soul. At the same time, He permeates the soul and the image He has evoked before the soul. It is the image that the soul beholds first ... *The form of prayer is less highly valued than the others, because a visible image appears in it;* but this form of prayer is, nonetheless, I believe, a wonderful incentive, bestowed by the grace of God, to restore and quicken the powers and capacities of the soul ..."

Text 89 (Christine Lucie, diary entry of 10 September 1883. 137): "... the grace of his Holy Presence ... is of a oneness and simplicity that the human spirit is struck silent with amazement ... The soul is then drawn into Him, into the centre that is safe against any foreign influence. And if I am not mistaken, God protects the soul in this wonderful state also from the snares of Satan. *What are the pitfalls the tempter could then devise? Could it be words? The soul does not listen to any. Could it be images? The soul does not behold any in this state. From which side could the imagination be tackled in this mental state?* God appears to fill the soul so entirely that there is no room for anything or anyone but God ..." [All translations provided. Italics as added by Albrecht. – FKW.]

The Basic Structure of the 'Imageless Vision'
["Das Grundgefüge der bildlosen Schau"]

Our phenomenological approach is currently focussed on the types of 'vision' with reduced pictorial content intending to advance to the type of 'vision' that is entirely without any image. We began our enquiry with the analysis of 'pictorial visions' and proceeded with 'visions' with sparse visual content. Now we are going to survey 'mystical visions' that are entirely devoid of any image. It is important to add, however, that the spectrum surveyed encompasses phenomenologically only a representative range of 'mystical visions'. Moreover, the current considerations do not include an account of the process of 'emptying' the mind from any item of 'content' achieved by a conscious mental process and, as such, part of the incipient stage of 'introversion' [viz., 'contemplation'], which usually precedes a mystical experience. Over and beyond this, an 'imageless vision' is a mystical event often ranked highest on the scale of mystical experience, but as such it does not necessarily indicate a certain stage of a mystic's spiritual growth. Given that we are, for the time being, exclusively concerned with the phenomenological structure of mystical states, we must refrain from including any value judgement of image-based versus non-visual modes of mystical experience. It is only when we shall shift our perspective and look at the varieties of 'mystical vision' from a gnoseological point of view that we are required to assess and evaluate their significance and gnoseological rank. The criteria for this assessment will inevitably be based on the established principles of discretion handed down from mystical traditions. And from the beginnings of mystical theology in the early Middle Ages, spiritual theology has assigned to the *visio intellectualis* a higher gnoseological rank than to the *visio corporalis* and the *visio imaginaria* (or *spiritualis*).

To begin with, we need to specify the distinctive features of the 'imageless vision'. The traditional concept termed *visio intellectualis* is appropriate, albeit rather diffuse, as it includes diverse phenomena by which the threshold to other types of 'vision' are partly obscured. Therefore, we need to clarify the concept by delineating the pivotal phenomenological characteristics. To achieve this aim, we must split up the overall concept and explore the specific phenomena of which it is composed. One is the 'mystical insight', which has already been defined. As the 'mystical insight' is an act of instant recognition, it is not an experiential characteristic of a 'mystical vision' but rather a corollary and/or after-effect of a mystical experience and as such an integral part of a 'mystical vision'. Furthermore, any visual varieties of mystical experience need to be grouped together in a separate unit; they constitute a transition zone between the type of 'pictorial vision' and the 'imageless vision'. The 'imageless vision' is, by definition, devoid of even the slightest vestige of an image. On the other hand, we should be aware that Teresa of Avila's conception of the *visio intellectualis* encompassed both 'mystically infused insights' and the awareness of spatiality in experiencing the 'mystical Presence'. Most of Teresa's visions are, in fact, composed of these two components.

The 'imageless vision' can be defined phenomenologically only from the subjective vantage point of the perceiver. Thus, there is the experiencing subject perceiving an 'object' 'arriving' in the vista of 'inner sight'. The formal structure of an inner visionary experience is the same, irrespective of whether it is a *pictorial* vision, or an entirely *imageless* one – that is to say, the basic formal mental structure and the function of 'inner sight' operating in it is the same when the perceiver beholds a 'pictorial vision' or when he/she is faced with the pure and unfathomable empty space, or Nothingness. From this it follows that *the term 'vision' can justifiably be applied to a concrete mystical experience if it is sustained throughout by the phenomenological structure of visionary perception* [i.e., as long as there is an 'experiencing I' beholding a 'mystical Object' in 'inner sight'].

The phenomenological structure of a 'mystical vision' can best be illustrated by resorting to findings of the psychology of consciousness. The [ideal] mental setting for an 'inner vision' to occur is a homogeneous state of consciousness, which has been vacated from any sense perceptions, discursive thoughts, object-related feelings and any other content that might interfere with the pure emptiness and perfect calmness within. The 'perceiving I' is immersed in this serene state of inner calm, in which all active functions of the 'waking consciousness' have been stilled, and the only 'active function' of the otherwise purely receptive 'I' is the function of 'inner sight', conventionally termed 'inner eye'. The 'perceiving I' is alert and radically 'open' to behold only phenomena 'arriving' in the vista of 'inner sight'. The *'mystical I'*, in other words, is passively open to receive and respond to the 'arrival' of the 'All-encompassing'. The phenomenological structure of this receptive state of consciousness is unique in that it is inexorably directed at the 'arrival' of the one singular 'mystical Object'. In the experiential sphere of a mystic who is gratified with a 'mystical vision', there is always the concomitant awareness that the focus of his/her receptive attitude is visual – not aural, emotional, tactile or somatic. The 'inward eye' is cleansed and open to receive, and, over and beyond this, abiding in tranquillity, it is looking into a specific direction. Hence, it is two vital features that are combined in a 'mystical vision': The 'openness' of the 'beholding I', and second, a certain 'directedness' of the 'inner eye' at [something 'arriving' from beyond the confines of the individual self]. (In parenthesis we should add that the word 'directedness' is understood neither in a metaphoric nor in a spatial sense here.)

It may happen, however, that the 'experiencing I', cognizant of having to look in a certain direction while awaiting the 'arrival' of the 'mystical Object', is faced with nothing but blank emptiness, devoid of any object. Though in this case the phenomenological structure of the 'vision' is clearly given, including the special 'directedness' of the perceiver's alertness, this is not a state of 'imageless vision' but a glimpse into the vacant condition of consciousness, in which no 'object' has yet 'arrived'. It is, in other words, an 'imageless vision' in which the 'mystical Object' is absent. An 'imageless vision' that is to be qualified as a 'mystical vision', it does not suffice that the vacated 'quiet state of alertness' is fully developed; it requires inalienably that the 'mystical Object' has 'arrived' in 'inner sight'. Without the presence of a 'mystical Object', the imageless state of 'inner sight' has no gnoseological value at all.

This means that the term 'imageless mystical vision' is not only understood as the emptied state of mind [termed 'quiet state of alertness'], but also an indispensable requirement that the 'mystical Object' is present in as – regardless of whether the 'mystical Object' is experienced as 'arriving', or as already 'having arrived' at the onset of the 'mystical vision'. Thus, the mere knowledge that the 'All-encompassing' is something real when the 'inner eye' is facing the void, does not qualify as an 'imageless mystical vision': Only when the 'All-encompassing' is experienced with absolute certainty as a [non-visual] living Presence does the term 'imageless mystical vision' apply. Therefore, it can be claimed that *the pivotal phenomenon of the 'imageless mystical vision' is the interlinking of the vacated state of quiet inner alertness with the assured experience of the 'mystical Presence'*. In this mystical event it does not matter where the evident knowledge about the 'Presence' of the 'All-encompassing' has come from or is coming from. The certainty that the 'All-encompassing' is present here and now is evident and undeniable and is instilled by the various modes involved in experiencing the 'mystical Presence'. The only exception here is the phenomenon termed *'vision* of the Presence': This is a special type of 'vision' which differs from other varieties in that it is the only one that falls outside the experiential spectrum of the 'imageless vision'. Although in 'the vision of the Presence' the phenomenological structure of the 'vision' is joined with the awareness of 'Presence', it is not a *pure* variety of 'imageless vision', because the 'Presence' beheld in it has a clearly spatial quality.

We have tried to approach the real core of the phenomenon of mystical recognition cautiously. In the foregoing critical analysis, we had to consign the individual elements of cognition encountered to the peripheral sphere of mystical recognition. This means that we have not yet succeeded in isolating a single element from the core of mysticism. For this reason, it is justified to be suspicious of any new aspect addressed from a new perspective. There are two fundamental questions that arise from a sceptical viewpoint: Is the phenomenon in which two elements are interlaced – i.e., the formal structure of consciousness of 'quiet alertness' as yet devoid of the 'mystical Object', and the evident knowledge about the concrete presence of the 'All-encompassing', which derives from experience – really an essential phenomenological part of the core of mystical recognition, which we have been looking for? Have we really reached the threshold of the essence of visionary mystical experience, or does the part separated from the core contain no genuine phenomenon at all, but rather merely a fabricated construct? These queries demand that we examine critically the alleged essence of mysticism from various changing perspectives. This demand is, however, is rather daunting, not least because we have, as yet, no concrete indication of what the essence of the phenomenon is that we are going to explore, as we have so far only identified a small fraction, which has, over and beyond this, been more or less arbitrarily separated from the entire structural whole. The cognitive perception of 'Presence' is composed of two elements: the experience of someone 'being present', and the experience of what/who is 'present'. Separating the two elements is a requirement imposed by methodology only, and therefore does not comply with empirical reality. The reasons why our enquiry must remain focussed (for the time being) on the 'isness' of the 'All-encompassing' and not on its 'whatness', will become clear later. The intertwined phenomenon of the pure structure of 'vision' and the knowledge of something/someone being 'there', which originates from experience, is phenomenologically fractured because it excludes the fact that any cognitive experience of the 'Presence of the 'All-encompassing" presupposes a minimum awareness of its 'whatness'. Otherwise it would be impossible to recognize that what is perceived as 'present' is the 'All-encompassing'.

Our critical examination of the isolated fraction of the 'imageless mystical vision' will begin with the established finding that the experience of 'Presence' is a multifarious phenomenon. There is a 'vision of Presence', but this is the smallest component within the entire structure of experiencing 'Presence'. This aside, a mystic may experience the 'Presence', or its 'arrival', either indirectly in that he/she *infers* the 'Presence' from the impact effected by it, or from the concurrent event of 'locutions'; or he/she may experience the 'Presence' directly by the concomitant experience of 'mystical effects', which we have, however, not yet sufficiently elucidated. The latter is indeed an arduous undertaking, since the experience of 'mystical effects' can hardly be grasped by the scientific concepts of the psychology of consciousness. This means that what is understood by the impact and/or feeling and/or somatic awareness of 'Presence', viz., the 'sense of Presence', is not adequately captured by resorting to emotional and/or somatic terms. Even sparser is the phenomenological structure of the 'mystical experience of Presence', which is part of the innermost core of mystical experience, which largely eludes phenomenological description. The psychological-phenomenological concept introduced [in *Psychology of Mystical Consciousness*] to denote this elusive mode of mystical experience is 'non-visual awareness of the presence of the It'. By identifying this phenomenon, we have reached the threshold of psychological expression and enquiry, and must acknowledge that the sparse, unspectacular and vague term 'awareness' refers indeed to a mystical event that has paramount existential significance. The 'awareness of the presence of the It' is inevitably linked to the experience of evident truth, resulting in the perceiver in the absolute conviction of the truth and realness of the mystical event.

This summary of insights gained in our previous study supplies the epistemological foundation for exploring the 'double phenomenon' of the spatial 'vision' of the non-visual 'mystical Object' and the concurrent experience of 'Presence' sustained by an unflagging sense of certainty. This means that if the structure of the 'vision' is combined with the experience of 'Presence', *then* a decisive new level in experiencing an 'imageless mystical vision' is reached. 'Then' in this sentence is not to be understood temporally but consecutively, i.e., it does not signify that the 'vision' has initially an 'empty' structure without any 'object', which is hereafter followed by the 'arrival' of the 'All-encompassing', but 'then' refers to a superior stage in grasping the phenomenological relationship within the domain of mystical recognition that occurs when the 'double phenomenon' is encountered. The overall structure of the 'imageless vision' is significantly modified by the various elements involved in a given experience of the 'Presence'. The mode in which the 'Presence' becomes manifest determines the overall nature of the experience and thus the impact on the perceiver and hence his/her individual response. For instance, when the 'Presence of the 'All-encompassing'' is perceived *indirectly* in that it is inferred from the impact effected in the 'experiencing self', this perception does not terminate the perceiver's alertness and the openness of his/her 'inner sight'. However, if the 'mystical Presence' is experienced sensibly in a real encounter, 'hitting' (as it were) the perceiver and operating within him/her and causing somatic changes and/or shifting emotional states, the awareness of the 'tangible' presence, or proximity, of the 'All-encompassing' and/or of its 'intrusion, immanence and omnipresence' is significantly enhanced, but even these multiple modes of experiencing the 'All-encompassing' do not contain the full range of potential encounters with the 'Presence' that are revealed in an 'imageless vision'. In the latter, the 'mystical Presence' is instantly recognized with absolute certainty. Contrary to all expectations, the *'vision* of Presence', which is sustained by the knowledge about the spatial presence of the 'All-encompassing', and in which the 'Presence' is either felt to be in the space surrounding the perceiver, or known to reside within the perceiver, is less often intertwined with a visionary experience that is entirely imageless than the pure awareness of the 'invisible mystical Presence'.

The 'experiencing I', endowed with the faculty of beholding phenomena 'arriving' in 'inner sight', has discovered his/her 'mystical Object' and directs his/her alertness towards the 'All-encompassing'; in doing so, the 'experiencing I' is in turn affected by the 'mystical Object', thus establishing a mystical relationship in a concrete mystical event. The 'experiencing I', immersed in the medium of hyper-lucidity and the calmness within, perceives the full potential of the 'mystical vision'. What previously had only been perceived in a fractured manner has now evolved into a comprehensive 'vision', in which the subjective pole is complemented by the objective pole. The 'mystical relation' between perceiver and the 'mystical Object' perceived, has become empirical reality. With these observations in mind, we may now propose the essential features of the 'imageless mystical vision' in thesis 64, though we must admit that the structure of the 'imageless vision' as stated in this thesis is not exhaustive, as it does not embrace the complete range of phenomena that can potentially be encountered in empirical reality.

THESIS 64: *The basic structure of the 'imageless vision' is composed of both the phenomenological framework of 'inner sight' directed at a 'mystical Object', and the contiguous perception of the 'mystical Presence'; this intertwined structure enables the cognitive mystical act of glancing at what is present.* – In brief: The perception of the 'mystical Presence' and the structure of 'inner sight' become fused, resulting in a united mode of 'inner vision', which is termed 'imageless vision'.

We have proceeded on our phenomenological path towards types of vision with more and more diminishing visual components. We have now reached the liminal stage in which the vision is almost entirely imageless. Retrospectively we may state: So long as the vision is pictographic, i.e., when the 'mystical Object' still appears in it in a pictorial manner, the gnoseological relation between the perceiver and the 'mystical Object' is fully developed, because the 'subjective pole' has a clear focal point in the 'objective pole', i.e., the image perceived. The fact that the pictorial object is not the 'All-encompassing' itself, but merely a pictorial representation, does not matter when assessed from *this* perspective: A *'pictorial vision' does not necessarily require a concurrent cognitive experience of Presence*. This means that the fewer the visual components perceived, the more the 'objective pole' seems to disappear. The risk for it to become entirely extinguished can only be obviated by the intrusion of the burgeoning 'Presence'. Already in the borderline area between 'pictorial visions' and the 'vision of physiognomic appearances', i.e., the perception of isolated gestures and physiognomic expressions which are not integral part of an image, is hardly conceivable without the simultaneous presence of the 'Object' revealing itself in them. The pure and genuine 'imageless vision' is, in other words, essentially a 'vision' without an object and as such it depends on the knowledge of the presence of the 'All-encompassing', which is grounded in prior experience. Otherwise the alertness of the 'perceiving I' could not plausibly be directed at a specific 'object'. It is therefore the concrete awareness of an existing relationship between the perceiver and the 'Presence' that establishes an 'imageless mystical vision' in empirical reality, irrespective as to whether what is perceived as 'present' in 'inner sight' is visible or invisible.

The 'Inward Vision' Directed at the Invisible ["Die Schau auf ein Unsichtbares"]

The fact that at the beginning of each new chapter the same considerations are reiterated does not result from monomaniac persistence, but springs from the fear that the constant focus on varieties of 'mystical visions' might lead to a flawed assessment of their phenomenological significance within the overall context of mystical experience. The 'mystical visions' are, however, only one mode of mystical experience amongst many others, and it is, moreover, intertwined in empirical reality with diverse other kinds of mystical perception. Over and beyond this, the process of diminishing image-based content in 'mystical visions' is inevitably linked to increased interaction of diverse modes of mystical experience. Obviously, the *iconographic*, viz., 'pictorial vision' can easily be singled out as an isolated phenomenon. The type of *'imageless vision'*, by contrast, is an empty phenomenological structure, which will collapse if it is removed from the entire framework in which it occurs in empirical reality. If we wish to understand the phenomenon of the 'vision' in all its facets, we are therefore required to consider it not just individually, but together with other modes of mystical experience with which it is interlaced. By adopting this approach, we shall be able to advance gradually towards the phenomenological threshold at which the term 'vision' no longer applies, and must not be used anymore, when the perceiver encounters the invisible mystical phenomenon.

Our current approach continues to adhere to the theoretical concept of the 'vision', which will inevitably require us to separate the phenomenon from the complex fullness it has in empirical reality. We shall try to probe into the phenomenological structure of the 'vision' until we get to its uttermost threshold. We have earlier observed a similar discrepancy between the rank attributed to the category of 'visions' and the rank attributed to any of the other [non-visual] varieties of mystical experience when exploring the experience of 'Presence': It has turned out that the 'vision of Presence' is not the most viable mode of experiencing facets of the presence of the 'All-encompassing'. The diminishing importance of the visual mode of mystical experience becomes even more evident when we enter the domain of the cognitive perception of the 'whatness' of the 'mystical Object'. However, at the current stage of our enquiry, I do not dare to make any prediction as to whether a *'vision'* of the 'whatness' of the 'All-encompassing' is possible at all. It might well be that the 'imageless vision' terminates when faced with the unfathomable abyss of darkness.

The assumption that the 'mystical vision' is probably not a proficient medium for discerning something of the essence of the 'All-encompassing' has been one of the reasons why we bypassed the question relating to features of the 'whatness' of the 'All-encompassing' that might become manifest in a visionary experience. Such an isolated focus would be just as artificial and removed from empirical reality as separating visionary experience from the overall framework of mystical experience. After all, the vision of the presence of the 'All-encompassing' inevitably requires that features of the 'whatness' of the 'All-encompassing' are recognized; otherwise it would be impossible to recognize that what is 'present' is indeed 'all-encompassing'. This means that the decision to bypass aspects of the 'whatness' in our analysis of the 'vision' derived from methodological reasons. And we are required to adhere to this method on our path for the time being, although the cognitive structure of the 'whatness' will demand increasingly to be integrated into the analysis of the entire whole of mystical experience.

We have now paved the way that should enable us to understand the special variety of the 'imageless mystical vision' that we have termed 'glancing into the abyss of darkness'. Whoever is faced with this unfathomable abyss will be overwhelmed by the naked profundity of this impenetrable depth, unable to see anything of the essence of the abyss, and will be lost in the nothingness of the darkness, but – and this is a thrilling experience, one that has crucial existential significance – from within this abysmal darkness, the stream of 'Presence' begins to glow like lava. There is an uncanny and yet fascinating discrepancy between the purely receptive glance lacking any object, and the assured conviction that within this impenetrable darkness, at which 'inner sight' is riveted, the fullness of what has been searched for has indeed 'arrived' and become empirically 'present'. The insuperable juxtaposition of these two opposite poles of the experience is the hallmark and core of the 'imageless mystical vision'.

Considering the fact that even a fragmented portrayal of the 'imageless mystical vision' (imposed by methodology) can open up such deep insights into the existential relevance of the entire phenomenon, we may wonder how much more profound and adequate our understanding will become if we add to it the two prerequisites of any genuine mystical experience: The givenness of the 'quiet state of alertness' in which the perceiver is absorbed in 'inner sight', intent on witnessing the 'arrival' of the 'All-encompassing', responding to the 'nearness' of it with intense numinous feelings and assurance. This 'vision' into the vast abyss and impenetrable darkness arouses instantly an intense numinous response: it is simultaneously awe-inspiring and deeply blissful, both annihilating and ineffably gratifying; the 'vision' into the immeasurable abyss is at the same time a vessel for the fullness of light, which – though invisible – is cognitively grasped as 'being there'. All the numinous concepts that we have identified so far in our enquiry prove to be valid as appellations for the qualities of what is present albeit invisible: It is an encounter with the *mysterium tremendum*, with the unapproachable, the wholly-other, the sacred, the alluring *mysterium fascinosum*. We have stated that the term *majestas* is an exception amongst the numinous concepts because it does not denote an evaluation but an experiential quality. The circumstance that the 'mystical Object' of the 'imageless vision' is imbued with the quality of *majestas* is experienced by the array of diverse effects upon the perceiver, which are concrete manifestations of the overwhelming power and omnipotence that are inherent in any genuine mystical event.

As we have seen, it has proved helpful, if not crucial, for the progress of our enquiry to analyse the 'imageless mystical vision' individually and separated phenomenologically from the compound structure it usually has in empirical reality. The 'imageless vision' is likewise extremely sparse when viewed from a gnoseological perspective, but it is, irrespective of this fact, also the core of mystical experience and has as such ultimate existential relevance. *The 'imageless mystical vision' is a glimpse into an impenetrable darkness in which nothing can be discerned, yet in this unfathomable darkness that the perceiver has been searching for. Hence this mode of inward perception is at the same time an act of clinging to something unconditionally, of adhering to it in a direct, incomparable manner, not obscured or disrupted by any image.*

Phenomenologically, the 'imageless mystical vision' is sparse, and therefore there is very little that can be said about it. And the little that can be said is, paradoxically, at variance with the fullness of its existential significance. Therefore, we will try to continue to revolve around this phenomenon for some time by contrasting it to other mystical phenomena. We have used several expressions in describing the characteristics of the 'imageless mystical vision' that might give rise to misunderstandings: 'glancing into the abyss of darkness', 'the naked profundity', 'unfathomable abyss'. These expressions appear to echo phrases used by mystics in the medieval Christian tradition of 'negative theology' for describing a similar mystical experience; such descriptive expression can be found, for instance, in the mystical writings of Pseudo-Dionysius Areopagita, Eckhart, Tauler, Suso or Ruysbroeck. However, we must be cautious here not to jump to conclusions: From the use of the same or closely similar phrases and ideograms for designating the Numen, we cannot necessarily conclude that they have the same origin, and it is imperative to ascertain whether these expressions originate in a genuine mystical experience, or if they are merely borderline concepts resulting from philosophical and/or theological reflection. There is obviously a philosophical borderline situation reaching out into the realm of the Transcendental, and which must resort to negative terminology or even to paradox when referring to the Unknown, the Incomprehensible, or the '[All-]comprising'.[104] The notion of the Transcendental as being infinite, all-comprising and incomprehensible is particularly thrown into relief when it is juxtaposed with what is known, limited and intelligible. Negative theology, as expounded by Pseudo-Dionysius and his followers, derives from such a borderline situation in thinking, and is thus not grounded in mystical experience.[105]

Analogous appellations of the Numen can be found in religion – for instance, when the spiritual bond between the believer and the Divine has become so purified and firm that the use of an anthropomorphic expression would be inadequate and is therefore dispensed with. In certain mystical events, however, the experience of a current relationship

---

104 [Note: The German term used by Albrecht is "das Umgreifende"; it was originally coined by Karl Jaspers and adopted by Albrecht – though he does not indicate the source in Jaspers's works, nor does he give a bibliographical reference. Albrecht studied the works of Jaspers extensively; he quotes from Jaspers repeatedly in *Psychology of Mystical Consciousness*. To obviate terminological confusion with Jaspers's "das Umgreifende" ('the [All-]Comprising'), Albrecht opted for the alternative term "das Umfassende" ('the All-encompassing'). – FKW.]

105 [Note: This is a rather controversial apodictic claim of Albrecht's which is likely to provoke criticism on the part of mystical theology. – FKW.]

to a 'radical Otherness', or to an entity that is unintelligible, incomprehensible and mysterious, expressions are employed which reflect the given phenomenological characteristics appropriately. Such expressions may include items of the imagination which may be part of the 'stream' of numinous feelings. We stated earlier that the perception of a numinous relationship is not identical with the relationship experienced in a mystical event. Thus, the expression 'glancing into the abysmal depth of darkness' refers to the imageless 'beholding' of the Numen perceived as *present* and has nothing in common with a rational reassurance that there is a Transcendental Reality, nor has it any shared characteristics with the words inspired by a hypostasized experience of the *mysterium tremendum*, or the numinous stupor aroused by the encounter with the 'wholly Other'. In describing the 'imageless mystical vision', the words 'darkness', 'depth' and 'abyss' mirror appropriately the phenomenological sparsity of the mystical experience; and although this mystical event has great existential relevance, the sparsity of the experience is reflected in the sparsity of linguistic expression.

The following selected passages from the writings of mystics in the tradition of 'negative theology' are quoted for illustration. It is difficult to decide, however, which of these texts are indeed authentic records of an imageless mystical experience, which of them are merely grounded in philosophical speculation, and which of these accounts render merely a numinous event. Both Pseudo-Dionysius and the medieval German mystics were undoubtedly gratified with genuine mystical experiences; nevertheless, it seems to me that most of their idioms and terms appear to originate from rational reflection and theological tradition. When reading these texts we also have to consider some other aspects critically: These mystics advocate a path of contemplation guided by the teaching that any visual image must be overcome and that the mind must be vacated from anything 'beneath God' if spiritual prayer is to be successful; moreover, the instruction to proceed from the 'visible' towards the 'Invisible' also applies to the entire path of the mystical ascent, hence to the process of 'purification' and spiritual transformation. To achieve this goal the mystics of the apophatic tradition ultimately demand the 'annihilation' of 'I-hood' resulting in the complete 'detachment' of the contemplative from worldly desires. However, a contemplative following this path may nonetheless be gratified on the way with the special gift of a 'mystical vision' that is not 'imageless'. These are vital aspects in the works of spiritual guidance of the mystics of the 'apophatic tradition'. The following texts thus must be read against this theological background, and descriptions of 'imageless mystical visions' must be assessed individually.

> *Text 90* (Dionysius Areopagita, *Mystical Theology*)[106]: [Ch. 1] "Trinity, which exceedeth all Being, Deity, and Goodness! Thou that instructeth Christians in Thy heavenly wisdom! Guide us to that topmost height of mystic lore which exceedeth light and more than exceedeth knowledge, where the simple, absolute, and unchangeable mysteries of heavenly Truth lie hidden in the dazzling obscurity of the secret Silence, outshining all brilliance with the intensity of their darkness, and surcharging our blinded intellects with the utterly impalpable and invisible fairness of glories which exceed all beauty! Such be my prayer; ...
>
> [Ch. 5] Once more, ascending yet higher, we maintain that It is not soul, or mind, or endowed with the faculty of imagination, conjecture, reason, or understanding; nor is It any act of reason or understanding; nor can It be described by the reason or perceived by the understanding, since It is not number, or order, or greatness, or littleness, or equality, or inequality, and since It is not immovable nor in motion, or at rest, and has no power, and is not power or light, and does not live, and is not life; nor is It personal essence, or eternity, or time; nor can It be grasped by the understanding since It is not knowledge or truth; nor is It kingship or wisdom; nor is It one, nor is It unity, nor is It Godhead or Goodness; nor is It a Spirit, as we understand the term, since It is not Sonship or Fatherhood; nor is It any other thing such as we or any other being can have knowledge of; nor does It belong to the category of non-existence or to that of existence; nor do existent beings know It as it actually is, nor does It know them as they actually are; nor can the reason attain to It to name It or to know It; nor is it darkness, nor is It light, or error, or truth; nor can any affirmation or negation apply to it; for while applying affirmations or negations to those orders of being that come next to It, we apply not unto It either affirmation or negation, inasmuch as It transcends all affirmation by being the

---

106   [Note: Albrecht's quotation is from the German translation of Pseudo-Dionysius's mystagogical treatise *De theologia mystica*: "Von der Mystischen Theologie." *Die Angeblichen Schriften des Areopagiten Dionysius*. Trans. J.G.V. Engelhardt. Suzbach: Seidel, 1823. Albrecht does not give page references, but the passages quoted can be traced – as indicated above – to the beginning of chapter 1, and in part to chapter 5. The English translation has been taken from <www.hoye.de/theo/denistxt.pdf>. – FKW.]

perfect and unique Cause of all things, and transcends all negation by the pre-eminence of Its simple and absolute nature-free from every limitation and beyond them all."

Text 91 (Meister Eckhart)[107]: "And this is most wholesome to the soul: *unknowing* entices her to aspire to something wonderful and animates her to chase it! For she feels clearly *that* it is, but does not know *how* and *what* it is … This knowing by unknowing entices the soul to persevere in her quest and to continue her pursuit. – The more you become emptied and void inside, and ignorant of all things, the closer you will get to it. – You can only see Him in 'blindness', in not-knowing, without any form, or sound or rational comprehension. If there were no earthly image in the notion of God any more, God would be seen pure as He is. – Nothing else can impart perfect bliss into the soul than being exposed in the desert of the Godhead, in which there is neither any activity nor image – where the soul gets lost and absorbed in contemplation and annihilated so that she becomes indifferent to all created things, as if they did not exist. God is born in this 'nothingness'. – The divine essence is devoid of any image and shape, which would enable the soul to comprehend it. When the soul has turned away from everything that is familiar to her and towards that which is *beyond* earthly existence – for this is what is understood by 'becoming indifferent' and detached from worldly things – she is bestowed with the likeness of the formless nature of God, whose true nature is never revealed to any creature as long as it is confined in the body. This is the secret access to the divine nature granted to the soul. For when the soul is deprived of everything on which she might rely, she has been purified and attained the likeness of God. This is what is meant by the expression that 'nothing is approaching nothingness'."

Text 92 (Johannes Tauler)[108]: "Exalt your feelings to the ultimate heights and into the desert within. – This spirit penetrates the ground, leaving all images and forms behind, until it – formless and without image – has moved

---

107 [Note: Albrecht has taken passages from Eckhart's writings from various sources: BÜTTNER, Hermann, ed. *Meister Eckharts Schriften und Predigten*. 2 vols. Jena: Diederichs, 1919. Vol. I. 81, 104, 148; KARRER, Otto. *Meister Eckehart Spricht: Gesammelte Texte*. Munich: Mueller, 1925. 136; 143; 144. English translation provided. – FKW.]

108 [Note: The passages from Tauler's sermons quoted by Albrecht are from: TAULER, Johann. *Predigten*. Leipzig: Insel, 1923. 60; 61; 69; 86; 55; 150; 175. – English translation provided. – FKW.]

beyond itself. – Those who have become detached are bestowed with [the gift of the Divine Spirit] in the concealed abyss, in the secret kingdom, in the blissful ground, in which the precious image of the Holy Trinity lies hidden. The ineffable abyss of God must be the abode of His reception, not a part in His creatures. – The powers of thy spirit will be stretched out into a wilderness, about which nobody is able to speak, into the hidden darkness of the formless essence. The spirit will be guided into the oneness and eventually it will become united with the formless Oneness, in a manner that all awareness of any difference is eroded; for in the state of union all multiplicity is suspended; union annihilates all multiplicity. – The abyss created is unfathomable; engulfed by the depth of the uncreated abyss and uncreated nothingness, both flow into each other resulting in a unified oneness, nothing afloat in nothing. – This is indeed the hallmark of the entire experience: becoming inexplicably absorbed in unfathomable nothingness."

These textual passages can unfortunately contribute but little to advancing our understanding of the 'imageless mystical vision', as they do not offer any conclusive phenomenological descriptions of the same. These texts are rather a mixture of theological reflections based on or inspired by the spiritual teaching of 'negative theology', of ideas derived from Christian Neoplatonism, and, arguably, of descriptions derived from personal mystical experience. There is an intricate linguistic pattern of metaphoric accounts of the 'content' of imageless visionary experiences, intertwined with concepts of 'negative theology' and theological reflection which can hardly be disentangled for the purpose of disclosing viable data for phenomenological analysis. Even if we concede that these accounts are in part grounded in personal mystical experiences of 'Nothingness' and/or in imageless visions of the Divine, it is reasonable to suppose that these mystics preferred to resort to established theological concepts and the approved terminology of apophatic mysticism and Neoplatonism for rendering and interpreting this ineffable mystical event.

There is yet another striking fact about these accounts: The 'imageless vision' appears to be closely affiliated with the upsurge of feelings of ecstasy. This is remarkable because in the 'imageless mystical vision' the subject-object-division is usually more pronounced than in any other mystical experience, whereas in an ecstatic experience the subject-object-split is only given in the incipient stage, but otherwise it is eroded (either gradually or abruptly).

The third aspect that should be noted is that in the writings of Eckhart and Tauler the 'imageless mystical vision' is also related to the mystic's progress on the spiritual path. Vacating the mind and becoming detached from the 'things in this world' are indispensable requirements of the process of 'purification'. This means that the texts quoted address three different aspects of the mystic's spiritual struggle against interfering images: 1. The texts refer in part to the experience of an 'imageless mystical vision', in which the contemplative's 'inner sight' is directed at the unfathomable, inscrutable and invisible Presence; 2. the accounts are also imbued with the authors' knowledge of philosophy and mystical theology (especially in the tradition of 'negative theology'), in which the Divine essence is claimed to be entirely 'unknowable', 'ineffable', 'invisible'; 3. spiritual growth is inexorably linked to a process of 'emptying the mind' and of divesting the soul from all images of God. Thus we may discern three notions of 'imageless emptiness': The 'Nothingness of the Godhead', the unfathomable abyss between perceiver and the Divine, and the nothingness of the seeker's soul, termed 'a barren desert' by Tauler; the mystic, immersed in the Nothingness of the Godhead, perceiving in the 'imageless vision' the 'abyss of his soul', is faced with a borderline situation, which evokes the mystical theorem of the identity between the perceiver (subject) and the 'mystical Object'. The notion of the 'oneness' of the perceiver and the Object perceived is at the root of the Christian mystic's conviction that he may advance to the 'ground of the soul' the more he/she has become immersed in a state of pure emptiness, devoid of any image, in which he/she may ultimately be gratified with the gift of being 'oned' with the formless and imageless essence of the Godhead.

The End of the State of 'Vision'

The 'imageless vision' is a glimpse into the darkness, but it is not a vision of the dark. It is a 'vision' in which nothing is seen, but it is not a 'vision' of Nothingness, for the 'vision' in which the perceiver glimpses into the darkness and the act of beholding nothing are always inextricably intertwined with the concomitant awareness that the 'mystical Presence' is secretly 'there'. The darkness is, as it were, the vessel for the whole fullness of the 'all-encompassing It' to become manifest. The experience of the 'Presence' and the persevering state of 'vision' are two mystical relations that depend on each other. *The concept of the 'imageless mystical vision' comprises necessarily the cognitive perception of Presence, and the experience of Presence acquires its full mystical dimension only, if the 'inner eye' is alert and intent on perceiving incoming phenomena in the hyper-lucid state of inner calmness; only if this serene and calm mental condition is sustained is the core-phenomenon of mysticism – the clear juxtaposition of subject and 'mystical Object' –given expression in the purest manner possible.*

The mental condition in which an 'imageless mystical vision' occurs is thus, phenomenologically, a borderline situation. Or to put it differently: The 'imageless vision' as described above has reached its final state. The words 'borderline' and 'final state' are to be understood strictly in phenomenological terms. These terms do not denote that the 'imageless vision' is specifically related to an existential or noetic threshold, nor do they mean that an ongoing imageless visionary experience must necessarily terminate the state of 'inner sight'. The latter cannot apply because it is possible that during an 'imageless mystical vision', visual and other phenomena may surface or intrude without disrupting the state of 'inner sight'. It is possible, for instance, that during an 'imageless mystical vision' a 'vision of light' may suddenly intrude, or that physiognomic appearances or gestures may emerge from the darkness. The 'final state' or 'end' of an 'imageless vision' is reached phenomenologically, when the term 'vision', viz., 'inner sight', no longer applies, i.e., when the clear distinction between 'experiencing I' and 'mystical Object' is no longer sustained. In this case, the concept 'imageless mystical vision' must be substituted by a different term.

The phenomenological characteristics of the 'imageless vision' identified by our enquiry permit the following conclusions: First, the 'imageless vision' turns out to be phenomenologically blurred in the peripheral and/or transitional zones. The state of 'vision' is transitory, tending to disintegrate and to be replaced by other varieties of mystical experience. Second, the 'imageless vision' may dissolve or be instantly superseded by a sudden, overwhelming mystical event.

Third, the 'imageless vision' may gradually change over into a 'pictorial vision', in which metaphoric shapes and effigies appear, which are ideograms of entirely different items of 'content' which come from a domain outside the realm of visionary experience. We have previously stated that the state of 'vision' may gradually change and/or merge with non-visual modes of mystical experience (like inner hearing); we will later refer to a few more such varieties of composite mystical experience.

The abrupt end or sudden disintegration of the state of 'vision' is a psychological phenomenon identified in our previous study as an instance of the 'ecstatic consciousness'. By this occurrence the 'quiet state of alertness' (i.e., a hyper-lucid, calm, alert and fully integrated homogenous state of consciousness and ideal medium of 'inner sight') is immediately destroyed and supplanted by the 'ecstatic consciousness'. In this event, the 'experiencing I', immersed in the tranquillity of the 'quiet state of alertness', with the function of 'inner sight' being directed at the vast darkness concealing as yet the presence of the 'All-encompassing', is unexpectedly overwhelmed by feelings of ecstasy; the perceiver is struck as if by lightning and at the same time shattered by the deafening noise of thunder. In this liminal event the 'vision' is no longer merely dazzling, but entirely dispersed. The impact of this overwhelming 'blow' terminates the state of 'vision'. It does not only affect the perceiver as 'perceiving I'; in addition, it has persevering repercussions on his/her whole existence. The perceiver becomes the 'vessel' of phenomena impinged on him/her and which he/she is required to suffer. He/she is inundated by a torrent of somatic, visionary, emotional, auditory and tactile phenomena culminating in a single composite ecstatic mystical experience. The perceiver is overpowered and the capacity of 'inner sight' is eroded, dazzled by the 'all-encompassing It', which had been hidden by the darkness. This is the paradoxical borderline experience and psychological-phenomenological substratum that has inspired the paradoxical expression 'dazzling darkness'[109].

---

109 [Note: In western mysticism the oxymoronic expression "dazzling darkness" can be traced to the writings of Pseudo-Dionysius and the influence of the *Corpus Dionysiacum* in the High and Late Middle Ages and beyond. The English phrase is,

Identifying the defining moment at which the state of 'vision' switches to the state of ecstasy is of paramount importance not only for our enquiry, as it marks the transition from one pivotal mystical domain [i.e., mystical experiences witnessed in the 'quiet state of alertness'] to the other core phenomenon of mysticism [i.e., mystical experiences occurring in the 'ecstatic state of consciousness'], but also because it is at the same time the decisive point at which the 'vision' of the mere 'isness' of the 'All-encompassing', i.e., the awareness of the 'mystical Presence' becomes an experience of the essence of the 'All-encompassing'. The impact of being 'dazzled' by the mystical event which has burst in upon the perceiver from 'over there', where something was perceived as present, albeit concealed by the darkness, which could be identified with absolute certainty as an 'all-encompassing Entity', indicates persuasively that the awesome power of the *majestas* has been experienced.

The phenomenological threshold of the 'vision' is transgressed whenever phenomena appear in the vista of 'inner sight' that can no longer be appropriately attributed to the realm of visual experience. A mystical 'vision' may terminate in three different ways – two of them have already been outlined, and the third will be delineated below. The third way does not involve (as in the first) a gradual process in which the state of 'vision' changes over into neighbouring kinds of mystical experience, nor does it entail the instantaneous destruction of the state of 'vision' (as in the second way), but it consists of a peculiar 'decline' of the state of 'vision' into modes of pictorial vision, which do not, however, result from a *primary* encounter with a 'mystical Object', but from secondary visual representations of concurrent non-visual components of the given mystical event. The word 'decline' has been used deliberately, as it is meant to emphasize that in this kind of 'vision' the 'mystical Object' is missing, though a wide variety of visual phenomena are beheld. The images beheld have metaphoric or symbolic import;

---

for instance, expressly used by the Welsh Metaphysical Poet Henry Vaughan (1621–1695) in his poem "The Night": "There is in God, some say, /A deep but dazzling darkness" (ll. 49–50). For an anthology on the tradition and use of this motif in western mysticism see GRANT, Patrick, ed. *A Dazzling Darkness: An Anthology of Western Mysticism*. Grand Rapids, MI: Eerdmans, 1985. – FKW.]

they surface in the vista of 'inner sight' and are related metaphorically to the ongoing 'stream' of impressions passing through consciousness.

This rather uncommon phenomenon can best be approached when it is divided into its main phenomenological components. The point of departure is again the lucid 'quiet state of alertness' in which the perceiver's 'inner sight' is directed at the 'mystical Object'; this state of 'vision' is intertwined with the cognitive awareness of 'Presence' – in other words, the point of reference is the basic phenomenological framework of the 'imageless vision'. It is a 'vision' reaching out into the darkness, in which the 'All-encompassing' is known to be 'present'. Yet there is a new element: The 'All-encompassing', viz., the 'It', which is cognitively grasped as 'present', has a nonpareil sensible impact on the 'experiencing I'. The perceiver is deeply affected by the 'It' – emotionally, somatically, and mentally. The perceiver's relation to the 'It' is experienced in terms of a multi-layered cause-effect relationship, which may find concrete expression, for instance, in a dramatic change of the emotional condition, somatic symptoms such as the sense of being touched, or directed by an overwhelming Power.

We will further explore these somatic, tactile, emotional and other non-visual sensible modes of mystical experience later. At this stage of our enquiry, the important issue is the fact that the perceiver is exposed to a mystical encounter with a 'stream of empirical phenomena' that occur outside the realm of a visionary experience. And this 'stream of phenomena' affecting the perceiver foreshadows metaphorically certain characteristics of the essence of the mysterious 'Presence', which is felt to dwell secretly in the darkness. As the function of the 'inner sight', viz., 'inward vision' is fully alert, diverse shape-like images may appear in it, in which the 'object' encountered may manifest itself metaphorically. Once the 'vessel' of 'inner sight' is prepared to 'receive', it will comprehend images and symbols that can be claimed to be fitting metaphors for what has been experienced on the level of somatic, tactile and/or auditory perception. Thus, something is experienced of the 'mystical Object' outside the realm of visual phenomena, though visual phenomena become manifest in 'inner sight', which are, however, merely appropriate representations of the underlying mystical experience and not a 'vision' of the 'mystical Object' itself. In this transitional zone, there is an ongoing fluctuation between visionary and non-visionary modes of perception. Yet this borderline zone does not correspond anymore to the concept of 'vision' as defined, as the lucid state of 'vision' has declined into a mere corollary in a mystical event dominated by non-visionary experience. There are two major reasons why I have considered it indispensable to elaborate on this liminal transitional phenomenon in some detail: First, it allows us to discern clearly the difference between the visual perception of metaphoric images in 'inner sight' which are merely ancillary to a non-visionary mystical experience, and genuine mystical phenomena encountered in a true 'mystical vision'. Both the image 'beheld' in a genuine 'pictorial mystical vision' (which is a picture 'infused', 'arriving' from beyond the confines of the individual consciousness) and the invisible 'Presence' grasped cognitively while shrouded in darkness in an 'imageless mystical vision', are items of the 'subject matter' instilled in a 'mystical vision' that cannot possibly be mistaken for a metaphoric image surfacing in 'inner sight'.

Second, it is important to acknowledge that there is a large realm of mystical relations beyond visionary mystical experiences in which the 'mystical vision' is embedded, by which it is sustained and by which it is enfolded like by something primeval. Just as there is an 'undifferentiated' primeval realm of sensory experience, there is likewise an 'undifferentiated' sphere in the domain of mystical experience, from which the auditory and visual modes of experience have sprouted (as it were).

We have now come to the outermost threshold of the state of 'vision': Though intensive search might perhaps yield a few more phenomena by which the thresholds of visionary experience could be delineated, I think the ones described above are enough to illustrate the distinctive characteristics of the genuine variety of the 'mystical vision'. By way of conclusion, we will summarize the findings before proceeding to the sustaining ground of all genuine mystical experiences.

The phenomenon dealt with last, the 'declining' state of 'mystical vision' resulting in a mode of 'vision' without a 'mystical Object', displaying visual items which are merely metaphoric representations of ongoing non-visual mystical experience, is nonetheless an important link between visionary and non-visionary mystical experience. The process of disintegration of the visionary state is very difficult to describe but can be well illustrated by authentic records of such an experiential occurrence. The following quotations are from documents retrieved from spontaneous utterances spoken by a person while absorbed in the 'quiet state of alertness':[110]

> *Text 93* (Personal document, dated 14 June 1950; spoken by a subject while immersed in the 'quiet state of alertness'): "I was filled with joy. It was a daring gamble, when I tried to offer this joy to Him. The place where I was situated radiated with a light that was brighter than anything I had ever seen before. The awareness of His nearness was constantly all about me and a fact beyond any doubt. There were circles put around me, which – increasing in diameter – reached out into the infinite. I was granted to touch the area encompassed by the first circle so that soft waves began to develop, which, becoming smaller and smaller eventually extended into the domain where everything was open for Him.
>
> I wanted to become absorbed in prayer and searched for the many things in me that have not been purified, hoping that I could offer them to Him in devout surrender. But he sealed my eyes, and I could not find anything that I was allowed to pray to Him for. I could discern the grey panel with an inscription that seemed so holy. Yet the immensely moving message 'I love You!' lost its devastating heaviness. I took the panel and leaned it against the big dark rock of 'Thou'. – I did this perhaps because I wanted to honour it, or else, because I wanted to be permitted to shut my eyes.
>
> Meanwhile, I knew that I was ablaze. The flames could not be seen flickering, but they were ablaze inside, flaring from all the countless life-points of my body; I felt the flames burning steadily and intensely inside. It was so uncanny that the overpowering impressions stayed close with me

---

110   [Note: The following testimonies of spontaneous utterances, spoken while the 'experiencing I' was absorbed in the 'quiet state of alertness', are most probably autobiographical. All of Albrecht's experiences of 'locutions' and utterances spoken during his progress to the stage of "Versunkenheit" as well as during the state of "Versunkenheit" (viz., 'quiet state of alertness'), were documented by his wife. Endowed with the humility of a true mystic, Albrecht appears to have refrained from acknowledging authorship; however, the year stated, as well as the stylistic and phenomenological affinities with other spontaneous utterances quoted in Hans A. Fischer-Barnicol's edition of *Das Mystische Wort. Erleben und Sprechen in Versunkenheit* (1974), suggest that these testimonies are almost certainly Albrecht's. – FKW.]

and nearly became familiar objects. The experiences of empty space and of becoming extinguished by the overwhelming power of an all-devouring chasm, these thrilling forces were at first placed around me like objects, without the fire inside changing. And yet: I became aware that I was weeping inwardly. I was crying because I was poor and could not get hold of anything that I could offer as a sacrifice. I would have loved to be purged for Him, but He did not give me the chance to do so.

The grey panel and the dark 'Thou' and the emptiness were ground to dust by a mortar and pestle; and I inhaled the dust and the levity of my breathing was not impaired at all. I was ablaze but not consumed by the fire. The outlines of my shape were mirrored again and again in the purging flames burning evenly.

When I was released from the place of this rare hour, I was filled with silent joy within in a tremor that God had passed by me and that I had experienced the divine footstep like a foreboding."

Text 94 (Record dated 18 August 1950; spoken by a subject while immersed in the 'quiet state of alertness'): "A very big heavy key, glittering darkly, was turned around in my body. I can still see the bronze and golden glow of the mysterious ornaments on the key's surface. I had been unlocked, somehow, and I saw a seal imprinted inside in the middle of my body, stretched out in a bareness that was uncanny. I could not tell whether I was a body, or a big heap of crystal; but I knew and saw that everything had been turned into a blaze by the overwhelming power of flickering tongues of fire and that the vault of the night had burst by the upsurge of flames ... Everything was devoured by the flames, but since my body had become infinite, whatever was burning was not consumed. There were numerous splinters of my 'flawed I' scattered around, which I threw into the flames, seemingly indifferent and as if in passing. – Oh, if He had gratified me with a picture of Himself, or a sacred object in front of which I might have bowed my knees, only to have something placed between me and His invisible Presence that I could behold. Yet not even the infinite emptiness of the room could be transformed into an image of Him, because the room was as dense and solid as the earth.

I have to add that, inexplicably, a gust of wind blew through me, or from me, and that sometimes the solidity of the room had some affinity to the lethal hush before the imminent outburst of a thunderstorm at noon ..."

These recorded verbal utterances spoken by a person while absorbed in the 'quiet state of alertness'; these records show quite unmistakably that each of them has been evoked by a complex visionary experience. The 'experiencing I' is faced successively with a wide range of images and other visual impressions; however, these visual impressions are not items of a 'mystical vision' but merely metaphorical representations of an ongoing non-visual mystical experience, notably one affecting the perceiver emotionally, somatically and cognitively. Assessed in view of a genuine mystical relation, the visual phenomena witnessed cannot even be classified as mystically 'infused' images or symbols, let alone as self-revealing pictorial appearances, or as an immediate encounter with the 'invisible Presence'.

At this point of our enquiry, we need to return to an earlier stage. The peripheral phenomena of the 'vision' outlined above – i.e., the transitional zone in which the 'mystical vision' becomes blurred and is blended with adjacent phenomena, the occurrence in which the state of 'vision' disintegrates by the powerful impact of somatic, emotional, cognitive mystical effects, and the decline of the state of the mystical 'vision' into the 'inner sight' of metaphoric images – must not obfuscate our perspective when we approach the core of mystical experience from a new angle.

If we wish to come to a final assessment of the 'imageless vision', we are required to resort to unconventional terms and seemingly contradictory expressions. I am going to epitomize the phenomenon in the following theses and (apparent) anti-theses; the theses juxtaposed are, strictly speaking, not antinomies, since their propositions are not mutually exclusive, but they are helpful for elucidating the phenomenon from different aspects.

Thesis: *In an 'imageless vision' the ultimate visionary stage of the mystical relation finds expression.* – The state of 'vision' has developed in it in the purest possible manner, and the relationship to the 'mystical Object' is an immediate one.

Antithesis: *In the 'imageless vision' the turning point of visionary experience is reached. The state of 'vision' has evolved into a borderline situation, for which the term 'vision' no longer applies* because in an 'imageless vision' nothing is beheld anymore.

Thesis: *In the 'imageless vision' the subject-object-division has reached the ultimate degree.* The 'perceiving I', absorbed in a hyper-lucid state of consciousness, is instantly filled with the evident knowledge of the 'Presence' of the 'mystical Object'. The 'beholding I' and the 'object beheld' are distinctly juxtaposed. The 'beholding I' is solely focussed on the 'mystical Object', and there is no delusory mediating image placed in between.

Antithesis: *Visionary perception is a phenomenon rooted in a mental condition that is radically empty and without any image, and for this reason it is commonly placed close to the state of ecstasy. Hence the 'imageless vision' is seen as a transition zone between 'vision' and 'ecstasy'.* The 'perceiving I' is overwhelmed by the impact of feelings of ecstasy, while still adhering to the capacity of 'vision'; they are thus adjoining phenomena becoming blended. It is possible, however, that the state of 'vision' may prevail within the ecstatic consciousness, and to experience ecstasy while immersed in the state of 'vision'. The seam between the two phenomena is the point in which the most serene state of 'vision' is dazed by ecstasy and ultimately suffused by ecstatic rapture.

THESIS 65: *The core-phenomenon of the 'imageless mystical vision' is the unique fusion of the state of imageless 'inner sight' and the inalienable awareness of 'Presence'.* The state of 'imageless vision' and the sense of 'Presence' can only be distinguished phenomenologically. In the ultimate stage of the 'imageless mystical vision', the state of 'vision' is entirely pure and empty, without any visual content, and hence it has become a void, formal structure in which alone the capacity for 'inner sight' remains. This capacity, however, has reached the most serene and supreme degree that can be attained, and in this ultimately lucid mental condition the nearness of the 'mystical Object' is most intimately perceived, and thus the existence of a cognitive relation between perceiver and the 'mystical Object' is revealed most genuinely.

The fact that the actual core of mystical experience consists of the coexistence of the serene, imageless state of 'vision' and the cognitive awareness of the invisible 'mystical Presence', may explain why in the 'imageless vision' the primeval condition of the state of 'vision' appears to have become jumbled. Evidently, what is most commonly given in any visionary experience is the presence of an object that is beheld, but in the 'imageless vision' the object remains invisible, and only the awareness of its non-visual 'presence' is retained. And it is the latter that turns out to be the most significant element in this mystical experience. Conversely, what really matters in a normal visual relationship – namely, the relationship between the perceiver to what is seen – is entirely extinguished in this special relation of 'not beholding' in the 'imageless vision'. The gnoseological sparseness of the 'imageless vision' is, paradoxically, reciprocal to its existential relevance. Evidently, an object perceived as present, though nothing of its essence can be discerned, is obviously an experience to which the lowest rank in the gnoseological hierarchy must be attributed. The fact, however, that the 'imageless vision' of the invisible 'object' has supreme existential significance for the perceiver suggests that it is rooted in an experiential relation to the invisible 'Presence', which must be attributed a ranking in the topmost tier of all varieties of mystical experience. And if, over and beyond this, the inability to recognize and the impossibility to fathom the essence of the 'mystical Object' is understood as an authentic ideogram for the ultimate incomprehensibility and unintelligibility of what is perceived as 'present' in the 'imageless vision', then we may infer that no phenomena have been missed in 'inner sight' during the state of 'vision', but rather that something has been bestowed that corresponds to the essence of the 'Object' beheld.

The Spectrum of the 'Mystical Vision'

The spectrum of the 'mystical vision' covers the range between the two juxtaposed poles of the 'pictorial vision' and the 'imageless vision'. *The varieties of visionary experience occurring in between these two poles consist of two strands of phenomena rather than of only one; these strands are, however, structurally so closely intertwined with each other that the individual components can only be identified methodologically by an approach through psychological phenomenology.* Depending on which of the two poles we begin the phenomenological approach – starting either from the pictorial or the imageless state of vision – *the types of 'vision' are either marked by decreasing pictorial content advancing to zero, or, respectively, increasing pictorial content.* These processes of decreasing and/or increasing pictographic content are at the same time linked to an analogous process of an *increasing or, respectively, decreasing sense of 'Presence'.* The ratio between the two sequences of visionary experience is basically proportionate, though *the share of each is proportionally inverted*, i.e., in visions with increasing pictorial content, the concomitant awareness of 'Presence' is declining, whereas in visions with decreasing pictorial content, the concomitant awareness of 'Presence' is increasing.

THESIS 66: *The sequence of visionary mystical experiences with decreasing pictorial content corresponds to the sequence of experiences with increasing awareness of 'Presence'*. And this applies analogously to:

THESIS 67: *The sequence of visionary mystical experiences with increasing pictorial content corresponds to the sequence of experiences with declining awareness of 'Presence'*.

The 'vision' of an emblematic or allegorical image is a 'pictorial vision' without any awareness of 'Presence'. In this type of 'picture-based mystical vision' the allegorical image has been generated mystically and is beheld with clarity in a hyper-lucid state of consciousness. The image observed is the [only] object behold; the visionary experience is not accompanied by any awareness of the 'presence' of the 'All-encompassing'. The 'presence' of the 'All-encompassing' in this event is not required phenomenologically and is not part of the experience.

In the 'imageless vision' any image or any other visual content is missing. The visionary relationship is reduced to that between the 'experiencing I' and the invisible 'Presence'. In between the two extremes of the 'pictorial' and the 'imageless vision', the three phenomena addressed earlier are to be placed in stepwise arrangement. This means that the entire spectrum of the 'mystical vision' encompasses altogether varieties of 'visions' composed of five major elements: *Starting at the pole of the 'pictorial vision', the next stage is the visionary experience consisting of the double-phenomenon in which 'visual image' and sense of 'Presence' are intertwined*. In this variety of the 'vision' the perceiver's relationship is focussed on the symbol and/or allegorical image perceived, while the awareness of the presence of the Numen is cognitively grasped only in a subsequent act of experience. The Numen is perceived, as it were, as if it were 'behind', or 'beside' the image beheld. *The third variety of 'mystical vision' is that of the epiphanic pictorial manifestation*. Here the perception of 'Presence' is an integral part of the image. Though the image is only a picture-like representation and not the 'mystical Object' itself, the latter is somehow transparent *within* the effigy witnessed; or rather, the 'Presence', the effigy and the self-revelatory manifestation are merged into a single visionary experience. The fourth variety is that of the *'self-expressive pictorial appearance'*. Here the perceiver does not observe a fully developed image, but only a reduced, fragmented effigy in which only rudimentary outlines of a shape or picture can be discerned, which, however, may have mystical import and elicit intimations of the 'Presence'. This supports that claim that the awareness of 'Presence' becomes more powerful and distinct the more the pictorial quality of a 'vision' is reduced. The 'Presence' comes to the fore increasingly in experiences of declining visual content, and its manifestation becomes more and more untainted. In the final stage, the 'self-expressive gestures and epiphanic appearances' are removed, permitting the 'naked Presence' to take centre stage as the sole Object of the 'imageless vision'.

The dynamic phenomena indispensable for the sequence of visionary experiences to occur, which have been described in terms of declining into a transitory state, and of 'eroding' and 'obscuring' the 'state of vision', are part of the intermediate stages of these five varieties of mystical visionary experience and have for this reason been placed outside the phenomenological spectrum of the 'mystical vision'. These terms have only been introduced to indicate the dynamic process and to show that various types of 'vision' are only *one category* within the entire range of genuine composite mystical experiences encountered in empirical reality.

One visionary phenomenon stands out: The 'vision of light'. This is a special phenomenon which cannot clearly correspond to the concept of 'vision' as conceived above. Though it is true that in the 'mystical vision of Light' a visual object is obviously beheld in 'inner sight', it cannot easily be assigned a place within the spectrum in the 'mystical vision'. It goes without saying that the light perceived in this vision is not an allegorical image. The vision of the 'mystical Light' is moreover always imbued with the sense of the 'presence' of the 'All-encompassing'. Yet the merging of the two phenomena is so inextricable that the concept of the 'double-phenomenon of image and Presence' is not appropriate. One might be tempted to consider the 'mystical Light' as an image-like apparition, but this would again conflict with the fact that the 'mystical Light' is not an 'image', or a 'picture'. Though light obviously has in the widest sense some picture-like quality, this visual quality does not signify its essence. For this reason, it has been suggested to classify the 'mystical Light' in terms of a 'self-expressive epiphanic appearance'. But this notion is likewise inadequate because it is too vague and ambivalent in that it suggests much more about the nature of this 'light' than is represented by it. Although it is true that the 'Light' featuring in a 'mystical vision' reveals some ineffable quality of the essence of the 'All-encompassing', this is too little and too sparse to classify it in terms of an epiphanic revelation.

This means that *the 'mystical Light' must be assigned an eccentric place beyond the spectrum of the 'mystical vision', not only because it is phenomenologically rather close to the type of the 'self-expressive image' and that of the 'epiphanic image-like apparition', but also because it has an even closer affinity to the 'imageless vision' of the 'pure Presence'.* Yet this fact notwithstanding, the 'vision of Light' is surely not identical with an 'imageless vision'. The 'mystical Light' is, perhaps – and I must admit, I really don't know – a visible metaphoric phenomenon elicited as a corollary of another mystical event; as such it might disclose something about the 'mystical Object' envisaged that might otherwise have escaped notice. Seen from this perspective, the 'mystical Light' might be a token of the realness of a mystical event; in other words, without the perception of the 'mystical Light', an ephemeral mystical encounter might elude recognition.

Auditory Mystical Experience

Within the many varieties of mystical experiences, the 'vision' is only one specific mode of experiencing the Numinous, viz., the 'All-encompassing'. The aim of our investigation, however, is to explore phenomenologically the entire range of mystical experience, and therefore we shall proceed to a category complementary to the 'vision': 'audition', or auditory mystical experience (a phenomenon that we briefly referred to above). Auditory mystical experience has many affinities, both phenomenologically and structurally, with visual mystical experiences; in fact, 'visionary' and 'auditory' mystical experiences are often intertwined in concrete mystical events. It is therefore relatively easy to provide a phenomenology of the phenomenon of 'mystical hearing' by way of a contrastive analysis. The results of this approach should furnish us furthermore with important insights relating to our gnoseological considerations.

The claim that mystical 'visions' and 'auditions' are analogous types of mystical experience is substantiated by empirical fact: In the event of a 'mystical vision', 'inner sight', viz., the function of the 'inner eye', is highly alert to and directed at the perception of visual phenomena 'arriving' in its vista. Similarly, *in 'auditory mystical experience', the 'listening I' is alert to, and intent on the 'hearing' of words and/or sounds heard within, i.e., words or sounds heard inwardly, perceived as 'arriving' within the mind.* Both these modes of inner perception occur while the perceiver is immersed in the 'quiet state of alertness', which is the clearest, most alert and most tranquil and most perfectly emptied state of consciousness accessible to man. *Visions and auditions are highly differentiated modes of mystical experience and differ significantly from such diffuse, undifferentiated experiences as the awareness of mystical feelings and tactile and/or somatic mystical effects.* Both visionary and auditory varieties of mystical experience involve encounters with a 'mystical Object'. These experiences are relatively easily accessible to phenomenological analysis, by which reliable epistemological foundations are supplied for their critical gnoseological assessment.

The phenomenological range of 'auditions' is analogous to the phenomenological range of 'visions'. Because of this analogy it has been possible for us to analyse in a previous chapter the phenomenological characteristics jointly. In this context we have also stated that there is a 'dark' transition zone between visionary and auditory experiences, in which it is difficult to differentiate between the two phenomena.

The spectral range of auditory experiences begins in a zone of intermingled phenomena, in inner acoustic impressions that are perceived as if coming from external space. These aural impressions are therefore akin to hallucinations. In this hybrid zone we generally encounter 'voices' and 'locutions' that are identified as entering from a spatial area outside the individual self, rather than 'voices' and 'locutions' that are heard inwardly. Hallucinatory 'voices' and 'locutions' are perceived as intruding from 'outside' and are often intertwined with the perception of 'apparitions' – i.e., images and other visual phenomena appearing in external space. In fact, many of the records of visionary and auditory mystical experiences handed down by western mystical tradition can be traced to such hybrid experiences in which genuine mystical encounters are blended with pseudo-mystical phenomena. Accounts by mystics originating in this hybrid zone are not only interspersed with hallucinations, but also with explicitly pathological phenomena, waking dreams, eidetic images, split-off items of the unconscious or sub-conscious and other non-mystical phenomena. Ample evidence of the mixture of bogus and authentic mystical phenomena is provided by the chronicles of nunneries and by diverse spiritual autobiographies of female coenobites and anchorites. These documents are often replete with spurious religious and pseudo-mystical phenomena along with descriptions of genuine mystical occurrences. But the descriptions of the subject-matter and of the psychological structure of these 'visions' and 'auditory' experiences are phenomenologically rather crude and simplistic: Recurrent motifs are the Virgin Mary and other figures of the Holy Bible; Christ obviously takes centre stage, his life is contemplated from infancy to adulthood, and his external appearance is portrayed in a manner reminiscent of medieval paintings. But these spiritual diaries also provide accounts of the deceased relatives of individual nuns, as well as succinct lives of local saints and saints affiliated with the monastery; these figures may turn up in 'visions' and 'apparitions' in diverse locations of the monastery such as the cloister, the chapel or the nun's cell. The figures of the 'other world' featuring in the 'vision' and/or 'apparition' are not only 'seen', but the visionary also communicates with a saint, or with Jesus. In the recorded 'visions' of the nuns examined above [i.e., especially from the nunneries of Töss and Engeltal], the conversations between the sacred figure and the female visionary are often recorded 'verbatim'; the subject-matter usually revolves around thoughts, desires and aspirations of the coenobitic life.

In these mystographical documents, visionary and auditory experiences are closely intertwined. This applies to both external 'apparitions' and inward 'visions'. The scale of 'inner hearing' begins with listening to words and/or concise sentences perceived acoustically; the phenomenon of 'inner hearing' ends when no words or sounds are perceived anymore, resulting in a non-verbal cognitive mystical moment in which some insight is 'infused'. The former are imaginative instances of 'inner hearing'; the latter, however, are more appropriately to be assigned to the realm of 'mystically infused insight'.[111] The descriptions of joint aural and visual experiences in the works of Teresa of Avila quoted earlier can be claimed to be reliable and authentic as well as self-explanatory so that there is no need to illustrate the phenomenon of 'inner hearing' any further.

The differences in kind between 'inner hearing' and 'inner vision' can best be illustrated by contrasting the perspective of subject to that of the object, as well as by considering the specific modes of perception in each case. These issues are epitomized in the following thesis:

THESIS 68: *Both the structure of consciousness enabling the perception of 'inner hearing' and the structure of consciousness enabling the perception of 'inner visions' is an 'ultimate phenomenon', and as such entirely independent, and cannot be inferred from each other. 'Ultimate phenomena' can only be described phenomenologically, but not rationally inferred or explained.*

The '[mystical] Object' is either represented in the 'vision' by the image that has been 'mystically infused', or cognitively grasped to be 'present' somewhere in the darkness confronting the perceiver in the state of an 'imageless vision'. This means that the image beheld in a 'pictorial vision' is not the 'mystical Object' itself, but a picture 'imparted' by the 'mystical Object'; whereas the hidden 'Presence' that is the unseen 'object' in an 'imageless vision' is identical with the 'mystical Object'.

In an 'auditory experience', by contrast, regardless of whether the 'audition' consists of 'locutions' with full syntactic sequences,

---

111   Cf. TERESA of AVILA, *Vida*, 25–27; *Interior Castle*, VI; UNDERHILL, Evelyn. *Mysticism. A Study in the Nature and Development of Man's Spiritual Consciousness*. London: Methuen, 1911. 319–56 [i.e., the chapter on 'Voices and Visions'. – FKW.]

or snippets, or non-verbal thoughts conveyed silently, the 'mystical Object' is not directly encountered. *The object of 'inner hearing' is a message conveyed by an unknown entity that remains outside the experiential relationship.* Although 'locutions' are clearly perceived as [personal] 'messages' [addressed to the recipient] by an unknown entity, they are much further removed from the 'mystical Originator' than is the case in 'pictorial visions' of 'epiphanic self-expressions'. The remoteness of the 'mystical Object' from the 'listener' in auditory mystical experiences might be compared to the distance that 'infused images' in 'pictorial visions' have from the ultimate 'Source', unless the verbal message is perceived as something more immediately related to the 'Speaker' than is the case in visions of symbolic or metaphoric pictures. Though the symbolic pictures are perceived as 'instilled' or 'imparted', they do not reveal any quality of the 'Originator' of the pictures imparted. Thus, in our empirical spectrum, the 'voice' heard inwardly in an auditory mystical experience corresponds in the realm of visionary experience to a stage in between 'self-expressive appearance' and 'instilled' symbolic picture.

What is termed 'intellectual locutions' are a voiceless mode of 'inner hearing'; the perceiver does not hear any voice but is bestowed with an insight that is mystically 'imparted'. For this reason, 'intellectual locutions' are not classified as instances within the phenomenological pale of the 'inner hearing'. The more an occurrence of 'intuitive insight' is removed from acoustic inner perceptions, and the more it assumes the quality of an intellectual insight that is 'instilled' in the flash of a moment, the less an 'intuitive insight' can be seen as an instance of mystical self-revelation, or as a token of mystical self-expression.

THESIS 69: *Within the phenomenological range of* [mystical] *'visions', it is the 'imageless vision' in which a direct experiential relationship with the 'All-encompassing' can be found.*

THESIS 70: *Within the phenomenological range of 'auditory mystical experiences', all experiential relationships with the 'All-encompassing' are exclusively indirect (mediated).*

The third perspective from which 'auditions' can be approached focuses on the distinctive characteristics of the spoken utterances. The manner of speaking, notably the 'sound' of the voice as well as the 'tone' in which something is spoken, do have semantic import. The 'sound' is obviously only a feature in 'locutions' consisting of words or sequences of words that are distinctly heard inwardly. However, the 'tone' of a 'locution', i.e., the pitch and timbre in which the words are conveyed, thus the specific nature of the speech-act, is itself charged with meaning and may also comprise non-verbal expressions. Remarkably, the 'sound of voice' in genuine mystical 'locutions' does not have a special quality, or none the perceiver takes special notice of. In fact, during such an event the perceiver is unable to pay attention to the 'sound' of the voice, because he/she is passively overwhelmed by the event and only able to perceive the manner of speaking in addition to the message conveyed. The 'tone' and the features of the intonation of a mystical 'locution' are thus the distinctive features of genuine verbal mystical experiences.

The acoustic manner of speaking and the linguistic structure of what is spoken can be specified and described phenomenologically. Two main phenomenological strands can be distinguished:

1. *What is heard inwardly is clear, distinct, bright, unmistakable and terse,* free of any redundant expressions and confined to essentials; *the syntactic structure is logically coherent and without any error; the meaning is coherent and consistent throughout, free of any contradiction;* and each 'locution' fits harmoniously into the big stream of successive 'locutions'. Inherent consistency, absence of any ambiguity and contradiction as well as unique clarity, are the hallmarks of a genuine 'mystical locution'.

2. *'Locutions' draw special attention* because what is communicated in them is not only persuasive, irrefutable and unerring, but also significant and decisive. It is impossible to doubt what is stated in 'auditions'. *The listener is overwhelmed, rivetted while facing a hortatory situation.* The first sequence in our phenomenological classification contains the phenomenon of insights 'imparted' orally. In this case, insights are communicated verbally; 'locutions' of this kind may express 'revelations', or, when they occur jointly with a visionary experience, they may explain, for instance, the meaning of symbols or metaphoric images in a 'pictorial vision'. The second strand of phenomena relates to mystically imparted orders, directives and summons. In 'locutions' of this kind it is

the will of the 'mystical Otherness' that becomes manifest; these orders and instructions are understood by the listener as an express personal summons or a commandment in terms of "Thou shalt".

The nature of any genuine 'locution' of any of the two phenomenological varieties referred to above is unique and cannot be compared to anything that can be encountered outside the realm of mystical experience. The manner in which 'locutions' are communicated is incomparable and hints at a provenance that is located beyond all the known sources of human experience. It can thus be said that in the event of a 'locution' some message is conveyed, and when the 'locution' occurs in the context of a genuine mystical experience, it is a mystical message that is communicated.

The nature of the experience of 'being spoken to' is unique and cannot be compared with anything that might be experienced outside the realm of mysticism. The manner of speaking in mystical 'locutions' is incomparable and hints at an origin located beyond the known realm of empirical sources. In the event of a 'locution' a message is conferred, and if the 'locution' is genuinely mystical in origin, it is a mystical message that is imparted.

The phenomenological characteristics of auditory mystical experience identified by our enquiry support the claim of the mystics that it is possible to conclude from the spoken utterances whether a 'locution' is genuine or bogus. 'Locutions' are acknowledged as genuine by the mystics if they are perceived as coming from a 'space' beyond the individual self, felt to be 'eternal' and if the 'content' transmitted is 'absolutely true'.

The phenomenological range of 'mystical locutions' is not sharply delineated from adjoining areas. This statement may appear controversial at a first glance, since the phenomenon of 'locutions' has been shown to be an exceptional phenomenon that stands out within the entire range of phenomena encountered in mysticism. The unequivocal nature of 'locutions' is, however, limited to the core-phenomenon in which the act of 'hearing' and clearly discerning what is spoken is phenomenologically distinctly delineated. This is different with 'locutions' occurring in a transition zone with other, more obscure phenomena. One such transition zone has already been addressed:

that between 'inner hearing' and 'mystical insight'. Yet there are other transition zones, like the one merging with 'mystical effects', and another transition zone joined with the phenomenon of 'mystical guidance'. We have not yet dealt with the latter, which is discerned here for the first time as a potential element of the entire framework of mystical experience. The experience of being guided or 'governed' by a Will or Power greater than oneself is an exceptional, albeit also problematic and ambivalent, phenomenon.

When tracing the range of phenomena located between 'inner hearing' and 'somatic and emotional modes' of mystical experience, we will encounter an area in which a new phenomenon is situated: the sense of 'being whispered to', which we might call 'inner whisperings'. The phenomenon of somatic and emotional changes effected by a mystical encounter will be dealt with in subsequent chapters. The sense of being touched and other somatic mystical effects supply the broad empirical substratum from which the more specific varieties of mystical experience emerge. The process of the 'inner hearing' of an express summons or of spoken instructions is often preceded by modes of somatic and emotional mystical perception. What in the incipient stage is 'felt' to be a diffuse awareness of being affected and surrounded by a mysterious entity perceived as 'arriving' [from beyond the domain of the individual consciousness], and which is not yet recognized as something numinous, and/or as an entity that has mystical import. After this opaque initial phase, a more articulate 'stream of inner whisperings' tends to emerge, followed by distinctly verbalized 'locutions'. This then is the sequence in which the modes of 'inner hearing' develop in empirical reality. This process is sustained by a growing range of somatic perceptions and intertwined with a growing number of 'inner whisperings' inundating the perceiver like an incessant stream. At this intermediate stage it is still uncertain, however, if distinct mystical 'locutions' will surface from the cacophonous stream of 'whisperings'. This stage of the transition zone between somatic/emotional modes of mystical experience and 'inner hearing' is still encumbered by the perceiver's state of unrest and doubt, because of the question as to whether these 'whispers' and 'voices' are indeed genuine tokens of the 'mystical Other'. The listener is keen on discerning whether the 'utterances' heard inside are indeed genuinely mystical. This impasse is resolved when the perceiver has become fully immersed in the calmness of the 'quiet state of alertness' which enables him/her to listen to the words spoken inside and to grasp cognitively the truthfulness of a genuine mystical 'locution'; in such an event any doubt is dispelled and replaced by a deep sense of certainty and of the 'evident truth' of what is conveyed in the 'locution'.

The Sense of Being 'Touched': Somatic Modes of Mystical Perception ["Das mystische Spüren"]

When I first came across the expression 'being touched' mystically in the records of contemporary mystics, I did not pay much attention to the word, considering it too vague and obscure to qualify as a descriptive term for a special variety of mystical experience. In the course of our enquiry, however, we have indeed encountered this opaque, undifferentiated realm of mystical experience, which calls for a term that dispenses with clear-cut concepts. In effect, the phrase 'sense of being touched mystically' used jointly with the term 'somatic mode of mystical perception' turned out to be quite an appropriate expression to denote this opaque phenomenon. The terms refer to a single category of mystical experience, but we must be aware that the real core of somatic modes of mystical experience remains inevitably hidden in the dark undifferentiated flow of the 'mystical stream'; moreover, we also have to be aware that any endeavour to identify and isolate single elements in the 'sense of being touched' by the 'mystical Otherness' will be abortive. Our endeavour to describe this phenomenon will focus on the primordial mode of experiencing, which is holistic and eludes rational analysis and thus further differentiation. The individual components of the experience are only detailed facets of the whole. By approaching the entire phenomenon from different perspectives, we may elucidate a few aspects of 'mystical 'feelings' and 'somatic perceptions', but it is not possible to establish a coherent phenomenological structure of this opaque variety of mystical experience. In other words, it is beyond the reach of our method to specify phenomenologically, let alone in gnoseological terms, what the true nature of mystically 'instilled' feelings and somatic perception really is.

1. By the term 'touch', i.e., 'the sense of being 'touched', we understand *a rather undifferentiated mode of experiencing*. The phenomenological range of 'touching' is located between the primordial source of mystical encounters and the zone bordering on differentiated modes of visionary and auditory mystical experience. At the beginning, the encounter consists merely of a fleeting 'awareness' that the 'mystical Object' has emerged within the horizon of individual experience and evoked the sense of 'being touched' by something numinous. The initial stage of feelings emerging and the sense of 'being touched' being elicited has close affinities to processes identified by *gestalt* psychology in a so-called '*Vorgestalt* experience': Just as small figurines gradually emerge from a darkened room when light is dawning and are then perceived vaguely in rough outlines, though they cannot yet be seen with the physical eyes, the 'mystical sense of touch' is not only geared to the sense of 'Presence', but also to the 'content' foreshadowing visionary and/or auditory experiences. The 'experiencing self' is 'touched', 'affected' and 'attracted' by the initial encounter, is alert to visionary and auditory phenomena as well as the inner sense of 'touch', which is directed at 'in-coming' phenomena. The experiencing person eventually has a dim awareness that in the vista of 'inner sight' something has become manifest, or that something might 'arrive' in consciousness that might become the foundation of 'whisperings' becoming instilled in the mind.

2. *The 'sense of being touched' is a kind of empirical awareness hovering between appearance and reality*. Seen from this perspective, the 'sense of being touched' is located at a subliminal stage of recognition. The perceiver is not yet able to discern whether the entity by which he appears to have been 'touched' is indeed a genuine object of an actual empirical event, or if it is merely a fabrication of fantasy.

3. *The 'sense of being touched' involves the cognitive perception of the unknown 'Object'*. In this event there is some tactile contact, which is like touching someone's skin. This feature is typical of

the primeval character of the experience of 'being touched'. In the mystical experience of 'being touched' a clear awareness emerges in the perceiver that he/she is so close to the 'mystical Object' that he/she is even able to touch it. In this event he/she is overcome with the sense of 'being surrounded from all sides' by the 'mystical Object'; thus, something unknown is experienced that has 'approached' from an unknown distance, which is perceived as being 'present' because of the '*fluidum*', the special '*atmosphere*' and the '*aura*' emanating from it.

4. *The 'sense of being touched' is deeply imbued with responding feelings.* This corresponds with the 'Vorgestalts-experiences' as verified in experiments of gestalt-psychology, in which a strong emotional response is aroused in a subject when unseen figurines gradually emerge from the dark when the room is gradually lightened. The anticipation of the 'arrival' of the 'object' from the dark is analogous to the growing sense of the 'nearness' of the 'mystical Object', which is concealed by the darkness faced by the perceiver in 'inner sight'. The awareness of the 'nearness' of the Numen evokes an intense emotional response in which expectation, excitement and the sense of being overwhelmed coalesce with numinous feelings.

5. *There is a joint empirical realm between the 'mystical sense of being touched' and the experience of 'Presence'.* The empirical structure in which a subject becomes aware of the mystical 'Presence' contains an element (amongst several others) which we may call 'tactile sense of Presence'. It would be wrong, however, to consider the entire realm of 'the mystical sense of being touched' to be identical with the entire range of experiencing the 'mystical Presence'. For in the mystical experience of 'being touched', it is not only the 'isness', i.e., the 'Presence' of the Numen, that becomes accessible, but also its 'whatness' (as we shall see shortly). The cognitive awareness of 'Presence' is, however, unlike 'the sense of being touched', not an obscure, but a clear and lucid mode of mystical perception. Its phenomenological core is the non-visual awareness of the 'Presence' of the It.

6. *The mystical 'sense of touch' is permeated by quasi-sensory impressions,* which occur, however, outside the domain of the higher sense organs and are thus largely confined to the area of somatic perception. It is the entire body that is the receptacle of perceptions of touch and the 'organ' responding to the impact and influx of mystical phenomena.

7. *The mystical 'sense of touch' is inquisitive (as it were), searching and groping for the source of the tactile encounter.* The quest for the 'mystical Object' is either triggered by an initial 'mystical touch' or is initiated without any prior mystical impetus. In the incipient stage this quest is an undifferentiated intuitive, unreflective mystical search reaching out into the Unknown.

8. *The word 'touch' implies not only a tactile but also a cognitive relationship between the perceiver and the 'mystical Object', although the specific experiential modes involved in establishing this relationship remain concealed to the perceiver.* In this case, it is not the 'content' of the experience that is obscure and inscrutable, but the various modes of perception involved in the experience. It is opaque somatic and tactile encounters with a 'mystical Otherness' by which the sense of 'being directed' is evoked, and 'impressions' are imparted or somatic 'effects' generated, and by which the approach of the 'mystical Otherness' is cognitively grasped as approaching and experienced as a shaping 'Will' and determining 'Power'. In other words, it is in the 'sense of being mystically touched' that the concealed 'mystical Source' of the somatic and tactile effects becomes [temporarily] manifest.

THESIS 71: *The gnoseological significance of the mystical 'sense of touch' is slight.* One may even be tempted to question if this rather indistinct and incomprehensible phenomenon complies with the concept of 'mystical experience' at all. However, the scope of the term 'mystical sense of touch' is clearly broader than the scope of the experiential concept 'cognitive mystical relationship', and therefore it comprises varieties of mystical experience which, though without immediate cognitive import, are interlaced or contiguous with experiences in which a clear cognitive mystical relationship is perceived. From a phenomenological point of view, the following claim can be upheld:

THESIS 72: *The 'sense of being touched by a mystical Power' is the sustaining and fostering ground in which all other varieties of mystical experience are embedded and from which they emerge individually. As such it is not only the empirical ground from which singular mystical experiences arise, but also the primeval mystical Ur- experience which perennially encompasses and is concomitant with any individual mystical event.*

The Sense of 'Being Directed' by an Overwhelming Power

The experience of 'being directed' or 'guided' is a mystical phenomenon that is even further removed from the explicit clearness of 'mystical visions' than the 'mystical sense of being touched'. The sense of 'being mysteriously directed' is baffling, incomprehensible and uncanny for the mystic exposed to such an occurrence. The experience of 'being directed', moreover, largely eludes phenomenological description since its distinctive features are oblique, ambiguous and evasive. The experience of 'being governed' is an event by which the perceiver is passively overwhelmed; it is inflicted or imposed upon him/her – often against his/her will and 'out of the blue'. As such it belongs to the broad domain of 'emotional experiences'[112] resulting from an encounter. The occurrence of 'being governed' mystically even goes beyond a mere encounter, as the subject's will is not just overwhelmed but instantly annihilated.

The phenomenon of 'being governed' can best be understood by comparing it to the experience of 'locutions'. In a 'locution' the recipient is appealed to, accosted, summoned, ordered or exhorted to do something specifically. In this event the 'listener' is usually free to decide how to respond to the summons, and thus he/she is personally responsible for the progress of the mystical event; he/she is free to reject, or to comply with the given order. However, the response is not alone governed by the voice of reason, but also by the voice of conscience; the latter will

---

112 Cf. HARTMANN, Nicolai. *Zur Grundlegung der Ontologie*. 3rd ed. Meisenheim am Glan: Westkulturverlag, 1948. 178–83.

intervene as a critical corrective. Thus, the deliberate denial of an express command perceived in a genuine 'mystical locution' will inevitably evoke a deep sense of guilt. In the event of 'being governed', however, the command instilled intuitively and/or aurally, or both, is instantly executed; in other words, the command infused and the act of execution coincide. When 'being governed' by a mystical Power, the perceiver desires instantly to carry out the summons. He/she feels not only 'guided' but 'governed' by coercion, compelled to yield to the overwhelming Power, aware that he/she is helplessly exposed to It, with his/her own will having been suspended. When 'mystically governed', there is no room for freedom of choice, nor individual responsibility, resulting in an altogether uncanny mysterious occurrence. It is a highly opaque and unfathomable manifestation of an experiential mystical relationship. When it occurs, the perceiver is neither able to understand the reason, nor the purpose of the governing force imposed on him/her. The actions resulting from 'mystical governance' may even be at variance with the subject's previous pattern of behaviour and ultimately result in some unprecedented action that is entirely inexplicable to him/her and/or the social environment.

To a person exposed to 'being governed mystically', the experience is usually rather tormenting, frightening and alarming, as it tends to conflict with his/her personality, or contrary to his/her will, and thus involves the experience of coercion by being deprived of one's own free will. The experience is, moreover, painful because the subject is permanently haunted by the question as to whether the sense of 'being governed' is indeed elicited by a genuine mystical event, not least because this mysterious phenomenon is particularly ambivalent and likely to be dismissed as a bogus or even a pathological phenomenon. A person exposed to this experience is aware of its affinities to the neurotic, delusory or pathological varieties of compulsive action and is therefore keen on finding tangible criteria by which he/she may discern whether the experience is authentic and sane or false. Such a critical examination tends to pass through the following two stages:

1. A genuine experience of 'being governed' by a mystical Power differs fundamentally from pathological or neurotic varieties of compulsive action by the way in which the impulse or the sense of being governed surfaces in consciousness: In a genuine event

the perceiver recognizes instantly and with absolute certainty that the sense of 'being governed' has been 'impinged' on him/her and 'arrived' from a domain beyond the confines of the individual self; moreover, the perceiver is aware that the 'sense of being governed' mystically is always embedded in a composite framework of diverse mystical phenomena and effects, of which some are experienced concurrently with the event of 'being governed'. For instance, as soon as the sense of 'being governed' has been instilled, the recipient will become instantly aware of the *'fluidum'* of the numinous 'Presence'; moreover, he/she may perceive the 'countenance' of the 'mystical Presence' in a 'self-expressive visionary appearance' simultaneously with the sense of 'being governed', and grasp cognitively the non-visual presence of the 'All-encompassing' at the same time. On the basis of this composite mystical experience, the experience of 'being governed' is recognized to be unquestionably authentic. However, these objective indications by which the phenomenon is approved as genuine are not enough to overcome the state of disquiet and discord afflicting him/her after having executed the actions imposed. It is the voice of conscience that intervenes at this stage (which is an important difference from 'locutions', in which the recipient is free to object and refuse to obey the verbal summons). The perceiver is haunted by pangs of conscience for acting without having previously been able to decide if the actions are in line with conscience. The capacity for reasoning, and thus of taking personal responsibility for one's actions, is suspended when the perceiver is 'governed' by the mystical Power; he/she can merely trust at the onset of the experience that the coercion to act imposed by a will that is not his/her own, is genuinely mystical in nature. However, this vague sense of the potentially authentic origin of the experience cannot dispel the perceiver's misgivings.

2. These misgivings are eventually overcome after the mystical event, when the actions 'governed' by the mystical Power turn out to be meaningful and have positive after-effects on the perceiver. The lingering doubts disappear owing to these insights inferred in retrospect, and peace and inner harmony are restored. Yet the

fact remains that the experience of 'being governed' mystically is the most obscure and most ambiguous phenomenon amongst all varieties of mystical experience. As such it calls to mind that the gnoseological mystical relationship is embedded in diverse other mystical relationships that can be encountered beyond the sphere of recognition, which supply the broad sustaining ground in which it is rooted.

Person-like Features of the 'All-encompassing' ["Die personale Struktur des Umfassenden"]

We have now reached a crossroad in our phenomenological analysis. We have so far established a wide range of phenomena and modes of mystical experience which enable us to distinguish between different types of mystical encounters and grades of intensity. The main concern of this study is, however, the issue of mystical knowledge, i.e., what can cognitively be grasped in a mystical experience. It is not enough to merely classify different varieties of cognitive relationships, as such a taxonomy does not reveal anything about what is cognitively grasped of the 'mystical Object'. We have so far explored the cognitive relationship from the perceiver's subjective perspective and bypassed for the time being any attempt to approach the issue of recognition phenomenologically from the perspective of the 'mystical Object'. When dealing with cognitive aspects of the 'mystical Object' above, we have distinguished between its 'isness' and its 'what-ness'. Consequently, we have separated the cognitive awareness of 'Presence' from the perception of its 'what-ness'. This subdivision is obviously artificial, imposed by methodology. This became apparent when our attempt failed to exclude strictly any aspect of 'whatness' from a given experience of 'Presence'. It was impracticable to focus exclusively on the modes in which the 'mystical Presence' may become manifest in consciousness. In effect, we have tried to ignore (for the time being) the issue of the 'whatness' of the 'mystical Object', though a few components had to be addressed in passing, which, however, were not examined any further at this stage. However, it has turned out to be inevitable to refer to features of the 'whatness' when dealing with the 'vision of Light', the 'vision of self-expressive epiphanic appearances', the 'vision of symbolic pictures', and, especially, when exploring the phenomenon of 'locutions' and the phenomena of 'being governed' and of 'being touched' by the 'mystical Object', and even when dealing with the pure (non-visual) experience of the 'mystical Presence'. Obviously, it is impossible to become cognitively aware of the presence of the 'All-encompassing' unless there is a 'Presence' that is recognized as an entity that is 'all-encompassing' in nature. And it would likewise be impossible to speak of a 'message instilled' in a mystical event, or of an 'epiphanic self-expressive appearance' without affirming that in these mystical events something of the essence or 'whatness' of the 'mystical Object' is revealed. In the following, the focus of our enquiry will shift to aspects of the 'what-ness' of the 'mystical Object'.

Yet before we embark on this difficult task, we need to add an important preliminary remark. Any experience is inevitably linked with a concurrent hermeneutical process. In the realm of natural sense perception, the act of recognition is thus not alone based on a sensory perception but also accompanied by a simultaneous process of interpretation: An oak tree can only be recognized if it is identified as such, i.e., as a tree with special characteristics which differ from those (for example) of a birch tree or a poplar. *Similarly, any cognitive mystical event is inextricably and immediately linked to a concomitant interpretative process.* The concurrent interpretative process derives its notions and concepts from the knowledge that the perceiver brings to the experience rather than from the systematically ordered knowledge supplied by scientific disciplines.

The expression 'individual knowledge brought by the subject to the experience' refers to the specific wisdom and knowledge acquired individually from tradition and learning (whether by formal education, reasoning or speculative thinking), but it does not refer to empirical knowledge. The [mystic's] personal store of acquired knowledge may derive from two main sources: philosophy and theology. Eastern mystical traditions are deeply rooted in philosophical-metaphysical knowledge, whereas in western traditions of mysticism the sources of acquired knowledge are the teachings of Christian and/or Islamic theology.

The acquired knowledge that a subject is endowed with prior to his/her inaugural mystical experience is, strictly speaking, not scientific knowledge: It is rather philosophical and theological learning that has 'declined' into commonplace knowledge. The word 'decline' is meant to indicate that the knowledge and its concepts have become time-worn, and no longer comply with clearly defined scientific concepts and scholarly terms; hence it is superficial knowledge impaired by the lack of scientific standards. But the word 'decline' does not suggest that the knowledge inherited has any reduced claims to truth. When concepts and scientific knowledge of philosophy and theology are adopted by an individual, they are usually tinged with subjectivity; over and beyond this, they become more or less arbitrarily affiliated with items of knowledge deriving from diverse other sources than theology and philosophy and are thus distinctly circumscribed by individual subjectivity. The theological knowledge, by contrast, is scientific knowledge and thus part of perennial wisdom, and is understood to be supplied by the domain of the 'objective Spirit' and is thus related to the 'subject per se'.

The scholarly knowledge of metaphysics and theology, including the received teachings from religious and/or philosophical tradition, must clearly differentiated from empirical knowledge. The former is based on metaphysical or theological assumptions propounded *a priori;* and *a priori* postulates are rooted in a varied spectrum of premises, theories, axioms and beliefs, and have nurtured cultural as well as religious and philosophical traditions to this very day. Empirical knowledge, by contrast, has no other source than a concrete experience involving an act of recognition. The term 'experiential mystical knowledge' thus refers to empirical knowledge originating in genuine mystical experience that is imbued with acts of mystical recognition.

The juxtaposition of the claims of individual theological knowledge brought to a mystical event versus mystically infused knowledge grounded in mystical experience, has no bearing on the question of the truth of the knowledge upheld by these claims. By separating the theological knowledge that a subject has adopted and stored prior to a personal mystical experience from the knowledge that originates from mystical experience, we do not imply in any way that theological knowledge has lesser claims to truth than the knowledge deriving from mystical experience. Any such attempt would not only conflict with the fact that mystical experience is often intermingled with delusory or bogus phenomena, but also with the fact that the range of genuine mystical phenomena is surprisingly sparse.

The pivotal concern of our study is, however, to unfold the distinctive phenomenological characteristics of genuine mystical experience. Any authentic mystical encounter is inevitably based on an empirical relationship between the 'experiencing self' and the 'mystical Object', which is the central object of our enquiry. *However, the special items of the 'content' of an individual mystical experience are inextricably intertwined with items of the theological knowledge that the subject brings to the experience, or more specifically, with the knowledge that the subject recalls, or that surfaces during the mystical event.* For the purposes of a phenomenological analysis, it is imperative to separate the areas of acquired theoretical knowledge and the empirical knowledge instilled in a mystical event. This methodological requirement calls for two preliminary questions to be asked: 1. *Is it possible at all to grasp the person-like structure of the 'All-encompassing' in a genuine mystical experience, or are the person-like features that are cognitively perceived in a mystical event merely the result of the mystic's interpretation of received theological knowledge which he/she projects onto the mystical experience?* The second question, related to the first one, is equally important: 2. *Is it possible to infer from the 'whatness' of the 'All-encompassing' some immediate experiential knowledge, or is all knowledge about the 'whatness' derived from the knowledge that a subject brings to a mystical event and which is released during the mystical encounter?*

On the basis of the mystical records examined, it can be said that the extent by which a mystical experience is shaped and influenced by a subject's prior theological knowledge differs considerably between individual mystics and/or mystical experiences. If we consider the spectrum of mystical experiences in which the 'All-encompassing' is attributed qualities of a 'Persona', beginning with the imageless experience of 'pure Presence', and proceed with mystical experiences in which person-like qualities of the 'suchness' become more distinct, we will eventually arrive at a variety of mystical experience that has the fullest range of features of its 'whatness', it can be claimed that the sequence of increasing features of the 'suchness' experienced is equivalent to the sequence of the increasing share that *a priori* theological knowledge has in a concrete mystical event.

THESIS 73: *The more we experience of the 'suchness' of the 'All-encompassing', the more is the experience permeated by the knowledge and notions that a subject has acquired prior to a mystical experience.*

In retrospect, our differentiation between knowledge that has been acquired, and empirical knowledge that is 'infused' by a mystical event, justifies our methodological decision not to probe into the 'suchness' of a mystical experience. This also explains why we will, in the following, limit our considerations concerning the potential of recognizing the 'whatness' of the 'All-encompassing' to what is necessary in the given context. Obviously, any personal record of a variegated mystical experience is inevitably permeated by the mystic's private religious convictions and his/her bond to faith, which will colour and modify to some extent the core of the mystical experience. These clarifying preliminary remarks are important, because I would otherwise not have ventured to address the special mystical encounter in which the 'All-encompassing' is perceived as a 'Persona', explicitly by the personal pronoun "He"; in other words, I would otherwise never have dared to say something about the recognition of the person-like structure of the 'All-encompassing'.

At this point we will change the perspective. We will no longer focus on the psychological and phenomenological structure of consciousness in which mystical experience occurs, but we will shift our attention to the phenomenological characteristics of the 'mystical Object', i.e., to the 'atmosphere' and *'fluidum'* and the impact of the 'All-encompassing' on the experiencing subject. This means that the various stages in which aspects of the 'whatness' are discerned are first and foremost seen from the perspective of the 'mystical Object' and its impact on the perceiver; only secondarily shall we consider features of the 'whatness' from the perspective of individual 'modes of cognitive perception'.

There are three stages in which aspects of the 'whatness' of the 'mystical Object' are revealed: The first stage covers the cognitive awareness that the 'mystical Object' is an 'all-encompassing' entity; in the second stage various experiential effects elicited by the 'mystical Object' are recognized; and the third stage affords the cognitive insight that the impact on the perceiver is caused by a 'mystical

Otherness' that has all the pivotal characteristics of a 'Persona'.

Thus, on the lowest level of experiencing the 'whatness' of the 'mystical Object', the perceiver is bestowed with the cognitive awareness that the 'mystical Object' that has 'arrived' in consciousness is 'all-encompassing'; this recognition is an indispensable requirement for any cognitive experience of 'Presence'. I have had doubts as to whether the word 'all-encompassing' is indeed appropriate for denoting the most undifferentiated, universal quality of the 'mystical Object'; yet though this term has deficiencies, it is the best choice after all, as it aptly conveys that the 'object arriving' in a mystical event is indeed greater than anything known in this world: hence a total 'Otherness', beyond comparison and beyond rational comprehension. 'All-encompassing' thus suggests in a positive sense a whole range of qualities of the 'mystical Object', which could alternatively only be expressed by terms of negation.[113] In the broadest and most general sense, the encounter with the 'all-encompassing Otherness' – still untainted by any awareness of any impact of its *'fluidum'* or of other effects – is an encounter with an 'It', which is experienced as 'present', though the only quality of its essence that is cognitively grasped is that it is entirely incomprehensible. Yet this cognitive insight is instantly evident and known to be true with absolute certainty, though I am uncertain as to how to determine the specific mode in which this evident knowledge is imparted. I am inclined to suggest that it is most appropriately termed an 'imparted awareness', because it has some phenomenological affinities with an 'infused insight'. But if we accept this proposal, we would concede that a cognitive quality is involved that is usually only revealed on the second stage of experiencing the 'whatness'. If we stipulate, however, that the first stage in perceiving the 'whatness' of the 'mystical Object' is confined to the plain cognitive awareness of it being 'all-encompassing', we can

---

113 [Note: Albrecht appears to have the teaching of 'negative theology' in mind, which claims that since the Divine is ultimately unknowable and ineffable, it cannot be described in affirmative terms, but only by negation or apophatic expressions, e.g., by stating what God is *not*. Cf. SHELDRAKE, Philip, ed. *The New Westminster Dictionary of Western Spirituality*. Louisville, KY: SCM Press, 2005. s.v. 'Apophatic Spirituality'. – FKW.]

summarize our findings in a few sparse terms:

THESIS 74: *The quality of being 'all-encompassing' as an element of the 'whatness'* [of the 'mystical Object'] *is cognitively grasped only within the cognitive perception of 'Presence', in which non-visual knowledge is immediately imparted and known to be true with absolute certainty.*

As this aspect of the 'suchness' of the 'Presence' is inalienably intertwined with the cognitive perception of its 'isness', we may now – after having recognized this empirical fact – state more specifically:

THESIS 75: *The core of the cognitive perception of 'Presence' is the non-visual awareness of the 'Presence' of the 'All-encompassing'. Both, the 'isness' and the 'suchness', the 'Presence' and the naked awareness of it being 'all-encompassing', are given in this singular non-visual awareness in hyper-lucid clarity.*

The second stage, in which features of the 'suchness' of the 'mystical Object' are revealed, refers to the effects elicited in the 'experiencing self'; and in the third stage the person-like qualities of these impacts are revealed. To begin with, we must consider the two aspects together before we can contrast and compare them. The two stages are related to each other in a tier-like pattern consisting of several levels: The first level is marked by a cause-effect relationship; though this is entirely a-personal, it must be assessed against the background of the potential person-like qualities underlying a mystical encounter. A-personal experiences of effects caused by the 'mystical Object' have none of the qualities associated with a person. However, effects perceived initially in entirely a-personal terms may acquire person-like qualities when the overall mystical event is inundated, and eventually dominated by a personal 'Presence', which is cognitively grasped in the ongoing event.

The intertwining of person-like and a-personal characteristics can be described from a different point of view: Every cause-effect relationship is determined by some purpose or aim. The relationship between the determining force and the subject exposed to the impact generated by the determining power evidently differs when the latter is perceived in non-personal terms, and when it is perceived as a 'Persona'. It is not helpful to classify the various determining relationships by conventional patterns. For instance, the pattern of a-personal effects must not be explained in terms of causal determination, and, conversely, the impact attributed to a personal 'Other' must not be claimed to have a final determination. It seems to me that the principle by which personal and a-personal varieties of mystical experience are determined is entirely transintelligible.

The comparison between a-personal and personal varieties of mystical experience is exclusively carried out in our study within the area of phenomenology. This means that the nature of the relationship between a-personal and personal mystical experience can be explored also hypothetically, i.e., in terms of a situation of 'as-if', and therefore does not have to provide empirical evidence, or to infer its conclusions alone from empirical reality.

On the basis of our preliminary investigation, we may now survey the entire phenomenological range of mystical effects. Altogether we may discern ten categories by which mystical effects can be grouped:

1. The phenomenon of 'mystical effects as such', i.e., the entire phenomenological range of cognitively perceived effects claimed to have been 'instilled' in or 'impinged' on the perceiver. These impacts include intuitions, symbolic images and the sudden transformation of the state of consciousness (to name only a few).

2. The phenomenon of 'mystical impacts' triggering a significant change in the emotional condition, and a person's will, attitude and disposition.

3. 'Mystically infused insights', which 'arrive' intuitively.

4. 'Evoking of a sense of Presence'; the 'Presence' can be perceived cognitively in three ways: by means of somatic experience, notably by a tactile experience (sense of being touched); by a spontaneous intuition (cognitive insight) and by a visionary experience.

5. The vision of the 'mystical Light'.

6. The awareness of the *'fluidum'* or 'atmosphere' of the 'mystical Object', which is felt and cognitively grasped.

7. 'Infused images', which are 'beheld' in 'inner sight'.

8. 'Gestures and self-expressive pictorial appearances', which are observed in 'inner sight'.

9. The inner hearing of 'voices' and 'locutions'.

10. The 'experience of being governed', which is inferred from the sense of being 'directed' by a mystical Power.

'Mystical effects' and the structure of mystical experience are related to each other, but this does not mean that a specific effect can be attributed to a particular variety of mystical experience. In fact, a mystical experience is usually composed of multifarious empirical components – for instance, in a 'mystical vision' several 'mystical effects' are involved; on the other hand, a single mystical impact can elicit several modes of recognition at the same time.

The entire range of 'mystical effects' outlined must now be assessed with regard to the special varieties triggered by personal and a-personal varieties of mystical encounters. As we shall see, comparing these varieties will disclose some striking differences. The entire range of 'mystical effects' can be subsumed under the category of person-related mystical experience, whereas only a few 'mystical effects' can be related to a-personal mystical experiences. Thus, we may group the experiences of the 'mystical Presence', the 'mystical *fluidum*' and the 'mystical Light' in the same category, because they are commonly determined by the awareness of 'Presence' and of 'after-effects' elicited. This is different with 'mystically infused insights', symbolic and allegorical images and somatic and emotional 'effects', which all require an additional concept for classification: that of 'im-press-ion', i.e., they inevitably depend on a mystical impact triggered by a mystical occurrence, which, however, cannot unambiguously be identified as a personal mode of mystical experience. The difference between a 'mystically infused impact' and a 'corollary' or 'after-effect' of a mystical encounter can be explained as follows: In the latter the perceiver becomes aware of side-effects, when the 'mystical Presence' has 'arrived' in the sphere of inner perception, but the 'Presence' does not yet directly affect his mental state, whereas in a 'mystical impact' a somatic, emotional or cognitive impression is impinged on the 'experiencing self'. The transition zone between the two phenomena is not clear-cut; moreover, we should not attach too much importance to the proposed distinction between 'mystical impression' and 'side-effect' or 'corollary' of a mystical encounter. The other instances in which the impact of a mystical encounter is experienced (i.e., in 'self-expressive pictorial appearances', the 'inner hearing' of voices and locutions and the 'sense of being governed and directed' by a mystical Power) can reasonably be accounted for only when seen as phenomena *triggered* by a person-like 'mystical Otherness'. Whenever a mystical event occurs within the domain of an a-personal experience, we do not come across instances of 'inner hearing', or of 'the sense of being directed' or induced to act. Similarly, whenever a mystical event is rooted exclusively in the domain of an encounter with the 'mystical Other' perceived as a 'Persona', any of the 'impacts' or 'corollaries' are inevitably attributed to it. A mystic who experiences the 'All-encompassing' as an a-personal entity knows that he is part of a cause-effect relationship and is alert and able to perceive the 'arrival' of incoming phenomena and is thus 'struck' existentially by the event. A mystic who experiences the 'mystical Object' as a 'Persona' knows not only that he is situated in a wider domain of mystical experience, but also that he is not just affected by a mystical relationship, but also personally addressed, intended or 'meant'. Moreover, he becomes aware during the mystical encounter with the personal 'Presence' that he is looked at, spoken to and guided.

The difference between personal and a-personal [monistic] mysticism is, however, not merely a phenomenological one. The difference is also rooted in eschatological and metaphysical claims. Our concern is, however, to provide (as far as this is possible) a most comprehensive catalogue of individual components of the entire range of mystical effects as well as of the structure of all varieties of mystical experience. Here we might dispense with asking a critical epistemological question, but the given circumstances require us to consider and evaluate personal and a-personal mystical experiences from a gnoseological perspective. For this reason, we will propose some contentious theses propounded on the evidence of phenomena described in empirical accounts.

If proponents of a-personal mysticism do not acknowledge that personal varieties of mystical experience are genuine, they are obliged to explain by means of tangible criteria why personal mystical experiences do not qualify as genuine mystical occurrences. They will probably argue that the more a mystical experience is permeated by specific characteristics of the 'whatness' of the 'mystical Object', the less will be its cognitive value; they will, moreover, state that the features of the 'whatness' of the 'mystical Object' perceived in a mystical event are inevitably intertwined with religious and theological notions that the experiencing subject has projected onto the experience and which he/she has embraced prior to the mystical experience. From the viewpoint of a-personal mysticism, personal mystical experience is therefore merely seen as an amalgamation of empirical components originating from both a-personal experiences and received religious concepts and beliefs that surface during a mystical event and by which the mystical experience is interpreted. What is acknowledged as genuine by adherents of a-personal mysticism is confined to the a-personal experiences of the 'mystical Presence' as reflected, for instance, in the 'awareness of the presence of the It'; the non-visual sense of 'Presence', and, arguably, in the 'vision of Light' as a symbolic representation of the 'Presence', are acknowledged as the genuine core of mystical experience.

Representatives of personal mysticism will have to admit that phenomena that are not part of the core of mystical experience are potentially spurious and must therefore be subjected to a thorough scrutiny to establish their authenticity or inauthentic nature. However, from the perspective of personal mysticism, two counter-theses can be put forward against the claims of a-personal mysticism, which must be taken seriously:

1. The range of phenomena that would have to be excluded from the realm of genuine mystical experience as potentially bogus when applying the criteria of a-personal mysticism is so comprehensive, independent and varied that it appears rather arbitrary to dismiss all of them as delusive or as subjective projections and/or fabrications of the experiencer's mind. By utilizing this rigorous approach, all 'pictorial visions', as well as 'visions of self-expressive gestures

and appearances', 'locutions' and other phenomena of 'inner hearing', and the experience of 'being governed and directed' by a 'mystical Power' would have to be excluded from the area of genuine mystical experience. Over and beyond this, the entire range of phenomena classified as 'mystical effects' would have to be stripped of their inherent person-related qualities.

2. *The structure of mystically induced effects and the entire structure of mystical experience are a joint coherent whole and evidently a meaningful unity.* The blending of personal and a-personal qualities and phenomena in a concrete mystical event does not result from an accumulative process but occurs simultaneously. This unity is flawless, devoid of any inconsistency; its constituent elements are coherently related and sustain each other. And it is this perfect congruity and homogeneity that is ultimately stunning to the perceiver. This awe-inspiring experience instantly instils in him/her the immediate knowledge that the experience has indeed been genuine. Any endeavour to split up the common sustaining ground of mystical experience would seem to be entirely arbitrary. The critical demand that must be decided on from the perspective of personal mysticism is, rather: The *entire* empirical structure of mystical effects can only be either genuine in its totality or entirely bogus. Any attempt to compartmentalize and subdivide the sustaining ground of mystical experience is incompatible with the claim to its inherent unity, wholeness and meaningfulness.

The theses and anti-theses presented in our critical juxtaposition of personal vs. a-personal mysticism are apparently incompatible and split up the domain of mysticism into two dissenting areas. It is therefore inevitable to decide whether personal or a-personal mysticism is to be given the prerogative concerning its authenticity and genuineness. However, at the current stage of our enquiry, such a decision cannot be made and must be postponed to the final section of the book. However burning the question may be as to what extent a mystical encounter is informed by genuine cognitive mystical experience, and to what extent it is shaped or based on the perceiver's religious beliefs and theological knowledge, the attempt to find an answer to this vital question on a scientific basis must be deferred, as our investigation has not yet yielded sufficient insights by which a viable scientific and scholarly answer could be given. Moreover, finding answers to the queries addressed above should not be attempted unless every single mode of mystical experience has been examined critically, both with a view to its potential delusory nature and to its potential authenticity and gnoseological rank. But even if these epistemological conditions are supplied, it appears to be rather unlikely that we will succeed in separating the genuine cognitive and experiential components of a mystical event from the beliefs and the theological knowledge held by the perceiver prior to the mystical experience. Hence it remains to be seen if it is possible to decide whether personal or a-personal [monistic] mysticism is the one supreme mode of experiencing the 'All-encompassing'. At the present stage of our enquiry, I am rather inclined to think that the answer will be left pending in the end.

The Experience of the Mystical Relation ["Die Mystische Erfahrungsrelation"]

When exploring a phenomenon critically, it is indispensable to examine it again and again from different perspectives and to decide if a phenomenological pattern can be discerned and if this pattern is only apparent or delusory, or if it conforms to empirical reality. Moreover, an in-depth scientific scrutiny of any surface phenomenon will disclose the underlying ground in which a manifest phenomenon is rooted, and to which it can ultimately be traced.

Our specific concern here is the phenomenon termed the 'mystical relation' [i.e., the cognitive and experiential awareness elicited in the 'experiencing self' in a mystical event, of being related to the 'All-encompassing', viz., to an unfathomable 'mystical Otherness']. We have so far orbited various spaces in which the 'mystical relation' has become apparent; we have examined the phenomenon from different angles and have tried to establish whether the 'mystical relation' can indeed be claimed to be an 'ultimate phenomenon' rather than classified as a 'surface phenomenon'. For this reason, we have separated the structure of mystical experience from the structure of 'mystical effects' and divided them into different categories.

The phenomenological classifications secured in this way will later be linked to received concepts and established items of the 'content' of mystical experiences. This staunchly rational approach may, admittedly, distort or even destroy the unbiased discernment of the phenomena encountered. For instance, the great delight felt when perceiving phenomena 'arriving' in 'inner sight' disables temporarily the perceiver's capacity to glance at the abyss of the unperceived. But the pivotal question we are concerned with here is: *When a 'mystical relation' is experienced, does this mean that in, or 'behind' it, merely an ostensible phenomenological 'gestalt' is encountered which can be traced to other phenomena, or is the 'mystical relation' becoming apparent in this phenomenological 'gestalt' one of the 'ur-relations', whose existence remains disclosed to rational enquiry?*

The previous chapter has already shown that our particularizing analytical investigation in which phenomena are traced back to phenomena lying beneath, has reached a final boundary, and it has also demonstrated that our perspective must be re-adjusted and re directed at the whole of the phenomenon. The confines for approaching the phenomenon rationally seem to be defined by the space in which the core of our phenomenon resides. If we will henceforth focus on the totality of what is revealed in a mystical experience, as well as on the totality of what is 'incorporated' in the 'object arriving', the act of 'beholding' must surely be open and free from any bias, but it may also be based on the results of the foregoing phenomenological analysis. The ordered structure of the varieties of mystical experience and the ordered range of 'mystical effects' have supplied the foundations that enable us to single out the essence of the phenomenon. At the same time they provide, moreover, the yardstick for positive or negative assessments.

For this new perspective, by which we are going to explore the totality of the phenomenon through surface phenomena, a new methodological approach is called for. This new approach can be divided into two parts: In the first part we shall try to expand the concept of the 'cognitive mystical relation' so as to encompass the 'experiential mystical relation'; in the second part of our approach we shall try to transcend the domain of the 'experiential relation' as well, in order to reveal the sphere of the 'mystical relation'.

Thus, there are three separate concepts which can be distinguished, though the individual concepts are not placed side by side but arranged like concentric circles with different diameters. The smallest (innermost) circle encompasses the 'cognitive mystical relation', which is embedded within the zone of the 'experiential relation'. The 'cognitive relation', which comprises the sphere of 'rational recognition' relation' is, to a limited extent, accessible to phenomenological analysis, because it is already obfuscated by oncoming darkness. The 'mystical relation' embraces the circle widest in diameter. It is the hidden sustaining ground in which both the cognitive and the experiential relationships are rooted. The zone of the 'mystical relation' abides in complete darkness and cannot be elucidated any further by phenomenological enquiry.

In the previous chapters we have not always distinguished sharply between the concept of the 'cognitive relation' and that of the 'experiential relation'. This, however, has been done on purpose, because the preconditions required to permit a clearly defined differentiation between the two concepts have not yet been fully provided. So far, the main emphasis of our enquiry has been on establishing the phenomenological characteristics of the 'experiential relation', within which the sphere of the 'cognitive relation' has been the object of our enquiry. The establishment of a ramified classification of the phenomenology of several varieties of mystical experience has also brought to light some distinctive features of the 'cognitive relation'. In this way we have been able to delineate, step by step, the totality of mystical experience by identifying a series of individual modes of mystical perception, and to elucidate, in the wake of it, not only the structure of 'mystical recognition', but also that of 'mystical effects'. This differentiating phenomenological analysis was based on long-term research in the field of the psychology of consciousness, in which both the specific phenomenological structure of the 'quiet state of alertness' and of the 'mystical consciousness' could be established scientifically and rendered intelligible in phenomenological terms. By succeeding in providing an empirically based, ramified structure of the two crucial states of consciousness, the process of probing more deeply into the realm of mystical experience by rational analysis has made considerable progress. Yet we also had to acknowledge the fact that our scientific approach could only disclose phenomena of the peripheral sphere of the 'mystical relation', and that we could not get any nearer to the core of the 'experiential mystical relation'.

Due to our change in perspective, the enquiry now moves toward the opposite direction, i.e., it is now the rationally differentiated realm of the 'cognitive relation' that is the focal point through which we are going to probe into the unknown domain 'behind'. The 'thing questioned' becomes the 'thing inquired for'. The aim is that the 'experiential relation' in its entirety should become accessible phenomenologically. To achieve this goal, we must begin from a new starting point. This new point of departure, however, requires as a precondition a perfectly unbiased perceptive attitude: listening attentively, without bias or prejudice, to what the mystics tell us in their personal testimonies.

The mystical records examined thus far have been used exclusively for the purposes of phenomenological analyses: These texts have supplied authentic and, on the whole, conclusive materials for an in-depth phenomenological examination, yielding distinctive characteristics of diverse mystical experiences and the phenomenological structure of specific types of mystical encounters. The critical reader may have noticed that a few of the textual sources were less useful than others and that some were rather sparse in phenomenological detail. Therefore, we have to expand our textual corpus and turn to texts by mystics and visionaries in which the phenomenon of the 'wholeness' experienced in a mystical event is addressed. From the large number of especially suitable accounts, I have selected only two, which I consider particularly informative because of their richness in phenomenological detail. The first text is the autobiographical record of the late medieval Italian visionary and mystic *Angela of Foligno* [1248–1309]; the second text is from the *vita* of the late medieval German Dominican friar *Henry Suso* [c. 1295–1366], a disciple of Meister Eckhart. Both mystics are representatives of the apophatic mystical tradition of Pseudo-Dionysius the Areopagite. Though both of these texts are evidently real-life accounts, they were not written by the mystics themselves but by a confidant(e) or *amanuensis*. The life of Angela of Foligno was documented by the Franciscan friar Arnaldus, who affirms most emphatically: "I have written this record with great awe and reverence and taken utmost care not to add any notion of my own, or to insert a single word that has not passed from her lips. Moreover, I often asked her to repeat a word that she wanted me to write down."[114] Suso's account of his pivotal mystical experience was recorded by the prioress of the Dominican convent of Töss [Switzerland], Elsbeth Stagel [c. 1300–1360], who was Suso's spiritual disciple and confidante. There is no reason to doubt that her record of Suso's experience is absolutely truthful and that it has been communicated with utmost care. My impression is that both records are undoubtedly genuine as they have all the hallmarks of authenticity and ultimate sincerity.

The records of both Angela and Suso stand out within their own writings as differing strikingly from the rest of their works: There are exceptionally detailed and varied descriptions of the background in which their visionary, auditory and ecstatic experiences occurred, and against which the extraordinary mystical event in their lives is singled out in each case: There are numerous descriptions of diverse 'pictorial visions' and 'apparitions', i.e., accounts of 'visions' beheld in 'inner sight' as well as accounts of 'apparitions' seen in external space, and instances of visual clairvoyance. These visionary experiences are all intertwined with auditory experiences as well as 'intellectual locutions'; the auditory 'locutions' often consist of remarkably private mystical conversations [between Christ and the visionary]. Apart from these phenomena we encounter instances of illumination, in which some spontaneous cognitive insight is mystically instilled, as well as 'mystical imprints', i.e., mystical effects instilled spiritually, psychically and somatically in the visionary. There are also avowals of situations in which the 'experiencing self' is overwhelmed by feelings of ecstasy, as well as of moments of true 'compassion', i.e., supreme moments of affective devotion to the passion of Christ in which the visionary becomes a partaker of the Passion, physically, spiritually and emotionally. Both mystics had longterm experience in the practice of spiritual prayer, contemplation and affective devotion, marked by a rare capacity for empathy. In the light of this rich and colourful background of mystical life, it is astonishing

---

114 ANGELA von FOLIGNO. *Gesichte und Tröstungen der Seligen Angela von Foligno*. Trans. Jan van Arend. Mainz: Grünewald, 1924. [Note: Albrecht does not give a page reference; English translation provided. – FKW.]

that the pivotal mystical event in both should have been so sober and unpretentious in nature.

There are several reasons for beginning with the record of Angela of Foligno. Her record addresses numerous phenomenological characteristics illustrating 'cognitive mystical experience' as defined by us. Over and beyond this, her report includes magnificent descriptions of an 'imageless mystical vision'. In Suso's record, on the other hand, the variety of 'cognitive mystical experience' is only referred to in passing, whereas the mystical experience of 'oneness' is presented in detail. He gives a vivid account of the sustaining ground and of the wholeness of mystical experience beyond any particularization.

We have now entered the experiential dimension in which it is no longer appropriate to apply an analytical approach. Our focus is now on the totality of a mystical event. The endeavour to capture the phenomenological characteristics of such an event should no longer by determined by analytical reasoning, but by a purely perceptive stance – by the pure, humble and reverent 'glance' at what is encountered. Though I will briefly introduce the passages from Angela of Foligno and Suso, these prefatory remarks are inevitably analytical, but as such they are only intended to provide an intelligible frame of reference for the experience of the ineffable wholeness, which is beyond rationalization.

1. In Angela of Foligno's account the relationship to the 'Godhead' is especially underscored. This marks a stark contrast to many of her visionary experiences, which are replete with colourful, sensual detail. In the record quoted, Angela encounters the mystical 'Urgrund', experienced as 'present' prior to any sense of a person-like quality. The event described is a genuine 'imageless mystical vision'; it is a glance directed at what is concealed in the darkness, though the unknown 'something' has in some inexplicable and ineffable manner 'arrived' in the mystic's hyper-lucid state of consciousness. She is gratified with illuminations bestowed by a formless invisible benign Entity. During this mystical encounter we may discern religious thoughts surfacing in the mind of the perceiver, and we may also witness a dramatic transformation of her emotional condition elicited by mystical effects, especially the eruption of deep feelings

of bliss and joy. These indicate the mystic's bond with, or 'relationship' to the phenomenological mystery. The latter forms the core of the experiential relation, which seems to be the ultimate, genuine 'Ur-relation', irrespective of the fact that this experiential relation also becomes apparent on the surface level in a wide variety of sensible or overt modes of perception.

2. Seen from the perspective of psychological phenomenology, *Henry Suso's record* describes a mystical experience that occurs in the incipient stage in the state of consciousness termed 'quiet alertness', but the structure of consciousness is transformed during the event and inundated by feelings of ecstasy; hence there is a shift toward the 'ecstatic consciousness'. The perceiver is finally overwhelmed by the encounter with a vast, incomprehensible and abysmal 'wholeness', an experience that culminates in a borderline experience in which all self-awareness is annihilated in the perceiver, who desires to surrender passively to the 'wholeness'. The 'experiencing I' has become absorbed in the 'wholeness', savouring the moment of silent bliss and listening to and glancing at what becomes manifest in 'inner sight'. We may discern a genuine instance of a mystical glance at a Presence, at something that is exceptionally powerful and effective, although it is without form or image and has forcibly intruded into the calm and lucid condition of the perceiver's consciousness. Suso's mystical experience is, moreover, intertwined with the 'mystical vision of Light', in which the 'experiencing self' beholds the splendour of the mystical Light. It is also entwined with instances of 'locution', 'illumination', the awareness of mystical effects and accompanied by a lingering sense of the 'mystical Presence'. These components are all integral parts of a single, coherent, unified mystical experience which is sustained by an 'experiential mystical relation':

> Text 95 (Angela of Foligno, *The Book of Divine Consolation*, Treatise III, vision vii)[115]: "There was a time when my soul was exalted to be-

---

115 [Note: Albrecht's textual source is ANGELA von FOLIGNO. *Gesichte und Tröstungen der Seligen Angela von Foligno*. Trans. Jan van Arend. Mainz: Grünewald,

hold God with so much clearness that never before had I beheld Him so distinctly. But love did not see here so fully; rather did I lose that which I had before and was left without love. Afterwards I did see Him darkly, and this darkness was the greatest blessing that could be imagined, and no thought could conceive aught that would equal this.

Then was there given unto the soul an assured faith, a firm and certain hope, wherein I felt so sure of God that all fear left me. For by that blessing which came with the darkness, I did collect my thoughts and was made so sure of God that I can never again doubt but that I do of a certainty possess Him. Thus, is my hope now made certain, for now do I see so clearly that what I see can neither be told by the mouth nor imagined in the heart. And by that blessing (most certain and including also that darkness) have I attained unto all my hope, and inasmuch as now I see clearly, I have all that I desired to have or to know.

Here, likewise, do I see all Good; and seeing it, the soul cannot think that it will depart from it or it from the Good, or that in future it must ever leave the Good. The soul delighteth unspeakably therein, yet it beholdeth naught which can be related by the tongue or imagined by the heart. It seeth nothing, yet seeth all things, because it beholdeth this Good darkly – and the more darkly and secretly the Good is seen, the more certain is it, and excellent above all things. Wherefore is all other good which can be seen or imagined doubtless less than this, because all the rest is darkness. And even when the soul seeth the divine power, wisdom, and will of God (which I have seen most marvellously at other times), it is all less than this most certain Good. Because this is the whole, and those other things are but part of the whole. Another difference is, that albeit those other things are unspeakable, yet they do bring great joy which is felt even in the body.

But seen thus darkly, the Good bringeth no smile upon the lips, no fervour or devotion or love into the heart, for the body doth not tremble or become moved or distressed as it doth at other times. And the cause thereof is that the soul seeth, and not the body, which reposeth and sleepeth, and the tongue is made dumb and cannot speak. All the many and unspeakable kindnesses which God hath shown unto me, all the sweet words and all other divine sayings and doings are so much less than this which I have seen clearly through the darkness, that I do put no hope in them. Yea, even if it were possible that all these were not true, it would in no wise lessen the hope which I have in this and all other good.

1924. Liber XXVI, 73–77. The English quotation has been taken from the translation of *The Book of Divine Consolation of the Blessed Angela of Foligno*: Trans. from the Italian by Mary G. Steegmann. London: Chatto and Windus, 1909. 181–85. – FKW.]

Unto this most high power of beholding God ineffably through such great darkness was my spirit uplifted but three times only and no more; and although I beheld Him countless times, and always darkly, yet never in such an high manner and through such great darkness.

And when upon the one hand my body is wasted by infirmity, when the world with its thorns and bitterness chaseth me forth, and demons do likewise afflict me with much vexation, and do continually persecute me and molest me (because they have power over me and because God hath given me soul and body into their hands, so that I do almost seem to behold them falling bodily upon me), upon the other hand God doth draw me unto Himself with that Good which I beheld through the darkness, in which darkness I did doubtless behold the Holy Trinity. And to me it seemeth that I am fixed in the midst of It and that It draweth me unto Itself more than anything else the which I ever beheld, or any blessing I ever yet received, so there is nothing which can be compared to It.

All that I say of this seemeth unto me to be nothing, I do even feel as though I offended in speaking of it, for so greatly doth that Good exceed all my words that my speech doth appear to blaspheme against it.

When I behold and am in that Good, I remember nothing of the humanity of Christ, of God inasmuch as He was man, nor of aught else that had shape or form; and albeit I seem to see nothing, yet do I see all things.

When, however, I am separated from that aforesaid Good then is it given unto me to see Christ, who draweth me with such gentleness that sometimes He saith, 'Thou art I, and I am thou.' I see those eyes, and that face so gracious and so pleasing, which embraceth and draweth my soul unto itself with infinite assurance. And that which proceedeth from those eyes and that face is nothing else save that Good of which I spake before and which I beheld darkly, which proceedeth and issueth forth from within. And it is that Good wherein I delight so greatly that I can in no wise speak of it.

Being thus one with Christ the soul liveth. And in this God do I live more than in the darkness, and although He who dwelleth in darkness draweth me beyond all comparison ever so strongly, yet do I live so constantly in Christ that, inasmuch as I have been once and for all granted assurance of God, nothing can ever come betwixt me and Him."

Text 96 (Henry Suso, *The Life of the Servant*, from chapters II and III, 19–20)[116]: "At the beginning of his life in religion it once happened

---

116 [Note: The passage quoted has been taken from the English translation of

that on St. Agnes Day [21ˢᵗ January], after the midday meal in the refectory, he went into the choir. He was alone there and stood in the lower row at the right hand of the choir. At this time, he was very depressed by a great sorrow that weighed down upon him. As he stood there, disconsolate and solitary, he went into an ecstasy and saw and heard what was ineffable. It was without form or shape, and yet it bore within itself all forms and shapes of joyous delight. His ear was hungry and yet satisfied, his mind joyous and happy, his wishes were calmed, and his desires had died out. He did nothing but gaze into the brilliant light, in which he had forgotten himself and all things. He did not know whether it was day or night. It was a sweetness flowing out of eternal life, with present, unchanging peaceful feeling. He said then: 'If this is not heaven, I do not know what heaven is, for all the suffering that can ever be put into words, could not enable anyone to earn such a reward and for ever possess it.' This blissful ecstasy lasted perhaps an hour, perhaps only half an hour; whether his soul remained in his body, or was separated from his body, he did not know. When he came to himself, he felt just like a man who has come from another world. His body felt such pain in that short moment that he thought no one could possibly suffer such pain in so short a time, save in death. He then came to himself in some way or other, and sighed from the depths of his soul, and his body sank to the ground as if in a fainting fit. He cried out in his heart: 'Alas, God, where was I, where am I now?' and said: 'Beloved, this hour can never die in my heart.'

He walked with his body, and no one saw or noticed anything outwardly in him, but his soul and his heart were inwardly full of heavenly wonders. The celestial visions went in and out in his deepest depths, and he felt somehow as if he was hovering between in the air. The powers of his soul were filled with sweet heavenly scent just as if one pours a good balsam out of a box, and the box afterwards retains a sweet smell. This heavenly odour remained with him a long time afterwards and gave him a heavenly longing for God."

These two testimonies illustrate quite clearly that a concrete mystical experience has a much broader empirical scope than the one

---

Suso's *The Life of the Servant*. Trans. James M. Clark. Cambridge: Lutterworth, 1952. 19–20. Albrecht's textual source was the modern German edition of Suso's selected writings: SEUSE, Heinrich. *Deutsche Schriften*. Trans. A. Gabele. Leipzig: Insel, 1924. The account is rendered in the third person – a conventional device often encountered in autobiographical mystical writings; it signifies the mystic's deep humility and self-effacing devotion to God. – FKW.]

encompassed by merely a single strand, such as that of an instance of 'mystical recognition'. The experiences described do not only include cognitive perceptions, but also intimate emotional responses. It is true, however, that not everything that is experienced during the mystical event can be comprehended with the clarity of a 'gnoseological relation'. Much remains hidden in darkness, which is grasped in a non-cognitive, primordial mode of experiencing.

With these two phenomenologically conclusive mystical records in mind, we have already taken the phenomenological step from the sphere of 'mystical recognition' to the sphere of the 'empirical mystical relation'. The new perspective, however, calls for further corroboration by additional documentary evidence. Moreover, it appears to be necessary to reflect critically on our findings at this stage. It is therefore the purpose of the following chapter to provide some critical annotations and to subject the methodological approach and the findings yielded so far to a thorough critical scrutiny. In this way some supplementary explanations will be supplied, notably by contrasting the phenomenon of the 'experiential relation' to the phenomenon of the 'cognitive relation'.

Critical Considerations

No phenomenological enquiry should be concluded without providing a critical resume of its results. At the end of our previous empirical study, *Psychology of Mystical Consciousness*, we had to concede that by confining our phenomenological approach strictly to the domain accessible to the psychology of consciousness, only peripheral phenomena and not the core of the phenomenon of mysticism could be reached. In the present study, however, the limitations imposed by the phenomenological method and the discipline of the psychology of consciousness are overcome by applying a pluridisciplinary approach, i.e., combining psychological phenomenology with a philosophical (gnoseological) [and cross-cultural] as well as anthropological approaches. In doing so, a broader perspective permits us to explore all varieties of mystical experience beyond the level of phenomenology, and to assess their nature and existential significance from different scholarly and scientific viewpoints. The results achieved so far might even give the impression that the phenomenon of mysticism has been described authentically and truthfully, apparently without any bias or distortion.

This, however, is not the case. When surveying critically the findings, we must concede that our enquiry has still been curbed by some strictures, albeit ones that were self-imposed: *now it is no longer limitations imposed by psychology of consciousness, but limitations imposed by gnoseology*. A mystical encounter is in its entirety a pivotal experience, which has a persevering impact on an individual's existence and orientation in life. It is thus not merely an encounter that occurs on a cognitive level. Although we know that our concern is not just with the 'cognitive mystical relation', but with the 'mystical relation' as such, our phenomenological enquiry has been confined strictly to the cognitive domain. Any attempt to explore the 'experience of the mystical relation' is bound to extinguish the overall structure of mystical experience and to distort the perspective into two directions:

First, the gnoseological phenomenon will be deprived of its natural 'setting' and its natural 'form'. The 'gnoseological relation' is inexorably rooted in the 'experiential mystical relation', by which it is enfolded. For what would be left of the 'gnoseological mystical relation' if it were not grounded in a causal empirical relationship, which has an impact that goes far beyond the sphere of recognition? The cause-effect relationship experienced clearly goes beyond the realm of recognition because it comprises the relationship between the 'mystical Object' and the 'experiencing subject'. What would the structure of a mystical experience be like that is not embedded *a priori* in a condition of being that has perennially, and prior to any act of recognition, been affected by the 'mystical It'?

Second, the fact that the view on the totality of the mystical phenomenon is warped becomes apparent phenomenologically by the following facts: The mystics [of western/theistic traditions] do not place the 'mystical insight', viz., cognitive mystical encounters, at the centre of their mystical quest, but the experience of 'mystical union'. To these mystics the unitive experience and the transformation of the 'self' ('conversion') effected by it are the mystical events of supreme existential relevance. Therefore, I have come to realize that the core of the experience of 'mystical union', which has paramount significance in the life of a mystic, cannot be elucidated unless by resorting to ethical criteria and theology.

From the cognitive perspective we have not succeeded in grasping the phenomenon of 'mystical union'. Whenever we came across this liminal experience, it appeared to be a borderline event at the periphery, against which the area of cognitive mystical experience could be clearly thrown into relief. From the psychological perspective, the 'mystical union' has been classified as the ultimate stage of mystical ecstasy, in which the subject-object division is annihilated, the capacity of 'inner sight' suspended, and the clarity of consciousness eroded. From the gnoseological perspective, the event of the 'mystical union' appears to involve the complete [temporary] loss of the cognitive faculties. The more powerful the experience of the subject's 'self' becoming overwhelmed or inundated and annihilated by the union with the 'mystical Object', the more intense and persevering is the existential impact on the 'experiencing I', the less seems to be the gnoseological value of what is cognitively grasped in the event. It is not only the 'experiencing I', but the entire faculty of recognition as well as the capacity of 'inner sight' that are suspended temporarily by the powerful impact of the unitive event.

Therefore, it would seem imperative to ask if the theses propounded above can claim to be valid and been truthfully propounded. For if it is true that the 'mystical union' is the ultimate core of mystical experience, does this not require us to change the focus of our enquiry away from the sphere of recognition to that of the experiential core, and thus to search for the 'ultimate mystical phenomenon' ["mystisches Urphänomen"] in the experience of 'mystical union'? These fundamental questions must not be bypassed. In preparing an answer to these questions, I am going to quote passages from a letter by a scholar who wrote a critical review of my earlier study *Psychologie des Mystischen Bewußtseins*. The letter expresses quite explicitly the author's criticism of the phenomenological approach and presents an alternative point of view; therefore, the crucial passage deserves to be quoted in full:

> *Text 97* (From a letter by a critical scholar, dated 30 January 1955): "I come to the end of my letter ... The texts by Henry Suso and Angela of

Foligno quoted and analysed by you have convinced me that your investigations have indeed directed you near the core of 'mysticism'. I do not agree, however, with your claim that at this stage all phenomenological enquiry must end, and that the liminal ecstatic mystical event reported by both mystics should be accepted as it stands. For it seems to me that in this case you have left the ground of scholarly enquiry too early. It cannot be ruled out, after all, that a different approach might yield some further insights into the core of mystical experience.

I would like to propose, albeit with some hesitation, an alternative view ... Having followed the pathways of your thinking, I think that the final stage of your enquiry might be described as follows: The phenomenological sequence of inward visions consists of a series of continually declining pictorial features (but pictorial images are necessarily inappropriate in this context). At the same time, this sequence is marked by an increasing awareness of Presence. You have elaborated very clearly that the 'imageless vision' is the ultimate stage of the sequence of 'visionary experience' and as such it is close to the core phenomenon of mysticism which has paramount existential relevance. I think that it is at this point that a clear threshold is reached. And it is beyond that threshold that the ultimate mystical experience is located, namely the 'mystical union' of the soul with God, in which God reveals Himself mysteriously while remaining ultimately concealed, though his Presence is felt by inundating the soul with his essence and by drawing the soul into Himself.

The impact of such an experience is so powerful that it causes a *hiatus* in the individual consciousness, as Suso seems to state quite clearly, and this hiatus is the sudden switch into the ecstatic state of consciousness. The very moment of this shifting into the state of ecstasy signifies two things: the ultimate awareness of God's Presence, and the holistic perception of his pure Essence. This is the moment of the ultimate stage of mystical recognition, which, however, is bound to subside. The 'mystical union' while the transformation into the ecstatic state of consciousness occurs and is marked by the annihilation of the subject-object-split. As soon as the difference between subject and object is suspended, the capacity of knowing or of cognitive perception is likewise suspended. What the subject is still aware of is a deep sense of ecstatic bliss. Suso calls this stage a stage of [temporary] obliviousness, in which everything is forgotten and suspended, including the consciousness of oneself, except for a lingering sense of sweetness.

For this reason, it seems to me that the core of mystical experience is 'becoming oned', and hereafter abiding in 'oneness' with the 'All-encompassing', but not an act of cognition. The ultimate stage of recognition is reached when consciousness has switched into the state of ecstasy, but this stage lasts only for the flash of a moment. What endures, however, is the awareness of bliss; yet after the subject-object-split has been restored, some memory of the state of ecstasy can be retrieved, and therefore some insights can be derived from the unitive experience *ex post*. While I consider Suso's account convincing in all these respects, I don't think that the same can be said for the record of Angela of Foligno. Her account is more verbose, less focussed on specific experiential phenomena, and although she refers cursorily to the existential relevance of the mystical events, these remarks are less urgent and less immediate than in Suso's account. Her report seems to mirror mystical experiences that occurred while she was immersed in the 'quiet state of alertness', rather than in the state of ecstasy and, therefore, the subject-object-split appears not to have been entirely suspended, as the hyper-lucid condition of consciousness seems to prevail throughout.

When considering the difference of the existential impact that the mystical experience has on the two mystics individually, and relating them to the findings of your phenomenological research, I get the impression that Angela's experience is that of a visionary having reached the ultimate threshold of the 'imageless vision', in which the awareness of 'Presence' and the 'vision' of the essence of the 'All-encompassing' have almost reached a maximum – albeit only 'almost'. Therefore, I would assess Angela's visionary experience as a borderline phenomenon of the 'imageless vision' rather than an instance of the core mystical experience.

In summary, it seems to me that the core mystical experience is the one described and reflected in Suso's testimony. In parenthesis, I would argue that the very fact of God's infinity suggests that the awareness of His full Presence must inevitably transport the perceiver into the state of ecstasy. Don't you likewise think that the core of mystical experience – as I have tried to delineate – can after all be described and explained, at least to a certain degree? My impression is that this core experience is indeed a union with the Ultimate, albeit an Ultimacy that is to some extent still accessible to human reason and understanding."

In the considerations presented so far in this study, there is hardly a single chapter in which the phenomenon of the 'mystical union' has not been addressed or come into view. I have indeed tried not to bypass this pivotal phenomenon, even though the notion of the 'mystical union' has occasionally interfered with the progress of our enquiry, which required us for methodological reasons to deal first and foremost with mystical encounters this side of the state of ecstasy, in which the subject-object division is not suspended. This explains why the phenomenon of the 'mystical union' appeared, as it were, only on the horizon; but I must admit that, on the whole, the phenomenon of 'mystical union' has been placed at the periphery of our enquiry. Thus the 'mystical union' has repeatedly been referred to in passing and, more specifically, in the context of the experience of the 'mystical Presence'. It has been stated that the 'mystical Presence' can be perceived in several different modes, including the mode of somatic awareness, the mode of the 'imageless vision', or the mere 'sense of Presence'. And it goes without saying that the 'mystical Presence' is likewise a variety of the ecstatic experience of 'union'. Being overwhelmed by the immediate encounter with the 'Presence' and becoming 'united' with it is the core of mystical ecstasy [in theistic mystical tradition].

It is equally true that our phenomenological enquiry might alternatively have started from the focal point of the 'mystical union' rather than from that of 'mystical recognition'. And I am sure that it is possible to probe deeply into the secret core of mysticism when opting for this approach. However, I refrained from the audacity of opting for the lofty path by starting from the core phenomenon, preferring instead to take the less perilous lowly path. By sticking strictly to the demand never to stray from the course of rational reflection and logical analysis, we had to force our way through the gates of psychology and gnoseology. The drawback of this methodological approach was that the existential impact of a mystical event has occasionally been bypassed or not sufficiently considered. And I also must concede that the focus on the cognitive dimension of mystical experience may have shed some distorting light on other areas or components of mystical experience. Yet despite these deficiencies, the enquiry and the methodology chosen has nonetheless disclosed new vistas and yielded new insights. Should we not be grateful, after all, that we have been enabled, by proceeding along the path of scientific enquiry in search of the secret core of mystical experience, to elucidate to a considerable extent the cognitive dimension of the 'mystical relation'? Yet we must still always bear in mind *that the 'cognitive relation' is only a single segment of the whole phenomenon of mysticism.*

The perspective of our enquiry is determined by the spot from which we may direct our view at the phenomenon of mysticism. And the perspective by which we are advancing has a three-dimensional structure: In the foreground is the 'cognitive mystical relation', behind of which and embedded within it is the 'experiential mystical relation', and further afar, at a remote distance, our view will encounter the 'ultimate phenomenon' termed 'mystical relation', by which everything is encompassed and sustained.

There are two other phenomena which are integral parts of a mystical encounter, but which have not yet been explicitly addressed in our phenomenological enquiry: The mystical encounter with Supreme Beauty and the encounter with 'all-encompassing Love'. We have not yet elaborated on these two mystical phenomena, as we tried to establish first the distinctive features of the 'cognitive mystical relation' as clearly as possible before turning to phenomena pertaining to sense-related modes of 'inner vision'. The 'vision of Supreme Beauty' and the experience of 'all-encompassing Love' are, unlike 'cognition', more easily accessible to phenomenological analysis and have, for this reason, been placed at the end of the current chapter.

The *'vision of Beauty'* is a multi-layered phenomenon. The encounter with Supreme Beauty ["das Ur-Schöne"] is a visionary experience of 'Supreme Beauty' which is, however, imageless, ineffable and awe-inspiring. The fact that such an experience has indeed occurred is beyond all doubt to any perceiver. The 'vision of Supreme Beauty' is immediate, imageless since what is perceived in 'inner sight' is without any shape and image. The 'vision of Supreme Beauty' instantly triggers an unfathomable sense of bliss and joy; this ecstatic emotional response indicates that the 'vision of Beauty' is affiliated with mystical ecstasy. To illustrate the difference and/or the affinities between the 'vision of Sublime Beauty' and a 'pictorial vision' in which the notion of Sublime Beauty is inherent, I will quote two examples for illustration – one from the diary of Christine Lucie, the other from the *vita* of Angela of Foligno:

> Text 98 (Christine Lucie, diary entry dated 6 May 1883, 119): "My beloved Lord instantly revealed to me His Supreme Beauty, and my soul became completely absorbed in it. In this Beauty I beheld all the beauty created ... I beheld this Infinite Beauty, *Itself alone*, independent from all the beautiful things that have been created by it; however, I was unable to express in words what this Beauty is, because I only beheld it spiritually and worshipped it in prayer, without understanding ..." [Italics as inserted by Albrecht for emphasis]

Text 99 (Angela of Foligno, *The Book of Divine Consolation*, Treatise III, Second Vision.)[117]: "Upon a certain time when I was at prayer and my spirit was exalted, God spoke to me many gracious words full of love.

And when I looked, I beheld God who spoke with me. But if thou seekest to know what I beheld, I can tell thee nothing, save that I beheld a fullness and a clearness, and felt them within me so abundantly that I can in no wise describe it, nor give any likeness thereof. For what I beheld was not corporal, but as though it were in heaven. Thus, I beheld a beauty so great that I can say naught concerning it, save that I saw the Supreme Beauty which containeth within Itself all goodness."

The encounter with mystical Love is even more multi-faceted than the sudden irruption of Supreme Beauty. Mystical Love must not be mistaken for the languishing desire for the Divine felt by a person when advancing on the mystical path. Nor is 'mystical Love' to be equated with Platonic Eros: 'mystical Love' is spiritual Love, *agape* or *caritas*, not erotic love *(amor)*. Phenomenologically, 'mystical Love' has affinities with the experience of the 'mystical Light': Like Light, Love is all-encompassing, omnipresent and all-pervasive; but unlike Light, Love is not experienced by a 'mystical vision' but by the mode of 'mystical feelings'. An encounter with 'mystical Love' is moreover similar to the encounter of Supreme Beauty in that it likewise evokes deep feelings of bliss; but unlike the 'vision of Beauty', the emotional response aroused by 'mystical Love' is deeply imbued with reverent loving devotion. 'Mystical Love' 'arrives', i.e., is experienced as something instilled [coming from the realm beyond the individual consciousness], and this awareness evokes instantly intense feelings of love in response. This mutual interchange of love has likewise a parallel in the experience of 'mystical Light': the 'vision of mystical Light' produces a state of inward luminescence in that it generates a hyper-lucid state of consciousness in the perceiver, and thus a supreme condition of inner clarity and thus a most perfect setting

---

117 [Note: Albrecht's textual source is *Gesichte und Tröstungen der Seligen Angela von Foligno*. Trans. Jan van Arend. Mainz: Grünewald, 1924. The English quotation has been taken from *The Book of Divine Consolation of the Blessed Angela of Foligno*: Trans. from the Italian by Mary G. Steegmann. London: Chatto and Windus, 1909. 169. – FKW.]

for the faculty of 'inner sight'. By contrast, the response triggered by the experience of 'mystical Love' causes a shift from the serene state of consciousness into the realm of the 'ecstatic consciousness'; the responding feelings of loving devotion inundating consciousness may ultimately culminate in the ecstatic state of 'mystical union'.

From this succinct description of the phenomenological characteristics of 'mystical Love' it should become clear why our phenomenological enquiry has intentionally been focused on mystical phenomena outside its domain. These critical considerations have also shown that *the phenomenon of mystical experience is much broader than the segment of 'mystical recognition' elaborated in our enquiry appears to suggest.*

Finally, we consider it helpful to address yet another aspect – as an appendix or supplement to these critical annotations – namely results of *enquiries undertaken by the psychology of religion, and more specifically, the researches carried out by Werner Gruehn*[118]: Gruehn's approach to mysticism is largely based on the experimental methods of the psychology of religion developed by Girgensohn. Our methodology, by contrast, has initially been a psychological and phenomenological one, and subsequently, combined with the former, a phenomenological-gnoseological approach. In the first part of our investigation we utilized spontaneous utterances spoken during the state of 'quiet alertness' and mystical states of 'quiet alertness' as well as in the incipient stage of ecstasy; the empirical data, in other words, were in part provided by authentic mystical 'locutions' spoken during an ongoing mystical event; these recorded utterances are thus spontaneous and have not been verbalized retrospectively from memory. In the second part of our study, we examined a substantial corpus of historical records of mystical experience, which have enabled us to reveal essential features of the phenomenon of mysticism.

We are, however, also clearly aware of the limitations of our approach. Yet irrespective of the boundaries imposed by methodology and the ultimately inscrutable realm of mysticism, we think to

---

118 GRUEHN, Werner. *Die Frömmigkeit der Gegenwart. Grundtatsachen der Empirischen Psychologie*. Münster: Aschendorff, 1956. Especially 1–40, 107–42, 261–94 and 219–331.

have succeeded in outlining some significant phenomena of several segments within the totality of mysticism, and that the findings of our enquiry have also elucidated some facets of the core of mystical experience. Now we are going to enquire, if the discipline of experimental psychology of religion has achieved similar results. According to *Gruehn,* the concept of 'mysticism' is determined by three aspects: 1. Mysticism is a specific variety of religious experience in which the proportion between the 'function of the I' and thoughts of God is shifted compared to everyday religious experience. The term 'function of the I' derives from experimental psychology; it purports the claim that a test person will generate lively and real relational experiences to the subject matter dealt with in a given religious text, which he/she has been required to read; as a consequence the 'I' is inclined to accept and approve of the religious ideas presented, even to the extent of internalizing and becoming (as it were) 'one' with them. In mysticism this proportion is shifted unevenly in favour of the 'function of the I', to the extent that the input of the 'experiencing I' increases significantly whereas the share of religious thought is reduced. 2. In mysticism the experiential content is heightened and amplified. 3. Mystical experience does not occur in a hypo-lucid or normal waking state, but in a hyper-lucid, alert state of consciousness. The term 'hyper-lucidity' denotes – like the ancillary terms 'being alert', 'being enraptured', 'being transported into rapturous bliss', and 'state of ecstasy' – that there is no room any more in the consciousness of the subject for anything else but the 'thought of God'.

I think, however, that these propositions [of Gruehn] are too broad and inaccurate; they have substantial gaps and therefore cannot capture the pivotal phenomena of mysticism: Gruehn's experimental approach fails to encompass the broad and rich domain of 'visionary' and non-visionary mystical experiences (as outlined in our study), nor does it examine individual mystical events against the given state of consciousness or relate them to the cultural and religious context; over and beyond this, the vital function of inner calmness in the context of mystical experience, in particular, as an inexorable condition in both the 'quiet state of alertness' and the 'mystical state of quiet alertness', is not recognized or taken into consideration. Even more importantly, the awareness of the 'mystical

Presence', one of the most essential independent phenomena of [theistic] mysticism, has entirely escaped Gruehn's notice.

In addition to the experimental research of Girgensohn and Gruehn, I have become especially interested in the studies of A. Canesi[119] and Alfons Bolley.[120] In the papers of these scientists some valuable records of their experimental research are quoted, which contain descriptions of empirical events which can be regarded as antecedents or rudimentary modes of cognitive mystical experience. Canesi presents instances of 'pictorial visionary experience' as well as examples of the 'vision of Light'; at close analysis, however, i.e., if we apply the strict psychological and gnoseological criteria for assessing genuine modes of 'mystical recognition' established by our study, the mystical occurrences described by Canesi qualify at best as visionary experiences in the incipient stage. This aside, Canesi passes off accounts as genuine mystical visions of the Divine Presence which can clearly be identified as imaginative and/or subjective cognitive evocations of the presence of God.

The paper of Alfons Bolley discusses an example of an (alleged) 'pictorial vision', which is replete with subjective characteristics. Bolley himself is aware of this fact, conceding that the protocols of his experiments contain numerous descriptions of pictorial visionary experiences, which are strikingly focussed on and dominated by notions of the 'experiencing I'. At close analysis, the examples quoted by Bolley do not qualify as instances of cognitive mystical experience and can be identified as accounts of rudimentary imaginative representations of God, or merely of a conscious recognition of the reality of God. These shortcomings and misconceptions probably originate from the given experimental conditions. Any experimental environment is an artificial construct in which it is rather unlikely for a genuine mystical experience to occur.

I do not deny that these experimental studies may disclose some significant features of the phenomenon of mysticism, but I refute

---

119   CANESI, A. "Vorläufige Untersuchungen über die Psychologie des Gebetes." *Archiv für Religionspsychologie* 10 (1936): 13–72.

120   BOLLEY, Alfons. "Das Gotteserleben in der Betrachtung." *Geist und Leben* 22 (1949): 343–56.

the claim that these experiments can probe into the core of mystical experience. It would therefore be helpful if a cross-disciplinary discourse between the psychology of religion and the psychology of consciousness would commence so that the results, methodologies and aims pursued in each discipline could be critically assessed from both perspectives.

The Mystical Relation
["Die mystische Relation"]

We have now reached the half-way point along the new path of our enquiry. The structure of 'mystical recognition' has been encompassed by the broader sphere of the 'experiential mystical relation'. *Through the screening filter of reason, we have nonetheless been able to get a glimpse of the phenomenological space in which the impact of a wholeness hits upon a subject in a concrete mystical event, in which the subject experiences the effects of the impact that has 'arrived'* [in consciousness] *in a holistic act of recognition.* The crucial phenomenon is not the 'cognitive mystical relation', but the 'experiential mystical relation', in which the cognitive relation is rooted and sustained. This insight can be summarized in the following thesis:

THESIS 76: *The 'cognitive mystical relation' is rooted in the 'experiential mystical relation'. The former is the rationally structured apex of an expansive, undifferentiated realm of experience.*

The phenomenological space in which we have glimpsed herein the 'experiential mystical relation' is still a zone in the forefront of the actual core. Therefore, it is necessary to go beyond this zone if we wish to arrive at the realm in which the core phenomenon of mysticism resides and may be further explored. The 'experiential mystical relation' attempts to transgress its own domain from all sides. When referring to the encounter of an '*effective* wholeness', which is experienced in a holistic mode of perception, we point to the fact that there is a wide-ranging domain of mystical effects that are part of a concrete mystical experience, of which, however, only a small part is accessible to conscious mystical perception.

The term 'mystical relation' has been introduced to refer to a realm of mystical effects beyond rational enquiry and thus transintelligible;

this domain is stretched out between the 'mystical It' and the 'experiencing subject' who is affected by it. The term thus denotes a relation which is directed at something that cannot be recognized. Yet even the word 'effect' seems to me to be too specific, as it implies a cause-effect relationship which is more than can reasonably be said about it. On the empirical level we have been able to advance a few steps into the unfathomable realm of mysticism. Hence, we can state that the 'experiencing subject' can be 'affected' or 'stricken' by 'mystical effects' imposed, or imparted upon him, even though these effects are not perceived as 'objects' of some undifferentiated experience, let alone of an act of clear 'mystical recognition'.

Our investigation has so far been based on a highly differentiated, analytical phenomenological approach. This method resulted in a systematic classification of the phenomena of mysticism and in distinguishing individual phenomena clearly from each other by contrasting them and by outlining occasional affinities, as well as by pointing out analogies. Phenomenological research, however, must not confine itself to the task of critical analysis. The endeavour to highlight a complete coherent pattern of individual phenomena is but the first step in overcoming these confines. This may provide a new epistemological basis for probing more deeply into the realm of mysticism and permit us to get a glimpse into the space in which the '*ultimate* phenomenon' can be discerned. But without taking the first step, i.e., without engaging in analytical enquiries, we would have been deprived of the structured phenomenological reference-frame that has allowed us to exchange the perspective of the 'scientific observer' for that of the 'informed witness'. Because of the analytical preliminaries by which the distinctive features of all the major varieties of mystical experience have been identified, we may venture to glance at the phenomenon of the 'mystical relation'.

The attempt to elucidate the essential core of mysticism requires that we approach it from different perspectives. In the end, however, we shall recognize that from whichever perspective the core of mysticism has been approached, the 'mystical relation' is indeed the 'ultimate phenomenon' we have been searching for. Hence, we may state:

THESIS 77: *The 'mystical relation' is an 'ultimate phenomenon'. This insight has been empirically grasped in an 'imageless mystical vision' and is as such an evident phenomenological fact. Therefore the 'ultimate phenomenon' of the 'mystical relation' must be acknowledged as a 'givenness', although it eludes rational analysis or explanation.*

Before we provide a phenomenological description of the 'mystical relation' on the basis of the findings in the foregoing stages of our investigation, we need to interpolate an annotation to obviate potential misunderstanding: The 'ultimate phenomenon' of the 'mystical relation' is not a new phenomenon that is in any way higher-ranking than any of the other 'relations' we have so far identified and analysed, nor is it to be added to, or placed side by side with the other 'relations'. Instead it is the '*all-comprehensive* relation', which incorporates all the other 'relations' while at the same time being partly composed of all the other relations.

Our long-term endeavour to trace the phenomenon of mysticism to its essential core has culminated in the final phenomenological result of the discovery of an ultimate phenomenon we have labelled 'mystical relation'. The characteristic features of the 'mystical relation', which are accessible to rational analysis, have been disclosed layer by layer. But we must admit that the phenomenological characteristics of the essential core of mystical experience that have been revealed are rather sparse, vague and intangible.

Despite these inadequacies and limitations, it has at least been possible to uncover some distinct phenomena by approaching the 'mystical relation' from the two poles between which it is determined. Yet the two poles can only be named cautiously and hesitatingly and by way of preliminary terms: The one pole has been termed the 'mystical It'. From a phenomenological perspective, nothing more can be said about it than that the 'mystical It' is the only *identical and phenomenologically unequivocal* point of reference of any genuine 'mystical relation'. The other pole is much more multifarious, and all its distinctive features can clearly be described. This pole has been termed the 'sphere of individual experience', whereby the word 'experience' does not denote an experiential encounter as defined by the psychology of consciousness, but has a broader meaning extended by anything by which, as subject, can be passively [pathicly] affected. We have been able in our previous study [*Psychology of Mystical Consciousness*] to outline several varieties of 'pathic experience' from the perspective of the psychology of consciousness.

In the present study the confines of psychology have been transgressed by combining the psychological-phenomenological approach with a gnoseological one. The gnoseological perspective has revealed that the ultimate pole of the 'mystical relation' is wrapped in the attire of gnoseological structures which extend into the realm of experience. We could discern varied structures of mystical experiences residing in the sphere of experience. And we could see through these empirical structures and discern 'mystical effects' 'arriving'. The individual elements of the latter structure derive their purpose and meaning from the structure of experience, because there is (for the most part) a correlation between specific modes of recognition and the modes of 'mystical effects'.

The structure of 'mystical effects' can only be approached and understood from the 'sphere of experience'; 'mystical effects', however, point beyond the confines of the 'sphere of experience'. The term 'structure of mystical effects' indicates an item of the 'mystical relation' already; and this item is located, as it were, close to the pole of the 'sphere of mystical experience' ["mystische Erlebnissphäre"]. The term 'structure of mystical effects' suggests that the cognitive perception of the 'mystical relation' is in part contained in it; more specifically, that part of the 'mystical relation' becomes apparent in a perceiver in the event of a mystical experience, though the subjective characteristics of the experience are rather elusive and sparse. As for the 'objective pole', it would be inappropriate at the present stage of our enquiry to say something more specific about the essence of the 'mystical It' on the meagre empirical evidence of these fleeting intimations of the 'mystical relation' in the 'experiencing subject', which occur (as it were) still in the 'forecourt' of mysticism. It would thus be entirely misplaced at this point to claim that we have succeeded in outlining the phenomenological characteristics of the 'mystical relation'. The essence of the 'mystical relation' is, after all, inherently 'dark' and hardly tangible – and this does not only hold true ontologically and ontically (which are metaphysical issues that do not concern us here), but also phenomenologically (which is much more important for this enquiry). What we know at this stage about the 'mystical relation' is, first, that it embraces several single phenomena, which are epitomized by the collective term 'structure of mystical effects', and second, that we have clearly recognized that the entire structure of the 'mystical relation', in which the individual components are embedded, which can be grasped phenomenologically and gneoseologically, is ultimately indeterminable.

We may thus summarize the few phenomenological characteristics of the 'mystical relation' that can be recognized as follows: *The 'mystical relation' consists of a lucid 'inner 'sphere', which is clearly structured and accessible phenomenologically through the psychology of consciousness; this 'inner sphere' is surrounded by a less lucid 'pathic sphere' which can be experienced; after which follows a structural component of the 'mystical relation' which can be grasped gnoseologically; beyond these features only the [pivotal] fact can be ascertained that the 'mystical relation' is as such phenomenologically a confirmed verity, that does not require any additional phenomenological qualifications for its verification; and this proposition is inevitably likewise true of the objective reference-pole: the 'mystical It'.* We have introduced the concept of the 'ultimate phenomenon' to refer to this 'ur-relation', revealed in the 'mystical relation'. The concept of the 'ultimate phenomenon', though repeatedly addressed in passing above, calls for further explication and needs to be further corroborated. This will be done in the following chapter, and in this context, we shall survey once more the different 'relations' encompassed by the 'ultimate phenomenon' and try to establish the essence of the 'relation' identified as *mystical*.

The Concept of the 'Ultimate Phenomenon' ["Der Begriff 'Phänomenletztheit'"]

The concept of 'ultimate phenomenon' must be delineated against two other concepts: on the one hand, in relation to the term 'phenomenon' as such, and, on the other hand, in relation to the concept 'ur-phenomenon'. *Phenomena* are, by definition, primary units of order. They are inferred from a plethora of facts and adjoining individual incidents and circumstances; phenomena are thus the primary items identified, which prevail and are encountered again and again, and to which single mutable items can be traced, or from which the interpretation of individual items derives. Phenomena are universal and can be discerned by applying the human principle of classifying order. In the realm of nature, for instance, phenomena can be classified into physical, chemical or biological categories, and in the realm of the psyche, we may distinguish between psychic, spiritual and historical phenomena. Phenomena are thus primary systems of order. This fact indicates that phenomena are typically apparent, conditional and interim.

'Underneath' or 'behind' the apparent area of phenomena, the domain of *'ultimate phenomena'* opens up. This domain is open to scientific and scholarly enquiry by any discipline – whether by the natural sciences, the humanities, and above all philosophical thinking, which is especially suited to advancing to the level of the 'ultimate phenomenon'. The term 'ultimate phenomenon' refers to the result of dealing with phenomena in terms of tracing them as far as possible to their ultimate origin, which, however, remains beyond rational enquiry. In other words, 'ultimate phenomena' are phenomena that have *hitherto* [i.e., until now, at the present state of our knowledge] resisted rational explanation and any attempt to trace them back to an ultimate origin, or to infer them from other phenomena. 'Ultimate phenomena' are thus 'ultimate' entities only in relative terms, i.e., provisionally, so long as any attempt to infer it from an antecedent source or cause is unsuccessful.

Underneath the domain of 'ultimate phenomena' there is the layer of *'ur-phenomena'*. By this term we mean phenomena that are entirely trans-intelligible, i.e., entirely beyond the reach of rational thinking. They are primordially 'given' facticities, inexplicable, and can never be resolved by any human effort. Whereas the term 'ultimate phenomenon' implies the notion that it is tentatively open to scrutiny and is thus a provisional phenomenon, the term 'ur-phenomenon' refers to a definite, final and irretrievable fact.

Genuine 'ur-phenomena' are concealed 'behind' or 'underneath' many of the 'ultimate phenomena'. Science depends on provisional conditions and potentially mutable objects of enquiry. Therefore, we must establish a clear distinction of the phenomenon of the 'mystical relation' from the concept of the 'ur-relation'. The realm of 'ultimate phenomena' is a twilight zone, which needs to be properly elucidated if we wish to identify the 'mystical relation'. We know that 'ultimate phenomena' have so far resisted any attempt at being dissolved or explained rationally, but this does not categorically exclude the possibility that they might be explained and traced to antecedent phenomena by science in the future. Even so, we are required to pay due respect to any phenomenon currently acknowledged as an 'ultimate phenomenon', since it has proved to be something significant and enduring. Yet, on the other hand, any 'ultimate phenomenon' arouses the desire to probe further into the realm 'beyond' or 'behind' it. This means that the question as to whether a particular 'ultimate phenomenon' is in truth itself already an 'ur-phenomenon', cannot be decided by the mere perception of the 'ultimate phenomenon'.

'Ultimate phenomena' are the major topic of philosophy. In fact, the history of philosophy is the history of 'ultimate phenomena': There are eras in which 'ultimate phenomena' have been claimed to be 'explained' and disclosed rationally, but these claims have been proved false because the alleged 'ultimate phenomena' have prevailed and surfaced later in history. For instance, the 'ultimate phenomenon' of 'freedom' was for some time obscured in history by the fact that the human power of the will was traced to an unbroken sequence of predetermined motivation; the [ultimate] phenomenon of 'life' became eclipsed (as it were) when it was explained in terms of a blinkered mechanistic notion of man and traced exclusively to physiological and biochemical processes; the phenomenon of 'spirit' was dissolved by being explained merely by psychological and biological processes and assumptions. The phenomenon of "Dasein" – the fact of man 'being in this world' – was either converted entirely into a subjective notion, or dissolved and replaced by the concept of 'life'; the phenomenon of 'conscience' has been assigned ever new obscuring notions and camouflages: theologically, 'conscience' has been claimed to be the 'voice of God', psychologically, the voice of 'super-ego', and in existentialist philosophy 'conscience' has been claimed to be 'Being' appealing to Itself.[121]

---

121   Cf. HEIDEGGER, Martin. *Sein und Zeit*. 1927. 2nd ed. Halle an der Saale: Niemeyer, 1929, 275. [Note: Albrecht refers to the phrase "*Das Dasein ruft im Gewissen sich selbst.*" (i.e., ' "Dasein" appeals to itself in conscience'.) (275; italics in the original; translation provided.) — FKW.]

Reductionist and revisionist attempts of this kind to explain away 'ultimate phenomena' have proved abortive, since they kept returning in history and continued to surface on the horizon of human consciousness. *The 'mystical relation' is thus one amongst several genuine 'ultimate phenomena'.* It has been inferred from the domain of significant conspicuous phenomena encountered in our enquiry. The psychological journey toward its phenomenological identification has begun by establishing the structure of the 'quiet state of alertness', in which, especially, the phenomena of 'arriving' in the vista of 'inner sight' from beyond the 'sphere of the self', have proved to be of pivotal significance. However, the 'mystical relation' could just as well have been disclosed by searching for it by applying an historical approach – for example, by examining the lives of mystics and studying their accounts of the varieties of mystical experiences and their modes of thinking – and the 'mystical relation' could furthermore have been discovered independently as being inherent in religious phenomena, such as diverse forms of prayer and practices of spiritual life, in which ascetic exercises are combined with contemplation and states of ecstasy. The approach chosen for our empirical research in the preceding book [*Psychology of Mystical Consciousness*] was that of psychological phenomenology, because this method seemed to be, scientifically speaking, the most reliable and tangible one. And this psychological approach permitted us to advance as far as the 'ultimate phenomenon' termed 'mystical relation'.

PART TWO

Gnoseology of Mysticism

The first part of the present study has provided a psychological-phenomenological analysis of mystical phenomena and has disclosed as a significant finding that mysticism is rooted in an 'ultimate phenomenon' termed 'mystical relation'. As emphasized above, this special 'ultimate phenomenon' encompasses three aspects, which must be borne in mind: First, we have identified *the structure of cognitive mystical perception*, which is based on a gnoseological 'mystical relation'. Subsequently we recognized that the 'cognitive mystical relation' is embedded in a broad, undifferentiated *experiential relation*. The third approach revealed that the concepts of 'mystical recognition' and 'mystical experience' are insufficient, as they can only cover the 'surface' or 'foreground' of the 'mystical relation'. The 'ultimate phenomenon' of the 'mystical relation' as such encompasses a much broader sphere than the one embraced by the two more specific partial relations termed 'cognitive mystical relation' and 'experiential mystical relation'. In other words, the entire phenomenon identified as an 'ultimate phenomenon' is *the 'mystical relation' as such*. This is the sustaining ground of all other experiential mystical relationships, of which, conversely, only a few are involved in establishing a 'cognitive mystical relation'.

These terminological and phenomenological clarifications are important in view of the further progress of our investigation: Each of the following two parts of this study will be concerned with diverse aspects of the 'mystical relation'. Part II will focus on the 'gnoseological relation'. The second part of the book, in other words, will critically examine the cognitive potential of mystical experience and its veridical claims. In other words, Part II provides a critical evaluation of the insights obtained by 'mystical recognition', including a preliminary investigation about 'truth and error' in mystical experience. On the basis of this critical study of 'mystical discernment' we shall subject several varieties of mystical experience to an in-depth gnoseological analysis, which will establish a clear notion of the phenomenon of 'mystical recognition'.

Part III is concerned with the 'ultimate phenomenon' of the 'mystical relation' as such. In this part, considerations relating to the 'gnoseological relation' are bypassed in favour of an effort to probe as deeply as possible into the undifferentiated realm of mystical experience. In the final section the critical reflections will orbit exclusively around the key-phenomenon of the 'mystical relation' and expound in some detail on the philosophical relevance of this specific 'ultimate phenomenon'.

Delusion and Error in the Context of Mystical Experience ["Trug und Irrtum in der mystischen Erfahrung"]

Delusion and error may occur in diverse ways in the realm of mystical experience. If we wish to identify delusory and/or bogus phenomena, we need to rely on three concepts by which the three main types of error in a mystical event can be discerned: These are the concepts of 1. 'delusory mystical experience', 2. the 'erroneous belief, or conviction that a bogus phenomenon is mystical in origin', and 3. the 'flawed interpretation in mystical terms of a locution, visionary appearance or intuition'. These three types of error may overlap in a concrete mystical experience; therefore, they cannot be strictly separated, but the distinction is helpful as these three concepts place different points of emphasis for recognizing items of flawed perception.

The three concepts refer individually to a specific experiential situation, but each concept has a different degree of immediacy to the actual empirical occurrence: A 'delusory mystical experience' is an integral part of an individual act of mystical perception, and thus the error results from the flawed perception of a phenomenon. The 'erroneous conviction of the mystical origin' of an alleged mystical event, however, is not immediately linked to the act of experiencing, though it is part of an empirical event. In this case the error occurs in erroneously assigning a phenomenon perceived as 'arriving' in 'inner sight' to a mystical origin; here the error does not spring from a flawed act of experiencing, but from the false attribution of the provenance of the alleged mystical event. An 'invalid mystical interpretation of a locution or visionary appearance' derives from the misconception of a physiognomic gesture, visionary appearance or message heard inwardly. This error does not result from flawed perception, but from an error about the true origin of the given experience; the perceiver falsely identifies the 'effects' elicited by an empirical event with the 'effecting' Presence of the 'mystical Object' itself.

A 'delusory mystical experience' is the perception of an apparent mystical phenomenon. It is thus analogous to a delusory sense perception. A delusive mystical perception is necessarily bound to an individual act of perception, i.e., it consists either of a spurious vision or a delusory event of 'inner hearing'. For delineating more clearly the difference between 'delusion' and 'error', the criterion of experiential proximity – i.e., the claim that delusions are elicited during the cognitive act of experience – is not conclusive enough. There are two more criteria by which a 'delusion' can be distinguished from an 'error' in a mystical experience:

1. A delusion is suffered. This means it is so deeply rooted in the act of perception that it cannot be controlled *a posteriori* by an act of volition, or by rational judgement. Thus, a delusion cannot be obviated. It can, however, be diagnosed after it has occurred by subjecting the perception to a critical examination and be removed hereafter. There are criteria of authenticity by which the question of truth or delusion in a mystical experience can be decided. The critical analysis of mystical experience thus requires inevitably distinct criteria for substantiating the veracity of a mystical event.

2. A delusion occurs by mistaking two divergent experiential occurrences during the ongoing act of experiencing. The pivotal characteristic of a delusion, however, becomes apparent only if the misconception is gross and persevering enough. For example, the mistaking of a person seen in the street for a different person does not qualify as a delusory experience. A delusion occurs when a low-ranking object is identified with a higher-ranking one. The term 'rank' here does not imply a value judgement but refers to

the classification of the items perceived in a given experiential situation – for instance, if something unreal is mistaken for something real, or if a non-mystical object is mistaken in an alleged mystical experience for a mystical one. A delusion thus originates from a flawed perception, and/or in being deceived about the true nature of the object(s) experienced. That is to say, in a delusory experience a false experiential situation is thought to be a genuine one.

The sphere of the concept of delusion has the tendency to expand. This has led to fuzzy expressions such as 'conviction of the realness of a delusion' and 'belief in the delusory nature of an experience'. These terms are not helpful; it is more appropriate to use the word 'error' to refer to the phenomena described by the two fuzzy expressions. An 'erroneous conviction about the mystical origin' and the 'erroneous mystical interpretation of a visionary appearance or locution' are not instances of 'delusion' as defined by us, but rather instances of an error, based either on a flawed assumption or a misinterpretation. It is true, however, that these kinds of error cannot really be detached from a given experiential situation, as they are an integral part of the experience. Errors of this kind are not the outcome of a process of thinking but rather false convictions or flawed interpretations which accompany the process of experiencing.

Delusions and the two kinds of error addressed are misconceptions of occurrences in empirical reality and are as such inevitably linked to a genuine act of cognitive perception *a posteriori*. Both delusion and error call for an act of cognitive perception which is itself free from error and delusion. Without the real possibility of a genuine process of cognitive perception that is devoid of any error and delusion, the probability of a delusory experience occurring would not exist, either. In other words, *the occurrence of a delusory experience depends inevitably on the possibility that the given experience is true*. This means that the sphere of the concept of delusion ends where a mode of cognitive perception is bound to be categorically questioned. An enquiry into the nature of delusion and its critical assessment requires as a precondition that it is based on a sound and approved gnoseological structure. Anyone who denies beforehand that the modes of mystical perception are at all rooted in a gnoseological structure has no need to bother about its potential delusory nature. From this inherently agnostic perspective, any mystical experience is inevitably mere appearance and delusion or, gnoseologically speaking, non-existent.

Any epistemological enquiry into the nature of delusion and error in the context of mystical experience is likewise to be placed outside the realm of phenomenology. This applies to any approach aimed at a rational analysis of the empirical substratum of mystical experience, as well as to any research trying to establish empirical evidence for the various modes of mystical perception. The theory of epistemology, after all, presupposes that the primary gnoseological situation is devoid of delusion. This means, conversely, that an epistemological enquiry about delusion is carried out without recourse to the fundamental question as to whether the gnoseological phenomena encountered are to be credited to the theorems propounded by idealism, realism or monism.

Following these preliminary terminological considerations, we may now proceed with our enquiry on the issue of 'delusion and error in the context of mystical experience'. Our task is now to engage in a meticulous analysis of each of the individual modes of mystical experience and to establish criteria by which it is possible to discern genuine from erroneous and delusory instances of mystical experience. To begin with, we will distinguish the areas in which the prospect of delusion is fairly high, from the experiential domain which is relatively resistant to delusion and error. The second aim is to provide a new viewpoint from which it is possible to elucidate the phenomenon of 'mystical recognition' that is exempt from error and delusion.

We shall begin with the *phenomenon of 'mystical effects'* as this phenomenon, though diffuse, is a constituent empirical element in most varieties of mystical experience. And we need to repeat briefly what we have stated above on this opaque phenomenon from the perspective of the psychology of consciousness. The term "being effected" or "acted upon" ["Gewirktheit"] underscores an important existential and phenomenological fact: It implies that there is a distinction between an 'object', viz., 'impact' that 'arrives' in the perceiver's consciousness and which is grasped in an act of cognition, and another 'object' that remains outside the realm of the individual consciousness, and is the ultimate Source that has conveyed the 'object' which has 'arrived' in the perceiver's mind. The extra-mental Source remains unknown and concealed but is perceived as the effective cause and operative entity ["das Wirkende"] of the experience. The relationship between the 'operating cause' and the 'effects' or 'impact' perceived is determined, not accidental, though it is entirely inexplicable and irrational.

THESIS 78: *It is not possible to conclude from the mere occurrence of the phenomenon of 'effects' 'arriving' in consciousness and/or operating within the perceiver if they have been elicited by a mystical or a non-mystical cause.* This thesis has crucial significance for assessing the options of error in a mystical experience. The question as to whether such phenomena as the inner hearing of 'locutions', or the perception of appearances in a vision, or of the somatic experience of impacts of 'effects' imposed on the perceiver, or of the 'arrival' of 'intuitions', have indeed been 'effected' by the 'mystical It', or if they must be dismissed as delusory occurrences, can neither be inferred just from the phenomenon of 'arriving', or from the awareness that an impact or effect has been 'instilled' or 'impinged' by an agent or 'power' from outside the perceiver's 'sphere of the self'. This is because neither the 'object arriving' nor the impact 'effected' in the 'experiencing self' has any experiential or cognitive characteristics that would indicate where the 'object' or 'impact' has come from. This means that errors are mainly rooted in the fact that the only reasons why the experiencing subject is convinced that the phenomena experienced are mystical in origin are grounded in his/her conviction that the phenomena have 'arrived' and been 'effected' by a trans-subjective (extra-mental) cause.

Considering the phenomenon of 'mystical effects', we may therefore state: The question of whether or not an impact has originated in an act of genuine mystical experience must be decided on the basis of the cognitive qualities, which are encountered outside the realm of 'mystical effects'. There are (I think) four major distinctive features that may be used as the touchstone (individually or collectively) for assessing a mystical experience as genuine or bogus:

1. *The content of a genuine mystical event has unique characteristics*: For instance, the meaning of an image beheld in a 'pictorial vision', the meaning of a 'locution', the explicit summons

perceived in an 'auditory experience', or a 'cognitive insight' instilled by illumination – all these experiences are attributed an exceptional 'rank' by the perceiver; they have supreme value for him/her, which is why it is difficult to argue that these experiences have just surfaced from within the 'experiencing self'. It is more convincing to acknowledge them as the results of impacts imposed on the perceiver, hence as mystical in origin.

2. *If the impact or the 'effects' impinged upon a perceiver are perfectly consonant with the structure of the totality of the given mystical experience*, this can be taken as a reliable indication that the mystical experience is indeed genuine.

3. *If the experience of 'effects' operating in or upon a subject is accompanied by the simultaneous cognitive awareness of the mystical Presence*, the underlying experience can be claimed to be genuine. Two modes of mystical experience are coupled in this event: the unquestionably genuine 'mystical Object' [i.e., sense of Presence] is linked with the effects perceived, and this is a clear indication of the genuine nature of the mystical event.

4. Mystics have unanimously emphasized throughout history that *the experience of 'effects instilled' or of the sense of 'being acted upon' from outside the confines of the individual self, is inexorably combined with an exceptional, often instantaneous change of the emotional condition and the spiritual disposition*. The experience of 'love infused', of 'bliss instilled', or of 'passive purification', or of the sudden (often unsolicited) 'conversion', i.e., the decision or irresistible desire to devote one's life henceforth solely to the service of God, are all 'effects' of such rare quality that they cannot be persuasively accounted for, unless as instances of *'mystical effects'* resulting from a genuine mystical encounter.

Though it is true that these four criteria cannot be claimed to provide evidence of truth, they can be seen at least as relative criteria for the genuine nature of a mystical occurrence. But when these criteria are not applied in assessing the authenticity of a mystical event, the doors to error and misconception are opened unconditionally. These four criteria thus have not only the purpose of curbing errors about the assumed mystical 'source' of the 'effects' perceived, but also of identifying flawed characteristics germane to delusory mystical events.

The more 'obscure' a mode(s) and the 'darker' the 'content' of a mystical event, the less it is possible to discriminate between a genuine mystical experience and a delusory one. This twofold kind of gnoseological vagueness is especially inherent in somatic and emotional modes of mystical perception. Yet there is another mode of mystical perception akin to somatic mystical experience that is even more ambivalent and more likely to be mistaken for a delusory experience: the experience of 'mystical guidance', i.e., *the experience of being 'governed' and 'directed' by a Power situated beyond the sphere of the 'individual self'*. We shall begin with our critical assessment of the authenticity or delusory nature of mystical experience with the latter.

In the chapter above, we have already described all the major characteristics of the elusive mystical phenomenon of 'being governed' by a transpersonal Power which are relevant to a gnoseological assessment. We have emphasized that the awareness of 'being governed, directed, or acted upon' is a most sinister, opaque experience, which is ultimately inscrutable and unintelligible. Though it is true that the 'content' of a given instruction, i.e., of where the subject's will is 'directed', or to what ends his/her actions are 'governed' by the mysterious impulse encroaching upon the perceiver can be clearly identified, the underlying mental and somatic process escape any rational analysis: First, because the phenomenon occurs separated from a concrete composite mystical experience; the 'sense of being governed' by an intrusive Power surfaces in consciousness like a foreign, isolated object; second, because it is perceived like a drive, or even an 'obsessive drive', marked by the persevering sense of being 'driven' or 'compelled'. These features have (as noted above) an uncanny closeness to neurotic or pathological instances of compulsive disorders. Although we have stipulated two criteria by which mystical varieties of 'being governed' can be distinguished from non-mystical kinds – i.e., the criterion stipulating that a genuine phenomenon must be harmoniously integrated into the entire whole of a mystical event, and the criterion stating that a genuine instance of mystical 'direction' must have some positive impact on the perceiver's orientation in life, or positive after-effects on his/her future existence – these criteria provide clues but no evidence of the authenticity of the event. Nor can these provisos mitigate the mysterious, unintelligible nature of the experience of 'being mystically directed'. *Genuine mystical experiences of 'being governed and directed' and delusory experiences of the phenomenon are so empirically and phenomenologically akin that attempts at establishing substantial differences in their essence are non-conclusive and thus have no epistemological value.*

Because of the inherent opacity of the experience of 'being governed and directed by some mystical Power', it is assigned by us to the lowest rank in the gnoseological scale of mystical experiences. Above it in the gnoseological hierarchy, *the phenomenon of 'being affected by mystical feelings and the sense of being touched'* is placed. This is likewise an opaque and ambivalent experience in which the only item that is felt to be certain is *that* something has undoubtedly 'arrived' in consciousness. Yet it is still a rather vague experience, like 'groping in darkness', in which the perceiver becomes dimly aware of an impact affecting his/her emotional state and/or somatic condition. The perception of the 'object' 'arriving' is still hovering in the twilight zone between appearance and reality, and when the 'object' has 'arrived' in the vista of 'inner sight', the perceiver is still unable to discern what it is.

THESIS 79: *The delusory experience of 'being touched and/or affected emotionally' is rooted in misconceiving the apparent presence of a mystical object for its real Presence; in other words, it is first, the mistaking of something unreal for something real, and second, the mistaking of a real non-mystical object for the real 'mystical Object'.* As stated earlier, the domain of emotional and somatic awareness provides the undifferentiated sustaining ground for all differentiated modes of cognitive mystical perception. This is an important ontic fact, which however does not reveal anything about its gnoseological status. The fact that it is an undifferentiated variety of mystical perception rather suggests that it is to be assigned a low rank on the gnoseological scale. This means that in the realm of somatic and emotional modes of mystical perception it is impossible to distinguish conclusively genuine from delusory experiences. The four criteria of authenticity proposed can only be applied if some differentiated varieties of mystical experience have emerged from, or become affiliate with, the undifferentiated, amorphous ground of mystical perception.

The third tier in our gnoseological hierarchy is jointly occupied by the phenomenon of 'mystical intuition' [i.e., mystically infused insights] and the phenomenon of 'mystical auditions'. I will first consider the phenomenon of 'mystical intuitions', because 'auditory mystical experiences' are to a large extent based on, or concomitant with, 'mystical intuitions'. Whereas the sense of 'being directed' mystically, and the awareness of instilled 'mystical feelings' and 'somatic effects' are diffuse and sinister modes of mystical perception, the act of perceiving 'mystical intuitions' occurs in a state with an exceptionally high degree of clarity. But it is not only the act and process of perceiving that are marked by extraordinary lucidity; it is also the content conveyed in an intuition. Thus, the subject matter is clearly recognized, clearly structured, logically coherent and can be communicated in terms of an assessment or value judgement. These empirical conditions, and above all the supreme clarity of the state of consciousness during the event, are a certain safeguard against delusion. The fact that in this hyper-lucid mental condition there is no room for delusion has prompted many mystics to assign to 'mystically infused intuitions' the highest rank on the gnoseological scale. The mystics considered 'mystical intuitions' as an integral part of visionary mystical experience, and thus they classified 'intuitions' erroneously as a mode of mystical experience in which, allegedly, something of the true essence of the 'mystical Object' can be directly perceived. However, our enquiry has established that 'mystical intuitions' do not qualify as instances of 'experience': *Though the phenomenon of 'mystical insight' involves a cognitive process, this process of acquiring knowledge is not rooted in an experience*, evidence of which is that the 'mystical Object' is not present in the event of a 'mystical insight'; hence nothing of the 'mystical Object' can be revealed in it. In a 'mystical insight' some knowledge about the essence of an object is instantly instilled, or else of the perceiver's relationship to an object; but there is no need for the given 'object' to be perceived as present. A 'mystical insight' thus is not a mode of mystical experience. Therefore 'mystical insights' cannot be part of a delusory mystical experience, either. The question as to whether it is possible to err in interpreting a 'mystical insight', however, is something entirely different from the question as to whether it can potentially be the subject of a delusory experience.

Having ruled out the possibility of a 'mystical insight' to spring from a delusory experience, we must now examine if any of the two possibilities for error might occur in it. The 'cognitive content' transmitted at an instant in an 'insight' is surely not conveyed by way of an epiphanic vision of a 'self-expressive image or appearance'. This can be ruled out, as it would depend on a 'visionary experience'; in other words, a 'mystical insight' does not involve an experiential cognitive relation, hence there is no 'object' present that could be cognitively grasped. For this reason, neither a delusion nor an erroneous interpretation can occur in the context of an 'intuitive insight'. *This means that the only error that may occur in the event of a 'mystical insight' is the false conviction that the 'content' bestowed is mystical in origin. This means that the possibility to err can only occur in misconceiving 'mystical effects'.* Only if the knowledge conveyed by a putative act of 'mystical insight' is cognitively perceived as having been 'infused' or 'instilled' from outside the individual consciousness, the question may arise if the 'insight' has been 'infused' mystically or been imparted by some non-mystical cause.

The phenomenon of 'insight' is closely related to the phenomenon of 'mystical effects'. Both a 'mystical insight' and a 'non-mystical insight' have in common the distinctive awareness that the 'insight' has been 'instilled' or 'given', which is, phenomenologically, strikingly similar to the perception of a 'mystical impact'. The prevailing structural features of such an event are the following: It occurs in a hyper-lucid state of consciousness; some 'insight' 'arrives' unexpectedly and suddenly in consciousness; and the realness of the occurrence is grasped with an infallible sense of certainty. Taken together, all of these distinctive features may have prompted mystics to designate a moment of 'mystical insight' as a gratuitous act of 'illumination'. The distinct awareness of the 'givenness' of a 'mystical insight' has been valued by [theistic] mystics as a rare gift, or token of grace. When the 'mystical insight' is perceived, a recipient's role is entirely passive, which enhances the sense of its 'givenness'. If an 'insight' is, moreover, conveyed in an act of 'intuition' in the 'quiet state of alertness', the perception is additionally linked with the clear awareness of it 'arriving', or of 'having arrived'. In this case, the notion of the 'givenness' is intensified even more and endorses the conviction that the 'insight' has been 'effected' by a Power beyond the individual self. This shows that 'mystical insights' and 'mystical effects' are closely intertwined. This phenomenological affinity is, however, also a potential cause for error, because a given 'intuitive insight' may falsely be attributed to a mystical cause.

We know that mystical events are commonly [i.e., in theistic mystical traditions] supposed to have been 'infused', 'effected', or 'instilled', and this postulation has often resulted in the false notion that any 'effect' or 'impact' perceived is mystical in origin. However, as we have shown above, contrary to this erroneous claim, the mere perception of 'infused effects' does not provide any clue about the provenance of these 'effects'. *Therefore, we may stipulate: It is impossible to infer from the mere perception of the 'arrival' of an 'insight' that it has been 'infused' or 'effected' by the 'mystical It'*. If we wish to verify whether an 'insight' is mystical or non-mystical in origin, four additional criteria will have to be applied.

Such verification cannot be established merely by examining the 'content' of an 'insight'. The pivotal characteristics of any 'insight' are not only that they are truthful 'intuitions' 'arriving' fortuitously, perceived with highest clarity, and that they are recognized with a deep sense of certainty, but also that the quality of their message has supreme value. However, these characteristics alone do not suffice as criteria for deciding whether an 'insight' is the result of a genuine mystical impact. The criteria for assessing the 'form' of an act of 'illumination' must also be applied to the assessment of its 'content'. This means that it does not matter if the 'content' flashing up in the event of an 'insight' is some intelligence about the essence of the 'mystical Object' or not: even the 'content' of this kind does not allow us to conclude that the 'insight' conveyed is genuinely mystical in origin. There would be no such discipline as theology if it were impossible to comprehend intellectually the essential attributes of God and God's relationship to man without resorting to the realm of mysticism, i.e., without depending on the experience of God's Presence and the perception of his impact on this world. I think this fundamental critical judgement is significant. After all, a considerable part of so-called 'intellectual visions' [*visiones intellectuales*] consists of 'illuminations' of this kind. From our psychological and gnoseological perspective, 'intellectual visions', viz., 'intuitive mystical insights', do not qualify as varieties of mystical experience (for reasons explained above), but can, *in most cases*, not be traced to a mystical impact. This restrictive assessment, however, does not say anything about the truthfulness of an 'insight', because the knowledge conveyed in each case can be perfectly true and correct, even if the 'insight' has neither been experienced in a concrete flash of 'intuition', nor been mystically 'infused'.

The remaining three criteria for establishing that an 'insight' is mystical in origin can be presented jointly. An 'illumination' can be a single phenomenon within a composite experience of mystical effects; it can, second, be accompanied by the perception of the 'mystical Presence', and, third, a 'mystical insight' can simultaneously be an integral part of a mystical experience composed of diverse mystical effects, such as the sudden change of the emotional state of mind and/or the somatic condition. In the first instance, the 'insight' can be identified as genuinely mystical, because its mystical quality is given secondarily, as the 'insight' is embedded in a more complex mystical event. In the second instance, the 'insight' is perceived as 'arriving' from outside the realm of the individual consciousness from an unfathomable domain of a Presence enfolding the perceiver. In the third instance, it is the exceptional quality of being overwhelmed by an unknown sense of bliss and the awareness of inner purity that are affiliated with the event of 'mystical insight' – and the rare emotional and somatic responses aroused by the event cannot be explained and understood in any other way than as having been mystically 'infused'.

It must be admitted that the three latter criteria cannot be claimed to be absolute, reliable criteria of authenticity; however, they are sustained by phenomena so striking and significant that the perception of an 'intuitive insight' cannot reasonably be dismissed *a priori* from the domain of mysticism, and thus altogether be reduced to a non-mystical phenomenon. The problem of how we can reliably discern whether an 'insight' is mystical or non-mystical in origin thus admits ultimately only one alternative: either propounding the thesis that the phenomenon of 'mystically instilled effects' is altogether mere delusion, in which case the entire range of alleged 'effects' – not only 'infused insights', but also somatic and emotional effects, locutions and other auditory experiences, as well as mystical visions – must be classified as delusory experiences. Or, if '*mystical* effects' are acknowledged as potentially genuine mystical phenomena, one will have to concede the *possibility* that amongst 'insights' encountered in empirical reality, there are such as are imparted in a mystical event. It goes without saying that in the tradition of 'a-personal mysticism' [i.e., notably monistic mystical traditions], the notion of 'mystical effects' and thus the phenomenon of 'illumination', viz., 'mystically infused insight', are likely to be dismissed as pseudo-mystical phenomena. Hence, in 'a-personal mysticism', the perception of an 'insight' is excluded from the domain of mysticism. This negative stance on 'insights' by a-personal mysticism, however, implies that all the other phenomena claimed to originate from 'mystical effects' [i.e., auditions/locutions, visions and changes in somatic and emotional states] must be eliminated from the realm of mystical experience; as a consequence, a-personal mysticism will have to account for all these empirical occurrences in non-mystical terms. But the demand to provide an intelligible explanation for 'locutions' and other 'auditory experiences', as well as for 'mystical visions' and 'mystical effects', seems impossible, unless the empirical ground of all mystical experience is eliminated altogether, and these phenomena reduced entirely to natural causes within the 'experiencing subject'. By adopting such a reductionist approach, however, the fact that 'insights' are encountered in empirical reality cannot be explained. The occurrence of an 'insight' will prevail and remain unaffected if its alleged mystical origin is refuted. The fact that a 'mystical insight' is a perennial phenomenon that cannot be traced to the subjective sphere of the self but is 'given from outside' the individual consciousness, cannot be denied. The question about the potential [transpersonal] source of an 'infused insight', however, has been answered differently. Instead of tracing the 'mystical insight' or 'illumination' to the impact of the 'mystical It', it is considered [outside theistic mysticism] as knowledge deriving from the sphere of the objective Spirit and coming fortuitously to the perceiver. These unique attributes of the phenomenon of 'insight' can be epitomized in the following theses:

THESIS 80: *The 'content' of an 'insight', i.e., the knowledge instilled incidentally in an 'insight', continues to exist independently and is unaffected by the sphere of delusion potentially inherent in an act of cognitive mystical perception.* This means that what is cognitively grasped by an 'illumination' or 'insight' can be logically flawed and the knowledge attained may even be untrue. Insofar, a 'mystical insight' is subjected to the same processes of critical examination that apply equally to non-mystical acts of thinking. Any genuine 'intuitive insight' will inevitably be confirmed subsequently by acts of discursive thinking.

THESIS 81: *Owing to the fact that an 'intuitive insight' is not based on an act of cognitive experience, the possibility of a delusory perception is ruled out.*

THESIS 82: *Erring in the context of a 'mystical insight' is merely based on the mistaken conviction about its mystical origin; an 'insight' may be attributed to a mystical or to a non-mystical cause, and therefore result in a flawed attribution.*

THESIS 83: *The possibility for error in a 'mystical insight' is equal to the possibility for error in the domain of 'mystical effects'.*

As I begin this section, which deals with the issue of erring in the context of mystical experience, I dare to propose the following claim as valid: *The more explicit the person-like characteristics in a singular phenomenon within the area of mystical effects, the more it is exposed to potential delusion.*

In the phenomenological area of an 'insight', the person-like quality hinges alone on the perception of 'mystical effects', but this applies only potentially, not inevitably. What is recognized in a given 'insight' is acknowledged as objective truth; therefore, there is no need to decide whether it has come from an a-personal or a personal source. In the event of a *'mystically* infused insight', there must also, by definition, be a relation to the 'mystical It' which has bestowed the 'insight'. Yet this fact notwithstanding, there remains the *possibility* that the 'insight' has not been imparted by a mystical Persona but derives merely from a-personal determination.

'Locutions' consist of phenomenological elements which are akin to 'mystical insights'. There is, however, a significant difference between the two phenomena: *It is much more difficult to remove the person-like qualities from a 'locution' than from an 'insight'.* In a 'locution', the person-like quality is attached to all phenomenological components: The act of being spoken to, the awareness of its 'givenness', i.e., the perception of words 'arriving' from beyond the individual consciousness – all these features are related to a person-like entity; moreover, the message conveyed cannot be detached from a person-like speaker. It is true that there is a zone of transition between 'locutions' and 'insights', in which the 'content' of the words perceived consists of objective truths, which are heard inwardly. The pivotal issue of the phenomenon of 'locutions', however, is that the given message is either an express 'summons' directed individually to the perceiver, or even an intimate personal address intended, for instance, to offer some consolation, comfort, reassurance or protection, or it may consist of an offer of future guidance in life. The option of succumbing to an error in listening to a 'locution' differs significantly from the possibility of erring in 'intuitive insights'. 'Locutions'– unlike 'intuitive insights' and 'pictorial visions' beheld in 'inner sight' – are not based on experiential 'mystical effects'. In 'locutions', the 'awareness of being acted upon' subsides and is suspended in favour of the clear awareness of 'being spoken to', i.e., the infallible sense of a verbal message 'arriving' inwardly, which is in essence a mode of self-expression by the 'mystical It'. Thus, error may occur on the level of 'locutions' by misconceiving items of its 'content'. Erring in this context thus results from the flawed interpretation of the mystical origin of the 'acoustic' mode of self-expression. A summons or a consoling verbal utterance can, for example, be a token of sympathy, love, goodness, sovereignty, power, or beauty. However, not only the understanding of the message of a 'locution' but also the 'sound of voice' may be a cause for error about the mystical origin of the auditory experience.

The ways of erring described so far are, of course, not exhaustive; there are other kinds of errors which may occur in the twilight zone between mystical and non-mystical 'locutions'. It seems to me that we have so far surveyed only a peripheral area of errors, whereas the main cause of succumbing to error is really rooted in delusive mystical experiences. The terms 'delusive auditory experience' and 'error about the mystical origin of an act of self-expression' refer to different aspects of one singular and indivisible occurrence. It is therefore justifiable to apply the term 'delusion' to both kinds of flawed perception.

Wherever the phenomenon of 'locutions' is encountered, the possibility of delusion is inevitably given. In fact, the delusions are an essential element of the phenomenon of 'locutions', as anything that is spoken to a perceiver and listened to inwardly occurs in the twilight zone between delusion and reality. Throughout the history of mysticism, mystics have been upset when they are haunted by the sound of an inner 'voice', or 'visited' by a wordless summons or sinister intuition. For it is very difficult for the mystic to discern if the 'inner voice', or wordless command, is a genuine gift of God, or if these phenomena have been generated by the deep recesses of the mind, or his/her own subjective sphere. These phenomena might, for instance, be explained in terms of acoustic representations of a personal wish, or a verbalized intimation foreboding a future event, or a voice surfacing from a 'split-off' item of the subject's unconscious, or an instance of a split personality addressing his/her double. Moreover, how should it be possible to distinguish the 'inner voice' of a 'locution' from an eidetic phenomenon, or from the hallucination of a morbid mind? Considering the enormous potential for delusion in the domain of 'inner hearing', it is not possible to examine individual cases critically here. For the purposes of our study it is enough to have established that the realm of 'locutions' is particularly predisposed to succumbing to delusory phenomena.

THESIS 84: *The perception of 'locutions', or the inner hearing of sounds and 'voices', is to a high degree prone to delusion.*

When perceiving a 'locution', there are different modes by which delusory phenomena may interfere, depending on whether it is a 'voice' or a voiceless intimation 'arrives', in which some 'intellectual content' or 'message' is conveyed. This means that it depends on whether the 'locution' is predominantly perceived in an auditory manner or in a voiceless mode, consisting of thoughts instilled into the recipient's mind.

The perception of an apparent 'inner voice' is a hallucination. This occurs when eidetic and/or acoustic phenomena of pathological origin are mistaken for mystical voices. In the case of an 'intellectual locution', a delusion occurs when a string of thoughts emerging from the 'sphere of the self' is mistaken for a genuine mystical 'locution'. In this instance, both delusory and non-delusive phenomena may be involved.

The peculiar position of the concept of 'locutions', on the one hand, and its proximity to delusion, on the other, as well as its potentially high cognitive value, results from the fact that it is particularly difficult with 'locutions' to be purged entirely from delusory phenomena, not least because of the high gnoseological significance of their semantic meaning. Mystics have therefore studiously tried to find criteria for discerning genuine mystical 'locutions' from delusory ones. By analogy, with the criteria established for assessing the genuine nature of 'mystically infused insights', the criteria stipulated include the demand that a 'mystical locution' must be free from inner contradiction and that the 'content' must have exceptional [moral, spiritual, cognitive] value as well as supreme clarity and sobriety. When a 'locution' has the character of an explicit 'summons', it carries close affinity to the phenomenon of 'mystical guidance and direction', and requires additional criteria of authenticity: a 'summons' or express command is considered genuine if the recipient is incapable of resisting or acting against it when it is later proved to be true and meaningful. Moreover, the *special mode* in which a 'locution' 'arrives' in the perceiver's mind is another hint at its genuine nature. A prophetic 'locution' is considered genuine when the prophecy turns out to be true. These criteria are, admittedly, not always unfailing nor are they exhaustive. But there are supplementary criteria, such as the sense of the 'givenness' and the rootedness of a 'locution' in adjoining 'mystical effects'. The supplementary criteria thus include the meaningful integration of a 'locution' into the entire whole of a mystical occurrence: the linking of a 'locution' with the concurrent awareness of the 'mystical Presence' and the concomitant occurrence of other 'mystical effects'. All these features indicate the experiential quality of the impact of a mystical encounter. These characteristics, in other words, reveal (in my opinion) very clearly that the 'experiencing self' is indeed exposed to 'mystical effects' in a composite mystical event sustained by the 'triad' of sense of the 'mystical Presence', 'pictorial vision' and 'locution'.

It should be possible (I think) to separate the genuine core of a 'mystical locution' from its potential intertwining with delusory phenomena. The effort seems to be especially justified and pertinent, because success or failure in achieving this aim is vital for the critical assessment of the 'locutions' whether the 'locutions' recorded in the history of humanity and which had a great impact on history and the individual life of a mystic, are genuine, or if they must be discarded as bogus. For instance, the auditory experience of Moses standing in front of the burning bush, recorded in *Exodus* (3.1–14) may be called to mind:

> 6. Moreover, he said, I am the God of thy father, the God of Abraham, the God of Isaac and the God of Jacob. And Moses hid his face: for he was afraid to look upon God …

14. And God said unto Moses. I AM THAT I AM: and he said, Thus shalt thou say unto the children of Israel, I AM hath sent me unto you. (*Exodus* 3.6; 3.13–14)[1]

There are numerous representative examples of 'locutions' in the history of Christianity. I would like to refer to the famous 'locution' recorded by Francis of Assisi, who heard the voice of the Lord commanding him: "Francis, go and repair my house, for as you see, it is falling into ruin."[2] Another famous example [albeit of an external 'locution'] is the 'summons' of Saul by Jesus on the road to Damascus: Saul was struck by the impact of the authoritative voice of Jesus addressing him, which caused his instant conversion:

3. And as he [Saul] journeyed, he came near Damascus: and suddenly there shined round about him a light from heaven. 4. And he fell to the earth, and heard a voice saying unto him, Saul, Saul, why persecutest thou me? 5. And he said, Who art thou, Lord? And the Lord said, I am Jesus whom thou persecutest: it is hard for thee to kick against the pricks. 6. And he trembling and astonished said, Lord what wilt thou have me to do? And the Lord said unto him, Arise, and go into the city, and it shall be told thee what thou must do. (*Acts* 9.3–6)[3]

Another example of a 'locution' that changed the course of history has been handed down from Jeanne d'Arc, in which she is commanded to save France by engaging in military action.

The endeavour to establish the genuine core of 'mystical locutions' has pivotal significance, not least because, if this effort failed, one of the pivotal empirical foundations of personal mysticism would be phenomenologically shattered.

---

1 [Note: Albrecht quotes only the crucial sentence "Ich werde sein, der ich sein werde" from the lengthy dialogue between God and Moses reported in *Exodus* 3.1–14, but he does not give any reference to the German Bible used. The English citation is from *The Authorized King James Version* [1611]. Oxford: OUP, 1976. – FKW.]

2 [Note: The passage quoted by Albrecht is from the German translation of the *Vita* of St. Francis by Thomas de Celano (no page references given): CELANO, Thomas de. *Das Leben des Heiligen Franz von Assisi*. Trans. Ph. Schmidt. Basle: Reinhardt, 1921. English translation provided. – FKW.]

3 [Note: From *The Authorized King James Version* [1611]. Oxford: OUP, 1976. – FKW.]

In the context of a 'mystical intuition', an error results from the false conviction about where an 'illumination' has come from. In the context of the inner hearing of 'locutions', errors may stem from the flawed perception of the verbal message in terms of a revelatory mode of 'self-expression' [of the Divine]. This kind of error thus results from a misunderstanding about the 'source' of the 'infused message'. The second major cause for error in the context of 'inner hearing', though connected with the causes referred to above, is a delusory experience in the full sense of the word. Whereas in a 'mystical intuition' the possibility of a delusory perception is ruled out (as outlined above), a flawed perception of a 'mystical locution' is, phenomenologically speaking, a delusory auditory perception.

In the context of a 'pictorial vision' there are several potential causes for error and delusion. Compared to 'locutions', however, there are (as explained above) some significant differences. Since the essential aspects relating to the potential causes for error and delusion in 'pictorial visions' have been addressed in the chapter on 'Pictorial Visions', only a few supplementary considerations are necessary at this point.

'Pictorial visions' can be divided into two phenomenologically distinct categories: the category in which the 'picture' featuring in a vision has 'allegorical' or 'symbolic' import; and the category in which the 'picture' appearing in a vision is an [epiphanic] 'pictorial self-revelation' [of the 'mystical Presence']. When an error occurs in perceiving an allegorical or symbolic vision, this has less bearing on the overall assessment of the validity of a mystical event than is the case with a 'self-revelatory pictorial vision'. We shall begin our critical examination with the former category, because the phenomenological structure of a 'symbolic image' is relatively plain and straightforward, and thus is more easily accessible to rational analysis.

A 'symbolic' or 'allegorical vision' inevitably calls for an interpretation; otherwise its meaning would remain obscure or undisclosed. However, any hermeneutic process is open to error and misunderstanding. But semiotic misunderstanding is something different from the phenomenological misreading of mystical phenomena. A plain symbolic image has no self-expressive or revelatory import, like an 'infused word' or a 'locution'. In a 'locution', it is not only the meaning of the words, but also the way in which it is uttered, as well as the sound of the 'voice', that tend to reveal something 'physiognomically' of the 'speaker' and/ or originator of the 'locution'. A 'symbolic picture' perceived as having been 'infused' in a mystical event is phenomenologically much closer to an 'intuitive insight' than to a 'locution'. The meaning conveyed by the symbolic image is not as fully autonomous from the phenomenon of 'mystical effects', which is the case with the sense of truth elicited in an 'infused insight'; symbolic images are to a certain degree autonomous and have only a rather vague 'physiognomic' relation to the originator of the 'vision'. This means that it is impossible to infer from an infused 'symbolic picture' where it has come from. *An error in perceiving a 'vision of a symbolic image' may result from the false conviction about the provenance of the 'infused image'*. The error, in other words, is rooted in the domain of 'mystical effects'. The fact that 'mystical effects' are the empirical ground in which all other mystical phenomena are rooted –most notably the 'mystical insight', 'mystical visions', and (in a modified manner) 'mystical locutions', all of which are effected by and related to the 'mystical It' – the same errors may occur in the context of 'pictorial visions' as may occur in perceiving 'mystical effects'.

In perceiving a 'revelatory self-expressive image', the chance of error and delusion occurring is considerably greater than when perceiving a vision of a symbolic or allegorical picture. In the vision of a 'self-expressive image', the appearance of a gesture or countenance of a figure from the 'other world' is embedded. It is a pictorial vision imbued with epiphanic import, since the 'effective cause' reveals itself more or less openly to the perceiver. *This means that an erroneous perception of a 'self-expressive visionary appearance' does not only arise from misconceiving the 'meaning' of what is displayed in the vision, but also (and even more importantly) from a flawed 'mystical interpretation of a self-expressive gesture or countenance'; it results, in other words, from a misconception of the ultimate source of the self-expressive visionary appearance*. This kind of error is transformed by and mingled with the false conviction about the provenance of the 'effects' imparted.

When considering the phenomenon of the 'self-revealing visionary appearance', a vital question is prompted, one which calls for an answer: Should we not concede that it is possible in a 'pictorial vision' to conflate a plain pictorial image with the real 'object' of mystical experience? Does not the sense of Presence that is inevitably inherent in an epiphanic visionary appearance entice the 'experiencing I' to assume erroneously that the 'visionary appearance' is the direct perception of the 'suchness' of what is cognitively grasped 'as present' in the concomitant awareness of Presence? Though it is true that it is theoretically possible to conflate the image or appearance of a 'pictorial vision' with the 'mystical Object', in a genuine mystical event such an error hardly ever occurs: every mystic knows, after all, that the image beheld in a visionary experience is just an image. The mystic knows, moreover, that a 'pictorial vision' is in part composed of elements surfacing from his/her own 'sphere of the self', that is, that the colours, garments, contours, and in fact any other visual elements featuring in the vision beheld inwardly are generated by images, ideas, memories and beliefs stored in the perceiver's mind.

In the special type of 'pictorial vision' termed 'self-revealing [epiphanic] appearance', the 'mystical vision' is so closely intertwined with the 'cognitive awareness of Presence' that the Numen becomes transparent in the appearance 'seen' in the vision. These two components of the visionary experience, however, are recognized as distinct and separate phenomena during the mystical event. The pictorial components of the vision are part of the subjective sphere [perceiver], whereas the 'sense of Presence' is part of the objective sphere [the 'mystical Object']. For this reason, it may happen only in exceptional circumstances that 'visual image' and 'non-visual mystical Presence' are conflated or identified in a visionary experience of a 'self-revealing appearance'.

THESIS 85: *Errors occurring in the context of a 'pictorial vision' are best understood (in analogy to errors encountered in mystical 'locutions') in terms of a delusory 'inner vision'.* In a 'delusory vision', the sensory perception of 'seeing' is conflated with the mode of 'beholding' by 'inner sight', that is, the mistaking of real space for imaginary space, or the mistaking of eidetic images for genuine images appearing in a 'vision'. We are certainly aware that a considerable number of alleged 'epiphanic mystical visions' are in fact merely perceptions of eidetic images. This kind of delusory misconception is analogous to the mistaking of a sense perception for the perception of images appearing in 'inner sight'. This means that there is an analogy between delusory visionary experience and delusive sense perception.

In empirical reality the phenomenon of delusory 'inner vision' is, however, more complex than has been epitomized in the theses above. For the purposes of our present concern, however, it is enough to repeat statements made in the chapter on the 'pictorial vision': 'A vision of Christ can be a hallucination, for instance, an eidetic image seen with physical eyes; or it can be a delusory sense perception of pathological origin; it can, moreover, be an image evoked by the perceiver's fantasy, and it can be elicited by the ardent practice of 'affective devotion'[4] centred on the Redeemer; it can furthermore be an archetype as conceived by C. G. Jung, and it can be an envisaged scene evoked by retrospective clairvoyance. Finally, a 'vision of Christ' can be a mystically 'infused' picture and, last but not least, a genuine instance of an epiphanic 'mystical vision'.'

The domain of 'mystical effects' perceived in terms of some impact 'arriving' or 'intruding' from beyond the individual self includes (apart from 'locutions', 'pictorial visions' and 'self-expressive appearances') another distinct, albeit opaque, phenomenon that must be subjected to careful critical scrutiny in view of its potentially delusive nature: the perception of 'mystically generated effects'

---

4 [Note: The practice of 'affective devotion' focussing on the Passion or on other stages in the life of Christ was especially popular from the High Middle Ages to the 17th century. 'Affective devotion' is linked to the tradition of 'bridal mysticism', initiated by Bernard of Clairvaux, and was an integral part of the tradition of 'mysticism of the Passion of Christ'. By the practice of 'affective devotion', "... feelings are not subdued, but love is directed towards God, who inspires it by his own tenderness and regard for us in the humanity and passion of Jesus. It is the prayer taught by Bernard of Clairvaux and evidenced in the Franciscans and the English mystics ... and is especially evident in the 17th century." (*Dictionary of Christian Spirituality*. Ed. Gordon WAKEFIELD, London: SCM, 1983, s.v. 'affective spirituality'). The practitioner of 'affective devotion' aspires through empathy to 'imitate' and re-live the passion of the Redeemer (*imitatio Christi*), hoping to be gratified in turn with the gift of true 'com-passion', by which the will of the devotee becomes perfectly harmonized with the will of God. Thus, the ultimate goal of a Christian's life – perfect conformity (*conformitas*) with Christ in will, thought and feeling – is achieved. – FKW.]

affecting the spheres of the body, volition and the emotions. This variety of 'mystical effects' differs significantly from the visual and auditory ones addressed above.

'Effects' [imparted mystically] that affect the perceiver's corporal, volitional and emotional spheres become apparent, for instance, in an abrupt change of the emotional condition, or in the surprising [not premeditated] reorientation of the perceiver's attitudes, dispositions and the direction of his/her will. This variety of 'mystical effects' causes an unexpected transformation of the perceiver's state of mind and/or orientation in life, and therefore differs strikingly, in phenomenologically speaking, from the 'mystical effects' by which 'locutions', 'pictorial visions' and 'self-expressive appearances' are triggered. In the latter the impact is cognitively grasped as 'arriving' from beyond or 'outside' the individual self and is thus perceived as an ingression from an 'objective sphere'. In the case of 'mystical effects' transforming the somatic, tactile, volitional and emotional condition, by contrast, the cognitive awareness that these changes are a response to impacts 'arriving' from beyond the perceiver's 'subjective sphere' is much less pronounced. When perceiving the latter type of 'mystical effects', subjective components tend to prevail over phenomena 'arriving' from the sphere of the 'mystical Object'.

This may explain why the mode in which non-visual and non-auditory 'mystical effects' are perceived as 'arriving' in consciousness are assigned a special place in the scale of mystically infused phenomena. As outlined above, 'mystical insights' 'arrive' in the consciousness in an instant, instilling knowledge or some 'illumination'. 'Locutions' are likewise perceived as 'arriving' and, moreover, elicit a clear sense of 'being individually spoken to'; 'pictorial visions' are perceived as having been 'infused', or 'given', and as coming from a foreign sphere beyond the individual self; hence there is a clear cognitive awareness that the 'inner voice' and the message heard do not originate from within the perceiver's 'sphere of the self'. If, however, 'mystical effects' are experienced by which the perceiver's emotions, volition and somatic state are significantly transformed, the distinctive mystical feature of 'arriving' is missing, since these alterations appear to originate from within the 'experiencing self'. For this reason, it is difficult to establish reliable criteria for distinguishing 'mystically instilled effects' from purely inner-psychic processes. As the distinct awareness of the 'arrival' of these effects from outside the perceiver is missing or hardly perceptible, the sense of the subjectivity of the ongoing alterations within the experiencing self persists even when the impact is instantaneous, awesome, and surprising, and even when these 'effects' have a unique quality, such as being unfamiliar, unintelligible or opposed to familiar patterns of previous experience.

In the event of a 'mystical locution', a 'pictorial vision' and a 'mystical insight', the sense of 'arriving' and thus the awareness that these phenomena have been 'mystically infused' is clear and pronounced, whereas there is no such certain knowledge when perceiving non-visual and non-auditory 'mystical effects'. This means that the 'mystical effects' of the latter variety are not immediately experienced but inferred after their occurrence from the unusual quality of the transformations caused in the perceiver.

THESIS 86: *An error in perceiving 'mystical effects' affecting the body, the emotions and the will, never results from a delusory perception.* The act of cognitive perception is as such invulnerable to delusion, because the instant awareness of the sudden change in one's emotional state and will is merely the immediate reflection of the current state of mind.

THESIS 87: *If an error in perceiving 'mystical effects' occurs, it always results from the flawed conviction about 'where' the impact has come from.* The error is thus, objectively seen, a false assumption about the ultimate source of these effects. This means that this kind of error can never be grounded in a delusory experience, because there is no immediate experience of the source of the changes elicited in the perceiver involved at all. *If an error occurs in the domain of 'mystical effects', it is triggered by the exceptional nature of the 'changes' experienced, which induce the perceiver to attribute them erroneously to a mystical source.* In the ambivalent twilight zone of explicable and inexplicable changes in feeling, will and somatic conditions, changes for which there is a rational explanation, are confused with changes that are altogether incomprehensible and which for this reason acquire the quality of having been 'infused' – hence they are claimed to be mystical in origin.

THESIS 88: *The perception of 'mystical effects' is a phenomenon that is highly predisposed to potential error, although the cognitive act of perception as such is exempt from delusion.* Here the error is first rooted in the uncertainties of self-assessment, and second in the vague phenomenological threshold between the subjective and objective phenomena involved in the changes effected in the perceiver. After all, who can state with absolute certainty, when he/she is overwhelmed suddenly by an unprecedented feeling of love, whether this emotion has been 'mystically instilled', or if it is the spontaneous response to the Numen perceived as present? Who could say for certain if the overwhelming feeling of love has been 'instilled' from 'outside', or if it is the manifestation of the perceiver's ardent desire, or an expression of loving gratitude, or a loving upsurge within a burgeoning state of bliss?

Considering the high potential for error and delusion, it is clear that 'mystical effects' of this kind cannot be assigned a high rank on the gnoseological scale. This means that the experience of somatic and emotional 'mystical effects', as well as those affecting the will, have individually no significant gnoseological value. Consequently, this phenomenon should be used sparingly as an additional criterion of critical mystical discernment. Despite these obvious limitations of the gnoseological value and the strictures on identifying these 'mystical effects' as authentic, it is all the more surprising that in mystical tradition the mystics have expressly used these 'mystical effects' as a pivotal criterion for assessing the authenticity of 'pictorial visions' and 'locutions'. As stipulated by the mystics, a visionary experience and a 'locution' can be claimed to be genuine if they arouse in the perceiver intense feelings of love and bliss, and/or if they trigger or advance a mystic's spiritual path and process of purification. But if a vision, locution or other encounter with an 'Otherness' elicits feelings of unrest, discord or even illicit sensual desires, all these responses are claimed to be unswerving evidence that the alleged mystical event is false.

By way of summary, we can state about our findings regarding our venture into the domain of 'mystical discernment': *The varieties of mystical experience and modes of cognitive mystical perception considered so far are all heavily burdened as regards their gnoseological rank.* The 'sense of being directed' or 'governed', as well as the awareness of a transforming 'impact' on the perceiver's emotional state, will and somatic condition, are all obscure modes of perception and therefore only marginally relevant for a critical assessment of the authenticity of a mystical encounter. Though the phenomenon of the 'mystical insight', and the 'inner hearing of voices and locutions', as well as the 'vision of mystically infused images' and the 'cognitive awareness of mystical effects' are all lucid modes of mystical perception, they are all rooted in the underlying phenomenon of 'mystical causation' [i.e., the awareness of some diffuse impact on the perceiver], and are all more prone to the possibility of error than any of the other varieties of mystical experience. This is the reason why their gnoseological rank is only slightly above that of the dim and obscure modes of mystical experience. Moreover, in two of these 'lucid' modes of mystical perception, i.e., 'mystical visions' and 'locutions', the potential for delusion is still inherent. We will only arrive at the genuine core of 'mystical recognition' if the modes of cognitive mystical perception analysed so far are assigned to the periphery in our gnoseological enterprise.

The cognitive perception of Presence[5] is the core phenomenon of mystical recognition. In this unique event the 'arrival' of the 'Object' of mystical recognition happens directly and not by way of an intermediate phenomenon. The fact that the 'Presence' is perceived immediately as 'arriving' from outside the sphere of the self, and the fact that there are no 'mystical effects' involved that might assume a mediating role, diminish considerably the possibility of error and delusion in experiencing the 'mystical Presence'. This means that in perceiving the 'mystical Presence', it is impossible to err about the source of its origin. It is possible, however, to misperceive the 'object' 'arriving'. The ability to decide about the origin of the 'mystical impact' depends on the recognition of the 'whatness' of the 'object' experienced as being 'present'. The opportunity for being mistaken in

---

5 [Note: When capitalized, the term 'Presence' refers to the awareness of the 'mystical Presence'. Albrecht distinguishes more specifically between mystical and non-mystical 'objects', either of which may evoke a 'sense of presence', viz., 'Presence'. Therefore, 'presence' spelt in lower case refers to a non-mystical experience and spelt in upper-case it refers to the 'mystical Presence'. When the reference is ambivalent, lower-case spelling is used. – FKW.]

this is, however, only present at the initial phase of a composite mystical event, in which 'mystical feelings' and other 'mystical effects' are involved. Yet the distinctive characteristic of the 'cognitive perception of Presence' is [paradoxically] precisely that the awareness of its 'whatness' is minimal. What is possible to discern cognitively of the 'suchness' is merely whether the 'object' perceived as 'present' is a mystical or a non-mystical object. This means that *the cognitive perception of Presence is exempt from delusion that might result from the misconception of its 'whatness'*. Since the 'cognitive perception of Presence' is a direct mode of mystical perception and, moreover, one that is exclusively centred on the 'Presence' as the only 'mystical Object', it is significantly more resistant to error and delusion than any of the indirect modes of mystical experience. The following survey of various levels of perceiving 'Presence' will, at the same time, enable us to assess the potential for error and delusion in each case:

1. *The 'sensory* [somatic, tactile] *awareness of Presence'* is in the same measure susceptible to error and delusion as the mystical experience of being somatically and/or emotionally affected by a Presence. Since this is a rather diffuse and obscure mode of mystical perception, the potential for delusion is considerable: It is possible to mistake the non-presence of the 'mystical Object' with its real Presence, that is to say, to confuse a real object with an unreal one; or to misconceive a non-mystical object with the 'mystical Object'. If the cognitive perception of Presence occurred exclusively on the empirical level of feelings and somatic modes of awareness, the potential for delusion would inevitably be profuse. But since the phenomenological core of the cognitive perception of Presence is sustained by the two lucid modes of mystical perception (i.e., non-pictorial vision and 'mystical insight'), the potential for delusion is reduced significantly.

2. *The* '[imageless] *vision of Presence*': This is a non-pictorial 'vision' of the 'spatial presence' of the 'mystical Object'. Psychologically, this type of 'vision' is, properly speaking, a 'mode of 'awareness' ["Bewußtheit"], i.e., the intuitive and instantly evident knowledge that 'something' is 'present' in a certain direction and

distance. This special mode of perceiving the 'mystical Presence' is potentially exposed to a special kind of delusion: There is a mode of sensing a presence that is pathological; patients suffering from mental illness tend to conflate a presence perceived by the physical senses with a delusory presence appearing in the mind. In a pathological experience of presence, the delusion is generated by transferring a natural sense perception into the realm of the imagination. Similarly, in the context of mystical experience, it is possible to transfer an imaginary awareness of presence into the realm of an alleged 'mystical vision of Presence'. But whereas in a pathological case the flawed sense perception can be verified empirically, this is not possible in the context of a non-pictorial 'vision of Presence'. The only criteria of authenticity that can be applied are those commonly used for distinguishing pathological from sane mental phenomena and, in addition, the criterion that a genuine 'mystical vision of Presence' must be coherent and can be meaningfully integrated into the totality of a given mystical experience.

3. The third mode of perceiving the 'mystical Presence' is termed the *'cognitive awareness of the Presence of the mystical It'* ["Bewußtheit von der Präsenz des mystischen Es"]. By this we understand a non-visual, hyper-lucid mode of recognizing the 'Presence', which is devoid of any spatial quality and sense of direction and phenomenologically extremely sparse, and yet unique; despite its phenomenological sparsity, it can clearly be distinguished from pathological varieties of 'sensing a corporal presence'. The cognitive 'awareness of the Presence of the mystical It' is a unique and independent mode of mystical perception that is entirely resistant to delusion or confusion with other modes of mystical experience. In it a gnoseological phenomenon becomes apparent. Though it is possible that the phenomenon can be refuted, ignored or not identified by a perceiver, as soon as it is consciously grasped and identified as a phenomenological fact, the experience cannot be dismissed as a delusion, but must rather be acknowledged as a phenomenon entirely impervious to error and delusion.

The structure of consciousness by which the 'awareness of the presence of the mystical It' is sustained is extremely sparse and as such a coherent, homogeneous phenomenological entity that cannot be dissected any further. This has inevitable consequences for the potential of delusion, which can be shown by juxtaposing this rigid singular perceptive structure to an instable, loosely structured one. In the realm of sensory perception, the act of visual perception is, in phenomenological terms, loosely structured; similarly, within the empirical domain of 'the quiet state of alertness', the act of 'inward beholding' [i.e., beholding with the 'inner eye'] has on the whole a slack structure. The formal structure that determines the essence of 'seeing' – respectively, the formal structure that determines the essence of 'inward beholding' – may merge with numerous interchangeable items. There are countless 'objects' that can be 'seen', and there is a wide variety of images that can be 'beheld inwardly' without the phenomenon of visual perception – respectively, the phenomenon of 'inward beholding' – to be wrecked.

On the other hand, a stable, unchanging structure of cognitive perception is given in the phenomenon termed 'cognitive awareness of the Presence of the mystical It'; thus, in this mode of inward perception no exchange of the items comprehended is possible. The spatial 'vision of presence', by contrast, and even more so the 'sensory awareness of a presence', have a loose, variable phenomenological structure. Consequently, in the latter two modes of perceiving a presence, it is possible that mystical and non-mystical phenomena are exchanged. Evidence of such an occurrence can be found in the records of Christine Lucie and Teresa of Avila quoted above [i.e., texts 50–53]. It is important to emphasize once more that in the third variety of perceiving a presence addressed here, the phenomenological structure is a stable coherent totality that cannot be dissected any further. Due to the fact that a delusion results from a flawed perception, a delusion cannot occur in the stable, coherent and unchanging structure by which the 'cognitive awareness of the presence of the mystical It' is sustained.

THESIS 89: *The perception of the 'mystical Presence' is, in its phenomenological core, exempt from delusion.* Only in the peripheral sphere of perceiving a presence may delusory phenomena surface. This applies especially to somatic and emotional modes of perceiving a presence, in which the 'object' perceived as present is falsely identified as the 'mystical Presence'. In the context of an imageless 'vision of the Presence', a delusion may occur if the visionary experience is elicited by a pathological condition and believed to be a genuine manifestation of the 'mystical Presence'.

At the end of this critical examination I would like to emphasize once more that *any scientific examination on the potentials for delusion in the domain of mystical experience inevitably demands to be based on a foregoing enquiry into the 'gnoseological relation'*. Such an enterprise depends on a penetrating phenomenological analysis. The question, however, as to whether the results of the phenomenological examination are valid, i.e., whether the gnoseological phenomenon identified can be claimed to be genuine, which applies if it cannot be traced to any antecedent or subservient phenomenon, is not an issue to be addressed in the context of this critical examination of delusory experiences, though it will briefly be referred to at the end of the current chapter. The validity of the findings and their gnoseological value of the claim that a mode of mystical perception is 'resistant to delusion' thus depends inexorably on the quality of the preceding phenomenological investigation.

The term 'impact of mystical effects' implies the awareness of the 'mystical Presence'. The impact of a mystical event and the after-effects of an encounter with the 'mystical Object' in the perceiver are phenomenologically closely affiliated with the cognitive awareness of Presence. However, the share of the 'awareness of Presence' and the share of the perception of 'mystical effects' in a given mystical event may differ; either the former or the latter may prevail, or both perceptions can be equally balanced. For instance, the vision of the 'mystical Light'[6] is clearly intertwined with the cognitive awareness of Presence. Moreover, it appears to me that the epiphanic 'vision of a self-expressive appearance' is intertwined with an almost pure 'vision of Presence', whereas the sensory perception of the *'fluidum'* and the *'aura'* is linked with, or even identical

---

6   To facilitate understanding, we will consider in this chapter the phenomenon of the 'mystical vision of Light' within the category of 'mystical effects'. In empirical reality, however, the mystical experience of 'Light' is a unique phenomenon. For further details see the chapters above on the phenomenon of 'Light' in mystical perception.

with, the 'tangible awareness of Presence'. Because the cognitive perception of Presence is inextricably embedded in the perception of 'mystical effects', the joint perception of 'mystical effects' and 'Presence' is in part a safeguard against delusion. Consequently, a delusion about *the real presence* of the 'effective cause' can only occur within the confines in which a delusion is possible in an isolated perception of 'Presence' at the periphery of the gnoseological spectrum. Delusion in the context of 'mystical effects' may thus occur only when it is rooted in a flawed perception of the 'suchness' of the 'mystical Object'. This means that every single 'mystical effect' is potentially exposed to a different cause of delusion.

I. In the chapter about the *'vision of the mystical Light'*, we have come across the mistaking of the non-mystical 'light', which is merely a luminous reflection of the hyper-lucid state of consciousness with a perception of the 'mystical Light'. The former is merely a visual corollary of the serene mental condition known as 'quiet state of alertness', which functions as the 'medium' of 'inner sight' in which – amongst other phenomena – the 'mystical Light' may become manifest. This kind of erroneous misconception, however, is, strictly speaking, no delusion, but only a flawed interpretation or a cognitive misconception, because it is not rooted in a flawed experience, but is truly an error of understanding, originating from the metaphysical assumptions the perceiver holds prior to the alleged mystical occurrence. Delusory experiences in the context of perceiving the 'mystical Light' are in fact rare in empirical reality. It is possible, though, that an occult metaphysical light may surface in the vista of 'inner sight', which is erroneously identified with the 'mystical Light'; in this case, the inner perception of an occult meta-physiological light is conflated with an alleged 'vision of the mystical Light'. Another potential cause of delusion is the false identification of an eidetic sensation of light with a genuine 'vision of the mystical Light'. A conflation of this kind is, however, merely a hypothetical option, since such instances have hardly ever been recorded in empirical reality. The 'mystical Light' encountered in a visionary experience has unique phenomenological characteristics, and experiencing it evokes a deep sense of authenticity and certainty, which is why it has been allocated a very high gnoseological rank in mystical traditions.

THESIS 90: *The vision of the 'mystical Light' is highly resistant to delusion.* In fact, it is more resilient to delusion than almost any other variety of mystical perception. *This finding has prompted the claim that* [the mystical] *Light is the most genuine form of manifestation of the 'All-encompassing'.*

II. As stated in thesis 59 above, *'a self-expressive appearance' is a three-dimensional pictorial vision in which the shape-like appearance and all its specific traits and movements are the physiognomic self-expression of a Presence that is experienced simultaneously.* In perceiving a 'self-expressive appearance' in a vision, a delusion may occur and is, as such, rooted in the awareness of spatiality adhering to this visionary experience. Because the perception of spatiality is phenomenologically akin to two pseudo-mystical (pathological) phenomena, it is vulnerable to delusion: these pathological phenomena are the imaginary inward awareness of 'corporeal presences', and hallucinations in which images of the imagination are projected into external space.

A vision of a three-dimensional 'self-expressive appearance' is sustained by an almost entirely untainted spatial vision of the 'Presence'. The potential for delusion inherent in this spatial vision is thus transferred to the vision of a 'self-expressive appearance'. This kind of delusion springs from mistaking the bogus awareness of a 'corporeal presence' for the real awareness of the 'mystical Presence'. A flawed vision of a 'self-expressive appearance' inevitably destroys its gnoseological value.

THESIS 91: *In a 'vision of a self-expressive appearance', delusion may first occur if the concurrent 'vision of Presence' is flawed.* This kind of delusion, however, is rare when a genuine experiential mystical relation is involved. But if a delusion of this kind does happen, it is pathological, generated by a morbid condition of the psyche. A pathological perception of the mystical relation, however, does not affect a genuine vision of a 'self-expressive appearance'.

Another, even more important kind of delusion may be generated by the perception of spatiality inherent in the 'vision of a self-expressive appearance': As all spatial visions are composed of subjective and objective elements, the possibility of conflating the two spheres is given. The 'mystical vision of a self-expressive figure' is a faded residue of a 'pictorial vision' in which vestiges of the pictorial quality appear. This opens up the potential for delusion, since a pictorial image may be 'mystically instilled', but it may likewise surface from the imagination or be caused by a hallucination. The ambivalent status of pictorial visions is a worrisome issue in many records of visionaries and mystics; they have propounded meticulous criteria for distinguishing genuine epiphanies from bogus 'pictorial visions' and, especially, of visions featuring a dynamic 'self-expressive appearance'. The question as to whether the *movements* shown in a 'vision of a self-expressive figure' can be acknowledged as genuine, mystically 'infused' phenomena (e.g., a sacred figure moving away, or coming closer to the perceiver, or shaking his/her head, or nodding at the perceiver as a sign of assent, or stretching out protecting arms) has occupied mystics and mystagogues throughout history. The same applies also to changes in the *facial expression* of the figure featuring in a 'self-expressive appearance' (e.g., a stern countenance suggesting authority, or sovereignty, or facial expressions signifying benevolence, compassion, or love). All these dynamic pictorial visions can be genuine instances of mystical experience, as tokens of affection and loving care of the Numen, elicited by the real perception of the 'mystical Presence', but these gestures and dynamic phenomena might just as well be generated by the perceiver's desire and loving devotion, or they can be self-induced phenomena projected onto the dim awareness of the unfathomable darkness of the Presence.

THESIS 92: *Second, in a 'vision of a self-expressive figural appearance' delusion may occur if items arising from the subjective sphere and items deriving from the objective sphere are conflated. A case of complete delusion is a hallucination passed off for a real mystical vision; a partial delusory experience occurs when features emerging from the subjective sphere are projected onto a genuine mystical vision of a personage or a countenance. In other words, in the latter event the 'suchness' of the 'mystical Object' is adulterated by* subjective items imposed on the visionary experience, but the cognitive awareness of the 'mystical Presence' remains unaffected; the 'awareness of Presence' continues to be genuine and untainted.

III. The third category of 'mystical effects' includes sensory 'emanations' of the 'mystical Presence' termed *the 'aura' and the 'fluidum' of the mystical Presence*. 'Aura' and *'fluidum'* are sensory phenomena perceived visually and somatically by the sense of touch, emotionally and (less frequently) by the senses of smell and taste. These are rather diffuse modes of perception and are therefore highly susceptible to delusion. Though the possibilities for succumbing to delusion in the domain of 'mystical effects' involving the sense of touch have been addressed above, the tactile olfactory and somatic perceptions of the *'aura'* and the *'fluidum'* are rather intricate and need to be further elaborated. In particular, we shall consider four specific aspects:

1. The sense of being 'touched' is inevitably intertwined with the perception of both the *'fluidum'* and the *'aura'* of the present Numen: without the cognitive awareness of 'being touched' there would be no knowledge about this special variety of mystical impact, and vice versa; in other words, 'aura' and *'fluidum'* are phenomena that are perfectly consonant with, and often an integral part of, the mystical sense of touch.

2. The awareness of 'being touched' mystically is inherently linked to the intuition to originate from a primordial act of recognition. The perception of the *'aura'* and the *'fluidum'* are the harbingers of an impending mystical occurrence, and thus clandestine portents of mystical Reality; at the same time, they are a genuine manifestation of the essence of the latter. The 'vision of the mystical Light' is foreshadowed by the fleeting awareness of oncoming 'brightness'; the experience of 'mystical Love' is heralded by the gestures or the loving countenance in an epiphanic 'vision of a self-expressive appearance', though Love has already 'arrived' before, and in this antecedent stage love becomes manifest by the awareness of all-surrounding warmth, bliss and loving devotion.

In the incipient act of perception Love is already perceived and cognitively grasped for what it is in essence.

3. The primeval, sustaining and comprehensive essence of somatic and emotional 'mystical effects' may explain why certain effects are rarely encountered individually in cognitive mystical events. The awareness of somatic, tactile, or emotional 'mystical effects' is an integral part of any experience. The resilience against delusion of the entirety of a mystical experience is transferred in a concrete mystical event to the perception of 'mystical effects'.

4. The perception of the *'fluidum'* and the *'aura'*, and the 'sensual awareness of Presence' are two modes of mystical experience which can be separated only phenomenologically and theoretically, but they are indistinguishable in empirical reality. This means that the phenomena of *'aura'* and *'fluidum'* are tangible harbingers of the 'mystical Presence', signifying in a genuine mystical event that the 'mystical Presence' is really 'there'.

THESIS 93: *The sensual perception of the 'fluidum' and the 'aura' is, on the one hand, inevitably highly susceptible to delusion since the high potential for delusion is inherent in any somatic, tactile, visual and emotional mode of mystical perception. On the other hand, the perception of the 'fluidum' and the 'aura' is shielded against delusion, as it is rooted in the full integrated, overarching realm of mystical experience, which is resistant to delusion.*

THESIS 94: *The perception of the 'fluidum' and the 'aura' can thus be claimed to be a variety of mystical experience that is relatively resilient to delusion.* For this reason, it deserves to be attributed not too low a rank on the gnoseological scale.

The Gnoseological Pyramid
["Die gnoseologische Rangpyramide"]

In the preceding chapter, every single variety of mystical perception was examined in view of its potential propensity to succumb to delusion. As we have seen, individual types of mystical experience are vulnerable to delusion to different degrees. It is helpful to arrange in hierarchical order the various degrees to which individual mystical occurrences are susceptible to delusion. The ranking of individual modes of perception along this hierarchy will have far-reaching significance for the further progress of our enquiry. The model of a pyramid will be used to illustrate the gnoseological rank allocated to a given mystical phenomenon. We are aware, however, that this is a theoretical model that may not fully coincide with empirical reality. Despite this deficiency, the pyramid proposed should be a helpful tool by which relationships between individual modes of mystical perception and their cognitive value and the given susceptibility to delusion and error in each case can more easily be discerned.

The gnoseological pyramid consists of a main axis, the ascending levels of which indicate the gnoseological rank of a variety of mystical experiences and the degree of their susceptibility to error and delusion. We further distinguish between the central area of the pyramid and the peripheral areas. In the central area the core phenomena of mystical experience are located, whereas less significant elements are allocated to adjoining or peripheral areas of the pyramid. The pyramid is furthermore divided horizontally into three segments: The lowest segment is at the base of the pyramid and contains modes of mystical perception that are highly prone to delusion and error. On this level, diffuse and opaque modes of mystical experience are located: somatic, tactile, and emotional modes of mystical perception, which are primeval modes of mystical experience, but as such they are also the sustaining ground, the integral part of all varieties of mystical experience. At the periphery and subordinate to these varieties, the phenomenon of 'mystical guidance and direction' is placed.

The main area in the middle of the pyramid is occupied by a group of mystical experiences that are, by and large, grounded in, or affiliated with, 'mystical effects'. These varieties of mystical experience are considerably susceptible to error and delusion, but since they are classified as a group of lucid, cognitive modes of mystical perception and rooted in the overall structure of mystical experience, from which they cannot be removed without destroying its essential phenomenological framework and coherence, they are justly assigned to the middle area. At the three outermost zones of the middle part of the pyramid, adjacent to the peripheral areas, the 'pictorial vision', 'mystical insights' and 'locutions' are located. In the central part, positioned around the vertical axis of the pyramid, which represents the sustaining ground of all mystical experience, somatic, tactile and other non-visual and non-auditory varieties of 'mystical impacts' are placed. Mystics throughout history have considered somatic and emotional modes of mystical perception and 'mystical impacts' affecting the perceiver's will and moral and religious disposition, more important and gnoseologically more relevant than 'visions' and 'auditions'. Despite the distinctly subjective characteristics germane to the transformation of feelings and changes in the bodily condition, as well as acts of conversion triggered by some mystical impact, mystics have always attributed to mystical occurrences of this kind a high degree of authenticity (albeit one that is difficult to explain).

At the top of the pyramid, encompassing the third area, all varieties of cognitive mystical experience are placed, which are highly resistant to error and delusion: The topmost rank is attributed to the pure (non-visual) 'cognitive awareness of the mystical Presence', which is (as demonstrated above) an extremely sparse albeit translucent phenomenon entirely invulnerable to delusion. This variety of perceiving the 'mystical Presence' is the only one that can be claimed to be exempt from delusion. The penultimate rank is occupied by the 'imageless vision', which is affiliated with the 'pure awareness of the mystical Presence', though in it the share of visionary perception is larger. In essence an 'imageless vision' consists of the contemplation of the unfathomable darkness encountered in 'inner sight', in which the Presence is concealed; it is a variety of mystical experience that is likewise exempt from delusion. Beneath this rank three varieties of cognitive mystical experience are situated, which are generated by the impact of the Numen, or the 'mystical Presence': the 'visionary of the mystical Light', which is placed just below the 'imageless vision'; it is largely resilient to delusion, albeit not entirely. In a 'vision of the mystical Light' the perceiver not only perceives sensations of light, but he/she is also enabled to grasp intimations of the 'mystical Presence'. The zone beneath it accommodates the sensory experiences of the *'aura'* and the *'fluidum'* of the 'Presence', which is indissolubly intertwined with the sensual perception of the nearness or the 'touch' of the 'mystical

Presence'. It is probably because of the unusual awareness of 'being touched mystically' that this dark variety of 'mystical effects', which as such is located at the lowest tier of the gnoseological pyramid, ascends to the highest layers and becomes intertwined with all other modes of mystical experience. Thus, the perception of the *'aura'* and the *'fluidum'* are bestowed with a high degree of resistance to delusion. One tier below, in the transitional zone to experiences that are prone to error and delusion, the visionary experience of 'self-expressive mystical appearances' is situated, along with – and inextricably intertwined with– the 'vision of the mystical Presence'. Both varieties of mystical experience are significantly more vulnerable to delusion than the 'vision of the mystical Light', and even more so than the 'imageless vision'. Yet despite this propensity to delusion, the two modes of cognitive mystical experience are allocated a higher gnoseological rank than any of the phenomena elicited by 'mystical effects'.

The gnoseological diagram in the shape of a pyramid permits us some illuminating findings and important inferences, namely:

THESIS 95: *In the hierarchy of the gnoseological pyramid, visionary mystical experiences are located on diverse rankings depending on the extent of the pictorial content: in general, it can be stated that the sparser the visual pictorial structure, the more resilient is the visionary experience to delusion.* A 'pictorial vision' is least resistant to delusion, the vision of epiphanic 'self-expressive appearances' is less disposed to error and delusion; even less susceptible to delusion is the 'vision of the mystical Light'. The 'imageless mystical vision' is entirely impervious to delusion.

THESIS 96: *The more a mystical vision contains features of the 'whatness' of the 'mystical Object', the more it is exposed to error and delusion.* This is why, at the top of the gnoseological pyramid, only imageless modes of perceiving the 'mystical Presence' are situated. Beneath the uppermost gnoseological rank, we may find varieties of mystical experience which are scarcely susceptible to delusion, such as the 'vision of the mystical Light', and the somatic and/or emotional and cognitive perception of the *'aura'* and the *'fluidum'*; in them, much less of the 'whatness' of the 'mystical Presence' is revealed than in a 'pictorial vision' or in a 'locution', which, however, are for this reason highly vulnerable to error and delusion.

THESIS 97: *The more a mystical experience is imbued with person-like qualities, the more is it susceptible to delusion.*

The only varieties of mystical experience that are entirely untainted by delusion are varieties that are entirely a-personal. Moreover, the 'vision of the mystical Light' and perceptions of the *'aura'* and the *'fluidum'* do not disclose any specific personal qualities and may thus be considered a-personal modes of mystical perception as well. Personal qualities become manifest only at the level of the epiphanic vision of a 'self-expressive appearance', and even more explicitly in 'pictorial visions' and in 'locutions'. This therefore implies that 'personal mysticism' as such is generally burdened by the fact of its rootedness in modes of mystical perception that are considerably prone to error and delusion. For this reason, personal mysticism requires a criterion substantiating its truth and authenticity which is safe and sound. Such a criterion, however, cannot be derived from the gnoseological situation of a single mystical occurrence.

Error and Delusion in the Overall Structure of Mystical Experience ["Trug und Irrtum im Gesamt eines mystischen Erfahrungsgefüges"]

We have tried to disclose all the potential hideouts and ramifications of delusion and error in our examination of diverse varieties of mystical experience. We have been able to establish a differentiated scale for the potential propensity toward error and delusion of individual modes of mystical perception. We have, moreover, assigned individual types of experience to a particular level on the gnoseological pyramid, stipulating in each case the degree of its susceptibility to delusion. The results of this critical assessment, however illuminating, still provide a considerable challenge to our main task of disclosing the 'ultimate phenomenon' of the 'mystical relation' inherent in all varieties of mystical experience. The challenge is to establish whether there are modes of mystical experience that can be claimed to be exempt from delusion. As we have seen, delusion permeates nearly the entire range of mystical experience and most of its components. This fact invokes the crucial question: *Is it indeed alone the pure imageless cognitive awareness of the 'mystical Presence' that can be claimed to be entirely untainted by delusion, or is it possible to disclose yet another realm of mystical experience that is invulnerable to delusion?*

In the course of our investigation we have come to recognize an empirical fact, which can be claimed to be taken as a general rule:

The more complex the phenomenological structure of a mystical experience, the more resistant it is to delusion. In other words, the plainer the entire structure of a cognitive mystical experience, and the fewer its constituent elements, the higher the propensity in a mystical occurrence to succumb to error and delusion. To put it differently: the more varied, complex and involved the phenomenological structure of a mystical experience, the better is it shielded against delusion. This claim, however, is not supposed to be a natural law, but merely a basic rule inferred from empirical data, viz., from the evidence of the testimonies of the mystics. The claim thus does not necessarily apply to mystical experience in toto, but to individual mystical experiences witnessed in a concrete mystical event. Hence it is imperative to subject the proposed rule to the test with every single mystical event.

THESIS 98: *The content of an experience of doubtful mystical authenticity, i.e., if it is as yet uncertain whether the 'content' perceived has been mystically 'infused' or if it derives from a pseudo-mystical occurrence – one that is more likely to have been generated by the perceiver's subjective sphere – the plainer and more rudimentary the experiential relation is shaped. The more variegated the content and the structural framework of the experience, the lower the probability of it to have been fabricated by the perceiver, and the higher the probability that it results from a genuine mystical event.* The structure of a mystical experience is not the accumulation of several individual modes of mystical perception, but a real, coherently structured whole in which the individual components are mutually and meaningfully related and sustain each other gnoseologically. The core of mystical experience consists of four basic modes of perception: The 'cognitive awareness of Presence', the 'imageless vision', the 'vision of the mystical Light', and the (quasi-)sensory perception of the *'aura'* and the *'fluidum'*. When these four modes are meaningfully linked to each other, they form a coherent whole which establishes a genuine foundation for mystical knowledge. If any one of these modes of perception occurs individually outside the integral whole, the mystical experience is more or less exposed to delusion. Within the coherent multiple structure of a mystical experience, however, the individual experiential modes support each other by mutually establishing a criterion of genuineness.

The same rule applies to the peripheral phenomena of the gnoseological pyramid. Thus, it is never possible to ascertain with certainty whether the content of a 'pictorial vision' has been 'infused' mystically or generated by a non-mystical cause. Phenomena in which the mystical quality is exclusively rooted in the perception of effects felt to be mystical in origin are heavily susceptible to delusion. But when a 'pictorial vision' is intertwined with the concurrent perception of the 'mystical Presence', or when it is intermingled with a 'vision of the mystical Light', or an abrupt inexplicable change in the perceiver's emotional state, or with a striking transformation of the perceiver's will, a multi-layered experiential structure is lent, which can be claimed to be authentic. *Thus, the propensity toward error and delusion in perceiving 'mystical effects' is mitigated and/or transformed by the integrity of the coherent whole of the mystical experience and counterbalances the disposition toward delusion of a singular mode of perception.*

This concludes our enquiry into the nature of 'error and delusion' in the context of mystical experience. Yet one final word on the statements above is on order from a wider perspective. Our considerations have been focussed on criteria sustaining the genuineness of a mystical experience and, more specifically, on the pivotal criterion that a concrete mystical event is considered genuine if it is grounded in the coherently structured whole of the composite cognitive experience. That is to say that a genuine mystical event is sustained by a coherently structured framework of cognitive perception and/or elicited by the impact of a coherently structured whole of 'mystical effects'. We have thus identified two kinds of wholeness which are both phenomenologically unique and independent. This permits the inference *that the real phenomenon of mystical recognition is not disclosed by a single 'mystical effect' or perceived by a single mode of experience, but rather that two complex mystical structures are phenomenologically and contiguously juxtaposed:*

The overall structure of 'mystical effects' impinges on the overall structure of mystical experience.

Yet as soon as we no longer speak of a single experiential relation, but rather of the relation between the entire whole of two phenomenological structures, a critical examination can no longer be carried out by applying the concepts of 'error' and 'delusion'. The notion of 'delusion' is rendered void if applied to the entire structural whole of 'mystical effects'. The concept of 'delusion' inevitably requires binary options; thus, the choice is between two incompatible modes of experience, which, however, are contiguous or similar enough to be falsely identified or mistaken. In the case of 'mystical effects' to which the perceiver is exposed, a pivotal rational decision must be made in advance, one independent of the actual mystical event: specifically, to decide beforehand whether 'mystical effects' do exist at all. The question to be asked here is not: "Is the cognitive structure of the mystical experience exposed to the possibility of delusion?" The proper question is: "Is the structure of cognitive mystical experience falsely classified as a 'mystical' one?" Or, to put it differently, "Is it possible to trace the alleged 'ultimate phenomenon' termed 'cognitive mystical relation' to an antecedent cause and thus render it non-existent by postulating that all phenomena allegedly claimed to be mystical in origin are in fact merely fabrications of the perceiver's mind?" If the latter question is answered affirmatively, the reasons will have to be supplied. *Those who support the affirmative claim are obliged to explain how the richly textured, meaningful whole of a mystical experience and its homogeneity, which is devoid of any contradiction and sustained by phenomena that mutually corroborate each other, could have emerged entirely from the perceiver's 'sphere of the self'.* It is, of course, possible to dodge this challenging question by allocating it to the realm of idle speculation, or by maintaining that an alleged mystical experience arises from the realm of the 'unconscious'. But if one is prepared to assess without any bias the uniqueness, exceptional beauty, clarity and existential relevance of a genuine mystical encounter, the reductionist claim that all this originates from the subjective realm of the 'unconscious' is not persuasive and will be refuted.

Critical Analysis of the Structure of Mystical Recognition ["Kritische Analyse der mystischen Erkenntnisstruktur"]

The 'experiential mystical relation' encompasses and sustains the 'cognitive mystical relation'. The latter is that part of the mystical relation that is accessible to rational analysis. On the basis of the phenomena germane to the 'cognitive mystical relation', it is possible to provide phenomenological characteristics that pertain strictly to the domain of gnoseology. Within the realm of gnoseology the range of phenomena relating to mysticism can be identified and classified accordingly. In this way a new perspective is opened from which the ontological question can be approached. Gnoseology is clearly neither psychology nor ontology. The domain of gnoseology encompasses a range of phenomena germane to its own. Hence the first thing that must be clarified is the phenomenon of 'recognition', viz., of cognitive perception, and to demonstrate that it is an entirely autonomous phenomenon, which enables us to elucidate the entire range of mystical experience. My considerations on this issue are based on the studies of *Nicolai Hartmann*.[7] I have adopted his phenomenological-gnoseological analysis and will use it as the foundation for my subsequent considerations.

The primary purpose of knowledge is the cognitive perception of a 'thing that is', hence an object of being. The gnoseological relation differs significantly from an 'intentional act', by which a subject signifies an object by way of thinking, or by way of imagination, or by way of feeling. Though these items of consciousness are 'object-like' items, they depend on, and exist only because of the foregoing 'intentional act'. Knowledge, by contrast, is not a simple, straightforward phenomenon of consciousness; it cannot be explained rationally, not least because knowledge results ultimately from acts that transcend the confines of the individual consciousness.[8] In a gnoseological act, an object is intended and perceived, and this act is independent from

---

7 Cf. HARTMANN, Nicolai. *Grundzüge einer Metaphysik der Erkenntnis*. 2nd ed. Berlin: de Gruyter, 1925. 43–59.

8 Cf. HARTMANN, Nicolai. *Grundzüge einer Metaphysik der Erkenntnis*. 2nd ed. Berlin: de Gruyter, 1925. 103.

an 'intentional act' and from an 'act of recognition', and thus the object exists by itself, hence is a 'being-in-itself'. "From the perspective of gnoseology, the intended object is entirely immanent"[9]; the object of knowledge, by contrast, transcends consciousness.

The phenomena and modes of perception outlined so far are part of the primeval gnoseological-phenomenological inventory. This primordial stockpile of phenomena is given *prior to* any potential metaphysical-ontological interpretation, and also prior to any epistemological proposition, whether this is based on idealistic, realistic or monistic premises. The concept of 'being-in-itself' ["Ansichsein"][10] has strictly gnoseological import; thus, it does not imply anything about the ontological possibility of 'being-in-itself', which might correspond to the gnoseological notion of 'being-in-itself'. The 'cognitive relation' is methodologically delineated against two sides: first, against 'intentional acts', and second, against metaphysical-ontological structures. The critical assessment of the store of mystical phenomena, as represented in the varieties of mystical experience examined in this enquiry, must have in view both these bordering areas of the gnoseological domain.

Apart from these elementary delineations, there is another one which has a specific mystical character: In the structure of mystical experience, a wide variety of objects are comprised which can unanimously be classified gnoseologically as 'being-in-itself'. However, these objects of mystical recognition are not always identical with the 'mystical Object' itself. Within the range of cognitive experiences, we may encounter cognitive relations that refer to the 'mystical Object' itself, and there are cognitive relations that refer to a non-mystical object. The latter are for two reasons termed 'mystical' cognitive relations: first, because they are constituent parts of the entire structure of mystical experience, and second, because they have been 'mystically effected' and therefore have an indirect relationship to the 'mystical Object'. The

---

9   Cf. HARTMANN, Nicolai. *Grundzüge einer Metaphysik der Erkenntnis.* 2nd ed. Berlin: de Gruyter, 1925. 107.

10 [Note: The term "Ansichsein" derives from Heidegger. The standard English translation is 'being-in-itself', as stated in INWOOD, Michael. *A Heidegger Dictionary.* Oxford: Blackwell, 1999. 179. – FKW.]

term 'mystical-gnoseological being-in-itself' can only be attributed to an object of recognition that has indeed been recognized as the 'mystical Object'. It is true, however, that all the other objects within the structure of mystical experience have a gnoseological 'being-in-itself' as well, but not a mystical-gnoseological 'being-in-itself'.

On the basis of these preliminary remarks, we are sufficiently equipped to contrast the sphere of mystical phenomena to the sphere of gnoseological phenomena. The first results of this juxtaposition can be epitomized in the following theses:

1. *Mystical cognition is an empirical form of cognition.* This means that the structure of mystical cognition contains, in its essential core, a process of cognitive perception which belongs to the concept of knowledge *a posteriori*.

2. There is an analogy between the structure of empirical knowledge based on sense perception and the structure of the knowledge based on modes of mystical experience. *There is, in other words, a structural analogy between sense perception and mystical modes of visual and auditory perception.*

3. *From the proposition that the distinctive characteristic of mystical perception is* – by analogy with normal sense perception – *knowledge a posteriori, the following insight ensues:* [visual and auditory] *mystical perception recognises a real solitary occurrence – just as it is in its singular givenness.*

4. Every individual act *a posteriori* is supplemented by *a priori* acts of perception, and thus it is expanded into a fully developed process of knowledge. Empirical knowledge is never just an act of perception *a posteriori* but is always composed of both acts of perception *a posteriori* and *a priori*. Even the plain mode of visual and auditory mystical perception has (like natural sense perception) a multi-layered structure. *The whole structure of mystical cognition has an even more multifaceted structure which is composed of both of elements a priori and elements a posteriori.* This structural expansion of the entire phenomenon is gnoseologically

consistent, but it does not affect the essence of mystical cognition, because the latter is empirical knowledge. Mystical knowledge is sustained by an act of cognition in which an object is perceived *a posteriori*, which is, gnoseologically speaking, 'being-in-itself'. This means that the object is perceived in its singular 'givenness' ["Gegebenheit"].

Having stipulated some of the general characteristics of the cognitive mystical relation by claiming that this relation is grounded in experience and that mystical perception is an act of perception *a posteriori*, we have only disclosed a single element of the entire spectrum of gnoseological phenomena. In the following we shall need to highlight a few more gnoseological elements of the essence of the mystical relation if we want to assess the gnoseological idiosyncracies of the 'mystical relation'. The concept of *'the fabric of knowledge'* embraces a crucial element of knowledge: the imaginative notion of the 'object', perceived by the subject. This image of the 'object' must be distinguished from the transcendent object of cognition as 'being-in-itself'. It is, in other words, the objectified portion of the latter. In an act of cognition, the transcendent object is perceived as a fabric of knowledge that consists partly of subjective, and partly of objective elements, by which the object of cognition is created within the sphere of the subject. The object itself as 'being-in-itself' is seen from a gnoseological-phenomenological perspective, independent of the act of cognition (and continues to be so), and more or less adequately objectified in the given 'fabric of knowledge'. The homogenous and independent object of knowledge is split up into three spheres of cognitive perception: The first sphere is occupied by the process of objectification and encompasses the range between the portion objectified and the threshold of objectification; the second sphere is the trans-objective realm, which borders on the realm of the inscrutable. The trans-objective items indicate the features of the object that have not yet been recognized, though the object is not perceived as entirely inscrutable. The third sphere is the domain of the trans-intelligible. A pivotal characteristic of knowledge is that it inherently strives for ultimate knowledge, unleashing the desire to probe into the unfathomable domain of the Trans-objective.

Having provided a broadened perspective of the spectrum of gnoseological phenomena, we may now further explore individual mystical relationships. For this purpose, we will refer to the relevant issues elaborated earlier in this study and try to establish the gnoseological aspects in [visual and auditory] modes of mystical perception ["mystisches Gewahren"]. Our starting point is the important distinction between direct (immediate) modes of mystical experience (of which the 'cognitive sense of the mystical Presence' is the most significant one), and indirect (mediated) modes of mystical perception. The latter are all rooted in the phenomenon that they are perceived as having been 'effected' by some mystical impact. The category of these 'mystical effects' can more specifically be divided into 'mystical impacts' ["Einwirkungen"], 'infused mystical effects and/or 'after-effects' ["Auswirkung"] and [ongoing] 'mystical influence' ["Wirkung"].

We should emphasise at this point that the expressions 'Presence', 'mystical effects', 'mystical impact', 'mystical effects' and 'mystical influence' are only descriptive phenomenological terms and are as such only helpful for the purposes of psychological phenomenology, whereas their significance in the domain of gnoseology value is rather limited, or even questionable. But these terms must by no means be transferred to the area of ontology, as this entails the risk of preconceived metaphysical notions to intrude. By referring to the overall phenomenon of 'mystical effects', we indicate, however, that there is indeed some kind of extant relationship between the sphere of the 'mystical Object' and the 'impact' and/or 'influence' perceived in a concrete mystical event. But the semantic connotations of the words 'effect', 'impact' and 'influence' must not entice us to believe that we might be able to disclose the essence of the implied relation to the 'mystical Object', which is ultimately unknowable. We should, moreover, be aware, when speaking of 'Presence', that it does not denote an ontological entity: the word 'Presence' does not say anything about the state of being of the sphere of the 'mystical Object', nor about the 'causes' by which the perception of Presence is elicited. Truly, we do not know what the 'Presence' is ontologically. But we do know for certain from insights derived from a psychological-gnoseological perspective that in an empirical encounter with the

'Presence' a cognitive relation is alive, here and now, between the 'mystical Object' and the perceiver.

It is an undeniable fact that *the perception of Presence* is a genuine gnoseological act: In becoming cognitively aware of the 'Presence', the perceiver transcends the confines of individual consciousness and objectifies the 'mystical Object', which exists as 'being-in-itself', resulting in an act of cognitive perception. This is, gnoseologically, a very special mode of *cognitive perception of 'Presence'*. We would not expressly use the term cognitive mystical *perception* of 'Presence' ["Präsenz*erfassung*"] and assess it as the supreme variety of perceiving the 'mystical Presence' if we could not demonstrate that it differs significantly, in phenomenological terms, from any of the familiar varieties of *experiencing* the 'Presence' ["Präsenz*erfahrung*"]: When experiencing an object, we usually recognize its 'presence' empirically by perceiving cognitively its 'suchness' ["So-Sein"]. But the 'suchness' of an object can never be comprehended *a posteriori*, if the object is not really 'there' ["Dasein"]. Thus, it only makes sense to speak of the 'cognitive perception of Presence' if the sense of the real presence of the object prevails over the discernment of its 'suchness'.

In the 'cognitive perception of the 'mystical Presence' the structure of the cognitive process and the 'shape' of the object perceived are phenomenologically extremely sparse. We have described this sparseness earlier using the psychological term 'non-visual awareness' ["unanschauliche Bewußtheit"], i.e., the immediately evident knowledge about the presence of the 'mystical It'. This phenomenological term signifies the unity of this state of 'awareness', though it is in fact composed of several qualities of awareness, notably the awareness of the ultimate otherness, incomprehensibility and immeasurable vastness of the 'object' perceived in the encounter with 'Presence'. Consequently, the core of the cognitive perception of 'Presence' consists of a wide range of emotional responses. This, however, does not affect the extreme sparsity of the overall structure of this mode of perception. From a gnoseological perspective it is quite unusual that the object of cognition should be perceptible only in an extremely scant and elusive manner. It can be said that *the perception of the 'mystical Presence' is, gnoseologically, a largely vacated cognitive structure, consisting almost entirely of the formal framework of the act of mystical cognition.*

The exceptional gnoseological status of the 'non-visual awareness of the 'mystical Presence' has wide-ranging repercussions on all the other essential components of recognition:

1. The fact that the 'objectification' of the 'mystical Object' is reduced to a minimum alters the gnoseological situation for assessing its truth. If nothing else remains in an act of recognition than the awareness of the presence of the 'mystical Object', the knowledge gained of this Object can be untrue only to a very limited extent. The perception of the 'suchness' of the object perceived, i.e., a fully developed perception of the 'mystical Object', is a necessary precondition for answering the question as to whether the cognitive perception of the object corresponds to the real essence of the Object – that is, if the cognitive perception of the essence of the Object is true or untrue. *As mystical recognition is not a recognition of 'suchness', but the cognitive perception of the presence of the Object encountered* ["Dasein"], the gnoseological situation for assessing its veracity can be clarified by the answers to the following two vital questions: Is the Object referred to real? And: Is the cognitive perception of the Object truly a perception of the *'mystical* Object'? The answers to these questions are suggested by the finding established earlier that the imageless cognitive perception of the 'mystical Presence' is relatively invulnerable to delusion and error.

2. The sparsity of the 'image' by which the perception of the Presence of the 'mystical Object' is represented entails not only that the sphere of its objectification is extremely scant, but also the unusual phenomenon that the gnoseological sphere of the object 'being-in-itself' is entirely suspended. This means that *the threshold of objectification coincides with the threshold of recognition. The area of the trans-intelligible Object borders immediately on the sphere of objectification.* In the event of mystical recognition (as manifested in the pure imageless perception of Presence) *there is no progress,* i.e., there is no successive progression in what is cognitively perceived. *Seen from the perspective of the cognitive perception of Presence, mystical recognition is not only*

sparse and scant, but also knowledge conveyed and terminated in a single act of recognition. The question as to whether these propositions, which have all been inferred from the phenomenon of the cognitive perception of Presence alone, are also valid for the entire range of mystical recognition, can only be answered after the analysis of all the other varieties of experiential mystical relations. We will proceed by examining the 'pictorial mystical vision', which is the variety of mystical experience that is phenomenologically most distant to the imageless mode of cognitive perception. By this contrastive analysis the phenomenological and gnoseological differences between the non-visual awareness of Presence and the most graphic variety of mystical experience can most clearly be demonstrated. The 'pictorial mystical vision' can yield gnoseological insights which will enable us to understand better the phenomenon of 'mystical impacts' and the items of recognition conveyed by it, as well as the various modes of mystical experience involved.

To begin with, we must distinguish between the 'vision of a picture' and a mental image of a picture. The latter is an intentional act. Without an 'intentional act' the image has no 'being-in-itself'. The image 'beheld' in a 'vision', however, is undoubtedly a genuine 'object of cognition'; the image perceived in the vision thus corresponds to the 'object of cognition'. As we have demonstrated in our previous study, visionary experiences do occur in empirical reality; thus, the phenomenon of 'images' 'arriving' in the vista of 'inner sight' ["Innenschau"] is an empirical fact. The 'object' that 'arrives' in 'inner sight' is clearly distinct from the mode of inner perception; and 'the object arriving is thought to be an extra-mental wholeness, of which the perceiver becomes increasingly aware in a successive series of visionary encounters.' *This means that the image perceived in a 'pictorial mystical vision' cannot be claimed to originate from the perceiver's fantasy or imagination, nor to have been evoked by an 'intentional act', but the 'image' perceived in a 'mystical vision' is an object that has become manifest and recognized in an act of 'inner sight'.*

Despite these empirically established facts, a 'pictorial vision' has a number of special gnoseological features by which it is clearly distinguished phenomenologically from the 'cognitive perception of Presence': The cognitive perception of the image, i.e., the picture beheld in the visionary experience, is phenomenologically not sparse at all, but, on the contrary, is rich in illustrative detail and (often) even sumptuously crafted. However, the object of recognition – of which the picture perceived in the vision is, gnoseologically speaking, a graphic 'representation' – is not an object as 'being-in-itself', of which a segment has been objectified in the picture 'beheld' in the vision. It is, rather, the picture itself, which has had some 'being-in-itself' of some kind in the realm outside the perceiver's consciousness 'before' it was represented in the 'vision'. Our persistence in adhering to the disparity between the picture featuring as 'object' of cognition in 'inner sight' and the object of recognition as such is not only justified because the picture 'arrives' successively in the process of visionary perception, but also because the picture as 'being-in-itself' can only have 'arrived', in part, so that the result is inevitably an incomplete, fragmented and veiled picture.

The peculiar circumstance that the structure and content of the picture featuring in the vision is identical with the object 'arriving' in the vista of 'inner sight' will be better understood by considering the following point: It goes without saying that the object of recognition thought to reside outside the realm of the individual consciousness is also rooted ontologically in 'being-in-itself', which is beyond human comprehension, and of which we cannot even say whether it has anything to do with the 'psychological', 'physiological', 'physical' or any other structures. However, the very special status of the gnoseological sphere, which is at issue here, becomes apparent precisely in the fact that, in the act of cognitive visual perception, the ontological sphere of the object perceived is not at issue at all. In the process of visual perception, the act of recognition is directed only at the picture that 'arrives' from 'outside' the individual consciousness, but not at the object on which the pictorial object beheld in 'inner sight' might be grounded. From the general perspective of gnoseology, we are here faced with a contraction of the phenomenological sphere, which is akin to that encountered in the realm of natural sense perception.

This phenomenological peculiarity of the 'pictorial vision' means that an additional cognitive relation is required that is linked to it, as otherwise the picture could not be fully cognitively grasped. Every picture, whether perceived inwardly or seen by the physical eyes, is endowed with meaning of some kind, which must be unravelled in a cognitive hermeneutical process. Every picture expresses something or is a visual message of something, either of which must be interpreted to be understood. Thus, the linking of the cognitive act of perceiving a picture [in the vista of 'inner sight'] and the act of interpreting or grasping the meaning of the picture perceived, is imperative.

By way of summary we can, from a gnoseological perspective, state the following about the distinctive features of the 'pictorial mystical vision': *1. The 'pictorial vision' is a genuine act of recognition that is based on a process of perception a posteriori. 2. The scope of gnoseological phenomena is condensed, because the picture perceived cognitively* [in 'inner sight'] *and the object of recognition are largely identical*. Thus, the question of truth does not depend on the truthful representation of an object as 'being-in-itself' in the individual act of cognitive perception, but instead hinges only on the more or less detailed quality and clarity of the 'pictorial vision'. *3. The primary act of the cognitive perception of the 'pictorial vision' is overlayed by another cognitive relation, which is an act of interpretation by which the meaning of the 'pictorial vision' is disclosed to understanding.* The latter cognitive relation, however, falls outside the scope of gnoseological issues considered in the context of this study.

The gnoseological analysis of the phenomenon of the 'pictorial vision' is left incomplete when merely stating that it is a visionary experience of a picture conveyed in a cognitive process *a posteriori*, in which the picture is recognized, and when claiming that it is supported by and intertwined with an act of understanding, by which its meaning is disclosed. Yet in a *'mystical* pictorial vision' a further essential element is involved, which must be taken into account: the image 'arriving' in 'inner sight' is cognitively perceived as having been 'infused' mystically; the 'pictorial mystical vision' is thus imbued with the cognitive awareness of 'mystical effects'. This finding requires us to assess at this juncture the gnoseological significance of 'mystical effects' in the context of mystical experience in general.

The question as to whether 'mystical effects' can be immediately perceived cognitively in the event of a 'mystical pictorial vision' *is open to debate*. If 'mystical effects' are indeed perceived during a 'pictorial mystical vision', this could only occur if the perceiver, while absorbed in 'inner sight', would instantly and immediately become aware that the picture has been 'infused' by the mystical It. And this awareness would also have to elicit a sense of absolute certainty. *Such an intuitive act of recognition, however, would not only be problematic but also irrational*, not only in regard to its apposite structure and underlying relation, but also in regard to the appropriate criteria of its veracity. It seems to me that the knowledge that the picture beheld in the mystical vision has been 'infused' can be persuasively explained without presupposing that it derives from a direct act of recognition. *The knowledge about the effects of a 'mystical impact' is inferred knowledge.* That is to say, for instance, that the extraordinary characteristics of a symbolic image, and its place in the entire framework of a given mystical occurrence, along with the concomitant 'cognitive awareness of Presence' and the concurrent manifestation of special 'effects' on the emotional state of the perceiver – all these are sufficient singular experiential features for eliciting in the perceiver the conviction that the 'pictorial vision' has indeed been mystically instilled. *It is therefore unnecessary to presuppose that this knowledge is grounded in an immediate act of recognition, in which the 'mystical impact' is directly identified.* This aside, such an immediate act of recognition could hardly be verified phenomenologically.

The phenomenon of 'mystical impacts' affecting the cognitive, somatic and emotional condition of the perceiver is linked with several other phenomena subsumed by the category of *'mystical effects'*. As we have emphasized earlier, the phenomenon encompassed by the generic term of 'mystical effects' consists of subordinate phenomena termed 'impact' and 'transforming effects', 'influence' and 'after-effects'. All these terms are, however, vague, ambivalent and overlapping in part, and are therefore not really helpful as descriptive phenomenological concepts. Moreover, their psychological-phenomenological meanings are at risk, as these concepts have also been used in metaphysics and theology and, therefore, are in part charged with philosophical and theological meaning. *However, the generic term and the supporting concepts are only meant to signify that the 'content' of an empirical occurrence is related to the 'mystical Object', and that this relation is structured somehow in a manner that is determined and shaped by the 'mystical It'. But it is entirely transintelligible and inscrutable of which kind this dependence is in essence.*

We have chosen to distinguish between 'impacts' ["Einwirkungen"] and 'after-effects' ["Auswirkungen"], because this allows us a provisional *deictic* phenomenological classification. The pivotal question in making this distinction has been whether, in the process of perception, some empirical content is encountered, which could likewise have occurred with being intertwined with the concurrent awareness of the 'mystical Presence', or if the awareness of the 'Presence' is inalienably linked to experience of a 'mystical impact'.

The term 'after-effect' is appropriate if the components of the experience, e.g., the 'vision of a 'self-expressive appearance', or the perception of the *'fluidum'*, or the 'vision of the mystical Light' are so closely and intimately coupled with the 'sense of Presence' that it seems impossible to separate it from any of these varieties of mystical experience. *The concept of mystical 'after-effects'* ["Auswirkungen"], *viz., experiential 'corollaries' of a mystical impact, is inseparably joined to the simultaneous perception of Presence. The term 'mystical impact', by contrast, refers to the individual effects elicited by the impact on the perceiver, which are not bound to the concurrent awareness of the 'mystical Presence'*. Therefore, it is possible that in a 'pictorial vision' a 'pure' *symbolic* or *allegorical* picture becomes manifest that is perceived as having been mystically 'infused', although the act of perception is not accompanied simultaneously by the cognitive perception of the 'mystical Presence'. An *'epiphanic mystical vision'*, by contrast, is inevitably fused with the simultaneous perception of Presence, though the linking of the two experiences is not as close and intimate as in genuine mystical 'after-effects'. This shows that the phenomenological areas of 'after-effects' and mystical 'impacts' are merged. *The two concepts may be helpful in delineating them phenomenologically, but the distinction is hardly relevant gnoseologically, and it is entirely irrelevant ontologically.*

The fact that this claim is true can be corroborated by analogy with examples from physical sense perception: For instance, when a patient is repeatedly exposed to intense x-ray treatments, the excessive x-ray dosage will cause an inflammation of the skin. Thus the 'impact' of the x-ray treatment has caused a wound in the skin. The term 'impact' is thus appropriately applied because the x-ray treatment, being the cause of the physiological response and the 'impact' on the patient's skin, are remotely related in time and place. Or to cite another example: a rose, concealed to the perceiver, can still be recognized as 'present' by the fragrance emanating from it. This is an experiential situation that is close to the phenomenon of 'after-effects' or 'corollaries'. The fragrance of the rose provides the experiential basis for the act of recognition and is evidence of the realness of the event as well as of the invisible presence of the rose, although the fragrance will linger for some time after the rose has been removed. Though these analogies can only serve as approximate illustrations for the difference between an 'impact' and an 'after-effect' or 'corollary' of a mystical occurrence. But the ontological realm in which these phenomena of mystical experience are rooted has not been addressed by these illustrations.

I would not have ventured this digression into the mundane area of sense perception (which is indeed rather inadequate for elucidating the nature of mystical experience) if I had not intended to demonstrate the inadequacies of the various concepts relating to the category of 'mystical effects'. In our enquiry, we shall no longer employ these concepts, since they are entirely useless in the context of ontological and metaphysical considerations; indeed, we are going to move beyond the threshold of psychological phenomenology and enter the realm of gnoseology.

We shall now subject the phenomenon of the 'mystical vision of Light' to the criteria of our gnoseological enquiry. To begin with, we must call to mind that in our phenomenological analysis above we have failed to render intelligible the essence of the 'mystical Light'. We have referred to various explications by so-called 'mystics of Light' and other visionaries, but we have not been able to determine which of the proposed explications by the mystics is the one that is phenomenologically most persuasive. The pivotal question is: *Is the 'mystical Light' indeed a visual manifestation of the 'All-encompassing'?* If this question is answered affirmatively, it would imply that the 'vision of mystical Light' would have to be placed on the same level as a 'vision of Christ'. In both instances it would be a 'mystically infused image' that is sustained by the simultaneous perception of Presence. The 'image of Light' is cognitively perceived in the act of 'inner sight' and is phenomenologically independent from this perception; the Presence is cognitively perceived simultaneously in a separate act of recognition. The gnoseological structures that are involved in the cognitive perception of the 'Light' 'arriving' in 'inner sight' would then be the same as those identified in our analysis of the 'pictorial vision' and of the 'cognitive perception of Presence'. This tentative approach to the understanding of the phenomenon of 'Light' is, however, unsatisfactory, because it fails to acknowledge the special phenomenological status of the visionary experience of the 'mystical Light': In this mystical event the 'mystical Presence' and the 'mystical Light' are more closely intertwined than is the case in an epiphanic vision of a 'self-expressive appearance'. Therefore, we are required to pose another question: *What is it that is recognized in a 'vision of the 'mystical Light' – is it a feature of its essence, or the structure of the essence of the 'mystical Object' itself?* In other words, does the 'vision of the mystical Light' disclose a cognitive image that represents essential structures of the 'mystical Object' as 'being-in-itself? Is there – seen from the gnoseological perspective – a correlation between the 'mystical Object' and the 'mystical Light' similar to the correlation known from visual sense perception? Does the 'Light' 'beheld' inwardly represent specific features of the essence of the 'mystical Object' itself? Is the 'Light' perceived inwardly a symbol that surfaces during the act of cognitive perception from the sphere of the subject, always related to the same underlying structural entity of 'being-in-itself'? If all these questions are answered affirmatively, this would be equal to confirming that something of the 'suchness' of the 'All-encompassing' becomes directly manifest *a posteriori* in the act of 'inner sight'.

We might furthermore pose the question in the language of the mystics: *Could it be that the mystical Light is perhaps not the 'All-encompassing' itself, but only a corollary of the Presence, or, as it were, an 'attendant' or luminous harbinger arriving concurrently with the 'All-encompassing'?* Could it be that the light [rather than the 'Light'] is emanating from an 'angel', or a 'herald', and thus provides some proof of the realness of the encounter with the Presence? Translated into the language of gnoseology, this would mean that the primordial domain of the 'mystical Object' as 'being-in-itself' is somehow structurally and, as for its determination, connected with the sphere of 'light', which is likewise a self-sufficient sphere of 'being-in-itself'. In this case a 'vision of light' is not the immediate perception of the 'suchness' of the 'mystical Object', because the 'vision of light' is not fused with the cognitive perception of Presence. Instead, the 'vision of light' is rather a luminescent corollary of the Presence becoming manifest in the vista of 'inner sight' as radiant light. At the same time, however, in perceiving the Presence and the light as its corollary, the 'dark' and unfathomable 'mystical Object' is cognitively grasped.

The fourth fundamental question to be asked is: *Could it be that the 'mystical Light' is, in fact, no light at all, but only a metaphoric indication of the abrupt arrival of the Presence, which for the perceiver is an event of ultimate existential relevance?* If this applies, the gnoseological structure of the cognitive awareness of Presence outlined above would be sufficient for elucidating the mystery of the 'vision of light'. Though it is true that in the cognitive perception of the 'mystical Presence' only a minimal fraction of the 'suchness' of the 'mystical Object' is revealed, these sparse features are enough to be unambiguously recognized as the 'Numen'. The 'experiencing self' responds to the distinctive qualities of the 'All-encompassing' elicited at the onset of perceiving the Presence – notably its foreignness, otherness, finality and incomprehensibility – with numinous feelings. This mystical event is an encounter not only with the 'Presence' but also with total darkness, in which the 'arrival' of the 'Presence' also elicits an overwhelming impression of a dazzling, all-permeating light.

The fact that there are divergent views of this kind on the nature of the 'mystical Light' should be taken as a warning that the phenomenological analysis must not be pushed to extremes. Over and beyond this, it has become remarkably clear that the gnoseological benefit from these phenomenological considerations is rather limited. What is really significant gnoseologically has been sufficiently illuminated in the analysis of the perception of the 'mystical Presence' above.

The next logical step in the progress of our enquiry would be the study of the gnoseological structure of all individual varieties of mystical experience. We have decided, however, to skip this task for the following reasons: The gnoseological analyses of the 'pictorial vision', of the perception of 'Presence' and the 'vision of the 'mystical Light' and its ambiguities, have expounded in sufficient detail the fundamental mystical-gnoseological structures in which we are primarily interested. The insights gained from these analyses are unlikely to be further advanced substantially if we were to engage in similar enquires with all the other varieties of mystical experience, notably with 'locutions', the somatic and emotional perception of 'mystical effects', the visual perception of 'self-expressive appearances' and elusive sense-related modes of mystical experience. Since the relevant gnoseological structures have already been identified in the three representative varieties addressed above, the analysis of other varieties of mystical experience appears to be redundant.

The second reason for skipping further gnoseological analyses of individual types of mystical experience is the following: Our enquiries into the nature of error and delusion in the context of mystical experience have been a preliminary concern in advancing our investigation into the field of mystical gnoseology. After having clarified the nature of delusion in the context of mystical experience and established criteria for discerning genuine from bogus mystical phenomena, we have been able to propose a gnoseological pyramid in which individual varieties of mystical experience are assigned a particular rank on the basis of their potential for delusion and gnoseological relevance. As we have seen, individual modes of mystical perception are in different measure susceptible to delusion. We have also been able to show that there is a very limited range of cognitive modes of mystical perception that is unfailingly resilient to delusion. Gnoseological enquiries are scientific investigations. As such they depend on phenomenologically unambiguous empirical data. There are, however, varieties of mystical experience that are especially susceptible to delusion – these include 'locutions' and other auditory experiences, obscure, ambivalent experiences like the sense of being 'mystically touched' or emotionally affected – and which are from the outset unsuitable for gnoseological enquiry. *The results of our investigation into the nature of mystical delusion have permitted us to restrict the phenomenon of mystical recognition to a few varieties of mystical experience. Our gnoseological considerations have, moreover, led us to impose significant strictures on potentially bogus phenomena.* This double safeguard has resulted in removing all phenomena from the field of our enquiry that are not directly related to the *cognitive perception of the 'mystical Presence', which has proved to be the core-phenomenon for which alone it is worthwhile to engage in a critical gnoseological investigation.*

One might object that these two restrictions are too rigorous, as they exclude too many potentially mystical phenomena from the full range of mystical experience. As a result, only a small number of phenomena have remained that have been acknowledged as authentic. This objection, however, calls for an emphatic answer: In this part of the book we are expressly concerned with gnoseology and no longer with an enquiry into the phenomenology of all varieties of mystical experience. *The main concern in this section of the book is not with the phenomenon of mysticism in its entirety as an existential event, and even less with a theological evaluation of a mystical occurrence. The only thing with which we are concerned here is – by deliberately limiting the scope of our enquiry –finding an answer to the special question as to whether or not mysticism as a universal and perennial empirical phenomenon is indeed grounded in a genuine cognitive mystical relation.* Unless this question is answered in the affirmative, it will not be possible to detach the area of cognitive mystical experience from the realm of religious faith, with which it is inexorably intertwined.

In the course of our gnoseological enquiry we have repeatedly, and apparently without misgivings, used the terms 'mystical recognition', 'cognitive mystical structure' and 'object of mystical recognition' without having previously dealt with the important question of whether mystical perception can be justly termed 'mystical recognition' at all, i.e., if the phenomenon of mystical perception embraces all the pivotal features that are considered indispensable for a genuine act of recognition. The term 'knowledge' in the strict philosophical sense can only be used in instances in which it does not refer to an isolated individual experiential content, but to knowledge that is generally and universally valid and related to a 'subject as such'. It seems rather doubtful to me that mystical perception complies in the least to this concept of knowledge. Therefore, we need to examine the special gnoseological qualities individually to be able to answer this fundamental question. The knowledge conveyed in an act of *mystical recognition* – as understood in this study after having been removed from the potential for delusion – *is, in the gnoseological sense, incomplete knowledge*. The knowledge bestowed in a mystical encounter derives from a single object of recognition; but irrespective of this circumstance mystical knowledge surpasses the ordinary range of knowledge acquired in this world. The cognitive process in the realm of mysticism is grounded in a single act of recognition *a posteriori*. Knowledge *a priori* accompanies this act of recognition only insofar as it is required for the full development of the faculty of cognitive perception. In the realm of mystical recognition there is no progress of knowledge. This deficiency is a real fact, and as such, inevitably a pivotal feature of genuine mystical knowledge. Because of this deficiency it is impossible to elucidate rationally both the sphere of the 'mystical Object' and the potential relations of the 'mystical Object' to other objects of recognition.

Mystical knowledge is not only strikingly incomplete, but also *extraordinarily sparse*. Though the 'cognitive perception of the mystical Presence' is undoubtedly a genuine empirical process *a posteriori* in that it results in the immediate conviction of the realness of a given individual occurrence, it is also a rather rudimentary process insofar as only a few fleeting and sparse features of the sphere of the 'suchness' of the present 'Object' can be identified by it. Yet the sparse and minimal features of the 'suchness' that are grasped cognitively reveal enough of the essence of the 'Object' that it permits it to be identified during the event of the 'cognitive perception of the mystical Presence'. But it is true that what can be cognitively grasped in an act of mystical recognition is extremely sparse compared to any mundane acts of recognition *a posteriori*.

Mystical knowledge is, moreover, not only exceptionally deficient and sparse, but also *highly individualized*. The fact that there are no *a priori* acts of cognition obviates the development of items of knowledge that is generally valid and related to a 'subject as such'. Mystical knowledge is not knowledge that is 'inevitable', because this would require that it is sustained by an intersubjective identity *a priori*. For if an object is perceived in several identical acts of recognition as identical, it is impossible to confirm that diverging impressions of the same object are generally valid *a priori*. But even if we ignore the epistemological requirement of a given *a priori* and remain exclusively within the sphere of knowledge *a posteriori*, there is still an abundance of individual features. In this respect we may discern that there is a significant difference between mystical processes of cognitive perception *a posteriori* and processes of recognition in ordinary sense perception. In the latter, recognition *a posteriori* does not occur unless the sense perception conforms to the mental image of the object perceived, and is shared collectively by individual subjects. The features of the 'suchness' of an object experienced in sense perception are, in other words, intersubjectively identical. For example, the colour 'red' is recognized if it corresponds to the impression of the colour 'red' transmitted by the visual senses; similarly, the tune 'C' refers to a specific sound, the quality of which is universally identical and perceived in the same way by all individuals. In the context of cognitive mystical experience, however, the sphere of the 'suchness' of the 'object' is shrunk to a minimum; for this reason, the range of identical items of recognition shared by individual subjects is almost entirely effaced. These gnoseological characteristics persuasively endorse the fact that mystical knowledge, which is disclosed in a genuine act of mystical recognition and grounded in the pure cognitive perception of the 'mystical Presence', is highly individualized knowledge.

There are, however, more items to be considered by which the scope of the phenomenon of mystical recognition is even further limited. If we bear in mind that the process of mystical recognition cannot be verified in empirical reality by other subjects, which is an inevitable requirement in any other process of knowledge, we will realize the actual core of the gnoseological phenomenon of progressive effacement. An object recognized by way of sense perception can be verified by other observers present at the site of the act of perception at the same time. *The mystical Object, by contrast, is perceived individually and thus has a unique individualized relation to the perceiver, based on a single occurrence which cannot be repeated. Thus, mystical knowledge deriving from a unique act of mystical recognition is not only highly individualized, but also intimately private knowledge.* The items of intersubjective identity inherent in mystical knowledge are confined to two crucial facts: First, that the 'content' or subject matter becoming manifest in mystical experiences has [basically] been the same across widely different cultures and historical periods[11]; and second, the fact

---

11   [Note: This statement, as it stands, is controversial and apparently difficult to

that the 'content' of a mystical experience is cognitively grasped in the same manner as the 'mystical Object'.

After having imposed fourfold strictures and limitations on the cognitive perception of the mystical relation, we may rightly ask if this relation can still qualify as a source of mystical knowledge, viz., 'mystical recognition'. *Despite these restrictions, I still think that the terms 'knowledge' and 'mystical recognition' are appropriate and should be retained.* Where else should we allocate the special relation rooted in the act of 'cognitive mystical perception', which has been inferred from the entire phenomenon of the 'mystical relation', if not to the sphere of gnoseology? For the 'cognitive mystical relation' is truly a genuine gnoseological entity: In the event of a 'cognitive mystical perception', the individual consciousness is transcended and establishes a relation to an 'Object' that is, gnoseologically speaking, 'being-in-itself'. This fundamental act of 'cognitive mystical perception' differs significantly from any intentional act of cognition that is intrinsic to the individual consciousness. This act of 'cognitive mystical perception' cannot be categorized psychologically but must be assigned to the realm of gnoseologicy. This aside, an act of 'cognitive mystical perception' is bound to convey knowledge that is true and universally valid, despite the sparsity of cognitive detail. It is true that the knowledge transmitted by it is not knowledge about the 'suchness' of the Object perceived but is, instead, special knowledge about the nature of the underlying cognitive mystical relation. *The fact that the 'mystical Object' can at all be encountered in the*

---

reconcile with the fact that monistic and theistic mystical traditions are rooted in different kinds of mystical experience and thus mystical knowledge. Albrecht is of course aware of the essential phenomenological and cognitive differences between theistic and monistic mysticism. In the given context, however, he seems to have the psychological-phenomenological concept of mysticism in mind, as conceived in his study *Psychology of Mystical Consciousness*, in which mysticism is defined as the "arrival of the 'All-encompassing' in the quiet state of alertness and/or the ecstatic experience of an 'All-encompassing'." And it is this holistic understanding of mysticism as an experience rooted perennially in man's encounter with the 'All-encompassing' – whatever its concrete form(s) of manifestation are in the given cultural and/or religious context(s) – on which Albrecht's seemingly contentious claim is based. – FKW.]

structure of cognitive mystical perception of an individual is – though it is the only gnoseological sparse insight – it is also the most relevant and universally valid result of this unique act of mystical recognition. If individual events of 'cognitive mystical perception' did not occur again and again, there would be no knowledge about the inherent possibility of man to have access to cognitive perception.

If a phenomenon is reflected on from diverse angles and without prejudice, it is permitted for methodological reasons to approach it, for the time being, from a single perspective. If the narrowing down of the approaches is carried out by abiding by the principles of science and phenomenology, any phenomenon will itself reveal new vistas and unfold the full range of its distinctive features. A new perspective of this kind is opened if we confine the approach to a given mystical event more strictly for gnoseological reasons, and if we separate the domain that is accessible to rational analysis from the entire whole of the 'mystical relation'. From this new vantage point, the whole structure of cognitive mystical perception will become apparent in an entirely novel manner. The gnoseological sphere tends to expand beyond its confines and demands for an ontological reference-frame in support and invokes initially fundamental metaphysical questions. 'Behind' the cognitive mystical relation, pressing claims resonate from the sphere of 'mystical effects'. The pure relation established by the 'cognitive perception of the mystical Presence' is (like any other cognitive relation) rooted initially in the 'impact' originating from the Object of mystical recognition, termed the 'mystical It'. Yet all the other components of mystical experience identified earlier (albeit temporarily bypassed in our gnoseological enquiry), signal their phenomenological significance. These components can be instantly reintegrated into the overall context of mystical experience when we shift our focus and consider the phenomenon of 'mystical effects' from an ontological perspective.

This shift in perspective is suggested by and implied in the very nature of the cognitive mystical relation itself, which has been purged from all ancillary phenomena. If mystical knowledge disclosed in an act of 'mystical recognition' is indeed confined to the perception of a small segment within the full range of mystical experience, the terms 'knowledge' and 'act of mystical recognition' seem to be hardly appropriate anymore. But this signifies that the shifting of the perception of a cognitive relation into the fullness of the 'experiential mystical relation' is inherent in the 'mystical Object' itself. Experience does not only consist of knowledge gained in acts of 'recognition'; it arises also and is grounded in 'encounters' (in the general meaning of the term) of any kind, in which the perceiver is exposed to some impact or 'effects', often without being cognitively aware at the time.

Before concluding this chapter, two final remarks need to be appended:

1. Though we have carried out a critical analysis in the realm of 'mystical recognition', we have refrained from advancing into the area of epistemology. Epistemology is something entirely different from a gnoseological analysis: The theory of knowledge addresses general philosophical problems and questions about the metaphysical theorems in which knowledge can potentially be claimed to be grounded. Mystical knowledge retrieved from acts of 'mystical recognition' does not differ in this respect from other kinds of knowledge. Mystical knowledge as well encompasses the entire range of *aporias* that inevitably belong to the phenomenon of cognition, and mystical knowledge is likewise subjected to the crucial epistemological question as to whether its 'content' is to be interpreted metaphysically in idealistic, realistic or monistic terms.

2. Before departing from the sphere of gnoseology, we need to re-unite the components of the phenomenon of cognitive mystical perception, which has – for methodological reasons – been split apart. As stated previously: *The concrete mystical process of recognition never consists of merely a plain, sparse and vacant 'act of recognition', as outlined here in theoretical and abstract terms, since we were required to restrict our enquiry to gnoseological concerns*. The entire phenomenon of 'mysticism' encompasses a plethora of diverse experiential features in which the sphere of 'mystical recognition' is never entirely detached from metaphysical assumptions and/or religious knowledge and/or aspects of religious faith. In empirical reality, the act of 'mystical recognition' is rather tinged or even imbued with religious and metaphysical

notions that the perceiver brings to a mystical event. For instance, *in Christian mysticism the cognitive mystical experience is fused with the knowledge deriving from personal religious faith grounded in the revelations of the Holy Scriptures.* In a concrete mystical event, the limited framework of 'mystical recognition' is thus instantly filled with a rich variety of phenomena, arising from both the source of mystical recognition and the sources of prevenient religious knowledge: *The experiential perception of the 'mystical Presence' evolves into the event of a personal encounter on the basis of the religious knowledge that the Christian believer has brought to the event and which is elicited by the impact of the 'mystical Presence'.* We can see now that all the mystical-gnoseological issues which were shifted to the periphery in our gnoseological enquiry are relevant and of hermeneutic value. This does not only apply to the perception of the *'fluidum'* of Love, or of the *'aura'* of Beauty, but also to the experience of 'mystical effects', which are cognitively grasped as the impact effected by a mystical Persona [viz., Divine Thou], to the 'vision of Light', to epiphanic 'self-expressive appearances [of the countenance of Christ]' featuring gestures of loving care and consolation. It also applies to auditory mystical experiences, notably 'locutions' perceived by the recipient as an express summons or calling.

Seen from the perspective of an empirical mystical relation, *mysticism is always composed of two simultaneous and intertwined processes: To a small extent mystical experience consists of a genuine act of mystical recognition in which the 'All-encompassing' is encountered and perceived as present. To a larger extent, however, mysticism relies on an act of 'comprehending in faith', thus on a process fostered and sustained by the subject's religious belief.*

PART THREE

The Philosophical Relevance of the Mystical Relation

Philosophical thinking is inevitably provoked and spurred on by 'ultimate phenomena'. 'Ultimate phenomena' are real entities that elude rational explanation and therefore are a perennial challenge to all the branches of philosophy. From times immemorial, 'ultimate phenomena' have been subjected to ever-new approaches. Anyone who ventures to propose a new 'ultimate phenomenon' should know that this is likely to spark daunting and relentless responses by philosophical thinkers. *Claiming that the 'mystical relation' is a new 'ultimate phenomenon' means to transfer a new topic to philosophy, implying that it is imperative for philosophy to deal with it.*

The entire domain of philosophical thought is split up into numerous special thematic fields. The phenomenon of the 'mystical relation', however, is relevant for all branches of philosophy and thus must be be reflected on from all these perspectives. The impact that the proposed new phenomenon has on philosophy depends on the individual branch. The response to it may just be a caveat or an admonition which needs to be dealt with, or the endeavour to launch an enquiry into the novel phenomenon and to consider how it might be integrated into the overall philosophical context. And a serious reflection on the 'mystical relation' might open up a new path in metaphysical thinking. Eventually, each branch of philosophy will be required to approach the 'ultimate phenomenon' of the 'mystical relation' by its own special methodology, and along with it, deal with the phenomenon of 'mysticism' in general. However, each branch of philosophy will be obliged to apply a double path: One approach will be determined by scepticism, viewing the phenomenon from a distrustful stance and endeavouring to explain away this strange new 'ultimate phenomenon' and trace it to a familiar phenomenon by harmonizing it with known concepts. But if this sceptical approach fails, an alternative approach is needed by which the 'mystical relation' is acknowledged as an 'ultimate phenomenon' and given a definite place in philosophical discourse. We shall demonstrate in the following that the 'mystical relation' is indeed an 'ultimate phenomenon' that is relevant for all branches of philosophy, although the extent of this relevance differs amongst the individual philosophical disciplines. In the following we shall try to consider (albeit only briefly and cursorily) the significance that the 'mystical relation' is attributed in various branches of philosophy. This endeavour is surely not what might appear to be a presumptuous effort to inaugurate philosophical thinking about the 'mystical relation' as an 'ultimate phenomenon', but merely an attempt to illustrate the philosophical relevance of the 'mystical relation'. It goes without saying that *attributing a place for dealing with a novel phenomenon is something different from engaging in critical reflections on the phenomenon.*

Anthropology

The term 'anthropology' denotes the science and knowledge of humankind. In the widest sense, it comprises the entire knowledge of the nature and development of mankind, including the study of human societies and cultures and the data and findings yielded by any discipline concerned with any aspect of humanity. Each of the disciplines involved in the study of man has developed its own specific methodology. Thus, it can be said that there are as many individual versions of anthropology as there are disciplines of science. The various branches of science and the humanities include (without any claims to completeness) biological, medicinal, psychological and sociological anthropology, and amongst the humanities, especially philosophical and theological anthropology.

By the term 'philosophical anthropology' we understand all the teachings and theories on humanity which are not only concerned with establishing empirical knowledge about humanity and/or defining its distinctive features and man's superior status amongst the species, but involve the ultimate concern of 'philosophical anthropology', which is to tackle the utmost question of humanity: What is the *essence* of man? 'Philosophical anthropology' can be practiced in different ways: It can be based on empirical data, by which the unique position of man in creation is substantiated,[1] but it can also explore the nature of man without resorting to empirical data.[2] Whichever of the two paths 'philosophical anthropology' prefers to pursue, it is necessary to clearly define its purpose and thresholds to related disciplines, notably scientific disciplines of anthropology and theological anthropology. The latter infers its epistemological premises and conception of man from the historic event of the Revelation.

1. Modern[3] *biological anthropology* is no longer based alone on data supplied by anatomy, physiology and the history of evolution. Its methodological approaches and epistemological premises are rather based on predetermined notions of the nature of man, which rely on biological, sociological and psychological insights. Biological anthropology aims at establishing the distinctive bio-physical characteristics of humanity at large. This has resulted, for instance, in the finding that a striking feature of the human species is that – although originally conceived as a 'precocial animal' rather than a 'nestling' – infants are not endowed with the capacity of autonomous mobility; from this remarkable biological fact, biological anthropology has inferred the proposition that the new-born child is the outcome of a foreshortened period of physiological incubation, and thus the result of 'premature birth'. The biological purpose of this unusual physiological condition of human infancy is taken as an indication of man's inherent existential condition of being 'open to the world' ["Weltoffenheit"]. And 'openness to the world' is thus seen as one of man's outstanding attributes: The human being, conceived as a 'premature birth', is coerced into becoming immersed in 'historicality' ["Geschichtlichkeit"], which is thus an inalienable part

---

1 Cf. SCHELER, Max. *Die Stellung des Menschen im Kosmos.* Darmstadt: Reichl, 1930.

2 Cf. HÄBERLIN, Paul. "Anthropologie und Ontologie." *Zeitschrift für Philosophische Forschung* 4 (1949): 6–28; and HÄBERLIN, Paul. *Der Mensch: Eine Philosophische Anthropologie.* Zurich: Spiegel, 1941.

3 [Note: The historical reference frame here is the period from about 1900 to the 1950s. – FKW.]

of man's development as a 'precocial animal'. Biological anthropology argues that it would be impossible for a human being to develop the pivotal features of humanness, if the infant were not nurtured in and assimilated to the given social environment – especially by developing the ability of upright walking, by learning the language and learning to act reasonably and responsibly.[4]

This example has been chosen randomly for illustration of the practices and mode of thinking of biological anthropology. The example shows that biological anthropology obviously relies on findings and includes considerations derived from other branches of anthropology. Yet it seems to me that biological anthropology does not give appropriate attention to significant phenomenological items germane to the nature of man. Thus, such a supreme 'ultimate phenomenon' of humanity like that of 'the spirit' is given only peripheral consideration. It is rather peculiar that the phenomenon of the 'spirit' should have hardly any relevance in the research of biological anthropology. *The 'ultimate phenomenon' of the 'mystical relation' is located entirely outside the thresholds of biological research and is for this reason neither recognized as a new path for the understanding of the spiritual nature of man, nor as a cause for criticism. The only heuristic function that can be attributed to the 'mystical relation' from the perspective of biological anthropology is this one: Since the 'ultimate phenomenon' of the 'mystical relation' is removed from the field of biological anthropology, it may function as a reminder directed at the discipline of biological anthropology that a most significant feature of the essence of man is beyond the reach of biological science.*

2. *Medical anthropology*[5] is a discipline which is from the outset situated in the blurred transition zone between physical and psychic processes. Its aim is to establish a concept of illness based on the anthropological notion of the mind-body unit, which, however,

---

4 Cf. PORTMANN, Adolf. *Biologische Fragmente zu einer Lehre vom Menschen.* 2nd ed. Basle: Schwabe, 1951.

5 Cf. WEIZSÄCKER, Viktor von. *Der Kranke Mensch. Eine Einführung in die Medizinische Anthropologie.* Stuttgart: Koehler, 1951.

cannot be grasped rationally. The research results of medical anthropology are as yet tentative and to some extent provisional. The endeavour to generate ever-more empirical data and analyses to be able to understand medical case histories – notably the intricate phenomena involved in the genesis of psychosomatic and somato-psychic illnesses, as well as the interdependence of psychic and somatic processes and their impact on health and well-being – cannot significantly advance the knowledge about the essence of man. The same is true of enquiries into the potential meaning of illness, or research relating illness to the biography of a subject and similar diagnostic and anamnestic enterprises. But all these empirical enquiries contribute very little to the understanding of the essence of humanity.

But as medicinal anthropology is inevitably co-determined by the laws of therapy, and thus is inevitably linked with the question of healing, i.e., what is understood by a successful and definitive process of healing, metaphysical notions come into view. Hence the therapeutic relevance of 'ultimate phenomena' that belong to the essence of man will have to be given serious consideration. *The widening of the perspectives in medical anthropology is thus imperative and will have to include not only the 'ultimate phenomenon' of the 'spirit', but also that of the 'mystical relation'.*

3. *Anthropological depth-psychology*: Just as depth-psychology has become an independent discipline after having become detached from medicine and the psychology of consciousness and has developed its own methodologies and brought to light a large number of new phenomena, *anthropological depth-psychology* has similarly become a branch of science in its own right. The conception of man upheld by this discipline is particularly open to the 'ultimate phenomenon' of the *'mystical relation'*. In fact, there is a mutual relationship between the 'mystical relation' and the tenets of anthropological depth-psychology: *The 'mystical relation' is relevant for the scope and perspectives of the research undertaken by depth-psychology, and conversely, the research results of this discipline have pivotal relevance for the conception of the 'mystical*

relation' and are, in fact, more relevant than the findings of any other discipline. The implications of this mutual relationship for the understanding of the 'mystical relation' will be considered later. The achievements of depth-psychology have been considerable; an astonishing range of important anthropological phenomena have been revealed, opening up new vistas for understanding the human psyche by elucidating the realm of the unconscious and the sub-conscious. The understanding of the psychological development of the individual has moreover been enriched by incorporating the history of an individual's life, and by exploring individual consciousness and its rootedness in the 'collective unconscious'. Archetypal patterns and formerly inscrutable dynamic psychic processes have been rendered intelligible, and new binary psychic opposites made apparent. All these results are not only illuminating and beneficial to anthropological depth-psychology, but also to the disciplines of psychology and psychotherapy. The 'mystical relation' as such, however, has never been explicitly addressed or identified by any of these disciplines.

The teaching of the 'collective unconscious' by C. G. Jung[6] and his teaching on archetypal images is particularly inspiring and thought-provoking, especially in view of the 'ultimate phenomenon' of the 'mystical relation'. According to Jung, images tend to surface from the unconscious in a person absorbed in 'inward perception', and, at times, images tend to intrude also in the waking consciousness. The visionary images are generally identical with images encountered in mythology. These images are claimed to be 'productions' of the unconscious, and in them an 'archetype' reveals itself. This means that the 'archetype' is not the image itself that has emerged from the unconscious, but the dispositional precondition for an image to surface in the mind. Archetypes are thus the collective potential of the imagination shared by all

---

6   Cf. JUNG, Carl G. *Über die Psychologie des Unbewußten*. 6th ed. Zurich: Rascher, 1943. JUNG, Carl G. *Psychologie und Religion*. Zurich: Rascher, 1940; JUNG, Carl G. *Psychologische Typen*. Parts 3 and 4. Zurich: Rascher, 1925, 587–691; JUNG, Carl G. *Psychologische Betrachtungen*. Zurich: Rascher, 1945, 380–416; and GEBSATTEL, Emil V. Freiherr von. *Christentum und Humanismus*. Stuttgart: Klett, 1947.

human beings to evoke mental images of symbolic import. The images surfacing in the mind are primordial, which means that they are not generated by or based on experiences in the life of a subject but are engrained and 'inherited' from perennial primeval ideas in which the effigies eventually emerge and materialize. The primeval images are received in consciousness; they may, for instance, take the shape of a saviour-figure, a harbinger or a demonic ogre. These pictorial impressions are perceived as an object 'arriving' in the mind. They may have a numinous quality and be experienced as overpowering and may have a transforming impact on the perceiver. One of these primeval archetypes [which can be traced throughout the religious and cultural history of humanity] is the archetype of the Deity ["Gottheit"]. This succinct summary of Jung's concept of 'archetypes' suggests that there seems to be an analogy or affinity between the perception of the 'mystical vision of Christ' or the visionary perception of the 'mystical Presence' in 'inner sight' as conceived in this study, and the Jungian 'archetypal image' of the Deity perceived in 'inner sight'. In other words, there seems to be an apparent analogy between the genuine phenomenon of the 'mystical relation' and the 'relation' perceived when the archetype of the Deity surfaces from the unconscious. *It is a phenomenological fact that there is an empirical relation between the conscious and the unconscious realms of the 'self', which evidently jeopardizes the 'mystical relation' as an independent, self-sufficient 'ultimate phenomenon'.* The claims of Jungian psychoanalysis thus provide a serious option to annulling the claim that the 'mystical relation' is an 'ultimate phenomenon' by reducing it to other psychological phenomena. Attempts to invalidate the 'mystical relation' as a genuine mystical phenomenon will and should be ventured again and again, not least because an 'ultimate phenomenon' can only be verified as genuine if it is repeatedly put to the test and exposed to a barrage of antagonistic approaches. We ourselves have not refrained in our enquiry from subjecting this 'ultimate phenomenon' to harsh critical scrutiny. The approach of Jungian depth-psychology has always been considered a potential threat to the notion of the 'mystical relation', and our considerations have had the arguments and adverse stance of Jung's depth-psychology in mind. We have tried to establish supporting evidence for the potential reductionist claim that the 'mystical relation' is merely an 'archetype'. The evidence has in part been supplied in the earlier study *Psychology of Mystical Consciousness* by delineating the unique phenomenological characteristics of the 'mystical relation' and establishing it as a certain empirical fact by contrasting it to similar phenomena identified in depth-psychology. The phenomenological-gnoseological enquiry carried out in the present study has, moreover, demonstrated persuasively that the 'mystical relation' is a genuine 'ultimate phenomenon', which has as such resisted any attempt to dissolve it by explaining the phenomenon by inner-psychic processes.

Hence, the claim that there is an empirical 'mystical relation' between the 'experiencing self' and the 'mystical It' and the claim of depth-psychology that there is a relation between the individual consciousness and the archetypal image of God are antagonistic and thus doomed to perpetual conflict. Depth-psychology will continuously endeavour to dissolve and eventually extinguish the mystical phenomenon. From the perspective of mysticism, depth-psychology is an intrusion into and violation of a doctrinal system. Thus, depth-psychological anthropology is an explosive wedge to the claim that the 'mystical relation' is a genuine 'ultimate phenomenon'.

4. This concise survey of the research results of various anthropological disciplines is, of course, not meant to be exhaustive; rather, it has been intended as a selective overview of the findings and methodological approaches in this field. The choice of studies has largely been determined by the relevance of the findings of an individual discipline for the concept of the 'mystical relation'. This explains why some seminal anthropological studies, such as the influential contributions by Paul Häberlin[7] and August Vetter's *Natur und Person*,[8] as well as Arnold Gehlen's *Der Mensch*,[9] have not been included in this selective review. Moreover, the

---

7   HÄBERLIN, Paul. *Der Mensch: Eine Philosophische Anthropologie.* Zurich: Spiegel, 1941; and HÄBERLIN, Paul. "Anthropologie und Ontologie." *Zeitschrift für Philosophische Forschung* 4 (1949): 6–28.

8   VETTER, August. *Natur und Person.* Stuttgart: Klett, 1949. Another important study by Vetter is *Die Philosophischen Grundlagen des Menschenbildes.* Leipzig: Klotz, 1942.

9   GEHLEN, Arnold. *Der Mensch. Seine Natur und Stellung in der Welt.* Bonn: Athenäum, 1955.

groundbreaking philosophical contributions to anthropology by Max Scheler[10] would have deserved more detailed commentary but have only been dealt with cursorily.

Max Scheler's main concern was to develop a systematic concept of *philosophical anthropology*. His final objective was to provide a comprehensive concept of the essence of man. Though Häberlin criticised Scheler's philosophical conception of man, claiming that it is impaired by being too heavily rooted in empirical reality, Scheler has significantly advanced philosophical anthropology by introducing new perspectives and categories for defining the essence of man, which have been overlooked by biological anthropology.

The main focus in Scheler's conception of humanity is on the 'ultimate phenomenon' of the 'spirit': It is the 'spirit' by which human beings stand out amongst other creatures, and by which man excels over the *'qualitas'* of the animal. An animal is sufficiently defined by the 'ultimate phenomena' of 'life' and 'soul', including the subservient phenomena of 'drives' and 'instincts' as well as the faculty of associative memory and even 'practical intelligence'. Despite these attributes, animals are confined to a given environment, whereas human beings are not. Humans are in an exceptional manner 'open to the world', owing to the power of the 'spirit'. Thus humans, unlike animals, have the whole world at their disposal. The 'spirit' of man is more than merely self-consciousness; it enables discursive thinking, creative imagination, the ability to perceive the essence of things, and, apart from these faculties of reason, it bestows the faculty of volition and emotional faculties, which are unique to the human species. Social feelings, for instance – like benevolence, love, remorse, or numinous feelings like reverent awe – are special properties of the human spirit. It is by the 'spirit' that a human being becomes, in essence, a 'person'.[11] *If we apply the 'ultimate phenomenon' of the 'mystical relation' to this conception of man as a being rooted in the 'spirit', a*

---

10   SCHELER, Max. *Die Stellung des Menschen im Kosmos*. Darmstadt: Reichl, 1930; and SCHELER, Max. *Vom Ewigen im Menschen*. 4th ed., *Gesammelte Werke*, vol. 5. Berne: Francke, 1954.

11   Cf. SCHELER, Max. *Die Stellung des Menschen im Kosmos*. Darmstadt: Reichl, 1930. 46–47.

new notion of a 'relation' between the individual and the 'spirit' emerges, which is confined to the realm of the individual. In this philosophical conception of man, the relation of the individual to the spirit is inherent and self-sufficient: *This relation is habitual, not embedded in or elicited by an empirical event: The ideational edifice of philosophical anthropology is in itself complete and does not require an orientation directed at a 'mystical relation', or an engagement in reflections as to whether the 'mystical relation' could potentially be an 'ultimate phenomenon'.* The 'mystical relation' has no relevance in the system of philosophical anthropology and appears to have been sidestepped altogether. *A critical response to the deliberate exclusion, a priori, of the notion of the 'mystical relation' from the domain of philosophical enquiry can only be provoked if the new mystical phenomenon can be shown to be a pivotal component of the nature of man.* It is not possible to ignore or overlook an 'ultimate phenomenon' for long. When a new 'ultimate phenomenon' is faced by science, it is likely to be dealt with sceptically, by questioning or refuting the real existence of the 'mystical relation'; a negative response, however, cannot erode the realness of the 'mystical relation', since, being an 'ultimate phenomenon', it will continue to surface in the history of humanity. It is the aim of the following sections to show that the 'mystical relation' cannot be dismissed as a speculative notion impinged on a spiritually biased conception of man, and to substantiate the claim that the 'mystical relation' is a unique distinctive feature of humanity grounded in empirical reality.

5. The discipline of *phenomenological anthropology* is aptly represented by the studies of *Ludwig Binswanger*. He has advanced anthropology to its full scientific potential and enabled it to become an independent albeit interdisciplinary branch of science, which is rooted in psychological sociology and in the fundamental ontology of *Martin Heidegger*. The claim that phenomenological anthropology is an autonomous discipline can be corroborated by two persuasive arguments: First, the studies of Binswanger do not only provide an inventory of psychological-sociological facts but establish anthropological foundations for psychological-sociological facts. It was Binswanger's endeavour to provide a systematic inventory that encompasses all individual manifestations

of being human. Second, the focus of Binswanger's studies is clearly anthropological rather than philosophical, despite his indebtedness to Heidegger's existential philosophy. His focus is not, like Heidegger's, on ontological issues. Heidegger's endeavour is to expound a 'hermeneutics of Dasein', i.e., hermeneutics of 'being-in-this-world', which is inevitably related to 'being as such', i.e., 'being' conceived as the ultimate ontological foundation of "Dasein". Binswanger, however, is, unlike Heidegger, both a phenomenologist and an anthropologist; therefore his main effort is to analyse and describe phenomenologically the fundamental forms of *being human* rather than to reflect on the ontological foundations of human existence.

After these introductory remarks, we may return to the main concern of this chapter, an exploration of the anthropological relevance of the 'mystical relation'. One potential answer to this question is provided by Binswanger's phenomenological anthropology, and we shall briefly try to summarize and assess it from different viewpoints.

As stated above, Binswanger's anthropology incorporates ideas from Heidegger's fundamental ontology. He developed, however, some of Heidegger's concepts further. Thus, he adopted Heidegger's concept of 'care'[12] ["Sorge"], meaning the inherent condition of man while 'being-in-the-world', and expanded the concept by applying it to both the act of procuring something and to man's caring relationship with fellow human beings.

As a phenomenological anthropologist, Binswanger is especially interested in the 'ultimate phenomenon' of love, which he juxtaposes to the 'ultimate phenomenon' of 'care'. He insists, however, that love is an entirely self-sufficient, independent phenomenon that can never be inferred or developed from the phenomenon of 'care'. The two phenomena, though independent entities, are nonetheless

---

12 [Note: In the English translations of Heidegger's works, the word "Sorge" is translated as 'care', although the German word denotes both 'care', meaning 'being concerned for the well-being of someone', and 'sorrow', feeling oppressed by grief, sadness, or worry. Cf. DAHLSTROM, Daniel O. *The Heidegger Dictionary*. London: Bloomsbury, 2013. – FKW.]

intertwined. For Binswanger, the essence of mankind is perennially determined by these two phenomena. In human existence the structure of love usually coexists simultaneously with the structure of care. But in individual situations of human existence it may happen that either 'care' or 'love' prevails, or that one or the other existential phenomenon is entirely missing. Hence it is possible to 'care' for someone without love; the behavioural pattern of being together with another human being without love is exclusively determined by 'care', while the emotional pattern of love is suspended at the time; conversely, the existential situation of being *together* in loving communion with a beloved person is obviously exclusively determined by love. And in true friendship, love and 'care' are ideally balanced.

Binswanger's achievement in highlighting the paramount anthropological significance of the 'ultimate phenomenon' of love and the essence of man can hardly be overrated. Yet it also has limitations, since his systematic analysis is strictly confined to the secularized viewpoint of anthropology. Any relation of love to a theological or metaphysical concept is excluded from his theoretical approach. Love as an 'ultimate phenomenon' of love is consequently attributed a neutral and isolated function in human existence. Though what Binswanger says about the phenomenon of love and the social pattern of 'we-hood' ["Wirheit"] created by it is apt and sensible, I cannot quite agree with the whole concept of anthropology proposed by him, which is essentially based on the intertwining functions of love and 'care'. He tends to give love superior significance over 'care', albeit not in terms of evaluation but in terms of its anthropological import. This stance implies that there is still a problematic situation that remains to be solved. This problem results partly from Binswanger's strictly secularized notion of love, and partly from his claim that love is inevitably intertwined with 'care'. This means that in Binswanger's anthropology, love is not attributed a special anthropological rank, as he does not place love in any hierarchical value system.

These considerations allow us to draw some significant conclusions: First, *the insight that a newly disclosed 'ultimate phenomenon' cannot arbitrarily be impinged on an established anthropological framework, like an attachment, as it were*. Since Binswanger's attempt has failed to incorporate satisfactorily the 'ultimate phenomenon' of love into the structural pattern of 'care', it can be claimed to be even more unlikely that the 'ultimate phenomenon' of the 'mystical relation' can be incorporated into, let alone harmonized with, any of the existing notions of anthropology. This much is certain: all the schemes of *anthropology* deriving from Heidegger's ontological analysis of "Dasein", and which are therefore based on the notion of 'care', are incapable of embracing the 'ultimate phenomenon' of the 'mystical relation'. The attempt to integrate love as an 'ultimate phenomenon', i.e., as an independent quality of human existence, and thus a human capacity that is not derived from the 'ultimate phenomenon' of 'care', has (I would contend) obviously overtaxed the basic assumptions of anthropology. Any further attempt to harmonize love within the given secular anthropological framework is inevitably bound to destroy them. Of course, anthropologists might object at this point that the 'mystical relation' is merely an offspring of theological thinking and therefore has no place in a secular, ideologically neutral scientific discipline. This objection, however, is flawed because the premise on which it is grounded is false: *The 'mystical relation' is not an offspring of theological thinking but an 'ultimate phenomenon' (one amongst several 'ultimate phenomena', like 'spirit' or 'love') that are inexorably part of empirical reality.* The term 'ultimate phenomenon' would not be justified if it referred merely to an abstract notion derived from theology. The term 'ultimate phenomenon' is, moreover, exclusively used to refer to a phenomenon identified by scientific rational analysis. *The 'mystical relation', however, has not only been established as an 'ultimate phenomenon' by scientific thinking, but is also grounded in 'experience', and in this sense it is a 'positivistic' concept.*

This brief survey of anthropological approaches to defining the essence of man has shown that *the 'mystical relation' is a unique phenomenon of man and thus eminently relevant for anthropology. As such it is not only a constant challenge but also an inevitable focal point for future research; the 'mystical relation' is not just a forgotten feature of humanity that demands to be retrieved and given proper attention, nor is it merely an antithesis to secular science, inciting strife, nor a divisive test for seasoned concepts of anthropology, but the 'mystical relation' provokes, most importantly, the fundamental question as to whether anthropology should not start its enquiry from it in the first place, and acknowledge the 'mystical relation' as an 'ultimate phenomenon' and as its ultimate fundament.*

Hermeneutics of "Dasein"

Our excursion into various areas of anthropology has ended in the realm of ontology, more specifically in the realm of Heidegger's existential philosophy. We have gained an insight (albeit a rather cursory one) into Heidegger's concepts of 'being' ["Sein"] and 'being-in-the-world' ["Dasein"], at which contemporary anthropology is directed. This does not come as a surprise if we consider that what Heidegger understands by "Dasein überhaupt", i.e., 'being-here-as-such', refers to the essence of the human condition in this world. 'Being-in-this-world' is the 'exemplary ground' ["exemplarische Grund"] in which any phenomenological enquiry into the condition of man is rooted. The structures of the essence of "Dasein" are the basis for the possibility of identifying seminal anthropological patterns.

The considerations above have touched upon Heidegger's analysis of "Dasein" and outlined some of the tenets of Binswanger's phenomenological anthropology. In retrospect, these considerations on both Binswanger and Heidegger need some further clarification, as we are now going to cross the thresholds of anthropology and enter the realm of Heidegger's 'hermeneutics of being'. Though Binswanger will continue to occupy us in the present chapter, not least because he was formatively influenced by Heidegger's fundamental ontology, the main focus will be on the philosophy of Heidegger. It was owing to Heidegger's influence that Binswanger expanded the discipline of anthropology beyond its frontiers into the domain of ontology.

What we need to clarify first is Heidegger's concept of "Dasein" and Binswanger's concept of "Wirheit" ['we-hood'].

To begin with, *the pivotal question to be asked at this juncture is: What is the relevance of the 'mystical relation' for a 'hermeneutics of being'?* In order to be able to answer this question, some *preliminary considerations from three different perspectives* are required: First, it is indispensable to define the concepts coined by Heidegger and used throughout his works and in his hermeneutical analysis of "Dasein" in particular. Second, we shall try to delineate Binswanger's notion of 'loving we-hood' and consider its *ontological* implications. Third, we will try to disclose the changes caused to the concept of "Dasein" when the 'ultimate phenomenon' of love is impinged on it.

When disparate ontological structures clash (i.e., the structure of 'care' clashing with the structure of 'love'), the impact has obvious repercussions on each of the structures involved. Binswanger imposed the notion of 'love' onto Heidegger's conception of "Dasein"; the consequences of this imposition demonstrate by way of analogy what is likely to happen if the 'ultimate phenomenon' of the 'mystical relation' is imposed on the received concept of fundamental ontology.

I. On the Terminology of Heidegger:[13]

Heidegger distinguishes, first and foremost, between the terms "*Seiendes*" ['entity', that which is] and "*Sein*" ['Being']. The former term refers to everything that is part of this world, i.e., whatever can be named individually, hence everything 'that we can talk about, everything we have in view, everything towards which we comport ourselves in any way, is being ...' (26). "*Sein*" ['Being'] 'is what determines the being of entities ...' (26). 'Being is always the Being of an entity' (29). However, "*Sein*" as such is not something like 'a thing that is'. And because the 'Being' ["Sein"] of the 'thing that is' ["des Seienden"] is not itself a 'thing that is', it is impossible to define the concept of 'Being': "Der Begriff des 'Seins' ist vielmehr der dunkelste." [3] 'So if it is said that 'Being' is the most universal concept, this cannot mean that it is the one that is clearest ... It is rather the darkest of all' (23).

The term "*Dasein*" [i.e., 'This entity which each of us is himself and which includes inquiring as one of the possibilities of its Being, we shall denote by the term "Dasein" (27)] must not be equated with 'the thing that is', because not every 'thing that is' can be subsumed under the concept of "Dasein". "Dasein" is an *ontological* term that is exclusively applied to a human being which can alone

---

13 Cf. HEIDEGGER, Martin. *Sein und Zeit*. 2nd ed. Halle a.d. Saale: Niemeyer, 1929. [Note: All page references to the German terms and quotations are to this edition and indicated in square brackets. – The passages quoted in English have been taken from the English edition of *Being and Time*. Trans. John Macquarrie and Edward Robinson. Oxford: Blackwell, 1962. All page references given in round brackets. – FKW.]

relate to 'Being'. Thus "*Dasein ist Seiendes, das sich in seinem Sein verstehend zu diesem Sein verhält.*" [53]. [This means, 'Dasein is an entity which does not just occur among other entities. Rather, it is ontically distinguished by the fact that, in its very Being, that Being is an issue for it. But in that case, this is a constitutive state of Dasein's Being, and this implies that Dasein, in its Being, has a relationship towards that Being – a relationship which itself is one of Being' (32)]. It is a primeval phenomenological fact that the 'being' of "Dasein" includes that "Dasein" is inevitably disclosed to the individual rooted in 'Being', and it is this pre-ordained structure of 'Being' that makes the venture of a hermeneutics of "Dasein" possible in the first place. The *'disclosedness'* [*"Erschlossenheit"*] of "Dasein" is a necessary condition for the possibility of understanding "Dasein". ['Understanding of Being is itself a definite characteristic of Dasein's Being. Dasein is ontically distinctive in that it is ontological' (32)]. The second way of defining the essence of "Dasein" can be expressed in this way: "Das 'Wesen' des Daseins liegt in seiner Existenz." [42], i.e., *'the essence of Dasein lies in its existence.* Accordingly, those characteristics which can be exhibited in this entity are not 'properties' present-at-hand of some entity which 'looks' so and so and is itself present-at-hand; they are in each case possible ways for it to be, and no more than that. All the Being-as-it-is ["So-sein"] which this entity possesses is primarily Being. So when we designate this entity with the term "Dasein", we are expressing not its 'what' (as if it were a table, house or tree) but its Being' (67). The third way of defining the concept of "Dasein" as stated by Heidegger is: "Das Sein, darum es diesem Seienden in seinem Sein geht, ist je meines ... Dasein ist je seine Möglichkeit." [42]. 'We are ourselves the entities to be analysed. The Being of any such entity *is in each case mine.* These entities, in their Being, comport themselves towards their Being ... in each case Dasein is mine to be in one way or another. "Dasein" has always made some sort of decision as to the way in which it is in each case mine. That entity, which in its Being has this very Being as an issue, comports itself towards its Being as its ownmost possibility. In each case "Dasein" is its possibility, and it 'has' this possibility, but not just as a property, as something present-at-hand would. And because "Dasein" is in each case essentially its own possibility, it can, in its very Being, 'choose' itself and win itself; it can also lose itself and never win itself; or only 'seem' to do so. But only insofar as it is essentially something which can be authentic – that is, something of its own – can it have lost itself and not yet won itself. As modes of Being, authenticity and inauthenticity ... are both grounded in the fact that any "Dasein" whatsoever is characterized by mine-ness' (68).

Another important ontological term is "Existential" [i.e., 'existential']. The term refers to the basic structures shared by every human being's way of living. Heidegger distinguishes three major 'existentials': first, the facticity that every human being is 'thrown into the world'; second, the fact that human existence is 'being-toward-death', and therefore is always directed toward the future; and, third, the existential of 'discourse', which means that every individual addresses the entities that show up in situations determined by 'care'. These three existentials define, according to Heidegger, human existence as a temporal unfolding.[14] The term 'category' is applied to 'things in this world' that are merely objects that are "vorhanden", i.e., are just present in this world but do not 'exist', since they are no items of "Dasein". A distinctive existential characteristic of "Dasein" is thus *'being-in-the-world'*. This does not mean that in Heidegger's thinking the separate phenomenological entities of 'the world' and of "Dasein" have been intertwined, but rather that Heidegger does not start from the conventional division of 'Being' between the 'I' and 'the world', but he goes further back to the primordial phenomenological notion of 'Being' epitomized in the claim: "Dasein" *is* 'being-in-the-world'. The term 'world' refers (according to Binswanger) to 'a structural moment of 'being-in-the-world.' "[15] Thus 'the world' is ontologically 'not a definition of the totality of what is 'in-the-world', or of what "Dasein" is *not* in essence, but 'the world' is rather a characteristic of "Dasein" itself' (64). Heidegger substitutes Binswanger's concept of 'the world' with the *term "Weltlichkeit"* ('worldliness'; 'worldhood'), which is an ontological concept referring to the structure of a constitutive moment of 'being-in-the-world'. This corresponds to Heidegger's notion of "Dasein" conceived as an 'existential'. 'Worldliness', in other words, is thus itself an 'existential'. But Heidegger not only applies *the term 'world'* to 'worldliness'; in addition, he sometimes uses it to signify ontically (not ontologically) the place *'in which'* "Dasein" 'lives' as a given fact. This means that the term 'world', as used in the latter sense, has a pre-ontological existential significance. The 'world' that is most intimately involved in man's "Dasein" in everyday life is the *'environment'*, i.e., the world around us (*"Umwelt"*): "Die nächste Welt des alltäglichen Daseins ist die Umwelt." [66]

---

14 [Note: Cf. AUDI, Robert, gen. ed. *The Cambridge Dictionary of Philosophy*. 2nd ed. Cambridge: CUP, 1999. 370–73. – FKW.]

15 Cf. BINSWANGER, Ludwig. *Grundformen und Erkenntnis Menschlichen Daseins*. 2nd ed. Zurich: Niehans, 1953. 32. [Note: All translations from Binswanger have been provided. – FKW.]

I wish to emphasize once again: The term 'existential' ["Existential"] is an ontological concept. It refers to the fact that 'being' has the capacity of 'being-in-the-world'; the term thus refers to a mode of 'being' represented by "Dasein", which, however, does not denote a mode of human behaviour encountered in empirical reality, but is to be understood in a purely ontological sense, in that "Dasein" as 'being-in-the-world' is an existential situation that is enabled only by the antecedent capacity of 'Being'. The 'existentials' specified by Heidegger include, apart from 'worldliness' and 'being-in-this-world', 'being-alongside-with' [other human beings, creatures and objects of creation], 'being-in-care' [for someone or something], 'being-together-with' [someone]; and further, "Befindlichkeit", i.e., the [emotional, mental, spiritual] state one is in, and "Verstehen", i.e., understanding and "das Verfallen" [i.e., lapsing into an inferior condition or state; 'degenerating', 'withering away']. These terms, however, must not be misunderstood in psychological terms, since they signify exclusively ontic qualities of "Dasein".

The term *"Faktizität"*, i.e., *facticity*, "... implies that an entity 'within the world' has 'being-in-the-world' in such a way that it can understand itself as bound up in its 'destiny' with the being of those entities which it encounters within its own world."[16] As such, 'facticity' is juxtaposed to the categorical concept of "Vorhandensein", i.e., 'just being there', 'being at hand', 'being available'. 'Facticity' thus denotes the 'factuality that one's own "Dasein" is a given fact', which is, in Heidegger's words, "... die Tatsächlichkeit der Tatsache des eigenen Daseins" (56). The facticity of "Dasein" is, however, 'dispersed' or 'split up' in some way or other, owing to "Dasein's" 'being-in-the-world'. The modes of 'being-in-the-world' are *dominated by the existential situation of 'being-in-a-state of-care'*. In this state, objects encountered and known 'to be at hand' (*"zuhanden"*) provide a means ('*tools*') for coping with and/or overcoming the state of 'care'. Second, *the modes of 'being-in-the-world' are inevitably states of 'being-together-with'* someone, which is actually the essence of "Dasein". 'Being-together-with' is thus another 'existential'. "By reason of this with-like ['*mithaften*'] Being-in-the-world, the world is always the one that I share with Others."[17] "... [T]hose entities towards which Dasein as Being-

---

16 [Note: INWOOD, Michael. *A Heidegger Dictionary*. Oxford: Blackwell, 1999. 218. – FKW.]

17 [Note: Quoted from the English translation of Heidegger's *Sein und Zeit*: *Being and Time*. Trans. John Macquarrie and Edward Robinson. Oxford: Blackwell, 1962. 155.

with comports itself do not have the kind of Being which belongs to equipment ready-to-hand; they are themselves Dasein. These entities are not objects of concern, but rather of *solicitude*."[18] This means that taking care of others or being concerned about something and 'being-together-with' someone, are all 'existentials'. Hence "Dasein" is essentially composed of 'existentials' of this kind; they are the pivotal components of 'being-in-the-world'.

Heidegger's analysis of human existence has resulted in numerous 'existentials', which in their totality are structural components of "Dasein". The structure of "Dasein" as entirely dominated by 'care' is epitomized by Heidegger in the famous formula: "Ahead-of-itself-Being-already-in (a world) as 'Being-alongside' (entities encountered within-the-world)."[19] In this formula the fundamental characteristics of "Dasein" are highlighted: The expression "ahead-of-itself" refers to existence, the phrase 'being-already-in' to the facticity [of man's "Dasein" in this world], and the formulation 'Being-alongside-with' denotes the inevitable process of decline to which man is exposed [since every human being is a 'being-unto-death']. This demonstrates that the whole of human existence is imbued with 'care' ["Sorge"]. 'Care' is a pivotal term in Heidegger's fundamental ontology, which [like the various 'existentials'] must be shielded from facile psychological interpretation. 'Care' is not a basic mood or an emotional state amongst other emotional conditions, but is rather a crucial *ontological concept denoting the human condition in "Dasein"* – of man's 'being-in-the-world'.

As stated earlier: To the condition of "Dasein" belongs essentially its state of 'disclosedness' ["Erschlossenheit"], i.e., the awareness of the gradual

---

The passage as quoted by Albrecht (343) is: "Auf dem Grunde dieses *mithaften* In-der-Welt-Seins ist die Welt je schon immer die, die ich mit anderen teile. (118)". – FKW.]

18 [Note: HEIDEGGER, Martin. *Sein und Zeit: Being and Time.* Trans. John Macquarrie and Edward Robinson. Oxford: Blackwell, 1962. 157. The quotation in Albrecht (343) reads: "Das Seiende, zu dem sich das Dasein als Mitsein verhält, hat aber nicht die Seinsart des zuhandenen Zeugs, es ist selbst Dasein. Dieses Seiende wird nicht besorgt, sondern steht in der *Fürsorge.* (121)" – FKW.]

19 [Note: HEIDEGGER, Martin. *Sein und Zeit: Being and Time.* Trans. John Macquarrie and Edward Robinson. Oxford: Blackwell, 1962. 364. The quotation in Albrecht (343) reads: "Sich-vorweg-schon-sein-in (der Welt) als Sein-bei (innerweltlich) begegnendem Seienden." (249) – FKW.]

'disclosure' of "Dasein" while 'being in this world'.[20] There are several ways in which "Dasein" can disclose itself, i.e., to 'lay itself open' to human existence: One is by way of '[intuitive] understanding', another by a particular 'state of mind' [*"Befindlichkeit"*]. The term 'state of mind' is not an ontic concept but an ontological term; it denotes a 'fundamental existential' ["fundamentales Existential", 134], i.e., a phenomenon rooted in human existence. "In having a mood, Dasein is always disclosed moodwise as that entity to which it has been delivered over in its Being; and in this way it has been delivered over to the Being which, in existing, it has to be" (173).[21] And the "... characteristic of Dasein's Being-this 'that it is' – is veiled in its "whence" and "whither", yet disclosed in itself all the more unveiledly; we call it the "thrownness" of this entity into its "there"; indeed, it is thrown in such a way that, as Being-in-the-world, it is the "there" (174). *The term 'thrownness'* "... is meant to suggest *the facticity of its being delivered over*" (174). It denotes a quality of 'Dasein'; ..."the fact that it 'it-is', which is disclosed in Dasein's state-of-mind, must rather be conceived as an existential attribute of the entity which has Being-in-the-world as its way of Being. *Facticity is not the factuality of the factum brutum of something present-at-hand, but a characteristic of Dasein's Being-one which has been taken up into existence, even if proximally it has been thrust aside.* The 'that-it-is' of facticity never becomes something that we can come across by beholding it" (174). The cognitive state of mind, however, by which 'Dasein' is most clearly disclosed is the state of *"angst"*. "The basic *state-of-mind of anxiety* as ... a distinctive way in which 'Dasein' is disclosed" (228). "So if the 'nothing' – that is, the world as such – exhibits itself as that in the face of which one has anxiety, this means that Being-in-the-world itself is that in the face of which anxiety is anxious" (232).

II. In the section above we have tried to provide a concise summary of Heidegger's hermeneutics of "Dasein". What needs to be added are a few important concepts and phenomena that are part

---

20 [Note: Cf. HEIDEGGER, Martin. *Sein und Zeit: Being and Time*. Trans. John Macquarrie and Edward Robinson. Oxford: Blackwell, 1962. 171. – FKW.]
21 [Note: Quoted from the English translation of Heidegger's *Sein und Zeit: Being and Time*. Trans. John Macquarrie and Edward Robinson. Oxford: Blackwell, 1962. 173. The quotation in Albrecht (344) reads: "In der Gestimmtheit ist immer schon stimmungsmäßig das Dasein als *das* Seiende erschlossen, dem das Dasein in seinem Sein überantwortet wurde als dem Sein, das es existierend zu sein hat." (134) – FKW.]

of Heidegger's conception of "Dasein". This includes the phenomenon of 'temporality' ["Zeitlichkeit"] by which "Dasein" is endowed with meaning; moreover, the existential concept of 'death', and thus the condition of man as 'being-unto-death', as well as the existential interpretation of 'conscience' ["Gewissen"] and the phenomenon of 'prevenient determination' ["vorauslaufende Entschlossenheit"], have not been elaborated on. However, these outlines of Heidegger's hermeneutics of "Dasein" are sufficient as an introduction to the subsequent considerations of Binswanger's ontological concerns and critical reflections on Heidegger.[22] Binswanger's *concept of love* is, like Heidegger's concept of 'care', not to be understood psychologically, for the primary meaning of the term is *ontological*: love denotes a universal *anthropological* phenomenon and as such is a vital 'existential' ["Existential"] of human "Dasein":

'Love' [according to Binswanger] is, phenomenologically – like the phenomenon of 'care' – an autonomous mode of being of 'Dasein'. Thus 'love' cannot be interpreted ontologically on the basis of 'Dasein's' structure of 'care' (55). 'Dasein' is inherently and perennially rooted in a loving encounter. The structural existential element of 'love' is, however, not something that can be inferred from a person's relationship to other human beings in 'Dasein', for instance as response to the situation of 'care', both for themselves and for fellow human beings, but 'love' is rather understood as a primordial ontological phenomenon by which 'Dasein' is imbued; hence it is a distinctive feature of 'Dasein' that eludes any further rational explanation (83–84).

For Binswanger, 'love' is the source of 'loving we-hood' ["liebende Wirheit"], *'enabling mutual togetherness'* ["Einräumung des Einander"]. 'Love' is an ontological verity, which 'encloses' 'Dasein' perennially and primordially, and thus love does not result from any detour via an encounter with the world or the self; 'being together' enfolded in love is an ontological facticity (29). "Ontologically, 'love' is not a phenomenon by which two independent individuals are bound together ... but 'love' is the prevenient openness of 'Dasein' for 'oneness', 'wholeness', or (if you wish) for the ur-condition of 'we-hood'" (30).

'Love' has a unique structure of temporality. 'Love' reaches out into

---

22 BINSWANGER, Ludwig. *Grundformen und Erkenntnis Menschlichen Daseins*. 2nd ed. Zurich: Niehans, 1953. [Note: all references are to this edition; English translations provided. – FKW.]

eternality ["Ewigung"]. 'The term *eternality* of 'love' means nothing else but being 'in this world' as being truly rooted in the essence of 'Dasein', which is 'we-hood' and 'encounter' (176). These qualifications endorse the difference between Binswanger's and Heidegger's conception of 'being-in-the-world' by highlighting *the fact that the structure of 'Dasein' determined wholly by love is something entirely different from the structure of 'Dasein' determined throughout by the phenomenon of 'care' alone.* To Heidegger's existential formula of 'Dasein' – couched in the terms quoted above ("Ahead-of-itself-Being-already-in [a world] as 'Being-alongside' [entities encountered within-the-world]") – Binswanger thus juxtaposes the structural formula of 'love': *Being together* (the two of us) in this world, as primordially immersed in ['love'], as beings *'being together'* in this world (which is equal to: being joined in Being)' (88–89).

III. At this stage of our considerations, a very significant fact becomes apparent: Binswanger's endeavour to consider the 'ultimate phenomenon' of love as an ontological entity had inevitable repercussions on Heidegger's conception of "Dasein" and even jeopardized its homogeneity and coherence. Binswanger was aware of the discrepancy between Heidegger's and his own conception of "Dasein" and the nature of human existence, which is clearly reflected in his writings:

"As it is impossible to substitute a single structural component within the oint of view conflicts entirely with Heidegger's ontological notion of 'being-in-the-world'. Though it is true that we likewise understand 'being-in-the-world' as a mode of being in which 'Dasein' is concerned *with itself*, the crucial point, however, is that we regard the 'self' not only as a factuality of the 'I-self' of 'Dasein', i.e., we think of it in terms of my own, your own, his own etc., but we also consider it in terms of the potential options of the 'we-self', which precede ontologically the individual 'self'; thus 'Dasein' is understood to be primordially 'ours', rooted in an ur-encounter ["Ur-Begegnung"]. This, however, means inevitably that the mode of man's 'being-in-this-world' determined by 'care', must be transcended by the mode of 'being-at-home-in-the-world' sustained by love." (Binswanger 101)

It is easy to recognize the methodological consequences that Binswanger's ontological conception of 'love' as an 'ultimate phenomenon' have on the progress of our quest for the 'ultimate phenomenon' of the 'mystical relation'. I will demonstrate this by classifying the individual elements [pertaining to the 'ultimate phenomenon' of 'love'] identified by Binswanger into three groups: The first group endorses the claim that the ontological structure of 'love' prevails over the ontological structure of 'care'. The second group is concerned with the problem of 'transcendence', and the third group refers to the relationship of 'Dasein' to its ultimate 'Ground'. We shall deal with each of these issues individually and reflect on them critically:

1. *The claim that the structure of 'being-in-this-world' determined by 'love' is superior to the structure of 'being-in-this-world' determined by 'care'*: 'Love' is a unique mode of being that is not merely juxtaposed to the mode of existence determined by 'care' – for instance, 'being-in-the-world' does not just involve caring for someone, or being together with other human beings, but offers also the possibility for loving encounters; thus the individual state of 'being' is placed next to the state of 'we-hood' in "Dasein", which may be coupled with 'love'; 'Love', however, is more than this: "Love must be understood as an inalienable principle of human existence in which 'being-in-the-world' determined by 'care' is overcome" (266) and elevated. "'Dasein' is in its ultimate ground of Being ... oneness, unity ... 'below' and 'above' the possibility of 'being-in-this-world' for some moments in the history of the world, there is the possibility of abiding in the 'eternity' of the moment of 'love'" (151). But this exalted view of 'love' does not mean that the existential structure of 'care' is extinguished by the existential structure of 'love': " 'Love' *is* only *there* jointly with 'care', or, to put it differently, "Dasein" can only be there as *an infinite entity, if it is finite*" (147). "Human 'Dasein' can only 'be', if it is constantly exposed to the *strife* between 'love' and 'care'" (482).

The critical question that needs to be asked at this point is: Is the asserted ontological primacy of 'love' over 'care' indeed valid? Does this not claim a veiled axiological statement – namely, the value judgement that 'love' is superior to 'care'? What can be said in response is, first, that 'love' is undoubtedly an established 'ultimate phenomenon' and as such an ontological fact, and second, that 'love' as an 'ultimate phenomenon' cannot be inferred from the existential structure of 'care'. However, these two facts do not sufficiently corroborate the claim that 'love' has *ontological* primacy over 'care'.

2. *'Dasein' conceived as 'being together' ('we-hood') transcends the horizon of 'being-in-the-world'.* The term 'transcendence' is not, in this context, to be understood as an epistemological concept, nor as understood by Jaspers, but is used in the sense as defined by Heidegger. In Heidegger's existentialist philosophy, "Dasein" is conceived as a state of 'being outside' [Being]. This means that 'being-in-the-world' is understood as an ongoing process by which "Dasein" is transcended.[23] But "Dasein" as 'we-hood' is not merely transcendence in the sense of 'being-in-the-world'. The structure of 'love' transcends, over and beyond this, the transcendence operating in the existential structure of 'care':[24]

> Since 'Dasein' *is* infinity and eternity and 'we-hood', "'Dasein' is *'being-in-this-world and beyond-this-world'* (136). "Transcendence as 'love' surpasses not only the current situation [in this world], but also the 'mineness' [the awareness of being mine] of 'Dasein'" (155). "In the process of transcendence, which is a pure act of going beyond, the trans-temporality or eternity of 'Dasein' becomes manifest in *exuberance*" (156). "The pure act of going beyond, of transcending, conceived as a movement of love, cannot plainly be dismissed as a 'mere fantasy' or illusion originating from 'care', because it is 'Dasein' itself that *responds* to it. An essential feature of the exuberance of 'love' is the *self*-transcendence of 'Dasein' in 'we-hood'..., i.e., the encounter with and self-response of 'Dasein' ... which becomes manifest in *being-lovingly-together*" (159). [Heidegger] furthermore adds a sentence which is of paramount significance for mysticism: "In this situation 'Dasein' is not experienced as finite from the perspective

---

23 Cf. HEIDEGGER, Martin. "Vom Wesen des Grundes." *Festschrift für Edmund Husserl*. Halle an der Saale: Niemeyer, 1929. 71–110. [Note: Albrecht does not provide any page references to the passages quoted. – FKW.]

24 [Note: In the following two paragraphs, printed in a smaller font, Albrecht summarizes passages from the writings of Heidegger, albeit without indicating the actual source(s). The page numbers given by Albrecht do not coincide with the page numbers in Heidegger's "Vom Wesen des Grundes" printed in the Husserl festschrift, which is referred to in Albrecht's bibliography. – FKW.]

of a transcendent Thou, but 'Dasein' is experiencing *itself*, conscious of its finiteness, as being an entity that is 'infinitely' transcending" (385).

The phrase 'going beyond' is meant ontologically, i.e., as an instance in which the disclosedness of 'Dasein' determined by 'care', is *overcome* by a *transcendent disclosedness*" (100).

These philosophical reflections undeniably have ontological import. *The structure of 'we-hood' clearly reveals phenomenologically that 'Dasein' is open*: 'Dasein' does not only transcend by means of the process of 'being-in-the-world', but also transcends by its very condition of 'openness' the state of 'being-in-the-world'. This verity, however, does not deter us from asking the critical question: *Is that which becomes manifest phenomenologically in the structure of love, indeed Love itself?* Could it not be – like in the phenomenon of 'fear', of which the underlying primordial state is 'angst', though 'angst' becomes first apparent as 'fear' and turns out to be in fact rooted in 'angst' only later – that in the phenomenon of 'love' an ontological 'openness' of 'Dasein' might become apparent that perennially precedes the 'openness' of 'love'? Could it not be that the 'openness' of 'love' for 'we-hood' is only an existential mode of this primordial 'openness'? Or might it perhaps be possible that the 'openness' of 'love' for 'we-hood' is not even an existential mode at all, but merely an ontic existential way of living that is grounded in existential 'openness'?

3. *The problem of 'being' rooted in, and destined for, the 'Ground'*: The elementary situation of man while 'being-in-the-world' is ontologically a mode of existential 'disclosedness' ["Erschlossenheit"]. In it the primary quality of 'Dasein' comes to the fore, which is termed *"Geworfenheit"* [i.e., 'thrownness'] by Heidegger. By 'thrownness', Heidegger understands the fact that man's 'being-in-this-world' is the result of having been 'thrown' into 'being here': "The expression 'thrownness' is meant to suggest the facticity of its being delivered over. The 'that it is and has to be' which is disclosed in Dasein's state-of-mind is not the same 'that-it-is' which expresses ontologico-categorially the factuality belonging to presence-at-hand. This factuality becomes accessible only if we ascertain it by looking at it. The 'that-it-is' which is disclosed in Dasein's state-of-mind must rather be conceived

as an existential attribute of the entity which has Being-in-the-world as its way of Being. Facticity is not the factuality of the *factum brutum* of something present-at-hand, but a characteristic of Dasein's Being-one which has been taken up into existence, even if proximally it has been thrust aside. The 'that-it-is' of facticity never becomes something that we can come across by beholding it."[25]

According to Heidegger, 'angst' is an *exceptional* mood. 'Angst' is, in fact, the fundamental frame of mind. The unique quality of 'angst' derives from the fact that, in it, the pure form of the 'ultimate phenomenon' of 'thrownness' is disclosed primordially. Thus "anxiety ['angst']"[26] is not only *afraid of the prospect of* 'being-in-the-world' but also *of* actually 'being-in-the-world'. In 'angst' the uncanniness of the facticity of 'Dasein' becomes apparent: In the state of 'anxiety' ['angst'] one feels 'uncanny'. Here the peculiar indefiniteness of that which Dasein finds itself alongside in anxiety ['angst'], comes proximally to expression: the "nothing and nowhere". But here 'uncanniness' also means 'not-being-at-home' ["das Nichtzuhause-sein"]. In our first indication of the phenomenal character of Dasein's basic state and in our clarification of the existential meaning of 'Being-in' as distinguished from the categorial signification of 'insideness', 'Being-in' was defined as 'residing alongside' ... This character of 'Being-in' was then brought to view more concretely through the everyday publicness of the 'they', which brings tranquillized self-assurance – 'Being-at-home', with all its obviousness – into the average everydayness of Dasein. On the other hand, as Dasein falls, anxiety ['angst'] brings it back from its absorption in the 'world'. Everyday familiarity collapses. Dasein has become individualized, albeit individualized in

---

25 [HEIDEGGER, Martin. *Being and Time*. Trans. John Macquarrie and Edward Robinson. Oxford: Blackwell, 1962. 174. – FKW.]

26 [Note: Heidegger's English translators render the German term "Angst" as 'anxiety', which is, however, inaccurate, since the German term refers to a persevering basic mood of human existence, not just to a temporary feeling of 'anxiety'; this aside, 'angst' has become an established loan-word in English (albeit spelt in lower case), whose meaning corresponds more closely to Heidegger's usage of the word than 'anxiety'. – FKW.]

the sense of 'being-inthe-world'. 'Being-in' enters into the existential 'mode' of the 'not-at-home'. Nothing else is meant by our talk about 'uncanniness'."[27]

Even more fundamental are Heidegger's statements on 'angst' in *Was ist Metaphysik?* – in which he claims that 'the state of 'angst' discloses 'Nothingness' ["In der Angst enthüllt sich das Nichts."] – And he adds that, 'in the state of 'angst', 'everything that is' ["das Seiende"] is as a whole rendered null and void.' ["In der Angst wird das Seiende im Ganzen *hinfällig*"].[28]

It is in these reflections that the fundamental problem of 'being-in-this-world', perceived as a mode of existence that inevitably advances towards the ultimate 'Ground', becomes manifest. At the same time, however, these considerations also indicate how thought-provoking the existential interpretation of 'being-in-this-world' in view of the 'ultimate Ground' can be, not least because it is precisely this ontological issue by which it should be possible to assess whether or not Heidegger's conception of 'Dasein' is sound and valid. Critics of Heidegger have taken up this issue and questioned the soundness of his conception of 'angst' by proposing alternative phenomena for the fundamental 'frame-of-mind' by which man's 'being-in-this-world' is determined. Some critics have proposed that the fundamental 'frame-of-mind' of human existence is neither 'angst' nor the 'uncanniness' of man's 'thrownness' into the world triggered by it, but rather the sense of "Geborgenheit" [i.e., reassurance, feeling secure and sheltered]. Other critics have argued that the 'Void' or 'Nothingness' that allegedly surfaces from the primordial condition of 'angst' is not the ultimate fundamental mood dominating human existence, but rather the awareness of the 'wholeness [and soundness] of the Ground'. These considerations are particularly relevant for our enquiry, since the key issue of human existence in this world addressed here in terms of an inalienable

---

27 [Note: The passage quoted is from the English edition of Heidegger's *Sein und Zeit: Being and Time.* Trans. John Macquarrie and Edward Robinson. Oxford: Blackwell, 1962. 233. – FKW.]

28 [Note: In the passage quoted, Albrecht does not use any quotation marks, though he refers to two different editions of Heidegger's inaugural lecture "Was ist Metaphysik?" as his sources: HEIDEGGER, Martin. *Was ist Metaphysik?* Bonn: Cohen, 1929. 18; and *Was ist Metaphysik?* Frankfurt a. Main: Klostermann, 1949. 14. – FKW.]

progress 'towards the Ultimate Ground' is also inherent to the concept of the 'mystical relation'. But before elaborating on this pivotal issue, we need to consider as a preliminary two more critical responses to Heidegger: one by Ludwig Binswanger, the other by Otto Bollnow.

> *Binswanger* emphatically argues that human existence is sustained throughout by love rather than haunted by 'angst': "Love is … in a twofold manner 'being unto the Ground' in that it is unconditional, unquestionable and a certain mode of 'being', and therefore a vital and triumphant instance shaping man's way of 'being-in-this-world' in view of the 'Ground'; love provides a dual-mode for abiding in 'Dasein' without 'angst' or anxiety, enabling 'Dasein' to be perceived as an infinite, eternal mystery … In 'loving we-hood' … we connect with each other as blessed beings, i.e., destined to touch without questioning the Ground by intuition" (482).[29] "In this situation the notion of the individual just does not arise, because 'you and me' repose in the Ground of Being that is perceived to be ours, and thus, we are gratified with the 'unproblematic' favour and fullness of 'Being'" (404). In Heidegger, by contrast, 'being-in-the-world' means having been 'thrown' as a 'powerless' being into 'Dasein' and thus into the 'foreign' nothingness of the Ground, hence, overpowered already before entering the world and dropped into its 'heaviness'. Against this we posit the notion of man's familiarity with 'Dasein' conceived as a gift and the awareness of one's perpetual repose in the comfort and shelter of 'Dasein', and its fruition as 'loving we-hood'" (96). "Whereas in the conception of 'Dasein' determined by 'care', the ultimate Ground is perceived as uncanny and equated with the overwhelming, overpowering Nothingness into which man is thrown, the conception of 'Dasein' determined by 'love' discloses *none* of these phenomena … the ultimate Ground is rather perceived as a 'homely', safe haven, and sheltered homestead, by which 'Dasein' is reclaimed from isolation by loving encounter, and with which it is *familiar* and in which it confides" (149). "In fact, 'Dasein' determined by love enables 'Dasein' to look right into the 'eye' of the Ground, and *to offer itself* and *surrender* to it in a *clandestine act of conception*" … "Here 'Dasein' is not at all understood from the perspective of this world … but rather from the ultimate Ground, and thus perceived as a gift, bequest or grace" (153). "In 'Dasein' determined by love, the circumstance that the Ground has not been created by 'Dasein' itself, is not seen as impotence or a deficiency or incapacity to

---

29 [All references in this paragraph are to BINSWANGER, Ludwig. *Grundformen und Erkenntnis Menschlichen Daseins*. 2nd ed. Zurich: Niehans, 1953. Page numbers as stated by Albrecht; English translation provided. – FKW.]

realize its potentials (= being guilty), but rather on the contrary, 'Dasein' is entirely devoid of any sense of inability and nothingness but is, quite the opposite, perfectly replete with the *fullness* of life" (152).

Turning to Bollnow's conception of 'Dasein' contrasted to that of Heidegger: Bollnow's approach is focussed on the phenomenon of 'trust' in 'being-in-this-world'. That is to say, in his anthropological approach he tries to establish a range of 'trusting patterns' encountered in the history of human behaviour and to develop from these findings an ontology of 'Dasein'. Unlike Heidegger, Bollnow starts from comprehensive empirical enquiries and anthropological data. The phenomenon of 'hope', he claims, has emerged as a pivotal existential phenomenon of humanity:

> "*Hope* belongs to the innermost essence of man ..." (85).[30] It "is the typical counterpart of despair" (24). Hope can be defined as "trusting in the future ... It is the sustaining relationship that extends beyond the presence and thus determines [man's] present and future relationship to the 'Ground of Being" (25). Thus, hope understood anthropologically as an existential condition of man is the ultimate foundation by which a number of further phenomena inherent in diverse modes of human existence are facilitated. These phenomena include *'composure'*, *'feeling comforted'* and *'patience'*, which become all intelligible phenomenologically only if they are grounded in hope.
>
> The ontological direction of Bollnow's anthropological approach becomes evident in such statements as: "The essence and relevance of hope cannot adequately be assessed, or discerned, if 'being-in-the-world' is claimed to be determined by 'angst'. Hope is rather an independent, self-sufficient condition of life which cannot be traced to any antecedent cause, and thus hope, like 'angst', is a primordial phenomenon. There are, however, persuasive reasons to substantiate the claim that hope is a more primeval phenomenon than 'angst'. It may be claimed that hope is indeed the ultimate condition for the possibility of all human life." (99) Elsewhere, Bollnow states: "Over and beyond this, hope is a phenomenon that is more primeval than 'care' as well" (114). "Seen from this perspective, the results of the foregoing enquiry can be summarized as follows: The 'resoluteness of care' [i.e., the disclosing of 'care' in the temporality of 'Dasein'] must

---

30 BOLLNOW, Otto F. *Neue Geborgenheit. Das Problem einer Überwindung des Existenzialismus.* Stuttgart: Kohlhammer, 1955. [All page references are to this edition; English translation provided. – FKW.]

inevitably consume itself in futile adventurous enterprises as long as it does not envision a prospect of hope, in which 'care' is offered a horizon of potential options from which it may choose. Without hope, any resolution to act will lead nowhere and result in a state of despair ... in hope, however, the resolution to act has a sustaining ground, which it can never produce itself. From this follows that 'care' must inevitably be preceded by and rooted in the sustaining and all-embracing ground of hope" (115).

In the passage quoted, Bollnow purports in *anthropological* terms a psychological-phenomenological condition of 'Dasein'. But if this conception of 'Dasein' has any ontological import as well appears to me questionable.

Bollnow has furthermore explored in detail the polarity between the *mood of elation* and the *dark mood of depression*.[31] Obviously, this dichotomy has been suggested by the polarity between 'Geborgenheit' [comfort, security, well-being], as a sought-after condition of 'Dasein', and the distressing condition of 'care'. "Geborgenheit" is a condition of 'Dasein' that is imbued with happiness and elation, and which enables man to open up to existential phenomena other than 'angst'. Hence, being embedded in "Geborgenheit" facilitates the disclosure of the 'wholeness' and 'fullness' of the ultimate Ground in 'Dasein'.[32]

The question addressed above is becoming more urgent: *Are the anthropological phenomena of 'Dasein' outlined by Bollnow and Binswanger indeed instances of the fundamental mood of 'Dasein' as conceived by fundamental ontology, i.e., instances of the existential 'disclosedness' of 'Dasein'?* The answer to this question is clearly no: Neither the structure of 'love', i.e., "perceiving 'Dasein' as a gift and the experience of reposing eternally in the security and comfort of 'Dasein' elicited in the event of an 'encounter' [with Being in 'Dasein'], nor the structure of 'hope' can be classified as genuine modes of *existential 'disclosure'*, because 'Dasein' is not disclosed or encountered in them as a whole. On the other hand, it may be asked if the following statement by Heidegger might, after all, apply to the two anthropological

---

31   BOLLNOW, Otto F. *Das Wesen der Stimmungen*. 2nd ed. Frankfurt am Main: Klostermann, 1943.

32   Cf. BOLLNOW, Otto F. *Neue Geborgenheit. Das Problem einer Überwindung des Existenzialismus*. Stuttgart: Kohlhammer, 1955. 147ff.

phenomena addressed (particularly the second part of the statement): "In the case of phenomena of this kind any enquiry must be wary not to confuse the ontic-existential characteristics of the phenomena with the ontological-existential interpretation of the same, or to overlook the positive phenomenological foundations inherent in the former and their relevance for the latter."[33]

Our detailed analysis of the works of Binswanger and Bollnow has finally yielded some significant results. It is helpful to summarize them *by contrasting positive and negative critical responses*. This should prove useful for the progress of our considerations.

The positive findings can be epitomized as follows:

1. *Phenomenologically, the 'ultimate phenomenon' of 'love' has clearly and unequivocally been highlighted. The same applies to the phenomena of 'hope' and 'trust'.* With these phenomena anthropological modes of being have been identified as separate entities. The ontological relevance of this fact is obvious. Any future attempt at proposing an ontological hermeneutics of 'Dasein' will have to deal with these anthropological phenomena.

2. *The phenomenological structure of 'love'* – or, in Binswanger's terms, of 'we-hood' – *has enabled us to demonstrate hermeneutically* that an integral part of 'Dasein' is not merely the primeval process of transcendence of 'being-in-the-world', but also the fact that *'Dasein' is open to transcending the state of 'being-in-the-world'*.

3. *The distinctive anthropological features of 'love' and 'hope' include a phenomenological sign pointing to the fact that 'angst' is not the only underlying mood of human existence, and thus not the only mode of the existential 'disclosedness' of 'Dasein'.*

On the basis of these phenomena, which are unquestionably real, empirical facts, it is reasonable to ask if there is yet another perennial existential mood underlying man's 'Dasein'. The question as to what

---

33 [Note: Albrecht refers to 'page 184' but does not indicate the work of Heidegger from which he is quoting. – English translation provided. – FKW.]

the ontological status of this second mood might be, however, cannot yet be answered at this stage of our enquiry.

As for the negative responses to our critical analysis of the hermeneutics of 'Dasein' as conceived by Heidegger, Bollnow and Binswanger, we may state the following:

1. *It has not been possible to verify the primacy of 'love' over 'care' as the determining component of 'Dasein'.* The detailed phenomenological-anthropological analysis of "we-hood" has not yielded any tangible results to support this claim.

2. *It has not been possible to displace the phenomenon of 'angst' from its central ontological position as the prevailing fundamental mood of 'Dasein'. The critical analysis of all the pivotal phenomena pertaining to human existence has failed to disclose another fundamental mood that could be compared to 'angst'. The effort of finding an alternative fundamental mood, which is similarly dominant and persevering as 'angst', has not yet been undertaken.*

If we review our critical assessment, some important questions arise, which are relevant for the future course of our enquiry. There is, first of all, the question, *If the ontological existential structure of 'Dasein' might be dialectic – that is to say, if we review all the 'ultimate phenomena' encountered, could this effort not result in the discovery of binary opposites and, ultimately, in a final pair of opposed 'ultimate phenomena'?*

It is, after all, remarkable that many anthropological and ontological investigations into the nature of man rely on the assumption that the structure of human existence is dialectic. This applies, for example, to the binary opposites considered by August Vetter in *Natur und Person*,[34] as well as to Hermann Krings's study *Fragen und Aufgaben der Ontologie*,[35] in which the contrasted ontological

---

[34] VETTER, August. *Natur und Person. Umriss einer Anthropognomik.* Stuttgart: Klett, 1949.

[35] KRINGS, Hermann. *Fragen und Aufgaben der Ontologie.* Tübingen: Niemeyer, 1954.

pairs are "Wesen" [essence] versus "Existenz" [existence]. And in the works of Heidegger we encounter the binary opposites of "eigentliches" vs. "uneigentliches Seinkönnen" [i.e., the potential for authentic vs. non-authentic modes of existence].[36]

The findings of this critical survey have supplied reliable foundations for exploring the 'ultimate phenomenon' of the 'mystical relation' and for considering its relevance for the hermeneutics of "Dasein". By examining contemporary philosophical and anthropological studies in this field, I have tried to establish a sound epistemological basis for the subsequent enquiry. It must be emphasized, however, that my intention is certainly not to engage in an ontological investigation. I will not even be able to provide clearly established, coherent insights about the relevance of the 'mystical relation' for a new understanding of fundamental ontology. For this reason, I have continued to speak merely of the *potential* relevance of the 'mystical relation' for ontology. My endeavour, in other words, is confined to providing suggestions for potential approaches by which the essence of the 'mystical relation' might be identified and corroborated.

We shall proceed by surveying the mystical phenomena established in the previous study, which might be relevant to our quest for the 'mystical relation'. In a second step, we shall examine new perspectives, which should help us to explore the issue of the 'mystical relation' from different angles. It is an established fact that every ontic phenomenon germane to human existence can be examined with regard to its underlying anthropological structure and, conversely, that every anthropological structure can be viewed from an ontological perspective. Thus the 'quiet state of alertness' ["Versunkenheit", i.e., the most serene, most highly alert and most tranquil state of consciousness available to man], as well as the 'mystical state of quiet alertness' [i.e., 'the quiet state of alertness' in which mystical phenomena have become manifest in the 'vista' of the 'inner eye' or 'inner sight'] are, at the outset, to be assessed as ontic phenomena. For this reason, we have tried in our previous study to delineate these

---

36 [Note: Albrecht does not give a reference here. – Heidegger elaborates on the concepts of "Eigentlichkeit" vs. "Uneigentlichkeit" in "Dasein" in chapter II of *Being and Time*. – FKW.]

two distinct states of consciousness in great phenomenological detail [and to set them off against other mental states such as the 'waking consciousness', 'somnambulist mental states' as well as 'ecstatic states of consciousness']. The 'quiet state of alertness' has been defined as a fully integrated, unified, homogenously structured, hyper-lucid and emptied mental state in which the stream of consciousness is slowed down to near stasis, and in which the underlying mood is complete calmness; the only active function in this inherently passive, receptive state of consciousness is that of 'inner sight' or ["Innenschau"]. These empirical and phenomenological enquiries resulted in a 'narrow' and an 'extended' psychological-phenomenological definition of 'mysticism'. The 'narrow' definition states that "mysticism is the 'arrival' of an 'All-encompassing' in the 'quiet state of alertness.'"[37] [The 'extended' definition states that 'mysticism is both the 'arrival' of the 'All-encompassing' in the 'quiet state of alertness' and the ecstatic experience of an 'All-encompassing'."][38]

The two ontic phenomena, i.e., the 'quiet state of alertness' and the 'mystical state of quiet alertness', are unequivocally defined and clearly differentiated from each other so that they provide a reliable epistemological foundation for an in-depth structural anthropological analysis. We shall subsequently try to infer from this analysis some fundamental-ontological perspectives. There is a myriad of ontic phenomena that are relevant anthropologically. And from many of them it is possible to derive distinctive structural characteristics of human nature. However, it is only singular elements and special components that can be used for a complete, all-embracing conception of the condition of man. The element singled out first in our enquiry, and from which our systematic anthropological analysis will commence, is the 'quiet state of alertness'. Though this mental

---

37 [Note: Albrecht's footnote in the original text refers to pages 106 and 254 of the first edition of his *Psychologie des Mystischen Bewußtseins* (1951); the references here are to the English edition: ALBRECHT, Carl. *Psychology of Mystical Consciousness*. Trans., introd. and annotated by Franz K. Woehrer. New York: Crossroad, 2019. 373. – FKW.]

38 [Note: ALBRECHT, Carl. *Psychology of Mystical Consciousness*. Trans., introd. and annotated by Franz K. Woehrer. New York: Crossroad, 2019. 374. – FKW.]

state is admittedly only a very limited and isolated component of man, it is nonetheless an illuminating and innovative approach to exploring the mental condition and spiritual nature of man. We also must concede that this anthropological analysis is inevitably selective and fragmented, so that its findings can only claim to be of limited heuristic value. Moreover, the findings at this stage of our enquiry are to be taken as provisional results and as such do not yet allow ontological inferences, and thus do not qualify as the foundation for a new hermeneutic of "Dasein".

The 'structural anthropological formula' underlying the 'quiet state of alertness' is the condition of 'being-within-oneself' ["In-sich-Sein", i.e., inwardness; reposing within one's self]. In other words: *The existential mode of 'being-within-oneself' is the anthropological condition for the possibility of the 'quiet state of alertness' to unfold.* The word 'within' in this formula must be understood in a non-spatial sense, just like the word 'in' in the ontological formula of 'being-in-the-world', which has likewise a non-spatial meaning. The word 'oneself' has been deliberately chosen because it is unspecific enough to permit us to distinguish the anthropological formula clearly from the ontic-psychological statements. 'Being-within-oneself' is a structural condition of 'being-in-the-world', and as such it must be distinguished from the concrete experience of 'being absorbed within myself'.

Yet more important than this delineation from the realm of psychology is the juxtaposition of the formula of 'being-within-oneself' to the ontological formula of 'being-in-the-world' ["in-der-Welt-Sein"], which is at the same time (as we know) identical to an anthropological formula. The starting point for our considerations is this important fact: *Heidegger's thesis that the fundamental structure of 'Dasein' is 'being-in-the-world' cannot be shaken.* Nor can this thesis be undermined or challenged by the existential mode of 'being-within-oneself': The fact remains that 'worldhood' ["Weltlichkeit"][39] as

---

39 [Note: Albrecht adopts Heidegger's term "Weltlichkeit", which in the English edition of *Being and Time* is appropriately translated as 'worldhood', rather than as 'worldliness'. The Heideggerian neologism "Weltlichkeit" refers to the fact that man in 'Dasein' is surrounded by things and other entities and is required to deal with them. Heidegger elaborates on this concept in detail in chapter III of *Being and*

a structural feature of 'being-in-the-world', and 'worldhood' as an existential condition of 'Dasein' is an ontological facticity and can thus never be suspended. Anyone or anything dwelling in 'Dasein' is inevitably part of 'being-in-the-world'. 'Worldhood', however, is not entirely static (as Heidegger insists) but is open to modification: "Worldhood itself may have as its modes whatever structural wholes any special 'worlds' may have at the time, but it embraces in itself the *a priori* character of worldhood in general."[40]

From this we may infer that *'being-within-oneself' must be understood as a mode of 'being-in-the-world'*. By stating this important epistemological thesis, we have taken a significant step forward, since it points in the direction in which our enquiry must proceed.

To begin with, we need to clarify the term 'mode', and along with it, the more specific term 'deficient mode', which is frequently used by Heidegger. If 'being-within-oneself' is a mode of 'being-in-the-world', it logically follows that the situational condition of 'being-within-oneself' must be encompassed by the existential condition of 'being-in-the-world'. The term 'mode' cannot only be applied if the basic pattern recurs in all its parts, but also if the structural pattern remains partly 'concealed'. If the latter applies, Heidegger employs the term 'deficient mode', and he contrasts it to the former 'mode', which is occasionally referred to as the 'full mode'. Thus a 'deficient mode' of 'being-in-the-world' is one in which several essential aspects of 'being-in-the-world' are either missing or concealed. That is to say, in the 'deficient mode' 'being-in-the-world' becomes apparent only in a fragmented, rudimentary manner. The fact that individual components of the overall structure are missing in the 'deficient mode', however, does not change or affect the essence of the whole structure, but the missing components are rather clear indications of the contemporaneous 'givenness' of the entire structure.

'Being-within-oneself' is thus a 'deficient mode' of 'being-in-

---

Time, entitled 'The Worldhood of the World'. Cf. HEIDEGGER, Martin. *Being and Time*. Trans. John Macquarrie and Edward Robinson. Oxford: Blackwell, 1962. 63ff. – FKW.]

40 [HEIDEGGER, Martin. *Being and Time*. Trans. John Macquarrie and Edward Robinson. Oxford: Blackwell, 1962. 93. – FKW.]

the-world'. This is an undeniable and immutable fact: First, because in the mode of 'being-within-oneself' the existential structure of 'care' is missing [i.e., *suspended*] along with the *concrete* situation of 'being-with-others', and second, because the existential 'world-hood' of the individual immersed in the state of 'being-within-him-/herself' is an evident fact. Though the *mundane* awareness of 'being-in-the-world' is suspended during the 'quiet state of alertness', the existential condition of 'being-in-the-world' persists for as long as the perceiver continues to 'be-in-this-world'.

It is important to add that the word 'deficient' does not have any negative connotation, nor does it imply a value judgement. It is a proven fact that a phenomenon can be a 'deficient mode' of another phenomenon, and exist as an independent phenomenon, and as such be ontologically and anthropologically equal or even superior to the 'partner-phenomenon'. This means the 'deficient mode' of any phenomenon needs to be examined as to whether it contains any additional 'out-standing' ["über-ragende"(sic!)] qualities that are not encompassed by the 'partner-phenomenon' from which it derives. Over and beyond this, we need to ask what relevance the distinctive additional quality of the 'deficient mode' of a given phenomenon has for our enquiry.

The starting point of our analysis, then, is the inalienable fact that 'being-within-oneself' is a 'deficient mode' of 'being-in-the-world'. The crucial question to be asked at this juncture is: Is it at all possible to identify individual components in the structure of 'being-within-oneself' that have some bearing on our hermeneutical conception of the condition of 'Dasein' without, at the same time, removing the existential condition of 'being-in-the-world'? The answer is yes. And the phenomenon that can be singled out here as a prototypical example is *the phenomenon of calmness*.

The distinctive psychological characteristics of the state of inner calm have been outlined in our previous study *Psychology of Mystical Consciousness*. The state of inner calmness has been shown to be a unique emotional state sustaining the serene 'state of quiet alertness'. Compared to any of the other emotional qualities germane to a human being, the calmness within is the only one that is instilled not only with the quality of 'encompassing' or 'enclosing' everything, but also with the quality of being something 'ultimate' and 'perennial'. Calmness, in other words, is a unique phenomenon that cannot be traced to any prior source. The 'quiet state of alertness' is the quintessential experience of inner calmness. Calmness is, moreover, not only the fundamental mood in which all other modes of experience are embedded and in which the 'perceiving I' is immersed, but the special attributes of calmness – notably its serenity, lucidity and vacuity – permeating consciousness, generate the tranquil space for the encounter with, or 'arrival' of, incoming phenomena [i.e., phenomena 'arriving' in the vista of the 'inner eye']. Our empirical research has furthermore shown that the calmness by which the 'quiet state of alertness' is inundated is the only emotional state of man that may acquire 'all-encompassing' quality. Hence, calmness is the ideal mental setting for a 'mystical encounter'. The state of 'all-encompassing calmness' allows the 'perceiving I' in the 'quiet state of alertness' to become entirely absorbed in it, even to the extent that any sense of self-awareness is extinguished. The distinctive phenomenological characteristics of the 'calmness within' suggest that calmness is most likely not just ontically *a fundamental mood* of the 'quiet state of alertness', but can indeed, when assessed from an ontological-anthropological perspective, be claimed to be a *genuine primordial state of mind*.

As stated above, it is impossible to doubt or deny that 'angst' is a genuine primary emotional condition or state of mind. Hence the question that arises – whether 'calmness' is on a par with 'angst' when classified as a genuine primordial state of mind – prompts the additional question of how the relationship between the 'angst' and 'calmness' is to be understood. The distinctive characteristic that must be explored first if we pursue these considerations is the phenomenological quality termed 'encompassing', which we have inferred from the calmness within, and in particular the qualities inherent to it, namely that the state of calmness is entirely devoid of any object and is thus imbued with a deep sense of 'emptiness'. The 'all-embracing' quality of calmness may acquire a mystical quality, which may spontaneously be imparted. There are numerous modes of feeling as well as moods that may be embedded in the experience of 'all-embracing calmness': These include reassurance, hope, consolation, composure, or patience. However, this relationship cannot be reversed: there is no phenomenological evidence that any of the feelings and emotional states that are embedded in the experience of calmness could ever encompass the state of inner calm, even if these feelings and emotional states are not just passing, temporary moods, but persevering emotional conditions, none of which is perceived as being 'encompassing' or 'all-comprising'. Though it is true that in the incipient stage of its emergence in consciousness 'calmness' may be evoked by such feelings as hope or consolation, or be elicited by a mental [meditational] technique, or arise spontaneously from the sphere of the body, 'calmness' can never be superseded by any other emotional state once it has attained all-inclusive quality. The 'calmness' inundating the 'quiet state of alertness' can therefore be claimed to be an 'ultimate phenomenon', which cannot be surpassed by any other emotional condition. Neither hope, nor the sense of being whole and secure, nor the state of consolation, nor the state of composure, let alone patience, can ever develop to the point of attaining the 'all-comprising' quality germane to inner 'calmness'. The various emotional modes of being referred to contain a limiting structural reference frame: in all of them we may discern some lingering awareness of being related to some other entity or being embedded within another phenomenon; this applies to hope, the feeling of reassurance, consolation, the state of composure and to patience. Even if these relational qualities are understood in very broad and abstract terms, they can never reach the 'complete emptiness' of 'calmness'. Thus, 'calmness' is the only existential phenomenon that can 'stand on its own' (as it were): 'calmness' can repose within itself and abide in the clarity of its own emptiness. 'Abiding', in this context, does not mean 'waiting for'. Since the state of 'calmness' is devoid of any desire, there is nothing to be waited for, nothing to be expected – 'calmness' is a state of mind without expectation. All these features indicate that 'calmness' is (as we will demonstrate later) the perfect vessel of passive receptivity and creativity.

The second important fact by which the course of our considerations is determined is the insight that 'calmness' is the only existential phenomenon that can compare with and be juxtaposed to 'angst'. In fact, 'angst' and 'calmness' are the only existential phenomena encountered in human 'Dasein' that are 'all-comprising'. It can thus be stated that *'angst' and 'calmness' are juxtaposed at the same level*, and that no other mood or emotional state encountered in empirical reality is phenomenologically on a par with 'angst' and 'calmness'. This claim can be illustrated by two examples: Bollnow[41] has placed 'hope' side by side with 'angst'. However, 'hope' cannot entirely extinguish 'angst', since there can still be 'hope', even when 'angst' culminates in an encounter with 'nothingness'. By analogy, 'restlessness' may be juxtaposed to 'calmness' and can, hypothetically, be classified as a phenomenon at the same existential level with 'calmness'. But 'calmness' may dispel the state of unrest, or else unrest can be absorbed by 'calmness' and thus be removed from a given state of consciousness. 'Restlessness' may intrude from the periphery of consciousness and temporarily disrupt the state of 'calmness'. It can only destroy the state of repose if 'restlessness' is sustained by 'angst'. In such an instance a seizure of 'restlessness' is the manifestation of an interference from beyond the confines of the individual consciousness, a cypher for the presence and/or impact of more high-ranking [disruptive] ontological entities.[42]

'Calmness' and 'angst' are phenomenological opposites and mutually exclusive, which proves that they are indeed on a par as existential phenomena.

There is a third aspect by which the thesis stated above is corroborated. The juxtaposition of 'elated mood' versus 'depressed mood' is a genuine phenomenological polarity,[43] which has anthropological relevance. The fact that these two pivotal moods are opposites, however, does not help us in our search for an answer to the ontological problem about the essence of the 'fundamental mood'. The 'elation mood' is as such not directly opposed to 'angst', and the 'depressed mood' is not

---

41 BOLLNOW, Otto. *Neue Geborgenheit. Das Problem einer Überwindung des Existenzialismus*. Stuttgart: Kohlhammer, 1955.

42 [Note: By this cryptic remark Albrecht seems to refer to the state of restlessness, which is often described by mystics, notably when a contemplative is harassed by demons, the fiend, or other subversive forces. These 'tribulations' occur especially when a mystic is exposed to the 'spiritual combat' between self-will and the Will of God at the initial stage of 'purification', and again when the advanced contemplative has reached the final stage of the mystical ascent, in which he/she is exposed to the process of 'passive purgation'. – FKW.]

43 Cf. BOLLNOW, Otto. *Das Wesen der Stimmungen*. 2nd ed. Frankfurt am Main: Klostermann, 1943.

directly contrasted to 'inner calmness' either. This indicates that 'angst' and 'calmness' are ontologically to be assigned a higher rank than any of the emotional moods, like elation or depression. The validity of this claim can be demonstrated by an example: The 'fundamental mood' of 'calmness' can be intertwined with both varieties of elated mood (like joy, happiness or bliss) and with varieties of depressive feelings (like depression, sadness or even melancholy gloom). This corroborates the claim that 'calmness', like 'angst', is a fundamental existential state of mind, which cannot be reduced to a mere passing mood.

Even if this claim is only accepted with some reservation, it is reliable enough to allow the following statement: *If there is any other 'fundamental existential state of mind' besides 'angst' at all, which can claim to be ontologically on the same level with 'angst', this can only be the phenomenon of 'calmness'.* In fact, the 'calmness' encountered ontically in the 'quiet state of alertness' and in 'mystical consciousness' [i.e., the mystical experience of 'all-encompassing Calmness' within the 'quiet state of alertness'] is the only possible ontological 'partner' of the phenomenon of 'angst'.

However, if this claim is valid, the question arises: If 'calmness' is indeed an existential state of mind and a mode of the 'disclosedness' of 'Dasein', does this fact not demand that there should be a special method for 'disclosing' 'calmness'?

If we search for an answer to this question, it is helpful to call to mind the ontic horizon, which contains the phenomena from which we may try to delve into the realm of ontology: Our starting point is the psychological-phenomenological structure of the 'quiet state of alertness'; this is a clearly defined state of consciousness that is composed of three pivotal phenomena: the sustaining mood of 'calmness', the function of the 'inner eye' ('inner sight', "Innenschau") and the 'object arriving' in the vista of 'inner sight'. Up to this point, we have only addressed the ontological aspect of 'calmness'. Now we need to proceed by examining the ontological import of the function of 'inner sight' and of the 'object arriving'.

We have shown above that 'calmness' and 'angst' are phenomena that are ontologically on the same level and that these two existential states of mind are diametrically opposed. These statements, however, must not lead to the flawed conclusion that 'angst' is equal to 'restlessness', or, conversely, to identify 'calmness' with 'fearlessness'. In our enquiry the view must remain open, and we need to consider not just the complementary aspects of the two phenomena, but focus as well on their significant differences. Though 'angst' is, by definition, not directed at (or caused by) a concrete object, it is nonetheless related to 'something' of which one is afraid. While 'angst', unlike 'fear', is not directed at an 'object' or person existing in this world, it surfaces surreptitiously and suddenly from the mere fact of 'being-in-this-world'. There is neither an item 'about which' nor a situation 'of what' one is afraid of. In other words, 'angst' as an existential state of mind has an exploratory function: in 'angst', the uncanniness of 'Dasein' and the condition of 'not-being at home' are disclosed; in 'angst', the awareness of one's 'thrownness' into this world becomes manifest; and 'angst' is also the response to the 'Nothingness' in which 'Dasein' as a whole is rooted.

Unlike 'angst', 'calmness' is an 'existential state of mind' that is not a component of the 'disclosedness' of 'Dasein'. Hence, 'calmness' has no exploratory function of 'Dasein'. In 'calmness', situations like those encountered in 'angst', i.e., 'of what' or 'about what' one should be afraid, or, in this case, 'calm down', do not occur. *Thus 'calmness' is not an emotion disclosing an understanding of 'Dasein'.* This means that the ontological structure of 'calmness' cannot reveal the 'disclosedness' of 'Dasein', but it can only disclose what becomes apparent within its phenomenological pattern. And this is something entirely different, namely the *'openness' of 'Dasein'*. When immersed in 'angst', one is transferred into the process of 'disclosing'; *'calmness', by contrast, is a receptive condition: 'being-immersed' in a state of 'openness'*. And the state of 'openness' is a necessary condition *for becoming 'receptive' within* [i.e., receptive to 'in-coming' phenomena, 'arriving' in the vista of 'inner sight']. 'Angst' permeates 'Dasein' in that 'being-in-the-world' is imbued by it. 'Calmness', by contrast, emanates from the individual's state of 'reposing within him-/herself', and this experience does not 'disclose' any aspect of 'Dasein', but rather enables the state of *'openness' as such, i.e., 'openness' that has the potential to be 'receptive'*.

We have thus revealed that 'angst' and 'calmness' are two different and independent phenomenological structures of human existence. The ontic phenomena of experiencing, recognizing and understanding have two foundations: They are, first, rooted in the 'disclosedness of Dasein', which is constituted by the 'current state of being-oneself', and a primordial mode of understanding. Second, they are rooted in the 'openness of Dasein', which is constituted by the ontological element of 'calmness', which we have termed 'receptivity'.

We also must recall that we wanted to substantiate the claim that 'being-within-oneself' is a mode of 'being-in-the-world'. 'Being-within-oneself' is a 'deficient mode', as it is a mode of 'being-in-the-world' in which the mind has [temporarily] been 'emptied' from all items belonging to this world. On the other hand, this 'deficient mode' is at the same time an 'outstanding mode', because it is identical with the state of 'openness of Dasein' as such.

A more thoroughgoing enquiry might provide a more differentiated picture and a better understanding of the anthropological structure of 'being-within-oneself'. This could be achieved methodologically by relating and comparing the many ontological characteristics of 'care', as conceived by Heidegger, to the ontic phenomenon of the 'quiet state of alertness'. For pursuing this approach, the Heideggerian *existential* phenomena of 'thrownness', of 'being-towards-death', as well as of 'conscience as an appeal to Dasein by calling it to its ownmost potentiality-for-Being-its-Self', and of 'being guilty as a structure of the essential nullity of Dasein', would be best suited. However, such a comprehensive analysis would go far beyond the scope of this study. We must confine our enquiry and, therefore, can examine only two existential phenomena: that of 'Dasein's authentic vs. inauthentic potentiality for being 'a-whole','[44] and that of the temporality of 'Dasein'. The considerations of these two phenomena should enable us to advance further in our phenomenological-anthropological analysis of 'calmness'.

Authenticity and non-authenticity are fundamental components of 'Dasein'. This means that 'Dasein' is primordially situated in the

---

44 [Note: Heidegger deals with this issue in chapter III of *Being and Time*, entitled 'Dasein's authentic potentiality-for-being a-whole, and temporality as the ontological meaning of care'. Cf. HEIDEGGER, Martin. *Being and Time*. Trans. John Macquarrie and Edward Robinson. Oxford: Blackwell, 1962. 349–82. – FKW.]

facticity of 'being-in-the-world'; thus 'Dasein' is forever placed in the potentiality of being authentic. The inauthentic being of 'Dasein' implies succumbing to the world, getting lost in the public sphere of 'everyman', which inevitably causes the loss of self-hood. Authentic potentiality of 'Dasein' is marked by the determination to deal with such issues as the condition of man as a 'being-towards-death', the call from one's forlorn condition, the acceptance of the 'thrownness' into this world. We cannot elaborate on these Heideggerian concepts any further, as our critical analysis has been confined to the two modes of being that occur in the 'quiet state of alertness'.

From an anthropological point-of-view, 'being-within-oneself' is not a mode of inauthentic 'Dasein'. Yet 'being-within-oneself' is not a mode of authentic 'Dasein', either. The 'quiet state of alertness' is, from an ontic-psychological perspective, a state of consciousness that is detached from the world outside and all 'innerworldly' relationships are [temporarily] suspended. It is an 'empty' state of consciousness, i.e., the mind has been vacated from all sense perceptions, drives, acts of the will, acts of discursive thinking and object-related feelings. The 'quiet state of alertness' thus does not contain anything that permits the underlying condition of 'being-within-oneself' to be disrupted, or, to put it differently, to be substituted by an anthropological mode of existential inauthenticity. The 'quiet state of alertness' is thus a mental condition in which all active functions of the 'ego' are [temporarily] suspended: The 'experiencing self' is alone receptive to 'in-coming' phenomena arriving in the vista of the 'inner eye'. These features of the ontic structure of the 'quiet state of alertness' indicate that 'being-within-oneself' as such does not qualify as a mode of existential authenticity because just being fully immersed in the 'calmness' within is not enough to establish an 'authentic mode of being'. Though any awareness of 'care' and of a caring relationship to the world 'outside' is suspended, these qualities are not unique and apply equally to other modes of being. This means that 'being-within-oneself' can neither be assessed as a mode of inauthentic 'Dasein', nor as a mode of authentic 'Dasein'. From this follows, however, that the state of 'being-within-oneself' must be rooted in a third mode of 'Dasein' which differs phenomenologically from the modes of authentic and inauthentic 'Dasein', which is independent from the other two modes. This specific anthropological mode of 'being-within-oneself' is the state of 'inner calmness'.

The word 'calmness' as used here is a psychological-phenomenological term, which refers to two aspects: On the one hand, 'calmness' denotes the underlying, all-permeating mood by which the 'quiet state of alertness' is inundated and sustained; 'calmness' refers, second, to the entire mental condition signified by the term 'being-within-oneself'. 'Calmness' is the outcome of the process by which the 'quiet state of alertness' is generated; this process involves, psychologically, the progressive elimination of any object-related 'content' from consciousness. And the result is a perfectly unified, homogeneous, fully integrated mental state imbued with perfect peace and calmness. From this fact we may infer the claim: *'Being-within-oneself' is 'calmness' per se*.

But 'being-within-oneself' is (as stated above) at the same time a mode of 'being-in-the-world'. And *'being-within-oneself' is 'calmness' per se*: this is the new structural formula that has emerged from our enquiry. The apparent contradiction between the two formulas above is resolved if the outstanding mode of 'being-within-oneself' while 'being-in-the-world' is understood in terms of *a 'reposeful' state of 'being-in-the-world'. Thus 'Dasein', determined by 'calmness', transforms 'Dasein' governed by 'care'*. 'Calmness' does not only transform components of the structure of 'being-in-the-world', but the entire structural framework is temporarily transformed and removed from the familiar state of 'being-in-the-world'. Thus 'calmness' does not change the condition of 'Dasein', but the situation of 'being-in-this-world' is for the time being transferred into a state of perfect repose and tranquillity. Yet the state of 'being-within-oneself' does not get its special relevance for the ontology of 'Dasein' from the fact that it is determined by 'calmness'; the exciting ontological aspect is rather that 'calmness' as a mode of being proves to be at the same time a state of supreme 'openness'. Hence *'being-within-oneself' is not only 'calmness' as such, but also 'openness' as such*.

Heidegger has done away with the 'vulgar' commonplace understanding of time, in which the notion of 'subjective time' is contrasted to 'objective time'; instead he derives the concept of time from the primal phenomenon of the 'temporality' of 'Dasein'.

'Temporality' is an integral part of 'Dasein', and 'time' only emerges from the condition of 'Dasein'. Time is thus a mode of the temporalization of 'temporality'. The notion of temporality is addressed in Heidegger's existential structural formula of 'care': "ahead-of-itself-Being-already-in (a world) as Being-alongside (entities encountered within-the-world)".[45] The expression "temporality is the meaning of care"[46] indicates that the structure of 'care' as a whole can only be understood if it is related to temporality, since the structure of 'care' is made possible in the first place by temporality. Temporality becomes manifest in such phenomena as primordial future, primordial past and primordial presence. The existential situation of being tied *a priori* to the structure of 'care' is only made possible by the phenomenon of the future. If it were impossible for 'Dasein' to approach itself right from the beginning, it could never be understood as something that has been ahead of time. The situation of 'being-already-in' is grounded in 'having been', thus in the second primordial phenomenon of temporality: 'Dasein' is thus inevitably Being as 'having been', because it has always been in advance of any human being before being 'thrown' into the world. The condition of 'thrownness' and 'fallenness' likewise pertains to the structure of 'care'. This awareness arises from the temporality of 'being present'. Primordial future, primordial 'having been' and primordial 'being present' are temporal manifestations of temporality; in Heidegger's terms they are the *'ecstases'* of temporality.[47] In them 'Dasein' 'stands

---

45 [Note: Albrecht does not give any reference here. – The passage can be traced to *Sein and Zeit*. – The English quotations have been taken from: HEIDEGGER, Martin. *Being and Time*. Trans. John Macquarrie and Edward Robinson. Oxford: Blackwell, 1962. 364. – FKW.]

46 [Cf. HEIDEGGER, Martin. *Being and Time*. Trans. John Macquarrie and Edward Robinson. Oxford: Blackwell, 1962. 377. – FKW.]

47 [Note: Albrecht is summarizing passages from *Being and Time*, chapter III, in which Heidegger elaborates on the three 'out-standing' modes of temporality: past, present and future. Heidegger plays with the literal meaning of the Greek word *'ekstasis'* ('to stand out'): "The future, the character of having been, and the Present show the phenomenal characteristics of the 'towards-oneself', the 'back-to', and the 'letting-oneself-be-encountered-by'. The phenomena of the 'towards …', the 'to …',

out'. The 'standing out' of 'Dasein' within Being becomes manifest in the three existential phenomena: 'Being perceived as understanding', 'Being perceived as thrownness', and 'Being perceived as fallenness'.

The essential theses elaborated in our enquiry so far can thus be summarized: 'being-within-oneself' is a mode of 'being-in-the-world'; and 'being-within-oneself' is 'calmness' as such. And 'calmness' transforms 'care', in that the structure of 'care' is 'calmed down' or laid to rest in the state of 'being-within-oneself'. This provokes the question regarding what this conception of 'Dasein' entails for the phenomenon of temporality and its manifestation in temporalization ('having been-ness'). When the structure of 'care' becomes suspended in 'calmness', temporality is, as it were, without temporalization. In this case, temporality is no longer 'ec-static' [i.e., it does not 'stand out' any longer] but has rather *absorbed in itself* all modes of temporalization. 'Being-within-oneself' is thus a very special, outstanding mode of 'being-in-the-world'; it is a [temporary] mode of being sustained throughout by inner calmness, which is not only diametrically opposed to 'angst' [i.e., eroding 'angst' for the time being], but it also transforms the underlying mood of 'care'. Moreover, the 'calmness' of 'being-within-oneself' is also a special mode of temporality (though I have, admittedly, no appropriate term for it). I can only circumscribe this unique mode of temporality when immersed in the 'calmness' of 'being-within-oneself': *'calmness' is temporality without ecstatic temporalization*. This description denotes quite clearly that 'Dasein's' condition of 'being-within-oneself' is being 'within-itself', but not being 'outside-of-itself'.

It is this special mode of *temporality without 'ecstasis'* that may offer an explanation not only for the ontic phenomenon of 'the [apparent] cessation of time' but also for the mystical phenomenon of the 'Eternal Now'. Yet even more important is the discovery that the phenomenon of 'non-ecstatic temporality' can be supportive for

---

and the 'alongside …', make temporality manifest as the ἐκστατικόν, pure and simple. Temporality is the primordial 'outside-of-itself' in and for itself. We therefore call the phenomena of the future, the character of having been, and the Present, the 'ecstasies' of temporality." HEIDEGGER, Martin. *Being and Time*. Trans. John Macquarrie and Edward Robinson. Oxford: Blackwell, 1962. 377. – FKW.]

delineating more specifically the condition of 'being within-oneself', and thus for enabling us to better understand the essence of the phenomenon of 'calmness'. If the 'calmness' while 'being-within-oneself' is at the same time 'openness' as such, the phenomenon of 'openness' must likewise be rooted in some way in the mode of temporality. However, the results of our enquiry established so far are not yet conclusive enough as to allow us reliable inferences.

We should therefore pause at this stage and review critically the insights gained so far: We have critically examined the 'quiet state of alertness' and tried to identify its underlying anthropological structure. We have been able to establish the condition of 'being-within-oneself' and to specify three of its seminal components: of 'being absorbed within-oneself', 'calmness' and 'openness'. We have, moreover, in the foregoing critical discussion of Ludwig Binswanger considered his ontic conception of 'love' and its underlying anthropological structure. This has revealed that the phenomena termed 'being-lovingly-together' and 'we-hood' by Binswanger are specific and phenomenologically independent modes of existence. The structure of 'Dasein' determined by 'love' rather than by 'care', as claimed by Heidegger, has been expressed by the formula: 'being-preveniently-already-being-with-one-another'. This concept of 'being-in-the-world' offers a modified understanding of 'Dasein' [compared to Heidegger's], rooted in a special mode of existence directed 'towards the [ultimate] Ground', involving a form of 'transcendence' by which the structure of 'care' is overcome. And we have always considered Heidegger's notion of 'care' to be a pivotal critical touchstone and inexorable reference-frame for the fundamental-ontological conception of 'Dasein'. Our anthropological enquiry has finally disclosed three distinct, albeit contiguous, structures of 'being-within-oneself', 'calmness' and 'openness', which are independent and cannot be derived from each other.

It is not evident how the three individual structures might be joined to form a single coherent structure, or to put it more precisely, how the underlying fundamental-ontological condition of being could be disclosed. We can only explore the complex domain of fundamental ontology peripherally, since the aim of our investigation is confined to establishing the philosophical relevance of the 'mystical relation'. Within this limitation, we wish to explore a further aspect: By examining the anthropological structure of the 'quiet state of alertness' individually, we have divorced it from the ontic phenomenon of 'mysticism', with which it is closely linked, since numerous varieties of mystical experience become manifest in the 'quiet state of alertness'. Now the time has come to probe more deeply into the *mystical* state of 'quiet alertness'.

In *Psychology of Mystical Consciousness* we have provided a psychological-phenomenological definition of mysticism, in which a pivotal quality of the 'object' encountered is that of being 'all-encompassing'. The mystical 'object' is perceived as 'arriving' in the 'quiet state of alertness' from a 'sphere' beyond the individual self, and as coming from an alien source that is ultimately unfathomable and unknowable. The 'All-encompassing' that 'arrives' thus has the experiential quality of coming from a foreign sphere, and of being a unique 'Otherness', something wholly 'Ultimate' and 'Incomprehensible'.

The [narrow] psychological definition of mysticism proposed in our previous empirical study has been: "Mysticism is the 'arriving' of an 'All-encompassing' in the 'quiet state of alertness'."[48] This psychological-phenomenological definition of mysticism has not been sufficiently satisfactory for the purposes of the present study. Therefore, a phenomenological-gnoseological analysis of the 'structure of mystical experience' has been applied, which has enabled us to probe more deeply into the core of mystical experience. By this approach we have indeed been able to considerably expand the range of phenomena pertaining to the realm of mysticism. Our focus has no longer been the 'content' of mystical states of consciousness, but the domain beyond the confines of the individual consciousness. This new perspective has enabled the insight that mystical experience is ultimately grounded in a 'mystical relation' that has cognitive import. What has been identified as the 'mystical mode of arriving' on the psychological level corresponds on the level of 'mystical recognition' to a gnoseological relation, which is perceived to be 'close' to the gnoseological sphere of mystical experience in terms of empirical effects. What

---

48 [Cf. ALBRECHT, Carl. *Psychology of Mystical Consciousness*. Trans., intro. and annotated by Franz K. Woehrer. New York: Crossroad, 2019. 373. – FKW.]

have been identified on the psychological level as 'forms of arriving', correspond on the gnoseological level to a composite structure of cognitive perception, which enables us to assess and differentiate between various types of mystical effects. And what, on the psychological level, has been classified as the phenomenon of 'the arrival of the All-encompassing' becomes manifest on the gnoseological level as 'cognitive awareness of the mystical Presence'. And, finally, what on the psychological level of mystical experience has been termed the 'All-encompassing', marked by such qualities as 'alienness', 'otherness' and 'ultimacy', is on the gnoseological level perceived as the 'remote, incomprehensible source' of the mystical impact and diverse effects the 'experiencing self' is exposed to in a mystical occurrence.

We have furthermore taken a third phenomenological step by transcending the sphere of gnoseology in our pursuit of the 'ultimate mystical phenomenon'. This has resulted in the disclosure of the 'ultimate phenomenon' termed the 'mystical relation'. It has been demonstrated phenomenologically that the 'mystical relation' is a real ontic relation between a human being and the 'mystical It'. However, though the realness of this relation is an empirical fact beyond any doubt, it has been impossible to examine its essence, which has thus remained largely in the dark. The only aspects of the 'mystical relation' that can be grasped rationally and empirically are the gnoseological components inherent in the impact and after-effects on the perceiver. Any of the other facets of the 'mystical relation' elude any further elucidation; this includes especially the [transpersonal] structure by which the experience is determined, and any knowledge about the ultimate source of the given mystical effects. The ultimate source of the mystical impacts, in other words, remains eventually inscrutable. What can be perceived by the 'experiencing self' in a concrete mystical event is thus merely the impact or effects impinged upon the perceiver and the awareness of the 'presence' of the 'mystical focal point' to which the 'experiencing self' is related. But the essence of this 'mystical focal point' *cannot* be perceived directly; indirectly it can be grasped empirically by the 'impacts' effected on the perceiver.

The psychological and the gnoseological concepts of mysticism elaborated in the present study finally permit us to propound some pivotal claims of anthropological import: Human existence is inevitably bound to 'worldliness' (in Heidegger's terminology), and this is the reason why the 'mystical relation' is ontically inherent in the 'world'. This is evident from the fact that the phenomenon of 'arriving' and the experience of being 'stricken' or affected by a [mystical] 'impact' occur inevitably within the sphere of 'worldliness'. However, what is, anthropologically speaking, encountered within the domain of 'worldliness', which is ontically an 'innerworldly' encounter, hints at a 'focal point' that eludes entirely any description or qualification by familiar 'modes of being'. This corroborates the validity of the phenomenological claim: The concept of 'worldliness' is at variance with the qualities of 'alienness', 'otherness' and 'ultimacy' germane to the ultimate 'focal point' of a mystical encounter. The concept of 'worldliness' thus fails to extend to the psychological and gnoseological remoteness of the 'mystical focal point'.

It is our endeavour to employ all the established phenomenological components pertaining to the 'mystical relation' for an anthropological concept of 'being', and subsequently for fundamental ontological reflections. In the field of anthropology, existentialist terms and their meanings are not as clearly delineated and strictly defined as is demanded by the branch of fundamental ontology. Thus, it may be granted to speak about the modes of human existence in provisional terms by arranging accumulated data systematically and joining them in a general concept of the human condition. A provisional concept of this is naturally broad and ostensible and must be further specified by additional existential characteristics.

The phenomenon of 'mysticism' is resilient to any attempt to 'explain' it in anthropological terms and renders abortive any effort to incorporate it into the structure of 'being-in-the-world': The existential feature of 'being-with-innerworldly beings' cannot substantiate the claim that the 'mystical relation' is a real potential of human 'Dasein', nor can it account for the rational and non-rational modes of manifestation of the 'mystical relation'. Moreover, the state of 'being-within-oneself' – though it is an outstanding mode of 'being-in-the-world' – can only help us to verify in anthropological terms that the serene state of consciousness termed 'quiet state of alertness' is an empirical fact, but merely acknowledging its phenomenological framework is not enough to substantiate the phenomenon of mysticism. Any attempt to assess seriously the entire established range of mystical phenomena from an anthropological perspective will, on the one hand, be faced with the requirement of sustaining the validity of the structure of 'Dasein' as 'care', and, on the other hand, with securing the claim of 'mysticism' for a place within the anthropological conception of man. Such an enterprise would call for a structural existential framework in which two opposed elements become apparent. The binary anthropological concept of this kind might be described in the following way: *Being human is inevitably 'being-in-the-world', and being human is inevitably a condition of 'Dasein' rooted a priori in a non-worldly relationship*. This formula is both captivating and thought-provoking. Yet this twofold polarity might provoke the false assumption that the *existential* determination of 'Dasein' is likewise governed by a binary pattern, perhaps even by a dialectic one. However, the closer we get to the realm of *existential* determinants, the more pressing becomes the need for careful critical reflection. From the perspective of fundamental ontology, for one, questions like these must inevitably be considered: Does not the formula *'being human is inevitably 'being-in-this-world', and being human is inevitably a condition of 'Dasein' rooted in a non-worldly relationship'* already transgress the confines of anthropology? Does this claim not transcend by far and violate what can responsibly be said from the perspective of anthropology? Does not this statement imply a clandestine ontological step beyond the domain of existential clarification? Does not the expression 'non-worldly-relationship' insinuate speculative notions?

We have stated above that our anthropological formula has been deliberately conceived in provisional and preliminary terms. Thus, it must obviously be further qualified to comply with the tenets of fundamental ontology. It is clear that we must go beyond the bi-polar conception if we wish to find a genuine existential element. Therefore, *the existential concept of 'mysticism'* is only permitted to comprise mystical phenomena that have been approved by *ontological* enquiry, and thus it seems to me that *the only term that can appropriately be applied for denoting the 'mystical existential' is "Offenstand"* [i.e., 'standing open', the state of being unconditionally open and receptive to the realm of

Being]. This key concept will be corroborated in detail after we have expanded the mode of 'being-within-oneself' as a special mode of 'being-in-the-world' by the phenomenon of 'mysticism'.

'Being-within-oneself' is 'openness' [i.e., 'being inwardly open', being alert and receptive to 'in-coming' phenomena]. This mental capacity has been identified ontically as a unique and distinctive feature of the 'quiet state of alertness'. But as a mere feature of the 'quiet state of alertness', 'openness' is just an 'innerworldly' phenomenon, since 'being-within-oneself' means being 'open' within the horizon of this world. But when 'openness' is sustained by the serene and all-pervasive 'calmness' of the 'quiet state of alertness', the term 'openness' applies appropriately – referring to 'openness *as such*'. Hence, the appropriate wording of the formula is: 'Being-within-oneself' is 'openness *as such*'. 'Being-within-oneself' is thus exhaustively characterized by the concept of 'openness'. The structural relationship between the capacity of 'inner sight' and the 'object arriving' in the vista of 'inner sight' within the phenomenological framework of the 'quiet state of alertness' is the ontic form of 'openness as such'. But this anthropological fact can be expanded significantly if the phenomena pertaining to the realm of mysticism are examined in view of the potential condition(s) of their occurrence. When taking this approach, we will realize that the 'openness' encountered when 'being-within-oneself' is merely an 'existential', since it can be shown that 'behind' the anthropological condition of 'openness' an ontological element can be discerned in which not only the anthropological possibility of becoming absorbed in the 'quiet state of alertness' is grounded, but also the anthropological opportunity for mystical experience. It is this ontological element that is understood by the term 'openness' ["Offenstand"], and, as indicated above, we understand by it that 'being-in-the-world' as such is 'being open'.

'Openness' is an anthropological term derived from the ontic phenomenon and is classified as an 'existential' as understood by Heidegger. "Offenstand" is *the condition for the possibility of 'openness'*. 'Being open', understood as an 'existential', is thus not a specific mode of being of an individual, but is an integral part of 'Dasein' *a priori*. As such, 'openness' *is* inevitably an attribute of 'being-in-the-world'. Hence, 'being-in-the-world' is inexorably bound to 'being open'.

'Dasein', however, does not mean 'being-in-the-world' on one occasion, and 'being open' on another. This would be an ontological notion of 'Dasein' resulting from a lapse into the ontic sphere, and it would deprive the term 'existential' of its ontological import. For 'Dasein' is inexorably and perennially rooted in 'being-in-the-world'. And the mode of 'being-in-the-world', hence 'Dasein', is (and has always been and will forever be) bound to the condition of receptive 'openness'.

If we relate these propositions once again to the entire scope of mystical phenomena, we may state: In the mystical state of 'being-within-oneself' the capacity for 'openness' ["Offenheit"] is a mode of the existential condition of 'standing open' ["Offenstand"]. In 'being-within-oneself', the existential situation of 'being-in-the-world' reveals itself as a mode of 'being-in-the-world' that is 'standing open': the 'worldliness' of man being endowed with a 'window'.

The term "Offenstand" has been chosen thoughtfully, which may be endorsed by such metaphoric expressions as the following: Thus 'standing open' does not suggest an opening like a door, or a gate through which one may pass to and fro, nor does it denote an opening like a crack in a wall through which one could pry, but "Offenstand" refers to the inexorable ontological-existential condition for the ontic possibility of man to be affected mystically within this world.

The concept of "Offenstand" is thus a liminal term that denotes the ultimate that can be expressed in language by the standards and the criteria of science. Any serious 'hermeneutics of Dasein' must remain within the sphere of 'Dasein', and abstain from transcending its thresholds, or from adopting notions from foreign 'spheres of being'. The proposition, however, that the 'worldliness' of 'Dasein' is indeed 'open' and 'standing ajar to' the realm of Being, and that in this state of 'standing open' an existential of 'Dasein' has become apparent – that is, to state it more precisely, an existential of mystical import seems to me to be a cogent conclusion from the scientific analyses of a substantial corpus of mystical texts provided in this study.

'Dasein' is and has forever been mystical. This fundamental ontological determinant has been intelligibly expressed by the following formula: *'Dasein' conceived as 'being-in-the-world' is inevitably a condition of 'being open'*. 'Dasein' is a 'windowed' reality of 'worldliness'.

As stated above, this proposition is the ultimate borderline of what we are permitted to express verbally about mysticism as a mode of being in 'Dasein'. This, however, provokes the question as to whether we have abandoned our enquiry into the nature of the 'ultimate phenomenon' of mysticism too early. If 'Dasein', seen from an anthropological perspective, is indeed being situated in a non-worldly relationship, can we then be satisfied with having merely established the condition of 'standing open' as an outstanding feature of being human, rather than probing more deeply into its cognitive potential? Being situated in a non-worldly relationship should, after all, yield more insights than the one that 'worldliness' means 'standing open'. However, the pivotal mystical phenomenon of the 'arrival' of an 'All-encompassing', or the awareness of it 'having arrived', as well as the experience mystical effects impinged upon a recipient and acting on and within him/her, appear to call for an ontological designation which is more comprehensive and conclusive than the term "Offenstand".

Being placed in a non-worldly relationship means being exposed to and/or affected by what has 'arrived' or is about to 'arrive'. Is it possible to uphold this proposition? The claim that the faculty of 'standing open' is the precondition for the possibility that one can ontically be affected [by 'in-coming' phenomena] is persuasively sustained by the foregoing considerations; thus, there would be no need for any further explication. Unless it is true that the 'mystical existential' is the condition for the possibility of a mystical event to occur, our critical reflection would have been abortive. By expanding the ontological formula by the concept of 'being affected', we do not merely include an ontic phenomenon which has already been incorporated; rather, we enlarge the concept of 'existentiality' itself. We do not merely reiterate the claim that 'Dasein' can be affected ontically owing to its faculty of 'standing open', but we instead maintain that 'Dasein' is, and has perennially been, 'being' inevitably exposed to 'being affected'. What we are proposing is that the existential of "Offenstand" is to be supplemented by the existential of 'being affected' ["Betroffenheit"]. I concede, however, that proposing this conception of 'Dasein' transgresses the boundaries of what can responsibly be inferred from the established understanding of 'Dasein', for it contains metaphysical notions 'borrowed' from a domain outside the ontological analysis of 'Dasein'. For this reason, I will confine my conclusions to the concept of "Offenstand". It is not necessary to emphasize once more that the faculty of 'standing open' in 'being-in-the-world' must not be understood in the sense that 'Dasein' is enabled by it, to step out of this world (as it were) ontically by an act of recognition or any other activity. *'Standing open' only denotes the condition of the possibility for becoming 'affected' ontically by an extra-worldly occurrence but does not denote a condition for the possibility of being ontically transferred into an extra-worldly state of being.*

Finally, a conclusive question remains to be considered: We have dealt in some detail above with Binswanger's anthropological structure of 'we-hood', which he developed from the 'ultimate phenomenon' of love. This proposition raises the following question: Could our endeavour to conceive the 'ultimate phenomenon' of mysticism in anthropological-ontological terms open an opportunity for incorporating the structure of 'loving we-hood' into a whole coherent ontological concept of 'Dasein'? The response is, disappointingly, negative, for it seems to me that we have not advanced a single step further in this effort. And the reason for it is that *the ontological foundation for the 'ultimate phenomenon' of love is still missing. Neither the structural unit of 'care', nor the structural unit of 'being-within-oneself-in-the-state-of-openness' are a prerequisite for the possibility of love.*

This fact is obviously ontologically relevant, and at the same time to be understood both as a cautioning and a criticism. It is a cautionary reminder that we must not value too highly the proposed anthropological concept deriving from mysticism, and that we must not presume to have succeeded in providing a universally valid, final concept of the essence of humanity viz., the ultimate nature of being human. The fact that we have been unable to trace love to its ultimate ontological foundation, thereby confirming it to be an 'ultimate phenomenon', is an essential point of criticism which provokes the fundamental critical query: *Is it possible at all to provide adequate ontological foundations for being human on the basis of a 'hermeneutics of Dasein'?* Is the 'hermeneutics of Dasein', which is rooted in the existential conception of 'Dasein' as a mode of understanding itself within the context of 'Being', not inherently entrapped within itself and thus inevitably a biased approach to the essence of human existence? *Should it not be imperative for ontology, which after all aims at disclosing the foundations of humanity, to go beyond the frontiers of a 'metaphysics of Dasein' and to advocate a metaphysics that takes its point of departure from other realms of being?*

CONCLUSION

The fundamental question addressed above does not only open a new perspective but is also based on a change of attitude. We have reached a door that is situated at the boundary between two realms: Behind us is the area in which we were in part occupied with philosophical thoughts, though these reflections cannot claim to be a genuine mode of philosophical thinking. Ahead of us is the area in which recurrent perennial metaphysical problems are encountered, which have been calling for answers from times immemorial. What we have tried to achieve so far by referring to received positions of philosophy is, first, to cleanse the 'cognitive mystical relation' by subjecting it to a critical epistemological scrutiny so that it is brought to light without any bias; and, second, we have introduced the 'mystical relation' as a new 'ultimate phenomenon' into the field of philosophical-anthropological discourse. Here as well our achievement is merely to have allocated the 'mystical relation' to the position where it must be situated if a serious philosophical discourse is expected to commence. That is to say, what we have accomplished is merely a preparatory study [for an in-depth understanding of mysticism], though it also provides in one respect a concluding result in that the 'mystical relation' has been identified as an ontic reality and shown to be a new 'ultimate phenomenon'.

As we have seen, philosophy – understood in the true meaning of the term as 'love of knowledge' and 'pursuit of wisdom' – is placed and moving about in the open and infinite demesne of metaphysics. By introducing the 'ultimate phenomenon' of the 'mystical relation' into philosophical discourse, innovative perspectives might be broached and new questions about the nature of man might be pursued, and thus new answers to ancient metaphysical questions and problems might be supplied. Adopting old-fashioned terms, we may state that the 'ultimate phenomenon' of the 'mystical relation' might have some significant bearing on such fundamental philosophical problems as the nature of the 'soul', of 'freedom' and, ultimately, the quest for 'God'.

Yet there are also metaphysical questions pointing in a different direction. The 'mystical relation' itself must be subjected to an in-depth scrutiny for the purpose of disclosing its concealed ontological foundation. Though the capacity of the mind ends at the thresholds of the intellect, reason cannot be prevented from progressing beyond the confines of rational enquiry and from probing into the realm of the unknown, the unfamiliar and trans-intelligible. Philosophy, in dealing with the 'mystical relation', will inevitably be confronted with such pivotal questions as what the 'mystical relation' is ontologically, and what the ultimate source of 'mystical effects' is, which have been established as empirical fact.

The task of our investigation has been a limited one in that it does not expand into the realms of metaphysics and theology. Our study has been confined to establishing the 'mystical relation' and to substantiate the claim that the 'mystical relation' is both an 'existential' and an 'ultimate phenomenon', hence the capacity for experiencing it is inherent in human nature. Yet by having provided persuasive evidence for the realness and philosophical relevance of the 'mystical relation', our scientific enquiry has reached its final goal.

At this point the question might be asked if there should not also be provided an enquiry dealing with the *theological* relevance of the 'mystical relation'. To this question we would respond that theology, unlike philosophy, has been concerned with the phenomenon of 'mysticism' throughout history. And though the theological conception of 'mysticism' has naturally always been tinged by faith and religious teaching, this means that in the theological concept the 'pure core' of the phenomenon of mysticism appears transformed by received notions inherited from tradition. For this reason, a new phenomenological approach might yield new insights and suggest a new way of dealing with and assessing the theological relevance of the 'mystical relation'. This task, however, falls clearly within the compass of theology, and thus outside our scientific enterprise.

We have taken great care and paid meticulous attention to disentangle in our empirical enquiry the 'mystical relation' from the framework of faith with which it is inevitably intertwined. This approach was an inevitable requirement of scientific objectivity, since the goal of our scientific enquiry was to disclose the 'mystical relation' as a potential capacity inherent in man, and thus to corroborate that it is a potential [empirical and cognitive] certainty, 'accessible' to humanity at large. In this way we have been able to transfer mystical experience phenomenologically from the domain embraced by theology and religion to the area of scientific and philosophical thinking.

This transfer in approaching the phenomenon of mysticism from the field of theology to that of philosophy might provoke the question of whether the alleged rift between philosophical and theological thinking is, after all, not as deep as is commonly claimed, or even if the alleged rift does not exist at all. Philosophy must inevitably adhere to its principles, yet the mystery of the 'mystical relation' will surely trigger a new kind of philosophical thinking. And it is even possible that this innovative philosophical approach might entail a new mode of thinking, which is itself mystical. This, however, would not only require that thinking is concerned with a 'mystical object', but also that thinking itself is transformed into a mystical mode of thinking. Since 'mystical thinking' is subjected to an arduous process of 'catharsis', it is obliged to pursue a pre-ordained goal by which the subject's original intentions are transformed. This purified mode of thinking is governed throughout by a concomitant process of '*catharsis*', and therefore inescapably bound to truth, righteousness, punctiliousness, prudence and fair-mindedness. At the end of this process of mystical thinking the summons is instilled into the subject, that is, the call to abandon verbalized thought and to suspend thinking altogether, and to abide in silence. 'Mystical thinking' thus ends with the subject residing in reposeful silence, immersed in the state of pure receptive 'openness'. He/she will then be perfectly receptive to the 'arrival' of a sublime gift, which though ineffable, is best rendered by 'Love'.[1]

---

1 [Note: This final paragraph is clearly based on Albrecht's own mystical experiences and long-term experience with 'mystical thinking', though he – endowed with the true humility of a mystic – does not expressly say so. But there is evidence from his letters and 'spontaneous mystical utterances', published in ALBRECHT, Carl.

Das Mystische Wort. Erleben und Sprechen in Versunkenheit. [1974]. Ed. Hans A. Fischer-Barnicol. Preface by Karl Rahner. Mainz: Grünewald, 1986, in which Albrecht confirms that large parts of the current book, and key passages of his earlier study *Psychologie des Mystischen Bewußtseins*, resulted from 'mystical thinking'. This means that he articulated spontaneously the thoughts passing through his consciousness while immersed in the 'quiet state of alertness' and recorded these spoken utterances on tape or had them recorded by his wife or another confidante. The final paragraph may be seen as a succinct testimony of a process of 'mystical thinking', culminating in the state of mystical silence and loving bliss. – FKW.]

BIBLIOGRAPHY

List of Works Cited by Albrecht

ADALSTEN, Karola. *Licht aus dem Norden. Die Heilige Birgitta von Schweden.* Freiburg i. Br.: Lambertus, 1951.

ALBRECHT, Carl. *Psychologie des Mystischen Bewußtseins.* Bremen: Schünemann, 1951.

AMMANN, A. M. *Die Gottesschau im Palamitischen Hesychasmus: Ein Handbuch der Spätbyzantinischen Mystik.* 2nd ed. Würzburg: Augustinus, 1948.

ANGELA of FOLIGNO. *Gesichte und Tröstungen der Seligen Angela von Foligno.* Trans. Jan van Arend. Mainz: Grünewald, 1924.

ANONYMOUS. *Erzählungen eines Russischen Pilgers.* Luzern: Stocker, 1944.

ARSENIEW, Nikolaus von. *Ostkirche und Mystik.* Munich: Reinhardt, 1943.

BALFOUR, G. F., Earl of. "A Study of the Psychological Aspects of Mrs. Willett's Mediumship, and of the Statements of the Communicators Concerning Process." *Proceedings of the Society for Psychical Research* 43 (1935): 41–318.

BALL, Hugo. *Byzantinisches Christentum.* Munich: Duncker & Humblot, 1923.

BALTHASAR, Hans Urs von. *Die 'Gnostischen Centurien' des Maximus Confessor.* Freiburg i. Br.: Herder, 1941.

BENDER, Hans. *Parapsychologie – Ihre Ergebnisse und Probleme.* Bremen: Schünemann, 1953.

BERNHART, Joseph. *Philosophische Mystik des Mittelalters von Ihren Antiken Ursprüngen bis zur Renaissance.* Munich: Reinhardt, 1922.

BERNHART, Joseph. *Das Mystische.* Frankfurt: Knecht, 1953.

BIHLMEYER, K. "Mystik." *Kirchliches Handlexikon.* Ed. Michael Buchberger. Munich: Allgemeine Verlagsanstalt, 1912. s.v. "Mystik."

BINSWANGER, Ludwig. *Grundformen und Erkenntnis Menschlichen Daseins.* 2nd ed. Zurich: Niehans, 1953.

BÖHME, Jakob. *Schriften Jakob Böhmes.* Ed. Hans Kayser. Leipzig: Insel, 1923.

BOLLEY, Alfons. "Das Gotteserleben in der Betrachtung." *Geist und Leben* 22 (1949): 343–56.

BOLLNOW, Otto. *Das Wesen der Stimmungen.* 2nd ed. Frankfurt am Main: Klostermann, 1943.

BOLLNOW, Otto F. *Neue Geborgenheit. Das Problem einer Überwindung des Existenzialismus*. Stuttgart: Kohlhammer, 1955.

BREMOND, Henri. *Falsche und Echte Mystik*. Ratisbon: Pustet, 1955.

BUBER, Martin. *Ekstatische Konfessionen*. Leipzig: Insel, 1921.

BUCKE, Richard M. *Kosmisches Bewußtsein*. Ed. and trans. E. v. Brasch. Celle: Kampmann, 1925.

BÜTTNER, Hermann, ed. and trans. *Meister Eckeharts Schriften und Predigten*. 2 vols. Jena: Diederichs, 1919.

CANESI, A. "Vorläufige Untersuchungen über die Psychologie des Gebetes." *Archiv für Religionspsychologie* 10 (1936): 13–72.

CELANO, Thomas de. *Das Leben des Heiligen Franz von Assisi*. Trans. Ph. Schmidt. Basle: Reinhardt, 1921.

CHENEY, Sheldon. *Vom Mystischen Leben. Geschichte der Mystik in den Verschiedenen Zeitaltern*. Wiesbaden: Limes, 1949.

'CHRISTINE, Lucie' [Boutle, Mathilde]. *Geistliches Tagebuch* (1870–1908). Ed. Auguste Poulain, SJ. Trans. Romano Guardini. 3rd ed. Mainz: Grünewald, 1952.

DIONYSIUS AREOPAGITA. "Von der Mystischen Theologie." *Die Angeblichen Schriften des Areopagiten Dionysius*. Trans. J.G.V. Engelhardt. Sulzbach: Seidel, 1823.

DIONYSIUS AREOPAGITA. *Des Heiligen Dionysius Areopagita Angebliche Schriften über die Beiden Hierarchien*. Trans. J. Stieglmayr. 2nd ed. Munich: Kösel, 1911.

DOM, Der. *Bücher Deutscher Mystik*. 13 vols. Leipzig: Insel, 1920–1923.

DRIESCH, Hans. *Leib und Seele. Eine Untersuchung über das Psychophysische Grundproblem*. Leipzig: Reinicke, 1923.

DRIESCH, Hans. *Parapsychologie: Die Wissenschaft von den 'Okkulten' Erscheinungen*. 3rd ed. Zurich: Rascher, 1952.

DÜRCKHEIM-MONTMARTIN, Karlfried, Graf von. *Im Zeichen der Großen Erfahrung*. Munich: Barth, 1951.

FRISCHEISEN-KÖHLER, Max. "Realitätsproblem." *Philosophische Vorträge, Kant-Gesellschaft* 1 and 2 (1912): 1–98.

GEBSATTEL, Emil Viktor, Freiherr von. *Christentum und Humanismus*. Stuttgart: Klett, 1947.

GEHLEN, Arnold. *Der Mensch – Seine Natur und Seine Stellung in der Welt*. Bonn: Athenäum, 1955.

GIRGENSOHN, Karl. *Der Seelische Aufbau des Religiösen Erlebens. Eine Religionspsychologische Untersuchung auf Experimenteller Grundlage*. Leipzig: Hirzel, 1921.

GROETHUYSEN, Bernhard. "Philosophische Anthropologie." *Handbuch der Philosophie. Abteilung III*. Ed. A. Bäumler and M. Schröter. Munich and Berlin: Oldenburg, 1931.

GRUEHN, Werner. *Die Frömmigkeit der Gegenwart. Grundtatsachen der Empirischen Psychologie.* Münster: Aschendorff, 1956.

HÄBERLIN, Paul. *Der Mensch: Eine Philosophische Anthropologie.* Zurich: Spiegel, 1941.

HÄBERLIN, Paul. "Anthropologie und Ontologie." *Zeitschrift für Philosophische Forschung* 4 (1949): 6–28.

HARTMANN, Nicolai. *Grundzüge einer Metaphysik der Erkenntnis.* 2nd ed. Berlin: de Gruyter, 1925.

HARTMANN, Nicolai. "Zum Problem der Realitätsgegebenheit." *Philosophische Vorträge, Kant-Gesellschaft* 32 (1931): 1–97.

HARTMANN, Nicolai. *Neue Wege der Ontologie.* Stuttgart: Kohlhammer, 1947.

HARTMANN, Nicolai. *Zur Grundlegung der Ontologie.* 3rd ed. Meisenheim am Glan: Westkultur-Verlag, 1948.

HEIDEGGER, Martin. *Sein und Zeit* [1927]. 2nd ed. Halle an der Saale: Niemeyer, 1929.

HEIDEGGER, Martin. "Vom Wesen des Grundes." *Festschrift für Edmund Husserl.* Halle an der Saale: Niemeyer, 1929. 71–110.

HEIDEGGER, Martin. *Was ist Metaphysik?* [1929]. Freiburg i. Br.: Klostermann, 1943.

HEILER, Friedrich. *Urkirche und Ostkirche.* Munich: Reinhardt, 1937.

HELLPACH, Willy. *Grundriß der Religionspsychologie.* Stuttgart: Enke, 1951.

HEPPE, Heinrich: *Geschichte der Quietistischen Mystik in der Katholischen Kirche.* Berlin: Hertz, 1875.

HERRIGEL, Eugen. *Zen in der Kunst des Bogenschießens.* Munich: Barth, 1951.

HESSEN, JOHANNES. *Religionsphilosophie.* 2 vols. Freiburg i. Br.: Chamier, 1948.

HILDEGARD von BINGEN. *Schriften der Heiligen Hildegard von Bingen.* Selected, ed. and trans. J. Bühler. Leipzig: Insel, 1922.

HILDEGARD von BINGEN. *Wisse die Wege. Scivias.* Ed. and trans. Abbess Maura Böckeler. Salzburg: Müller, 1955.

HUMPHREYS, Christmas. *Zen Buddhismus.* Munich: Barth, 1951.

HUXLEY, Aldous. *Die Ewige Philosophie. (Philosophia Perennis).* Trans. Henry R. Conrad. Zurich: Steinberg, 1949.

JAENSCH, Erich. *Die Eidetik und die Typologische Forschungsmethode.* Leipzig: Quelle & Meyer, 1925.

JAENSCH, Erich, et al. *Eidetische Anlage und Kindliches Seelenleben.* Leipzig: Barth, 1934.

JAMES, William. *Die Religiöse Erfahrung in Ihrer Mannigfaltigkeit: Materialien und Studien zu einer Psychologie und Pathologie des Religiösen Lebens.* Trans. Georg Wobbermin. Leipzig: Hinrichs, 1907.

JASPERS, Karl. "Über Leibhaftige Bewußtheiten (Bewußtheitstäuschungen), ein Psychopathologisches Elementarsymptom." *Zeitschrift für Pathopsychologie* 2 (1913): 150–61.

JASPERS, Karl. *Allgemeine Psychopathologie*. 5th ed. Berlin: Springer, 1948.

JASPERS, Karl. *Der Philosophische Glaube*. Munich: Piper, 1948.

JELKE, Robert. *Grundzüge der Religionspsychologie*. Heidelberg: Jedermann, 1948.

JOHANNES vom KREUZ [JOHN of the CROSS]. *Sämtliche Werke*. Ed. Aloysius ab Immac. 5 vols. Munich: Kösel, 1924–1952.

JUNG, Carl G. *Psychologische Typen*. Parts 3 and 4. Zurich: Rascher, 1925.

JUNG, Carl G. *Psychologie und Religion*. Zurich: Rascher, 1940.

JUNG, Carl G. Über die Psychologie des Unbewußten. 6th ed. Zurich: Rascher, 1943.

JUNG, Carl G. *Psychologische Betrachtungen*. Zurich: Rascher, 1945.

KARRER, Otto. *Meister Eckehart Spricht: Gesammelte Texte*. Munich: Mueller, 1925.

KARRER, Otto. *Die Große Glut. Textgeschichte der Mystik im Mittelalter*. Munich: Müller, 1926.

KARRER, Otto. *Gott in Uns. Die Mystik der Neuzeit*. Munich: Müller, 1926.

KERNER, Justinus. *Die Seherin von Prevorst: Eröffnungen über das Innere Leben des Menschen und über das Hereinragen einer Geisterwelt in die Unsere*. Leipzig: Reclam, 1930.

KÖNIG, Josef. *Der Begriff der Intuition*. Halle: Niemeyer, 1926.

KRINGS, Hermann. *Fragen und Aufgaben der Ontologie*. Tübingen: Niemeyer, 1954.

LANGEAC, Robert de [Delage, Augustin]. *Geborgenheit in Gott. Aufzeichnungen eines Zeitgenössischen Mystikers*. Trans. H. Härder. Einsiedeln: Benziger, 1952. Series Licht vom Licht, n.s. 2. 26.

LAUER, Hans Erhard. *Die Wiedergeburt der Erkenntnis in der Entwicklungsgeschichte des Menschlichen Erkenntnisstrebens*. Freiburg i. Br.: Novalis, 1946.

LERCHER, Ludwig. "Grundsätzliches über Mystik und Theologie." *Zeitschrift für Katholische Theologie* 42 (1918): 1–45.

MAGER, Alois. *Mystik als Lehre und Leben*. Innsbruck: Tyrolia, 1934.

MAGER, Alois. "Mystik." *Lexikon für Theologie und Kirche*. Vol. 7. Ed. M. Buchberger. Freiburg i. Br.: Herder, 1935.

MARTIN, Bernhard. *Von der Anthroposophie zur Kirche. – Ein Geistiger Lebensbericht*. 2nd ed. Speyer: Pilger, 1950.

MENGE, Gisbert. *Die Beschauung der Mystik*. Paderborn: Junfermann, 1943.

MERKEL, Rudolf F. *Die Mystik im Kulturleben der Völker*. Hamburg: Hoffmann & Campe, 1940.

MOSER, Fanny. *Der Okkultismus: Täuschungen und Tatsachen.* 2 vols. Munich: Reinhardt, 1935.

NEBEL, Gerhard. *Das Ereignis des Schönen.* Stuttgart: Klett, 1953.

OESTERREICH, Traugott K. *Die Religiöse Erfahrung als Philosophisches Problem.* Berlin: Reuther & Reichard, 1915.

OESTERREICH, Traugott K. *Einführung in die Religionspsychologie als Grundlage für Religionsphilosophie und Religionsgeschichte.* Berlin: Mittler, 1917.

OTTO, Rudolf. *Das Gefühl des Überweltlichen. Sensus Numinis.* Munich: Beck, 1932.

OTTO, Rudolf. *Das Heilige: Über das Irrationale in der Idee des Göttlichen und sein Verhältnis zum Rationalen.* [1923]. 26th to 28th ed. Munich: Biederstein, 1947.

PABEL, Reinhold. *Athos, der Heilige Berg. Begegnung mit dem Christlichen Osten.* Münster: Regensburgsche Verlagsbuchhandlung, 1940.

PARAM[A]HANSA, Yogananda. *Autobiographie eines Yogi.* Munich: Barth, 1950.

PFÄNDER, Alexander. *Die Seele des Menschen – Versuch einer Verstehenden Psychologie.* Halle: Niemeyer, 1933.

PFÄNDER, Alexander. *Philosophie der Lebensziele.* Göttingen: Vandenhoeck & Ruprecht, 1948.

PLASSMANN, Joseph, ed. and trans. *Vom Göttlichen Reichtum der Seele – Altflämische Frauenmystik.* Cologne: Diederichs, 1951.

PLOTINUS. *Plotins Schriften.* Trans. Richard Harder. 5 vols. Leipzig: Meiner, 1930–1937.

PORTMANN, Adolf. *Biologische Fragmente zu einer Lehre vom Menschen.* 2nd ed. Basle: Schwabe, 1951.

RAHNER, Karl. *Hörer des Wortes. Zur Grundlegung einer Religionsphilosophie.* Munich: Kösel, 1941.

RÉCÉJAC, Edouard. *Essai sur les Fondements de la Connaissance Mystique.* Paris: Alcan, 1897.

RHINE, J. B. *Neuland der Seele.* Trans. Hans Driesch. Stuttgart: Deutsche Verlags-Anstalt, 1938.

RHINE, J. B. *Die Reichweite des Menschlichen Geistes: Parapsychologische Experimente.* Ed. R. Tischner. Trans. Karl Hellwig. Stuttgart: Deutsche Verlags-Anstalt, 1950.

RINTELEN, Fritz Joachim von. "Sinn und Sinnverständnis." *Zeitschrift für Philosophische Forschung* 2 (1947): 69–83.

ROLLAND, Romain. *Der Götter-Mensch Ramakrisha und das Universale Evangelium des Vivekananda.* 3 vols. Zurich: Rotapfel, 1929.

RUISBROECK, Jan van. *Die Zierde der Geistlichen Hochzeit.* Ed. and trans. Markus Huebner. Leipzig: Insel, 1924.

SCHELER, Max. *Die Stellung des Menschen im Kosmos.* Darmstadt: Reichl, 1930.

SCHELER, Max. *Vom Ewigen im Menschen*. 4th ed., Gesammelte Werke, vol. 5. Berne: Francke, 1954.

SCHMIDT, Bernhard. *Das Geistige Gebet*. Diss. U Breslau, 1916. Halle: Karras, 1916.

SCHMIDT, Heinrich, and Justus STRELLER. *Philosophisches Wörterbuch*. 12th ed. Stuttgart: Kröner, 1951.

SCHMÖGER, Karl E. *Das Leben der Gottseligen Anna Katharina Emmerich*. 2 vols. Freiburg i. Br.: Herder, 1870.

SERTORIUS, Lili. *Katharina von Genua Lebensbild und Geistige Gestalt. Ihre Werke*. Munich: Kösel, 1939.

SEUSE, Heinrich. *Deutsche Schriften*. Ed. and trans. A. Gabele. Leipzig: Insel, 1924.

SMOLITSCH, Igor. *Leben und Lehre der Starzen*. Vienna: Hegner, 1936.

STEGMÜLLER, Wolfgang. "Die Ontologie und Anthropologie von Paul Häberlin." *Zeitschrift für Philosophische Forschung* 2 (1947): 364–81.

STEIN, Edith. *Kreuzeswissenschaft*. Freiburg i. Br.: Herder, 1954.

STEINBÜCHEL, Theodor. *Mensch und Gott in Frömmigkeit und Ethos der Deutschen Mystik*. Düsseldorf: Patmos, 1952.

STEINER, Rudolf. *Wie Erlangt man Erkenntnisse der Höheren Welten?* Berlin: Philosophisch-Anthroposophischer Verlag, 1922.

STEINER, Rudolf. *Die Rätsel der Philosophie*. 2 vols., 6th ed. Dornach: Philosophisch-Anthroposophischer Verlag, 1924 and 1926.

STEINER, Rudolf. *Theosophie: Einführung in Übersinnliche Welterkenntnis und Menschenbestimmung*. New ed. Freiburg i. Br.: Novalis, 1946.

STEINER, Rudolf. *Philosophie der Freiheit. Grundzüge einer Modernen Weltanschauung*. New ed. Stuttgart: Behrendt, 1947.

STEINER, Rudolf. *Die Geheimwissenschaft im Umriss*. New ed. Stuttgart: Freies Geistesleben, 1948.

STEINER, Rudolf. *Wahrheit und Wissenschaft*. New ed. Freiburg i. Br.: Novalis, 1948.

STEINER, Rudolf. *Grundlinien einer Erkenntnistheorie der Goetheschen Weltanschauung*. New ed. Freiburg i. Br.: Novalis, 1949.

STIGLMAYR, Josef, ed. *Des Heiligen Dionysius Areopagita Angebliche Schriften über die Beiden Hierarchien*. Trans. J. Stiglmayr. 2nd ed. Kempten: Kösel, 1911.

SUZUKI, Daisetz T. *Die Grosse Befreiung*. 3rd ed. Constance: Weller, 1947.

SWEDENBORG, Immanuel. *Theologische Schriften*. Trans. Lothar Brieger. Jena: Diederichs, 1904.

SYMEON the New Theologian. *Licht vom Licht: Hymnen*. Trans. Kilian Kirchoff. Munich: Kösel, 1951.

TAULER, Johannes. *Predigten*. Leipzig: Insel, 1923.

THERESIA von JESU [Theresa of Avila]. *Sämtliche Schriften. Neue Deutschsprachige Ausgabe.* 6 vols. Munich: Kösel, 1935–1958. *Vida* (Leben). Trans. Aloysius Alkofer. Vol. I. Munich: Kösel, 1952.

TISCHNER, Rudolf. *Ergebnisse Okkulter Forschung.* Stuttgart: Deutsche Verlags-Anstalt, 1950.

TRILLHAAS, Wolfgang. *Grundzüge der Religionspsychologie.* Munich: Kaiser, 1946.

TYRRELL, George N. *The Personality of Man. New Facts and Their Significance.* West Drayton: Penguin, 1948.

UNDERHILL, Evelyn. *Mystik. Eine Studie über die Natur und Entwicklung des Religiösen Bewußtseins im Menschen.* Trans. Helene Meyer-Franck and Heinrich Meyer-Benfey. Munich: Reinhardt, 1928.

URBAN, Hubert. *Über-Bewußtsein ("Cosmic Consciousness"). Nach Bucke and Walker Bearbeitet.* Innsbruck: Tyrolia, 1950.

VETTER, August. *Die Philosophischen Grundlagen des Menschenbildes.* Leipzig: Klotz, 1942.

VETTER, August. *Natur und Person. Umriss einer Anthropognomik.* Stuttgart: Klett, 1949.

VILLER, Marcel, and Karl RAHNER. *Aszese und Mystik in der Väterzeit. Ein Abriss der Frühchristlichen Spiritualität.* Freiburg i. Br.: Herder, 1939.

VOLKELT, Johannes. *Die Gefühlsgewißheit. – Eine Erkenntnistheoretische Untersuchung.* Munich: Beck, 1922.

WALTHER, Gerda. "Die Bedeutung der Phänomenologischen Methode Edmund Husserls für die Parapsychologie." *Psychophysikalische Zeitschrift* 2 and 3 (1955): 22–29; 37–40.

WALTHER, Gerda. "Die Innerseelische Seite Parapsychologischer Phänomene." *Neue Wissenschaft: Zeitschrift für Parapsychologie* 6 (11/12) (1956): 364–73; and 6 (13) (1957): 408–22.

WALTHER, Gerda. *Phänomenologie der Mystik.* 2nd ed. Freiburg i. Br.: Olten, 1955.

WARCOLLIER, René. *Mind to Mind*: New York: Creative Age Press, 1948.

WEIN, Hermann. "Von Descartes zur Heutigen Anthropologie." *Zeitschrift für Philosophische Forschung* 2 (1947): 296–314.

WEIN, Hermann. *Das Problem des Relativismus: Philosophie im Übergang zur Anthropologie.* Berlin: Francke, 1950.

WEINHANDL, Margarete. *Deutsches Nonnenleben. Das Leben der Schwestern zu Töss und der Nonne von Engeltal.* 2 vols. Munich: Recht, 1921.

WEIZSÄCKER, Viktor von. *Der Kranke Mensch. Eine Einführung in die Medizinische Anthropologie.* Stuttgart: Koehler, 1951.

WILKINS, Sir Hubert, and Harold M. SHERMAN. *Thoughts Through Space. A Remarkable Adventure in the Realm of Mind.* New York: Creative Age Press, 1942.

WITZENMANN, Herbert. "Intuition und Beobachtung." *Die Drei: Monatsschrift für Anthroposophie, Dreigliederung und Goetheanismus* 18.1 (1948): 36–51.

WITZENMANN, Herbert. "Vom Denken, Fühlen und Wollen." *Die Drei: Monatsschrift für Anthroposophie, Dreigliederung und Goetheanismus* 18.2 (1948): 118–28.

WÜST, Joseph. "Physikalische und Chemische Grundlagen der Menschlichen Aura." *Neue Wissenschaft: Zeitschrift für Grenzgebiete des Seelenlebens* 4 (1954): 193–200; 257–66.

List of Works Cited in General Introduction and Notes

ALBRECHT, Carl. *Das Mystische Wort. Erleben und Sprechen in Versunkenheit.* [1974]. Ed. Hans A. Fischer-Barnicol. Preface by Karl Rahner. Mainz: Grünewald, 1986.

ALBRECHT, Carl. *Psychology of Mystical Consciousness.* Trans., intro. and annotated by Franz K. Woehrer. New York: Crossroad, 2019.

ANGELA of FOLIGNO. *The Book of Divine Consolation of the Blessed Angela of Foligno.* Trans. Mary G. Steegmann. London: Chatto and Windus, 1909.

AUDI, Robert, gen. ed. *The Cambridge Dictionary of Philosophy.* 2nd ed. Cambridge: CUP, 1999.

BALTHASAR, Hans Urs von. "Zur Ortsbestimmung Christlicher Mystik." Ed. Werner Beierwaltes, Hans Urs von Balthasar, and Alois M. Haas. *Grundfragen der Mystik.* Einsiedeln: Johannes, 1974. 37–71.

BÄUMER, Bettina. *Abhinavagupta. Wege ins Licht. Texte des Tantrischen Śivaismus aus Kaschmir.* Zurich: Benziger, 1992.

BÄUMER, Bettina, ed. *Mysticism in Shaivism and Christianity.* New Delhi: Printworld, 1997.

BERINGER, Kurt. *Der Meskalinrausch. Seine Geschichte und Erscheinungsweise.* Berlin: Springer, 1927.

BIBLE. *The New English Bible with the Apocrypha.* Oxford Study Edition. New York: Oxford UP, 1976.

BLANNBEKIN, Agnes. *Leben und Offenbarungen der Wiener Begine Agnes Blannbekin († 1315).* Ed. and trans. Peter Dinzelbacher. Göppingen: Kümmerle, 1994.

BOCK, Eleonore. *Die Mystik in den Religionen der Welt* [1991]. 2nd ed. Münster: Principal, 2009.

BRENTANO, Clemens, ed. *Das Marienleben. Nach den Betrachtungen von Anna Katharina Emmerich.* Munich: Literarisch-Artistische Anstalt, 1842.

BRENTANO, Clemens, ed. *Das Bittere Leiden Unseres Herrn Jesu Christi. Nach Betrachtungen der Gottseligen Anna Katharina Emmerich, Nebst dem Lebensumriß dieser Begnadigten* [sic]. Munich: Literarisch-Artistische Anstalt, 1864.

BUCKE, Richard M. *Cosmic Consciousness. The Evolution of the Human Mind.* New York: Dutton, 1901.

BÜHLER, Johannes, ed. and trans. *Hildegard von Bingen. Wisse die Wege.* Frankfurt a. Main: Insel, 2008.

CONZE, Edward. *Buddhist Meditation.* London: Unwin, 1972.

COULTER, Dale M. *'Per Visibilia ad Invisibilia': Theological Method in Richard of St. Victor (c. 1173).* Turnhout: Brepols, 2006.

DAHLSTROM, Daniel O. *The Heidegger Dictionary.* London: Bloomsbury, 2013.

DAWKINS, Richard. *The God Delusion.* London: Bantam, 2006.

DAWKINS, Richard, Daniel DENNET, Sam HARRIS. and Christopher HITCHENS. *The Four Horsemen. The Discussion That Sparked an Atheist Revolution.* Foreword by Christopher Fry. London: Bantam, 2019.

ECKHART, Meister. *Meister Eckehart. Deutsche Predigten und Traktate.* Ed. Franz Pfeiffer. 2nd ed. Göttingen: Vandenhoeck & Ruprecht, 1908.

EGAN, Harvey, S.J. *Christian Mysticism. The Future of a Tradition.* New York: Pueblo, 1984.

ENOMIYA-LASSALLE, Hugo, S.J. *Meditation als Weg zur Gotteserfahrung. Eine Anleitung zum Mystischen Gebet.* Mainz: Grünewald, 1972.

ENOMIYA-LASSALLE, Hugo, S.J. *Zen und Christliche Spiritualität.* Munich: Kösel, 1987.

FORBES, Christopher. "Early Christian Inspired Speech and Hellenistic Popular Religion." *Novum Testamentum* 28 (1986): 257–70.

FÜHRKÖTTER, Adelgundis, and Angela CARLEVARIS, eds. *Hildegardis Bingenensis Scivias.* Turnhout (Belgium): Brepols, 1978.

GRANT, Patrick, ed. *A Dazzling Darkness: An Anthology of Western Mysticism.* Grand Rapids/MI: Eerdmans, 1985.

HARPER, Douglas. *Etymological Dictionary Online.* Web. 14 March 2018. <https://www.etymonline.com/word/numen>.

HART, Columba, and Jane BISHOP. *Hildegard of Bingen: Scivias.* (Classics of Western Spirituality). New York: Paulist Press, 1990.

HEIDEGGER, Martin. *Being and Time.* Trans. John Macquarrie and Edward Robinson. Oxford: Blackwell, 1962.

HEISENBERG, Werner. *Ordnung der Wirklichkeit.* Ed. K. Kleinknecht. Munich: Springer, 2019. (Kindle ed.)

INSTITUTE of CARMELITE STUDIES. <https://www.icspublications.org/>

INWOOD, Michael. *A Heidegger Dictionary.* Oxford: Blackwell, 1999.

JAMES, William. *Varieties of Religious Experience. A Study in Human Nature. Being the Gifford Lectures on Natural Religion Delivered at Edinburgh in 1901–1902.* [1902]. New York: Random House, 1929.

KRABBE, Caspar F. *Erinnerung an die Selige Anna Catharina Emmerich, Augustinerin des Klosters Agnetenberg in Duelmen*. Münster: Regensburg, 1860.

LEVENSON, Michael R., and Carolyn M. ALDWIN. "Mindfulness in Psychology and Religion." *Handbook of the Psychology of Religion and Spirituality*. Ed. PALOUTHIAN, Raymond, and Crystal L. PARK. 2nd ed. New York: Guilford Press, 2013. 580–91.

McGINN, Bernard, and John MEYENDORFF, eds. *Christian Spirituality I. Origins to the Twelfth Century*. New York: Crossroad, 1985.

McGINN, Bernard. *The Presence of God. A History of Christian Mysticism*. Vol. I, *The Foundations of Mysticism*. London: SCM, 1991.

NEWMAN, Barbara, ed. *Voice of the Living Light. Hildegard of Bingen and Her World*. Oakland/CA: University of California Press, 1998.

NEWMAN, F. X. "St. Augustine's Three Visions and the Structure of Commedia." *Modern Language Notes* 82 (1967): 58–61.

NISHIDA, Kitaro. *Kitarō Zenshū* [*Complete Works of Nishida Kitarō*]. Tokyo: Iwanami, 1987–89.

O'BRIEN, Astrid M. *A Mysticism of Kindness: The Biography of 'Lucie Christine.'* Scranton/PA: University of Scranton Press, 2010.

O'MURCHU, Diarmuid. *Quantum Theology. Spiritual Implications of the New Physics*. Revised and Updated Edition, with Reflective Questions. New York: Crossroad, 2004.

PARAMAHANSA, Yogananda. *Autobiography of a Yogi*. [1946]. 13th ed. Preface by W.Y. Evans-Wentz. Los Angeles/CA: Self-Realization Fellowship, 1998. E-book.

PENG-KELLER, Simon. *Gottespassion in Versunkenheit. Die Psychologische Mystikforschung Carl Albrechts aus Theologischer Perspektive*. Würzburg: Echter, 2003.

PEZ, Bernhard, ed. *Ven. Agnetis Blannbekin Vita et Revelationes Auctore Anonymo Ord. FF. Min. Accessit Pothonis. Liber de Miraculis Sanctae Dei Genitricis Mariae. Primum Edidit R.P. Bernardus Pez*. Vienna: Monath, 1731.

PLOTINUS. *The Enneads*. Trans. Stephen MacKenna. 2nd ed. rev. by B. S. Page. London: Faber & Faber, 1956.

POULAIN, Auguste, ed. *The Spiritual Journal of Lucie Christine (1870–1908)*. London: Paul, Trench, Trubner & Co., 1920.

PSEUDO-DIONYSIUS AREOPAGITA. *The Mystical Theology* <www.hoye.de/theo/ denistxt.pdf>

RUH, Kurt. *Geschichte der Abendländischen Mystik*. 2nd ed. Vol. 1. Munich: C. H. Beck, 2001.

SAKAGUCHI, Alicja. *Sprechakte der Mystischen Erfahrung: Eine Komparative Studie zum Sprachlichen Ausdruck von Offenbarung und Prophetie*. Freiburg im Breisgau: Alber, 2015.

SCHULTZ, J. H. *Das Autogene Training (Konzentrative Selbstentspannung). Versuch einer Klinisch-praktischen Darstellung*. Leipzig: Thieme, 1932.

SHELDRAKE, Philip, ed. *The New Westminster Dictionary of Western Spirituality*. Louisville/KY: SCM Press, 2005.

SLOTERDIJK, Peter, ed. *Mystische Zeugnisse aller Zeiten und Völker. Gesammelt von Martin Buber*. Munich: Diederichs, 1993.

STACE, Walter T. *Mysticism and Philosophy*. London: Macmillan, 1960.

Stanford Encyclopedia of Philosophy. 6 March 2018. <https://plato.stanford.edu/entries/medieval-haecceity/>.

STANLEY, Gordon, W. K. BARTLETT, and Terri MOYLE. "Some Characteristics of Charismatic Experience: Glossolalia in Australia." *Journal for the Scientific Study of Religion* 17 (1978): 269-77.

SUSO, Henry. *The Life of the Servant*. Trans. James M. Clark. Cambridge: Lutterworth, 1952.

TERESA of AVILA. *The Life of St. Teresa of Jesus of the Order of Our Lady of Carmel. Written by Herself: St. Teresa of Avila*. Trans. from the Spanish by D. Lewis. 3rd ed. London: Baker, 1904.

UNDERHILL, Evelyn. *Mysticism. A Study in the Nature and Development of Man's Spiritual Consciousness*. London: Methuen, 1911.

WAINWRIGHT, Gordon, ed. *Dictionary of Christian Spirituality*. London: SCM, 1983.

WALSHE, Maurice O'C., ed. and trans. *The Complete Mystical Works of Meister Eckhart*. New York: Crossroad, 2009.

WOEHRER, Franz K. "*The Cloud of Unknowing*: A Late Medieval Example of Apophatic Spiritual Guidance." *Studies in Spirituality* (Louvain, Belgium) 7 (1997): 113-44.

INDEX

A

Abhinavagupta, xliv, xliv n.6, xliv n.7
Absence (of God), 105, 199, 223 (*see also* Dark Night of the Soul)
Albrecht, Carl, (works, first editions) *Das Mystische Erkennen* (1958), xvii, xxvii, xxx, xxx n.5, xxxi, 2 n.2
    Das Mystische Wort (1974), xxx, xxx n.5, xxx n.6, xxxii, xxxii n.11, xxxiii n.12, xlii, xlii n.4, xlv n.8, xlviii n.11, 269 n.110, 465 n.1
    Psychologie des Mystischen Bewußtseins (1951), xii, xviii, xxx, xxx n.7, xxxi, 1, 1 n.1, 3, 19, 39-40 n.49, 47 n.54, 139 n.49, 315, 436 n.37, 465 n.1
'All-encompassing, the', ["Das Umfassende"], xii, xix, liv, liv n. 19, 1-2, 19, 38, 41, 57, 58, 82, 93, 122, 184, 195, 203, 218, 221, 222, 249, 250-251, 274, 275, 276, 316, 436, 457
    characteristics of experiencing the A., 39-40, 60, 70, 71, 74, 98, 102, 129, 141, 143, 145, 148, 150, 156-157, 175, 187-188, 207, 213, 219-221, 223, 225, 228, 238, 250, 252-253, 255-256, 264-267, 280, 316, 317, 319, 392, 397 n. 11, 443, 451, 452
    cognitive awareness of, 90, 96, 101, 120, 145, 187, 205, 213, 215, 249, 290, 391, 400
    epiphanic vision of, 146, 152, 155, 235, 237, 238, 367
    person-like quality of, 74, 118, 209, 243, 291-303
    self-revelation of, 232-234, 238-239, 242, 390-391
Alvarez, Pedro, 172, 223
Angela of Foligno, xx, 306-311, 307 n.114, 309 n.115, 316-317, 319-320, 320 n.117
Angels, 23, 24, 28, 39, 82, 89, 91, 96, 154, 165, visions of, 100-102, 107-108, 110, 114-115, 118, 125, 170
Angst, existential condition of, 422, 427-431, 428 n.26, 432, 433, 434, 440-444, 449
Annihilation, (of 'I-hood'), 44-45 n.52, 208, 211, 259, 261, 288, 309, 315, 316
Anthropology, l, 3, 5, 404-416, 453, 454
Apophatic (negative) theology, xxiv, xxiv n.7, xxv, xxxix, xxxix n.22, 44 n.52, 72 n.6, 258-260, 262, 263, 296, 296 n.113, 306
Apparition (perceived with the physical and/or spiritual eyes as occurring in external space)
    (*see also visio corporalis*), 20, 79, 87, 103, 106, 108, 139, 227 n.99, 276, 278
Appearance, inward (pictorial vision perceived in 'inner sight'), 78, 88
    definition of, 89-90, 122, 145, 237, 238, 336, 337-339
    mystical a., 90-91, 101, 106, 147, 237, 245
    self-expressive epiphanic a. ["Ausdruckserscheinung"] 238-239, 241-244, 245, 275, 276, 280, 290, 292, 345, 355-356, 365, 367-369, 374, 389, 391
    non-mystical a., 72, 81, 86, 87-90
Archetype, 89, 91, 357, 408, 409
'Arriving', (as a key-phenomenon in altered states of consciousness; an object arriving' in the vista of 'inner sight'), ["das Ankommende"], xix, xl, xliii, l, 1-2, 4, 18-20, 38, 69-75, 78, 81, 86, 90, 95, 98, 106, 113, 117, 125, 141, 143, 146, 152, 175, 180, 184, 188, 212, 213, 214, 222, 226, 227, 228, 248, 249, 253, 268, 277, 283, 296, 304, 327, 331, 336, 340, 343, 345-347, 349, 350, 357-359, 361, 385, 386, 387, 391, 409, 440, 443, 444, 446, 451-453, 455
Ascent, spiritual, xxxvi, 26, 137, 233 n.101, 259, 442 n.42
Auditory mystical experience, ('inner hearing' of words, voices, sounds; sense of being spoken to), xlii, liv, 4, 111, 112, 116, 206, 209, 215, 220, 226-227, 229, 231,

479

233, 265, 267, 268, 276-284, 285, 307, 341, 344, 347, 348, (genuine vs. delusory) 350-351, 352, 354, 358, 380, 382, 400
Augustine, St., xxiii, liv n.18, 75, 179, 190, 233, (*De genesi ad litteram*) 75-76 n.8, 227 n.99
Autogenic Training, (J. H. Schultz), xix, xxxi, xxxvii
Awakening, spiritual, xxi, 73

B

Balthasar, Hans Urs von, xxxiii-xxxiv, xxxiv n.14
Bäumer, Bettina, xxxix n.23, xliv n. 6, xliv n.7
Beierwaltes, Werner, xxxiv n.14
Binswanger, Ludwig, 412-417, 419, 419 n.15, 423, 424, 425, 430 n.29, 432, 433, 434, 450, 458
Blannbekin, Agnes, 148-149, 149 n.54
Bliss, ineffable (elicited by a mystical event), xxvi, liii, 50, 51, 52, 53, 54, 56, 107, 108, 109, 120, 123, 127, 130, 131, 135, 139, 141, 145, 155, 173, 175, 197, 208, 211, 218, 219, 236, 261, 309, 316, 319, 320, 322, 341, 347, 360, 369, 466
Bock, Eleonore, xxxiv-xxxv, xxxiv n.16
Böhme, Jakob, xx, 49, 54-56, 55 n.65
Bollnow, Otto, 52-55, 52 n.59, 53 n.61, 53 n.62, 54 n.64, 430-433, 431 n.30, 434, 442, 442 n.41, 442 n.43
Brentano, Clemens, 83 n.13
'Bridal mysticism', 357 n.4
Buber, Martin, 55, 55 n.65, 59, 84 n.14, 98 n.21, 153, 153 n.57, 211 n.88
Bucke, Richard M., lii, 45, 48, 49, 52, 130, 131
   Cosmic Consciousness, lii n.16, 45 n.53, 48 n.55, 52 n.58, 130 n. 34, 130 n.35
Buddhism, xxi, xxxix, 60-61, 61 n.70, 61 n.71, 232 n.100
   jhana, stages of, xxxix, xxxix n.24
   samadhi, 49, 129
   satori, xxi, 60-61

C

Calmness, within (permeating the 'quiet state of alertness'), xxiv, xxxviii, xlvii, 2, 139, 171, 224, 248, 253, 264, 284, 322, 436, 439-440, 455, (as an existential condition) 440-447, 449-450

Cataphatic theology, xxiv n.7, xxv
Christ, xxv, 23, 81, 87, 90, 91, 104, 133, 135, 138, 183, 237, 278, 307, 311
   Passion of, 82, 84-85, 307, 357 n.4
   vision of, 81-82, 86, 91-92, 100-102, 116-121, 125, 141, 171-173, 175, 192, 211, 237, 244, 311, 357, 390, 400, 409
Clairvaux, Bernard, 357 n.4
Clairvoyance, (as a potential corollary of paranormal, visionary and mystical experiences), 13, 14, 15, 17, 51, 52, 54, 85, 91, 97, 307, 357
Clarity of consciousness, enhanced condition of, xxxvii, 77, 102, 104, 124, 126-127, 134, 148-149, 151, 153, 155-156, 171, 174, 183, 189, 190, 211, 213, 253, 274, 281, 297, 315, 320, 322, 344, 346, 352, 377, 440, 441
Cloud of Unknowing, The, xxxix n.22, 44 n.52, 72 n.6, 73 n.6
Cognition, *see* cognitive mystical experience
cognitio Dei experimentalis, xxi, 73 n.7
Compassion, *com-passio*, 307, 357 n.4, 368
Contemplation, xxxviii, xxxix, 44 n.52, 48, 73 n.7, 75, 75 n.8, 106, 182, 190, 193, 224, 233 n.101, 245, 247, 259, 261, 307, 331, 372
   contemplatio acquisita, 73 n.7,
   contemplatio infusa, xxxix, 73 n.7
Consciousness, mystical, xvii, xviii, xxxiv, xxxvi, xxxvii, xliii, 2, 46, 56, (characteristics of) 2-3, 305, 443
Conversion, xxii, 73, 207, 208, 314, 341, 353, 372

D

Darkness, unfathomable, xxii, 94, 105, 134, 138, 146, 200, 203, 213, 255-259, 262-265, 265 n. 109, 266, 267, 268, 279, 286, 305, 308, 310-311, 313, 343, 368, 372, 392
Dark Night of the Soul, (John of the Cross), xxii, xxiv
Dawkins, Richard, *The God Delusion*, li n.13, 186 n.74
Detachment (from this world), xxiv, 117, 232 n.100, 259
Devil, visions of, 24, 86, 89, 91, 100-107, 110, 118, 124, 170, 245
Devotion, affective practice of, 85, 91, 307, 357, 357 n.4

INDEX

Divine, the, xxi, xxvi, xliii n.5, 44 n.52, 74, 75 n.8, 87, 90, 115, 132, 136, 149, 183, 190, 192, 193, 227, 244, 258, 262, 263, 296 n.113, 320, 323, 354, 400

E

Eckhart, Meister, xix, xxix, xxix n.1, xxix n.2, 44 n.52, 258, 261, 261 n.107, 263, 306

Ecstasy, state of, xxvi, xxxiii, 1, 12, 99, 106, 152, 156, 262, 265, 266, 307, 309, 316, 317, 321, 322, 331
    mystical state of, 1, 51, 95, 108-109, 113, 127, 183, 191, 192, 218, 237, 272, 312, 315, 316-317, 318

Egan, Harvey, xxxv, xxxvi, xxxvi n.18

Emmerich, Anna Katharina, xx, 83-85, 83 n.13, 85 n.15

Emptying of consciousness, process of, (*see also* 'introversion') xxix, xxxi, xxxiii, xxxvii, xxxviii, xxxix, xli, 232 n.100, 247, 263

Enlightenment, xxi, 61, (*see also* awakening, spiritual)

Enomiya-Lassalle, Hugo, SJ, xxx, xxxi, xxxi n.9, xxxi n.10, xxxii, xxxv

Existentialist philosophy, xiii n.4, xviii, l, li, lvi, 40, 204 n.87, 330, 426, 453

Extrasensory perception, (ESP), 13-14, 17

F

Faith, religious, (influence on mystical experience), xii, xiv, xix, xxv, xlv, 47, 87, 161, 171, 173, 190, 191, 194, 210, 227, 295, 310, 394, 399, 400, 465

Fischer, Roland, xxxiii n.13

Fischer-Barnicol, Hans A., xxx n.6, xxxii, xxxiii, xlii, xlviii, 269 n.110, 465 n.1

Francis of Assisi, St., 353 n.1

Freud, Sigmund, li n.13

G

Ghazali, Abu Hamid al-, xxvi, xxvi n. 9

'Ghost-Seer', 10, 21-23, 25, 27, 29, 32, 97

Gilbert (Wibert) of Gembloux, 97, 97 n.20

'Givenness' (of a mystical phenomenon/event), ["Gegebenheit"], xxxiii, 73, 86, 110, 118, 120, 218, 227, 242, 326, 345, 349, 352, 380, 381, 438

'Glimpse of God', (as a variety of religious mystical experience), 124, 135, 150, 192, 210, 232, 234-238, 240, 241

Glossolalia, xlii, xliii n.5

Gnoseological Pyramid, (in discerning mystical phenomena), lv, 370-374, 376, 393

Gnoseology, xviii, xliv, l, liii, 20, 43, 47, 57, 112, 231, 314, 318, 333-400, 381, 452

Gnosis, xxi, 59, 132

God, xiv, xxi, xxii, xxiii, xxiv, xxvi, xxix, xxx, xxxiii-xxxiv, xliii n.5, xlvi, 44 n.52, 45 n.52, 50, 51, 55, 73 n.6, 73 n.7, 98-99, 107-109, 114, 115, 116, 127, 132, 133-134, 136, 142, 148, 149-151, 154, 161, 173, 181-183, 186, 189-194, 210, 211, 221-224, 227, 228, 233 n.101, 234-237, 244, 246, 259, 261-262, 263, 266 n.109, 270, 296 n.113, 310-312, 312 n.116, 316, 320, 322-323, 330, 341, 346, 351, 352, 353 n.1, 357, 410, 442 n.42, 464

Godhead, the, 44 n.52, 55, 173, 192, 193, 260, 261, 263, 308

Grace, (gift of God, *gratia gratis data*), xxxiii, xlv n.8, xlvi, 11, 21, 69 n.13, 73 n.6, 73 n.7, 83, 85, 96, 104, 107, 115, 133, 137, 172, 173, 181, 211, 233 n.101, 235, 236, 246, 345, 430

Grassi, Ernesto, xiii n.4

Gregorius Palamas, 133-135

Gruehn, Werner, 160 n.62, 321 n.118, 322-323

H

Haas, Alois M., xxxiv n.14

Hartmann, Nicolai, 30, 30 n.30, 65-66 n.1, 288 n.112, 378, 378 n.7, 378 n.8, 379 n.9

Heidegger, Martin, xiii n.4, l, lvi, 52, 204, 379, 412-413, 415-431, 429 n.28, 432, 434, 437, 438, 445-450, 453, 455
    Hermeneutics of "Dasein", l, lvi, 52, 416-450, 456, 458
    Sein und Zeit / Being and Time, 52 n.60, 330 n.121, 379 n.10, 413 n.12, 417 n. 13, 435 n.36, 437 n.39, 437-438 n.39, 438 n.40, 445 n.44, 448-449 n.45-47

Heiler, Friedrich, 132 n.36, 133, 134 n.38, 135

Heisenberg, Werner, xlviii, xlix, xlix n.12

Heschel, Abraham J., xvii, xvii-xviii n.1

Hesychasts, the, xix, 131-134, 132 n.36, 142-143, 153

INDEX

Hildegard of Bingen, xix, 92-95, 94 n.16, 95 n.17, 97, 97 n.20, 98-100, 106, 109, 116, 187
Hinduism (Hinduist mystical tradition), xx, xxi, xxxix, xliv, 129-131, 232 n.100
Holy Spirit, xxxii n.11, 55, 73, 138, 191
Husserl, Edmund, 18, 426 n.23, 426 n.24

I

Illuminantion, xxii, xlii, xlviii, xlix, lvi, 125, 126, 127, 131, 141, 142, 146, 147, 148, 150-151, 189, 190, 192, 194, 208, 346, 347, 354
    infusa illuminatio, (mystically instilled i.) 187, 187 n.75, 195, 210, 307, 309, 341, 345, 347-349, 358
'Inner eye', *see* 'inner sight'
'Inner sight' /'inward perception' ["Innenschau"] xl, xlii, 1, 2, 19, 38, 56-57, 60, 71, 75, 81, 83, 87-90, 93, 95, 98, 100, 106, 108, 110-113, 117, 118, 120, 121, 122-123, 126, 128, 130, 140-143, 145, 146-152, 158, 163, 165, 168, 170, 175, 179-180, 183-185, 212-213, 216, 226-228, 232, 237, 242, 248, 249, 252-254, 256, 263-268, 272, 273, 275, 277, 285, 286, 299, 304, 307, 309, 315, 319, 321, 331, 336, 343, 350, 356, 366, 372, 385-388, 390-392, 409, 435, 436, 443, 444, 455
Insight, mystical, xxi, 183-195, 186 n.74, 216-217, 225, 228, 229, 230-232, 248, 283, 314, 344-349, 355, 358-359, 361, 362, 372
Introspection, ["Versenkung"] (*see also* process of emptying consciousness), xix, xxxi, xxxvii, xxxviii-xxxix, xli, l, 247, 263
Intuition, xii, xlii-xlviii, 5, liv, 34, 35, 36, 36 n.48, 37, 57, 111-112, 340, 344, 347, 351, 430
    mystically infused (*see also* insight, mystical) lvi, 20, 74, 179-180, 185, 186-188, 190, 192, 194, 196, 210, 216-219, 226, 228-230, 241, 291, 344, 345, 354, 369

J

James, William, lii, lii n.15, 48 n.55, 54 n.63, 102, 166, 168, 170, 174, *Varieties of Religious Experience*, 48 n. 55, 102 n. 23, 136, 167 n.66
Jaspers, Karl, 39-40 n.49, 160, 160 n.60, 161, 161 n.63, 162 n.64, 258 n.104, 426

Jesus, *see* Christ
Jesus Prayer, 133, 135
John of the Cross, xx, xxiv, 44 n.52, 73 n.7
Jung, C. G., xxii, 89, 91, 357, 408-409, 408 n.6

L

Light, as a mode of visionary experience, liv, 4, 51, 55, 58, 95, 97, 101-102, 105, 122, 126, 132-139, 141-142, 152, 154-156, 157, 189, 238, 269, 301, 353, 372, 400
    as "Lichtschau", (inner visionary perception of light), 121-145, 150, 152, 155-156, 171, 189, 206, 238, 264, 291, 312, 323, 366, 392, 400
    mystically infused l. (lux vivens, uncreated mystical Light), 96-100, 101, 114-115, 118, 119, 132, 133, 134-139, 140-141, 143-146, 150-156, 157, 183, 189, 206, 222, 232, 275-276, 298-299, 309, 320, 365-367, 365 n.6, 369, 372-376, 389-391, 392, 400
    l. as a medium of 'inner sight', 99, 146-153, 172, 191
    as a paranormal (occult) phenomenon, 12, 33, 50-51, 52, 100, 102, 104, 109, 130-132, 139, 141, 155
Locution(s), (*see* utterances mystical, and auditory mystical experience)
Logos, xliii, xlviii
Love, all-encompassing (mystical), xxix, lvi, 55, 58, 59, 115, 124, 148, 151, 154, 183, 222, 223-224, 236-237, 241, 246, 319-321, 341, 369-370, 400, 465
Lucidity (of consciousness) *see* Clarity
'Lucie, Christine' [aka Boutle, Mathilde] 100-104, 100 n.22, 103 n.25, 114-120, 114 n.28, 122, 123-125, 136, 141, 149-151, 171, 174-176, 175 n.69, 181-183, 189-193, 189 n.77, 210, 221, 221 n.93, 223, 235-236, 246, 319, 364

M

Maritain, Jacques, xii n.2, xxxiv n.14
McGinn, Bernard, xi n.1, xxx, xxx n.5, xxxv, xxxix n.21
Mescaline, experiments with, and mystical experience, lii, 54, 54 n.63
Metaphysics, l, lvi, 62, 127, 144, 204, 293, 388, 458, 459, 463

INDEX

Mindfulness, (as a serene condition of consciousness), xi, xv, xxxviii-xxxix, xl, 232 n.100
Miracle, 134, 137, 138
Misotheism, li n.13
Moses, 352-353, *Exodus* 3.1-14, 352-353, 353 n.1
Mystagogue, 72 n.6, 189
Mystery, sacred / unfathomable, xlvii, xlviii, 44 n.52, 137, 144, 193, 197, 201, 203, 205, 208, 232, 233 n.101, 309, 392, 430, 465
Mystical experience, xi-xiii, xv, xvii, xviii, xviii n.1, xix-xx, xxi, xxi n.3, xxiii, xxv, xvi, xxxii, xxxiii, xxxv, xxxvii, xl, xli, xlii n.2, xliv, l, li, li n.13, liii, liv, liv n.19, lv, 1, 3-5, 25, 38- 40, 42-43, 47, 59, 60, 61, 63-329, 333-401 (*see also* 'glimpse of God', 'auditory mystical experience', Light, mystical, and Presence, mystical)
    apersonal modes of, xxv, 243, 297-303, 348, 349, 374, (*see also* monistic mysticism)
    cognitive content of, (*see also* intuition and insight, mystical) xviii, xxi, xxii, 21, 34, 41-43, 47, 65-69, 106-107, 141, 158, 163-165, 177-183, 185, 195, 203, 206-207, 218-219, 225, 230, 231, 250, 291, 293, 305, 313-314, 324-325, 335, 339, 345, 361, 376, 378-400, 451, 458
    compared to prophetic experience, xiv, xxi, xxii, xxiii n.5, 227, 352
    emotional impact / effects on the perceiver, 51, 72, 78, 109, 139, 144, 155, 196-197 n.82, 197, 198, 175, 201-204, 207-210, 212, 214, 216, 218, 266, 286, 299, 300, 313, 319, 320, 358, 359, 342, 383
    extrovertive vs. introvertive, liii, liii n.17
    language as a mode of, *see* utterance, mystical and word, mystical birth of
    life-transforming impact / influence on volition, xx, xxvi, xxxvii, xli, 4, 19, 20, 28, 31, 66, 67, 71, 72, 73, 87, 89, 93, 97-98, 115, 116-117, 159, 173, 175, 183, 187, 191, 209-210, 214-222, 224, 225, 243, 244, 251, 252, 265, 267, 287, 295-298, 314-318, 324, 339-343, 345-347, 348, 352, 353, 357, 359, 361, 365, 369, 372, 376, 382, 388-390, 398, 399, 400, 407, 409
    oneness, sense of, 36, 54, 56, 127, 192-193, 195, 246, 262, 263, 308, 316, 423, 425
    person-like modes of, xl, liii, 74, 123 n.30, 182, 211, 235, 241-243, 260, 269, 270, 291-303, 311, 320, 349, 353, 400, 427, (*see also* theistic mysticism)
    potential for delusion and error in, 336-377
    somatic varieties of, xlii, liii, liv, 4, 15, 67, 68, 74, 107-109, 111, 112-113, 116, 155, 175, 176, 177, 180, 181, 209, 210, 213, 215-217, 225, 241, 249, 251, 252, 265, 267, 271, 277, 283, 284-290, 298, 299, 300, 318, 340, 343-344, 347-348, 358-362, 364, 369-373, 388, 393, 407
    spatiality, perception of in, 30, 31, 159, 169-171, 174-175, 177, 234, 248, 367, 368
    ultimate incomprehensibility of, xxiv, xl, 2, 36, 125, 134, 138, 140, 143, 144, 197, 200, 242, 258, 259, 273, 287, 288, 296, 309, 359, 383, 392, 451, 452
    ultimate ineffability of, xii, xxi, xxiv, xxiv n.7, xxvi, xl, liii, lvi, 44 n.52, 50, 51, 52, 54, 61, 109, 115, 124-127, 135, 137, 140, 143, 145, 149, 151, 155, 183, 190, 196, 208, 221, 233 n.101, 236, 262, 263, 276, 296, 308, 312, 319, 465
'Mystical relation' ["mystische Relation"], xix, xli, xlii, xlvii, li, liii-lvi, 3-5, 12, 16, 19, 38, 42, 43, 58, 62, 67, 68, 86-87, 93, 94, 121, 144, 157, 159, 161, 183, 207, 253, 271, 314, 318-319, 331, 335-336
    experience of, defined as an 'ultimate phenomenon', xlvii n.10, 3 n.3, 303-313, 324-328, 329, 335, 367, 374, 377, 378, 381, 394, 397, 398, 399
    philosophical relevance of, 400-465
Mystical relationship, xlii, 184, 253, 287, 288-289, 291, 300
Mysticism, xi, 4, xiii, xxv, xxx, xxv, lvi, 12, 13, 15, 38, 142, 144, 156, 195, 231, 327, 351, 395, 464-465, definitions of, liv, liv n.19, 1-3, 165, 250, 321-323, 400, 436, 451-452, 453
    and empirical enquiry, xiii-xiv, xvii, xviii, xxx, xxxii, xxxiv, xxxvi, xliv, 3, 43, 186 n.74, 207-209, 216, 321, 347, 353, 400

and psychedelic drugs, xliii, lii, 54
and philosophy, xi, l, lii, liii n.17, 3, 5, 35, 40, 144, 200, 204, 263, 292, 293, 330, 403-465
and theology/religious faith, xii, xxiv, xxxii, xxxiii, xxxiv, l, 44 n.52, 72 n.6, 73, 125, 144, 179, 189 n.76, 190, 204, 221, 227 n.99, 247, 258, 258 n.104, 259, 260, 262, 263, 292, 293, 296 n.111, 315, 346, 388, 415, 464
Christian tradition of, xxi, xxiii, xxiv n.7, xxv, xxx n.5, xxxii, xxxv, xxxviii-xxxix, xxxix n.21, xxxix n.23, liv n.18, 24, 44 n.52, 72-73 n.6, 73 n.7, 75, 81, 90, 141, 179, 187, 189 n.76, 190, 227 n.99, 232 n.100, 233 n.101, 243, 258, 353, 357 n.4, 400
gnoseology of, (*see* gnoseology)
Islamic m., xxii, xxvi, 292
Jewish tradition of, xxi, xviii, (*see also* Buber, Martin)
Monistic (a-personal) m., 35, 36, 243, 300, 301-303, 348, 379, 396-397 n.11, 399
phenomenology of, xviii, xxxvi, xlix, l, liii, 18-20, 42, 45, 81, 101, 144, 156, 206, 207, 216, 240, 242, 243, 244, 250, 264, 266, 282, 313, 314, 316, 318, 321, 322, 324, 325, 326, 335, 346, 378, 394, 399, 451-453, 454, 463
psychological-phenomenological approach to, xiii, xxxv, li, 3, 18-20, 42, 45, 59, 60, 69, 81, 92, 264, 353, 410, 436, 451, 452
theistic (personal) m., 220, 224, 243, 301-303, 314, 318, 323, 345, 346, 348, 353, 374, 396-397 n.11
Mystology, lvi

N

Negative theology, *see* apophatic theology
Neo-Atheism, 186 n.74
Neoplatonism, 132, 262
Nicodemus of Naxos, 135
Nishida, Kitaro, xxix, xxix n.3, xxxix, xxxix n.25
Nothingness, xxiv, xl, xlvii, 62, 248, 256, 261, 262, 263, 429, 430-431, 442, 444

Nous, 132
Numinous experience, 144,
aura, liv, 17, 18, 20, 26, 33, 131, 168, 241, 286, 365, 369-370, 372, 373, 374, 375, 400
fluidum, 241, 286, 290, 295-296, 298-299, 365, 369, 370, 372, 373, 375, 389, 400
majestas, 123, 123 n.30, 125, 197, 203, 208-215, 235, 257, 266
mirum, 197, 203, 208
mysterium fascinosum, 144, 197, 202, 203, 208, 257
mysterium tremendum, 144, 197, 199, 202, 203, 208, 209, 257, 259
sanctum, 197, 203
sensus numinis, 195 n.79, 196 n.81, 200-202, 204-206

O

Occultism (*see also* pseudomysticism), 9-20, 21, 45
Ontology, l, 47, 378, 382, 412, 413, 416, 417, 421, 431, 432, 435, 443, 447, 450, 453, 454, 458
'Openness to receive', ["Offenstand"], (prerequisite for perceiving phenomena 'arriving' in consciousness), xix, 44, 165, 232, 232 n.100, 248, 249, 252, 407, 444, 445, 450, 454-456, 457-458, 464
Otto, Rudolf, 195, 195 n.79, 196-199, 200, 201, 202, 203, 208, 209, Das Heilige 195 n.79, 199 n.83, 199 n. 84, 200, 201 n.86, Das Gefühl des Überweltlichen. Sensus Numinis, 195 n.79, 196 n.81, 201, 203, 208, 209
ousia, 134

P

Param(a)hansa, Yogananda, xx, 12 n.5, 49-51, 49 n.57, 58, 129-130, 129 n. 32, 130 n.33
parā vāc, (Sanskrit), the 'transcendental mystical word', xliv
Peng-Keller, Simon, ix, xiii n. 4, xiv n. 5, xv
Plotinus, 59, 59 n.66, 59 n.67, *Enneads*, 59 n. 67
Prayer, spiritual, xxxviii, xxxix, xl, 73 n.6, 73 n.7, 105, 114, 115, 119, 122, 132-134, 132 n.36, 135, 153, 171, 173, 187

n.75, 192, 222, 223, 224, 236, 246, 259, 260, 269, 307, 319, 320, 331, 357 n.4
Presence, mystical (sense of, beholding of, and cognitive awareness of), xii, xl, xlii, xlvii, li, liii-liv, 2, 4, 20, 44 n.52, 60, 74, 87, 88-91, 96, 101, 102, 102-103 n.23, 110, 118-120, 121, 123 n.30, 131, 133, 141, 145-146, 156, 157-183, 184, 188, 192, 193, 199, 206, 207, 210, 219-222, 228, 229-231, 233-235, 238-239, 241, 243-246, 250-256, 263-264, 266-268, 270-275, 279, 285, 286, 290-292, 296-299, 300, 301, 309, 316-318, 323, 337, 341, 343, 346, 347, 352, 354, 356, 361, 361 n.5, 362-370, 372, 373, 375, 376, 382-386, 388-392, 394-396, 398, 400, 409, 452
Pseudo-Dionysius, Areopagite, the, xix, xxiv n.7, xxxix, 23 n.15, 44 n.52, 72 n.6, 258, 259, 260 n. 106, 265 n. 109, 306
Pseudomysticism, (pseudomystical phenomena), lii, liii, 3, 7-62, 162, 189 n.76, 278, 348,
Psychology, transpersonal, xx
Purification, active (as a self-imposed part of the spiritual quest), xxxvii, 34, 232 n.100, 259, 263, 360, 442 n.42
    passive (effected by a mystical impact), 26, 27, 44, 73, 155, 208, 341

Q

'Quiet state of alertness', ["Versunkenheit"], xv, xxix, xxxiii, xl, xliii, l, liv, liv n. 19, 4, 19, 49, 69-71, 112, 117, 127, 139, 141, 142, 147, 151-152, 155, 185, 196, 207, 213, 226, 226, 249, 256, 265-267, 269, 269 n. 110, 270, 277, 284, 305, 317, 322, 331, 345, 366, 435-437, 439-441, 443, 445-447, 450-451, 453, 455, 465 n.1, definition of, xxxiii n.13, 1-3, 56-57, 60, 139 n. 49
    speaking in the state of, (*see also* utterance, mystical) xlii, xxxi, xxxvii, xli, xli n. 1, xliii-xlv, xlv n.8, xlvii, lii, 5, 25, 47, 269-270, 269 n. 110, 280-283, 321, 465, 465 n.1

R

Rahner, Karl, SJ., xxx n.6, xxxii, xxxii n.11, xxxv, 132 n.36, 465 n.1

Rainach, Adolf, xxvii, xxvii n.10
Recognition, mystical, *see* cognition and cognitive mystical experience
Revelation, moment of (as a component of a mystical event), xxii, xlii, 97, 101, 110, 120, 140, 145, 152, 174, 183, 232, 233, 235, 239, 242, 244, 246, 276, 280, 354
Richard of St. Victor, 187 n.75
Rolle, Richard of Hampole, 127 n.31

S

Sai Baba, Sathya, 12 n.6
Sakaguchi, Alicja, xvii, xxxv, xlii n.2, *Sprechakte der Mystischen Erfahrung*, xxii n.4, xxiii n.6, xxv n.17
Scaramelli, Giovanni B., *Direttorio mistico*, 198 n.76
Scheler, Max, 18, 405 n.1, 411, 411 n.10, 411 n.11
Schultz, J. H., xxxi, xxi n.8, xxxvii
Seeress of Prevorst (*aka* Hauffe, Frederike), 24 n.19, 24 n.20
Sivaism (Shaivism), Tantric, xliv, xliv n.6, xliv n.7
Sophia of Klingnau, 153-154
Stace, Walter T., liii n.17
Steiner, Rudolf, lii, lii n.14, 22, 24, 25, 26-43
Subject-object-split (division), (eroded in a mystical event), l, 49, 51, 56, 95, 262, 271, 315-317
Suso [aka Seuse], Henry, 258, 306-308, 311-312, 312 n. 116, 315-317
Suzuki, Taisetz, xx, 61 n.71, 62 n.73
Swedenborg, Immanuel, 24, 24 n.18
Symeon, the New Theologian, 132, 133-138, 137 n.45, 137 n.46, 139-142, 147, 147 n.52, 148, 148 n.53, 153-154, 154 n.58, 154 n.59, 174, 211-212

T

Tauler, Johannes, xix, 44 n.52, 258, 261, 261 n.108, 263
Telepathy, (as a potential corollary of paranormal, visionary and mystical expierences), 13-15, 16, 17-20, 166 n.65
Teresa of Avila, xix, xxv, xxv n.8, 73, 100-110, 108 n.26, 108 n.27, 113-114, 120, 122-123, 123 n.29, 124-125, 136, 141-

144, 170-174, 171 n.67, 189-192, 211, 222-224, 223 n.94, 224 n.96-98, 236, 245-246, 248, 279, 279 n.111, 364

Theosophy, lii n.14, 26 n. 21-24, 27 n. 26-28, 32 n. 31, 35

Transfiguration, experience of, 51-52, 133, 146, 147, 153-157

U

'ultimate phenomenon', ["Phänomenletztheit"], xiii, xix, xxxvi n.19, xlvii, l, lii, liv-lv, 3, 4, 5, 19, 48, 144, 146, 165, 279, 303, 319, 325-326, 335-336, 374, 377, 403, 404, 406-416, 417, 424-425, 428, 433, 435, 441, 452, 457, 458, 463-464, (defined) xxiii n. 5, xlvii n.10, 2-3 n.3, 328-331

Underhill, Evelyn, 48 n.55, 279 n.111

union, mystical, (*unio mystica*), 45 n.52, 314-318, 321

Utterance(s), mystical, (*see also* speaking as a mode of mystical experience), xx, xxxi, xxxvii, xli, xli n.1, xlii, xlv n.8, xlvi, xlviii, lii, 5, 25, 47, 269, 269 n.110, 270, 280, 282-283, 321, 350, 465 n.1

V

Vaughan, Henry, 266 n.109

"Versenkung", *see* 'introspection'

"Versunkenheit", *see* 'quiet state of alertness'

visio corporalis, liv, liv n.18, 75-76, 75 n.8, 78, 80, 139, 227 n.99, 244, 247

visio Dei, xxi, 233 n.101

visio imaginaria (*spiritualis*), (*see also* pictorial vision) liv, liv n.18, 19, 75, 75 n.8, 172, 227 n.99, 244, 247

visio intellectualis, (*see also* insight, intellectual) liv, liv n.18, 75, 75 n.8, 103, 125, 179, 190, 195, 227, 227 n.99, 247-248

Vision, allegorical, 92-100
    imageless (non-pictorial), xx, xxi, liii-lv, 4, 75 n.8, 76, 90, 107, 132, 145, 146, 157-158, 168-169, 174-175, 177, 179-181, 184, 188, 192-195, 215, 219, 220, 222, 225, (defined) 226-230, 227 n.99, 232-235, 240, 245, (phenomenological structure, of) 247-264, 267, 268, 271-276, 279, 280, 294, 308, 316, 317
    pictorial, xx, liii-liv, 4, 73, 75-92, 93, 96, 100-102, 104, 106, 108-111, 113-122, 125, 140, 145, 155, 157, 168, 170, 171, 174, 175, 177, 187-188, 191, 193-194, 206, 210-211, 222, 225-227, 227 n.99, 229, 231, 232, 234, 237-240, 244, 245, 246-248, 254, 255, 265, 266, 268, 273-275, 279-280, 281, 300, 301, 307, 316, 319, 323, 340-341, 350, 352, 354-360, 362, 367-368, 372-374, 376, 385-389, 391, 392
    of Christ, 117-121, 125, 140
    of Light, *see* s.v. Light

Void, the, *see* Nothingness

W

'waking consciousness', ["Wachbewußtsein"], xv, xxxi, xxxvii, 2, 56-57, 60, 68, 133, 185, 196, 248, 408, 436

Walther, Gerda, 9 n.1, 17 n.9. 17 n.10, 18-20, 18 n.11, 20 n.13, 20 n.14, 166 n.65

Will, transformation of (as an impact of a mystical occurrence), 71-73, 197, 217, 224, 259, 298, 308, 314, 316, 358, 372, 376

Words, 'arriving' in mystical consciousness, (birth of the mystical word), (*see also* 'utterances, mystical', and auditory mystical experience), xlii-xliii, xliii n.5, xliv, xlvi, xlvii, 99, 116, 119, 176, 183, 191, 210, 215, 227, 259, 277, 281, 349, 350, 354

Y

Yogi, xx, 12, 12 n.5, 49, 49 n.57, 51, 129, 129 n.32, 130, 130 n.32, 139, 174

Z

Zen, xx, xxi, xxxi, xxxi n. 10, xxxviii-l, 60-62, 61n.70, 61 n.71, 62 n.73

www.ingramcontent.com/pod-product-compliance
Lightning Source LLC
Chambersburg PA
CBHW022005300426
44117CB00005B/43